Landscape Innovation and Nostalgia

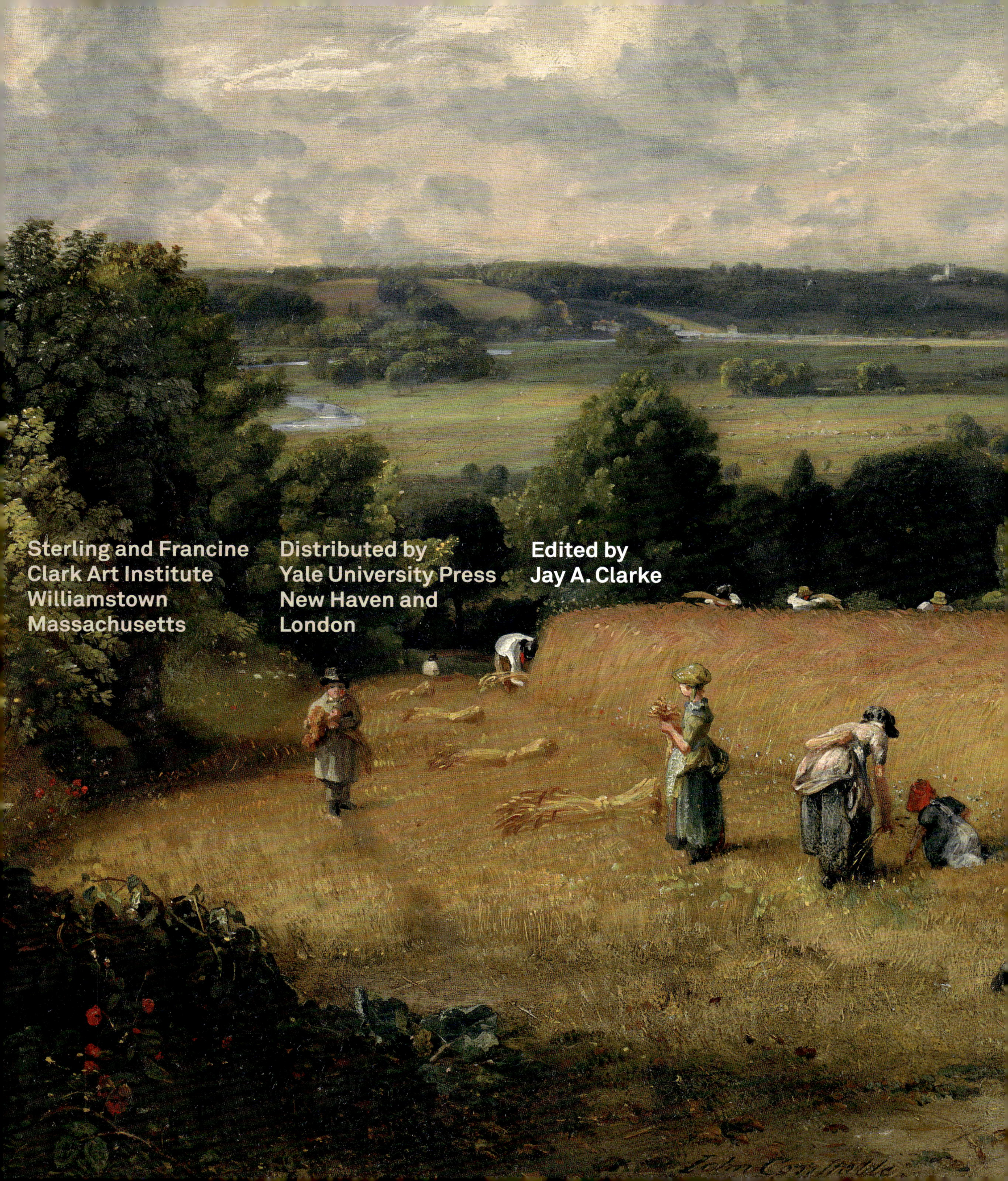

Sterling and Francine
Clark Art Institute
Williamstown
Massachusetts

Distributed by
Yale University Press
New Haven and
London

Edited by
Jay A. Clarke

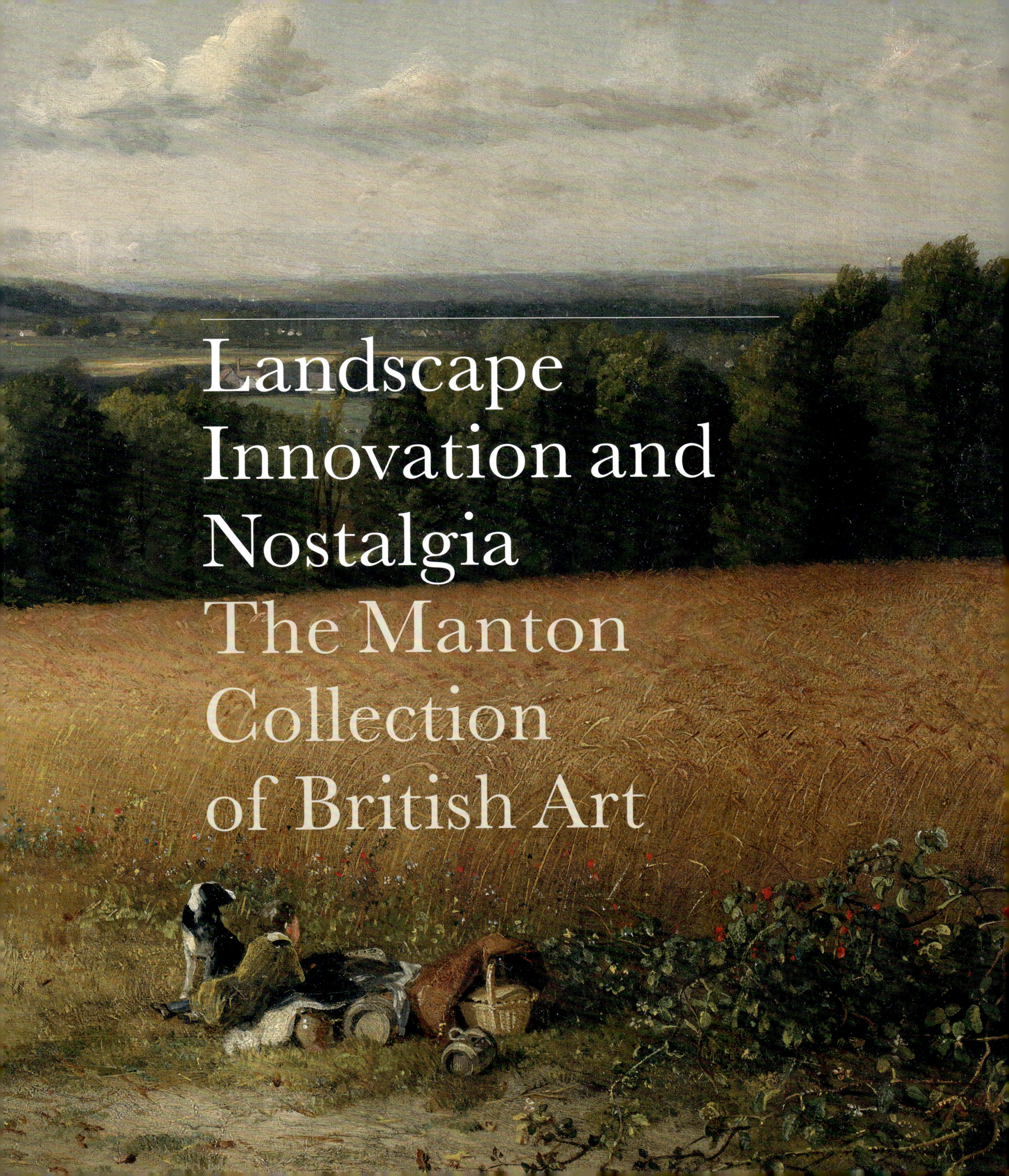

Landscape Innovation and Nostalgia

The Manton Collection of British Art

Produced by the Sterling and Francine Clark Art Institute, 225 South Street, Williamstown, Massachusetts
www.clarkart.edu

Curtis R. Scott, Director of Publishing and Information Resources
Anne Roecklein, Managing Editor
Dan Cohen, Special Projects Editor

Copy edited by Audrey Walen
Designed by Studio Blue, Chicago, Illinois
Indexed by Kathleen M. Friello
Printed on PhoenixMotion Xantur and Finch Opaque Smooth White Text by Meridian Printing, East Greenwich, Rhode Island

Pages 2–3: John Constable, detail of *The Wheat Field*, 1816
Pages 50–51: John Constable, detail of *Leathes Water (Thirlmere)*, 19 Sept. 1806
Pages 112–13: Joseph Mallord William Turner, detail of *View off Margate, Evening*, c. 1840
Pages 166–67: Richard Parkes Bonington, detail of *Coast with Beached Boats and Figures*, c. 1823–24
Pages 226–27: John Constable, detail of *Willy Lott's House* (recto), c. 1812–13

Distributed by Yale University Press
New Haven and London
www.yalebooks.com/art

Printed and bound in the United States of America
10 9 8 7 6 5 4 3 2 1

Library of Congress Cataloging-in-Publication Data
Sterling and Francine Clark Art Institute.
Landscape, innovation, and nostalgia : the Manton collection of British art / edited by Jay A. Clarke.
pages cm
Includes bibliographical references.
ISBN 978-1-935998-07-5 (Clark hardcover : alk. paper)
— ISBN 978-0-300-17966-8 (Yale hardcover : alk. paper)
1. Art, British—18th century—Catalogs. 2. Art, British—19th century—Catalogs. 3. Art, British—20th century—Catalogs. 4. Manton, Edwin, Sir, 1909–2005—Art collections—Catalogs. 5. Manton, Florence, Lady, 1911–2003—Art collections—Catalogs.
6. Art—Massachusetts—Williamstown—Catalogs.
7. Sterling and Francine Clark Art Institute—Catalogs.
I. Clarke, Jay A. (Jay Anne) II. Title.
N6766.S74 2012
759.2074'7441—dc23
2012010680

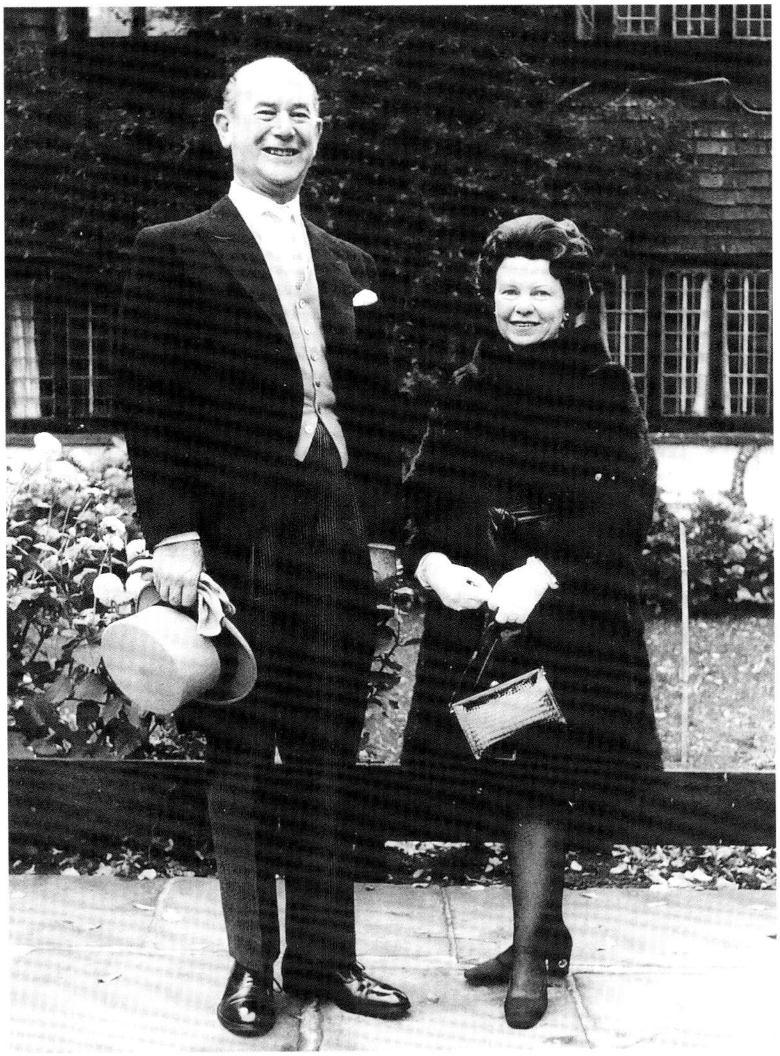

Dedicated to the memory of Sir Edwin and Lady Manton

Contents

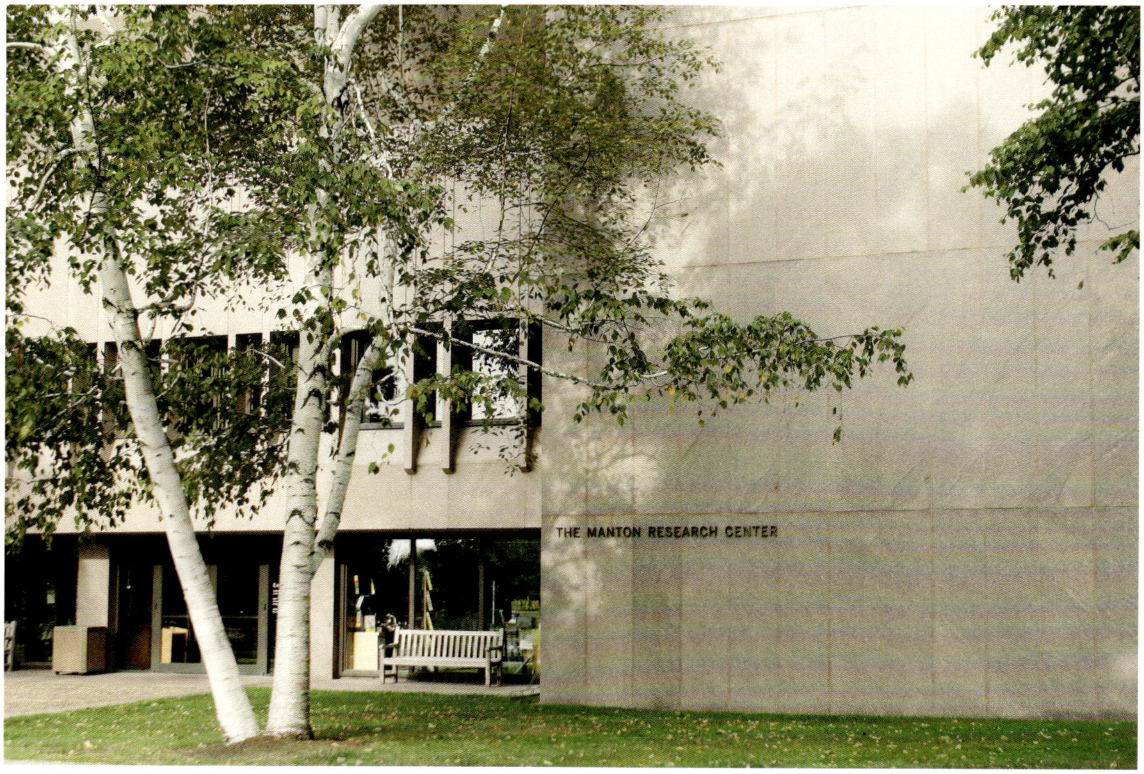
THE MANTON RESEARCH CENTER

Director's Foreword

Sir Edwin and Lady Manton and Sterling and Francine Clark shared similar approaches to collecting. Both bought for pleasure, doing so without the aid of curators or professional advisors, favoring works that could be best appreciated in intimate spaces. They kept their collections largely out of the public eye. The Clarks unveiled their works for the first time with the opening of the Institute, in 1955, and the Mantons did so posthumously at the Clark just over fifty years later. In June 2007, selections from the Manton Collection went on display for the first time, revealing the breadth and depth of this very important but largely unknown collection of eighteenth- and nineteenth-century works. It was a transformational moment for the Clark in ways that can barely be expressed in a brief introduction like the one I pen here.

The path leading to this extraordinary gift began only a year earlier when the trustees of the Manton Foundation visited the Clark to see its campus and gain a firsthand understanding of the depth and seriousness of its collection and research and academic programs. Following Jim Manton's wishes, his Foundation's trustees wanted to place the collection where it would not only be shown regularly, but incorporated into a museum's education and teaching mission – not to get lost, as Manton had once said, in a "huge, cavernous repository." Given the deep respect Manton had for art historical scholarship, the trustees realized that the Clark library, guest scholar program, multifaceted conferences and symposia, the Williams graduate program housed at the Institute – not to mention the depth of the Williams undergraduate art history curriculum – made Williamstown and the Clark the right location for the collection.

The trustees also realized that the Manton Collection fit seamlessly into the holdings of the Clark, given the Institute's intimate character and its special focus on nineteenth-century landscape, both in paintings and works on paper. The Clarks provided a representative collection of British art with works by Turner, Gainsborough, and Constable, but the Manton gift deepened this emphasis with its extensive holdings in early nineteenth-century British art. The gift now allows the Institute to present a broader and more inclusive story of nineteenth-century European art in its galleries.

In recognition of the donation of over three hundred works and a substantial endowment directed at supporting not only the collection but also the research and scholarly activities of the Clark, the Institute proudly named its red granite building the Manton Research Center in August 2007. This building houses the activities of the Research and Academic Program and the library and will also be the home of the new Manton Study Center for Works on Paper and renovated Manton galleries, where selections from the Manton Collection will be exhibited regularly.

The incorporation of the Manton Collection within the Clark has catalyzed a series of ongoing and powerful conversations, both scholarly and personal, as it has also generated a number of new discoveries, many of which are chronicled in this volume. These essays summarize our current appreciation and understanding of the works that comprise this significant collection. We know, however, that research on the Manton works will continue at the Institute, providing future generations of students and scholars the opportunity to study and reinterpret. New empirical evidence will advance our knowledge. The reinterpretation of works by future generations of scholars will demonstrate the value of the collection's place in this special academic center, one whose commitment to scholarship and the understanding of the visual arts is second to none among art institutions in this country.

Michael Conforti
Director

Acknowledgments

When the Clark first embarked on this project, we found ourselves at an exciting moment in the history of museum publishing, with many arguing that online publishing had rendered collection catalogues obsolete. Recognizing the advantages and limitations of both traditional and electronic catalogues, we knew that we wanted to create something different for this very special collection. Under Sir Edwin Manton's support and direction, four volumes focusing on important sections of the collection had already been privately published. Written by esteemed scholars in the field – Leslie Parris, John Hayes, and Andrew Wilton – these handsome books are artist-based: *Constable* (1994); *Gainsborough and Rowlandson* (1998); *Constable: Supplement* (1998); and *Turner, Girtin, and Bonington* (2001). They include complete catalogue entries on each object as well as exhibition, provenance, and publication histories. Because this crucial work had already been done, the Clark was free to consider more experimental options to publish the collection in its entirety; in other words, to rethink what a collection catalogue could be.

In the fall of 2009, the Clark convened a colloquium of publishers, academics, and curators to address the future scope of this project. These included curators from the United States and the United Kingdom: Cassandra Albinson, David Blayney Brown, Jay Clarke, Anne Lyles, Patrick Noon, Elizabeth Pergam, Richard Rand, and Conal Shields; academics from the United States and Australia: Hollis Clayson, Marc Gotlieb, Kay Dian Kriz, and Mary Roberts; editors and publishers Gillian Malpass and Curtis Scott; and additional members of the Clark staff. Before the colloquium we took the opportunity to put the Manton works online, a pilot project for a future web-based launch of the Clark's entire collection. After viewing each object in the collection and puzzling over several attributions, the group met over two days to discuss the most forward-looking and appropriate format for the Manton Collection publication.

Because the Clark is both a museum and a research institute, and the range of participants reflected the range of our publications, we decided on a hybrid form. The conclusions reached at the colloquium reflect precisely what you now hold in your hands. The introduction tells the story of Sir Edwin and Lady Manton's lives: a tale woven through a tapestry of interviews with family, friends, dealers, curators, academics, and former business associates. A chronology of Sir Edwin and Lady Manton's collection was gleaned from the rich archival sources available at the Clark. The second section of the book takes a different direction. These nine essays address issues in the field of British studies through works in the Manton Collection. Each essay focuses on one work, one artist, or a group of works, organized around a particular topic. In this way the collection serves as a sounding board for current issues in British art, be they based on material culture, artistic biography, or historiography. The last section of the book provides, for the first time, a complete illustrated checklist of the collection, with revised media descriptions and full provenance.

The research conducted for the publication would not have been possible without the help of numerous individuals at the Clark and beyond. Assuring that the provenance and media descriptions were correct in relation to the forthcoming *Nineteenth-Century European Paintings at the Sterling and Francine Clark Art Institute*, Sarah Lees and Dan Cohen were assiduous in confirming consistency. Leslie Hill Paisley conducted a thorough survey of all of the works on paper, which served as the basis for the revised media descriptions in the checklist, and Sandra Webber worked with us to ensure the most complete and accurate descriptions of paintings. Paul Provost, Sarah Yoder, and Rosemary Luddy helped with questions about works that were sold at auction. Several scholars generously helped to resolve attribution questions: Hugh Belsey, David Blayney Brown, Lowell Libson, Anne Lyles, Andrew Moore, Patrick Noon, Susan Sloman, Paul Tucker, and Stephen Wildman. We also owe a debt of gratitude to the aforementioned authors of the original Manton publications, who were the first to put their eyes and pens to issues of authorship.

For their help with the beautiful images that grace this book, we thank photographer Mike Agee, as well as Merry Armata, Laurie Glover, Carly Hansen-Decelles, and Julie Walsh. Paul Dion, Tom Merrill, and Monique LeBlanc facilitated the movement of the art for photography and conservation, while John Carson helped with a number of computer crises. Donna Chenail carefully transcribed the taped interviews into text form. Elleree Erdos assisted with a number of thorny research questions and provided valuable assistance with the provenance research, as did Susannah Wang and James Pilgrim. Karen Bucky worked to help us track down hard-to-find books and auction catalogues. Katie Frisina, James Ganz, Deborah Giroux, Maureen Hart Hennessey, Mark Ledbury, Kathleen Morris, Teresa O'Toole, Richard Rand, and John Skavlem all worked on this publication in a wide variety of areas. Clark director Michael Conforti championed this publication from its inception.

Many individuals shared their knowledge of the Mantons by offering interviews and accepting phone calls: Judy Caruso, Florence Davis, Deborah Gage, Dennis Keene, Lowell Libson, Patrick Noon, Charles Rhyne, Nicolas Serota, Marjorie Shelley, and Andrew Wilton. E. J. Johnson was not only helpful in this regard, but was also instrumental in his early introduction of the Manton Foundation trustees to the Clark.

The authors of the insightful essays included in this book deserve special thanks. Their fresh ideas and enthusiasm for this project were inspiring. These scholars include: Tim Barringer, Ann Bermingham, Mary Broadway, David Blayney Brown, Antony Griffiths, Anne Lyles, Patrick Noon, Leslie Hill Paisley, Amelia Rauser, and Sam Smiles. The book greatly benefited from the careful and intelligent eye of our outside reader, Martha Tedeschi.

Several individuals worked diligently on this catalogue, checking every detail numerous times. Sarah Hammond and Susannah Blair spent countless months creating the checklist, verifying information, and hunting down a host of facts and numbers. Audrey Walen took special care to clarify our prose and ensure the accuracy of the lengthy checklist. Cheryl Towler Weese, Silja Hillmann, J. Brad Sturm, and Megan Deal of Studio Blue took on the elegant design of the catalogue with great sensitivity to the works of art. Daniel Frank of Meridian Printing printed the book with exceptional attention to detail and color. Curtis Scott oversaw this publication with care and enthusiasm, always keeping the Clark's high standards at the fore. Anne Roecklein went to every length to ensure the book's consistency and beauty, from the title page to the index, always with a smile. We thank June Cuffner for her careful proofreading and Kathleen Friello for preparing the index. As well, I would like to thank my family: my parents, and John, Liam, and Cora Bradley.

The greatest debt of thanks goes to the Manton family. Without their generosity this book would not exist. Diana and Hugh Morton, Sandra Niles, and Julia Krapf were beyond generous in providing interviews and answers to my countless e-mails and phone calls, answering questions about family history and how the collection was displayed and stored, and sharing treasured family photographs. The Manton Foundation's decision to entrust these works of art to the Clark, and their continuing engagement with all that we do, is a testament to their belief in our mission and the enduring resonance of our collections. The institution-changing gift they made to the Clark in 2007 allows us to share their vision with visitors, and to carry innovative research forward into the next generation. Most of all, it is our hope that Sir Edwin and Lady Manton would have approved of this book. The passion that went into the book's production, we hope in some small way, parallels the passion they took to build their collection.

Jay A. Clarke
Manton Curator of Prints, Drawings, and Photographs

Landscape and Nostalgia

Sir Edwin and Lady Manton as Collectors

Jay A. Clarke

Writing to his friend and patron Rev. John Fisher in 1821, the artist John Constable opined, "I should paint my own places best; painting is but another word for feeling. I associate 'my careless boyhood' ... to all that lies on the banks of the 'Stour'."[1] The same could apply to Sir Edwin Manton's fifty-year engagement with British art, particularly his collection of works by Constable. Manton pursued representations of his "own places" as a way to connect visually and emotionally with his "careless boyhood," which also passed not far from the banks of the River Stour. Having left England at the age of eighteen, never to live there again, seascapes and landscapes of his native country remained powerful and visceral links to the places he loved. An altogether private and highly personal enterprise, the Manton Collection was built carefully and quietly, with powerful but modest-scaled works that paralleled their own personalities.

Family, Work, and Philanthropy

Born Edwin Alfred Grenville Manton in 1909, Sir Edwin was nicknamed "Sunny Jim" by one of his favorite aunts.[2] The name stuck, and he was known as Jim or Jimmy his entire life. He was born in Earls Colne, Essex, a place that remained a touchstone throughout his life. Though he spent the majority of his adulthood in America, he never gave up his British citizenship or his ties to England. Soon after Manton's birth the family moved to Westcliff-on-Sea, in a setting with views of the Thames estuary; a location, as Tate Director Sir Nicholas Serota opined, that "encouraged his enduring affection for expanses of sea and sky."[3]

Sir Edwin's father John had been a banker, but left to serve in the armed forces during World War I. Manton's Uncle Edwin took responsibility for the family, moving them to Shaftsbury, a picturesque town in a bucolic setting in Dorset. Manton entered the Shaftesbury School, where he remained as a boarding student when the family moved to London. Here he nurtured a love of sports on the cricket field and strength as a communicator in the classroom (fig. 1).[4] Despite the offer of a scholarship to Cambridge University in 1926, Manton apprenticed with an insurance firm, partially to help support his family as his father had difficulty returning to work after the war.[5] In 1927, at the age of eighteen, Manton moved to Paris to take up a position with the Caledonian Insurance Company, where he became fluent in French.[6] Six years later he was offered a post at the then-small American International Underwriters (AIU) in New York, later known as the American International Group (AIG).

Manton was instrumental in building AIU into a premier overseas property-casualty company, rising through the ranks over a seventy-year career to become chairman from 1969 to 1975, and remaining involved as honorary director and senior advisor until his death in 2005.[7] By the time of Manton's passing, he had seen his efforts help AIU/AIG's New York office grow from a modest space employing a small number of underwriters in 1933 to a stunning Art Deco skyscraper on Pine Street (fig. 2) with thousands of employees.[8] Begun by the legendary businessman Cornelius Vander Starr in Shanghai in 1919 as American Asiatic Underwriters in a two-room, two-clerk office, the company would eventually transform into a trillion dollar business with annual revenues of $110 billion, a global presence in over 130 countries, and a roster of 97 thousand employees worldwide.[9]

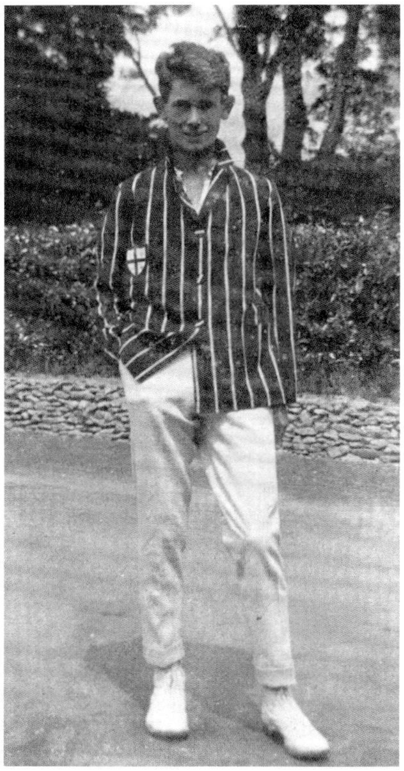

Florence Davis, a former AIG employee, remembers how deeply Manton's wisdom and experience was valued even into his nineties. Manton was consulted often by colleagues when it came to corporate history and protocol.[10] Shrewd and armed with a wonderfully wry sense of humor, he was kind and approachable, rare traits in a competitive business environment. When the French furthered their insurance privatization program in 1998 with the sale of the publically owned GAN insurance group, Manton, then age 89, was sent with an AIG delegation to conduct due diligence. He brought both language fluency and his still-sharp skills as a negotiator to the table. In part due to the immense respect he garnered in the field both nationally and internationally, Sir Edwin was inducted into the Insurance Hall of Fame in 1999, and was awarded an honorary degree from the American College of Insurance in 1994.

Upon his arrival in New York at the age of 24, Manton not only began a superb job but also met the love of his life, Florence Vivian "Gretchen" Brewer. As many single businessmen did, Manton lived in a long-term hotel, the St. George, until plans for a possible move to AIU's operations in Shanghai were solidified. One day he walked into the lobby and invited a beautiful woman working at the front desk to dinner. She declined because employees were not allowed to date guests. So Jim Manton picked up his bags, moved to another hotel, and returned to invite the striking Gretchen out again.

Fig. 1 Jim Manton in his cricket uniform at Shaftesbury School

Fig. 2 The former AIG headquarters on Pine Street: an Art Deco skyscraper designed by the architects Clinton & Russell, Holton & George. Collection of the Skyscraper Museum, New York

Gretchen, Lady Manton, was born in California and raised on a farm in Iowa. An aspiring actress, she began her theatrical work by mounting plays for civic organizations. She would come to a town that was planning a fundraiser, build the sets, create the costumes, and produce and direct the plays. After attending junior college in Iowa, she moved to New York to pursue acting. This glamorous portrait photograph was likely taken soon after her arrival (fig. 3). Jim and Gretchen Manton wed in 1936 (fig. 4), and welcomed a daughter, Diana (fig. 5), in 1938. Clearly a gregarious woman, Lady Manton was also willing to take risks. She left her small Midwest community to move to New York, married a British man, and was prepared to move to China with him. The move never happened: due to political changes in China, AIU closed down its insurance operations in the country.

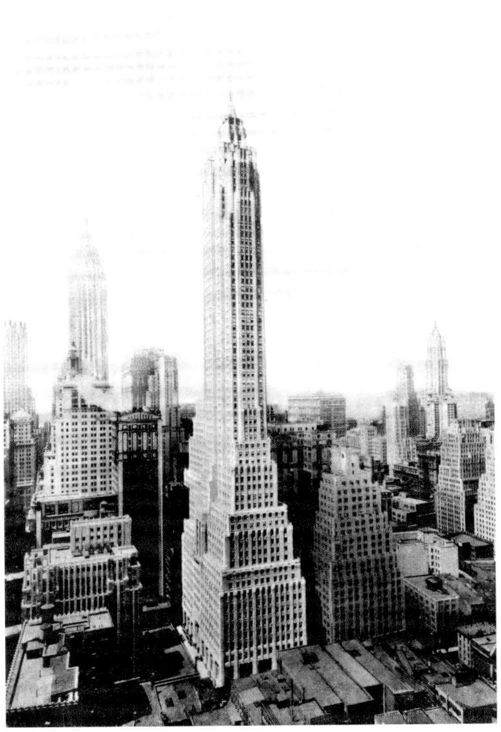

The couple lived in a modest apartment on Fifth Avenue in Greenwich Village most of their married life (fig. 6). They loved the diversity of their community, and the proximity of their apartment to the Church of the Ascension, where they were active members. Manton served as treasurer, warden, and vestryman.[11] Their financial generosity was unparalleled in the history of the church. They gave quietly and without conditions. As part of their intense interest in music, evident in their near-weekly visits to the New York Philharmonic and the Metropolitan Opera, the Mantons sponsored the first recording of the church choir and orchestra, *Voices of the Ascension*. Travel also brought the couple great pleasure, and business trips to Bermuda, Asia, Paris, Hawaii (fig. 7), and Stowe, Vermont, were perks of being part of the AIG community. They even lived for six months in 1956 in pre-revolutionary Cuba. During the summer months, Jim and Gretchen enjoyed close access to the sea at their summer cottage in Westport, Massachusetts.

It is safe to say that the largess of their philanthropy will never be known: the Mantons always gave anonymously. In researching this essay, it seemed that with each interview

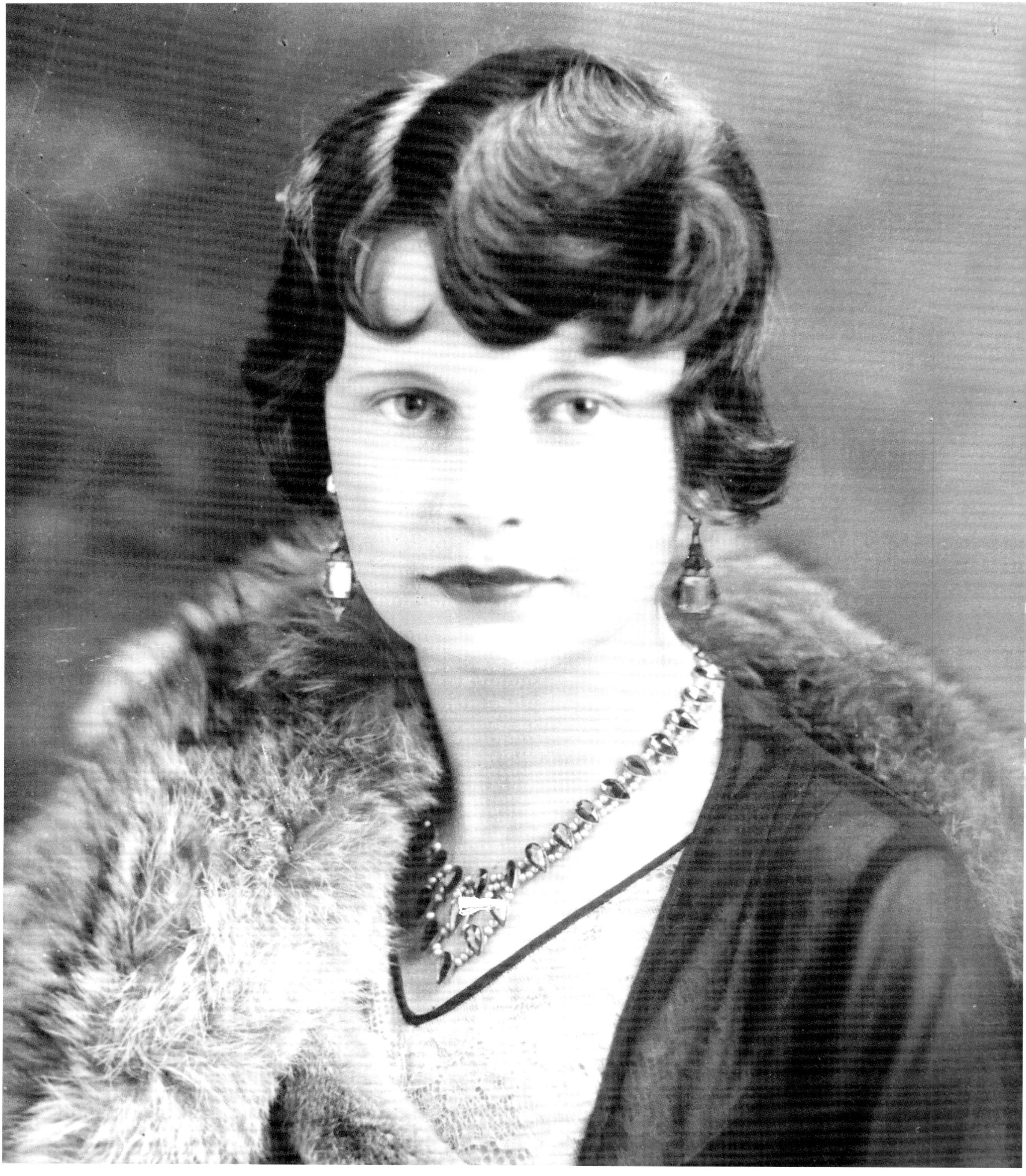

Left page:

Fig. 3 Florence Vivian Brewer in the 1920s

Right page, clockwise from top left:

Fig. 4 Jim and Gretchen Manton on their wedding day, 1936

Fig. 5 The Mantons with their daughter Diana on the beach, c. 1941

Fig. 6 The Manton's apartment building on Fifth Avenue, next door to the Church of the Ascension

Fig. 7 The Mantons in Hawaii at an insurance convention, c. 1950

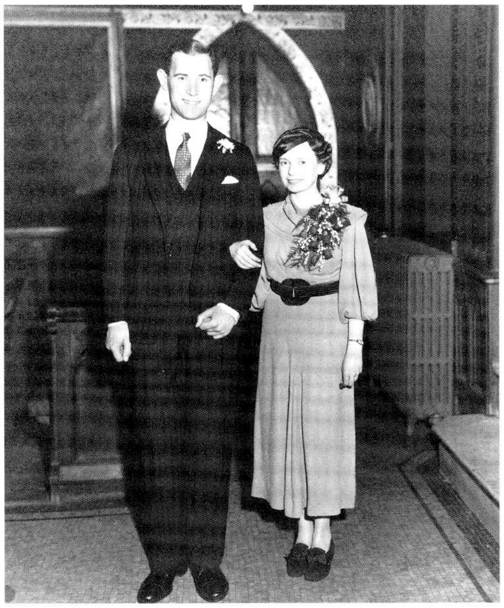

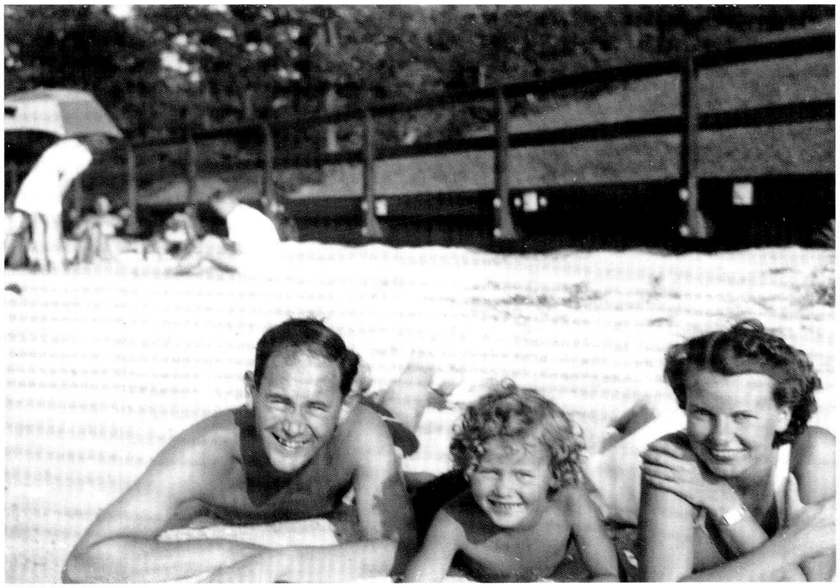

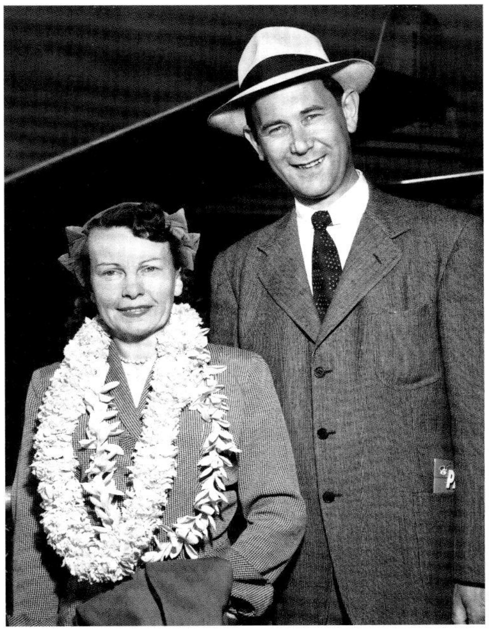

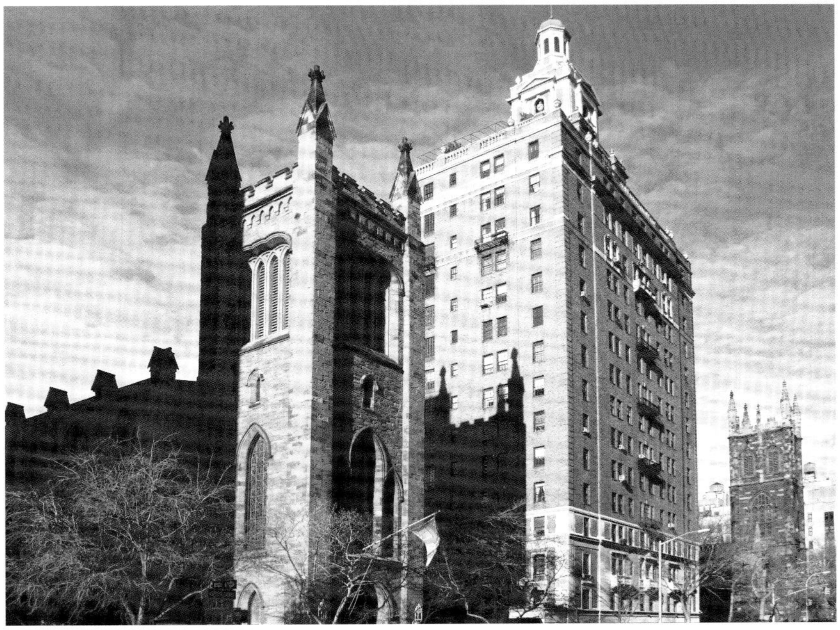

subject new and heretofore little-known facets of the Mantons's giving would be revealed, from reframing the art collection at Reed College to a 13 million pound gift to the Tate. It took a host of journalists several months to figure out who was the Tate's "mystery" donor. Sir Edwin was a member of the Board of Directors of St. Luke's-Roosevelt Hospital Center, a trustee of Beth Israel Medical Center, and on the Board of Directors of the Starr Foundation. Through the Starr Foundation, which he served from 1955 to his death, Manton directed scholarships to Reed, Smith, Dartmouth, and Williams colleges, and Columbia, New York, and Yale Universities, as well as scholarships for two American students to study at the Royal Academy in London.[12]

Despite their sophistication, generosity, and wealth, Sir Edwin and Lady Manton were humble people who enjoyed simple pleasures. Sir Edwin eschewed the luxury of a driver, instead eagerly walking three miles to and from work every day, until he broke his ankle. Even then he took the subway and walked part way. It was only after being mugged on the subway when he was in his nineties that he conceded to his associates' insistence that he get a driver. Both were autodidacts, although Lady Manton eventually earned her bachelor's degree from New York University. Her favorite hobby was reading; she devoured everything from the *New York Times* to her favorite magazines *W*, the *Enquirer*, and *Hello*.[13] Likewise, their interest in art was personally motivated, not driven by a need for status or investment.

Building a Collection: "A Clear Case of Nostalgia"

While the Mantons' life was lived as a couple, the acquisition of British art was the domain of Sir Edwin alone. Shortly after World War II, Sir Edwin began to focus on buying Constables, later explaining how "Hitler's fury" impacted his collecting:

As a victim of Stokes Adams Disease [a heart condition], I was rejected for military service. It was to be nine years before I could visit my native land again. It was during this period that my interest in Constable really took root. I'm sure that it was a clear case of nostalgia. What other artist can call so well to the exiled's mind the England of his youth?[14]

Over a period of fifty-five years he built a collection of more than three hundred works, a labor of love enacted one object at a time. His acquisitions were instinctive and highly personal, not accompanied by a flock of curators or consultants. Although this publication documents the collection as a synthetic entity, Sir Edwin never set out to create a well-balanced, representative grouping. As he once claimed, "none of this was planned, it just happened."[15] He bought what he liked out of pure affinity rather than to fill in gaps. The impressively organized, complete records of his purchases, which include voluminous correspondence with dealers, are not filled with highbrow discussion of art historical vagaries, but the stuff of everyday life like family, work, and paying taxes. Little is said about the fact that the vast majority of his collection comprised landscapes. His love for representations of the countryside of his childhood helped Sir Edwin remain spiritually close to a land that was far removed geographically.

In fact, his decades of acquiring art were so private that no one was able to see the entirety of the British collection until 2007, when the Manton Foundation gave the collection to the Clark. Asked about his tendency toward privacy, be it charitable giving or art purchases, Sir Edwin explained with characteristic humor and modesty: "I made my gifts anonymous to protect myself. It was not a noble feeling."[16] Sir Edwin and Lady Manton were fundamentally not interested in public recognition, but steadfastly avoided it.

Sir Edwin's first acquisition (fig. 8) was in 1949 from a now-defunct gallery and auction house in New York, Kende Galleries. Kende sold Manton a painting then attributed to Constable, a work now designated in the "style of" that artist. The story of his first acquisition has a rather surprising twist, which Manton enjoyed telling. In his typically self-effacing manner, Sir Edwin wrote in the 1994 introduction to the first publication on his Constable collection:

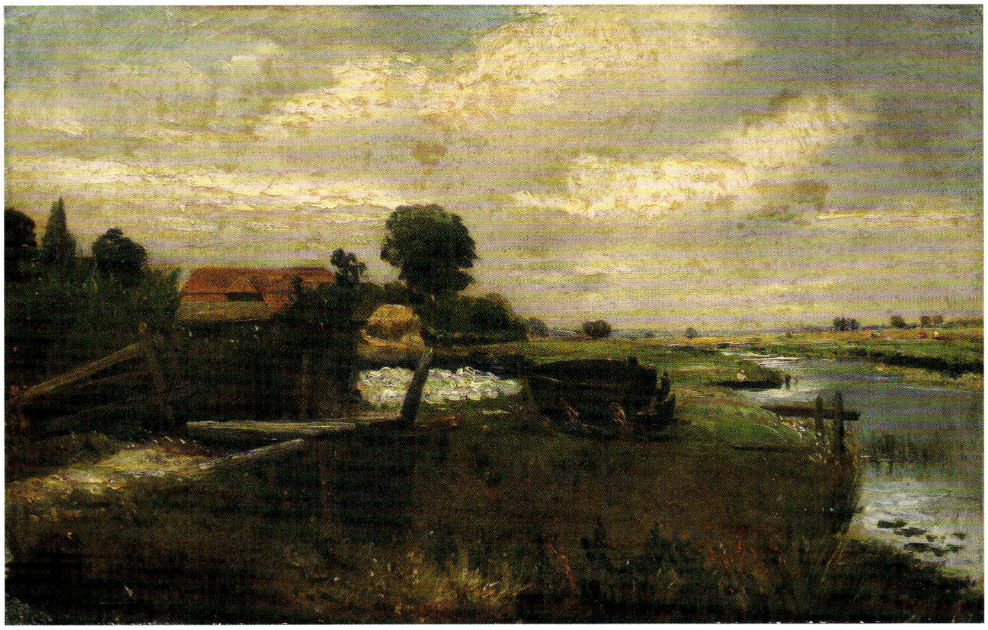

Fig. 8 Style of John Constable (British, 19th century), *River View*. Oil on canvas, 30 × 45.8 cm (no. 84)

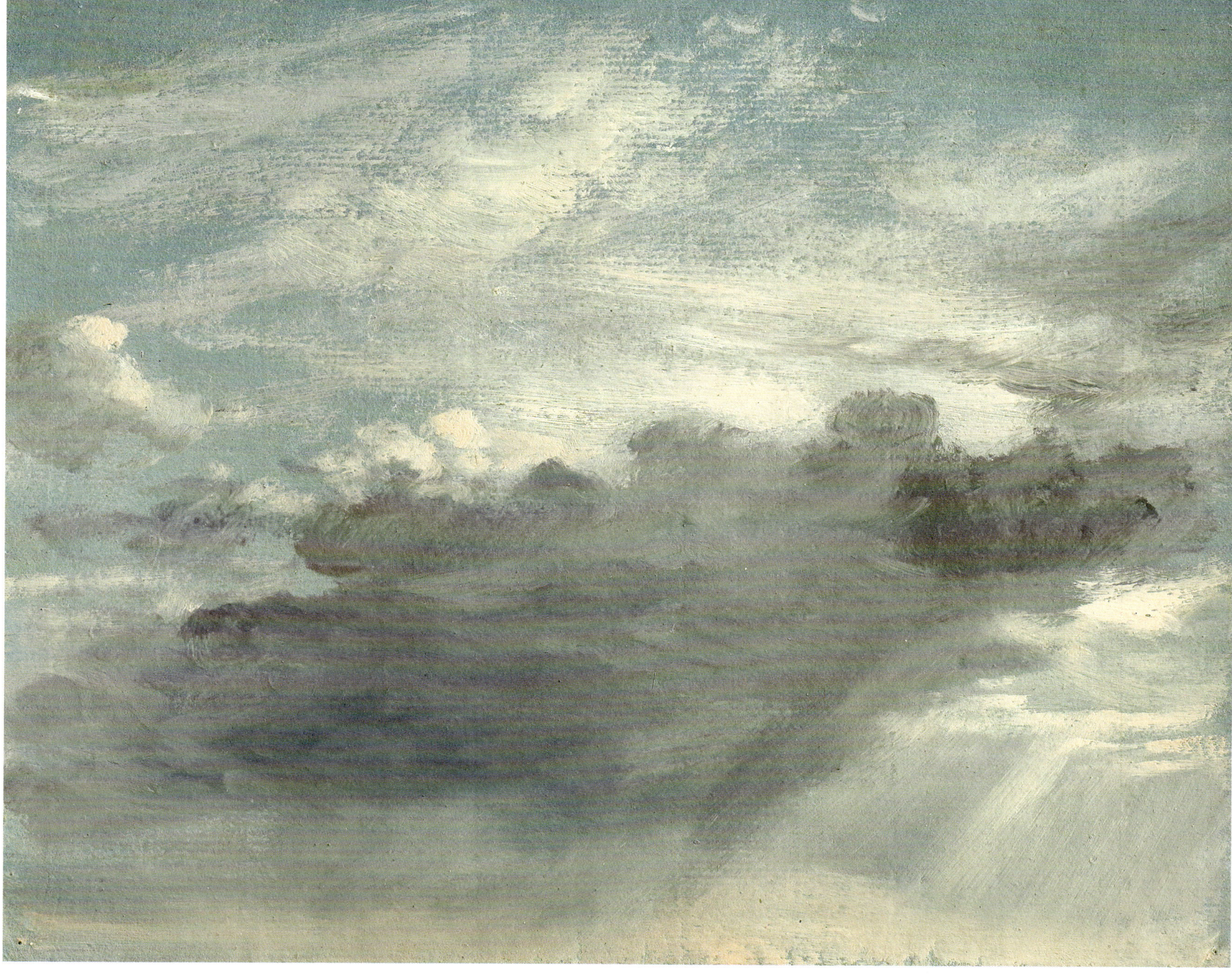

In the 1940s New York sported a reputable evening paper called "The Sun." One day my wife drew my attention to an article illustrated with a photograph of a Constable "View on the Stour"; from an Austrian collection seized by the Austrian state and deposited at the Linz Museum because the owner was Jewish. Liberated by the American Army Fine Arts Commission, it had been restored to the widow, who was shortly to sell it. I bought my first "Konstable" at the auction – not a very propitious beginning to my pursuit of nostalgia![17]

Fig. 9 John Constable (English, 1776–1837), *Cloud Study*, c. 1821–22. Oil on cream laid paper, mounted on canvas, 27.5 × 32.7 cm (no. 60)

Equally significant is the fact that Manton kept this "Konstable" all his life, even after he knew it was no longer signature. As he said in 1997, "I was right about fifty percent of the time," referring to his mistakes as "Constabiles."[18] As his granddaughter Sandra Niles explained, adventures with "the mistakes were as fun ... as the real things."[19] It was only in 1983, after acquiring over fifteen works by (or attributed to) the artist, that Manton connected with the Constable scholar and Tate curator Leslie Parris. They developed a close friendship and, over the course of three decades, worked through the various attribution puzzles. Although Parris did not direct Manton's decisions on what to buy, he connected Manton with numerous scholars to aid him in his quest to learn more about his growing collection.[20] Manton learned from his mistakes and went on to build one of the most important Constable collections in private hands. Rather than being embarrassed about his "Constabiles," he had an insatiable curiosity to learn more about them. In a letter to Parris in 1986 about the Constable scholar Ian Fleming-Williams then writing on *Flailing Turnip-heads* (see fig. 94), Sir Edwin mused: "I think it is marvelous to have a serious scholar write about pictures and thus develop a great deal more information about them than I could possibly learn on my own. I say this even though it sometimes lead[s] to a re-attribution!"[21]

The next Constable acquisition, made in 1958, was the luminous and atmospheric *Cloud Study* (fig. 9), from among a group of works the artist executed during the summer and fall months of 1821 and 1822 in Hampstead. Immensely sought after today as examples of Constable's virtuosic depictions of nature, in the 1950s these sketches had yet to be "discovered" by an art historical world obsessed with Impressionist plein air painting and its historical precedents.[22] As Manton wrote to Peter Johnson, then of Leggatt Brothers, after its purchase:

I am very pleased with the Constable sketch you sold me. You will be amused to know that the best place to look at it is lying on the floor, since one gets the best impression of the light coming from behind the clouds.... I am indeed interested in the sketches because

I think that they are the best part of Constable's work anyway, and not unimportantly, because his pictures [oil paintings] usually fetch prices beyond my reach.[23]

Manton would go on to acquire eight Constables that featured skies and over forty additional sketches from nature. His opinion that these sketches were "the best part of Constable's work" was not always prevalent. While historians have focused on the specific sites depicted and the evolutionary process from sketch to finished work, less attention has been paid to the market for the oil sketches. For most collectors around 1800, an age when verisimilitude and "finish" was in vogue, the open brushwork and fresh, annotative appearance of Constable's oil sketches were not greatly prized. The artist was also reluctant to sell them, remarking he would part with the corn (the final product) but not with the field that grew it (his outdoor sketches). But as the craze for "unfinish" developed from the 1880s onwards, the market and popular appreciation for Constable's oil studies grew steadily.[24] Related to this popularity was the rise of Impressionist painting and the scholarly connections made between them and Constable's plein air practice.

Manton was also interested in the conservation and scientific underpinnings of his collection. Constable was known to have inscribed the date and weather conditions at the moment of their execution on the back of his cloud studies. A work in the Yale Center for British Art, *Study of Altocumulus Clouds* (1821), is annotated by the artist: "Septr 13th. One o'clock. Slight wind at North West, which became tempestuous in the afternoon. With rain all the night following."[25] Many years after purchasing *Cloud Study*, Manton brought the sketch to Marjorie Shelley, Paper Conservator at the Metropolitan Museum of Art, to whom he often turned for assistance with conservation or with questions about technique. He wanted to inquire if there was any way to see the annotations on the back of the sketch, which had been mounted to canvas. Upon consideration she explained that the only way would be with an infrared camera, which the department did not have. After Manton asked how much one would cost, and was given the figure, "in no time flat he had sent a check to the museum to purchase it.... Having that piece of equipment transformed this department."[26] On another occasion, Shelley told him about Raman Spectroscopy, a spectroscopic technique in which light vibrations are studied by looking through a device, thereby avoiding the need to take samples. Unsolicited, Manton asked Shelley to send him a proposal and, soon thereafter, he bought one for the paper lab. This gift made the Metropolitan Museum of Art the first museum in North America to own such a costly piece of equipment. Possibly as a nod to his affection for the paper conservators and the knowledge they imparted about his drawings, Manton also donated funds to the museum to acquire an important watercolor by Thomas Girtin, *St. Paul's Cathedral from St. Martin's-le-Grand* (c. 1795).[27] Manton's interest in methods, materials, and the science of conservation exemplifies his endless curiosity and desire to educate his eye.

Another early "Constabile," purchased in 1962, which later was proven to be by the amateur soldier-artist James Gubbins Archer-Burton and was retitled *Woodlands, Emsworth, Hampshire* (fig. 10), shows how Manton enjoyed using art historical evidence to slowly learn about his acquisitions over time. The painting was originally presumed to be a depiction by Constable of Rockstone Place in Southampton. Woodlands was the home of Constable's cousin Mrs. Lancelot Archer-Burton (née Gubbins), Archer-Burton's mother. He was said to have been taught to paint by Constable or Constable's son Lionel. In 1983 Manton began corresponding with Archer-Burton's heir, and the attribution was corrected from annotations on the back of the canvas.[28] The descendant even provided the name of Archer-Burton's dog "Beau," depicted in the right foreground. As Manton opined of his efforts to nail down this tricky attribution, it "led to a delightful exchange of correspondence with his descendant Lt.-Col. James Archer-Burton, O.B.E."[29]

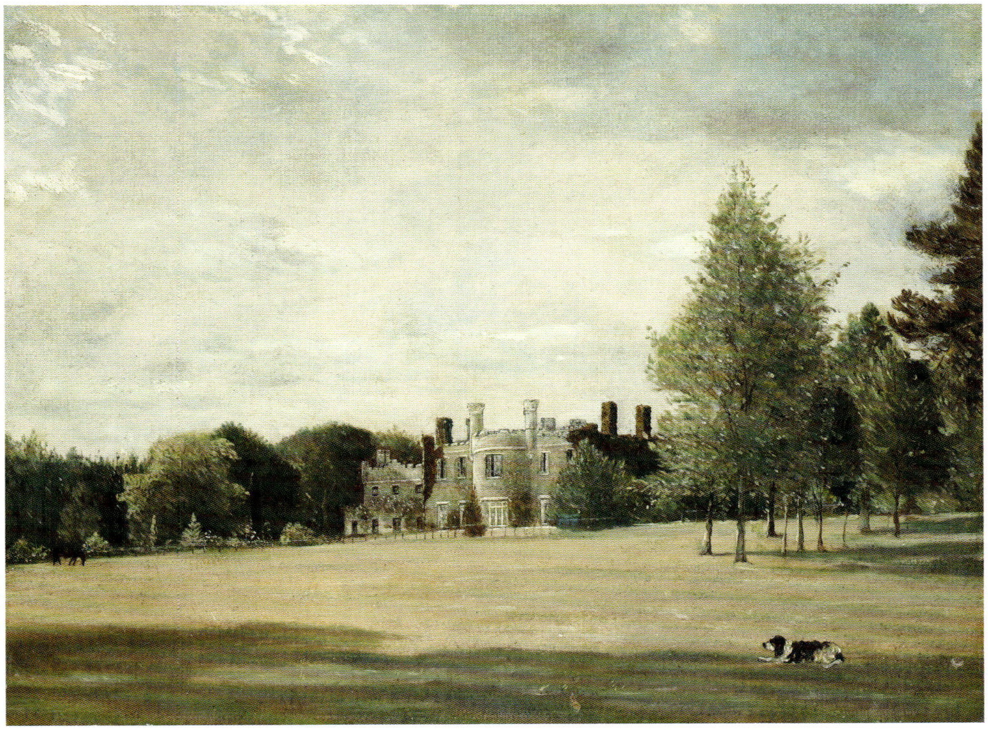

Fig. 10 James Gubbins Archer-Burton (English, 1800–1875), *Woodlands, Emsworth, Hampshire*, c. 1850. Oil on wood-pulp board, 22.8 × 30.3 cm (no. 1)

This "delightful" correspondence and personal elucidation of his picture was more important to Manton than de-attribution of the Constable.

Following these initial purchases in New York, Manton shifted gears and began to buy from highly regarded dealers specializing in British art based in London. It is entirely possible that he shifted attention to British dealers after having bought spurious works in New York. Or perhaps the British dealers simply had more inventory. The fact that his core group of dealers remained small points to the importance he placed on these relationships. Manton's primary contacts between the 1950s and 1980s were the Leggatt Brothers Gallery, Oscar and Peter Johnson, Ltd., Ackermann, Spink and Son, Spink-Leger, and Leger. He occasionally bought at auction from Parke-Bernet in New York, using his dealers as representatives to maintain his anonymity.[30]

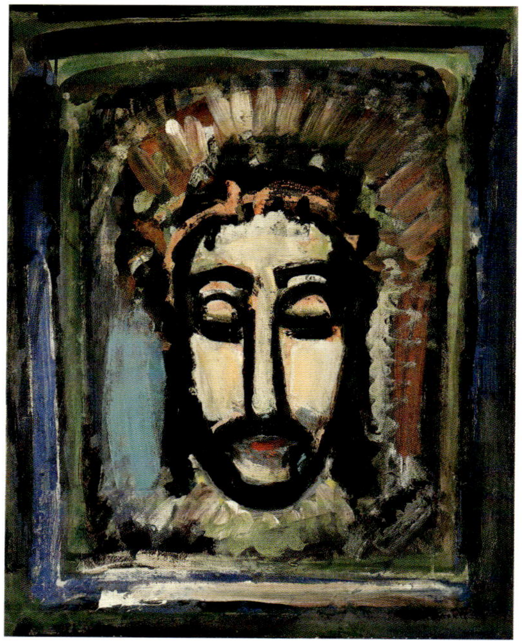

As Lowell Libson, formerly of Spink-Leger, explained of his buying trips: Manton would "arrive on the morning train at Victoria and wander across the park and hitch up at the gallery at about 9 o'clock in the morning ... unannounced, and he'd look at whatever we had, probably buy something, and wander off ... but it was a very sort of informal, easy relationship. He was a really sweet and delightful man."[31] There was no agenda of forming a representative collection, filling in holes, or trophy hunting. His purchases were instinctive and made for pure enjoyment, rather than from an academic or intellectual perspective. While dealers would try to sell him a drawing or oil sketch they "thought" would appeal to him, Manton only bought what he liked, and was never swayed by art historical arguments alone. As Libson recalled, "he was buying British pictures purely for his own enjoyment, and as a hugely private activity, which was a form of nostalgia for the England that he'd left behind many decades before."[32]

During this early period of collecting Sir Edwin was not the only one buying art. The Mantons also acquired works by other schools, including prints, drawings, and paintings by modern European and Japanese artists. For example, in the 1950s they acquired the oil painting *Christ of the Incas* (fig. 11) by Georges Rouault.[33] They also acquired an unusual seascape by Gustave Courbet painted on a palette (fig. 12). In 1972 Parke-Bernet held a benefit auction of duplicate prints from the Brooklyn Museum, when Sir Edwin and Lady Manton bought four prints, among them Manet's *The Spanish Singer* (1861). As always, they selected works based on instinct and preference, and their broad and eclectic tastes are evidenced by the diversity of their collection.

Lady Manton had a special interest in Asian sculptures and works on paper, nineteenth-century printed portraits of artists, and Odilon Redon floral still lifes, which largely comprised the art adorning their home.[34] The British collection was mostly kept in the AIG vaults. The Asian art included *netsuke*, Japanese miniature sculpture, eighteenth- and nineteenth-century Chinese and Japanese hanging scrolls, and Japanese ukiyo-e color woodblock prints. The portrait prints ranged from Édouard Vuillard's *Portrait of Cézanne* (1914), Redon's *Portrait of Maurice Denis* (1903), and Georges Rouault's *Gustave Moreau au Petit Chapeau* (1932), to Tsuguharu Foujita's drypoint *Self-Portrait with Cat on Shoulder* (1927), and Leonard Baskin's *Portrait of Courbet* (1969). Lady Manton always wanted a Redon floral still life and, by 2000, they owned the oil painting *The Rose and the Daisy* and several lithographs by the French Symbolist.[35]

Manton remained prudent about his purchases into the 1990s. He knew the market well, and dealers avoided overcharging him. His dealer correspondence is full of amusing anecdotes about prices, payments, and taxes. For example, in 1965 he wrote to Peter Johnson about a Gainsborough: "Please reserve it and I will pay you when my ship comes in (the S.S. Good Fortune currently estimated to dock on or about December 10)."[36] Writing the following year of the payment due for Constable's sensitive wash drawing *Caister Castle, Norfolk* (no. 66), he added, "Now I'm going to look for the gold at the end of the rainbow to pay for my castle."[37] Even after he reached the point when he had the means to acquire more readily, Sir Edwin remained cautious. As he wrote to Parris in 1991, a dealer "has just offered me a tiny Bonington sketch at £300,000 [then over $500,000]. I think he has a nerve!"[38] On the occasion of the Tate's major Constable retrospective in 1991, Manton had to establish insurance values for his works prior to travel. As he relayed to Parris and Serota, he was shocked by the rising prices of Constable's work, and lamented the fact that he may no longer be able to afford them.[39] Writing a year later to former Yale Center for British Art Curator Patrick Noon, he informed him of a happy discovery: "Last week I went to pick up a number of Rowlandson drawings that [Marjorie Shelley] had been attending to and received a most pleasant surprise. The first Rowlandson I ever bought [in 1958] is a chophouse scene, *Mutton Chops in Maiden Lane*

Fig. 11 Georges Rouault (1871–1958), *Christ of the Incas*, c. 1930s. Oil on paper mounted on canvas, 65.1 × 50.2 cm. Smith College Museum of Art, Northampton, Mass. Bequest of Florence V. Manton, through the generosity of Sir Edwin Manton and Diana Morton (Diana Manton, class of 1960) SC 2003:28

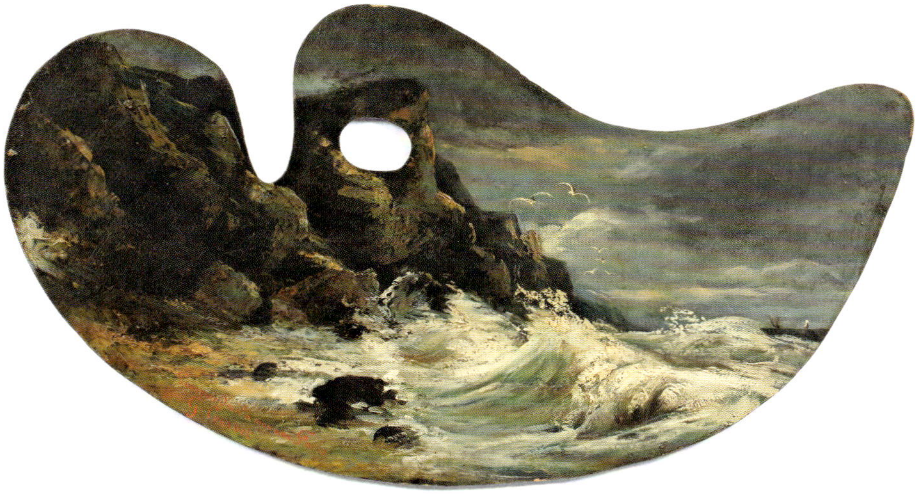

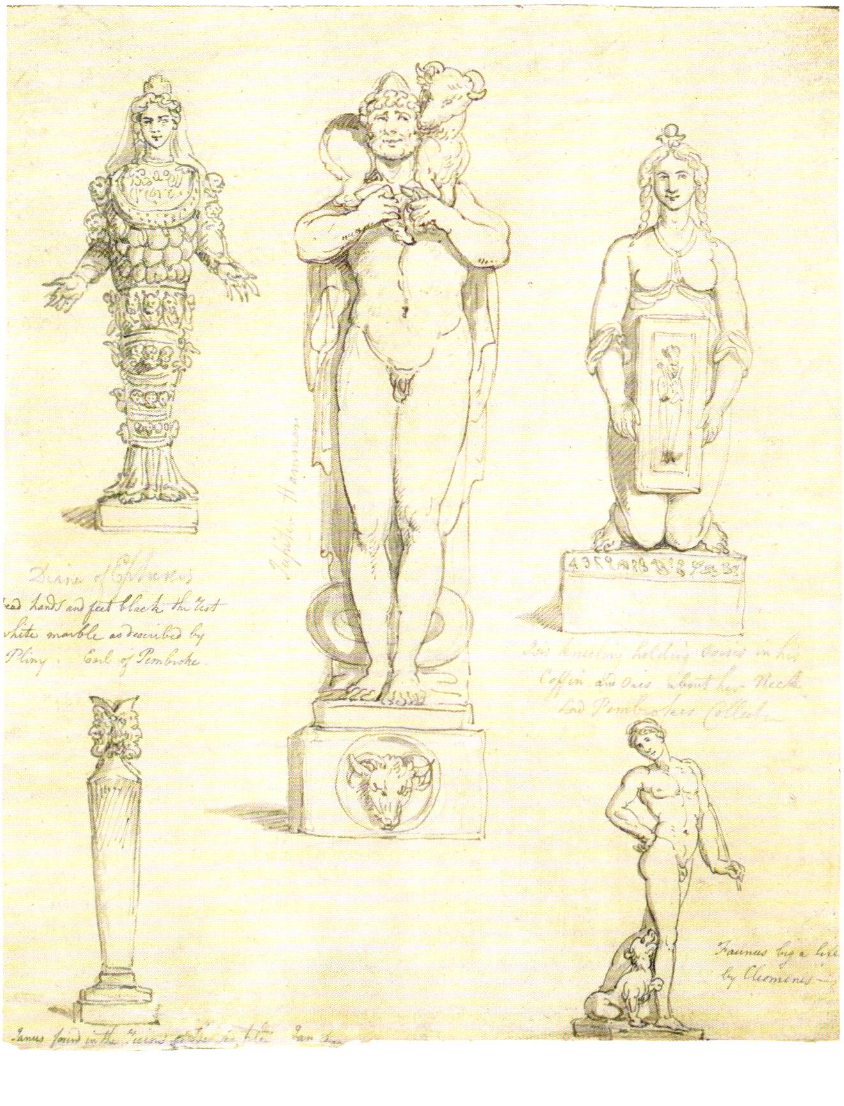

Diana of Ephesus
head hands and feet black the rest
white marble as described by
Pliny . Earl of Pembroke
Jupiter Hammon
Isis kneeling holding Osiris in her
Coffin and Osiris about her Neck
Lord Pembrokes Collection
Faunus big a life
by Cleomenes

(see fig. 73). Lo and behold, Marjorie found on the back a study of classical figures (fig. 13) beautifully drawn. I remember paying something like £200 [then about $325], and to find that I purchased two for the price of one is a stroke of good fortune."[40] This attention to monetary care perhaps came from his modest upbringing, as well as professional fiduciary reserve.

Sir Edwin, as Libson recounted was "extremely humorous. And he loved a good joke. He had the drollest and driest sense of humor ... and I think that some of the more subtle drawings by Rowlandson of character and incidents immensely appealed to his incredibly good-humored view of life."[41] Upon first glance, the impressive group of Rowlandson sheets may seem anomalous in the collection. However, Rowlandson has always exemplified a typically British sense of humor, especially to those of Manton's generation. In Rowlandson's work, the variety and complexity of British character is described through caricatural episodes, perhaps representing the nature of what it means to be British more realistically than the most serious history painting.[42] *Peregrine Rescuing Emilia from the Inn Fire* (fig. 14), which depicts a scene from Tobias Smollett's novel *The Adventures of Peregrine Pickle* (1751), includes all the elements of Rowlandson's caricatural inventory: a dog pulling on a vain French officer's long braid, a man leering up a woman's skirt, a gout-ridden older gentleman, and a chamber pot being unceremoniously emptied on an unassuming person's head.[43] Manton also admired the more rare non-caricatural Rowlandsons, such as the luminous *Wooded Hilly Landscape with Cottage and Figures* (no. 201) of 1809. The artist's bravura use of wash heightened with marks in squiggly vermillion ink must have appealed to Manton as a collector of landscape drawings.

Another collector and philanthropist who shared a love of Rowlandson and many of the artists Manton collected was Paul Mellon (1907–1999).[44] The son of Andrew W. Mellon and heir to the Mellon Bank fortune, he began buying British art in the 1930s, and his efforts gained momentum in the 1960s, at which time he promised his collection to the Yale Center for British Art and donated funds to construct the Louis Kahn building to house it. It was precisely in the heyday of Mellon's collecting that Manton first recalled being thwarted by this man with deeper pockets. As Manton reported of this time:

My inexperience was not the sole obstacle to reaching the goal of acquiring a modest Constable collection ... I had come up against Mr. Mellon, who so successfully wielded a vacuum cleaner for a number of years on amassing a museum full of English pictures, which I now have the privilege of visiting from time to time to shed a tear at what might have been.[45]

Fig. 12 Gustave Courbet (French, 1819–1877), *Waves Crashing on a Rocky Shore*, c. 1875. Oil on panel, 36.5 × 67 cm. Private collection

Fig. 13 Thomas Rowlandson (English, 1756–1827), *Studies of Classical and Egyptian Figures*, c. 1817–21. Pen with brown and gray inks, graphite, and watercolor on cream wove paper, 27.8 × 21.7 cm (no. 196, verso)

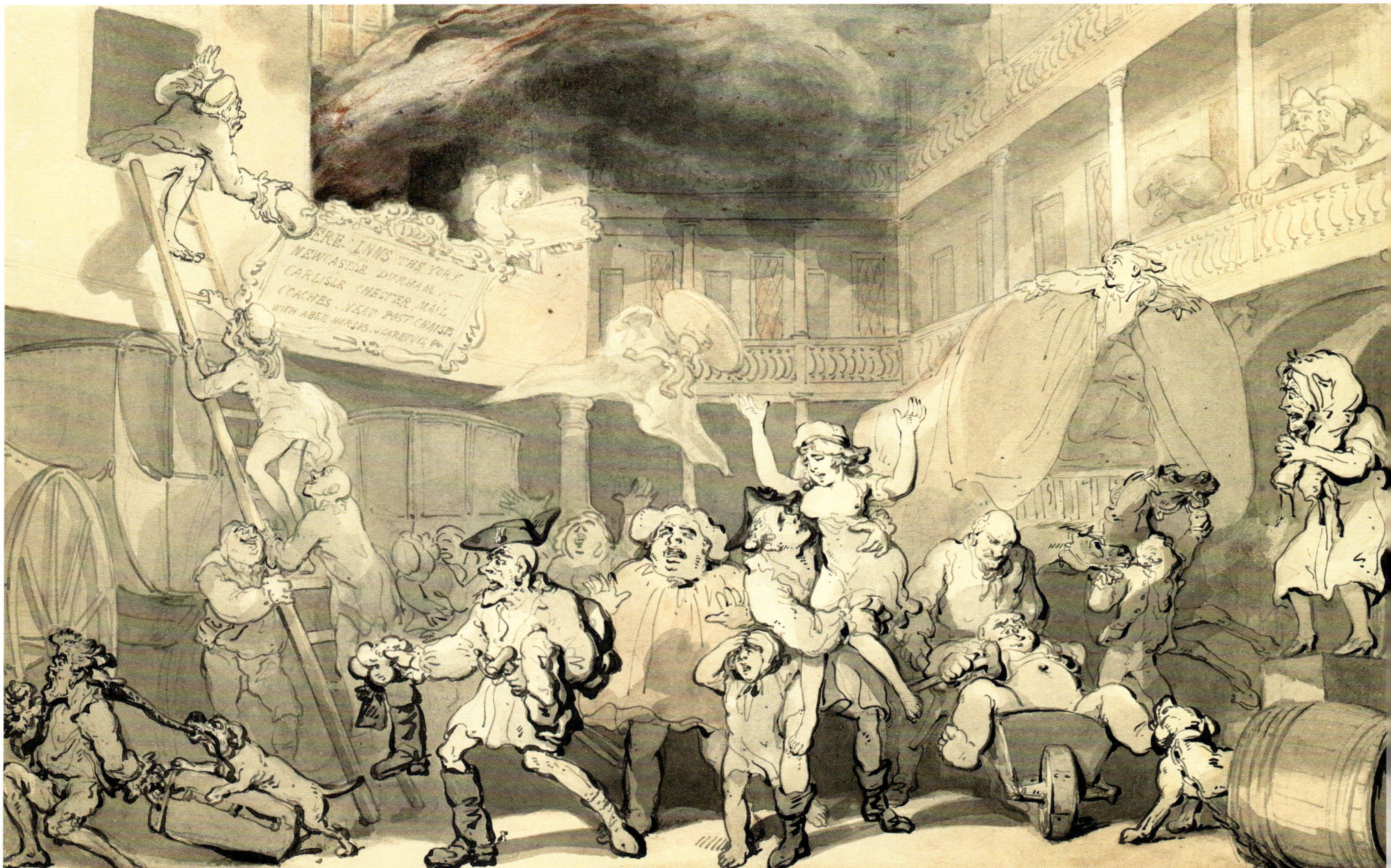

NEWCASTLE DURHAM
CARLISLE CHESTER MAIL
COACHES . NEAT POST CHAISES

As he further remarked in 1963, "I supposed that if you have Mr. Mellon's money almost anything is possible."[46] With characteristic humility, Manton never presented himself to the Yale Center for British Art, despite many visits to his granddaughter Julia, who attended Yale in the 1980s and early 1990s for her Bachelor and Master degrees. However, he did forge a friendship with Noon, a curator at the Center working on the 1991 retrospective of Bonington. As Noon remarked: "Mellon was never ostentatious and Jim never was ... [both were] very dignified and serious collectors. And people who were passionate about what they were collecting, which is crucial."[47] This combination of passion and self-effacement are the hallmarks of Sir Edwin as a man and as a collector.

Fig. 14 Thomas Rowlandson, *Peregrine Rescuing Emilia from the Inn Fire*, c. 1786. Pen and black and gray inks and watercolor over graphite on cream wove paper, 21.6 × 32.8 cm (no. 191)

In some ways Manton's collecting trajectory fit the formula of his generation, and in other ways his choices were less obvious. Throughout the twentieth century, enormous holdings of British art were built by Mellon, Henry Huntington, and others.[48] While their acquisition strategies were ambitious and extravagantly funded, Manton's ambitions were of an entirely different sort. As the dealer Deborah Gage remarked, "he was always an Englishman. In his heart and his emotion he was always an Englishman."[49] Manton's collecting was personal; each artist he collected in depth held special significance to the country of his birth. He related to Constable in particular not only geographically but also because of what Manton perceived as their similar temperaments. Gainsborough's facility as a draftsman was something Manton admired, and he revered "the Englishness of Gainsborough who depicted ... the romantic England [Manton] still imagined was there." Unlike the diverse natural romanticism of Gainsborough or Constable, Manton "went to Turner for excitement ... he was moved by Turner and found in him an evocative, stirring painter."[50] Although his financial circumstances changed over time, Manton's humble origins as a British subject continued to be mirrored in the acquisitions he favored.

During a brief period from 1977 to 1983 Manton expanded his area of collecting to include works by Edward William Cooke and Albert Goodwin. Cooke's atmospheric *Venice at Sunset* (no. 90) exemplifies the artist's debt to Bonington's technique and Turner's subject matter, which he had admired in London.[51] Goodwin's *Afterglow on the Nile* (fig. 15) and *Sinbad the Sailor* (no. 150) connect to the few non-Western subjects in the collection (Goodwin traveled extensively in India and Egypt). *Afterglow on the Nile*, with its high-keyed color, impressionistic approach to facture, and heavily scratched surface, likewise evidences the painter's immense debt to Turner. Another connection can be seen in Goodwin's close friendship with the art critic, amateur artist, and avid Turner apologist and collector John Ruskin.[52]

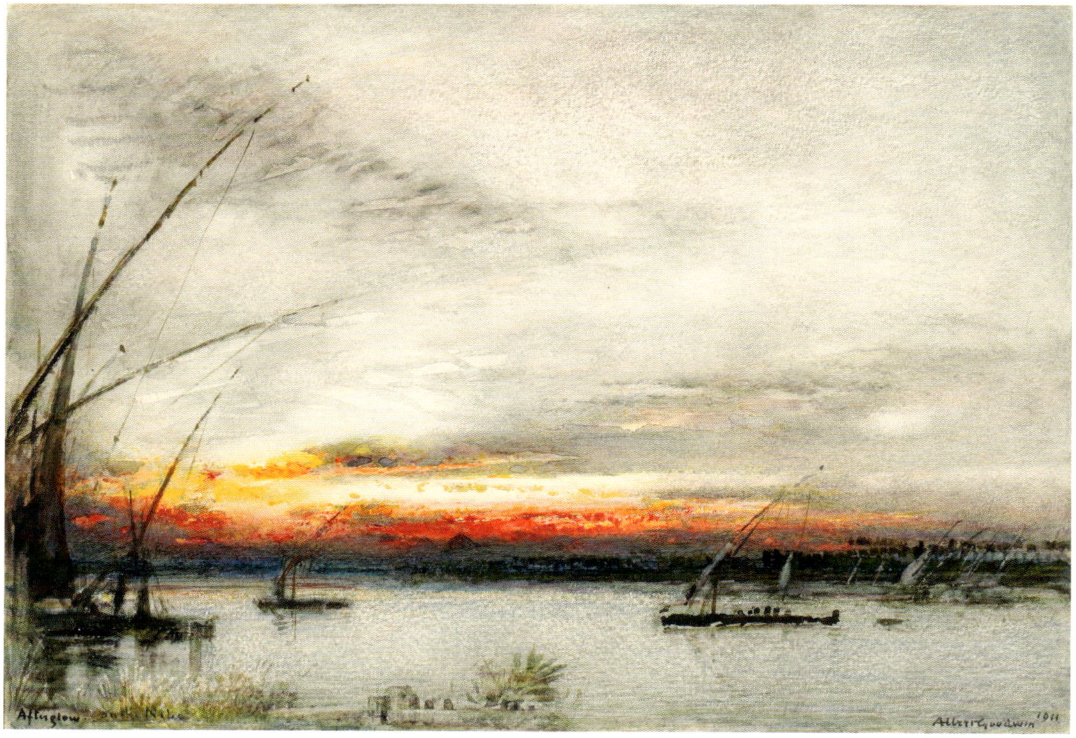
Albert Goodwin 1911

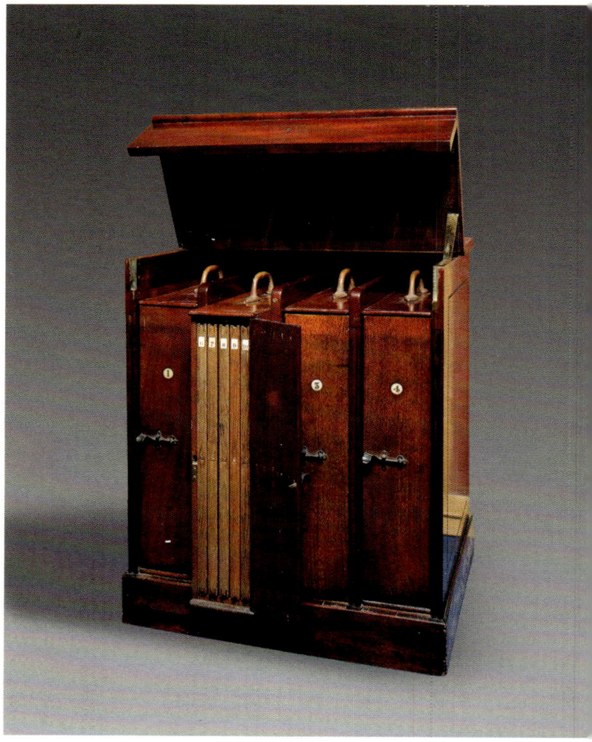

Despite being separated by history, Ruskin and Sir Edwin shared a direct and powerful connection in their admiration for Turner. Additionally, Manton owned not only a drawing by Ruskin (no. 206) but also a rare Turner cabinet designed by Ruskin (fig. 16). An avid collector himself, Ruskin became aware of the deleterious effects of light on watercolors. Starting in the 1860s, he designed and commissioned the production of mahogany cabinets with sliding vertical drawers that could be pulled out to view drawings.[53] As Manton was equally sensitive to conservation concerns, he kept his Turner watercolors in this antique cabinet. In letters and discussions with dealers and conservators, he made numerous requests that they mat a work to "fit" Ruskin's cabinet.[54] As he said to Libson of Turner's *Tower of London* drawing, it "is destined for Ruskin's cabinet, where it should feel at home since Ruskin used it for his Turners."[55] The cabinet was a touchstone to Manton both in his love for the past, a Ruskinian gesture if there ever was one, and his sense of responsibility to preserve these works for future generations. Manton kept his Turner cabinet at home in the living room.

The intensity of Manton's collecting increased over the years in line with his growing interest, financial abilities, and available leisure time. He bought five works in the 1950s, eighteen in the 1960s, twenty two in the 1970s, and fifty two between 1980 and 1992. In the late 1970s Manton's managerial role at AIG shifted from chairman to honorary director and senior advisor, which meant that although he still worked every day, the demands on his time lessened. This period also coincided with a staggeringly exponential increase in the value of his AIG stock holdings. Not only had the value of each share increased, but in the period between 1986 and 2000 the stock split eight times. A single share worth $122 in 1986 had grown to approximately twenty-three shares in 2000, with a value of $2,250.[56]

Sir Edwin's continued focus on Constable, Gainsborough, Rowlandson, and Turner remained strong, but the price points and overall quality of the works he sought to acquire went up a notch as his financial situation improved and his already superb eye gained even more expertise. Works acquired during this period include Rowlandson's *The Cat-astrophy, or Crash to My Grandmother's Old China* (see fig. 74) and *Underwriters or Bad News at Lloyd's Coffee House* (no. 199), a sheet that must have amused him given its reference to the insurance business. The slow and methodical attention he paid to Bonington was boosted by the purchase of a fresh and powerful sheet, *A Fisherman on the Banks of a River, a Church Tower in the Distance* (see fig. 135). Several new, impressive Gainsboroughs were added to the mix, including the magisterial *Rocky Wooded*

Fig. 15 Albert Goodwin (English, 1845–1932), *Afterglow on the Nile*, 1911. Watercolor and gouache, with scraping, on white wove paper, 28.5 × 38.8 cm (no. 149)

Fig. 16 Designed by John Ruskin (English, 1819–1900), made by William and Edward Snell, *Turner Cabinet*, 1861. Mahogany, 77 × 63.4 × 51 cm. Ruskin Foundation. The Manton Turner cabinet is similar to this one, housed in the Ruskin Library at the University of Lancaster.

Fig. 17 John Constable, *Dedham Vale from the Road to East Bergholt: Sunset*, 1810. Oil on paper, mounted on board, mounted on panel, 15.4 × 26 cm (no. 45)

Landscape with Winding Track (see fig. 30). Manton's admiration for Gainsborough signaled his attraction to the mystery of the unfinished, the romantic fascination for the openly evocative, non-descriptive sketch.

Sir Edwin's steady admiration for Turner's jewel-like watercolors continued with the purchase of *View of La Riccia (Ariccia)* (see fig. 86) and gained a new geographic perspective with *Hoolay Deedy, Seringapatam* (see fig. 85). He acquired his second Turner oil, the atmospheric *View off Margate, Evening* (see fig. 93) in 1998. The speed with which he acquired the Turner oil suggests the immediacy of Manton's decisiveness. When Libson brought the canvas to New York, Manton walked into the space and "he looked at it for about three or four minutes, I . . . gave him my oft totally unnecessary art historical build . . . and then he said to me, 'It's an awful lot of money Lowell [about $1.3 million].' And I said, 'Well, I'm afraid it is.' He thought about it for about ten seconds and then remarked, 'And when would you want to be paid?' And I simply told him and he looked at the picture for four or five minutes more and then begged to leave. I was slightly confused. I said, 'Jim, do you want it?' 'Yes, of course,' he said, 'send me the invoice.'"[57] This charm and decisiveness characterized all his acquisitions, from the smallest to the most impressive and costly.

Fig. 18 John Constable, *Yarmouth Jetty*, c. 1822–23. Oil on canvas, 32.4 × 51.1 cm (no. 64)

Manton's passion for Constable's oil sketches continued unabated. These numerous works ranged from the small-scale oil study of a farmer returning from the fields at day's end, *Dedham Vale from the Road to East Bergholt: Sunset* (fig. 17), to the larger, finished seascape *Yarmouth Jetty* (fig. 18). During this period Sir Edwin also bought seminal, singular statements by artists not yet represented in the collection. One of these is Samuel Palmer's evocative and visionary exhibition piece *The Setting Sun* (fig. 19), which marks not only Manton pushing the bounds of his Romantic watercolor holdings, but also his moving further into the century while still maintaining a devotion to landscape.

The personal and unceremonious manner in which he enjoyed his collection transferred to his acquisition process. When Manton made the decision to buy a major watercolor by Girtin, *The Gatehouse of Battle Abbey, Sussex* (see fig. 114), he remarked on his reasons to Anthony Spink in 1999:

My choice, I think, would be Girtin's Battle Abbey *for two reasons. I know the Abbey pretty well because my brother lives at Battle, and I have a few Girtins, and adding this item would enrich the collection and costs much less than the others. My problem at the moment is that I am confronted by two great obstacles – my obligation to remit to you [about $53,000] in the next few days and a presently unknown income tax payable in April.*[58]

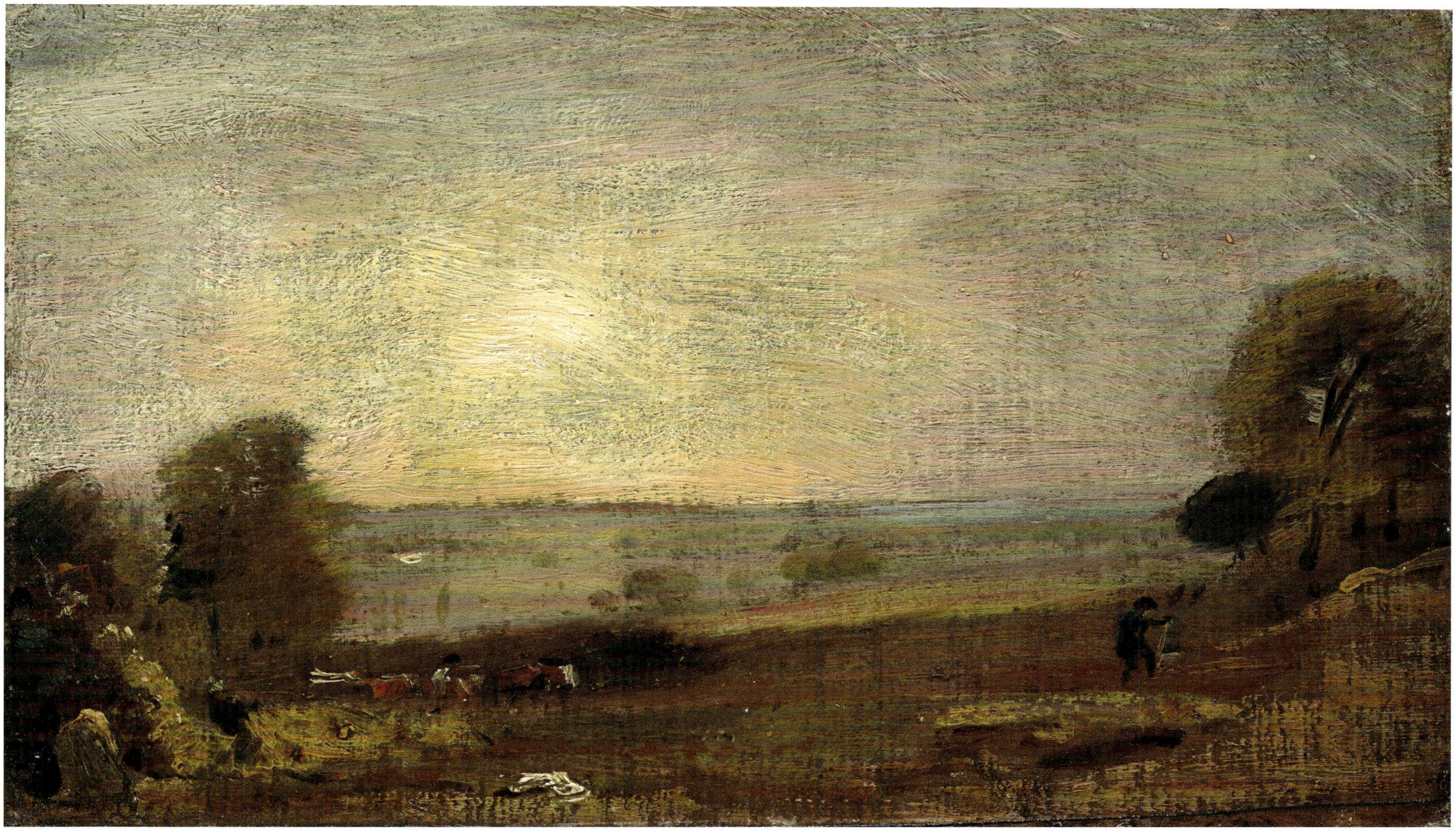

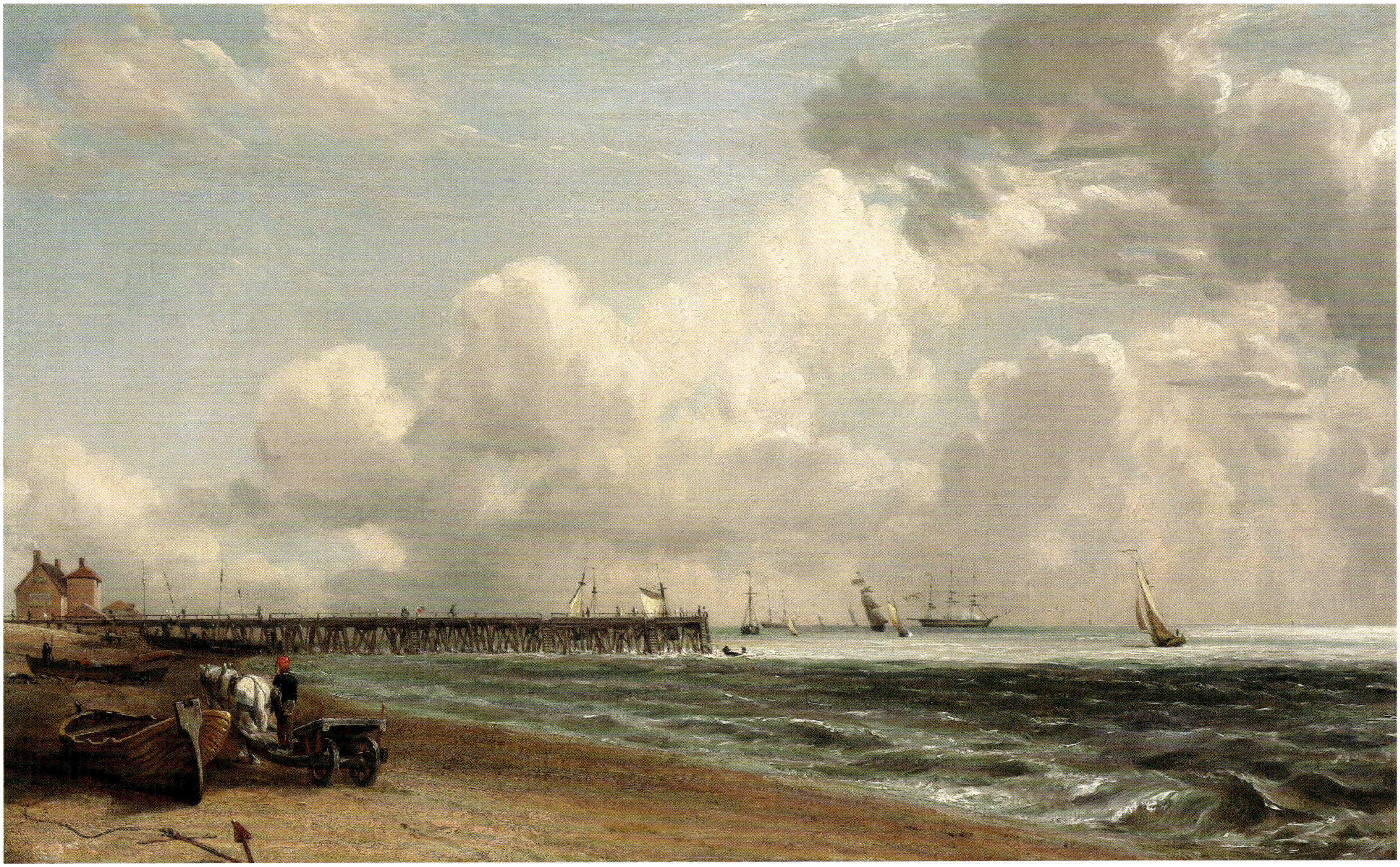

Fig. 19 Samuel Palmer (English, 1805–1881), *The Setting Sun*, c. 1862. Watercolor and gouache, with touches of shell gold and scraping, on cream wove paper, 52.5 × 72.5 (no. 187)

Fig. 20 Thomas Girtin (English, 1775–1802), *Lydford Castle*, c. 1800. Watercolor and gouache over graphite on white laid paper, 31.8 × 52.1 cm (no. 145)

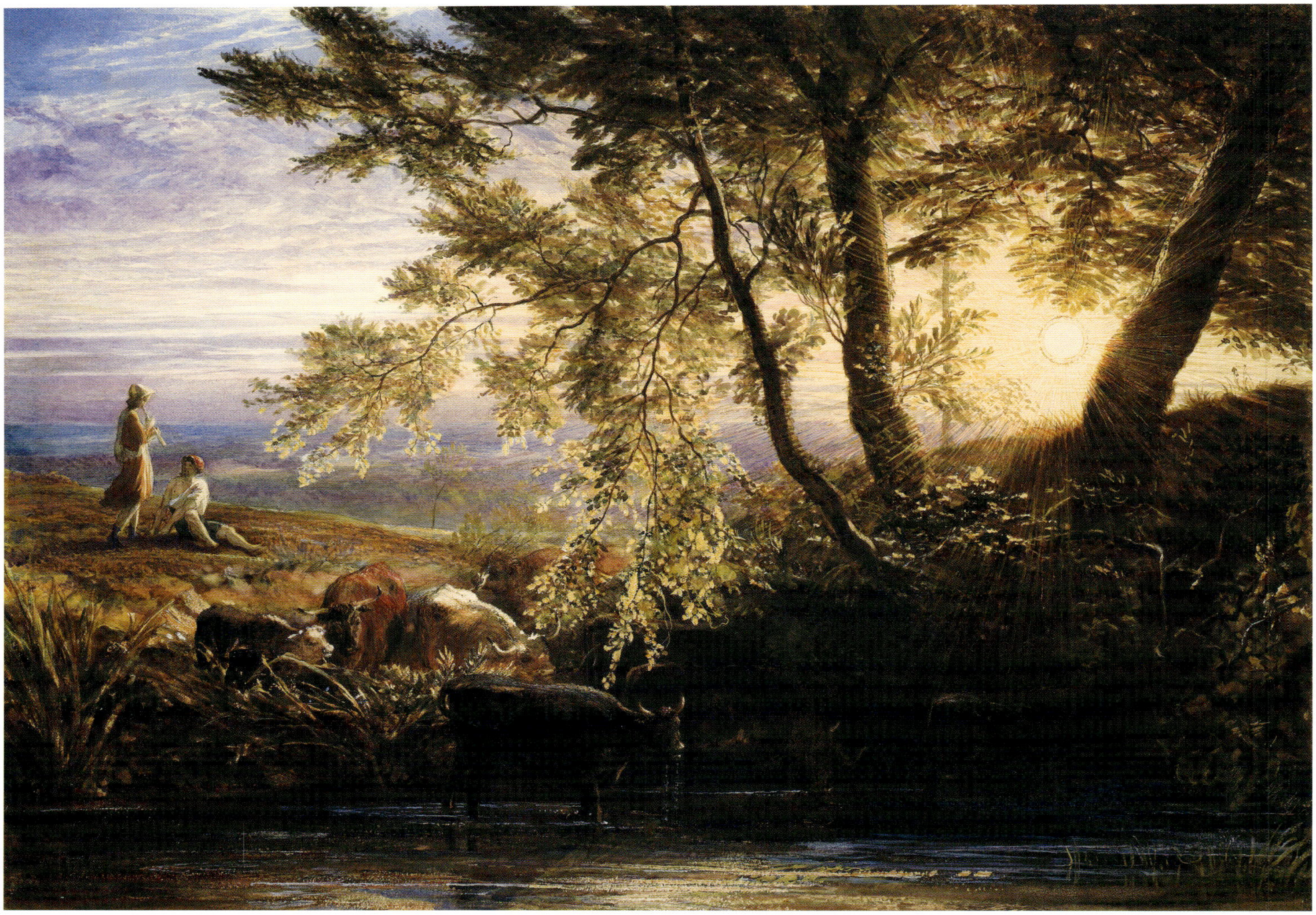

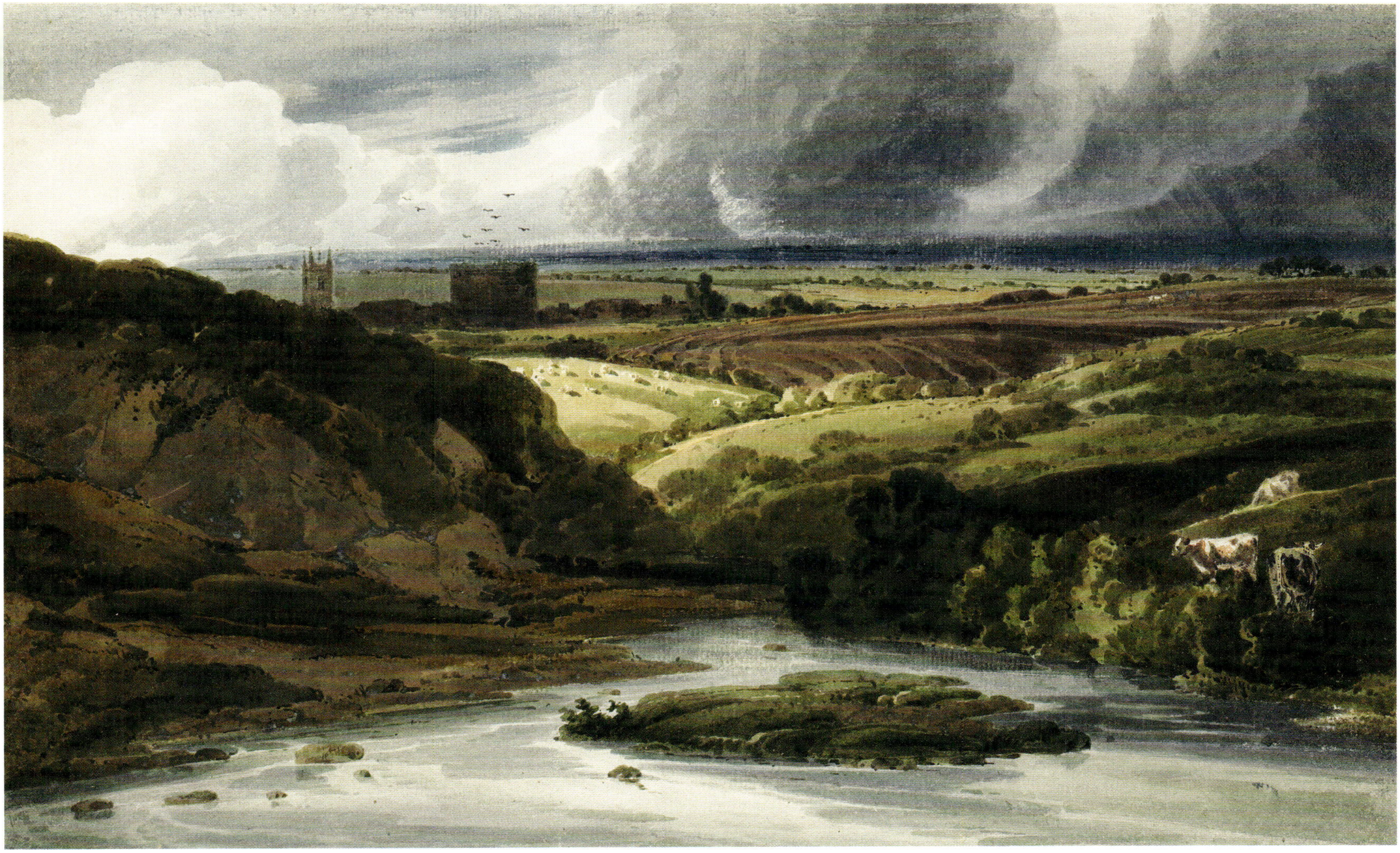

The basics are covered in this letter: his personal experience of seeing Battle Abbey on visits to his brother, admiration for the artist, and the pesky issue of tax payments. It is interesting to note that nine years prior, when Manton bought the magnificent Girtin watercolor *Lydford Castle* in 1990 (fig. 20) for twelve times the price of *Battle Abbey*, there was no mention of the tax man. He simply loved the work and bought it.

The care Sir Edwin took to maintain his privacy and the modest and unassuming manner in which he and Lady Manton lived was paralleled in the way they displayed and stored their collection of British art. Most of the collection was kept in a large vault in the basement of the AIG building, which one of his grandchildren affectionately referred to as the "Fortress." AIG's founder had a similarly rich art collection, so this facility was climate and humidity controlled with built-in security systems. Only a few of the paintings and drawings were hung in their home, the limited number being confirmed by the 2000 inventory and reports by family members.[59]

The British art collection was brought out and discussed frequently at the AIG headquarters. Dealers and curators fondly recall visiting his spacious and light-filled office for lunch, where there would be scores of framed objects propped against the walls for discussion about attribution puzzles. When the art dealer Deborah Gage broached the topic of installing more art in his home around 2000 in order to enjoy it daily, he replied, "I do. Judy brings them up every day."[60] By this he meant that his assistant, Judy Caruso, would retrieve objects from the vault upon request for viewing. Noon recalls his first visit to the office: "He had a big office and [on] two or three of the walls in the office were ... stacked on the floor facing in against the wall, framed drawings, five or ten deep."[61] The curator and the collector simply went through them, one by one, and then they were returned to the vault.

Only once did the Mantons exhibit a significant portion of their collection. In 2000 the Salmagundi Club mounted a show that included over thirty of their Constable paintings, oil sketches, and drawings. The club, among the oldest arts organizations in America, was an important social outlet for them. Mounted to mark the 130th anniversary of the club, *Constable at the Salmagundi Club* was curated by two artist members and accompanied by a small catalogue.[62] As the preface to the modest publication stated: "The Salmagundi Club is unique. It is a place where people can view exhibitions of working artists of today, as well as the past, in a conversational environment."[63] As former Tate curator Andrew Wilton said, "he went public there in a way he never did otherwise. So he would go to the Salmagundi as, in a sense, an extension of his own drawing room."[64] It was in this elegant yet unassuming environment that Manton showed the world, or at least New Yorkers, his art for the first time.[65]

It was not just early British pictures that Manton acquired in his later years, he also had an interest in contemporary art. In 1983 he bought a painting by the famed British portraitist John Wonnacott from the Marlborough Gallery titled *Thames Estuary Window: High Summer* (fig. 21). In a letter several years later to the artist, Manton explained his very personal reaction to the picture:

You might like to know it depicts a scene familiar to me as I lived nearby as a boy. One of my earliest memories related to the Great War. In the summer of 1914, a R.[oyal] N.[avy] squadron visited the mouth of the Thames and my parents had promised to take me to a firework display put on by the fleet. Alas, it never took place, as Churchill, the First Lord, ordered them to sea in anticipation of the War's outbreak. The painting now graces the wall of my office. If you come to New York, you must come to lunch and look at it.[66]

Manton and Wonnacott lunched in his office soon after the letter was sent, and one can imagine them looking at the painting and reminiscing, Manton of his childhood, and Wonnacott of the girl with the "glorious head of red hair" that walked across the center of the canvas.[67] The connections were further strengthened by the fact that Wonnacott's studio was situated overlooking the Thames Estuary, just as was Manton's boyhood home.[68] Artist and patron became friends, and Wonnacott did several drawings and three unfinished oil sketches of Manton from life. In 2006, a group of donors asked Wonnacott to complete one of these portrait sketches (fig. 22), which they then donated to the Tate in recognition of Manton's immense generosity to the museum. In it, the *Thames Estuary Window: High Summer* painting is visible behind his head. This portrait, perhaps more than any other of the collector, captures his kind and affable nature.

Sir Edwin and Lady Manton created the American Fund for the Tate Gallery in 1987, a restricted endowment to acquire contemporary art from North and South America. This long and fruitful relationship with the Tate began through Manton's friendship with Parris, who, in 1987 suggested that the Mantons donate funds for the Tate to acquire Constable's *The Opening of Waterloo Bridge ("Whitehall Stairs, June 18th, 1817")* and thus save it from export. It was fitting that the museum should approach them, as the Mantons owned two studies for the large canvas.[69] Afterwards the couple established the American Fund with a large gift of AIG shares. Tate director Serota explains this gesture as a "natural expression of Jim being English and wanting to reconnect ties

Clockwise from top left:

Fig. 22 John Wonnacott, *Portrait of Jim Manton*, 2000. Oil on canvas, 61 × 51 cm. Tate, London

Fig. 21 John Wonnacott (English, b. 1940), *Thames Estuary Window: High Summer*, 1980–82. Oil on canvas mounted on board, 106.8 × 182.9 cm, Private collection

Fig. 24 Sir Edwin Manton with a bust of Henry Tate, Tate, London, c. 2000

Fig. 23 Louise Bourgeois (American, b. France, 1911–2010), *Cell (Eyes and Mirrors)*, 1989–93. Marble, mirrors, steel, and glass, 236.2 × 210.8 × 218.4 cm. Tate, London. Presented by the American Fund for the Tate Gallery, 1994. Art © Louise Bourgeois Trust/Licensed by VAGA, New York

between the U.S. and the U.K."[70] Both Sir Edwin and Lady Manton came to every meeting, encouraging this cultural exchange both monetarily and through service work. Over time, the fund had has supported the acquisition of major works by Louise Bourgeois (fig. 23), Philip Guston, Ellsworth Kelly, David Smith, and Dorothea Tanning.[71] The Mantons were particularly pleased with the purchase of Tanning as she lived in their building in Manhattan. In addition, they bequeathed a major Constable painting, *Glebe Farm* (c. 1830), which was given to the Tate upon Sir Edwin's death.

Their generosity continued in the form of monetary gifts to the Tate's centenary building projects, particularly the construction of Tate Britain, where the Constables, Gainsboroughs, and Turners Manton so loved hang in great number. All told, the astounding munificence Manton showed to the Tate made him the most significant benefactor to the institutions since Henry Tate himself (fig. 24). In 1994, in recognition of his charitable services to the Tate, Manton was knighted in a ceremony presided over by the Queen.

Ironically, what began as a private friendship and admiration for Parris brought Manton very public recognition. As one headline in London's *Times* read, "Shy Millionaire Finally Explains Pounds 7 M[illion] Gift to the Tate." The article went on to say that though he "craved anonymity," Manton provided this large gift to the Tate because "he was indebted to a member of the Tate's staff [Parris] whose advice stopped him from buying a fake Constable. A further motive for the gift was avoiding taxes."[72] With customary wit and self-deprecation, Manton only revealed his identity to the press when he found out a journalist (who dubbed him "the mystery millionaire") was going to write about his knighthood.[73]

This move away from anonymity also saw the publication of four privately produced catalogues of his collection between 1994 and 2001.[74] The books were written by major scholars in the field of British art, Leslie Parris, John Hayes, and Andrew Wilton, and focused on those artists he collected most in depth, Constable, Gainsborough, Turner, Girtin, Bonington, and Rowlandson. Each work was illustrated and given its own entry. These handsome catalogues were distributed to friends, dealers, and family members. As Wilton, one of the authors detailed, Manton gave the scholars free reign to select works and organize the volumes as they wished, and employed Parris's wife Pippa to create the subtle yet elegant design.[75] Sir Edwin and Lady Manton's names were not printed in the first volume, although intimate friends and colleagues knew their identity.

While some argue the publications were the brainchild of Parris that Sir Edwin agreed to as a scholarly favor, in the end Manton was extremely pleased with and proud of them.

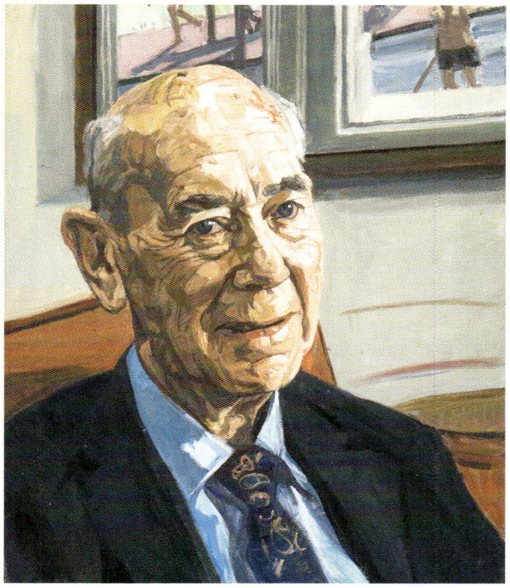
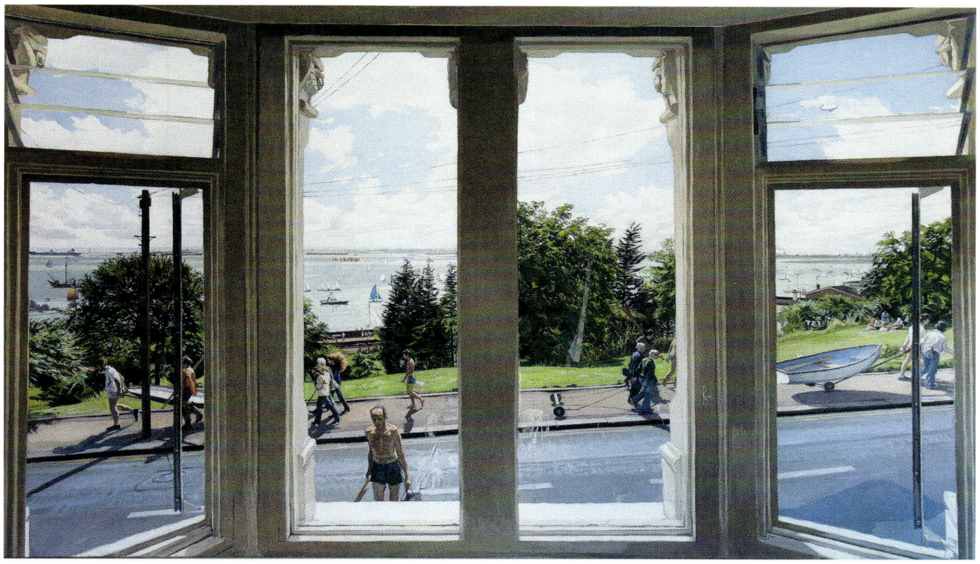
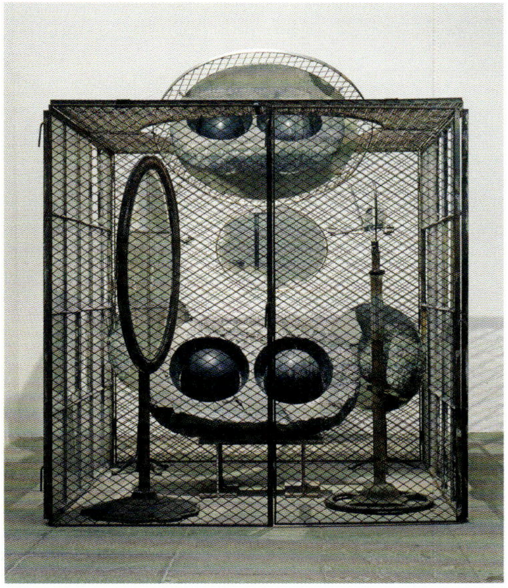
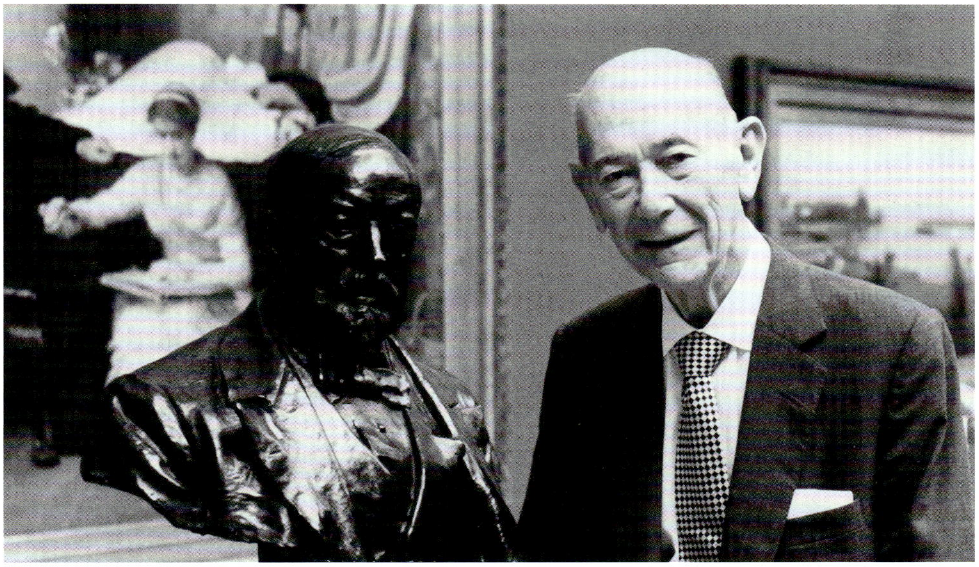

Fig. 25 Thomas Gainsborough (English, 1727–1788), *Wooded Landscape with Herdsman and Cow*, early 1780s. Brush and black and gray wash with black and white chalks on cream laid paper, fixed with skim milk and/or gum, 26.7 × 35.6 cm (no. 124)

As Gage recalls: "I remember when he gave me my copies, because he invited me to lunch and he was so proud. And then we looked at every single page together, and actually it was lovely because one would talk to him about each drawing or each painting.... So it meant a huge amount to him."[76] The excitement that built from volume to volume coincided with the increase of Sir Edwin's honors and public recognition, just as the initial volume had a preface cryptically signed "E. A. G. M.," while in the last three volumes it was signed "Edwin Manton" – without his royal title.

The last decade of Manton's life did not see any slowing of his passion for buying. Between 1993 and 2003 he acquired over sixty works of art, among them the most signature of his fifty-year engagement with buying. Within the years 1998 to 2001 he acquired Girtin's *The Gatehouse of Battle Abbey, Sussex* (see fig. 114); Gainsborough's evocative *Wooded Landscape with Herdsman and Cow* (fig. 25); Turner's *What You Will!* (see fig. 80); and Constable's *The Wheat Field* (see fig. 117) as well as the artist's highly unusual and rare *Paint Box* (fig. 26), and many more.[77] In addition to the dealers with whom he had worked for decades, Sir Edwin began to buy frequently from the Salander-O'Reilly Galleries in New York, who had forged a close relationship with the Constable estate.

Fig. 26 John Constable, *Paint Box*, c. 1825, Tin box with hinged lid, and seventeen compartments containing oil paints and varnishes, 8.6 × 5.1 × 33 cm (no. 82)

The London dealer Deborah Gage became a close friend and advisor to Manton during his later years, encouraging him to refine and reenergize his collecting, suggesting that he pursue only the very best. This period coincided with a sense of destiny for the collector, a feeling that the time had come to buy what he had always wanted. As he said time and again to Gage: "First of all there was Mr. Mellon, and every time I was after something Mr. Mellon got there ahead of me and paid more. And then there was Mr. [David] Thomson [a Canadian collector] ... I just had to wait my turn."[78] Mellon passed away in 1999 and Thomson had taken a pause in his impressive series of acquisitions, so Manton felt it was "his turn." During the last years of his life he seemed to thoroughly enjoy the right he felt this turn exercised.

Fittingly enough, among the very last works Sir Edwin acquired in 2003, when his health took a turn for the worse, was the large-scale, stunning Rowlandson watercolor, *The Subscription Club Room* (fig. 27). The raucous image chronicles the misfortune that has struck two young men at the gaming table. The standing youth raises his fist in despair at a bad toss of the dice while the distraught gentleman in the foreground sinks in despair, his head in his hand. The room contains a vast array of social groups ranging from well-born gentlemen to ragged looking thieves. As Manton once said in one of his few

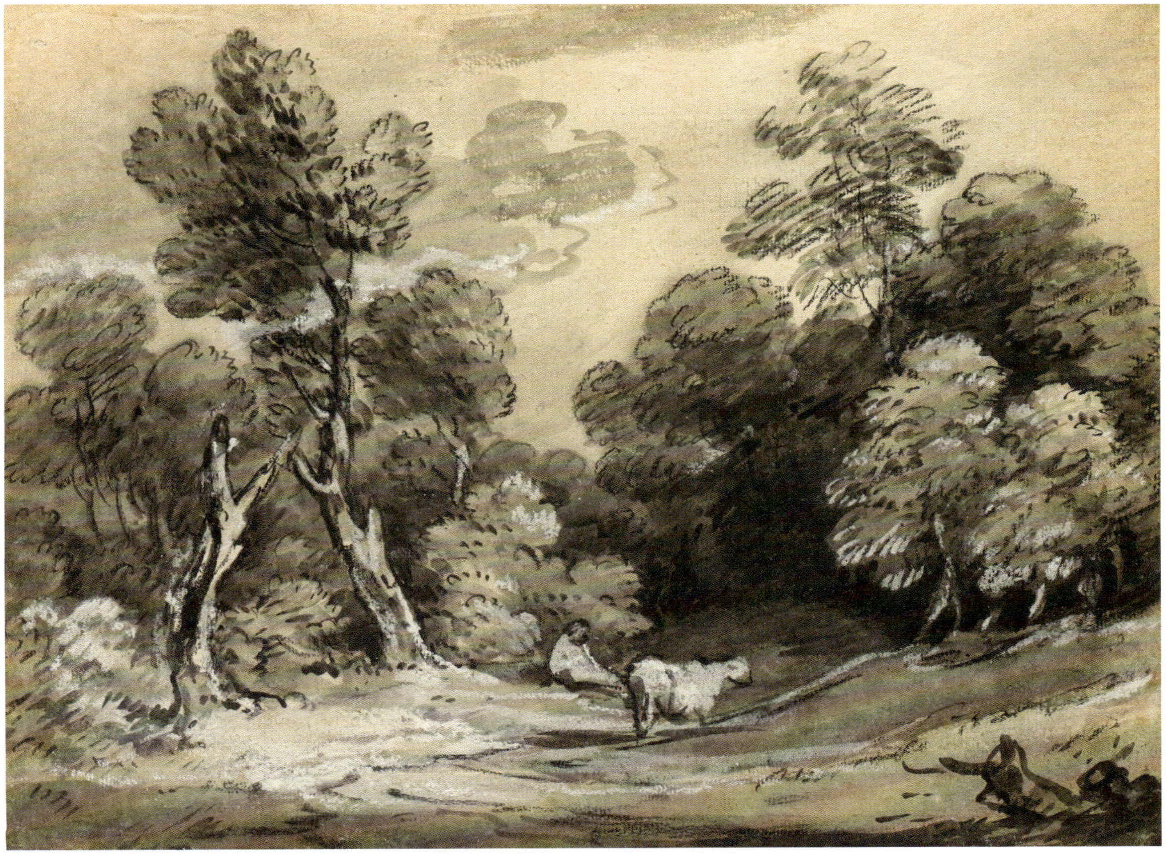

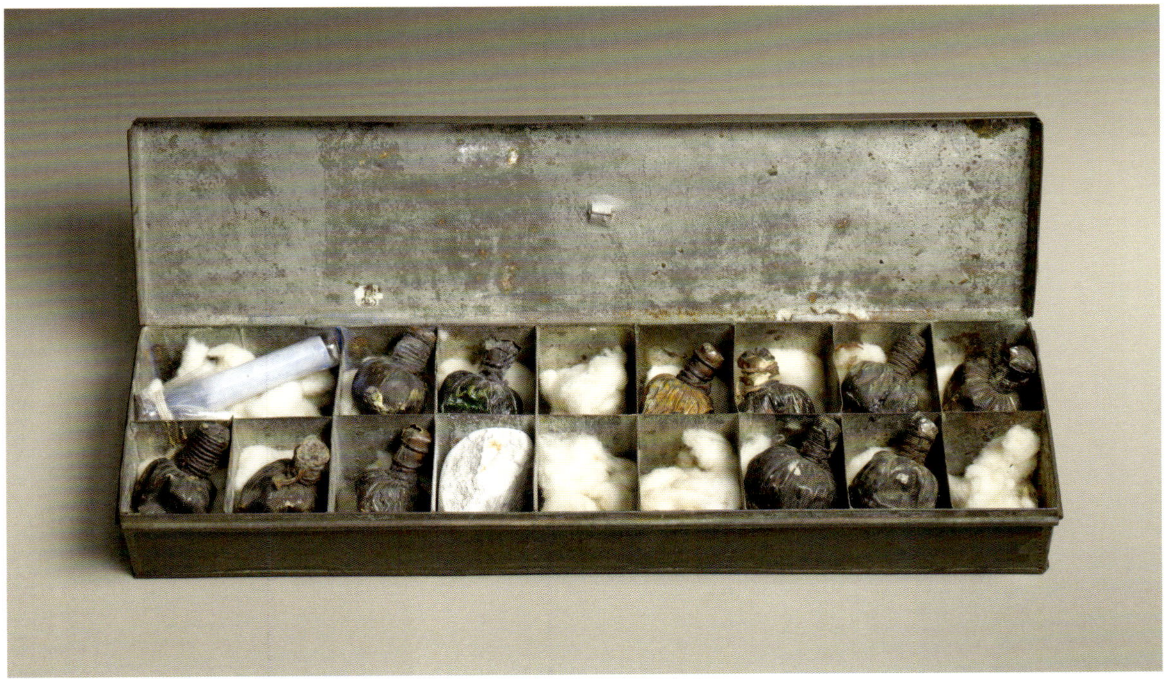

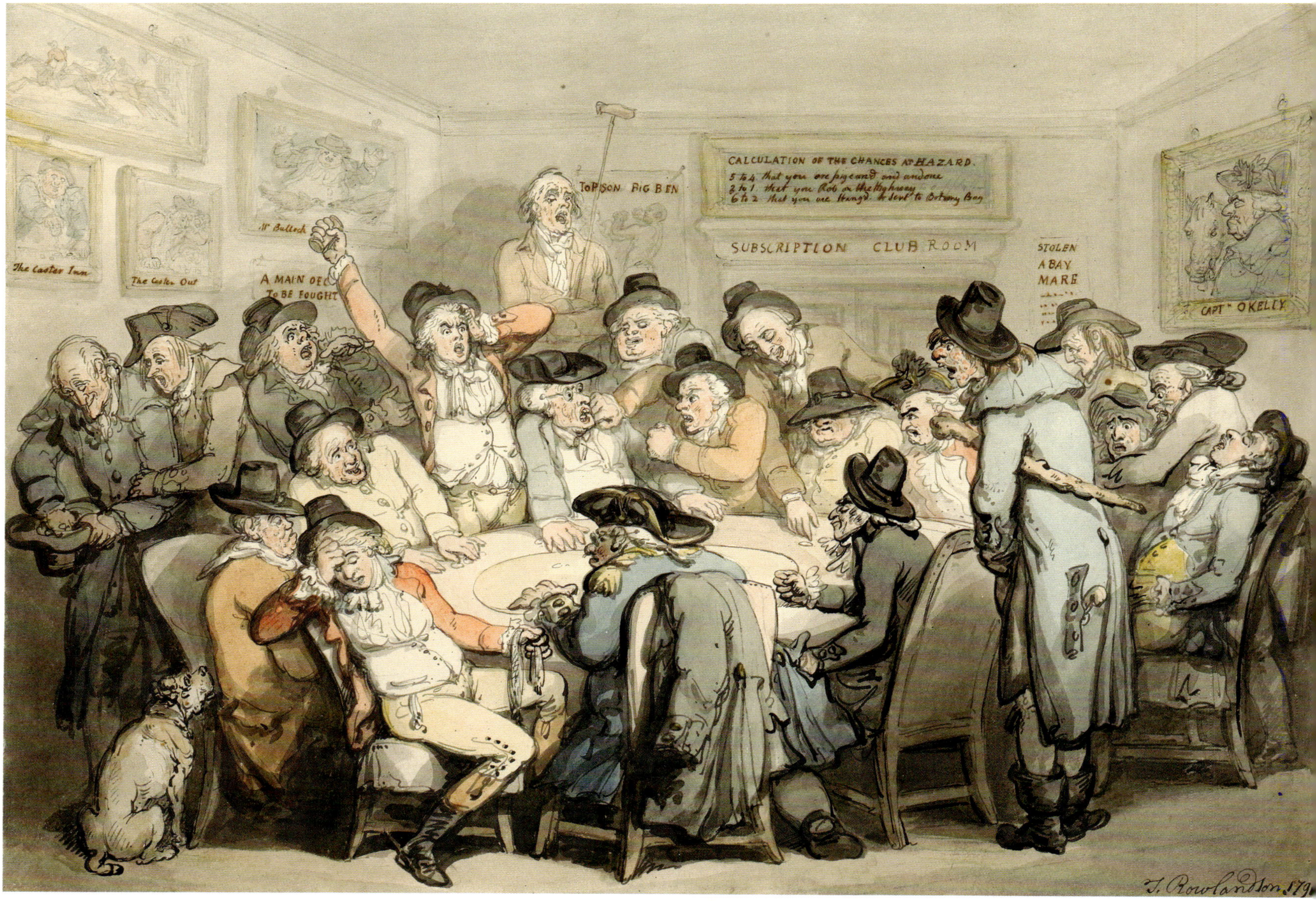
The Castor Inn
The Castor Out
Mr Bullock
A MAIN OF C
TO BE FOUGHT
TOP SON BIG BEN
CALCULATION OF THE CHANCES AT HAZARD.
5 to 4 that you are pigeon'd and undone
2 to 1 that you Rob on the Highway
6 to 2 that you are Hang'd or sent to Botany Bay
SUBSCRIPTION CLUB ROOM
STOLEN
A BAY
MARE
CAPTn OKELLY
T. Rowlandson 179

statements to the press, he was "addicted to buying watercolors.... I'm a compulsive buyer. I do not look upon [art] as an investment. It's better to buy art than bottles of Scotch."[79] While many characters in this sheet were no doubt over-spending due to an excess of Scotch, their passion and verve for gambling was equal to Manton's obsession for acquisition. The grizzled countenances and fierce regret of Rowlandson's gamblers are worlds away from the reserved wit of Sir Edwin, but both shared the absorptive qualities of a hobby that brought them into community with others sharing the same interests. Sir Edwin and Lady Manton's private contemplation and intimate conversations about their art with a close-knit group of friends and scholars has been transformed at the Clark into an opportunity for a much broader appreciation and investigation by scholars, students, and the general public. The "Fortress" walls have been breached: what they experienced and encouraged privately can now be continued on a broader scale, available to all.

Fig. 27 Thomas Rowlandson, *The Subscription Club Room*, 1791. Pen with black and brown inks over graphite and watercolor with additions in pen and brush and black ink on cream wove paper, 32.6 × 46.5 cm (no. 194)

The stories in this introduction about the Mantons as people and collectors have been gleaned from the voluminous research files kept on their collection and from interviews with family, friends, dealers, and curators. Manton and his assistants Miss Doherty and Judy Caruso kept impeccable records, which allowed staff at the Clark to build a chronology of the collection and piece together the trajectory of the Mantons's likes and dislikes. This was augmented by the archive of letters and documents unrelated to the collection in the Clark library that has helped us create this narrative. Given that both Sir Edwin and Lady Manton were private and unassuming, it is fitting that most of the information in this brief history comes in the form of personal letters and conversations, not from published sources. Aside from the numerous honorific obituaries published upon Sir Edwin's death, and two short articles in the *Clark Journal*,* this is the first comprehensive look at the total collection and the couple that built it.

* Michael Conforti and James Ganz, "English Accents," *CAI: Journal of the Clark* 8 (2007): 16–25; and Jay A. Clarke, "A Closer Look at the Manton Collection," *CAI: Journal of the Clark* 10 (2009): 12–23.

1 Leslie Parris and Ian Fleming-Williams, *Constable* (London: Tate Gallery, 1991), 119.

2 His nickname referenced both his disposition and a popular cartoon figure from a cereal advertisement of the day. Interview with Diana Morton, daughter of Sir Edwin and Lady Manton, September 2011, Westport, Mass. All interviews for this essay were conducted by the author.

3 Nicholas Serota, "Obituary: Sir Edwin Manton: Businessman and Art Benefactor Who Donated Millions to the Tate Gallery," *The Guardian*, 17 October 2005.

4 "Obituary of Sir Edwin Manton, Essex-Born Multimillionaire Who Became One of the Most Generous Benefactors of the Tate Gallery," *Daily Telegraph*, 6 October 2005.

5 Interview with Julia Krapf, granddaughter of Sir Edwin and Lady Manton, September 2011, Carlisle, Mass.

6 Interview with Sandra Niles, granddaughter of Sir Edwin and Lady Manton, August 2011, the Clark.

7 "In Memoriam, Sir Edwin A. G. Manton: A Guiding Light for AIG," *AIG Contact* vol. 17, issue 3 (December 2005), n.p.; and Serota, "Obituary: Sir Edwin Manton"; *A Short History of AIG: 1919 to the Present* (New York: published privately by AIG, 2001).

8 Although Peter Bahra, Director of the AIG archives, was unable to help with information on the company's history, he confirmed Manton's titles and dates of employment: secretary 1937, vice president 1938, president 1942–69, and chairman 1969–75. As one former AIG employee opined, Manton was self-taught, elegant, and erudite; Ronald Kent Shelp, *Fallen Giant: The Amazing Story of Hank Greenberg and the History of AIG* (Hoboken, N.J.: Wiley, 2009), 113, 119.

9 http://www.aigcorporate.com/aigstory/index.html. See also J. David Cummins and Bertrand Venard, eds., *Handbook of International Insurance: Between Global Dynamics and Local Contingencies* (New York: Springer Science and Business Media, LLC, 2007), 248.

10 Interview with Florence Davis, Director of the Starr Foundation, October 2011, New York.

11 Telephone interview with Dennis Keene, Artistic Director and Conductor of the Church of the Ascension, October 2011. For more on their connection to the church, see http://ascensionnyc.org/worship/manton-organ.

12 The Starr Foundation makes grants in a number of areas, including education, medicine, healthcare, human needs, public policy, culture, and the environment.

13 Interview with Niles.

14 E. A. G. M. [Manton], "Introduction," in Leslie Parris, *Constable: A New York Private Collection* (New York: published privately, 1994), 9.

15 "Sir Edwin Manton," *Telegraph*, 6 October 2005.

16 Damian Whitworth, "Shy Millionaire Finally Explains Pounds 7 M[illion] Gift to Tate," *Times* (London), 22 July 1997.

17 E. A. G. M., "Introduction," 9. The painting, when attributed to Constable at auction, carried the title *View on the Stour, Suffolk*, which has been subsequently changed to *River View* as there is no evidence to support that the work depicts the River Stour. The *New York Sun* article Manton mentions, which illustrates the painting, is from Friday, 25 February 1949. The highly regarded Viennese collector Oscar Bondy (1870–1944) owned this painting until he was forced to flee Austria during the Anschluss. The work was restituted to his heirs, and then sold through Kende. The sale attracted quite a bit of attention in the press due to its connection with Hitler's seizure of art.

18 Whitworth, "Shy Millionaire," 22 July 1997.

19 Interview with Niles.

20 Interview with Lowell Libson, July 2011, the Clark.

21 Manton, letter to Parris, 22 July 1986. A Guide to the Records of Edwin Alfred Grenville Manton, 1927–2005, Sterling and Francine Clark Art Institute Records, Sterling and Francine Clark Art Institute, Williamstown, Mass.

22 For more on twentieth-century perceptions of his oil sketches, see Mark Evans, "Constable's Oil Sketches in the Twentieth Century," *John Constable: Oil Sketches from the Victoria and Albert Museum* (London: V&A Publishing, 2011), 9–11.

23 Manton, letter to Peter Johnson, 11 July 1958. A Guide to the Records of Edwin Alfred Grenville Manton, 1927–2005.

24 Clarke, "A Closer Look at the Manton Collection," 17.

25 Edward Morris, *Constable's Cloud Studies: Painting and Cloud Studies by John Constable* (Edinburgh: National Galleries of Scotland, 2000), 68.

26 Interview with Marjorie Shelley, September 2011, New York.

27 For an illustration of this sheet, see Greg Smith, *Thomas Girtin: The Art of Watercolor* (London: Tate Publishing, 2002), 101.

28 Manton, letter to Lt. Col. James Archer-Burton, 30 June 1983, and Archer-Burton, letter to Manton, 17 June 1983. A Guide to the Records of Edwin Alfred Grenville Manton, 1927–2005.

29 E. A. G. M., "Introduction," 10.

30 The first three galleries were connected through one family: Oscar Johnson began at Leggatt Brothers, as did his son Peter. In 1963 father and son founded Oscar and Peter Johnson, Ltd. In 1992 Peter Johnson merged their firm with Ackermann, which then became Ackermann and Johnson. A similar connection applies to Anthony Spink, who worked at Spink and Son, Spink-Leger, and Leger, and served as the main conduit of art for Manton along with Lowell Libson.

31 Interview with Libson.

32 Ibid.

33 *Christ of the Incas* exemplifies Georges Rouault's use of religious imagery to represent his own unique form of personal expression. This work was given to the Smith College Museum of Art as a bequest of Lady Manton in honor of her daughter Diana.

34 Interview with Krapf.

35 This collection was kept intact, and was not included in the gift made to the Clark. Many of these works were sold at the auction houses Skinner, Boston, and Christie's, New York, in a series of sales between 2007 and 2010.

36 Manton, letter to Johnson, 16 November 1965, in curatorial files.

37 Manton, letter to Johnson, 4 October 1966, in curatorial files.

38 Manton, letter to Parris, 2 October 1991, in curatorial files.

39 Manton, letter to Parris, 17 September 1990; letter to Serota, 13 August 1991; letter to Ruth Rattenbury at the Tate, 8 February 1990, in curatorial files.

40 Manton, letter to Patrick Noon, 2 December 1991, in curatorial files.

41 Interview with Libson.

42 For more on this topic, see Hope C. Saska, "Staging the Page: Graphic Caricature in Eighteenth-Century England" (Ph.D. diss., Brown University, 2009).

43 Andrew Wilton, *Turner, Girtin, and Bonington: A New York Private Collection: Paintings, Drawings, and Watercolors* (New York: published privately, 2001), 64–65.

44 Wilton, former curator of prints and drawings at the Yale Center for British Art, described Paul Mellon's love for Rowlandson's humor, recalling "Paul used to stand with a box of Rowlandson drawings and roar his head off." Interview with Wilton, October 2011, London.

45 E. A. G. M., "Introduction," 10.

46 Manton, letter to Johnson, 22 August 1963, in curatorial files.

47 Telephone interview with Patrick Noon, October 2011.

48 For more on these collectors and others of their generation, see Shelley M. Bennett, "The Formation of Henry E. Huntington's Collection of British Paintings," in *British Paintings at the Huntington* (San Marino, C.A.: Huntington Library, 2001), 1–15; John Baskett, "Paul Mellon: A Remembrance," *Paul Mellon's Legacy: A Passion for British Art* (New Haven, Conn.: Yale Center for British Art, 2007), 1–11; Malcolm Warner and Robyn Asleson, *Great British Paintings from American Collections: Holbein to Hockney* (New Haven, Conn.: Yale Center for British Art, 2001).

49 Interview with Deborah Gage, October 2011, London.

50 Ibid.

51 John Munday, *Edward William Cooke, 1811–1880: A Man of His Time* (Woodbridge, England: Antique Collectors' Club, 1996), 152.

52 Indar Pasricha, "Apparell'd in Celestial Light: Indian Paintings of Albert Goodwin," ed. Pauline Rohatgi and Pheroza Godrej, *Under the Indian Sun: British Landscape Artists* (Bombay: Marg Publications, 1995), 152–53.

53 For more on these Ruskin-designed Tuner cabinets, see Robert Hewison, Ian Warrell, and Stephen Wildman, *Ruskin, Turner, and the Pre-Raphaelites* (London: Tate Gallery Publishing, 2000), 194–98.

54 Interviews with Libson and Shelley.

55 Manton, letter to Libson (then of Leger Galleries), January 1995, in curatorial files.

56 My thanks to Paul Richardson for these calculations.

57 Interview with Libson.

58 Manton, letter to Anthony Spink, 15 March 1999, in curatorial files.

59 In 2000 the Mantons were concerned about the theft of several Constable paintings, so an investigation was conducted and an inventory done. The paintings were later found in one of the Manton's storage areas, and it was concluded that a theft never occurred, rather the works were simply misplaced. Documents in Manton archives: A Guide to the Records of Edwin Alfred Grenville Manton, 1927–2005.

60 Interview with Gage.

61 Interview with Noon.

62 The co-curators were Richard C. Pionk and Margaret Somer.

63 *Constable at the Salmagundi Club* (New York: Salmagundi Club, 2000), n.p.

64 Interview with Wilton.

65 Sir Edwin served as his own preparator, mounting, framing, and preparing his works for transport to the exhibitions to which the couple were always generous lenders. Manton did so in the "basement room where," he said, "I perform my own professional packing and unpacking." Manton, letter to Parris, 3 October 1991, in curatorial files.

66 Manton, letter to John Wonnacott, 27 October 1997. A Guide to the Records of Edwin Alfred Grenville Manton, 1927–2005.

67 Wonnacott, letter to Manton, 5 November 1997. A Guide to the Records of Edwin Alfred Grenville Manton, 1927–2005.

68 Serena Davies, "In the Studio: John Wonnacott," *Daily Telegraph*, 1 November 2005. The artist confirmed this and explained the genesis of the Tate portrait in a phone conversation, February 2012.

69 The dealer David Posnett, who had sold Manton a number of works from Leger, first introduced Parris to Manton in 1981 or 1982.

70 Telephone Interview with Serota, October 2011.

71 Serota, "Obituary: Sir Edwin Manton."

72 Whitworth, "Shy Millionaire." Another article, "The Art of Generosity: The Man Who Gave Pounds 7M to Tate," *Independent*, 8 July 1997, suggested that Manton's worth derived from four million shares of AIG.

73 "The Art of Generosity."

74 The four privately published catalogues were: Parris, *Constable: A New York Private Collection*; Leslie Parris, *Constable: A New York Private Collection: Supplement* (New York, 1998); John Hayes, *Gainsborough and Rowlandson: A New York Private Collection* (New York, 1998); Wilton, *Turner, Girtin, and Bonington*.

75 Interview with Wilton.

76 Interview with Gage.

77 Sarah Cove, "Mixing and Mingling: John Constable's Oil Paint Mediums (c. 1802–37), Including the Analysis of the 'Manton' Paint Box (1837)," *Painting Techniques: History, Materials and Studio Practice*, eds. Ashok Roy and Perry Smith (London: The International Institute for Conservation of Historic and Artistic Works, 1998), 211–16.

78 Interview with Gage.

79 Whitworth, "Shy Millionaire."

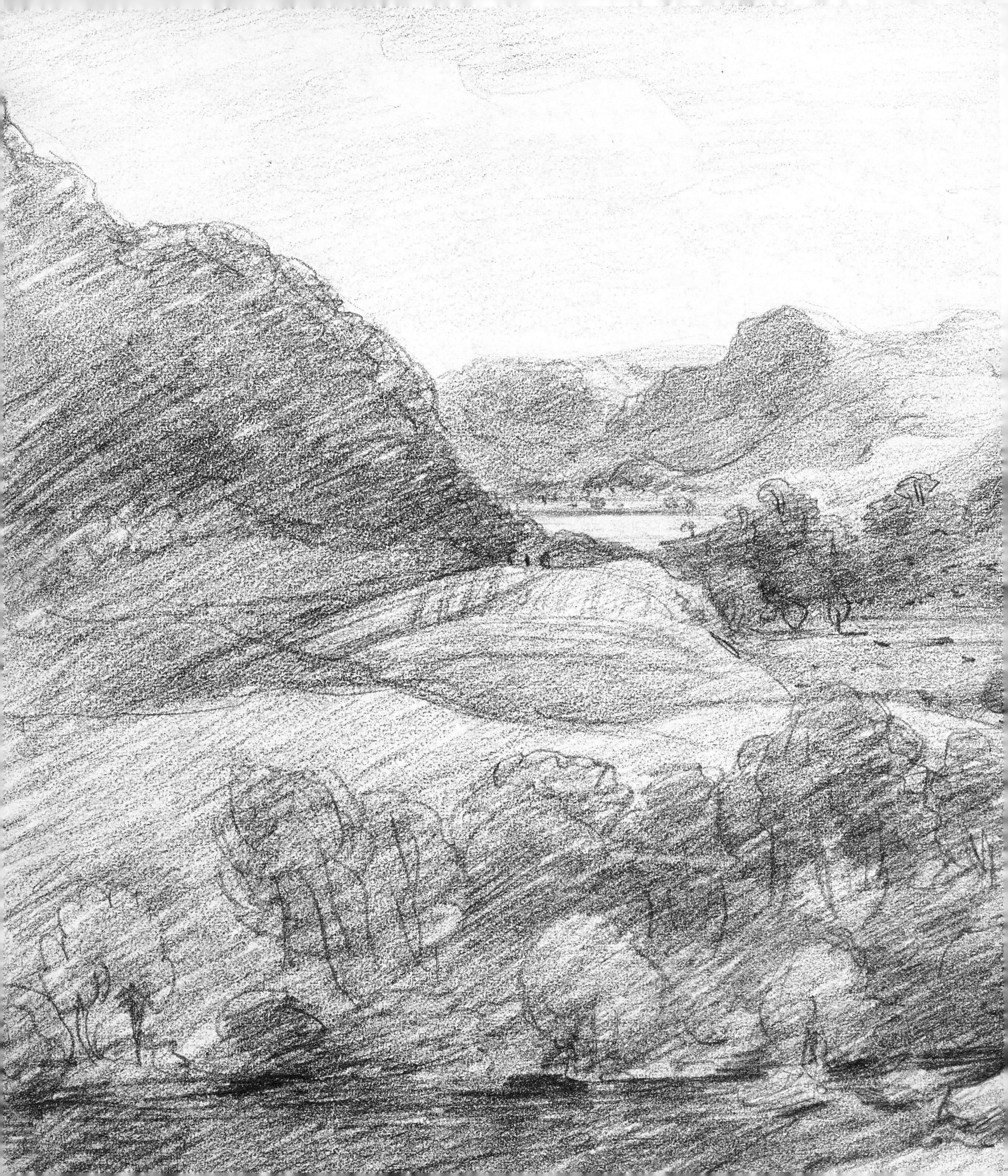

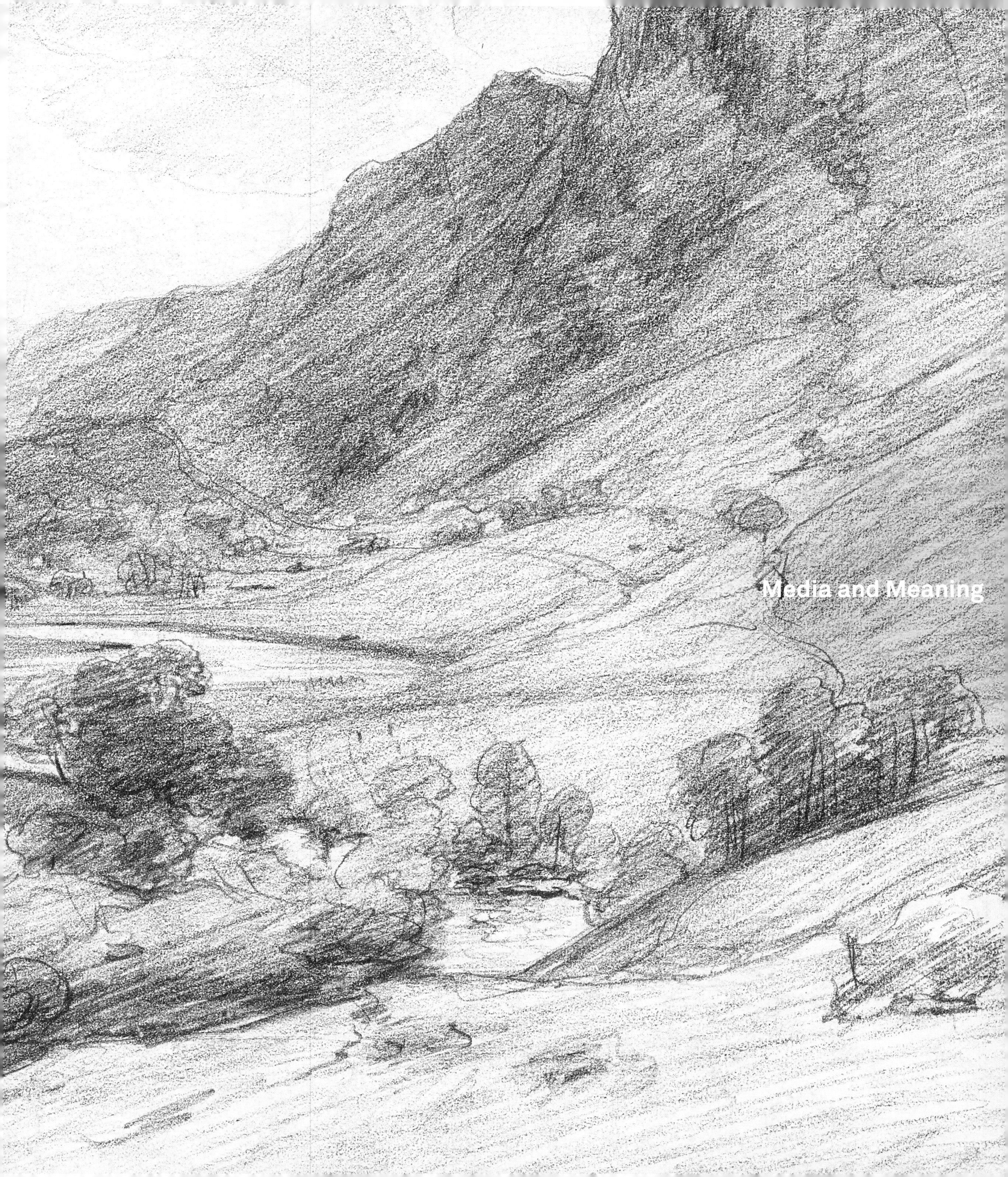

Media and Meaning

Daubings, Moppings, and Splashings

Gainsborough and the Drawing Masters

Ann Bermingham

Though revered by his eighteenth-century contemporaries as an unparalleled graphic genius, at the start of the nineteenth century Gainsborough was increasingly viewed as a dangerous influence. Those tempted to imitate his drawing style "will be apt to produce blots instead of drawings," warned one author, while another claimed that Gainsborough's facility with the pencil was "too dangerous ground even for a first rate Artist."[1] The most outraged voice came from an anonymous critic writing for the *Somerset House Gazette* who claimed that only "copyists ... dabblers ... polite idlers at Bath" imitated Gainsborough's style, vainly imagining that "because this rare genius could, by a sort of graphic magic, dash out romantic scraps" that they too could do the same. These deluded amateurs, he wrote, covered "their own conceit and incapacity, in their daubings, and moppings, and splashings."[2]

While Gainsborough's imitators might be conceited "idlers" too proud and lazy to subject themselves to the hard work of learning to draw properly, Gainsborough's own style, early commentators acknowledged, reflected his eccentric, passionate, and mercurial temperament. Allan Cunningham, in his *Lives of Eminent British Painters, Sculptors, and Artists* (1829–33), stated that Gainsborough's "drawings are numerous and masterly: no artist has left behind him so many exquisite relics of this kind.... They have all great length and singular freedom of handling."[3] Nevertheless, he went on to say that Gainsborough's

productions are sometimes disfigured by the impatience of his nature and the fiery haste in which he wrought. Wishing to do quickly what his mind conceived strongly, he often neglected in the dashing vigour of his hand, many lesser graces which lend art so much of its attractiveness. He felt the whole indeed, at once; he was possessed fully with the sentiment of his subject; he struck off his favorite works at one continuous heat of thought, and all is clear, connected, and consistent. But, like nature herself, he performed some of his duties with a careless haste, and in many, both his portraits and his landscapes, we see evident marks of inattention and hurry.[4]

Cunningham and others derived their psychological explanation for Gainsborough's unusual style from interviews with the artist's contemporaries and also from early written accounts. One contemporary, Edward Edwards, a fellow Royal Academician, recalled in his *Anecdotes of Painters* (1808) that Gainsborough was "capricious in his manners and rather fickle and unsteady in his social connections."[5] Others, such as an early friend and patron, Philip Thicknesse, recollected Gainsborough's "susceptible mind and benevolent heart," as well as his impatience and intemperance.[6]

Fig. 28 Thomas Gainsborough, (English, 1727–1788), *Wooded Landscape with Shepherd and Sheep, Winding River, and Tower*, mid- to late 1770s. Black and white chalks on brown laid paper, 18.2 × 21.8 cm (no. 122)

The peculiarities of temperament that could be tolerated in the drawings of a great artist – and all commentators acknowledged Gainsborough's greatness – became intolerable if imitated by an amateur, and reprehensible if found in the work of a professional. Gainsborough's style was so much a reflection of his particular nature that to imitate it was seen as taking something to which one had no right. It would be dishonest pretense, a form of masquerade.

It is worth pausing to analyze what it was in Gainsborough's work that critics saw as unique to him and dangerous to others. *Wooded Landscape with Shepherd and Sheep, Winding River, and Tower* (fig. 28) gives us some idea. This black-and-white chalk drawing from the mid- to late 1770s exemplifies what Cunningham called Gainsborough's "singular freedom of handling." The drawing was made on blue laid paper that, over time, has turned brown. Despite the discoloration of the support, the chalk media retains the characteristic energy of Gainsborough's handling. The outlines of the trees are suggested by loops, while their interiors are indicated through horizontal hatching. Other forms are similarly abstracted. The dozing shepherd is a dark curved form, while his sheep are nothing more than rounded mounds touched with white chalk. A pentimento at the top of the distant tower reveals that originally it was much taller; Gainsborough used white chalk to shorten the tower and to suggest a streaky, cloudy sky. As is typical of so many Gainsborough drawings, nothing is spelled out in detail; the whole composition works by suggestion rather than definition.

Another black and lead white drawing, *Landscape with Herdsman Driving Cows and Distant Buildings* (fig. 29), from the later part of Gainsborough's life, is equally free in its manner. As is characteristic of Gainsborough's mixed-media drawings, this one was started in gray wash. Black chalk was used to define the forms, and lead white was applied last to create highlights and make corrections. Despite this systematic way of working, the lights and darks appear dashed in, foliage is suggested by loops and zigzags rather than careful delineation, and the two leading cows bear the marks of spontaneous changes and adjustments. Such impatience in execution seems to be matched by an indifference to the actual look of nature. As in *Wooded Landscape with Shepherd and Sheep*, abstract shapes only gesture toward the objects they represent, but do not describe them. Moreover, there are strange improbabilities in the image, such as a dead tree in the left foreground that sprouts foliage, though how these leaves attach themselves to the tree's blasted branch is a mystery.

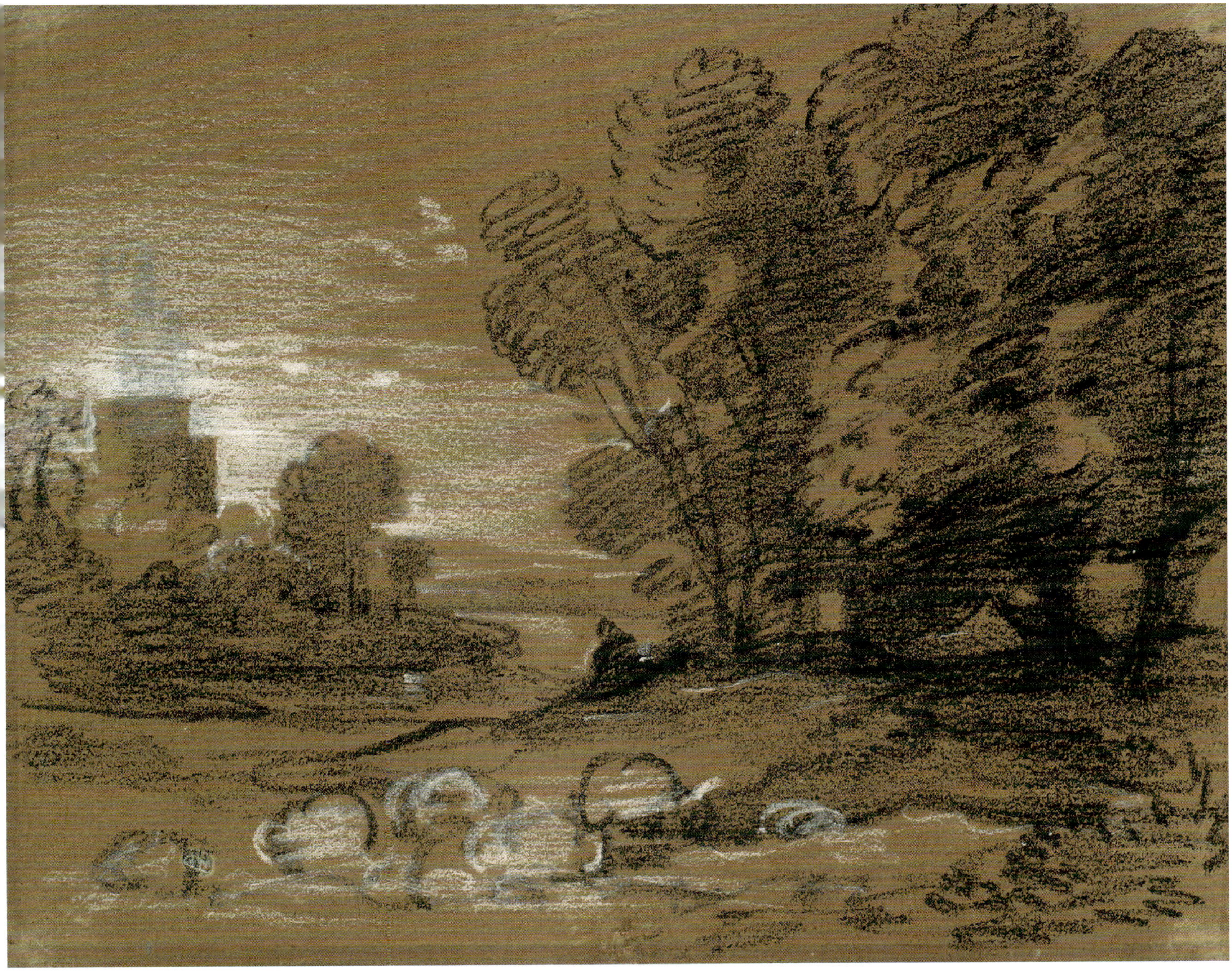

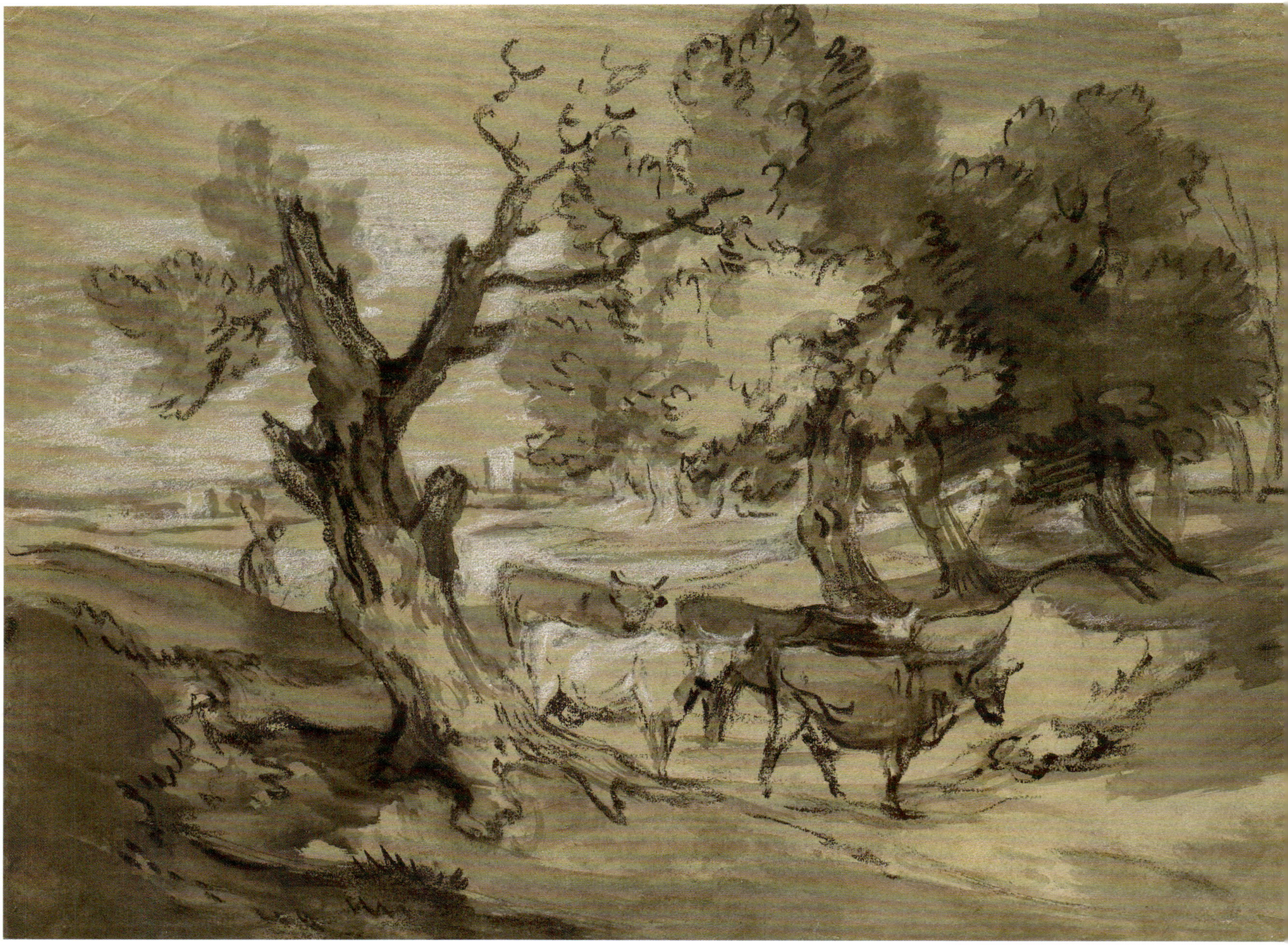

A late drawing, *Rocky Wooded Landscape with Winding Track* (fig. 30), executed in pen and ink with white chalk and wash, shares the same impatience with finish and indifference to creating a realistic representation of nature. Rocks, trees, and foliage are blocked in with gray wash, and their outlines are drawn in a sketchy, approximate manner. White chalk is again used to make corrections, in this case to lighten the gray wash tones in the middle ground. One prominent compositional element, a tree on the right hillock, appears to be a somewhat improvised afterthought.

Fig. 29 Thomas Gainsborough, *Landscape with Herdsman Driving Cows and Distant Buildings*, mid- to late 1780s. Black chalk over brush and gray wash with lead white on beige laid paper, fixed with gum (?), 24.6 × 32.4 cm (no. 130)

Gainsborough's impatience with finish and naturalistic detail was matched by a fascination with media. *Rocky Wooded Landscape with Herdsman Driving Cattle along a Valley and Distant Mountains* (fig. 31), from about 1783, is an unusual work in that it is drawn entirely with a brush with no evidence of pencil, pen, or other media that would produce clear, sharp lines. The resulting landscape sketch has a narrow range of gray tones and indefinite, melting contours. While it lacks the calligraphic definition of Gainsborough's chalk drawings, it nevertheless has a pleasing atmospheric softness.

Drawings such as these circulated widely after Gainsborough's death in 1788. A private sale of his studio contents was held in 1789, and further sales were held at Christie's in 1792; in 1797, following the death of the artist's nephew and pupil Gainsborough Dupont; and in 1799, following the death of Mrs. Gainsborough. In every case, drawings, in particular landscape drawings, made up a considerable number of the lots.[7] In addition to the sale of his original drawings, many of Gainsborough's landscape drawings were reproduced as prints immediately after his death. The artist Thomas Rowlandson reproduced five landscape drawings of Gainsborough in soft-ground etching and aquatint in his book *Imitations of Modern Drawings* (c. 1788). This was followed by John Thrane's publication in 1789 of four Gainsborough landscape drawings from the collection of Gainsborough's musician friend, Carl Friedrich Abel. The most ambitious of these reproductive enterprises was William Frederick Wells and John Laporte's *A Collection of Prints Illustrative of English Scenery from the Drawings and Sketches of Thomas Gainsborough* (1802), which included seventy-two soft-ground etchings after Gainsborough landscape drawings.[8]

Gainsborough's own experiments in printmaking were also published at this time. While the artist produced prints of landscape scenery throughout his career, he published very few of them.[9] Almost a decade after his death, beginning in 1797, John Boydell published twelve of Gainsborough's original prints from the original plates under the title *Etchings by the Late Mr. Gainsborough: Twelve Prints of Landscape Scenery, with*

Fig. 30 Thomas Gainsborough, *Rocky Wooded Landscape with Winding Track*, late 1770s. Pen and black ink with brush and gray wash and white chalk on blue laid paper, 26.7 × 34.4 cm (no. 123)

Fig. 31 Thomas Gainsborough, *Rocky Wooded Landscape with Herdsman Driving Cattle along a Valley and Distant Mountains*, c. 1783. Brush and gray wash on beige laid paper, 21.1 × 30.8 cm (no. 125)

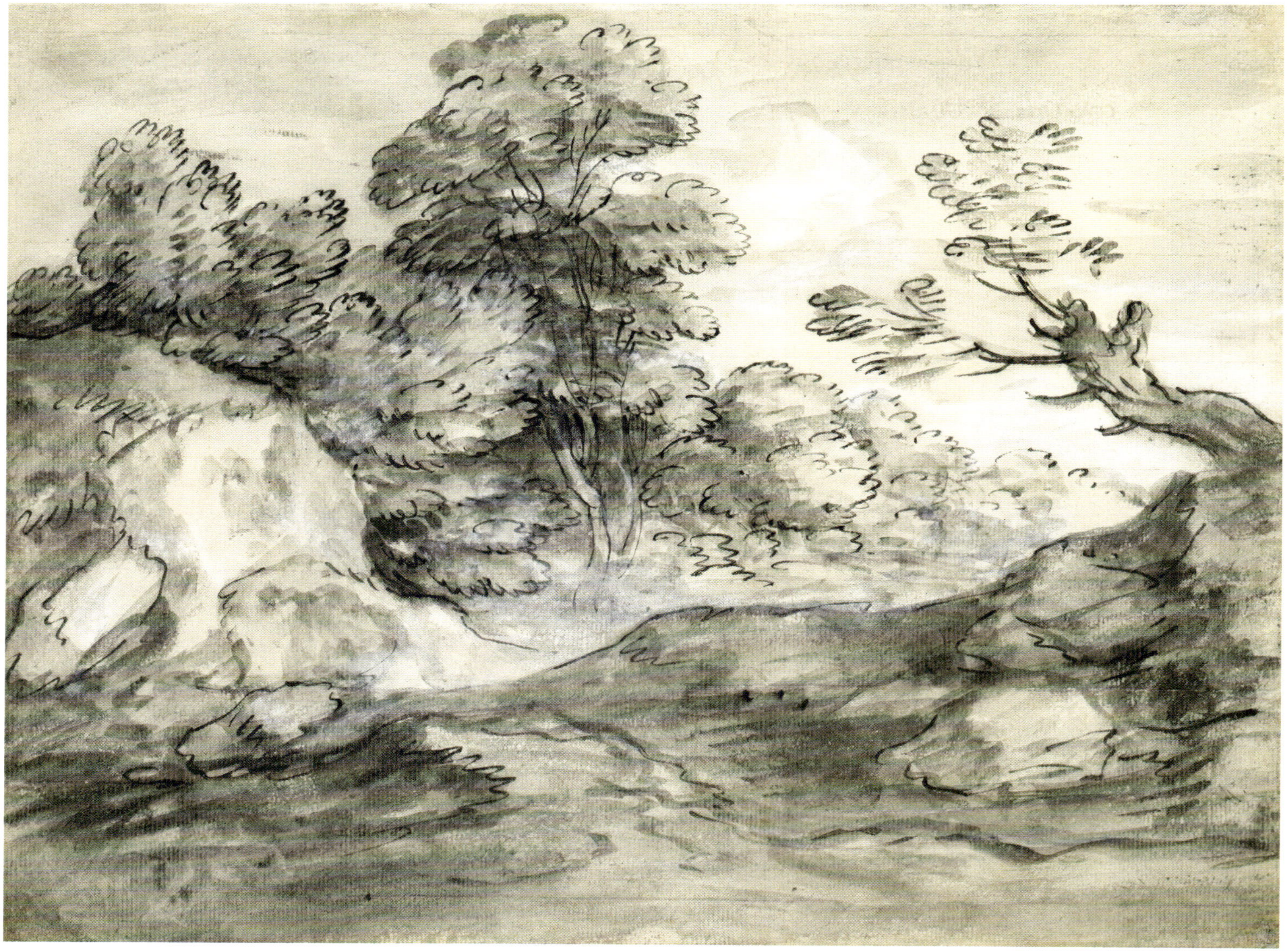

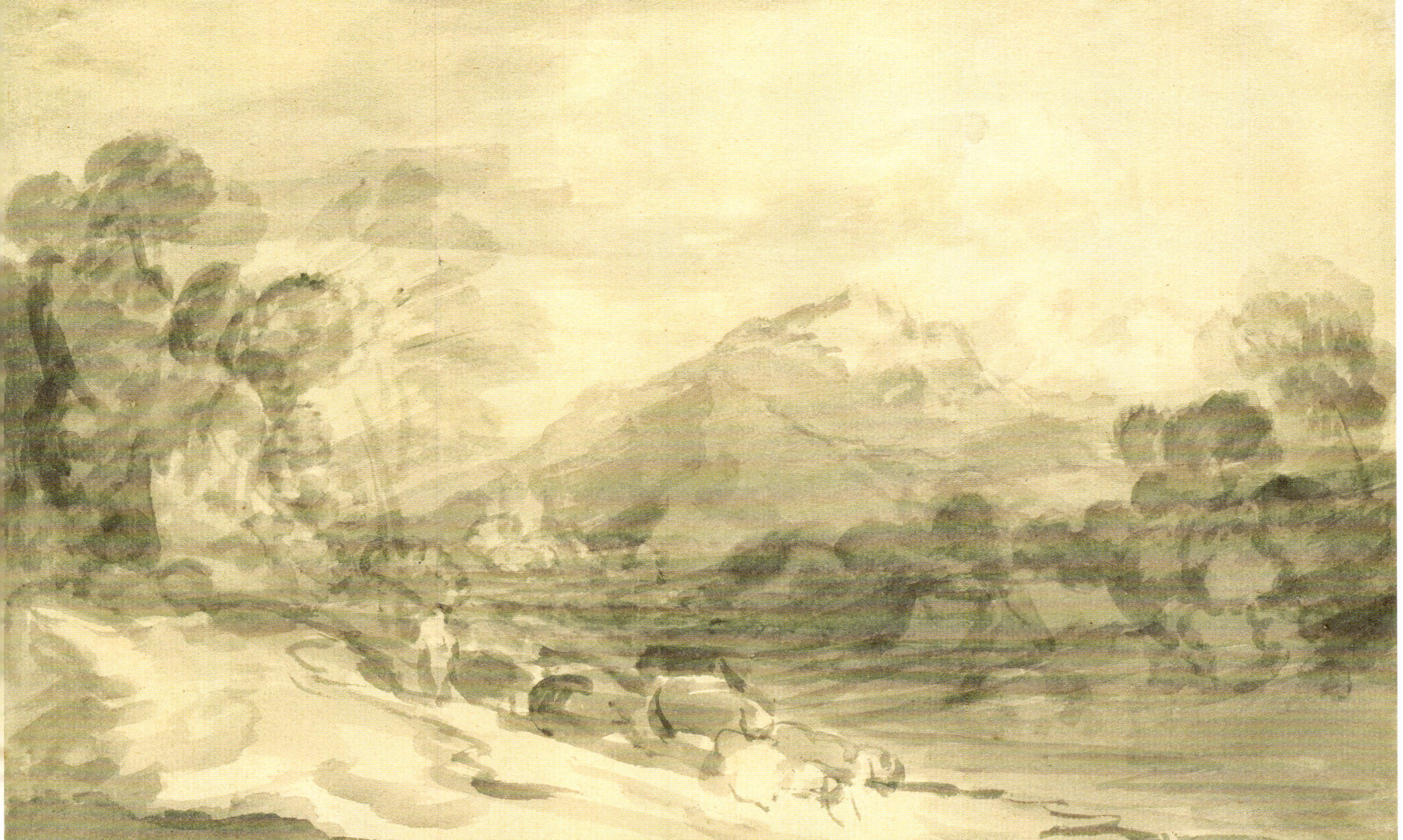

Cattle and Figures, Plates Have Never Been Worked upon by Any Other Artist. One of these twelve landscapes printed by Boydell (fig. 32) is based on the Manton drawing of *Landscape with Herdsman Driving Cows and Distant Buildings*.[10] When looked at side by side, the Boydell print has greater linear graphic definition. The interior of the forms, such as the blasted tree, are more elaborated, suggesting texture and dimensionality. This is true too of the figures of the shepherd and the distant buildings. The left and right edges of the Boydell print contain more sharply defined trees and buildings along the horizon, which give the landscape greater depth. However, with these changes, which tend to favor line over tone, certain aspects of the drawing that are important to the clarity of the composition disappear. In the drawing, the roots of the blasted tree meet the earth in a way that is more readable than in the print, due to its distinct tonal variations. The shading of the tree transitions from light at the lowest level to dark at the top, contrasting against the dark earth and the light sky. In the same way, the small hillock to the left of the roots is more comprehensible as a shape and a volume in the drawing than the print, through the greater range of tones used to define it.

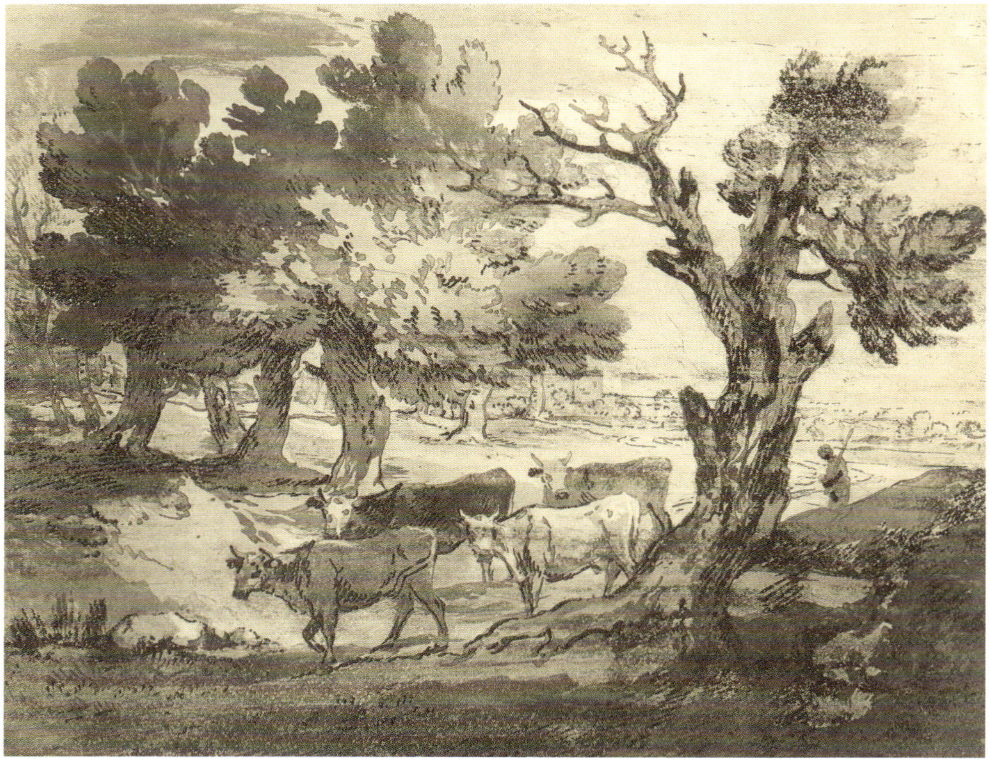

Fig. 32 Thomas Gainsborough, *Wooded Landscape with Herdsman and Cows*, 1797. Soft-ground etching and aquatint on cream wove paper, 27.9 × 34.9 cm (cropped inside plate). Yale Center for British Art, New Haven, Conn., Paul Mellon Collection

Throughout the 1790s, both Gainsborough's landscape prints and drawings and reproductive prints were collected and copied. The significance of Gainsborough's own prints was that he intended them to look as much as possible like his drawings. This was unusual, in that most artists had their work reproduced by professional printers in line engraving and mezzotint, whereas Gainsborough reproduced his own work in aquatint and soft-ground etching. Aquatint mimics the look of wash, and soft-ground the look of chalk. It was Gainsborough's drawing style rather than subject matter that his prints disseminated.

It must be noted that a large number of Gainsborough's nineteenth-century critics were drawing masters, and their warnings against his style were professionally motivated. If everyone was content to dash off slight drawings like *Wooded Landscape with Shepherd and Sheep, Winding River, and Tower* (fig. 28) or like many of those reproduced in Wells and Laporte, what would be the need of drawing masters? Examples of the kinds of amateur drawings they censured can also be found in the Manton Collection.

An oval graphite sketch of *A Wooded Landscape with a Village on a Hilltop and Figures on a Lane in Front* would seem to be cobbled together from motifs common to Gainsborough's landscape drawings (fig. 33). While gracefully composed so that the landscape elements mount vertically up the page, culminating with the church steeple on the hilltop in the central distance, the tones are not varied enough to give the space definition, and the silhouettes of the trees and foliage lack the energy of Gainsborough's vigorous handling. Finally, the church is too squat to really mark the apex and visual climax of the composition, and the figures are too indeterminate to add much to the overall effect. The total impression is of a somewhat confused and flaccid effort at imitation, one that wholly lacks the bright, lyric rhythms of Gainsborough's drawings. Moreover, it is a drawing that is unnaturalistic, not by choice, but by default.

A second example from the Manton Collection, *Rocky Landscape with Horseman and Packhorse* (fig. 34), shows what could happen if an amateur attempted to manipulate wash without having a good foundation in drawing and a secure sense of the medium and its qualities. When compared to Gainsborough's own wash drawings, such as *Rocky Wooded Landscape with Winding Track* and *Rocky Wooded Landscape with Herdsman Driving Cattle along a Valley and Distant Mountains*, this work appears crude in its execution, lacking the subtlety and refinement of Gainsborough's line and tonal structures. The horses and cliffs do not evince linear definition, and the ground and sky seem overworked with wash without resulting in spatial clarity or tonal interest.

Fig. 33 Style of Thomas Gainsborough (British, 18th century), *A Wooded Landscape with a Village on a Hilltop and Figures on a Lane in Front.* Black and white chalks with stumping on beige laid paper, 25.5 × 34 cm (no. 136)

Fig. 34 After Thomas Gainsborough (British, 18th century), *Rocky Landscape with Horseman and Packhorse.* Graphite over brush and gray washes on cream laid paper, 17 × 23 cm (no. 134)

At a moment when landscape artists, many of them drawing masters, were struggling to earn their livings and dignify their profession through a display of earnest hard work, "blots" like this could not be tolerated.[11] Too often, drawing masters argued, amateurs tried to reach excellence not through the careful study of nature but simply by imitating the work of other artists. One of the most outspoken critics of this kind of imitation was William Marshall Craig, a champion of naturalism in drawing who urged his pupils to draw from nature. In his *Essay on the Study of Nature in Drawing Landscape* (1793), he argued that, by imitating nature closely, in time and with experience, the beginner's laborious style would give way to a "perfect knowledge of the subject" and "facility in expressing it."[12] By contrast, the beginner who starts with a "bold and free manner" will end in difficulty and error.[13]

The example of Gainsborough himself can be used in support of Craig's theory, for as Edwards explained, Gainsborough's drawings fell into two phases:

In the first class, are those which he made in his youth, at which time he was attentive to rural scenery; and several of these early drawings possess a peculiar freedom of execution, accompanied by a judicious attention to the minutiae of nature, that is not surpassed by any productions of the Flemish masters in the same line of art; these were mostly in black lead, and some in black Italian chalk.... The second class consisted of those which he executed after he settled in Bath, where he adopted a very different manner, both of style and execution, the subjects being more romantic in their composition, and their execution more indeterminate, and (if the expression may be allowed) more licentious than those of the former class. These last were executed by a process rather capricious, truly deserving the epithet bestowed upon them by a witty lady, who called them moppings.[14]

Gainsborough created his "moppings," Edwards explained, by tying a small bit of sponge to a stick and using it to paint-in the shadows while using a lump of whiting held by a pair of tea-tongs to produce the highlights.[15] *Rocky Wooded Landscape with Winding Track*, with its loose gray washes and its vigorous heightening with white calcium carbonate, would seem to fit the description of a "mopping."[16] By contrast, Gainsborough's early style – preferred by Edwards and presumably by naturalists like Craig – is beautifully exemplified by the Manton Collection's *Study of Mallows* (fig. 35), a graphite drawing from the 1750s. The individual character of each leaf is described through the careful delineation of its contours and by the use of shading. The manipulations of contour and light reveal how the leaf turns in space, reflects light, and droops or springs from its stem.

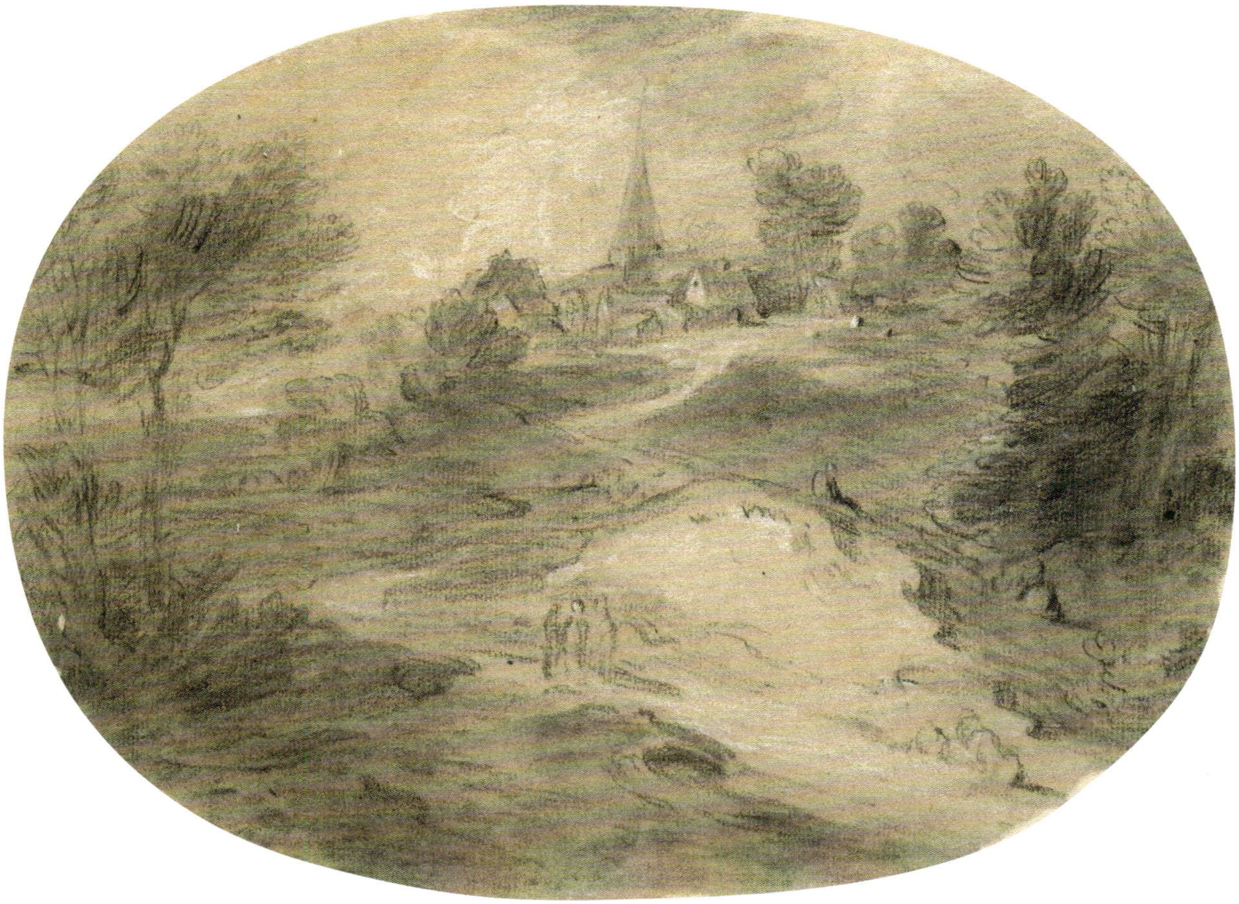

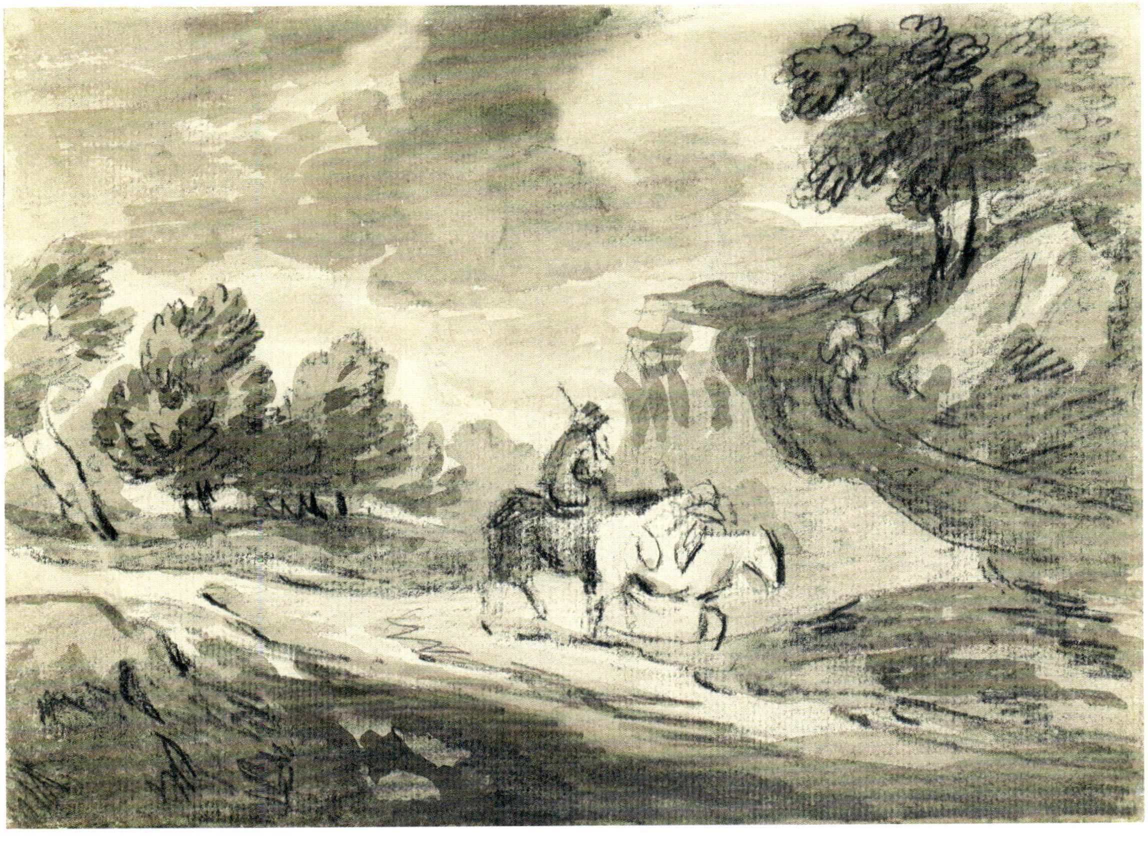

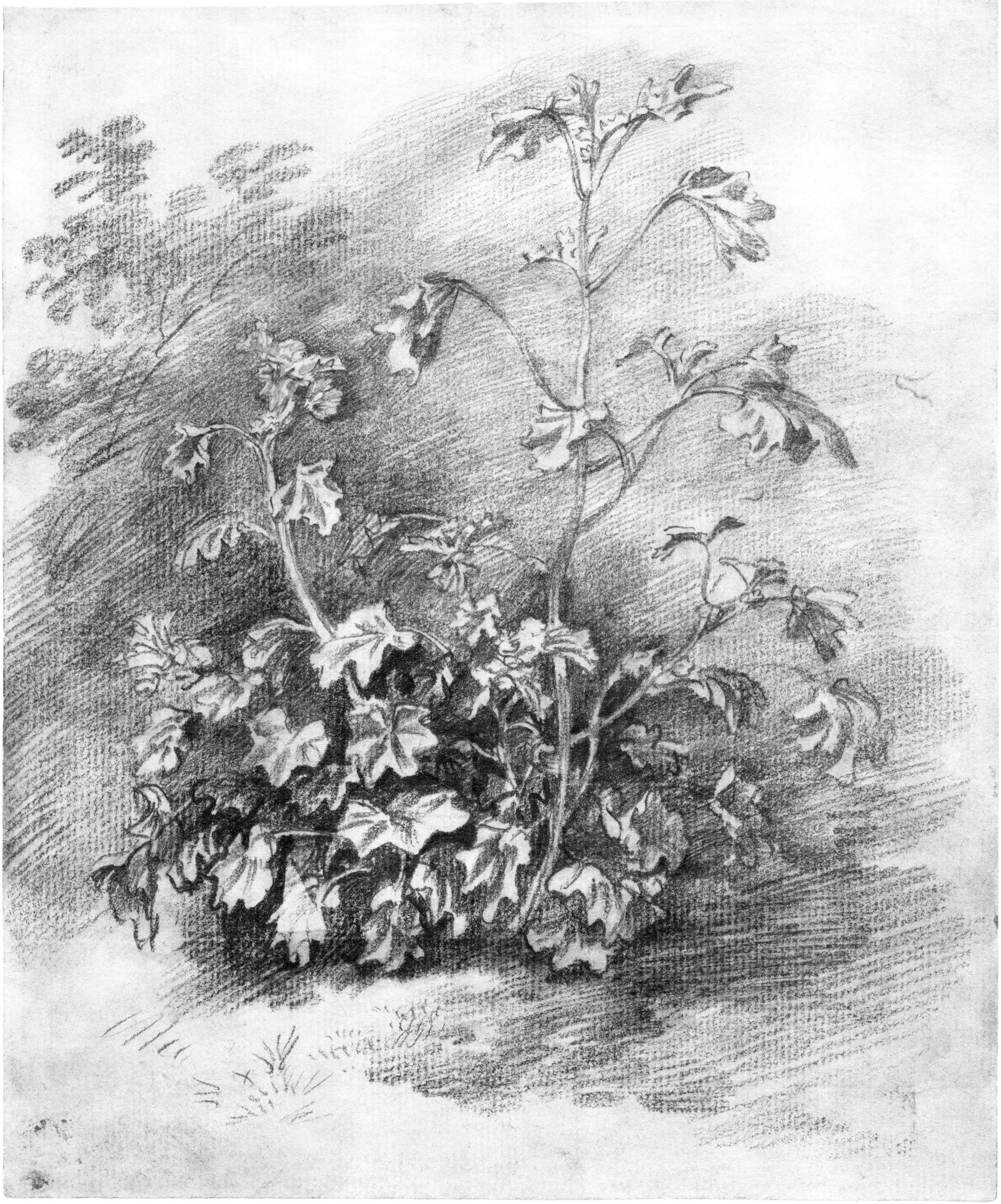

Here, Gainsborough's pencil is subjugated to what Edwards approvingly would call the "judicious attention to the minutiae of nature." The vigor of Gainsborough's hatching, characteristic too of his later touch, is restricted in this study to a landscape background, a suggestion that the study was sketched out of doors, directly from nature.

Fig. 35 Thomas Gainsborough, *Study of Mallows*, mid- to late 1750s. Graphite with stumping on white laid paper, with gum fixative, 19.3 × 15.5 cm (no. 117)

Early friends of the artist, like Thicknesse, wrote approvingly of the younger Gainsborough's attentiveness to nature, claiming, "friendship there was between him and dame NATURE . . . Nature sat to *Mr. G.* in all her attractive attitudes of beauty."[17] By contrast, the stories that circulated about the later Gainsborough tended to emphasize his studio-based and eccentric ways of working. In 1788 Sir Joshua Reynolds reported that Gainsborough brought branches, weeds, and animals into his London studio to incorporate into his landscapes, and that he even made small table-top landscape models that he then copied.[18] Edwards too remarked on this method of working, while Cunningham reported that: "He loved to sit by the side of his wife during the evenings, and make sketches of whatever occurred to his fancy, all of which he threw below the table, save such as were more than commonly happy, and those were preserved and either finished as sketches or expanded into paintings."[19]

Wooded Landscape with Rocks Overhanging a Pool (fig. 36), a black-and-white chalk drawing from the end of Gainsborough's life, displays the odd relationships of scale occasionally found in Gainsborough's drawings, which may have come from sketching natural objects indoors. The rocks in the foreground can be read as both small and large. They appear small when looked at in relation to the pool of water, and large when seen in relation to the trees. Similarly, a thin white line, to the right of the drawing, zigzags through a depression between the rocks. It reads like a path leading to a copse of trees, but if it is a path, then the rocks become enormous and wholly out of scale with the rest of the landscape elements.

Rather than careless errors, the late Gainsborough's indifference to rational scale and space and his impromptu execution signal a conscious embrace of artifice. His later drawings are not intended to look like nature but to look like drawings. Despite their oddities of scale, drawings like *Wooded Landscape with Rocks Overhanging a Pool* succeed visually because we view them as a whole; it is only when we break them down into smaller passages that we find inconsistencies and discrepancies and then wonder at these amazing, even playful sleights of hand. It is the visual truth of the whole rather than of the individual detail that Gainsborough values and presents to us. It is his artistry in interpreting nature, not accuracy in reproducing nature, that his drawing style calls to

Fig. 36 Thomas Gainsborough, *Wooded Landscape with Rocks Overhanging a Pool*, mid-1780s. Black chalk and lead white with stumping on beige laid paper, fixed with skim milk (?), 26.5 × 32.7 cm (no. 127)

Fig. 37 Thomas Gainsborough, *Extensive Wooded Landscape with a Bridge over a Gorge, Distant Village, and Hills*, c. 1786. Black and white chalks with stumping on beige laid paper, fixed with skim milk and/or gum, 25.9 × 34.8 cm (no. 128)

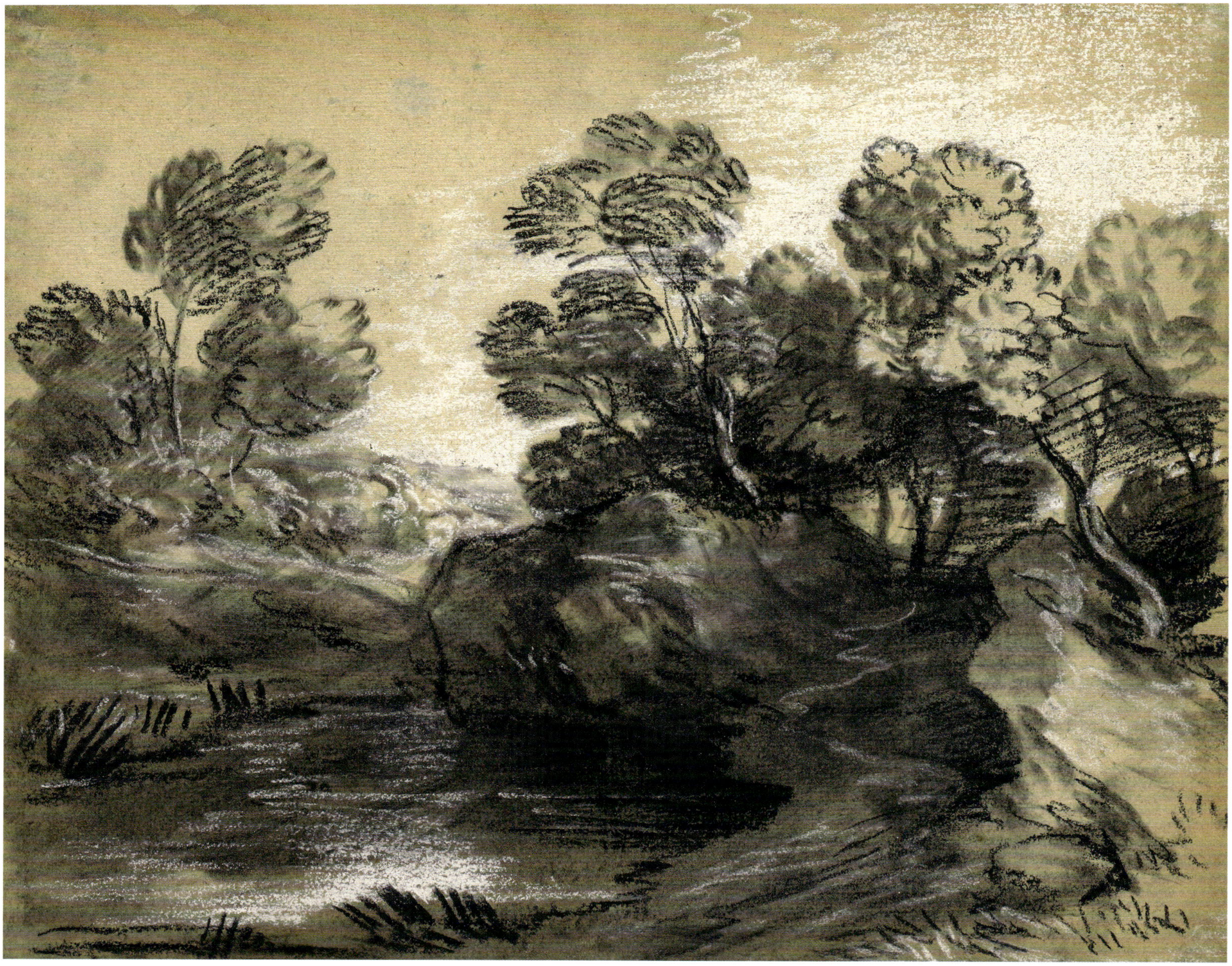

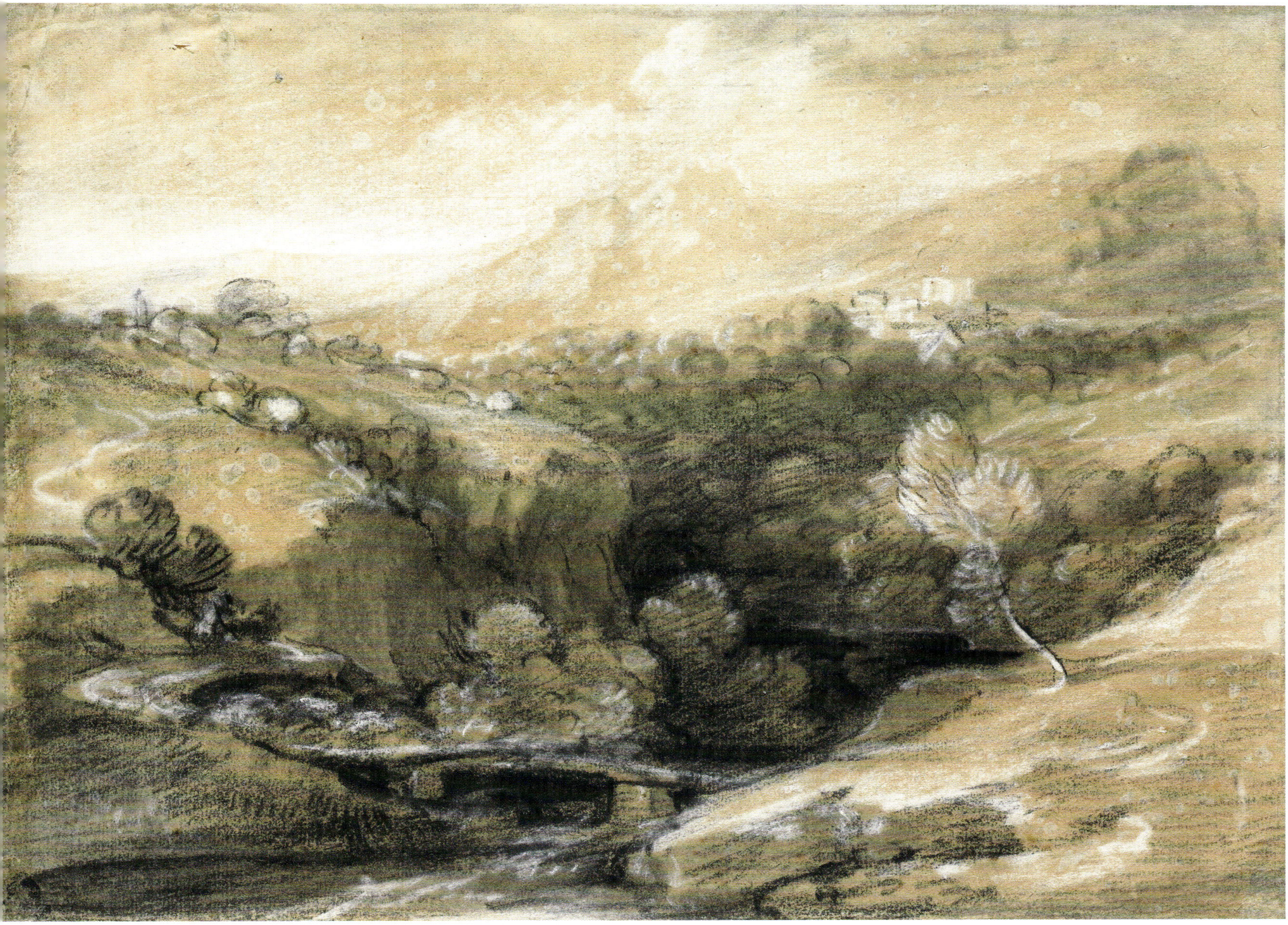

Fig. 38 John Constable (English, 1776–1837), *Study of an Ash Tree, East Bergholt*, October 1810. Black chalk on white laid paper, 17.7 × 11.4 cm (no. 44)

our attention. A great deal of the strength of his compositions has to do with the way in which he plays with light against dark in endless varying progressions: dark foregrounds against light distances, dark shadows against gray or white highlights. The rhythms of his tonal structures are like those found in the Baroque music he so loved. When examined with an eye to their abstract patterns, works such as *Landscape with Herdsman Driving Cows and Distant Buildings* reveal a masterful play of light and a happy diagonal placement of trees that energizes the composition.

Occasionally late drawings return to nature, but without the intensity of *Study of Mallows*. The extraordinary *Extensive Wooded Landscape with a Bridge Over a Gorge, Distant Village, and Hills* was most likely done while visiting the Lake District around 1786 (fig. 37). Here Gainsborough's characteristic freedom of handling combines with the suggestion of an actual place. The rugged landscape recalls Cumberland and Westmoreland, as does the small stone bridge in the foreground. The character of the place becomes an occasion for the artist to display his powers of composition. The dark tones gathered at the center of the composition pull the eye into the deep vertical gorge that extends into the foreground, ending at the horizontal bridge that spans this vertical space and serves as a counterweight to the rising mountains in the far distance. Despite the references to place, it is Gainsborough's powers of abstraction that draw our attention.

It was on the strength of early works such as *Study of Mallows*, and not late drawings like *Extensive Wooded Landscape with a Bridge Over a Gorge, Distant Village, and Hills* that artists and critics like Edwards could argue in the early nineteenth century for Gainsborough's continuing importance to younger artists. The early works they felt showed an earnest grappling with natural appearances that the later works, sketched from models seen in firelight or even from the imagination, lacked. For them, the later Gainsborough's fault as a draftsman lay in his distancing himself from nature, becoming ultimately indifferent to its actual appearance, which presented a dangerous example for young artists at the start of the new century.

At this time the young John Constable wrote to a friend declaring his determination to stop "running after pictures and seeking truth at second hand." His resolution, one that Craig would have heartily approved, was instead to "make some laborious studies from nature."[20] One of the artists Constable had run after was Gainsborough. Writing from Ipswich, a town where Gainsborough had once lived, the impressionable young Constable imagined seeing him "in every hedge and hollow tree."[21] The result of Constable's new-found determination to study nature directly can be seen in *Study of an Ash Tree, East*

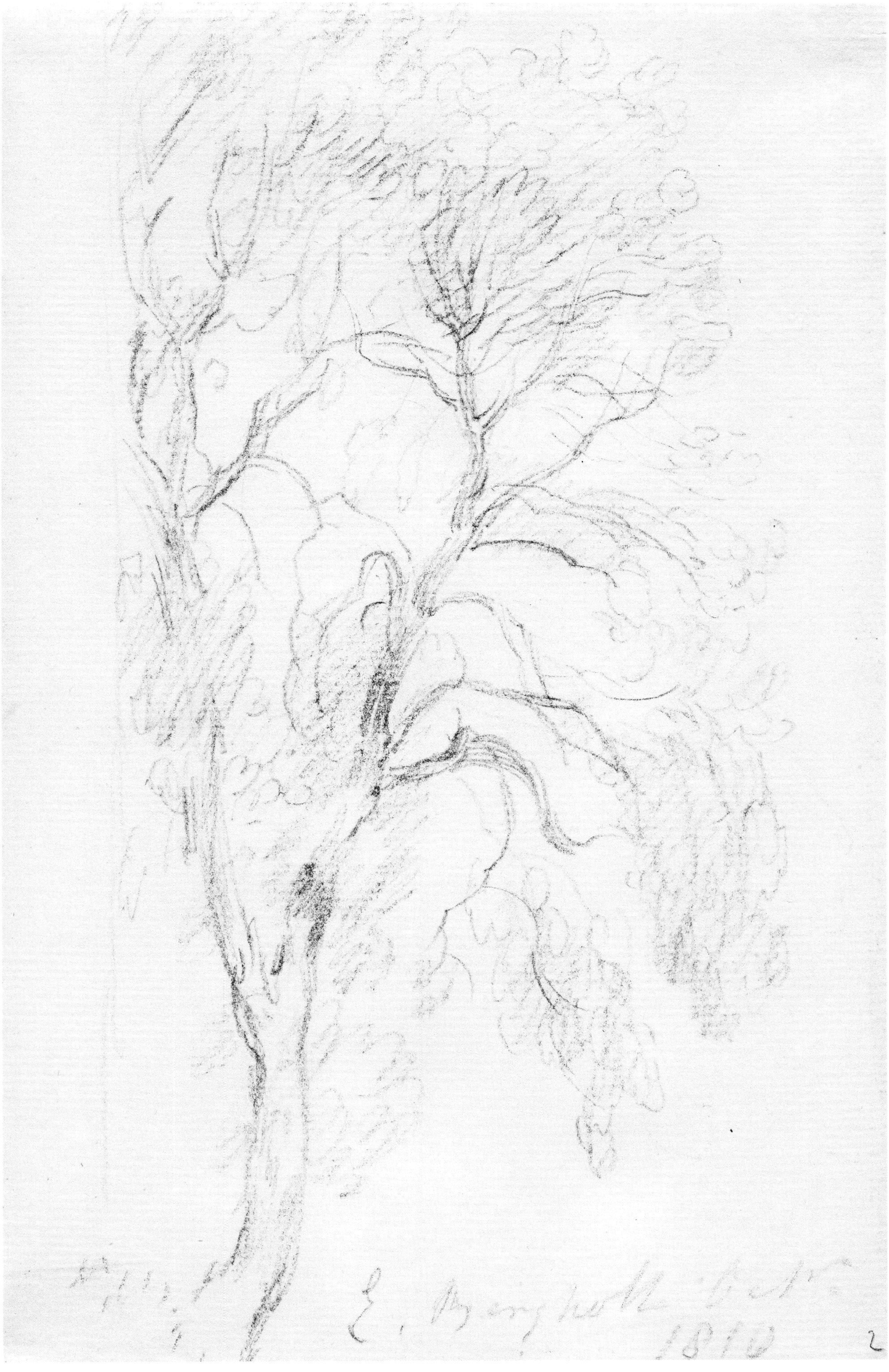

Bergholt from 1810 in which his black chalk searches out the particular linear branching system of the ash and the way the weight of the foliage causes the thinner branches to bend (fig. 38). The emphasis is not on decorative shapes and tonal patterns, but on the particular appearance of this individual tree. Like Gainsborough's *Study of Mallows*, it is a portrait of a singular object.

However, when we compare Gainsborough's and Constable's studies side by side we see significant differences not only between these two great landscape artists but between two great periods of landscape drawing and painting. Constable struggles to capture the individuality of the ash, to match his pencil's lines and shadings to the tree's branching patterns, to render as exactly as possible the tree's character and uniqueness. The result is a drawing that seems intended for no one's eyes but the artist's own, a study made to discipline the eye and the hand, and perhaps to serve as an *aide-mémoire*. Constable's labors to match as nearly as possible the drawing with the object should be contrasted to Gainsborough's efforts. Whereas Constable ignores background details to focus all his attention on the tree, Gainsborough suggests a background, thus rounding out the study of an object into a more complete landscape composition. Where Constable forgets everything except the ash, Gainsborough never forgets that he is making a drawing first and a study of a particular plant second; he is determined to make an interesting drawing from this humble clump of mallows.

Constable's emphasis on matching and Gainsborough's on making is the difference between the nineteenth century's romantic approach to landscape and the previous century's love of artifice.[22] The eighteenth century's sleights of hand, best seen in Gainsborough's calligraphic flourishes, tonal rhythms, and playful ambiguities of scale and space, give way in the early nineteenth century to a new sincerity with regard to the rendering of natural appearances. Landscapes like Gainsborough's that openly announce their artificial nature by drawing attention to their abstract elements and virtuosic management of line and tone might have been admired by later artists like Constable, but they were not imitated. A sea change in artistic taste and sensibility had come about. The rise of a new generation of landscape draftsmen like Constable, Thomas Girtin, Samuel Prout, John Cotman, David Cox, and J. M. W. Turner in the first decades of the nineteenth century announced a new attentiveness to natural appearances, and in the process an end to the "daubings, moppings, and splashings" that had so delighted Gainsborough and his followers.

1 Rudolph Ackermann, *A Treatise on Ackermann's Superfine Watercolours* (London, 1806), n.p.; and Huet Villiers, *Rudiments and Characters of Trees* (London, 1806), n.p.

2 *Somerset House Gazette*, 20 December 1823, 123. This anonymous essay, titled "On the Rise and Progress of Watercolour Painting," has been attributed to the artist William Henry Pyne.

3 Allan Cunningham, *Lives of Eminent British Painters, Sculptors, and Artists*, 5 vols. (London, 1829), 1:272.

4 Ibid., 1:273.

5 Edward Edwards, *Anecdotes of Painters* (London, 1808), 131.

6 Philip Thicknesse, *A Sketch of the Life and Paintings of Thomas Gainsborough, Esq.* (London, 1788), 42.

7 John Hayes, *The Drawings of Thomas Gainsborough*, 2 vols. (New Haven, Conn., and London: Yale University Press, 1971), 1:327.

8 See John Hayes, *Gainsborough as Printmaker* (New Haven, Conn., and London: Yale University Press, 1972), 26–27.

9 On Gainsborough's work as a printmaker, see Ibid.

10 There are two earlier states of this print, both printed by Gainsborough. The first is in the Staatliche Museen, Berlin, and consists of aquatint without any soft-ground. The second is in the Yale Center for British Art, and is inscribed: "Gainsbro by himself/presented to Sr. J. I. by Mrs. Gainsbro." This print was created with aquatint and soft-ground. Both Gainsborough prints are reproduced in Hayes, *Gainsborough as Printmaker*, 98–101. The Boydell print, an impression of which is also in the Yale Center for British Art, is more professionally inked and wiped. As a result, signs of hair and lint that appear in Gainsborough's second impression are eliminated in the Boydell impression, and certain passages, such as the foliage attached to the blasted tree, are more readable.

11 See Greg Smith, *The Emergence of the Professional Watercolourist: Contentions and Alliances in the Artistic Domain, 1760–1824* (Aldershot, U.K., and Burlington, Vt.: Ashgate, 2002), 112–25; and my own "System, Order, and Abstraction: The Politics of English Landscape Drawing around 1795," in W. J. T. Mitchell, ed., *Landscape and Power* (Chicago: University of Chicago Press, 1994), 77–101.

12 William Marshall Craig, *Essay on the Study of Nature in Drawing Landscape* (London, 1793), 19.

13 Ibid.

14 Edwards, *Anecdotes of Painters*, 138–39.

15 Ibid., 139.

16 Conservation notes by Leslie Hill Paisley on Gainsborough drawings in the Manton Collection on file at the Clark.

17 Thicknesse, *A Sketch of Gainsborough*, 14.

18 Joshua Reynolds, *Discourses*, ed. Robert Wark (New Haven, Conn., and London: Yale University Press, 1975), 250.

19 Edwards, *Anecdotes of Painters*, 135; and Cunningham, *Lives of Eminent British Painters, Sculptors, and Artists*, 1:269.

20 *John Constable's Correspondence*, ed. Ronald Brymer Beckett, vol. 2, *Early Friends and Maria Bicknell (Mrs Constable)* (Ipswich, U.K.: Suffolk Records Society, 1964), 31–32.

21 Ibid., 16.

22 "Making and matching" is Ernst Gombrich's famous formulation. See his *Art and Illusion: A Study in the Psychology of Pictorial Representation* (1960; repr. Princeton, N.J.: Princeton University Press, 1969).

Print Portfolios and Narrative Series

Blake, Turner, and Constable

Antony Griffiths

The Manton Collection contains prints from three of the most famous portfolios made in England in the first third of the nineteenth century. Turner's *Liber Studiorum*, Blake's *Book of Job*, and Constable's *English Landscape* (to list them in order of publication) form at first glance a miscellaneous group of disparate material. But they have some remarkably close links. All were made within a short period of time (1807–33), all three artists knew each other, and the artists would have known each other's work (though Blake had died before Constable's series was begun). All three series emerged from the same context of printmaking in London, and two of the series (those by Blake and Turner) were printed by the same plate printer, James Lahee (active 1811–1852), a man highly regarded at the time. Thomas Dibdin, the bibliographer, paid him a warm tribute: "He is among the most punctual men of business with whom I am acquainted; and in the mezzotint department of art the acknowledged '*facile princeps*' [first by far]."[1]

All three portfolios stand far outside the mainstream of print publishing of the time. They were published by the artists themselves or, in Blake's case, by a close friend, and were inspired by non-commercial considerations. Each was a very personal production, meant a great deal to their authors, and cost a great deal of time, effort, and worry. They each lost money, as the way in which they were produced was anything but businesslike. The artists' energy went almost entirely into making the prints, leaving little left over for marketing and selling. However, they resulted in what today are some masterpieces of printmaking of the period, and among the most important productions of the three artists concerned.

In discussing these series, it will be convenient to take Blake first, before Turner and Constable. Blake was much older than the others, and his *Book of Job* (fig. 39) was made at the end of his life, when he was living in near-indigence. The moderate success that he had in the eighteenth century as a reproductive engraver, trained as an apprentice of James Basire (1730–1802), was in the distant past; he and his wife had more recently spent their time on his now famous and then unsalable illuminated books. It was at this low point in his career that he was "discovered" by a group of young artists, among them John Linnell (1792–1882), a relatively successful landscape painter who was exhibiting at the Royal Academy. It was Linnell who formulated the idea of supporting Blake by commissioning him to engrave the *Book of Job*, and who paid all the associated costs. The project is remarkably well documented in Linnell's papers, and has been superbly published by modern scholars. As a result, we know more about it than about any other print series of the period.[2]

The figure of Job, a patriarch of the Old Testament with an entire book of the Bible devoted to his story, meant a great deal to Blake, who treated this subject frequently in his work from the 1780s onward. Blake clearly identified with this heroic man who was made the victim of a wager between God and the Devil, who cast him down from his prosperity and reduced him to destitution and misery. His final rescue in the Bible is almost as arbitrary as his fall. Blake, however, as many commentators have observed, changed the significance of the bleak Old Testament moral in his series of illustrations, replacing it with a form of personal redemption through understanding. The genesis of the series lay in a set of twenty-one watercolors that Blake had made for his patron Thomas Butts between 1804 and 1810.[3] These were borrowed back and traced by Linnell and Blake in 1821, and formed the basis for a set of reworkings of compositions by Blake in 1823.[4] It was in March of that year that Linnell drew up a contract with Blake to engrave the plates, which were printed in 1825. Each plate bore a publication line giving the date of 8 March, and a copyright line listing Blake as the publisher. In reality, Linnell had paid all the costs, including a fee to Blake, and in July 1826 Blake signed a receipt for one hundred fifty pounds from Linnell in return for the copyright and the plates. By this stage the printing of about three hundred fifteen sets had been finished, and distribution had begun to Blake's small circle of admirers. Linnell must have hoped the sales would cover his costs, although he still had copies available for sale in the 1860s.

The twenty-one plates were issued with a title plate, but without any letterpress. Instead, the text was contained within the printed images in the astonishingly original marginal decorations, which include not only a caption explaining which part of Job's story is being illustrated, but also Blake's own selections of comments from other stories in the Bible, both from the New Testament and the Old. These offer Blake's personal glosses that reinterpret the meaning of the story to give an explanation for Job's sufferings in a way that made sense of the story for Blake himself. *The Lord Answering Job out of the Whirlwind* (fig. 40), numbered plate 13 of the series at top right, incorporates text from the book of Job immediately underneath the central image, which serves both to caption the image and to identify which scene is being illustrated. Here the Lord (above) appears in the whirlwind to the kneeling figure of Job surrounded by his friends. The swirling lines of the composition extend beyond the central panel and connect it with the marginal decoration that contains additional text. The words at the top, "Who is this that darkeneth counsel," are spoken by the Lord, as are the ones below, "Hath the rain a father." But the words, "Who maketh the clouds his chariot," come from Psalm 104

Fig. 39 William Blake (English, 1757–1827), title page, from *Illustrations of the Book of Job*, 1825. Engraving on chine collé on cream wove paper, 20.2 × 16 cm (chine); 21.3 × 16.5 cm (plate); 50.6 × 34.2 cm (sheet) (no. 2)

Following spread:
Fig. 40 William Blake, *The Lord Answering Job out of the Whirlwind*, plate 13 from *Illustrations of the Book of Job*, 1825. Engraving on chine collé on cream wove paper, 20.6 × 15.7 cm (chine); 21.8 × 17 cm (plate); 51.2 × 34.5 cm (sheet) (no. 15)

Fig. 41 William Blake, *The Creation*, plate 14 from *Illustrations of the Book of Job*, 1825. Engraving on chine collé on cream wove paper, 20.3 × 15.6 cm (chine); 21.8 × 16.5 cm (plate); 50.8 × 34.5 cm (sheet) (no. 16)

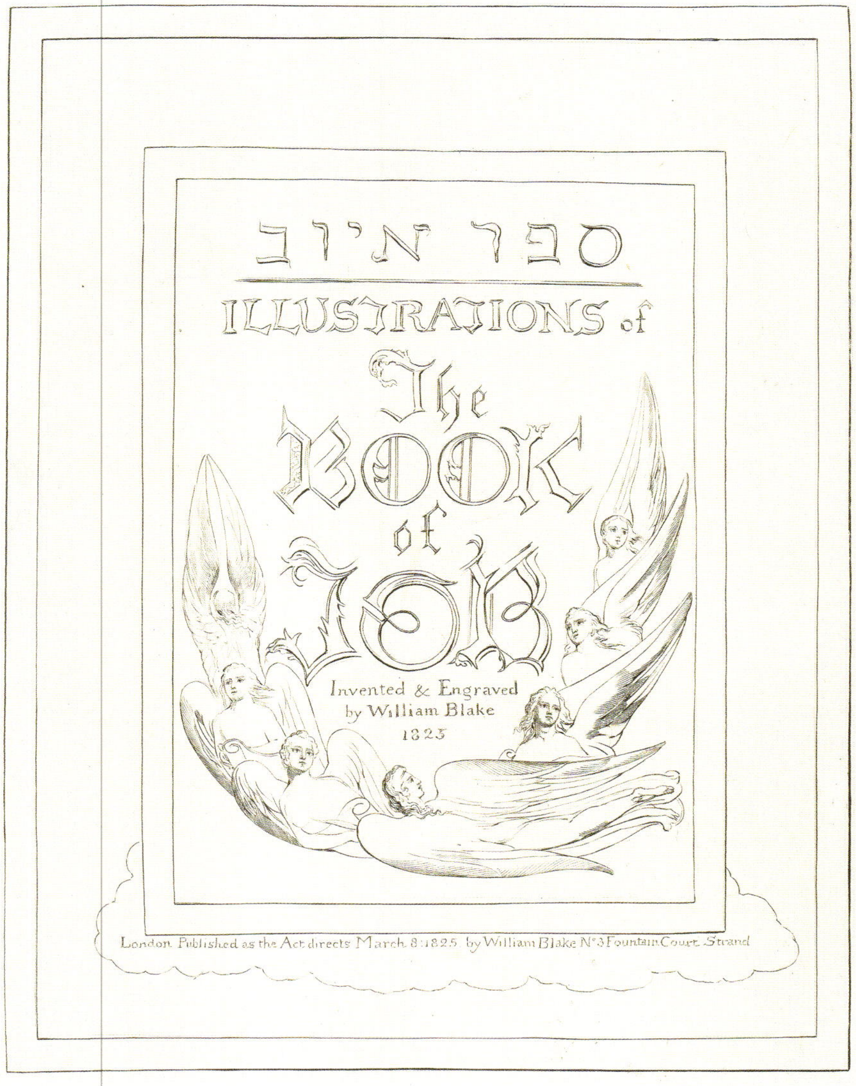

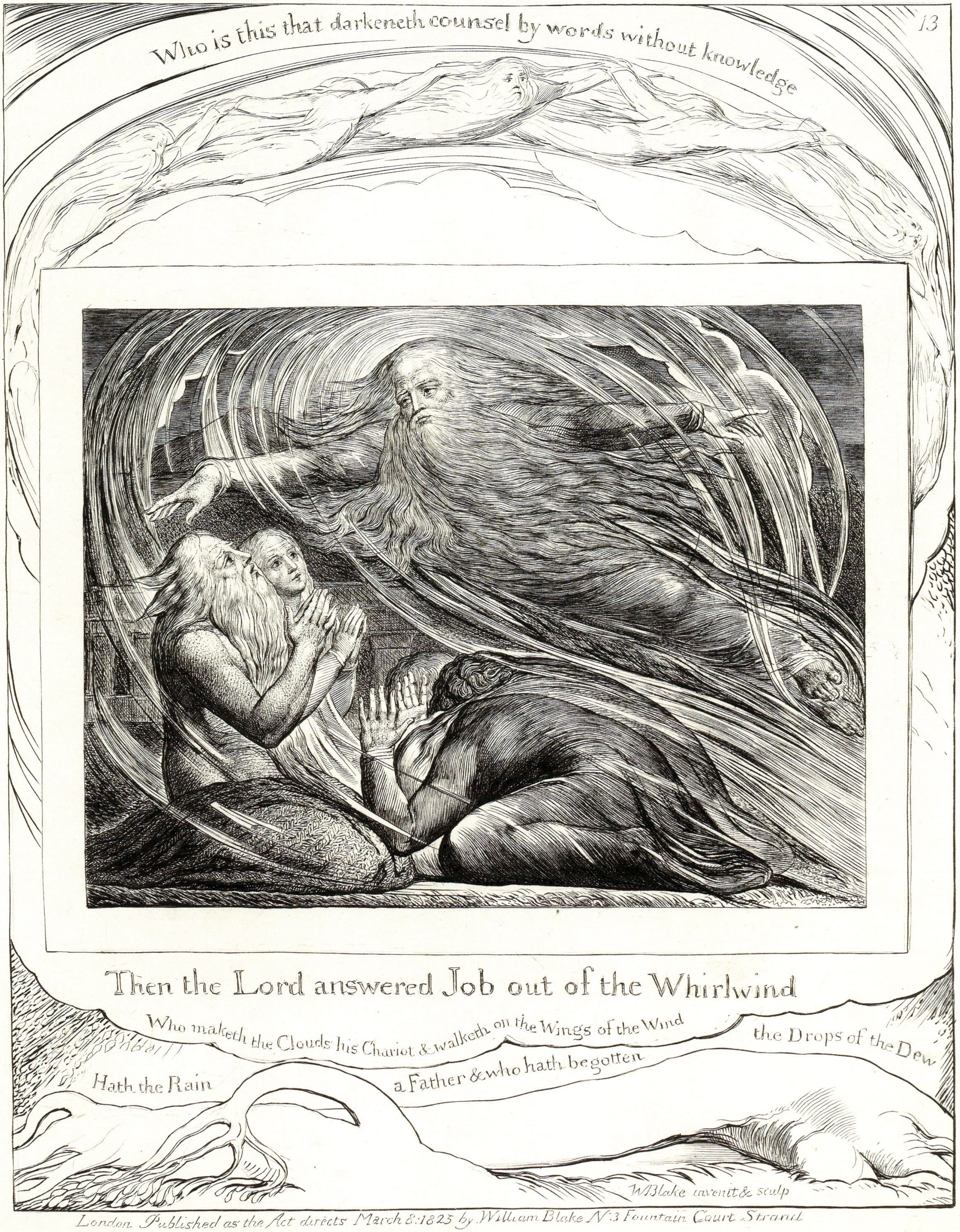
13
Who is this that darkeneth counsel by words without knowledge
Then the Lord answered Job out of the Whirlwind
Who maketh the Clouds his Chariot & walketh on the Wings of the Wind
the Drops of the Dew
Hath the Rain
a Father & who hath begotten
W Blake invenit & sculp
London Published as the Act directs March 8: 1825 by William Blake N: 3 Fountain Court Strand

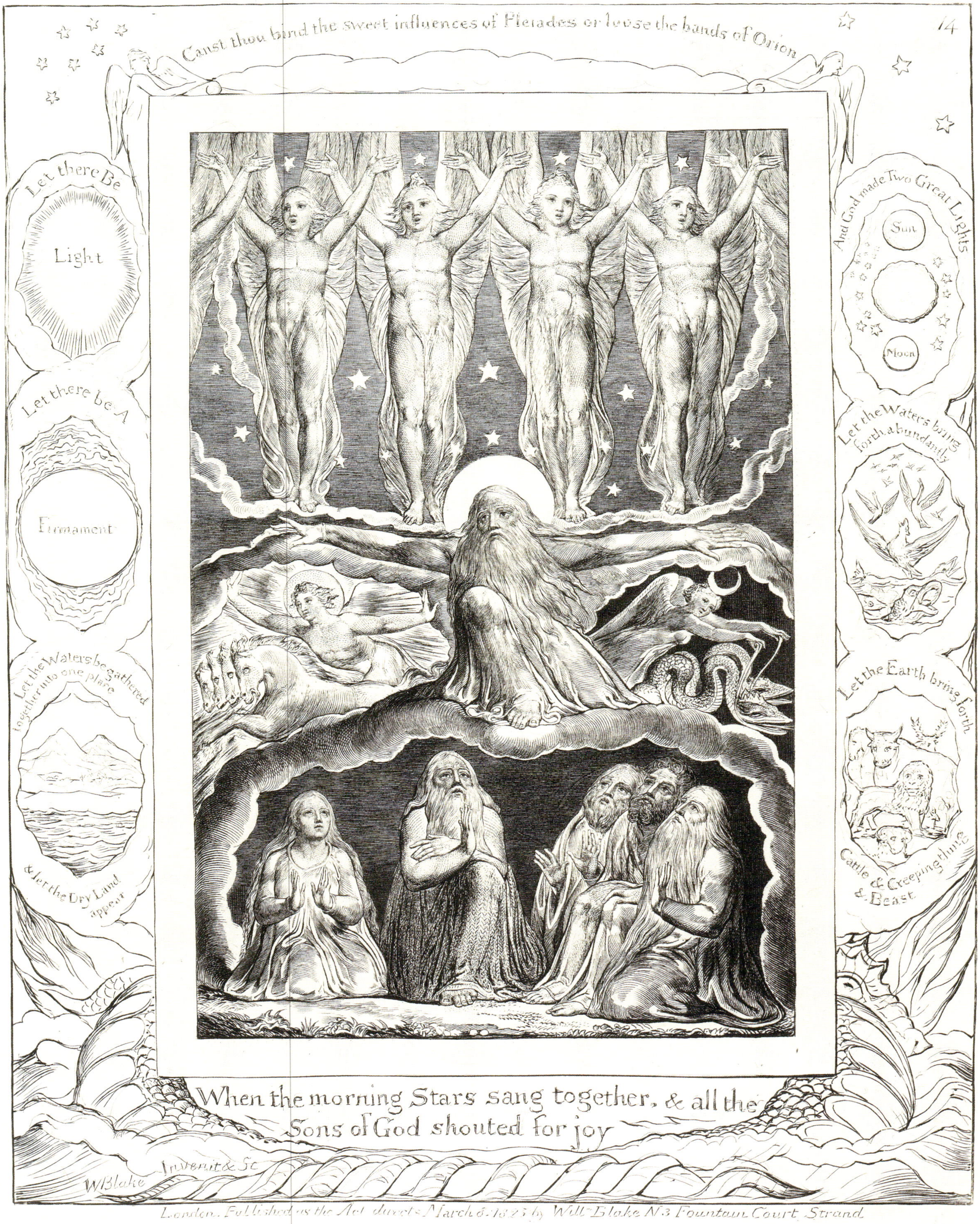
14
Canst thou bind the sweet influences of Pleiades or loose the bands of Orion
Let there Be
Light
Let there be A
Firmament
Let the Waters be gathered together into one place
& let the Dry Land appear
And God made Two Great Lights
Sun
Moon
Let the Waters bring forth abundantly
Let the Earth bring forth
Cattle & Creeping thing & Beast
When the morning Stars sang together, & all the
Sons of God shouted for joy
W Blake Invenit & Sc
London. Published as the Act directs March 8: 1825 by Willm Blake N 3 Fountain Court, Strand

and explain the way in which Blake has chosen to represent God. Along the bottom, the trees pressed to the ground by the passing whirlwind echo the figures of Job and his friends who are swayed but not broken by adversity. The following plate, number 14, *The Creation*, shows how Blake varied his formats (fig. 41). Here the composition is vertical, and down the sides are six of the acts of Creation keyed to the text from Job included along the bottom. At the top Blake added another text from Job to serve as his commentary on the scene, thus casting doubt on the rigidity of the prescriptions of the law of Moses. These compositional formats set the series far apart from more traditional illustrations tied to a narrative, such as Delacroix's illustrations to Goethe's *Faust*, which were made only a year later. Visually, too, the marginal decorations remove it from the nineteenth century into a medievalizing past, in the same way that Blake's chosen method of handling the burin looks back to sixteenth-century engravers and pays no attention to the eighteenth-century methods in which he had been trained.

If Blake was one of the least commercially successful artists of his age, Turner was one of the most successful, leaving an estate worth one hundred forty thousand pounds at his death. He was elected a full Royal Academician in 1802, at the age of 27, and was able to build his own exhibition gallery (the Turner Gallery) at 64 Harley Street, which opened in 1805. The following year he formed the idea of standing for the vacant position of Professor of Perspective at the Academy, and was duly elected in 1807. He found preparing the lectures a terrible burden (the first of them was only delivered in 1811), and we know from various sources that he would far rather have been a professor of landscape – a position that did not exist.[5] It is against this background that he began in 1807 the publication of a series of landscapes of his own composition under the title *Liber Studiorum* (fig. 42), which was originally intended to be issued in twenty parts, each of five plates. It was advertised only in Turner's Gallery, where a prospectus was on display (the text of this is lost), and there were apparently about one hundred twenty subscribers. Turner was the sole proprietor and paid all the costs. He made a new monochrome drawing for each plate, and most did not necessarily derive from an existing painting: many were new compositions. He also etched the outline design for each plate and corrected innumerable proofs after the mezzotinted ground had been added and scraped down.

This process can be seen in *Solway Moss*, published as part of the eleventh part of the series in 1816. Like the other plates, the published state carries only the title, the names of the artist and engraver (in this case Thomas Lupton), and the publication line of Turner himself in Queen Ann Street West. A first state in the British Museum shows the

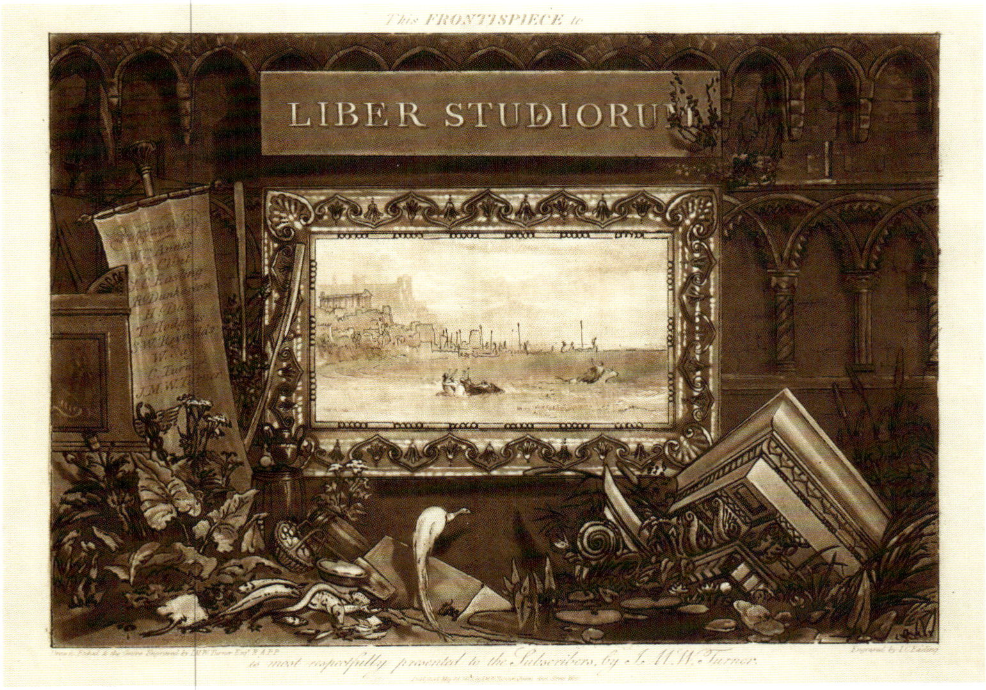

Fig. 42 Joseph Mallord William Turner (English, 1775–1851), frontispiece, from *Liber Studiorum*, May 1812. Etching and mezzotint printed in brown inks on cream wove paper, 21 × 29.3 cm (plate); 29 × 43.5 cm (sheet) (no. 213)

production process (fig. 43). Turner began by etching the outline after a preparatory wash drawing (this is now lost), and then sent a proof with watercolor and crayon overworking to Lupton. In the sky is Lupton's note suggesting that Turner might wish to add more etched lines to the plate before he (Lupton) adds the mezzotint layer. The final state was reached only after a long process of revision through successive corrected proofs (fig. 44). The top center includes the letter P, which introduces one of the oddities of the series. Every plate carries in this same position one of the letters H, M, P, A, or EP. Turner never stated what they meant, but the printed wrapper for each part gives a key: "Liber Studiorum, illustrative of landscape compositions, viz. Historical, Mountainous, Pastoral, Marine, and Architectural."[6] But M covers both "Marine" and "Mountainous," and EP was never explained. This still gives rise to controversy, though modern writers tend to favor "Elevated Pastoral."[7]

Solway Moss is a peat bog in Cumbria, near the English-Scottish border. The plate was coupled in the same part issue with four other plates: *Solitude* (no. 265); *Mill near the Grand Chartreuse* (no. 266); *Entrance of Calais Harbor* (fig. 45); and *Dumblain Abbey* (no. 268). These bear respectively the letters EP, M (for Mountainous), M (for Marine), and A. It is clear that Turner intended to arrange each part with a mixture of types, even though he

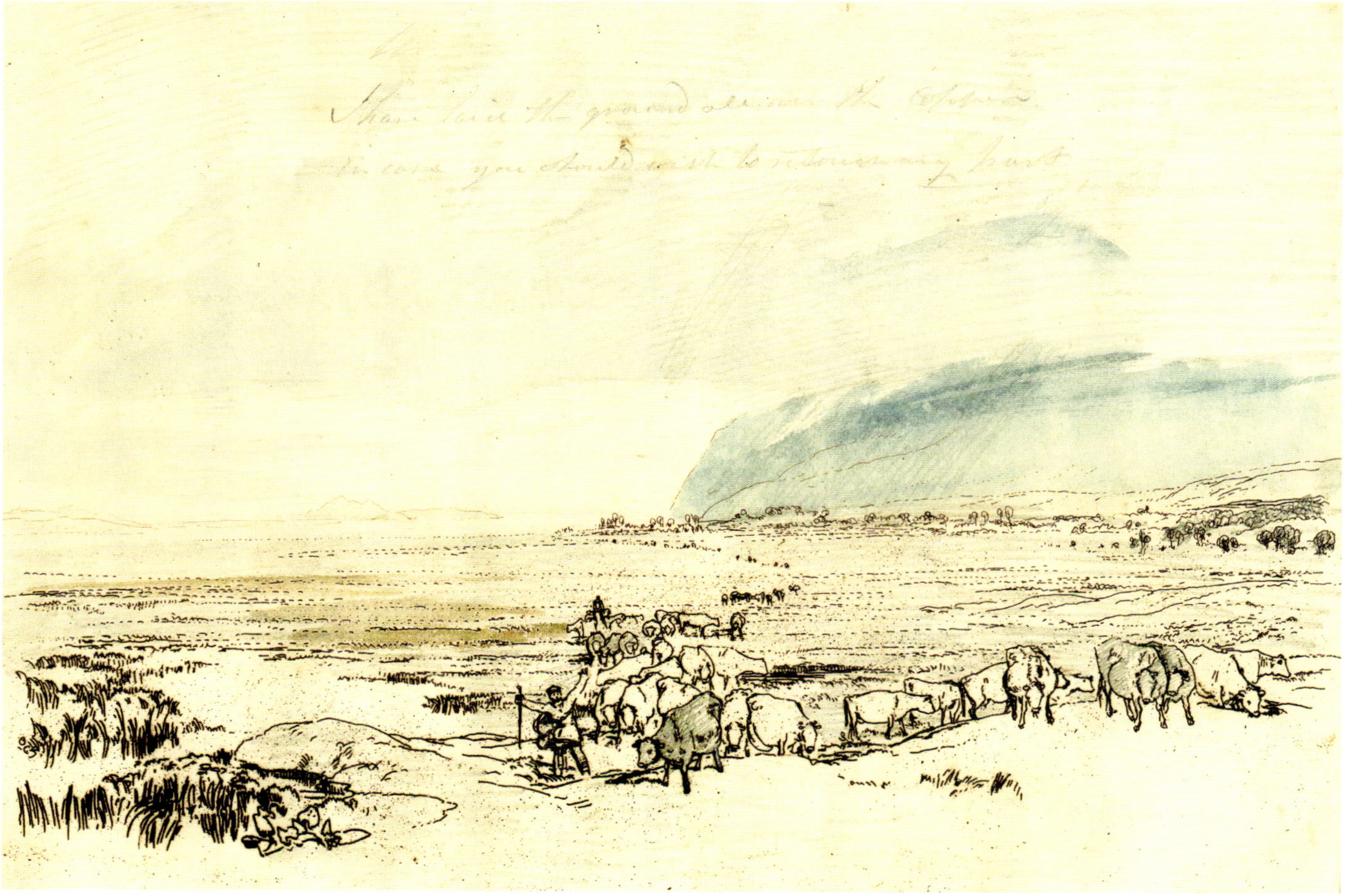

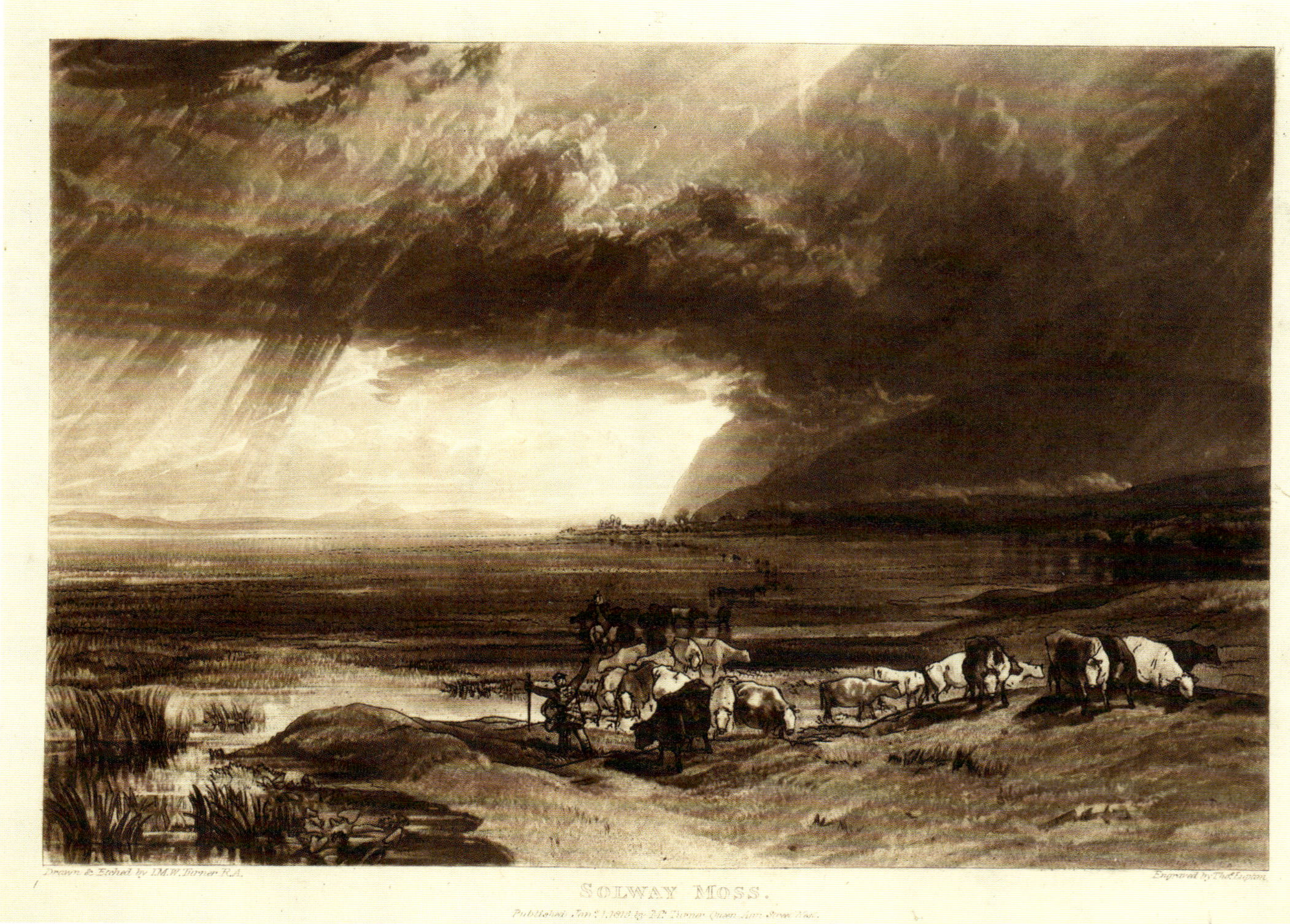
Drawn & Etched by J.M.W. Turner R.A.
SOLWAY MOSS.
Engraved by Thos Lupton

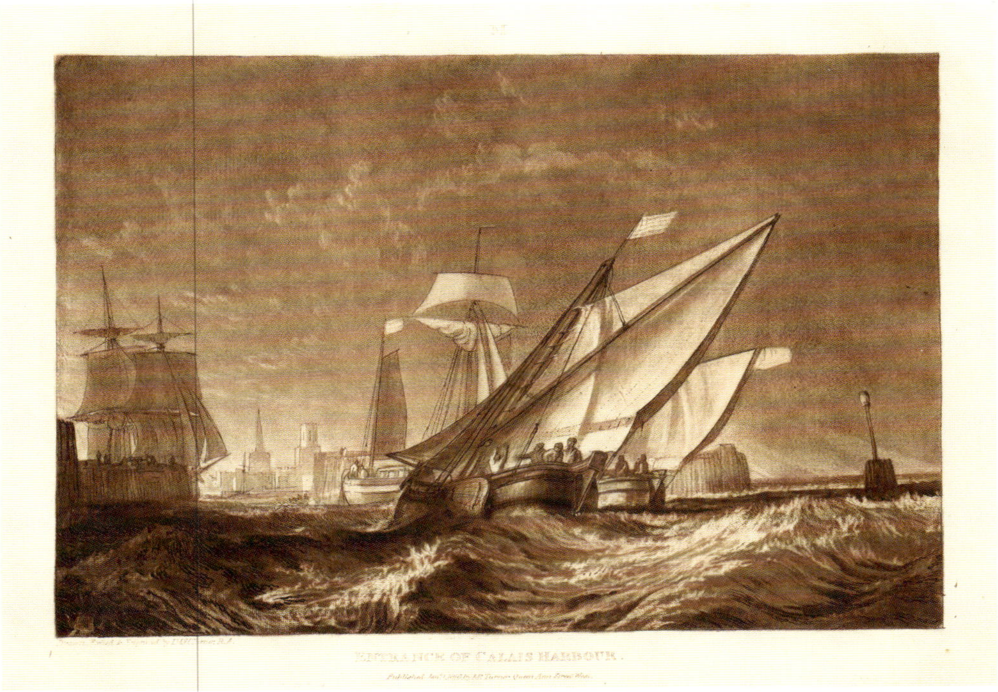

Fig. 43 Joseph Mallord William Turner, *Solway Moss*, from *Liber Studiorum*, working proof, 1816. Hand-colored etching on paper, 20.8 × 28.8 cm. British Museum, London

Fig. 44 Joseph Mallord William Turner, *Solway Moss*, 1 Jan. 1816. Etching and mezzotint printed in brown inks on cream laid paper, 20.9 × 29 cm (plate); 29.3 × 42.5 cm (sheet) (no. 264)

Fig. 45 Joseph Mallord William Turner, *Entrance of Calais Harbor*, from *Liber Studiorum*, 1 Jan. 1816. Etching and mezzotint printed in brown inks on cream laid paper, 21.9 × 30.2 cm (plate); 29.3 × 42.4 cm (sheet) (no. 267)

could not in practice do so, since he issued only five plates in each part, whereas he had six compositional types. Nevertheless, the series was intended to be read in a sequence, with different landscape compositions succeeding each other.

Initially Turner hired Charles Turner (not a relation) as his sole collaborator, and for a short period in 1808–9 employed him as distributor and manager of the project. They fell out over Turner's extreme miserliness; he was only prepared to pay eight guineas a plate for all the mezzotinting, printing, and delivery to subscribers. So Turner himself resumed the role of manager and recruited a group of ten replacement mezzotinters. But the project dragged more and more slowly, and was eventually broken off in 1819, after Turner's first visit to Italy. At this point seventy plates had been issued in fourteen parts, plus a frontispiece to the whole series.

Managing a project as complicated as this is a major undertaking, and Turner was neither prepared to pay another enough to do the work, nor had time or space to manage it himself. His extraordinary success as a painter led to his receiving as many commissions for watercolors to be engraved at the risk and expense of other publishers – either as book illustrations or as topographical series – as he could possibly handle.[8] Big printmaking projects generate great quantities of impressions, and keeping track of what belongs with what is a major undertaking in itself, demanding large areas of space for sorting and storage, space which Turner did not have available in his home. The problem was compounded by the fact that he issued the prints in different proof and print states, and by his demand for large (his publishers thought outrageous) numbers of impressions of all his other plates as part of his fee. When he died, the prints in his house filled two horse-drawn carts, and the sales of them at Christie's in 1873–74 contained more than seventy-six thousand impressions. So the question arises, why did he bother with the *Liber*?

To this there is no certain answer, as Turner never explained his intentions. But the division of the plates between his classifications of landscape, pastoral, elevated pastoral, mountainous, architectural, historical, and marine suggests that he wished to give a complete survey of landscape as he understood it, and thus demonstrate his mastery of the field. As has always been realized by those that know something about the history of prints, Turner was consciously matching himself against Claude Lorrain, and in particular his so-called *Liber Veritatis*. This was Claude's own record of his paintings, in a series of two hundred monochrome drawings mounted in an album, then in the collection of the Duke of Devonshire in Derbyshire.[9] Turner had almost certainly never seen the originals, but he knew the series well from the publication by Richard Earlom (fig. 46) that had appeared in parts between 1774 and 1777.[10] He deliberately followed Earlom both in technique (mezzotint over etching) and in color of ink (light brown, often described as sepia). Turner's title also echoes Claude's, whom he saw as the great model for the types of elevated landscape that he himself made. Turner took the variety and beauty of Claude's compositions as an implied challenge; once we see the *Liber Studiorum* as Turner's way of claiming his own place in the history of landscape painting, we can understand why the project meant so much to him.

Turner always saw his oeuvre as having an inner unity; he strove for it to be seen as completely as possible. This desire underlay not only the *Liber Studiorum*, but also his establishment of the Turner Gallery, and eventually the bequest of his studio to the nation.[11] In later life someone told him that a print dealer, F. Halsted, was breaking up the *Liber Studiorum* for sale as individual plates, as some plates sold better than others. At this he grunted out: "A pack of geese! A pack of Geese! Don't they know what Liber Studiorum means?"[12]

Turner's claim to his own position in the history of landscape painting, and his implied assertion of eminence if not preeminence in the field, inevitably acted as a challenge to his contemporaries and successors. Such was the case with John Constable and his *English Landscape*, a series of twenty mezzotints after his own compositions, made by David Lucas and published in five parts, each of four plates, between June 1830 and July 1832.[13] Constable began work on the series in September 1829, when he was 53 years old and had many of his greatest paintings already behind him. His wife had died in November the previous year, and Constable himself was far from well, and oppressed by the responsibility of raising seven children single-handedly. On the other hand, for the first time in his life he was financially secure through a bequest made to his wife shortly before her death in 1828, which gave the family an income of around one thousand pounds a year. This enabled Constable to embark on a project that we may reasonably assume he had long been contemplating. He met all Lucas's costs himself, from supplying the plates to the charges for proofing and printing the entire edition.[14] Constable also saw to the subscriptions and delivery of copies himself.

That the series meant a great deal to him can readily be understood from reading the succession of letters between Constable and Lucas that document the progress of the work,[15] and the extraordinary number of corrected ("touched") progress proofs

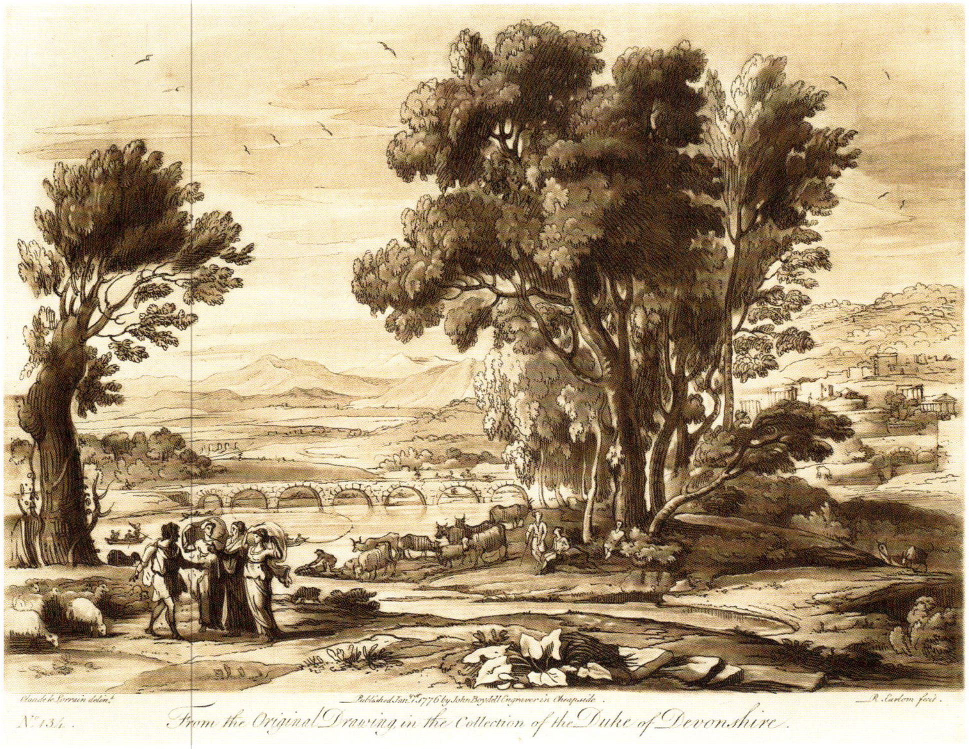

Fig. 46 Richard Earlom (English, 1743–1822), after Claude Lorrain (French, 1604/5–1682), *Landscape with Jacob and Laban with Laban's Daughters*, from *Liber Veritatis*, 1776. Mezzotint and etching on paper, 20.6 × 25.6 cm. Sterling and Francine Clark Art Institute, Williamstown, Mass.

Fig. 47 David Lucas (English, 1802–1881), after John Constable (English, 1776–1837), *Seabeach, Brighton*, from *English Landscape*, 1830. Mezzotint on paper, 19.0 × 25.3 cm. British Museum, London

Fig. 48 David Lucas, after John Constable, *Old Sarum*, from *English Landscape*, 1833. Mezzotint, trimmed to image and laid within false platemark, on cream wove paper, 13.6 × 18.4 cm (image) (no. 171)

with which he tormented Lucas.[16] Constable's mood alternated between despair when the proofs came out badly and exhilaration when all went well. Sales were poor, mainly because he never put any energy into trying to market the prints. Many sets were given away to friends and patrons, and others were left on a sale-or-return basis with his friend, the print dealer Paul Colnaghi.[17] But none of this added up to anything like a return on his outlay, which prompted a bout of self-recrimination as he blamed himself for robbing his children of their inheritance.

So again we have to ask why he undertook the series. Constable, unlike Blake and Turner, accompanied some of his plates with a separate sheet of explanatory text in letterpress. This was mostly written in 1833, after the series had been finished.[18] Though few of the plates had such a text, when they did the narrative could be very long. Constable constantly rewrote these texts, in the same way as he continuously changed his mind about the makeup of the four plates that went into each part. The two examples illustrated here follow each other in the order of publication. *Seabeach, Brighton* is, we learn from the text, set in the city of Brighton on the south coast of England, and Constable's text expounds both on the grandeur of an incoming wave and on the recent development and healthy properties of the town itself (fig. 47). This part of the text reads almost as though it might have been written by the local tourist office. For the next plate, *Old Sarum* (fig. 48), Constable provided a text of eight hundred fifty words, which

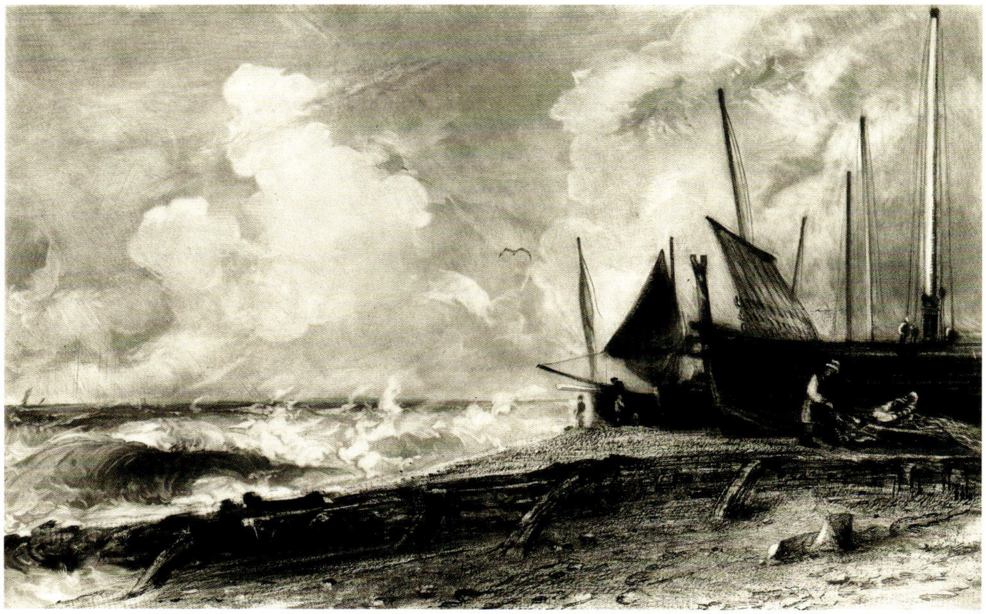

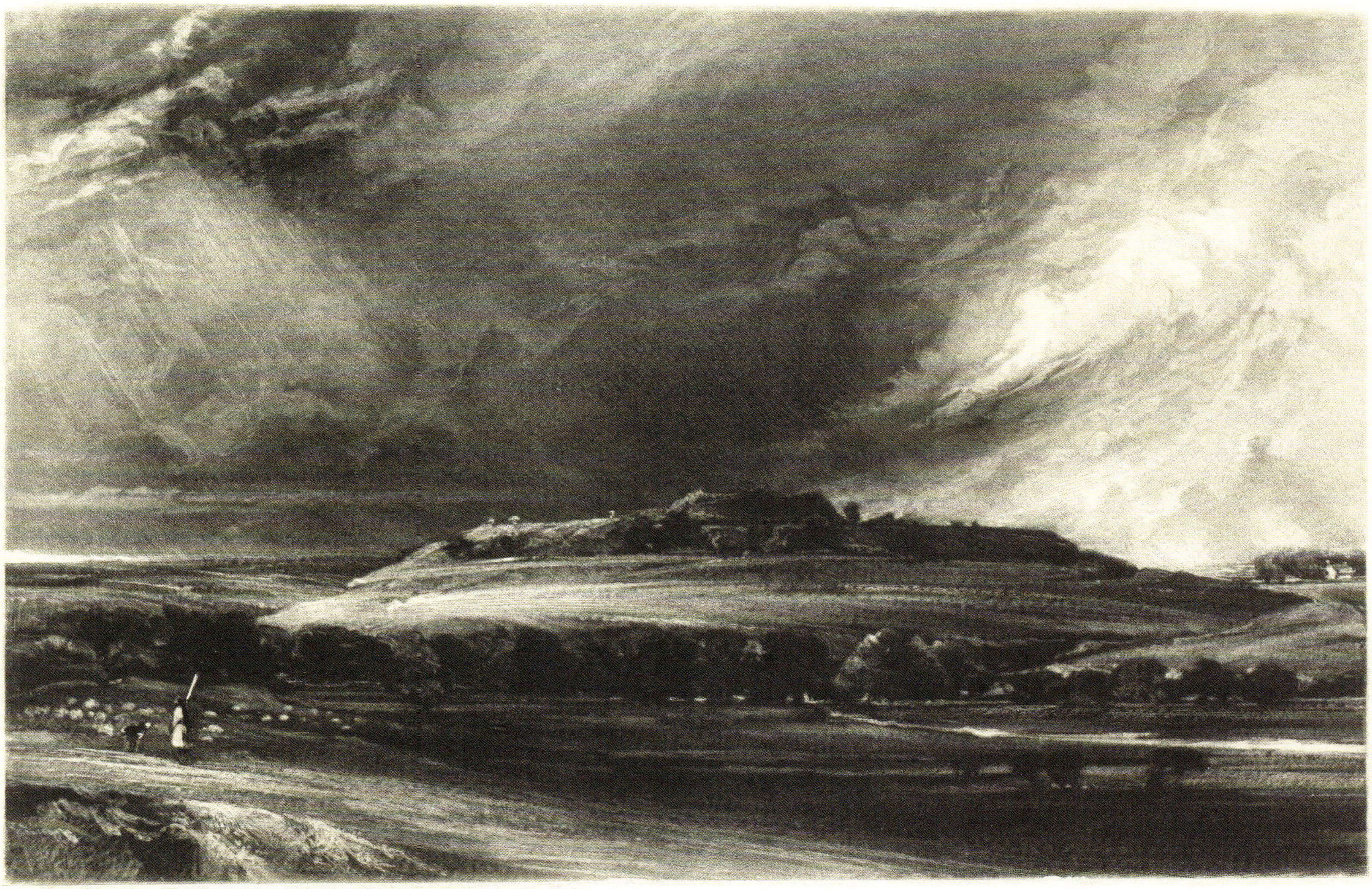

concludes with twelve lines from the poet James Thomson's *Seasons* (1726–30). It reveals Constable's emotional response to the passage of time: "The present appearance of Old Sarum – wild, desolate, and dreary – contrasts strongly with its former greatness." It also evokes the symbolic significance of the abandoned city: "This proud and 'towered city,' once giving laws to the whole kingdom ... It was on this spot the wild Conqueror, in 1086, confirmed that great political event, the establishment of the feudal system."[19]

Constable's account of the series would be unlikely to occur to the modern viewer, but it gives the best insights into his art: how it emerged from his love of the Stour Valley and the English countryside, and how he was attempting to convey the "chiaroscuro" of nature, which comprehended the different play of light on landscape at different seasons and times of day. This was far from the approach of Turner or Blake, who in one of the ferocious notes in his so-called Public Address wrote, "No man of sense can think that an imitation of the objects of nature is the art of painting, or that such imitation, which anyone may easily perform, is worthy of notice."[20] Constable's texts show how he wished to interpret and describe the series, but they do not explain why he wanted to make it. For this we need to go back to a remark he made in a letter to his great friend John Fisher in January 1825: "My reputation at home among my brother artists [is] dayly gaining ground, & I deeply feel the honour of having found an original style & independent of him who would be Lord over all – I mean Turner – I believe it would be difficult to say that there is a bit of landscape that does not emanate from that source."[21]

This statement provides a clue to the significance of *English Landscape*. Toward the end of his career, his reputation amongst his contemporaries now established, Constable wished to secure his position for posterity. To do this he had to lay claim to an area of landscape that was entirely his, and which owed nothing to the overwhelming presence of Turner. Thus the curious way in which he went about the project. Instead of creating a series consisting of purpose-made designs, as Turner had done, Constable selected a number of previous color studies in oil, some of which he had made years before, for the prints. None had been made with a print in mind, and by any conventional view were wildly unsuitable for the medium: it is notoriously difficult to translate color into tone.[22] Turner had made monochrome drawings for his *Liber Studiorum* as a guide for his engraver, but Constable's art was all about color, meaning that the "chiaroscuro" of nature to which he referred in his letterpress text had to be translated into the chiaroscuro of mezzotint by poor Lucas, a young man who had only just emerged from his years of apprenticeship with the famous mezzotinter Samuel William Reynolds

(1773–1835). The process involved innumerable proof stages, during which Constable rethought his compositions, sometimes going so far as to rework them drastically. *Summer Morning* (no. 179), for example, had new figures added, while *Stoke by Nayland* was radically altered in proofs. That Lucas succeeded so well was a miracle that owed much to Constable's tuition and constant exhortation; their collaboration ended with the charming compliment from Constable: "We have a bond of friendship . . . *a unison of feeling in art* and a mutual regard for the talents of each of which we have sufficient proofs in the lovely amalgamation of our works."[23] When after Constable's death Lucas took up other plates after his paintings, the results were nowhere near as impressive, showing how dependent he had been on Constable's improvements.

Today Blake's and Constable's prints are sought after and loved, while Turner's are more distantly admired. This was not always so: after Turner's death a vogue for the *Liber Studiorum* spread across Britain and America, founded on the frequent eulogies of the series in the writings of John Ruskin.[24] At that time, as the artist had intended, the prints served to convey Turner's art to places where the originals had not traveled, a function that is now served by color facsimiles of Turner's paintings and watercolors. But no one buys such facsimiles in series, and their effect is different. The concept of the series has been lost, and with it the idea that an artist should be judged by a wide range of his work. Neither Turner nor Constable would have wished their careers to be seen in this way. For them, their achievement was the sum total of what they had done, and the function of the print series was to distill the essence of that.

1 Thomas Frognall Dibdin, *Reminiscences of a Literary Life* (London: 1836), 619n2, quoted by John Gage, *Collected Correspondence of J. M. W. Turner* (Oxford, U.K.: Oxford University Press, 1980), 263.

2 David Bindman, ed., *William Blake: Illustrations to the Book of Job* (London: William Blake Trust, 1987). This magnificent three-volume boxed set was published in a limited edition of 387 copies, and contains all the documents and excellent essays by a number of scholars. I have referenced these volumes for all the information given herein, as well as Gerald Eades Bentley, Jr., *Blake Records*, 2nd ed. (New Haven, Conn., and London: Yale University Press, 2004).

3 These twenty-one watercolors are now held in the Pierpont Morgan Library, New York. Illustrations of all the drawings and prints may be found on www.blakearchive.org.

4 The tracings are mostly in the Fogg Museum, Harvard Art Museums, Cambridge, Massachusetts, while the pencil reworkings are in a sketchbook in the Fitzwilliam Museum, University of Cambridge, U.K.

5 Gillian Forrester, *Turner's "Drawing Book": The Liber Studiorum* (London: Tate Publishing, 1996), 29. Forrester's book gives the best introduction to Turner's *Liber Studiorum*, although I do not follow her description of it as a "drawing book," as this term has a precise application, and should be restricted to a well-recognized type of publication that was intended to teach the student how to draw.

6 Ibid., Fig. 3.

7 Ibid., 31.

8 Anne Lyles and Diane Perkins, *Colour into Line: Turner and the Art of Engraving* (London: Tate Publishing, 1989); and Luke Herrmann, *Turner's Prints: The Engraved Work of J. M. W. Turner* (Oxford, U.K.: Phaidon Press, 1990), give accounts of these projects.

9 The *Liber Veritatis* is now held in the British Museum.

10 Richard Earlom, *Liber Veritatis: Or a Collection of 200 Prints ... After Claude le Lorrain* (London: John Boydell, 1777).

11 The Turner Bequest is the posthumous gift in 1856 of the contents of Turner's studio, comprising nearly three hundred oil paintings and around thirty thousand sketches and watercolors (including three hundred sketchbooks), to the British nation, and is housed in Tate Britain.

12 William George Rawlinson, *Turner's "Liber Studiorum,"* 2nd ed. (London and New York: Macmillan, 1906), li, fn.

13 Andrew Wilton gives a good introduction in his *Constable's "English Landscape Scenery"* (London: British Museum Publications, 1979). The 1833 edition of the series was titled *Various Subjects of Landscape, Characteristic of English Scenery, Principally Intended to Display the Phenomena of the Chiaroscuro of Nature: from Pictures Painted by John Constable, R.A., Engraved by David Lucas*. The series is generally known by the abbreviated title *English Landscape*.

14 It was highly unusual for the engraver to print the edition, and attention is drawn to this in Constable's Prospectus of 1833: "To insure the whole of the impressions being perfect, they have been printed at the house of the Engraver only."

15 *John Constable's Correspondence*, ed. Ronald Brymer Beckett, vol. 4, *Patrons, Dealers, and Fellow Artists* (Ipswich, U.K.: Suffolk Records Society, 1966), 314–443. This has a very helpful commentary. The letters had previously been published by Andrew Shirley in *The Published Mezzotints of David Lucas after John Constable* (Oxford, U.K.: Clarendon Press, 1930), which also gives a catalogue of the prints.

16 The largest group of these is in the Fitzwilliam Museum at the University of Cambridge, U.K., but there are many more in other collections.

17 Beckett, *John Constable's Correspondence*, 4:159–65.

18 The various versions of the texts are printed by Shirley, *Published Mezzotints of Lucas after Constable*, 219–46; and in Ronald Brymer Beckett, *John Constable's Discourses* (Ipswich, U.K.: Suffolk Records Society, 1970), 1–27 and 82–85.

19 Beckett, *John Constable's Correspondence*, 4:24–25.

20 Geoffrey Keynes, ed., *Poetry and Prose of William Blake* (London: Nonesuch Library, 1927), 626.

21 *John Constable's Correspondence*, ed. Ronald Brymer Beckett, vol. 6, *The Fishers* (1968), 190–91.

22 For the concept of color in printmaking, see the writings of John Gage, especially *Colour in Turner: Poetry and Truth* (London: Studio Vista, 1969), ch. 2; and *Turner: A Wonderful Range of Mind* (New Haven, Conn., and London: Yale University Press, 1987), ch. 3.

23 Beckett, *John Constable's Correspondence*, 4:416 (in a letter dated 16 December 1834).

24 Marjorie B. Cohn, "Turner, Ruskin, Norton, Winthrop," in *Harvard University Art Museums Bulletin* 2, no. 1 (Fall 1993): 9–66, gives an excellent account of what the plates of the *Liber Studiorum* meant to the generation of Ruskinians in the late nineteenth century.

Up Close and Illuminated

Methods and Materials in the Manton Collection

Leslie Hill Paisley
and Mary Broadway

The eighteenth and nineteenth centuries in Britain witnessed unprecedented inventions in the production of artists' media, inspiring a wide range of new drawing styles and techniques. In preparation for this publication, conservators at the Williamstown Art Conservation Center studied the papers, materials, and experimental techniques of works in the Manton Collection, providing insights into the material history of drawing at the time.[1]

Paper

Works on paper in the Manton Collection are representative of the burgeoning interest in drawings, both amateur and professional, and the growth of paper manufacturing on a large scale at that time.[2] Laid papers, recognized by the linear grooves retained from the wire surface of the paper mold on which they were formed, were often chosen for their high quality (fig. 49). They were designed for holding ink, rather than for facilitating the dispersion of media such as pigment in a watercolor wash. In the middle of the eighteenth century, James Whatman developed smoother wove papers, more conducive to dispersion (fig. 50).[3] Watermarks, which can be seen via transmitted light and sometimes with the naked eye (figs. 51 and 52), allow a paper mill to be identified, and were used as indicators of quality.[4] Wove paper resulted in a support capable of holding up to extensive scratching, blotting, and rubbing. Though wove came to be the preferred paper for watercolor, laid papers remained in circulation, and were often intentionally selected by artists for their texture.

In addition to their importance for visual effect, paper choices were pivotal to ensuring the durability of the work, of interest to artists responding to the increasing commercial and exhibition values of drawings. Many watercolors in the Manton Collection are in excellent condition, having been executed on the finest paper available and carefully protected from the harmful effects of light. Watercolors made around the turn of the nineteenth century, including J. M. W. Turner's *Hoolay Deedy, Seringapatam* (see fig. 85), Thomas Girtin's *Melrose Abbey: The East Window* (see fig. 115), and Thomas Rowlandson's *A Review in Hyde Park* (no. 197) and *Laborers Laying a Pavement* (no. 204) are on fine-wove English papers watermarked using a Whatman paper mold.

Artists chose papers for their surface, working properties, convenience, or cost. As high quality papers became more readily available, there was also a proliferation of papers in different colors (figs. 53, 54, 55, 56). White paper might better define highlights, blue might be used for expanses of sea and sky, or blue-gray to set a mood for a landscape. Papers in the Manton Collection range from bright white to very dark brown.[5]

Clockwise from top left:

Fig. 49 Thomas Gainsborough (English, 1727–1788), detail of *Rocky Wooded Landscape with Winding Track*, late 1770s. Pen and black ink with brush and gray wash and white chalk on blue laid paper (no. 123)

Laid paper in raking light.

Fig. 50 Joseph Mallord William Turner (English, 1775–1851), detail of *Sky and Sea*, c. 1826–29. Watercolor and graphite on white wove paper (no. 280)

Wove paper; Examination in raking light reveals more about the surface texture than natural light alone.

Fig. 51 Thomas Gainsborough, detail of *Rocky Wooded Landscape with Herdsman Driving Cattle along a Valley and Distant Mountains*, c. 1783. Brush and gray wash on beige laid paper (no. 125)

Examination in transmitted light reveals the fiber distribution, paper thickness, and evidence of the paper mold upon which it was formed. Note the "LVG" watermark, which was copied by rival papermakers to impart a sign of quality to their papers.

Fig. 52 Thomas Girtin (English, 1775–1802), detail of *Melrose Abbey: The East Window*, c. 1796. Watercolor and graphite on cream wove paper (no. 143)

Note the "J Whatman" watermark.

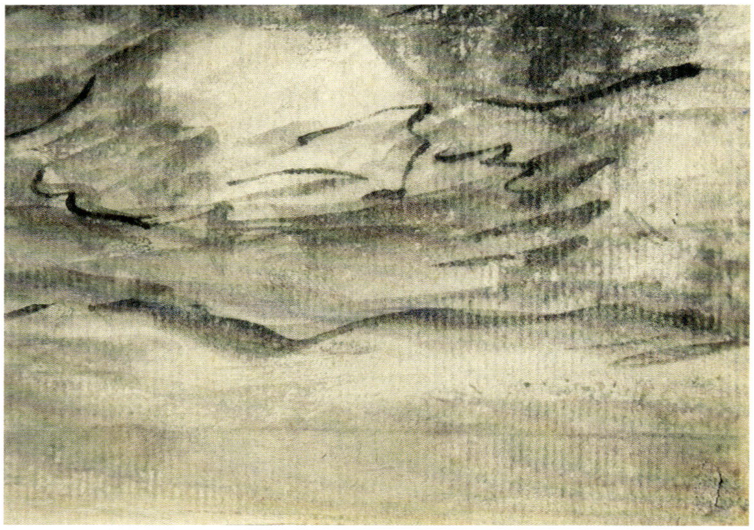

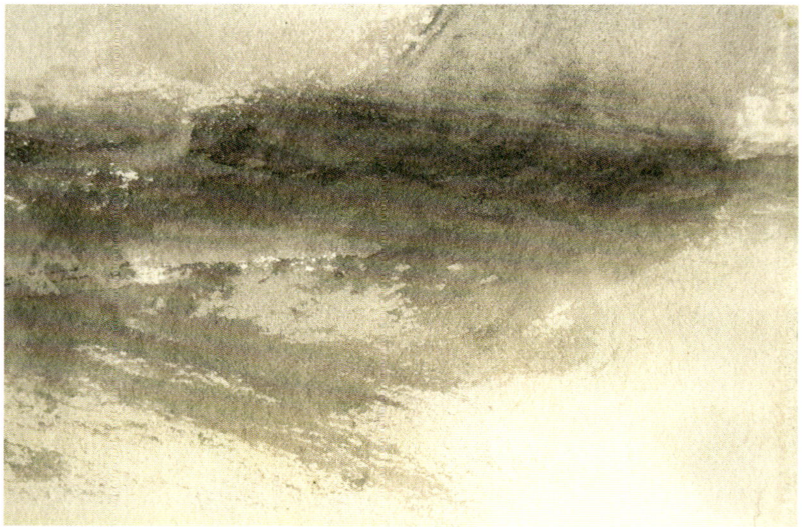

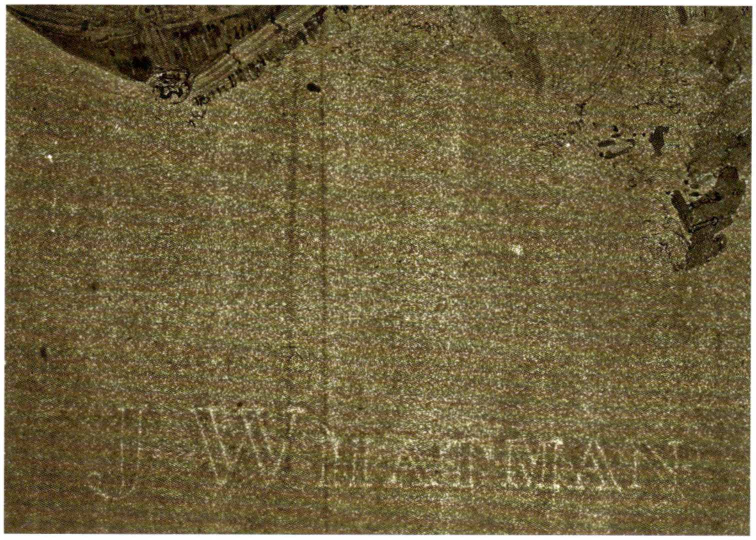

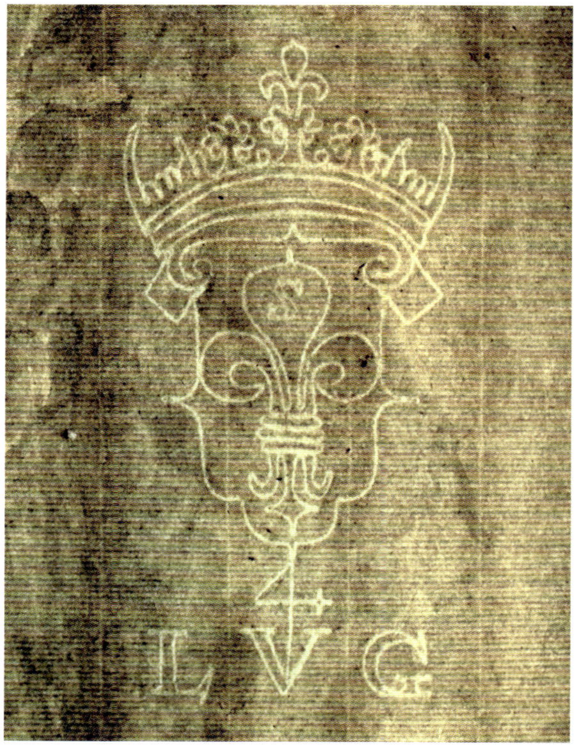

Different paper tones are used to achieve atmospheric effects.

Clockwise from top left:

Fig. 53 Joseph Mallord William Turner, *Sky and Sea*, c. 1826–29. Watercolor and graphite on white wove paper, 22.4 × 31.3 cm (no. 280)

Fig. 54 John Constable (English, 1776–1837), *Academy Study*, c. 1820. Black and white chalks on beige wove paper, 25.4 × 27 cm (no. 81, recto)

Fig. 55 Joseph Mallord William Turner, *Great Yarmouth Fishing Boats*, c. 1827. Gouache on blue wove paper, 24.6 × 18.1 cm (no. 282)

Fig. 56 Thomas Gainsborough, *Landscape with Herdsman Driving Cows and Distant Buildings*, mid- to late 1780s. Black chalk over brush and gray wash with lead white on beige laid paper, fixed with gum (?), 24.6 × 32.4 cm (no. 130)

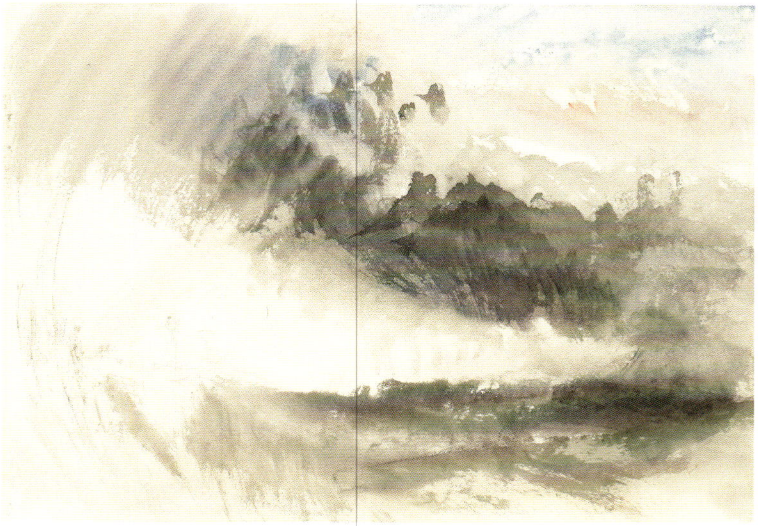

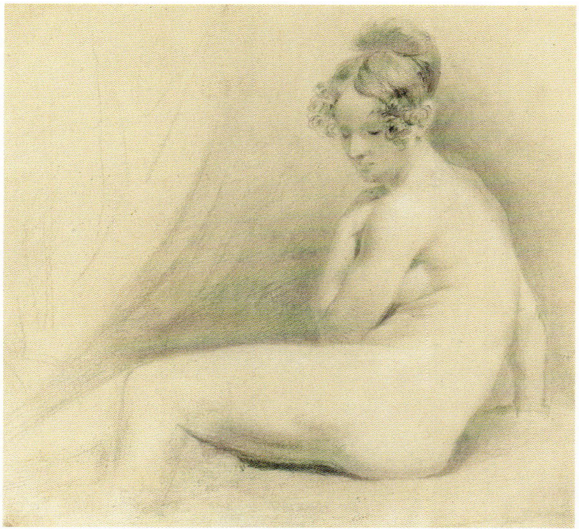

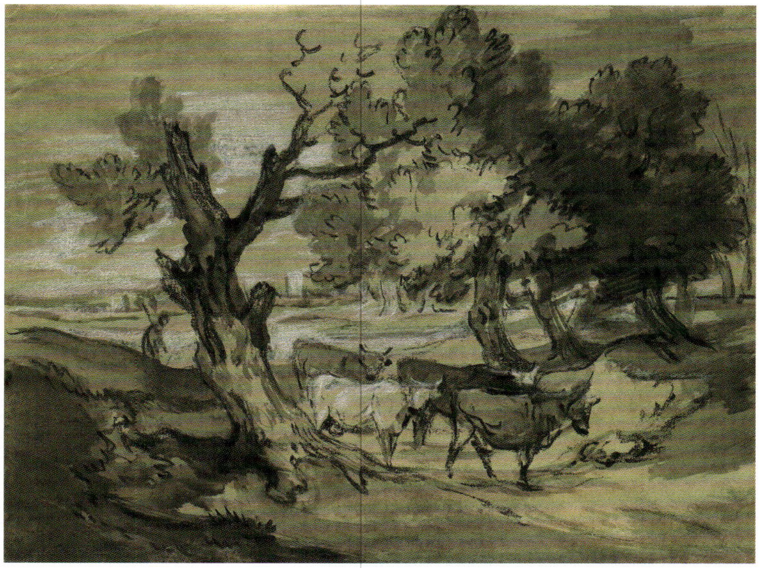

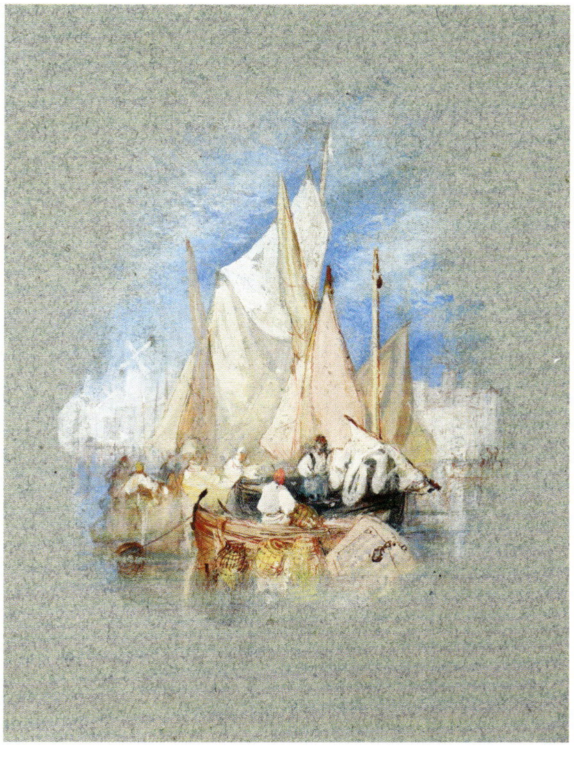

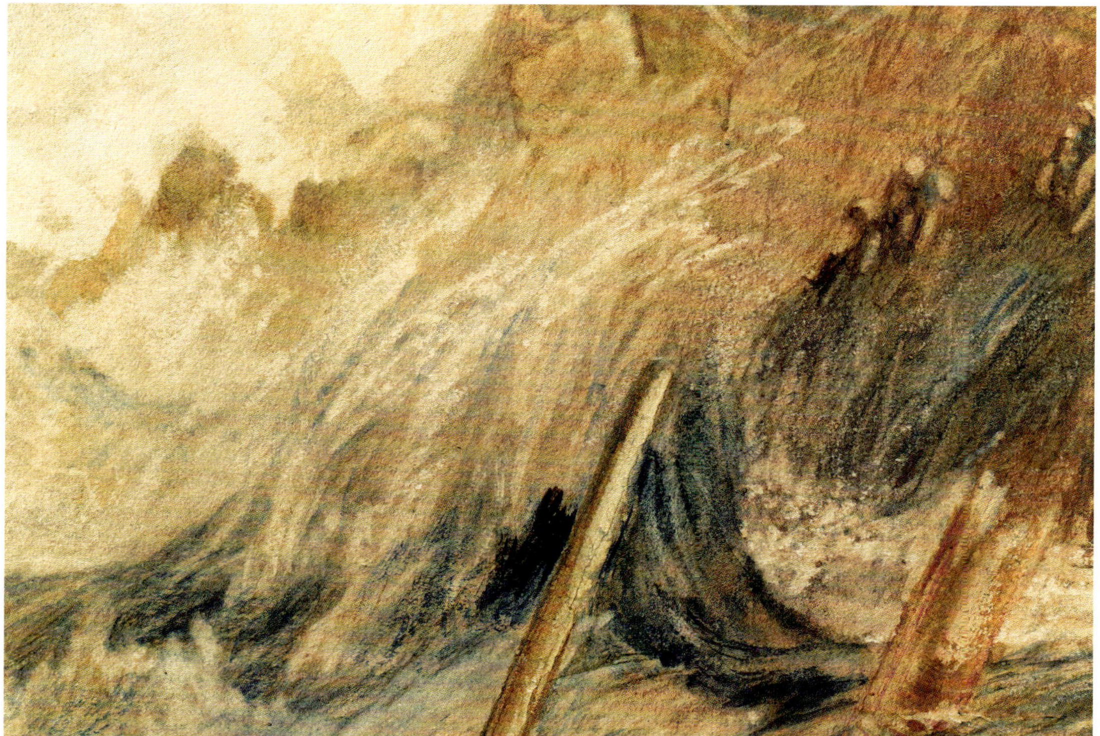

While Whatman wove watercolor paper was handmade from the whitest linen rags, pure water, and gelatin sizing, and because papermakers often added blue colorants to the pulp to counteract the effects of natural yellowing over time, many works made on this paper have retained their original color. However, drawings executed on paper produced from cheap hemp rope and linen rags more often have turned brown.[6] Papers made from fermented, processed rags from previously worn clothing, sails, and ropes contain more impurities than paper made from virgin linen fibers. As Peter Bower, noted British forensic paper historian, says, they are "full of rubbish."[7] A few of the papers in the Manton Collection reflect these typical impurities, and contain minute metallic inclusions from buttons, snaps, or hooks that escaped the rag sorting step (fig. 57).

Fig. 57 John Constable, detail of *Academy Study*, c. 1820. Black and white chalks on beige wove paper (no. 81, recto)

Wove paper in transmitted light showing paper impurities.

Turner took great care in choosing the type and quality of paper for his drawings. Close inspection reveals experimental, vigorous watercolor techniques involving extreme working of the paper both wet and dry, techniques that required papers capable of withstanding wetting and rewetting. Masking agents (such as wax) were used to leave white reserves,[8] followed by many colored washes laid onto wet paper so they would bleed and blend. Turner frequently moved the wash around and went back into the wet wash with a damp brush to remove color and create highlights. Most of his watercolors reveal full or partial fingerprints and evidence of dry scumbling and scraping (fig. 58). These would have been done last in order to preserve the remaining sizing in the sheet, as Turner knew exactly how to manipulate his media to avoid muddying or dulling his vibrant colors.

Fig. 58 Joseph Mallord William Turner, detail of *Entrance to Fowey Harbor, Cornwall*, c. 1827. Watercolor and gouache, with scraping, on cream wove paper (no. 281)

Note scraping that exposes lighter paper underneath the watercolor.

Charcoal and Graphite

In the eighteenth century, charcoal, made of carbonized vegetable matter, remained one of the more popular and inexpensive mediums available to artists.[9] Thomas Gainsborough made a number of drawings in charcoal, its relative friability prompting his significant experimentation with fixatives.

In the late eighteenth century, Gainsborough's loose, idealized landscapes influenced the work of Dr. Thomas Monro, the host of one of the more important, informal "schools" for British artists. Although the Royal Academy was the central educational institution for professional artists at the time, the study of drawing occurred in more casual contexts. A number of important artists of the day, including Turner and Girtin, spent significant periods copying Monro's collection of drawings, particularly those of John Robert Cozens.[10] In *A Wooded River Landscape with a Rock in the Left Foreground* (fig. 59), Monro began with a brief sketch in graphite, then completed it in charcoal. The imprecise, rhythmic curls of the foliage that he was able to create with the charcoal

Fig. 59 Thomas Monro (English, 1759–1833), *A Wooded River Landscape with a Rock in the Left Foreground*, c. 1800. Graphite and black chalk with watercolor on cream laid paper, 15.2 × 17.8 cm (no. 186, recto)

Fig. 60 John Constable, *Leathes Water (Thirlmere)*, 19 Sept. 1806. Graphite on cream wove paper, 25.1 × 38.8 cm (no. 36)

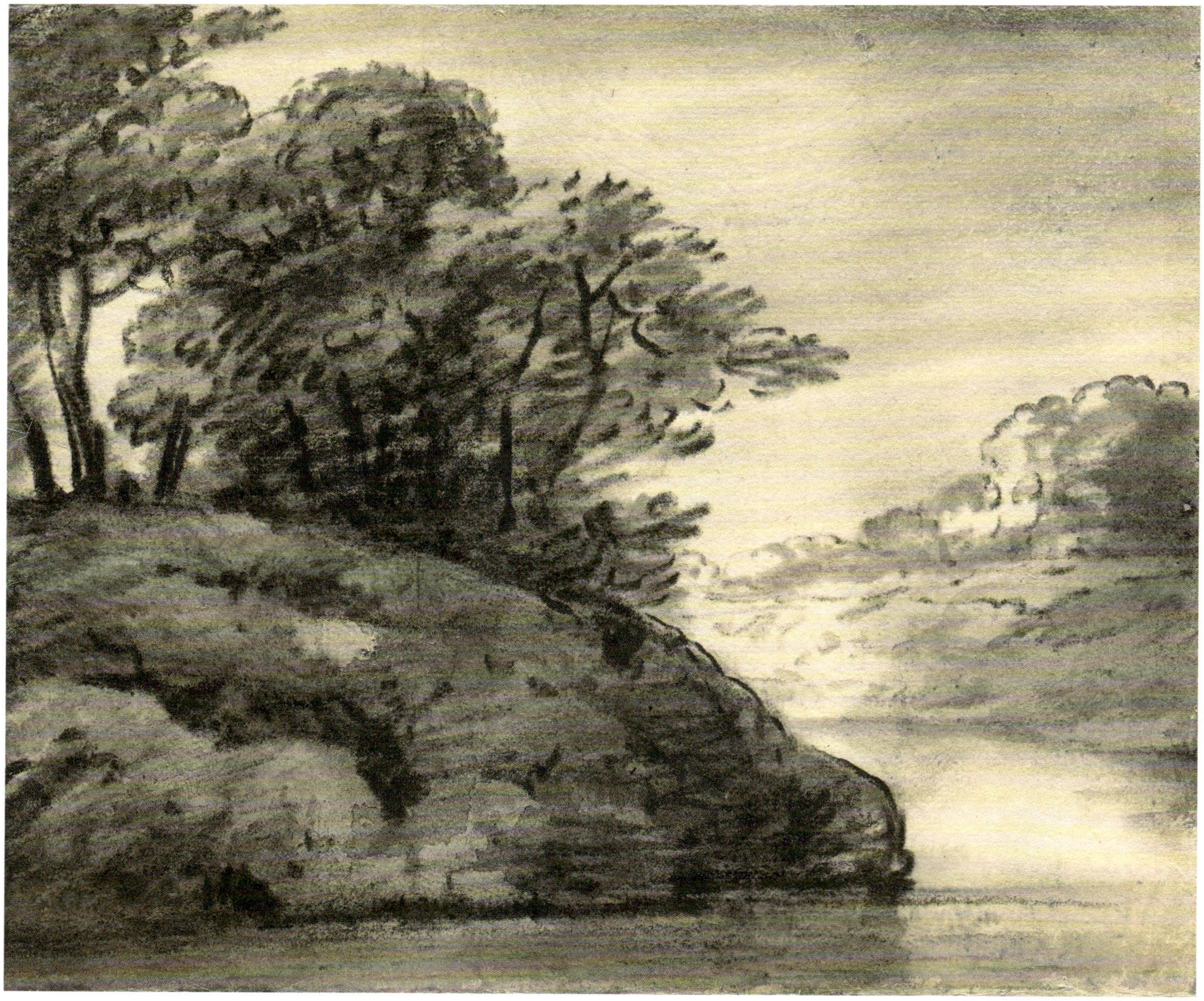

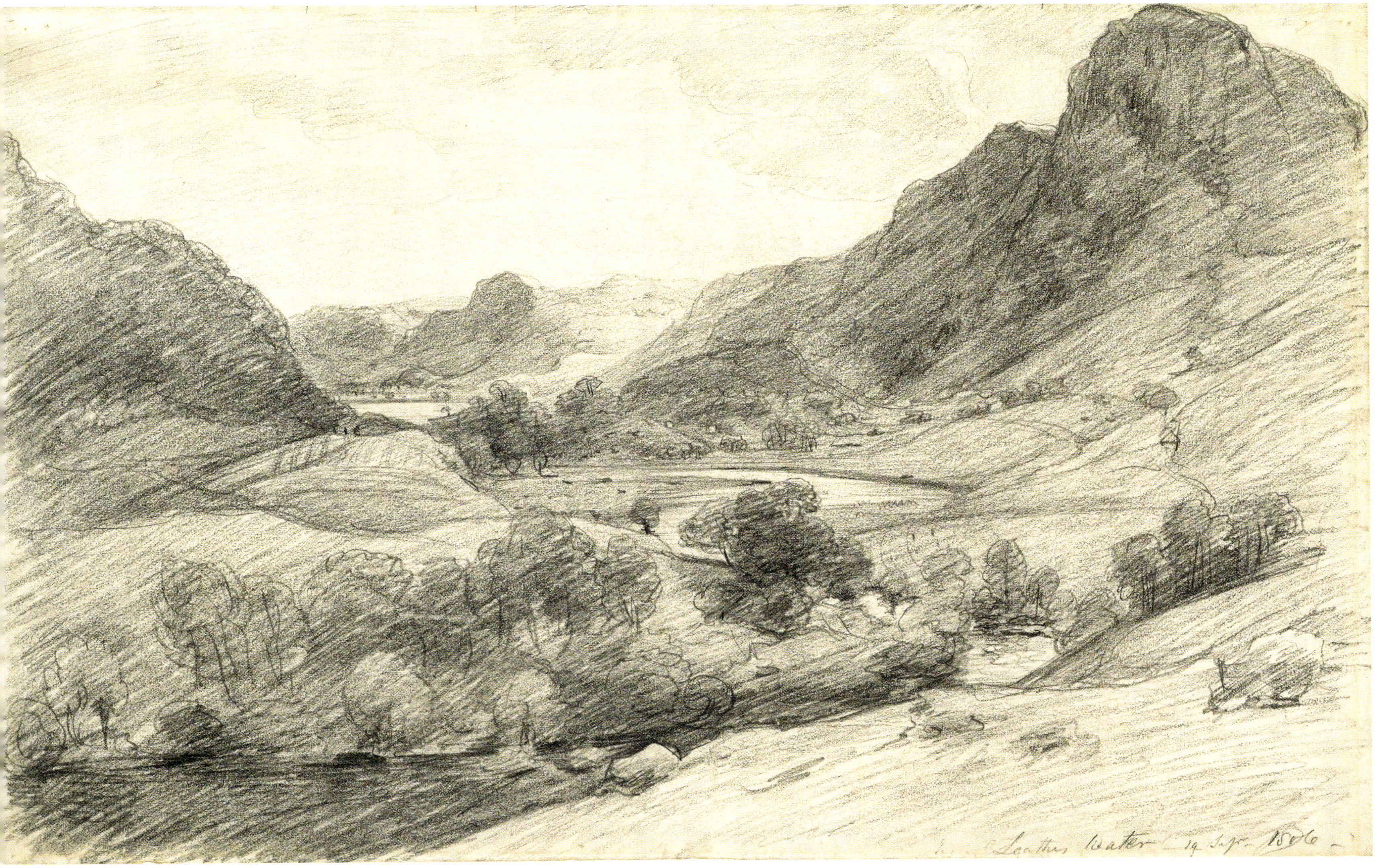
Leathes Water 19 Sepr 1806

Figs. 61 and 62 John Ruskin (English, 1819–1900), *Sunset over the Mountains*, c. 1845. Watercolor and gouache with graphite on beige wove paper, 14.3 × 22.2 cm (no. 206)

Above, the sheet is seen in natural light; *below*, an infrared image makes the inscription visible.

are reminiscent of Gainsborough's use of the medium. Charcoal allowed both artists to create evocative, Romantic depictions of nature.

Graphite was chosen for a number of reasons. Mined in Cumberland since the twelfth century, it had been discovered in Borrowdale in the sixteenth century, so it was readily available. Graphite offered artists sharper lines than chalk or charcoal, and its durability made it an ideal tool when traveling. Artists making topographical sketches were particularly partial to the precision graphite offered their naturalistic studies. Rowlandson and Girtin, among others, frequently used graphite to make a preliminary sketch underneath watercolor, its insolubility in water making it an excellent tool for this purpose. As Anne Lyles has noted, the new process of mixing graphite with clay developed by Jacques Conté and Joseph Hardtmuth in the 1790s generated more consistent degrees of hardness in graphite pencils, leading to their becoming more widely adopted. During this period, many artists used graphite to block out works before completing them in other media. In his maturity, Gainsborough abandoned graphite for chalk, preferring the softness and rapidity of the latter.[11]

Constable used graphite for most of his life. The Manton Collection includes thirteen graphite drawings made by Constable, including *Leathes Water (Thirlmere)* (fig. 60), made during his 1806 fall tour of the Lake District, which is among his most virtuosic. The trip took him close to the source of graphite, in Borrowdale, and many sketches from that trip make use of the medium. Characterized by soft outlines combined with rhythmic lines to create subtle modulations of tone, Constable created evocative, lyrical landscapes that demonstrate the atmospheric range possible in graphite.

The intriguing color notes in graphite beneath a sheet by art critic, collector, and artist John Ruskin on his *Sunset over the Mountains* (figs. 61 and 62) were difficult to decipher until photographed with infrared radiation. The pencil notes indicate that the watercolor portion of the composition was probably not executed on the spot, but colored later in the studio. Other small landscapes in the collection were taken from artists' sketchbooks and may have been made as study works used to encourage commissions, rather than being offered up for sale as potential finished works.

Pen and Ink

Artists also used ink as a drawing medium, often to accentuate outlines, as in Girtin's *The Gatehouse of Battle Abbey, Sussex* (see fig. 114). Occasionally artists worked exclusively in ink, choosing it for its fluidity and, when watered down and applied with a brush, to create wash tones. More commonly, though, it was used for writing.

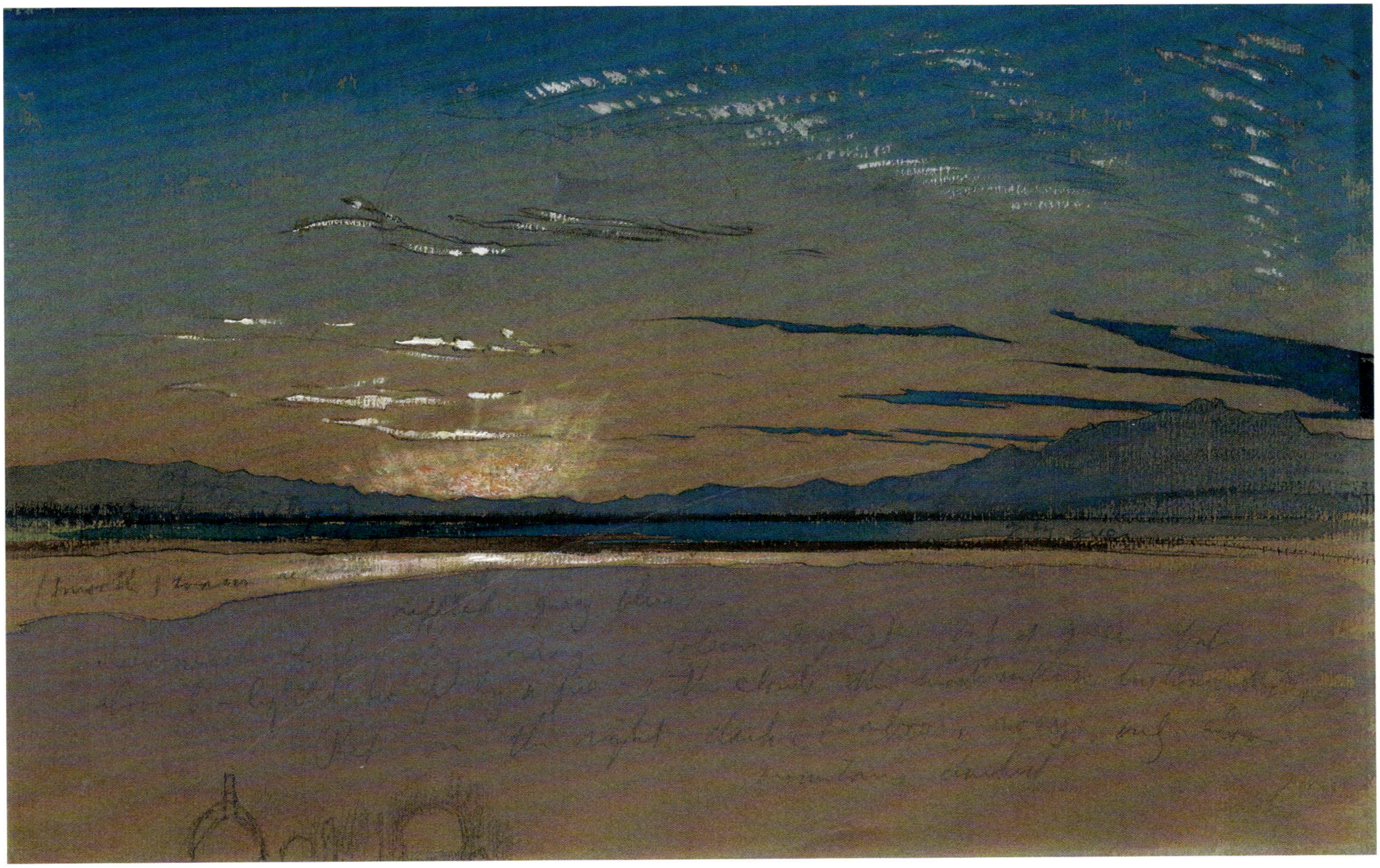

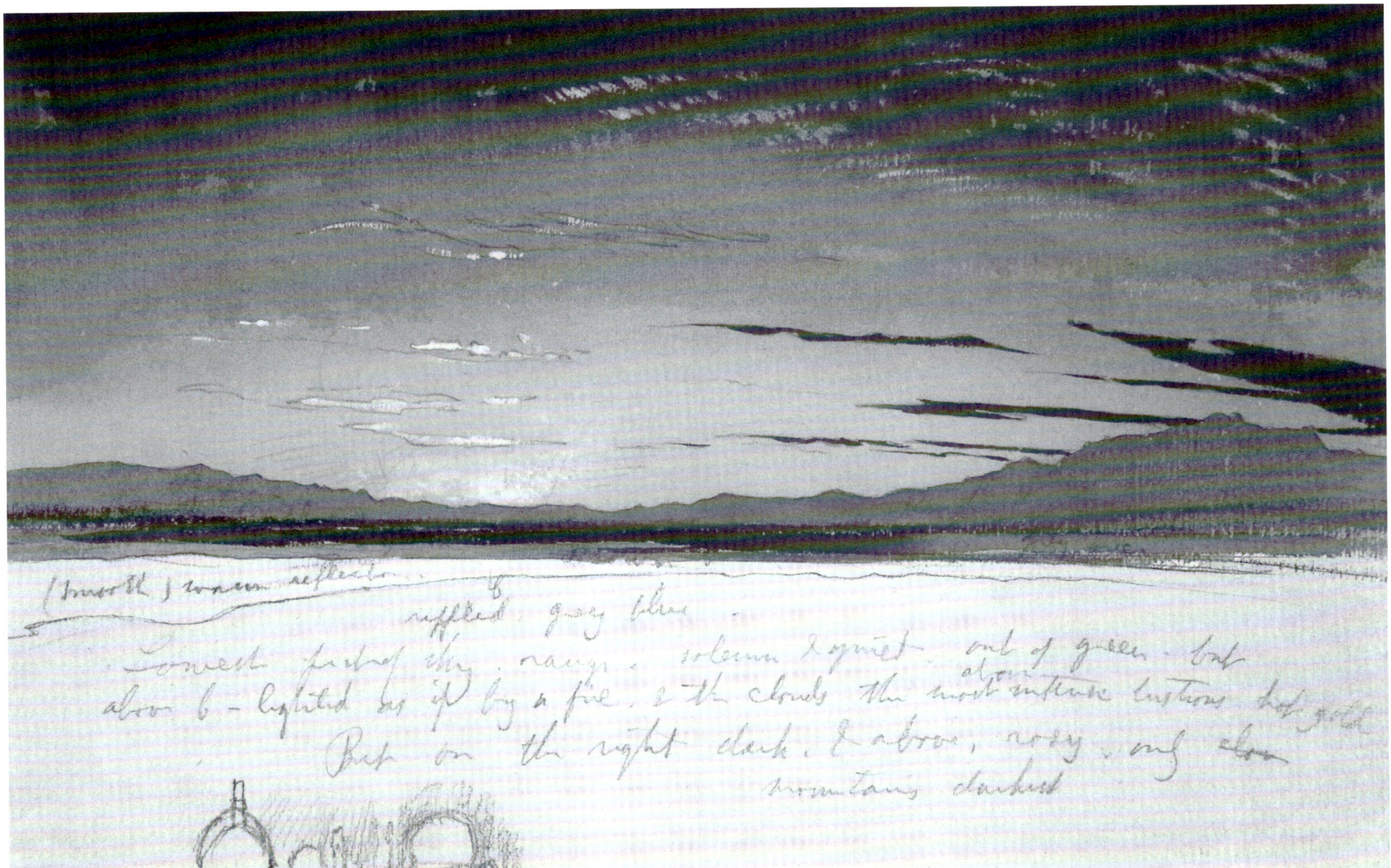

Fig. 63 John Constable, *Sheet of Sketches with Verses from Burns*, 23 Oct. 1832. Pen and brown ink and brush and brown wash on white laid paper, 19.4 × 15.7 cm (no. 77)

Constable's *Sheet of Sketches with Verses from Burns* (fig. 63) demonstrates the aqueous fluidity of ink and his particular dual use of the medium for both image and text. As Leslie Parris has suggested, it appears that Constable began transcribing verses from Robert Burns's poem "English Song."[12] While writing, he began to observe his surroundings, and then to depict the "very showry day" that appeared before him. Constable used the pen in his hand to quickly depict the rainstorm, using gestural lines to evoke cascades of water and the contours of clouds and landscape. He added small areas of tone with the same brown ink and a brush, highlighting the planes of the landscape and the underbelly of the clouds.

Many artists used a variety of media when drawing. Rowlandson built up his compositions with graphite, ink, and wash. His graphite underdrawing, visible in unfinished works, such as *A Review in Hyde Park*, reveals just a few squiggles to block out the perspective and compositional elements. He then followed with extensive sketching in gray or pale vermilion ink or thin watercolor outline applied with either a thin brush or a reed pen. Next came colored washes to fill in the shape and tone and delineate volume. His works are often finished with a quick staccato of deeper black or vermilion ink to create shadows and accentuate foreground action.[13]

It is also instructive to examine Rowlandson's watercolors that contain no graphite. He is known to have created counterproofs of his drawings as a preliminary step to further work on an idea or to create multiples, though few of these have survived.[14] The original drawing would have been dampened and pressed with another sheet of clean damp paper, pulling a reversal of the image. The cognate and the original would then be worked up further with new ink lines and washes.[15] *Underwriters or Bad News at Lloyd's Coffee House* (fig. 64) shows evidence of its having been used to produce a cognate. The deep red lines created by a vermilion and India ink mixture appear to have been added over fainter ink lines that appear to have bled at some point. This could have occurred when the ink was transferred from one sheet to another.

Watercolor

The diversity of works in the Manton Collection demonstrates the wide range of experimentation and possibilities in the medium of watercolor that emerged during the second half of the eighteenth and throughout the nineteenth century. Watercolor first came into widespread use in topographical studies, and grew in popularity as a preparatory medium for compositions in oil. Artists like Paul Sandby, John Robert Cozens, and Edward Dayes were instrumental in its use. By 1804 the status of watercolor had risen

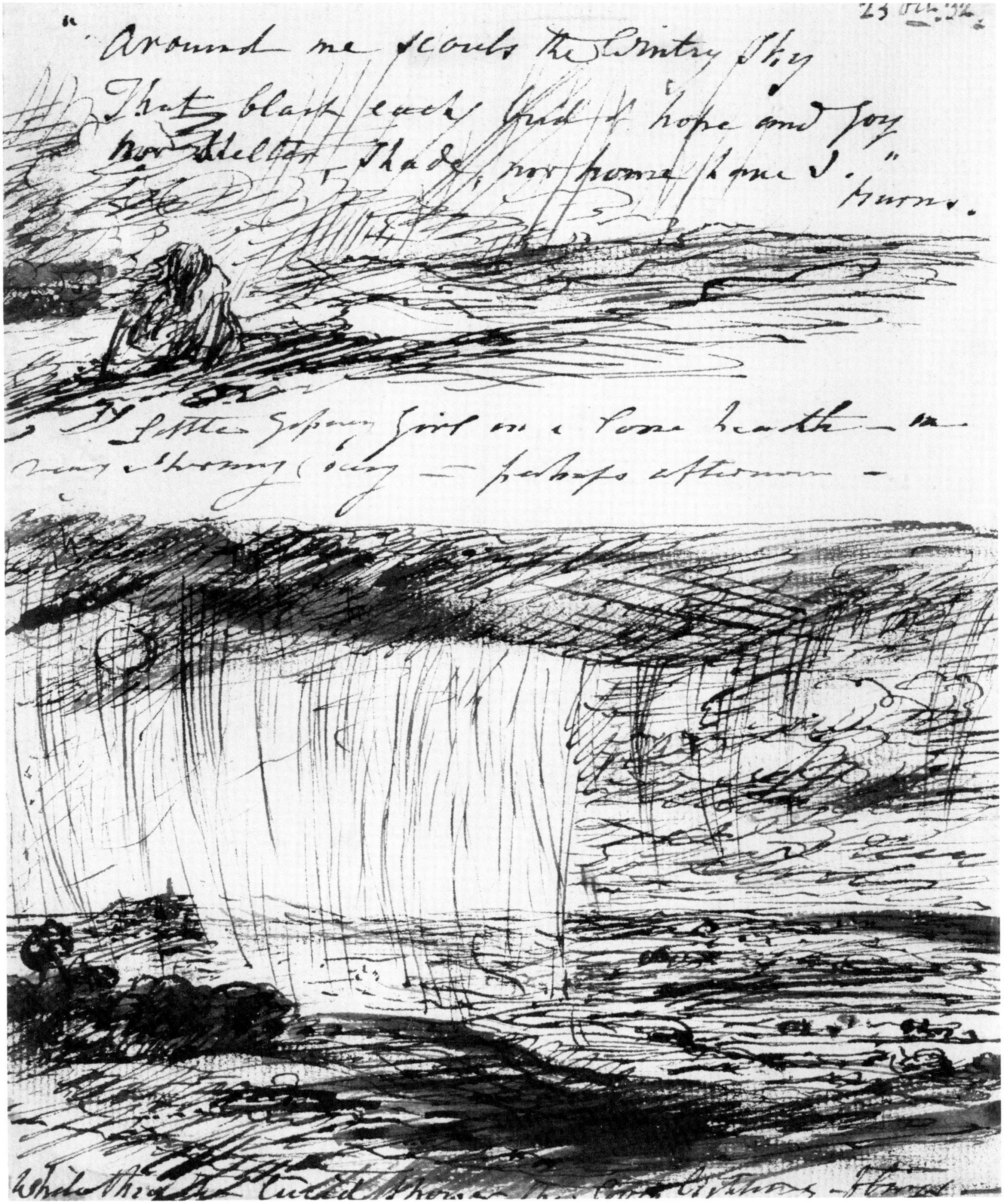
23 Oct. 32
"Around me scowls the Wintry Sky
That blasts each bud of hope and Joy
Nor Shelter, Shade, nor home have I."
Burns.

Fig. 64 Thomas Rowlandson, details of *Underwriters or Bad News at Lloyd's Coffee House*, c. 1800–10. Pen and vermilion ink with watercolor over graphite on cream wove paper, (no. 199)

Note the squared ink lines delivered with a reed pen. Some of the deep red ink lines on *Underwriters* appear to have bled at some point. What caused the bleeding is unclear, but it could have resulted from direct transfer.

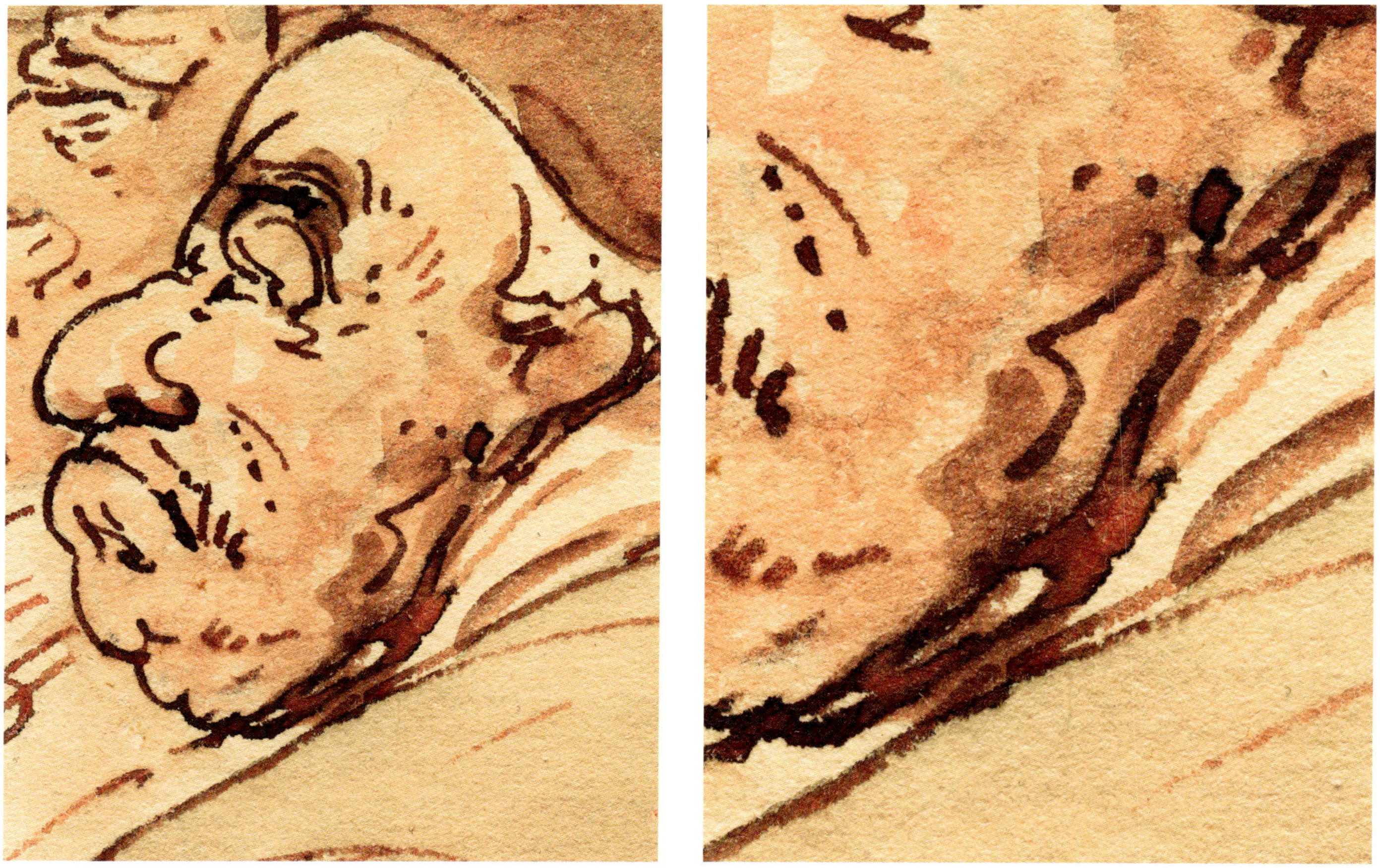

sufficiently to merit the foundation of the Society of Painters in Water Colours. Though not without stringent critical debates, in 1810 watercolorists were also admitted to the Royal Academy.[16] With the proliferation of watercolor came an intensification of rhetorical and visual arguments for the status of the medium, as well as specific demands for high quality materials.

Artists who sought to create exhibition pieces in watercolor entered a discourse dominated by oil painting, necessitating a move away from gouache to techniques that allowed for more transparent washes. Thus watercolor artists could consciously vie with the depth and transparency achieved in oils, seeking to supersede these effects with watercolor's particular aqueous transparent luminosity.

As the market for watercolors intensified, artists became increasingly concerned with the durability of their works. While paper selection was key, the stability of pigments proved equally critical. Nineteenth-century English watercolors in cake and tube form produced by respected colormen (specialists in watercolor preparation) such as Rowney, Reeves, and Son and Winsor & Newton were made from both light-sensitive colorants or dyes as well as durable pigments. Certain colors were particularly unstable; artists and colormen were often able to observe changes within their own lifetime. Efforts to produce more stable watercolors increased in the nineteenth century, but artists continued to use fugitive pigments for those effects that could not be achieved with substitutes.

The versos and previously covered edges of several objects in the Manton Collection reveal the original paper color and the fading characteristics of certain watercolors. Blue papers or blue-painted sky and water become green as paper yellows with age, just as foliage, once green, may fade to blue when the gamboge of the green wash fades more rapidly than the blue. John Constable's *Bow Fell and Langdale Pikes* (fig. 65) shows this fading where a portion of the watercolor was protected from light by a window mat: the sky area was once purple, but the blue component has faded, leaving the sky a rosy pink.

Fixatives and Varnishes

Fixatives and varnishes were necessary to ensure the stability of the work or to alter its appearance. The term "fixative" refers to a dilute liquid substance generally sprayed or dipped to adhere powdery pigment particles to paper, while "varnish" indicates a natural resin finish, often applied by brush, imparting a gloss. They were added during execution to protect the media from smudging, as well as upon completion to more closely approximate the varnished look of oil paintings.

Fig. 65 John Constable, *Bow Fell and Langdale Pikes* (and detail), 1806. Watercolor and graphite, squared for transfer, on white laid paper, 20.3 × 38.8 cm (no. 38)

Note the color shifts within the exposed central image area as compared to the outer edges that were protected from light with a window mat.

Fig. 66 Thomas Gainsborough, *Study of a House and Shed in a Wooded Valley*, c. 1783. Graphite on beige laid paper, fixed with gum, 14.1 × 18.9 cm (no. 126)

While several watercolors in the Manton Collection contain coatings applied over the watercolor washes, the nineteen Gainsborough drawings in the Clark's collection provide the largest, most intriguing group for study. Gainsborough considered the fixative process central to the final appearance of his pictures, and used an innovative method, particularly in his application of coatings in layers. The drawings fall into two groups: those with a matte surface, executed in graphite or black-and-white chalks; and more fully realized drawings with added watercolor and a glossy varnish. Even his drawings that present only dry media have one or more layers of fixative, as can be seen in *Study of a House and Shed in a Wooded Valley* (fig. 66). Both have an applied coating, most likely a water-soluble plant gum – such as gum arabic – in a binding medium. In a letter to his friend William Jackson, Gainsborough imparted his "secret" method of making a drawing look like a painting:

Make the black & white of your drawing, the Effect I mean, & disposition in rough, Indian Ink shadows & lights of Bristol [referring to white lead chunks produced in Bristol as opposed to London] ... when you see your Effect, dip it all over in skim'd milk ... correct your Effects with Indian Ink ... dip again.... Then tinge in your greens, your browns with sap green & Bistre, your yellows with Gall stone & blues with fine Indigo ... when this is done, float it all over with Gum water ... let that dry & varnish it 3 times with spirit varnish such as I sent you; tho only Mastic & Venice Turpentine is sufficient....[17]

In an effort to better understand the layered structure of Gainsborough's more complex, coated watercolors, initial research and analysis was carried out at the Williamstown Art Conservation Center on a group of four varnished drawings. They fit the criteria of the study not only because they appear to have been executed with similar materials and methods, but because they all contain thickly applied white media in need of consolidation, which provided open sample sites. The drawings were divided into pairs. One pair was acquired by Sterling and Francine Clark in the 1910s, the second was part of the Manton bequest.

At first glance it was clear that the first pair, *Herdsman and Cattle* and *Landscape with a View over a Distant Plain* (figs. 67 and 70), were significantly less yellowed than the second pair, *Landscape with Figures, Herdsman and Cattle at a Pool, and Distant Church* and *Wooded Landscape with Figures and Winding Track Leading to a Cottage* (figs. 68 and 69). Examination of the paper, media, and coatings confirmed much of Gainsborough's description of his working technique.[18] The artist in all four cases selected a fine quality,

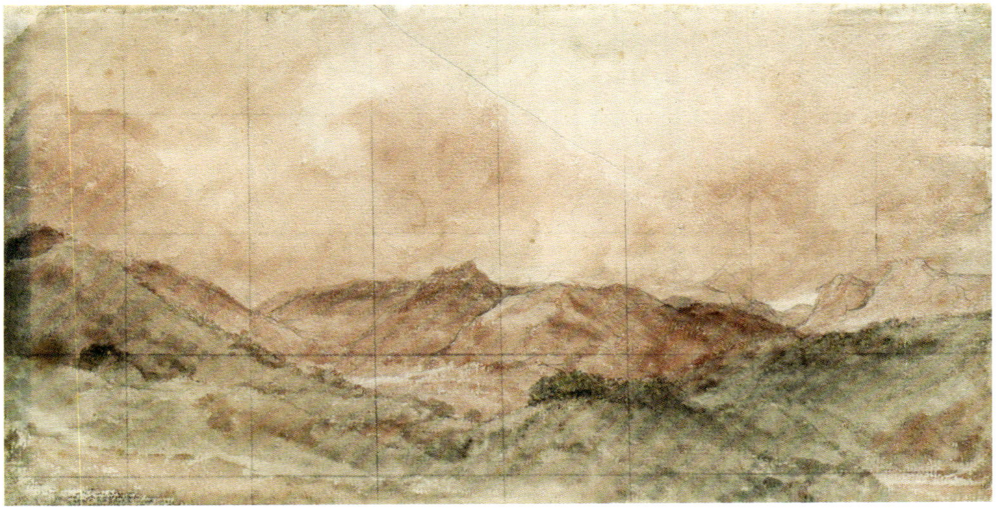

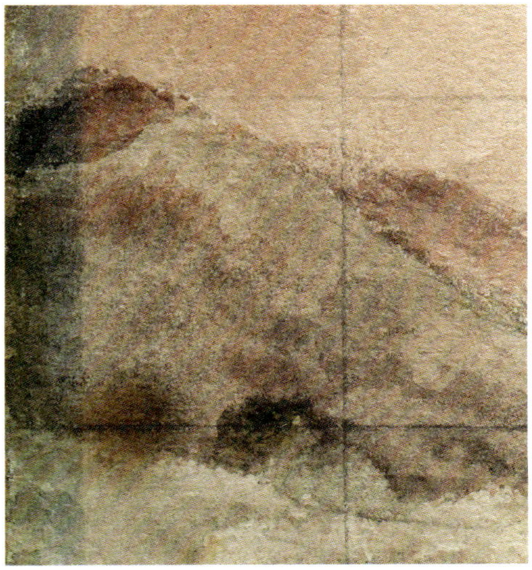

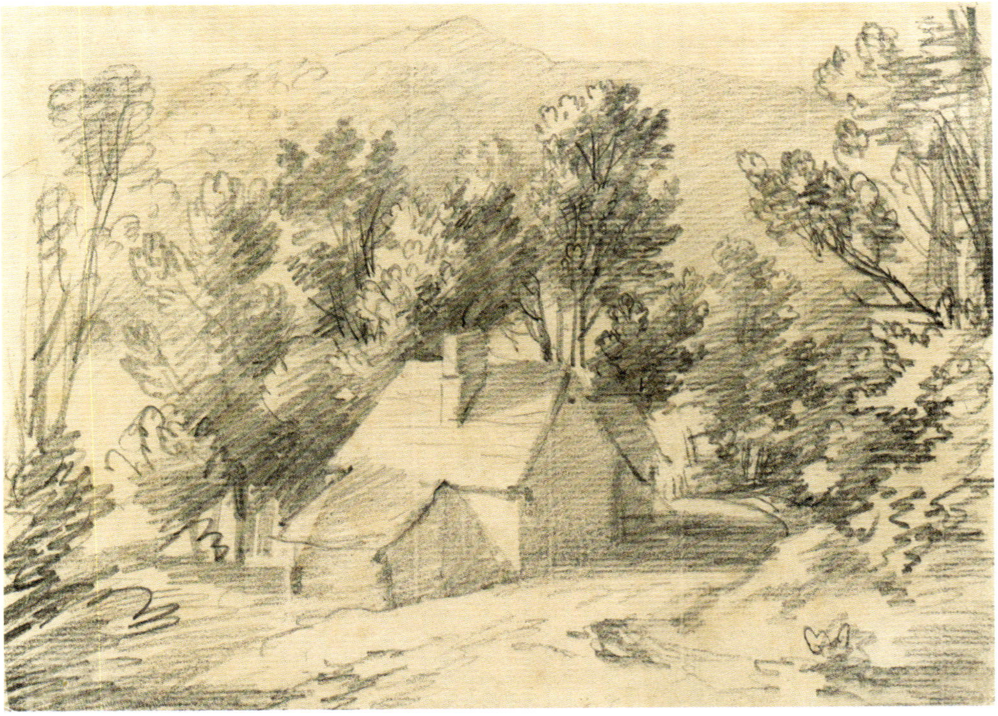

laid, linen-and-hemp-fiber writing paper, sized with gelatin. Gainsborough used graphite for the preliminary underdrawing, charcoal for linear detail, and stumped or smudged portions of the charcoal with a tool to infer the darkest darks and midtones. At this point, he brushed a plant-based gum, such as gum arabic, gum tragacanth, or almond gum, on the drawing, and then dipped it in skimmed milk depending on the friability of the media. This initial fixative held the charcoal in place and prevented it from sullying the white highlights, which were applied next. When working in dry media, Gainsborough preferred an opaque dry lead- or calcium-based white chalk, which he referred to as Bristol after its place of origin. In cases where dry and wet media were combined, Gainsborough applied the whites thickly; in some instances he may have done so directly from a tube of paint.

Once laid in, the highlights needed to be fixed to preserve their opacity and vibrant, fluffy quality. This fixative was likely the skimmed milk to which he referred in his letter. Preliminary cross-section analysis using fluorochrome dyes and visual evidence support this supposition. Using milk as a binder provided a film of natural fixative that would have been relatively tough and almost transparent once dry. For its application, Gainsborough preferred dipping, evidence of which became apparent when the drawings were viewed under ultraviolet light (UVA), showing areas the approximate size of a person's thumb (fig. 71), which likely indicate where the artist held the sheet of paper as it was gently submerged. Following the milk fixative, Gainsborough laid in any colored washes, first the yellows, browns, greens, and blues, then ending with reds and oranges, which were often vermilion based. This structure is confirmed by drawings such as *Wooded Landscape with a Cottage and Cows* (fig. 72), in which the pigment can be seen applied on top of white, and in which the lead-white highlights are protected by a skim milk coating.

Once the composition and colors were in place, the decision to varnish the drawings to make them look more like oil paintings was presumably made based on the quality of the work and its intended status and audience. For the varnish, Gainsborough preferred mastic resin and Venice turpentine, which could be brushed over the surface of the drawing. Often, more than one coat was used, producing an effect like an oil painting. Over time this natural resin varnish has yellowed and developed a fine crackle pattern, more so on the two works that received more light exposure. Future analysis on these coatings may help determine the exact composition and placement of the coating layers.

Four varnished watercolor drawings by Thomas Gainsborough. *On the left*, two drawings that have been part of the Clark's permanent collection since 1955; *on the right*, two drawings acquired by the Clark as part of the Manton gift in 2007.

Clockwise from top left:

Fig. 67 Thomas Gainsborough, *Herdsman and Cattle*, 1770–80. Brown chalk, watercolor, with touches of oil paint on beige laid paper, varnished, 22.5 × 31 cm (1955.1971)

Fig. 68 Thomas Gainsborough, *Landscape with Figures, Herdsman and Cattle at a Pool, and Distant Church*, mid- to late 1780s. Watercolor and gouache with lead white on beige laid paper, fixed with gum, varnished with mastic, 22.1 × 30.7 cm (no. 129)

Fig. 69 Thomas Gainsborough, *Wooded Landscape with Figures and Winding Track Leading to a Cottage*, mid- to late 1780s. Watercolor and gouache with lead white on beige laid paper, fixed with gum and skim milk (?), varnished with mastic, 22.1 × 37 cm (no. 131)

Fig. 70 Thomas Gainsborough, *Landscape with a View over a Distant Plain*, c. 1775. Brush and brown ink with touches of oil paint on beige laid paper, varnished, 21.6 × 30.7 cm (1955.1837)

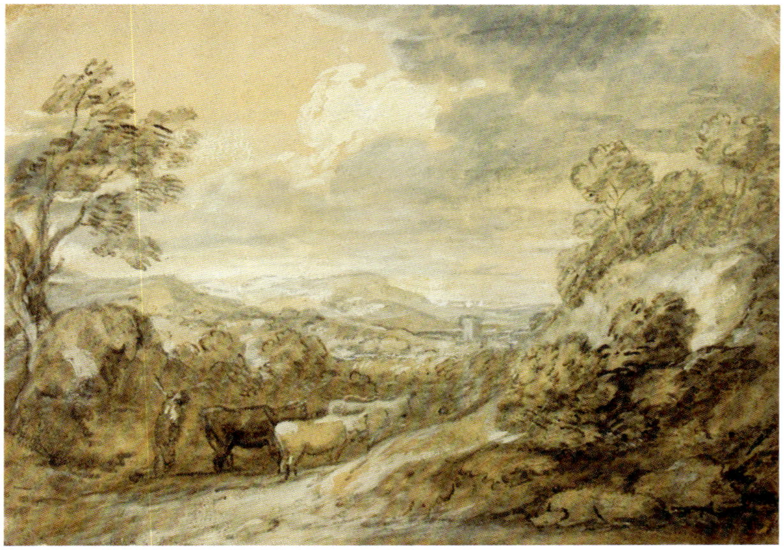
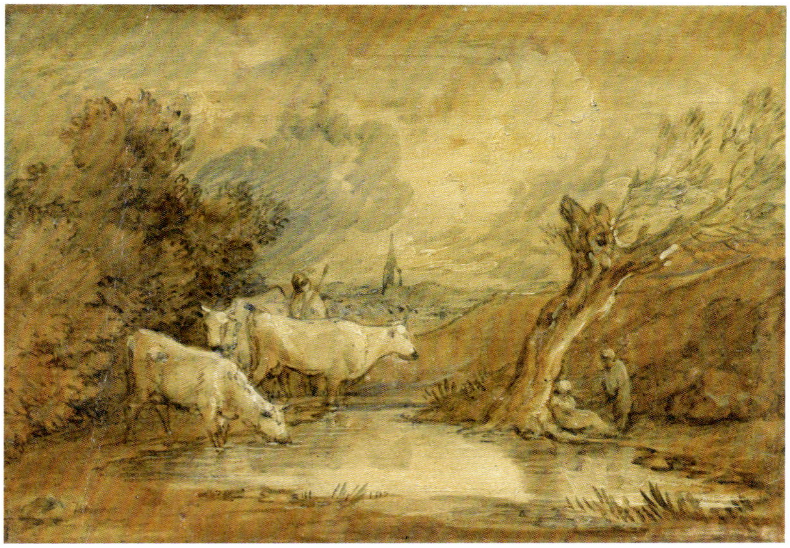
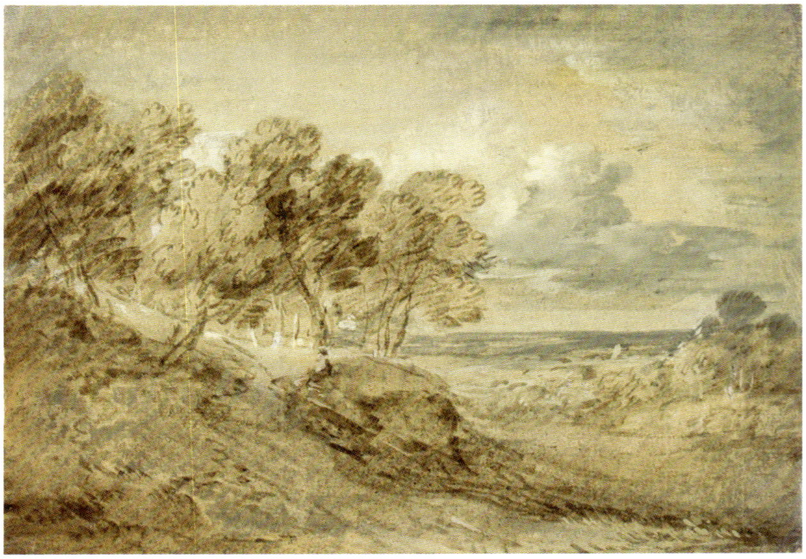
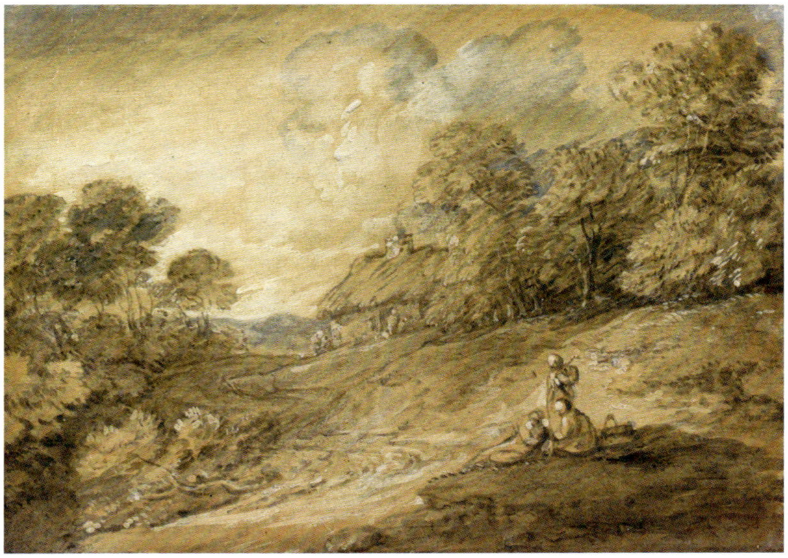

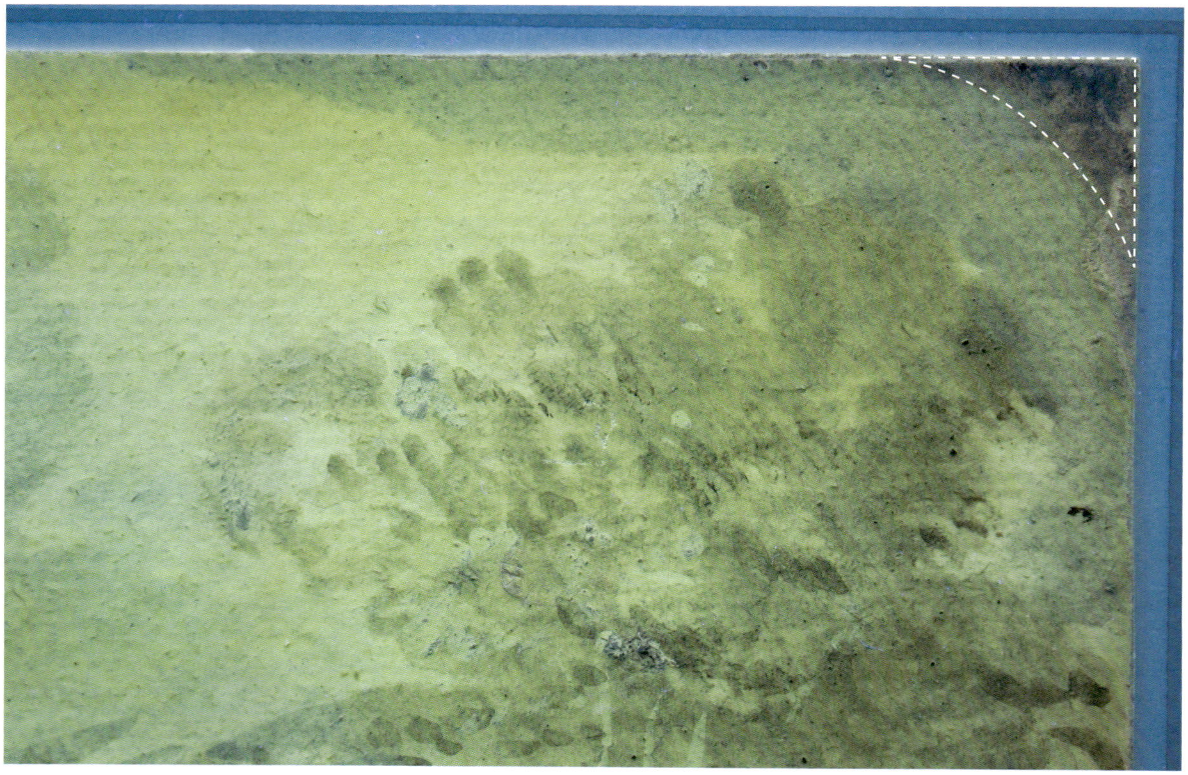

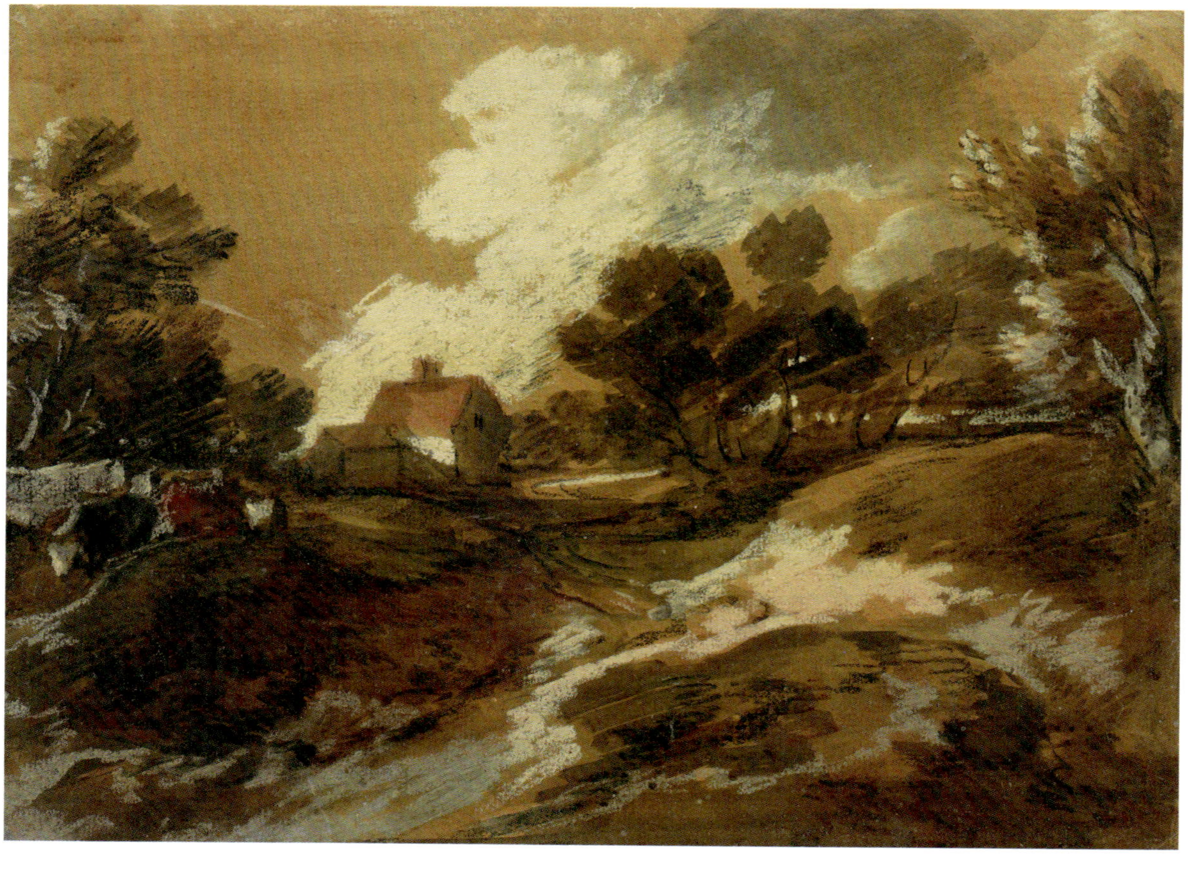

A true microcosm of British drawings from the eighteenth and nineteenth centuries, works from the Manton Collection will continue to excite further research and examination over time. As paper conservator Marjorie Shelley observed about her conversations with Sir Edwin: "What I remember about him most of all was his enthusiasm for works of art ... and his curiosity about the materials and techniques.... He was a truly unique [collector] in that regard...."[19] How fitting then that we include a consideration of process and materials with this series of essays. The mysteries these sheets have to reveal will continue in Williamstown and beyond.

Fig. 71 Thomas Gainsborough, detail of *Wooded Landscape with Figures and Winding Track Leading to a Cottage*, mid- to late 1780s. Watercolor and gouache with lead white on beige laid paper, fixed with gum and skim milk (?), varnished with mastic (no. 131)

A detail viewed under ultraviolet light (UVA). The top and bottom right corners each exhibit a curved area of little to no fluorescence. This indicates that one or more artist-applied coatings are absent from these areas, possibly where the paper was held or clipped while dipping.

Fig. 72 Thomas Gainsborough, detail of *Wooded Landscape with a Cottage and Cows*, mid-1770s. Brush and gray and red wash with black and blue chalks and lead white on tan laid paper, fixed with skim milk (?) and gum, varnished with mastic (no. 120)

Note the vibrancy of the lead white highlights, which have been protected by the skim milk coating.

Susannah Blair and Jay A. Clarke contributed significantly to this essay, and we are grateful for their suggestions and additions during the editorial process.

1 A thorough examination of the paintings in the Manton Collection has been undertaken by Sandra Webber, Paintings Conservator at the Williamstown Art Conservation Center. These findings will be included in *Nineteenth-Century European Paintings at the Sterling and Francine Clark Art Institute*, to be published in the fall of 2012.

2 For more on the social history of drawing in this period in England, see Ann Bermingham, *Learning to Draw: Studies in the Cultural History of a Polite and Useful Art* (New Haven, Conn., and London: Yale University Press, 2000). For more on the paper trade, see John Krill, *English Artists' Paper: Renaissance to Regency* (London: Trefoil, 1987).

3 Theresa Fairbanks Harris and Scott Wilcox, *Papermaking and the Art of Watercolor in Eighteenth-Century Britain: Paul Sandby and the Whatman Paper Mill* (New Haven, Conn., and London: Yale University Press, 2006).

4 Dated watermarks cannot be relied upon for dating, as the molds were repeatedly used many years past the date of the watermark. Also, some molds were acquired by papermakers secondhand, after their useful life expired. These papers may not be of the same quality as the original papers made with the watermark.

5 For a discussion of colored paper, see Peter Bower, "Blues and Browns and Drabs: The Evolution of Colored Papers," in *The Broad Spectrum: Studies in the Materials, Techniques and Conservation of Color on Paper*, ed. Harriet K. Stratis and Britt Salveson (London: Archetype Publications, 2002), 42–49.

6 See Marjorie Cohn, *Wash and Gouache: A Study of the Development of the Materials of Watercolor* (Cambridge, Mass.: Harvard University Press, 1977), 16–23.

7 Peter Bower, conversation with Leslie Hill Paisley, October 2009.

8 Peter Bower, *Turner's Later Papers: A Study of the Manufacture, Selection and Use of His Drawing Papers, 1820–1851* (New Castle, Del.: Oak Knoll Press, 1999).

9 Cohn, *Wash and Gouache*, 75.

10 Andrew Wilton, "The 'Monro School' Question: Some Answers," *Turner Studies* 4, no. 2 (Winter 1984): 8–23.

11 Anne Lyles, "The Landscape Drawings of Contable's Contemporaries: British Draughtsmanship c. 1790–1850," in *Constable, A Master Draughtsman* (London: Dulwich Picture Gallery, 1994).

12 Leslie Parris, *Constable: A New York Private Collection* (New York: published privately, 1994).

13 Joseph Greco, *Rowlandson the Caricaturist* (London: Chatto & Windus, 1880). "It is related that Rowlandson would saunter from his neighbouring lodgings in the Adelphi, round to the Repository of Arts, and, as the title of Mr. Ackermann's establishment was no misnomer, every possible appliance was therein found ready to hand. The artist would then order a saucer of vermillion, and another of raw Indian ink, ready ground, from the colourists room, with reed pens, and several sheets of drawing-paper; he would then combine his inks in the proportions he thought proper, in the flesh lines vermillion predominated, in draperies India ink, shadows were a warm mixture of the two and distant objects were faintly rendered in India ink alone."

14 Robert Wark, *Rowlandson's Drawings for the English Dance of Death* (San Marino, Calif.: The Huntington Library, 1966).

15 A. P. Oppé, *Thomas Rowlandson: His Drawings and Watercolors*, ed. Geoffrey Holme (London: The Studio, 1923). "There are in almost every collection, public and private, well-known drawings in which a soft, oily line, with unusual unevenness and blurs, suggests some such mechanical origin. There are also drawings in which the ink seems to have been sucked from the centre of the line leaving the edges dark."

16 For a history of the institutional development of watercolor, see Mathew Hargraves, *Great British Watercolors: From the Paul Mellon Collection at the Yale Center for British Art* (New Haven, Conn.: Yale Center for British Art, 2007).

17 Thomas Gainsborough to William Jackson, 1773, in Mary Woodall, ed., *The Letters of Thomas Gainsborough* (Greenwich, Conn.: New York Graphic Society, 1961), 177–79.

18 Research project on varnished Gainsborough drawings, on file at the Sterling and Francine Clark Art Institute, Williamstown, Mass.

19 Marjorie Shelley, interview with Jay A. Clarke, October 2011.

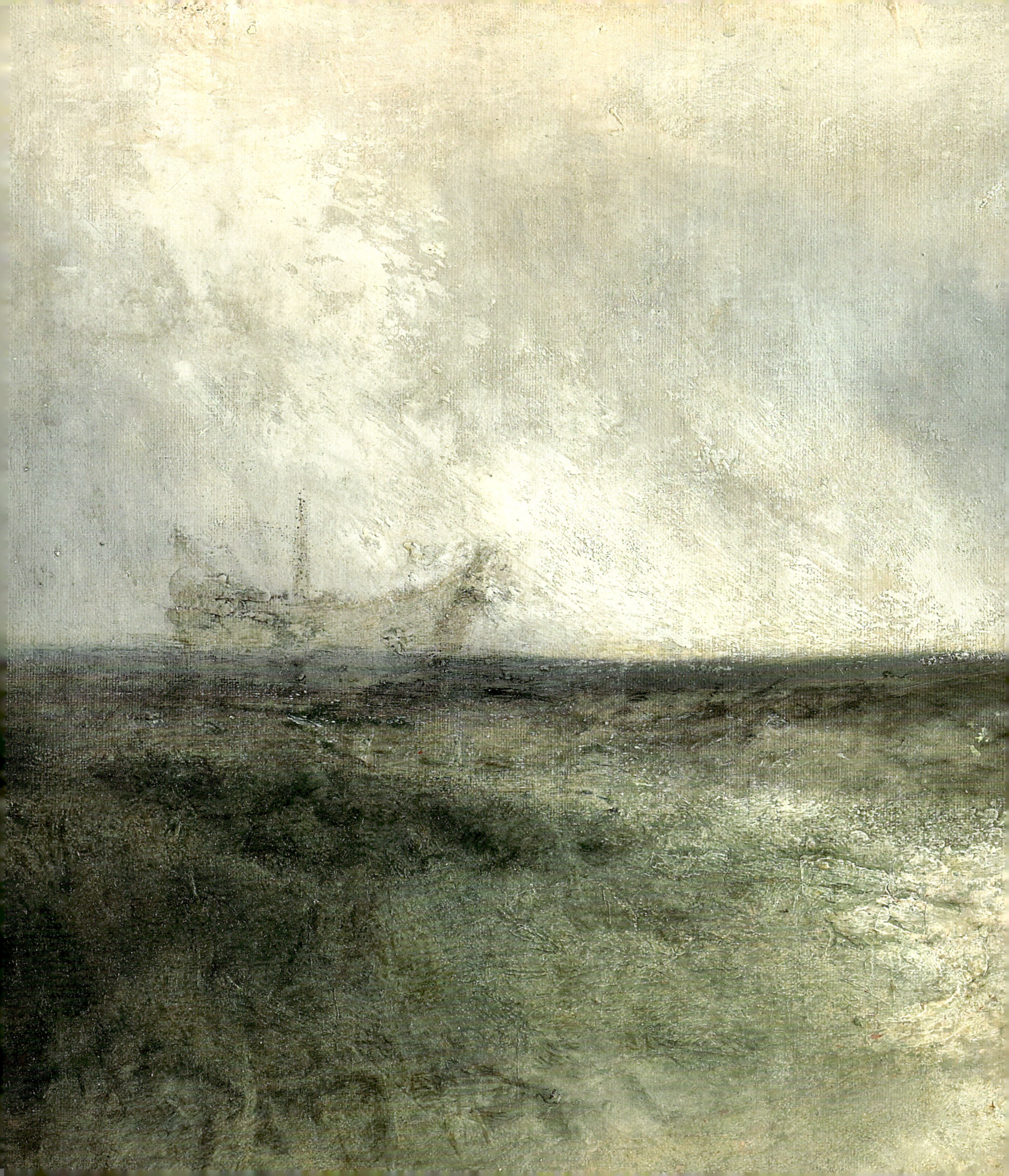

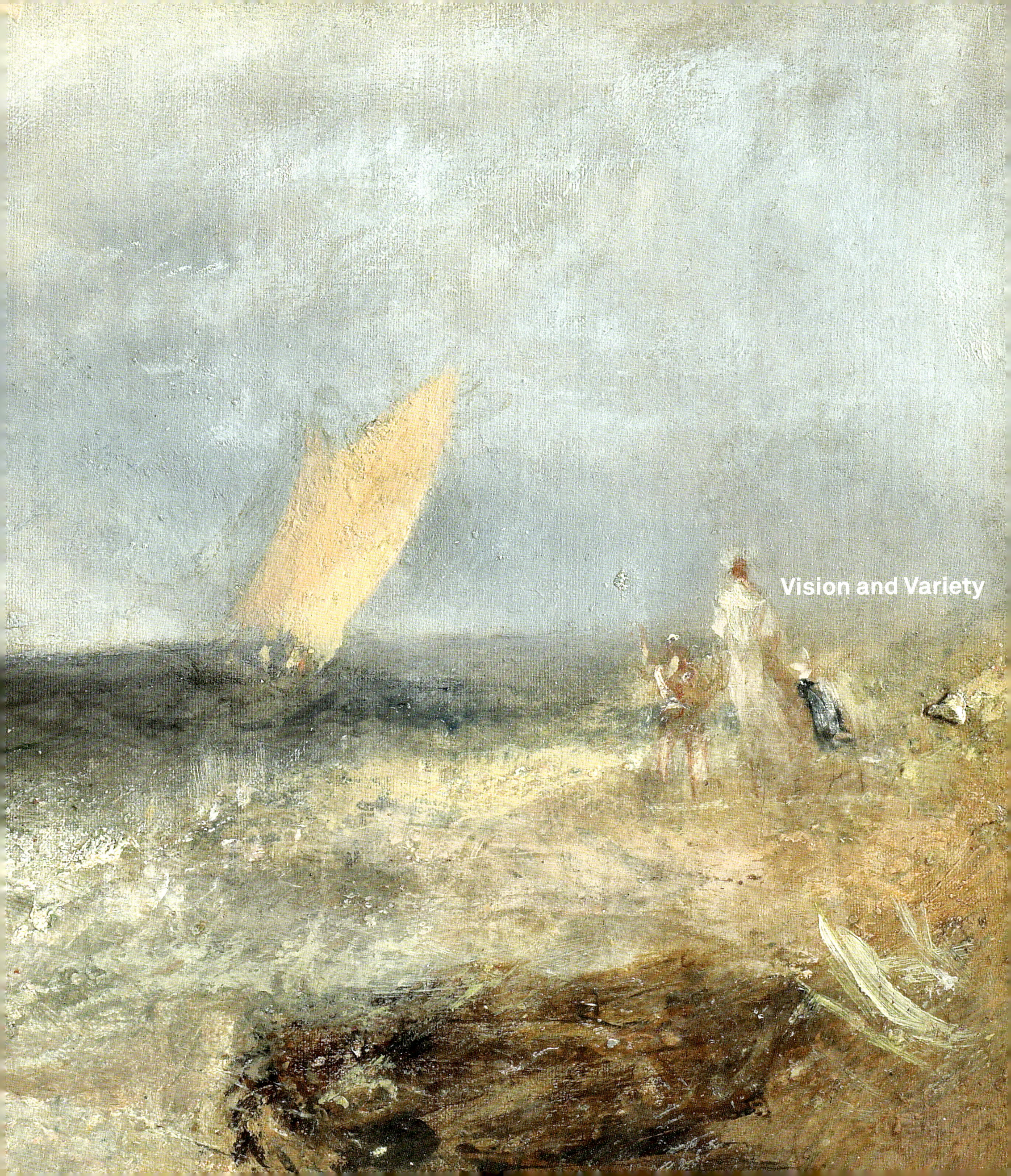

Vision and Variety

The Tyranny of the Bodily in Rowlandson's Art

Amelia Rauser

Thomas Rowlandson's watercolor, *Mutton Chops in Maiden Lane* (fig. 73), celebrates the pleasures of a good English chophouse. The male patrons sit, knife and fork at the ready, in comfortable booths at tables laid with white cloths, while a beautiful serving girl, buxom and pink-cheeked, carries in a plate of chops, and the boy behind her bears tankards of ale and a basket of bread. Conviviality, good health, and the satiation of bodily need are promised. For Rowlandson, such bodily pleasures – feasts for the belly and the eye – were unequivocal boons of London's civilization. But the degree of human refinement offered by such an establishment is not overly large; the lumpy, grinning, big-bellied man is but a short remove from the cheerful, panting dog at his feet: both salivate at the sight of the waitress.

The omnipresence, or even tyranny, of the body and its urges are the central and motivating theme in Rowlandson's work, and the main current of his satire.[1] In a drawing like *Mutton Chops*, the pleasures are straightforward and the achievements of human culture are to satisfy them. But Rowlandson's satire grew more pointed as the pretensions of civilization grew more elevated. In *The Cat-astrophy, or Crash to My Grandmother's Old China* (fig. 74), the elegant lady of the house, adorned with dangling earrings and a fashionable plumed coif, cries out in dismay as she watches her two pudgy, clumsy servants trip over the house cats and tumble down the sweeping staircase, crashing an elaborate china tea set to the ground. Refinement and sensibility have been cultivated in many ways in this household, from the architecture to the purchase of fine goods and the pursuit of refined habits. But sweeping staircases are made to be tumbled down, pets trip us up, and fine china is inevitably broken. Our unruly animal natures are always erupting, to our chagrin, betraying the ambitions of our little minds.

The broad humor created by the contrast between our intellectual and aesthetic ambitions and the embarrassing eruptions of our bodies has ageless appeal. But in the late eighteenth century, the relationship between aesthetics and embodiment was under particular scrutiny.[2] Perhaps, Enlightenment philosophers argued, the perception of beauty and excellence was not limited to the abstract mind, but rather located in the bodily sensations we feel as we experience the world. As "the new science of sensation," and an outgrowth of empiricism, aesthetic theory was developed to understand the mechanism by which base human sensations – perceptions of the world acquired through sight, smell, or especially touch – were converted into sensibility, an appreciation of beauty, and finally an understanding of virtue and excellence.[3] "New money" members of the rising middle classes in England aimed to refine their sensibility

Following spread:
Fig. 73 Thomas Rowlandson (English, 1756–1827), *Mutton Chops in Maiden Lane*, c. 1798–1810. Pen with vermilion and gray inks and watercolor on cream wove paper, 27.8 × 21.7 cm (no. 196, recto)

Fig. 74 Thomas Rowlandson, *The Cat-astrophy, or Crash to My Grandmother's Old China*, c. 1800. Brush and dark brown ink with touches of pen and vermilion ink and watercolor over graphite on cream wove paper, 34.5 × 26.2 cm (no. 198)

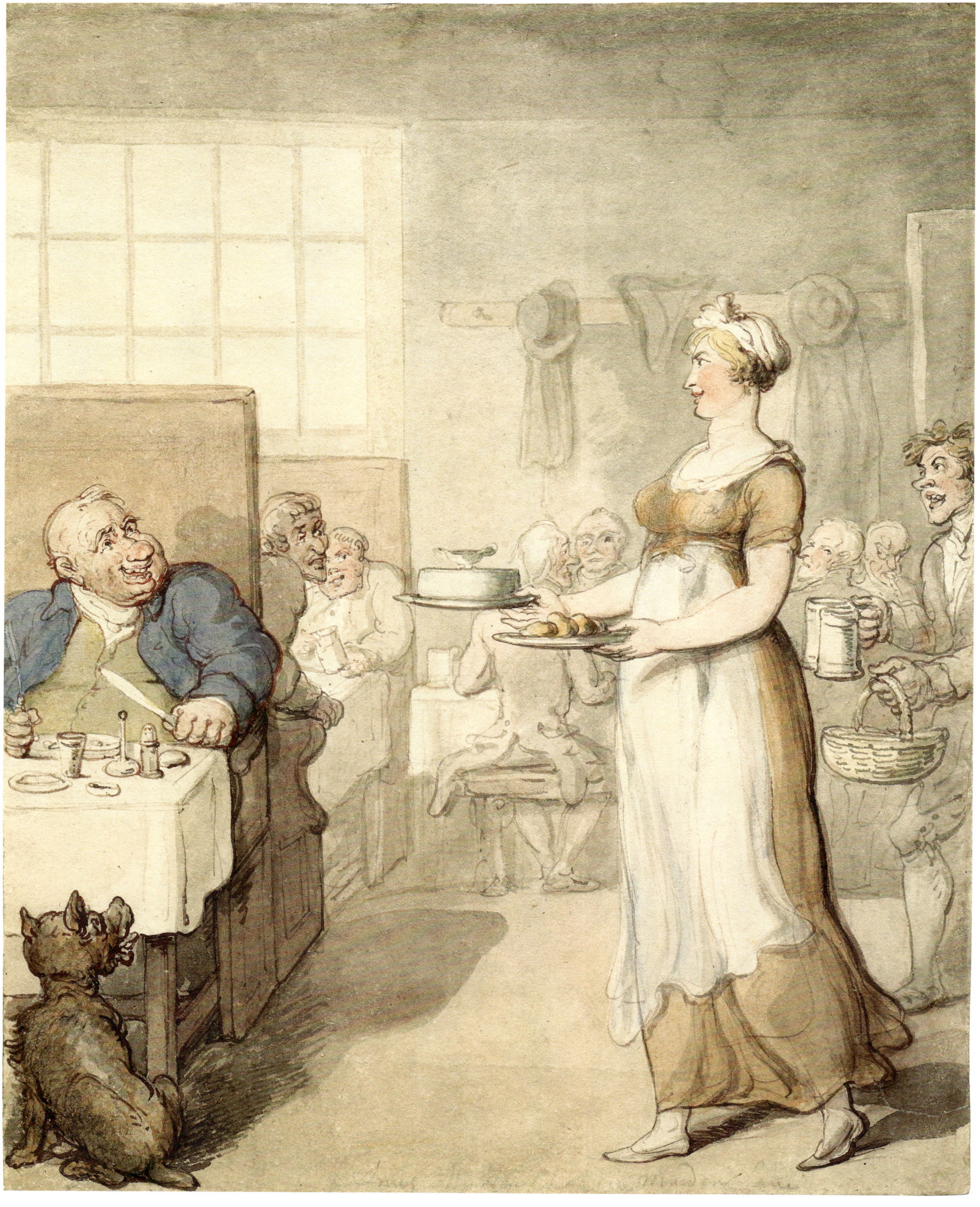

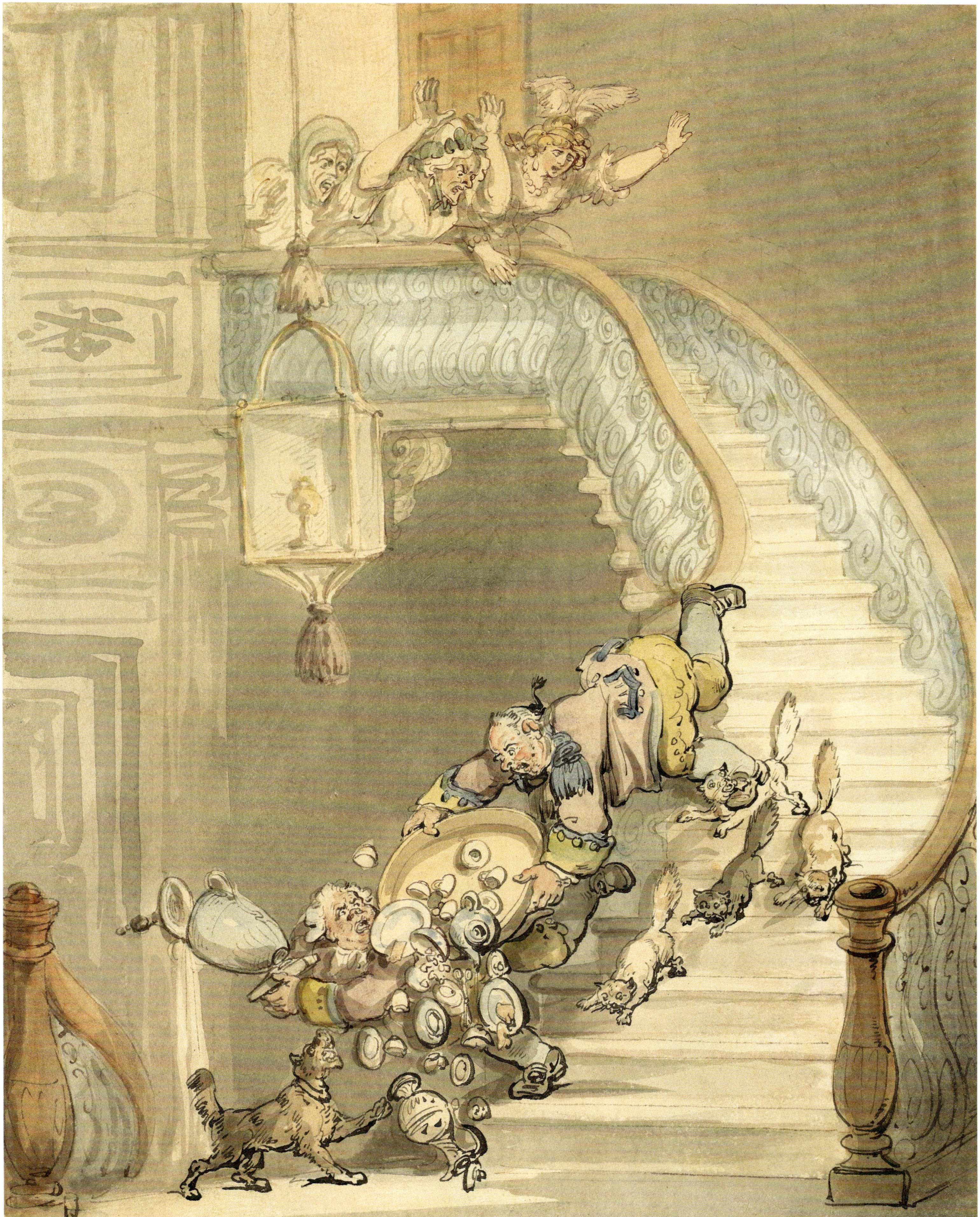

(and raise their social status) by contemplating and patronizing art, and contemporary aesthetic theorists like Johann Joachim Winckelmann, Gotthold Ephraim Lessing, and Johann Gottfried von Herder worked to specify the process that allowed the sensations of the body to be reconciled with the elevation of the mind and a sensational appreciation of nature. These philosophers' ideas were widely disseminated through more popular accounts of style and taste in periodicals like *The Gentleman's Magazine*, and influenced how people thought about the power of art to refine and transform.

Fig. 75 Thomas Rowlandson, *The Art Gallery*, c. 1790–98. Pen and brown ink over graphite and watercolor on white wove paper, 9.1 × 13.6 cm (no. 193)

But Rowlandson was highly skeptical of this purported elevation, and his satires relentlessly unmask cultural attempts to transcend the bodily. For him, the art world was perhaps the place in contemporary life where the veneer of refinement was most hypocritical and the social mask most deceptive. Rowlandson made a cottage industry of skewering the pretensions of connoisseurs, repeatedly asserting that what drove the production and consumption of fine art was nothing more than greed and lust. In what follows, I will discuss several of Rowlandson's satires of the art world to provide a context for the Manton Collection drawing, *The Art Gallery* (fig. 75). We will see that Rowlandson's general theory of the tyranny of the bodily found particularly juicy evidence in the case of the lust for art.

Thomas Rowlandson began his artistic career as a promising student at the Royal Academy, and spent time living in Paris as a young man. When his aunt died and left him an inheritance of two thousand pounds, his gambling surged until his fortune had dissipated.[4] For the rest of his life his artistic production seems to have been driven mainly by his need for cash. The print publisher Rudolph Ackermann was a frequent employer; Rowlandson's virtuoso facility made it easy for him to turn out salable prints, usually satires on social mores rather than political events, whenever needed.

Connoisseurs, a hand-colored etching (fig. 76), shows four bewigged men in a room filled with paintings in elaborate gold frames. Hunched over, they stare greedily at the image of a reclining nude on an easel. The elevated subject matter of the painting is suggested by the inclusion of a chubby, winged putto, but we suspect the connoisseurs are not contemplating the moral meaning of this history painting. As the seated connoisseur squints comically through his monocle, we notice that the men are not the only ones ogling the painted nude; the figures in pictures on the walls also seem quite interested in her. Indeed, little separates *this* connoisseurship from that of the old man in the Manton Collection's drawing, *The Courtesan* (fig. 77), which illustrates a prostitute enticing a passerby. In both cases, a squat older man ogles a beautiful young woman

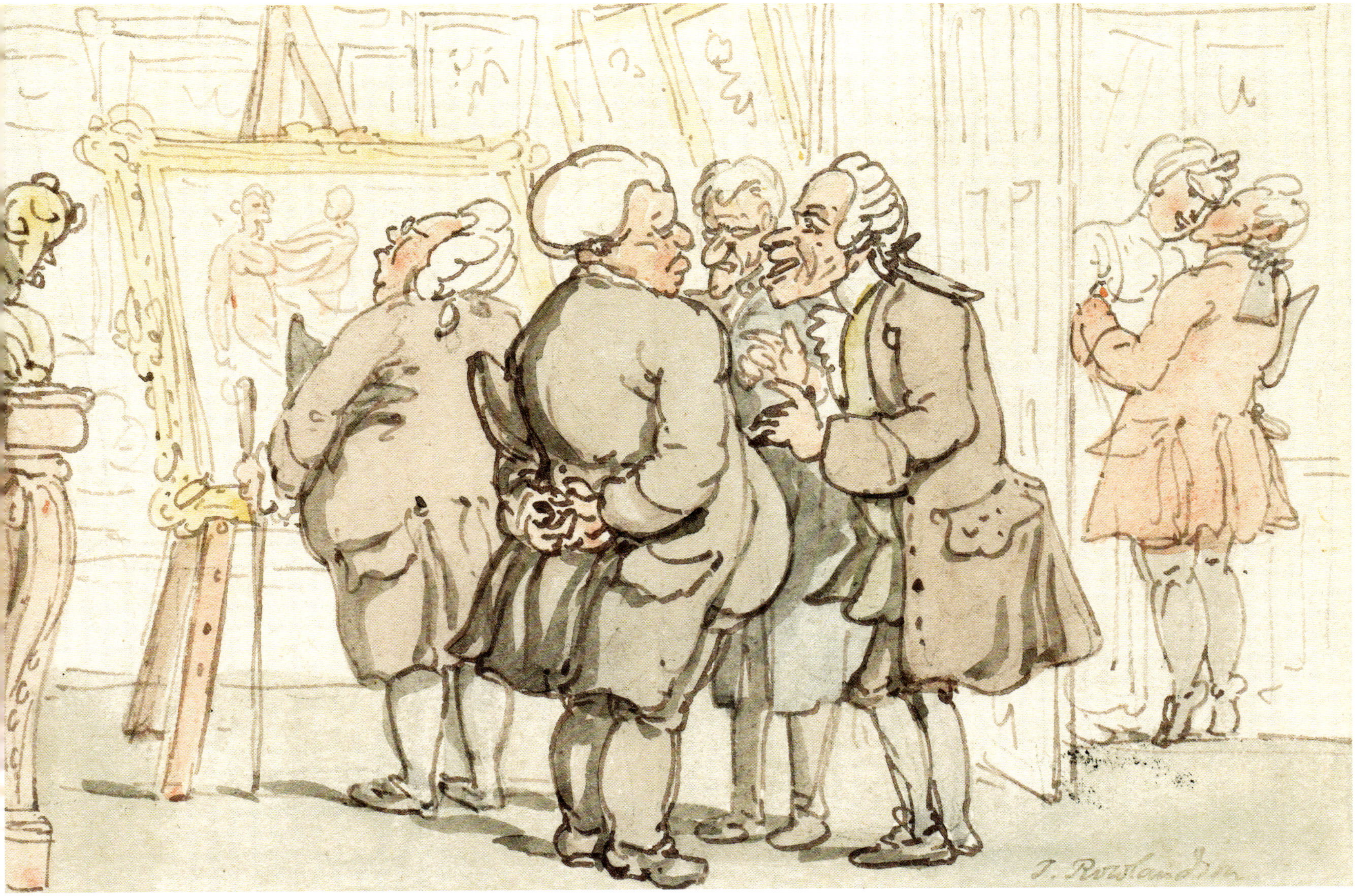
T. Rowlandson

Fig. 76 Thomas Rowlandson, *Connoisseurs*, 1799. Hand-colored etching, 25.9 × 19.5 cm. British Museum, London

Fig. 77 Thomas Rowlandson, *The Courtesan*, c. 1795–1800. Pen and gray ink and watercolor over graphite on cream laid paper, 10 × 11.6 cm (no. 195)

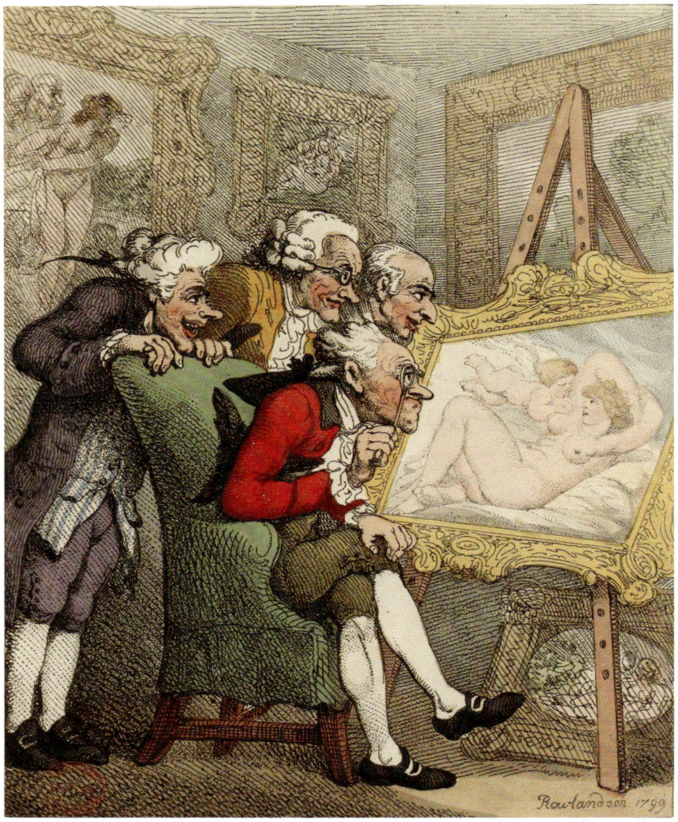

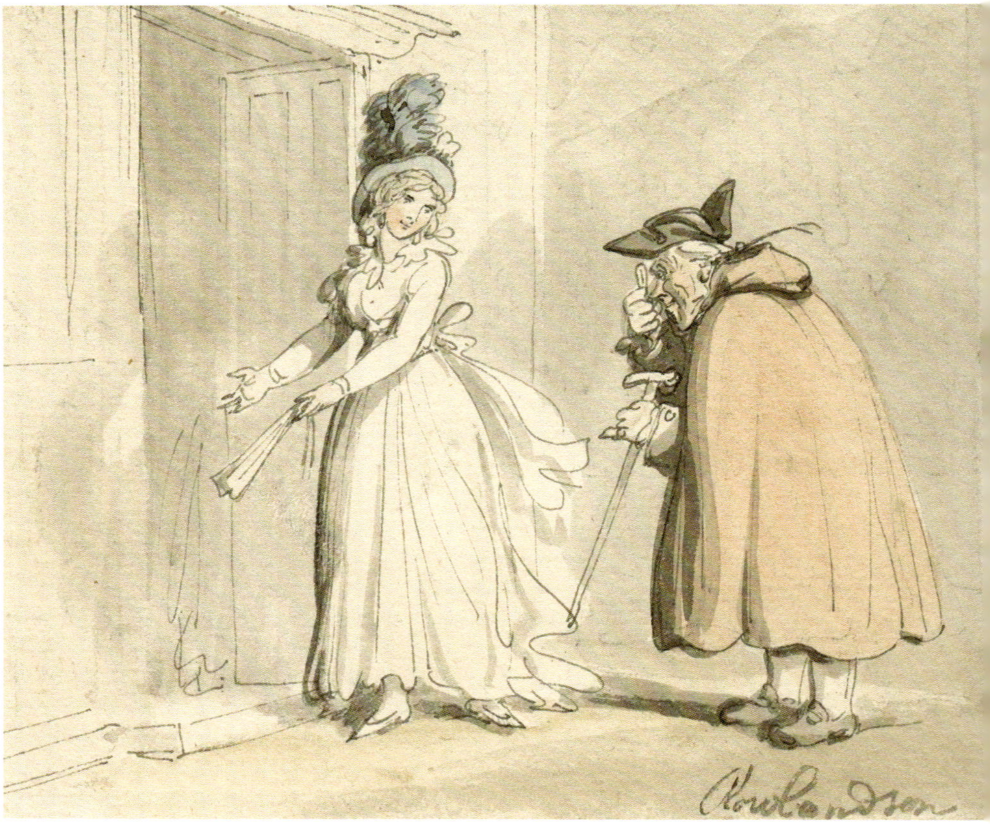

through a monocle. The main difference is that in *The Courtesan* the man's lust is straightforward, while in *Connoisseurs* it has the alibi of art appreciation. In both, we are, of course, the most privileged viewers. We can laugh at the men who are being made ridiculous by their lust, while we not only enjoy the nude picture but also feel amused by the spectators within the image whose own desire brings them low, and whose supposedly elevated, disinterested aestheticism is unmasked.[5]

This hierarchy of vision and visibility was a typical strategy for Rowlandson, as scholar James Sherry has observed.[6] Rowlandson often included a layering of spectatorship in his prints, beginning with those figures who exhibit their raw, human, bodily passions, followed by those who hungrily, although partially, observe them in the print, and surmounted by the bemused viewers of the whole comic scene: ourselves. *The Cat-astrophy* exhibits this hierarchy: the servants are made ridiculous by their headlong tumble, the women on the landing watch with dismay as the china is smashed, and we, the viewers, find ourselves amused not only by the servants' blunder but also by their mistress's discombobulation.

Sherry argues that this hierarchy of spectatorship has an important function: the creation of detachment, which is the key to Rowlandson's comedy.[7] Rowlandson's facile, bemused pencil and brush turn scenes of pain, degradation, or embarrassment into light, even superficial follies, distancing us momentarily from the chaos and anxiety of the world and our bodies with the irony of his perspective and the deflating strokes of his pen. But I would add that Rowlandson's ironic treatment of these subjects also enjoins us to recognize our common humanity. We laugh at these bodily eruptions not necessarily to feel superior to the satirized characters, but rather because we understand their pain and embarrassment. We are all, at bottom, animal creatures, no matter how elevated our status or our pretentions to civilization.

Accordingly, erotic desire might be considered an important step in the ladder from sensation to sensibility. Winckelmann's reverence for the formal perfection of nude classical sculptures, for example, was founded on their physical beauty and his desire for them, and the mental process of appreciation he described was largely a process of making the cold marble seem to come to life through the imaginative intervention of the viewer.[8] For his part, Lessing suggested that the classical sculptor chose a "pregnant moment" just before the decisive action of the implied narrative, and thus achieved two objectives: he avoided the depiction of an extreme emotion or action that would become distasteful to look at over time; and he enlisted the viewer by requiring him to complete

Fig. 78 Thomas Rowlandson, *The Gratification of the Senses: A la Mode François*, 1800. Hand-colored etching, 34.3 × 24.4 cm. Lewis Walpole Library, Yale University, New Haven, Conn.

Fig. 79 Thomas Rowlandson, *Lady H******* [Hamilton's] Attitudes*, 1800. Etching, 23.7 × 17 cm. British Museum, London

the narrative in his imagination, thereby enlivening the sculpture through mental and sensual stimulation.[9] Thus, the more a sculpture stimulates a viewer's imagination, the more engaged would be the viewer and the more lifelike the sculpture. The imaginative process of making the sculpture live in the eye of the beholder elevates the initial, base appreciation of physical beauty into a higher understanding of moral excellence.[10] In this way, desire became the spur for all higher aesthetic apprehension.

For many aesthetic theorists, the sensation of touch was the most important in this process of art appreciation. In Herder's influential formulation, the sense of vision, when looking at the plastic form of a sculpture, produces the memory of touch, which the imagination then uses to seemingly enliven the cold marble of the sculpture.[11] This is a reciprocal process of sublimation and appreciation, linking bodily sensations with intellectualized apprehensions of formal beauty. Through this process, the body and mind of the viewer are united, and physical sensation is thus transmuted into aesthetic sensibility. Rowlandson's images are not, of course, literal illustrations of such aesthetic treatises, but his consistent unmasking of aesthetic contemplation as just so much lust and greed demonstrates his familiarity with this cultural trope. The last step of Herder's process – the transmutation of the physical into the intellectual and moral – is the one never taken in Rowlandson's representations of aesthetic experience.

In the hand-colored etching *The Gratification of the Senses: A la Mode François* (fig. 78), Rowlandson explicitly addressed these ideas regarding the aesthetic animation of the senses by transmuting both the sensations and the art object of aesthetic theory into human, living form. The five senses are represented by five Frenchmen who orbit a beautiful woman in fashionable neoclassical attire, which constructs her as a kind of living statue clad in thin, revealing classical drapery. All the senses are focused greedily on her body, smelling, seeing – that monocle again – hearing, tasting; but the one with pride of place is "touch," Herder's haptic, the sense that conveys truth through sensibility, and which in turn sensitizes us to beauty. Yet Rowlandson is clearly having none of it. These aesthetes do not seem to be busily refining their sensibility or using their physical sensations as a spur to elevated moral understanding. Instead, the indulgence in sensation seems to make the men coarser, not more refined. Rowlandson deflates contemporary aesthetic theory by unmasking it as so much basic lust. The fact that these sensory-gratifiers are French, known to English viewers at the time as lusty and degenerate, makes the satire that much more appealing to a publication audience.

Not only connoisseurs, but also artists and patrons were motivated by lust, according to Rowlandson. His print *Lady H******* [Hamilton's] Attitudes* (fig. 79) makes a shrewd visual articulation of this nexus of artistic and sexual desire. Here, Sir William Hamilton, the British ambassador to Naples and renowned art collector, exhibits and unveils Emma Hart, his mistress and later wife, for the gaze of a handsome, young male artist. The artist again peers through a monocle (Rowlandson's visual shorthand for ludicrous short-sightedness) that is clearly inadequate to the grand voluptuousness of the woman in front of him. The pose of her body is mirrored by a female statue in the background that is part of an embracing couple; similarly, two bodiless busts seem to kiss at her feet. Art historian Ulrike Ittershagen has noted the evident desire of the artist in the way his pencil hovers over the pubic area of the drawn woman on his tablet, and in the embracing statuary couple, which looms above his head like a physical manifestation of his fantasy.[12] In typical style for Rowlandson, all the figures are unmasked (Emma, literally so: she is naked and holds a mask), and their high-minded pretensions are exposed as merely bodily urges in disguise. Emma is vain and promiscuous, cloaking her exhibitionism in artistic posturing; the artist is satisfying his desire to ogle under the guise of training his hand as an artist; and the old man is a fool, exhibiting his most prized possession in hopes of raising his status as a connoisseur, when in actuality he

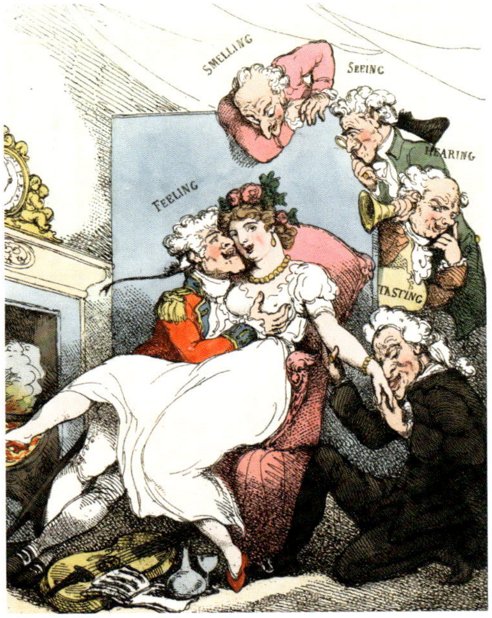

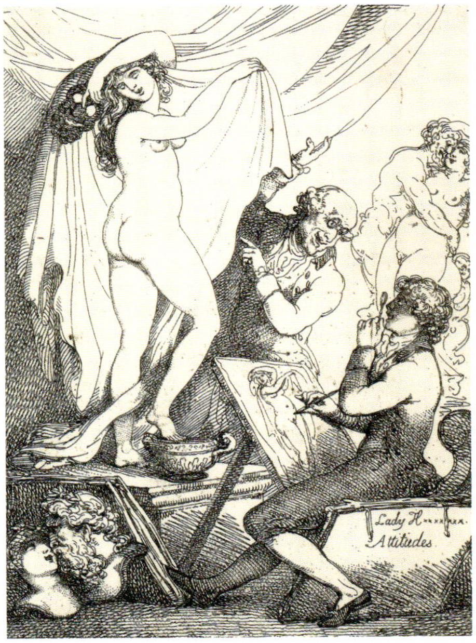

is being cuckolded visually. In Rowlandson's print, the line is blurry between a real woman posing for art, the art made depicting her body, and the art she mimics with her body, as well as between the scopic and physical pleasure in beauty itself.

In the Manton Collection's *The Art Gallery* (fig. 75), no one is using a monocle, but the otherwise standard elements of Rowlandson's art world satire are present and familiar. There is the squat older man staring too closely at the painted nude, and the opportunist who embraces the pretty girl standing off to the side. Three men in the foreground talk animatedly, while seeming to ignore the art lining the walls all around them. Are they discussing the taste of the collector? Society gossip? Or a pending financial deal? The prevailing belief among Londoners who bought prints, viewed exhibitions, and collected antiquities was that art was a prestigious pastime that would refine their sensibilities and elevate their minds. But here, Rowlandson contends that the space of the art exhibition is not a place where base sensations are transcended. On the contrary, as is made clear by the pairing of the man-enjoying-painted-woman with the man-enjoying-real-woman, pendants on either side of the central group, the art gallery is merely a high-status place where men can indulge their sensations while deceiving themselves about their motives. By the end of the eighteenth century, all commentators seemed to agree that the sensations of the body were the source of all truth and knowledge about the world. But authentically human bodily pleasure remained, for Rowlandson, more likely to be found in a London chophouse than in the fanciest art gallery.

1 For the best accounts of Rowlandson's work, see Ronald Paulson, *Rowlandson: An Interpretation* (New York: Oxford University Press, 1972); James Sherry, "Distance and Humor; the Art of Thomas Rowlandson," *Eighteenth-Century Studies* 11, no. 4 (1978): 457–72; Arline Meyer, "Man's Animal Nature: Science, Art, and Satire in Thomas Rowlandson's 'Studies in Comparative Anatomy,'" in *Humans and Other Animals in Eighteenth-Century Britain: Representation, Hybridity, Ethics*, ed. Frank Palmeri (London: Ashgate, 2006); and Bernard Falk, *Thomas Rowlandson: His Life and Art* (London: Hutchinson and Co., 1949). A new biography of Rowlandson is valuable for its thorough accounting of the chronology of his life and career: M. T. W. and J. E. Payne, *Regarding Thomas Rowlandson, 1757–1827: His Life, Work, and Acquaintance* (London: Paul Holberton Publishing, 2010). See also my essay on Rowlandson's political prints, "Amoral Humor: Desire and Mockery in Rowlandson's Comic Art," in *Thomas Rowlandson: Pleasures and Pursuits in Georgian England*, ed. Patricia Phagan (Poughkeepsie, N.Y.: Frances Lehman Loeb Art Center, Vassar College, 2011).

2 I have argued this with specific reference to a new model of subjectivity in *Caricature Unmasked: Irony, Authenticity, and Individualism in Eighteenth-Century English Prints* (Newark: University of Delaware Press, 2008), esp. ch. 5.

3 On the haptic in particular, see Mark Paterson, *The Senses of Touch: Haptics, Affects, and Technologies* (London: Berg, 2006); and *Sensible Flesh: On Touch in Early-Modern Culture*, ed. Elizabeth D. Harvey (Philadelphia: University of Pennsylvania Press, 2003).

4 Vic Gattrell, "Rowlandson's London," in *Pleasures and Pursuits in Georgian England*.

5 Notice, too, that one of these is a drawing, while the other is a published print. Some of Rowlandson's drawings were made to sell directly to collectors who valued his beautiful facility of line and wry humor; his more erotic drawings are certainly examples of this private patronage. Others were preparations or proposals for publication. Professional etchers and aquatinters employed by the print publishers would produce the prints from Rowlandson's drawings, which were then often hand colored before sale. Published prints needed to be (slightly) more decorous, narratively more resolved, and thus more broadly understandable, than drawings.

6 Sherry, "Distance and Humor," 467–70.

7 Ibid., 460.

8 See Alex Potts, *Flesh and the Ideal: Winckelmann and the Origins of Art History* (New Haven, Conn., and London: Yale University Press, 1994); and Whitney Davis, "Winckelmann Divided: Mourning the Death of Art History," in *Gay and Lesbian Studies in Art History*, ed. Whitney Davis (Binghamton, N.Y.: Haworth Press, 1994), 141–59.

9 Gotthold Ephraim Lessing, *Laokoon: An Essay on the Limits of Painting and Poetry* (1766). See also Karin A. Wurst's interesting essay on how these theories of imaginative animation translated into the spectatorship of other artistic performance, such as Emma Hamilton's attitudes, in "Spellbinding: The Body and Art/Art as Body in the Cultural Practice of *Attitüden*," *Lessing Yearbook* 33 (2001): 151–81.

10 Because of this theoretical preoccupation with animation, the myth of Pygmalion was a potent one in the eighteenth century. See J. L. Carr, "Pygmalion and the Philosophes: The Animated Statue in Eighteenth-Century France," *Journal of Warburg and Courtauld Institutes* 23, no. 3–4 (July–December 1960): 239–55.

11 Johann Gottfried von Herder, *Sculpture: Some Observations on Form and Shape from Pygmalion's Creative Dream* (originally published in Riga, 1778).

12 See Ulrike Ittershagen, *Lady Hamiltons Attitüden* (Mainz: Zabern, 1999).

What You Will!

Turner's Shakespearean Variety

David Blayney Brown

Joseph Mallord William Turner is the virtuoso of British art, a painter of unique range whose subjects span landscape and marine imagery, history and contemporary life, and British and European scenery; whose trajectory of style and technique took him from watercolor to oil, from somber homages to the Old Masters to vivid impressions of nature and light; and whose paintings have been admired by artists from Claude Monet to Mark Rothko. He is impossible to characterize save in terms of paradox. How else to explain an artist who kept an eighteenth-century interest in the classics, and reverence for tradition, longer than almost any of his contemporaries, yet also was the first to paint steamships and trains? Whose restless curiosity drove him to constant travel even as he aimed to create the definitive picture of his own country? Or who retained some of his best work for a posthumous Turner Gallery (he hoped at London's National Gallery), yet also mistreated it, using one canvas as a cat flap, or talking of using another as a shroud? Endlessly fascinating, at once familiar and unknowable, Turner's art has stretched the limits of critical discourse, and is a Holy Grail for collectors. Fittingly, he is a star of the Manton Collection, and at its heart is *What You Will!* (fig. 80), one of his most beautiful but also provocative and controversial pictures.

In 1822 the forty-seven-year-old Turner was at the summit of his profession. Sir Thomas Lawrence's assessment, as early as 1809, that he was "indisputably the first landscape painter in Europe,"[1] had never seriously been challenged in Britain. Turner was hard at work on a variety of commissions and projects, from literary illustrations to British and European topography, and planning a series of pictures recording King George IV's state visit to Scotland. That summer, Turner's Gallery reopened at his London house, refurbished and with a retrospective of pictures, and his watercolors were highlights of "the most splendid Collection ever exhibited of Drawings by English Artists," at the premises of the engraver-publishers George and William Bernard Cooke. Yet he was not doing much new painting, and although some of his greatest pictures still lay ahead, his exhibiting career at the Royal Academy had reached something of a lull. He had shown nothing at the Academy in 1821, and the following year sent only *What You Will!*, a small picture whose subject and appearance marked a surprising new departure while its title seemed a devil-may-care shrug at what was usually expected of him.

Was Turner going through some sort of midlife crisis? Hardly, to judge from the energy and consistency he brought to other aspects of his work. Was he taking stock, pausing to assimilate the effects of visits to Italy in 1819 and France in 1821? More likely; and on one level at least, *What You Will!* was his comeback to those of his critics

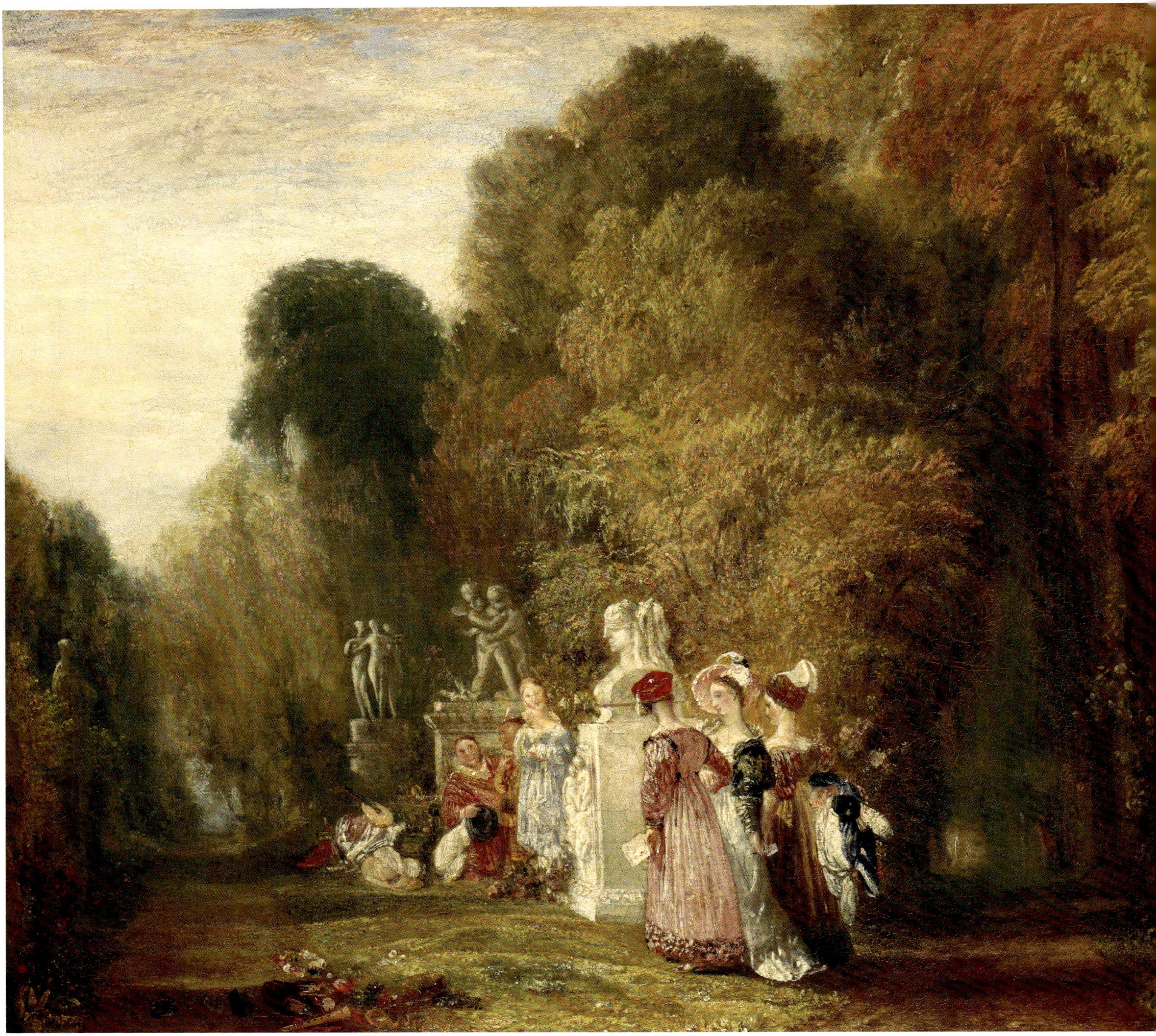

who had dealt rather harshly with his exhibit in 1820. *Rome from the Vatican: Raffaelle Accompanied by La Fornarina Preparing His Pictures for the Decoration of the Loggia* (fig. 81) had attempted to collect his impressions of the light, color, history, and architecture of Italy on a grand scale.[2] The move from a tribute to Raphael in the tercentenary of the master's death to an incident from Shakespeare's *Twelfth Night* painted as if seen through the eyes of Antoine Watteau was certainly a change of mood. And Turner had exchanged one of his largest canvases for one of his smallest.

What links these pictures? Both display Turner's growing interest in art history, complex perspective, and dazzling color, as well as a sense of narrative that bridges time and breathes intimacy into grandeur and elegance. In the Vatican loggia, Raphael shows off his art to his mistress, La Fornarina. In her garden in Illyria, Olivia holds a letter that will fool her majordomo Malvolio into thinking she loves him while Malvolio's tormentors, Sir Toby Belch, Sir Andrew Aguecheek, and Maria, lurk behind a statue. Just as Turner's Rome was not really Raphael's, since it includes Bernini's arcades, *What You Will!* was not a literal representation of Shakespeare's play. Turner's borrowing of Shakespeare's subtitle to title his painting seems to have escaped the critics in their hasty dismissal of the work. So, too, because more obvious when spoken in Turner's Cockney accent, did the implied pun on Watteau's name. For *The Examiner*, it framed a question to which there was only one answer: "Almost anything but what a picture ought to be." For *The New Monthly Magazine*, it was "worse than nothing, . . . an affront to the public taste."[3]

These reviews, written to amuse, miss the insouciance and sophistication of Turner's unexpected comedy. But the reviewers were right to intuit that his ideas about what makes a picture were changing. The emerging middle class, the print market, and popular "keepsake" publications wanted something different from the grand histories and mythologies that had made Turner's reputation in the Royal Academy exhibitions. If anyone it was Turner who was in touch with the public taste. This was the very period when Shakespeare was being rediscovered by the Romantic generation for his volatile mix of genres, characterization, and dramatic pace – especially in 1827, when English actors brought the bard to Paris. Theirs was also the generation that rehabilitated Watteau, in Britain and then in France, when the Restoration released him from the stigma of the *ancien régime*.

Turner's association of playwright and painter was intentional, and had already been made. *England: Richmond Hill, on the Prince Regent's Birthday* (fig. 82), exhibited at the Royal Academy in 1819,[4] depicts a garden party above the Thames on 23 April

Fig. 80 Joseph Mallord William Turner (English, 1775–1851), *What You Will!*, 1822. Oil on canvas, 49.8 × 54.3 cm (no. 278)

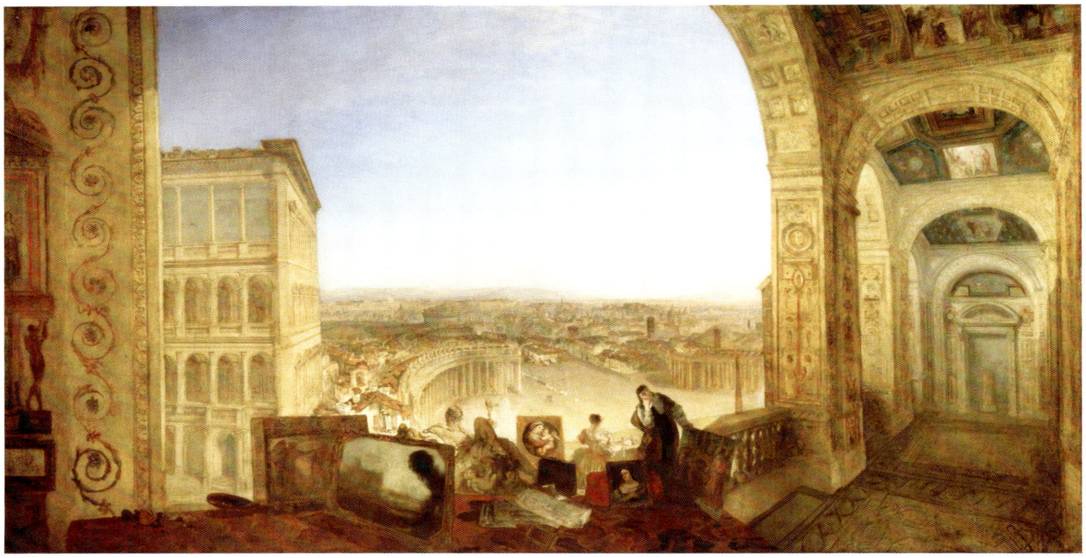

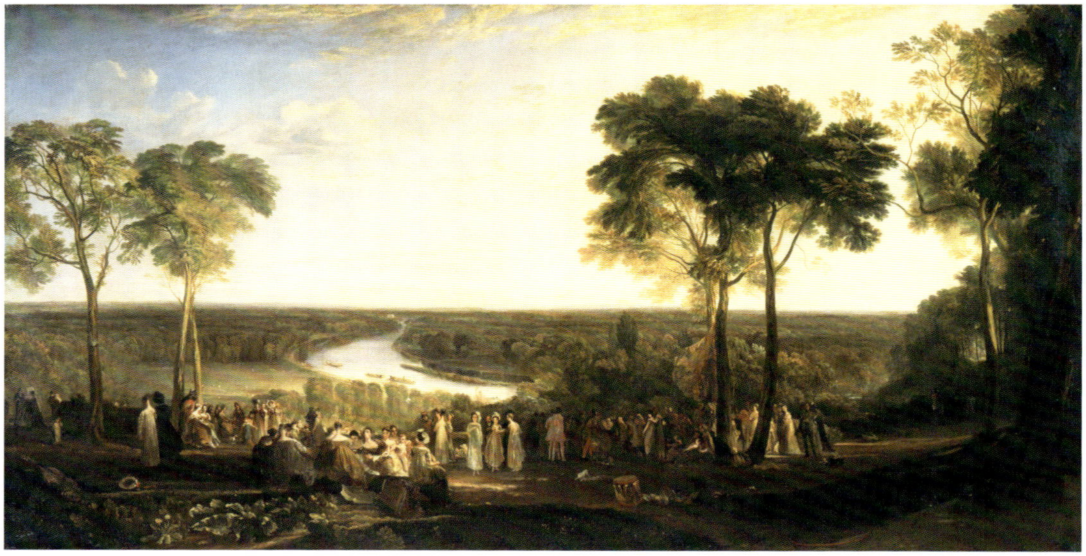

– also the birthday of Shakespeare and Turner. The scene is reminiscent of Watteau's *fêtes galantes* and especially his *Île Enchantée*, which was formerly in the collection of Sir Joshua Reynolds (whose house overlooked this view) and now belonged to Turner's friend, the watercolorist James Holworthy. *What You Will!* continues the Shakespearean connection and may have been partly modeled on Watteau's *Open Air Party* (now known as *Alte*, 1720) belonging to Turner's patron the Earl of Egremont;[5] Turner was certainly familiar with other works by Watteau in the collections of John Soane, Samuel Rogers, and the Dulwich Picture Gallery, as well as prints after Watteau published in the *Recueil Jullienne*.[6] In Paris in 1821 he copied parts of the Louvre's version by Jean-Baptiste Pater of Watteau's *Fête Champêtre: Réjouissance de Soldats* (c. 1730), perhaps believing it was by the master himself, and may have gained access to *La Perspective* (c. 1715) in a private collection.[7] Watteau was always an artist's artist; Turner is said to have declared he had learned more from Watteau than any other painter. One can see the results in the shimmering silks worn by Olivia and her friends, the shady avenues of her garden, and the golden autumn leaves.

Fig. 81 Joseph Mallord William Turner, *Rome from the Vatican: Raffaelle Accompanied by La Fornarina Preparing His Pictures for the Decoration of the Loggia*, 1820. Oil on canvas, 177.2 × 335.3 cm. Tate, London

In defiance of the critics, *What You Will!* was bought by a stalwart of the Academy, the sculptor Francis Chantrey. He and Turner were close friends, and had served together on the Academy Council since 1818. Both were self-made men with a shared sense of humor. Chantrey must have recognized the Roman origin of the sculpture in Olivia's garden, which Turner based on sketches he had made in 1819.[8] Perhaps he was amused by the blindfolded double herm, epitomizing the romantic concealments and confusions of Shakespeare's plot and representing the new directions in Turner's art: its capacity to look two ways at once, at past and future, England and abroad. In 1815 Chantrey had visited Paris with the painter Thomas Stothard,[9] who launched a popular sideline of imitations of Watteau with *Sans Souci*, exhibited in 1817.[10] Chantrey may have challenged Turner to better it. We can be sure that he saw in his friend's pathos-tinged comedy not only inspiration and invention, but a breadth of sympathy that matched his own. As a collector of his colleagues, Chantrey's tastes were diverse, spanning genre pictures by the likes of David Wilkie (also an enthusiast of Watteau) to a huge biblical subject by the now largely forgotten Henry Thomson. As an "unbounded" admirer of Turner, Chantrey "could well comprehend [his] mental scope" and "efforts of imagination."[11]

Fig. 82 Joseph Mallord William Turner, *England: Richmond Hill, on the Prince Regent's Birthday*, 1819. Oil on canvas, 180 × 334.6 cm. Tate, London

What You Will! exemplifies what Constable praised as Turner's "wonderful range of mind."[12] It was one of only two canvases and the last work by Turner acquired by Sir Edwin Manton. If at first it seems a surprising acquisition when viewed alongside Sir Edwin's

Fig. 83 Joseph Mallord William Turner, *Watteau Study by Fresnoy's Rules*, 1831. Oil on oak panel, 40 × 69.2 cm. Tate, London

Fig. 84 Joseph Mallord William Turner, *Saumur from the Île d'Offart, with the Pont Cessart and the Château in the Distance*, c. 1830. Watercolor and gouache with pen and black and brown ink over traces of graphite on blue wove paper, 12.7 × 19.2 cm (no. 283)

Turner watercolors of landscape and topography, we can soon identify common ground – in the artist's internationalism, historical and literary interests, and extraordinary technical development and capacity for reinvention, all propelled by a Romantic impulse to associate himself with his subjects and themes, whether through experience and observation or by leaps of the imagination. While the art historian Andrew Wilton has observed a "celebration of Englishness" in the Shakespearean origins of *What You Will!*,[13] no less striking are Turner's appropriations from classical antiquity and eighteenth-century France. Over time, these were joined by practice and theory drawn from Venetian colorists, French classicists, or more recent writings by Johann Wolfgang von Goethe. When in 1831 Turner painted *Watteau Study by Fresnoy's Rules* (fig. 83),[14] depicting the painter in his studio, he associated Watteau with the well-known treatise on painting to emphasize his qualities as a colorist, especially in relation to the role of white as a highlight or a means of projection or recession in pictorial space.[15] Described as a "white painter" for the airy pallor of some of his landscapes, Turner made increasing use of white grounds for oils and of the natural color of the paper – white, blue, or tinted – in his watercolors, adding white as a highlight on top of other colors. The painter portrayed in *Watteau Study* is a kindred spirit.

Saumur from the Île d'Offart, with the Pont Cessart and the Château in the Distance (fig. 84) dates from just earlier, being one of many views of the Loire made about 1830 for an ambitious project to depict the rivers of Europe.[16] Based on drawings made in 1826,

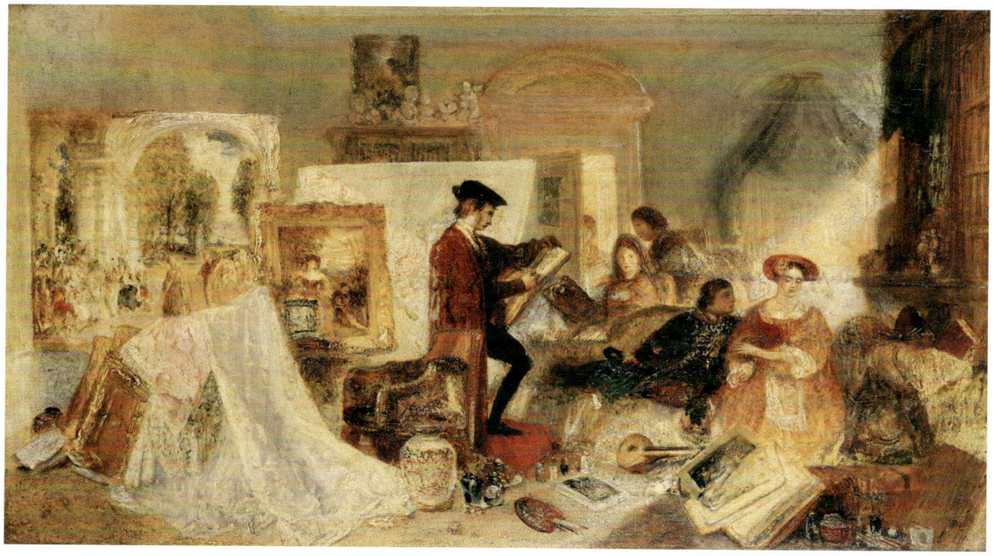

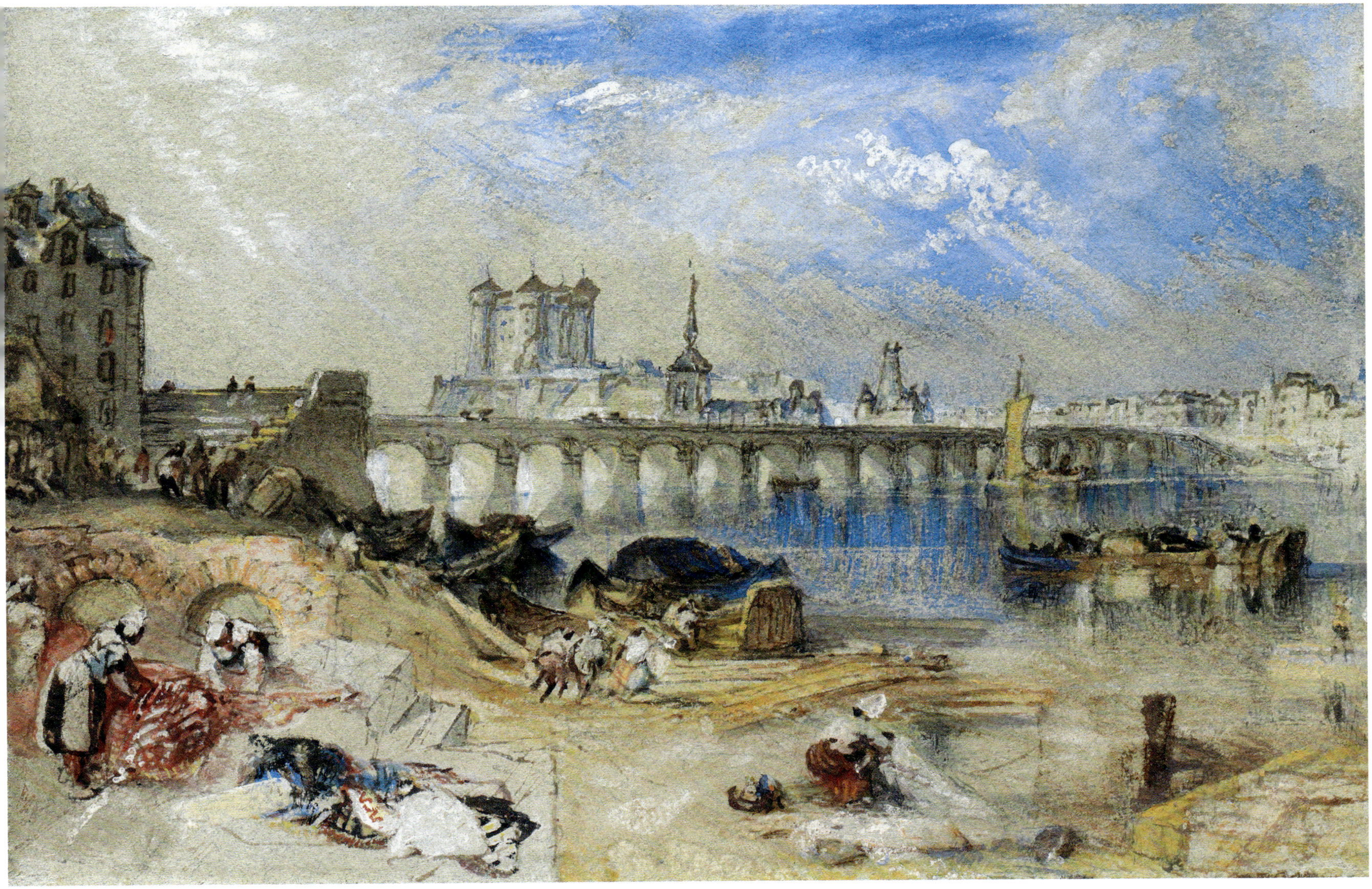

Fig. 85 Joseph Mallord William Turner, *Hoolay Deedy, Seringapatam*, c. 1800. Watercolor over graphite on white wove paper, 42.1 × 65.4 cm (no. 212)

Fig. 86 Joseph Mallord William Turner, *View of La Riccia (Ariccia)*, 1817. Watercolor and gouache, with scraping, on cream wove paper, 13.6 × 21.5 cm (no. 276)

it was engraved in 1833 for *Turner's Annual Tour – The Loire*. The publication stresses Turner as traveler, familiar with his continental subjects, while its design shows a parallel mastery of materials – brilliant local color and sparkling highlights applied with great economy over blue paper that pulls everything together. He used watercolor, gouache, and ink, black as well as white, and worked quickly, conveying the illusion of a first impression. By contrast, the early *Hoolay Deedy, Seringapatam* (fig. 85) is a tinted drawing, painted in flat washes that create stillness, even stasis. Perhaps Turner hoped to give the suggestion of enervating heat, for the subject (probably also intended for engraving) is Indian, one of a set recording General Baird's conquest of Tipoo Sultan's fortress of Seringapatam in 1799.[17] However, when this was painted about 1800, Turner had not yet been abroad, so had to work from materials prepared by a British military draftsman. While the watercolor is a feat of imaginative projection, it lacks the benefit of experience. Until his visit in 1819, this was true also of his views of Italy. *View of La Riccia (Ariccia)* (fig. 86), made in 1817 as an illustration for James Hakewill's *Picturesque Tour*, was based on an on-the-spot drawing by the author.[18] Although Turner could stipple and layer his washes to suggest mobile, shifting light, as with *Hoolay Deedy*, his northern eye could not yet envisage its true radiance.

The realities of a changeable, rain-prone continental climate are evoked with absolute conviction in *The Moselle Bridge at Coblenz* (fig. 87), one of fifty-one watercolors arising from a tour of Belgium and the Rhineland in 1817.[19] From a visit to Waterloo, where Napoleon had met defeat only two years prior to Turner's travels, the artist imagined the aftermath of the battle in *The Field of Waterloo* in 1818.[20] The watercolors were a more personal project, begun on site or developed from his sketchbooks. They are on a gray ground that sets the "subdued and regretful" tone that has been observed in the series,[21] but their local colors are rich and warm, lit up with glints of white gouache or highlights scratched into the paper where light catches buildings or reflects on water. Clouds or sunshine sweep over ancient bridges and castles as the modern Rhinelanders go about their business. The series is a landmark in Turner's humane topography, and he seems to have had only one client in mind – his friend Walter Fawkes, who already owned some of his best watercolors of the Swiss Alps from a visit made in 1802. After landing at Hull on the Yorkshire coast, Turner went straight to Farnley, Fawkes's country estate, where he pulled the "Rhine" watercolors from his coat pocket immediately on crossing the threshold. Knowing very well what was expected of him, Fawkes bought them for five hundred pounds.

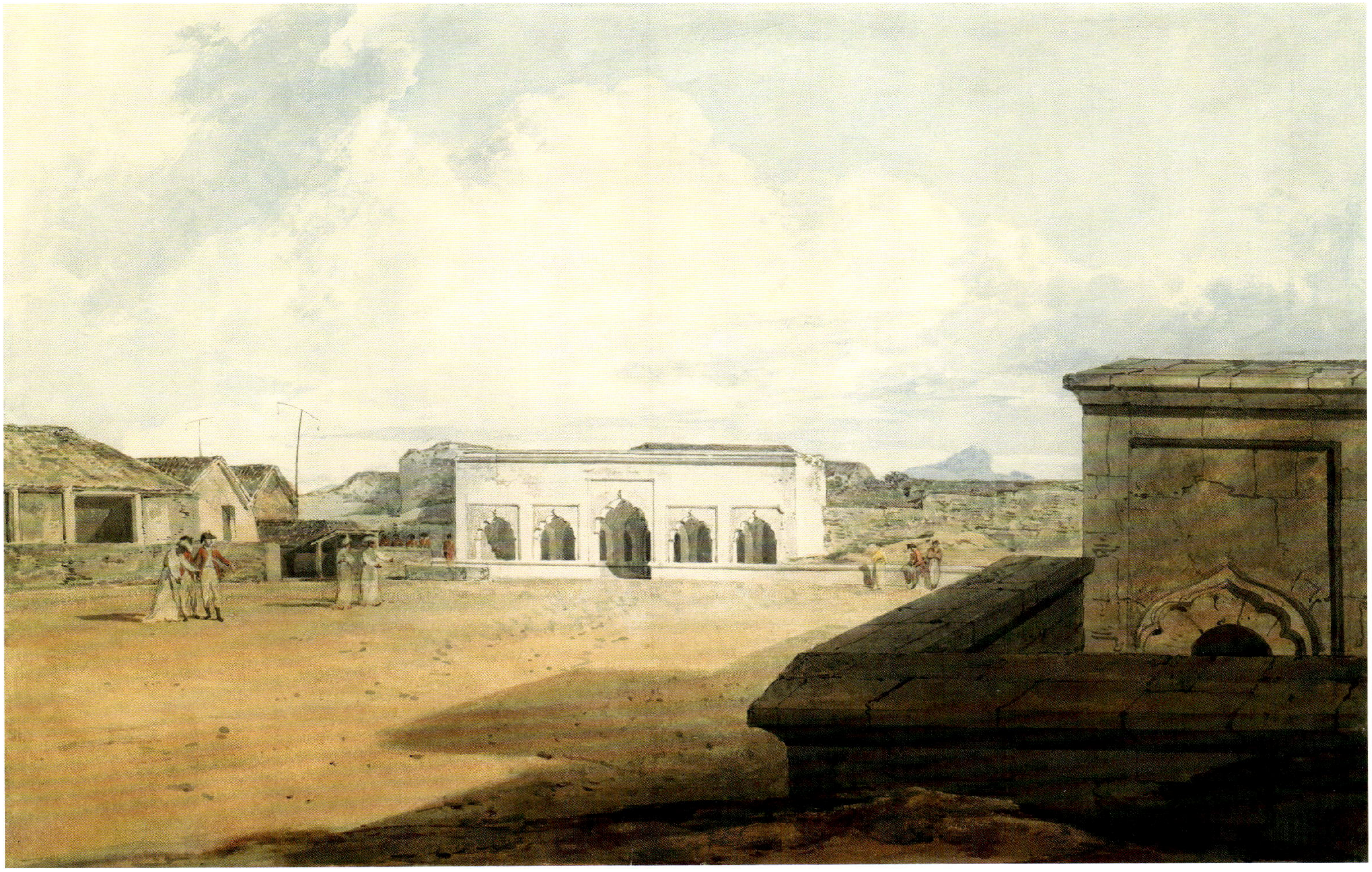

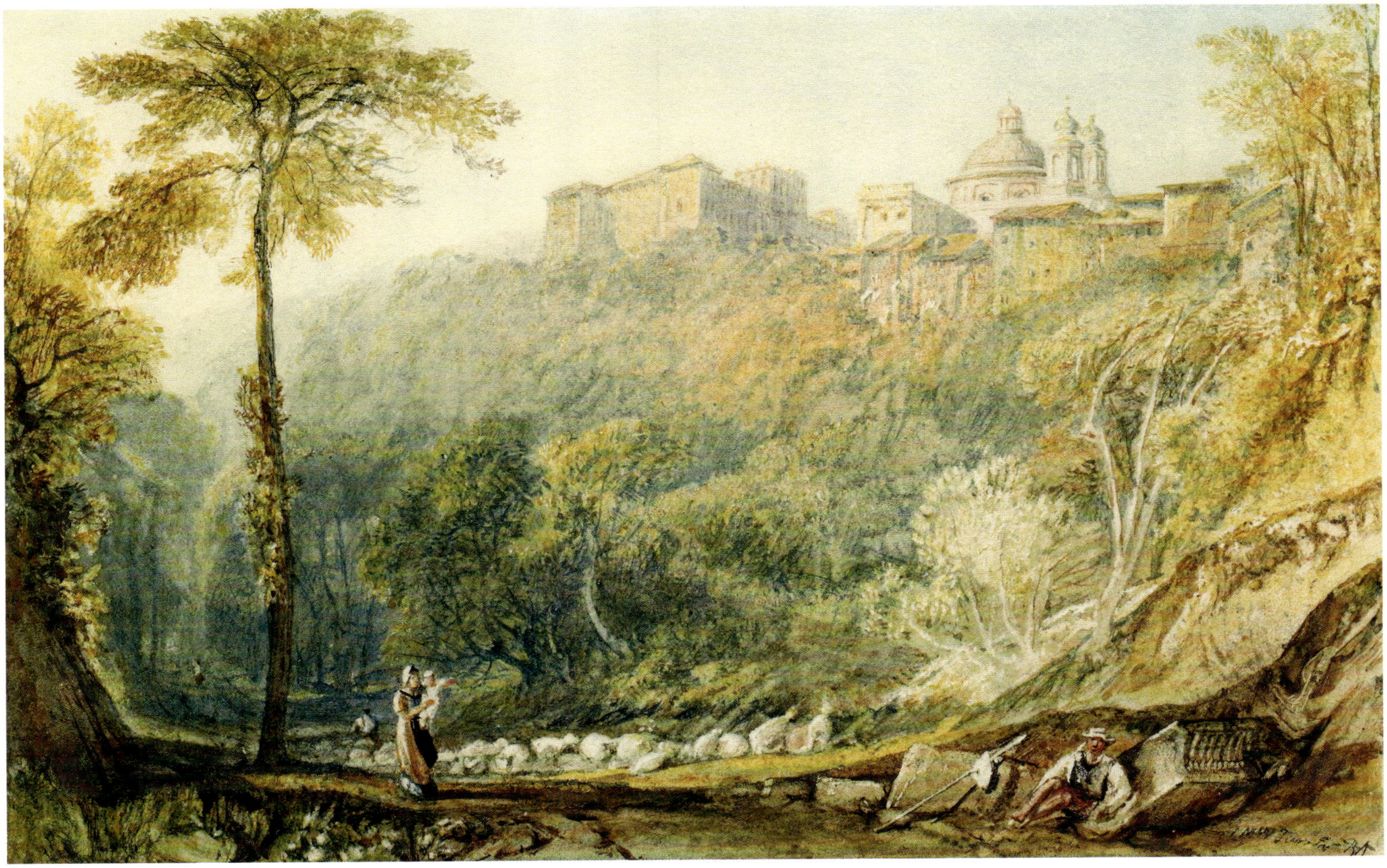

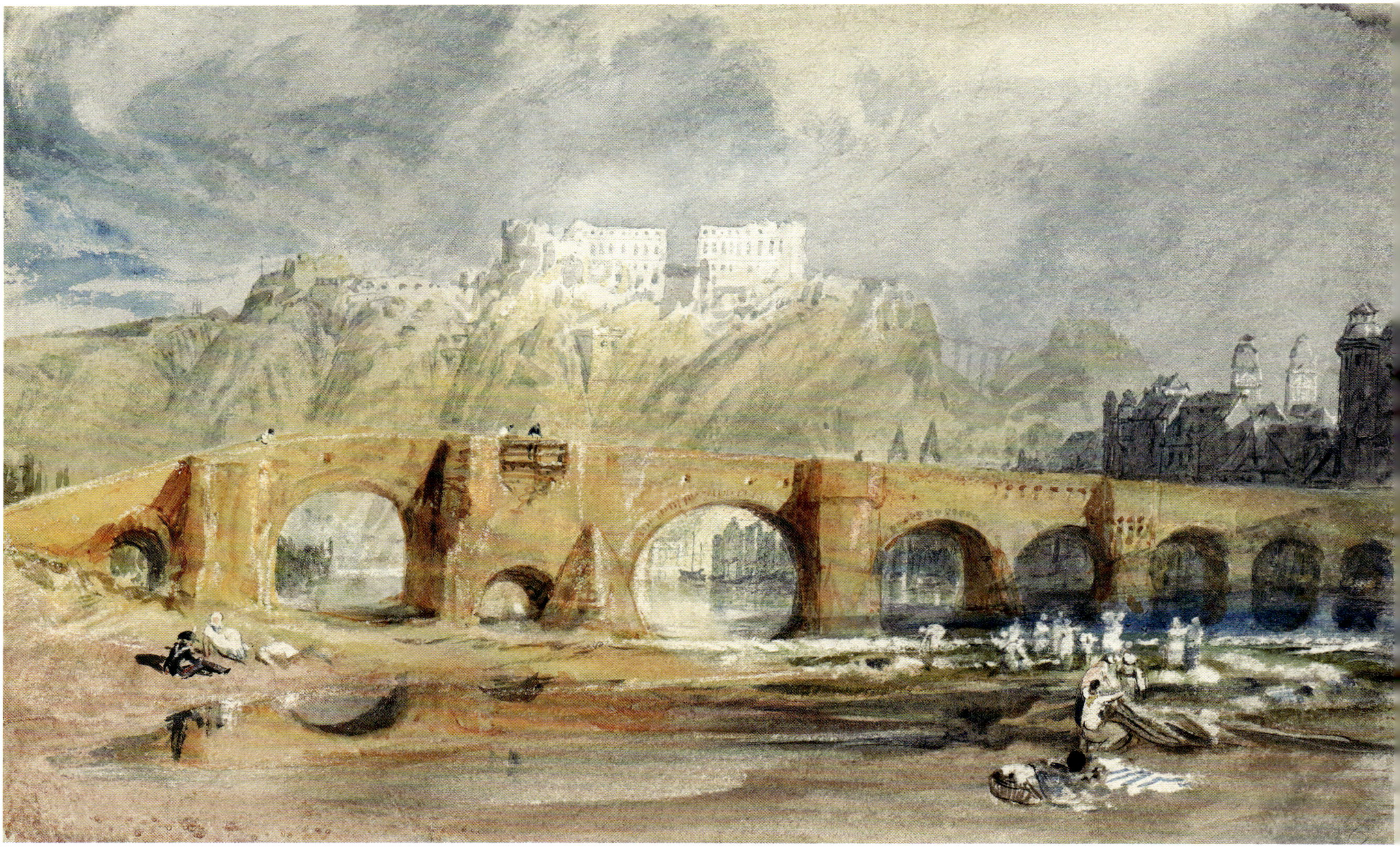

Fawkes was probably attracted to these subjects because they covered ground described by Byron in his recently published poem, *Childe Harold's Pilgrimage*, an association that was certainly intended by Turner, who attached Byron's famous "Waterloo stanzas" to his picture of the battlefield. The friendship between the Cockney artist and Yorkshire squire was warmed by shared interests, among them European history and English literature; in 1822 Turner embellished books in the Farnley library with watercolors illustrating Byron and his fellow poets Walter Scott and Thomas Moore,[22] a task that probably gave as much mutual enjoyment as painting the Shakespearean *What You Will!* for Chantrey. In *Melrose Abbey* (see fig. 115), taken from Scott's *Lay of the Last Minstrel*, a lone nocturnal visitor – poet, painter, or even patron – admires the abbey's great window, while on a fallen stone Turner has written an epigraph from the poem:

Who'er would see fair Melrose right
Must visit it by the pale Moon light

The moon's glimmer penetrates the bluish gloom of the ruins, making the image seem to rise like a ghost from the page.

This effect is even more striking in Turner's open-edged vignettes, such as *Genoa* (fig. 88), designed for the *Works of Lord Byron* (1831–33) issued by the poet's publisher, John Murray. It was engraved by Edward Finden who also used it for his *Landscape*

Fig. 87 Joseph Mallord William Turner, *The Moselle Bridge at Coblenz*, 1817. Watercolor and gouache, with scraping, on white wove paper, 20 × 31.4 cm (no. 275)

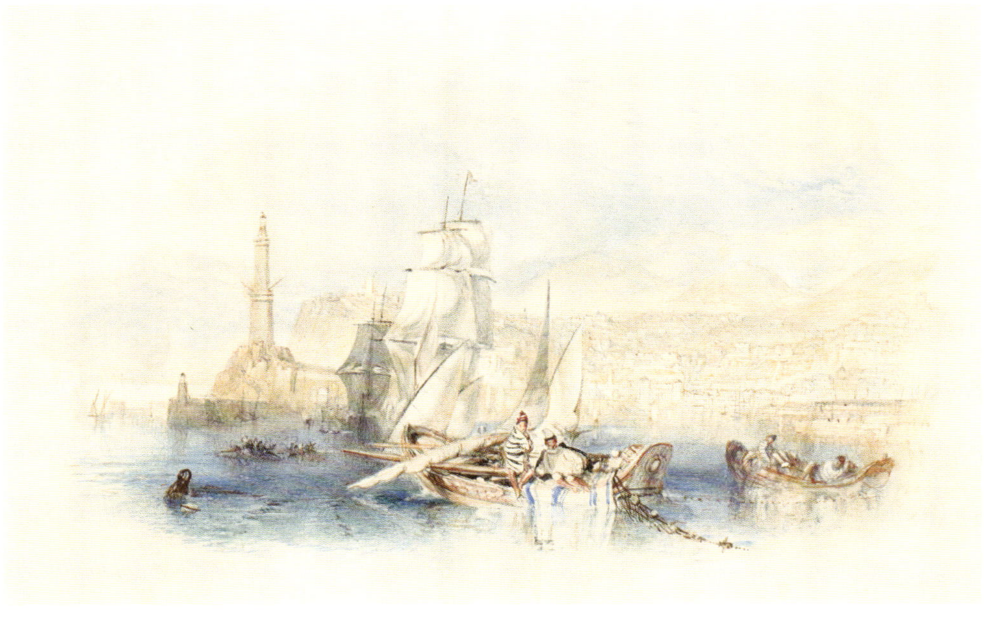

Fig. 88 Joseph Mallord William Turner, *Genoa*, c. 1832. Watercolor and gouache over graphite on cream wove paper, 12.7 × 21 cm (no. 284)

Fig. 89 Joseph Mallord William Turner, *Wolf's Hope, Eyemouth*, c. 1835. Watercolor and gouache over graphite, with scraping, on cream wove paper, 10.5 × 16.5 cm (no. 286)

Fig. 90 Joseph Mallord William Turner, *Distant View of Plymouth*, 1813. Oil on cream wove paper, 15.2 × 23.5 cm (no. 274)

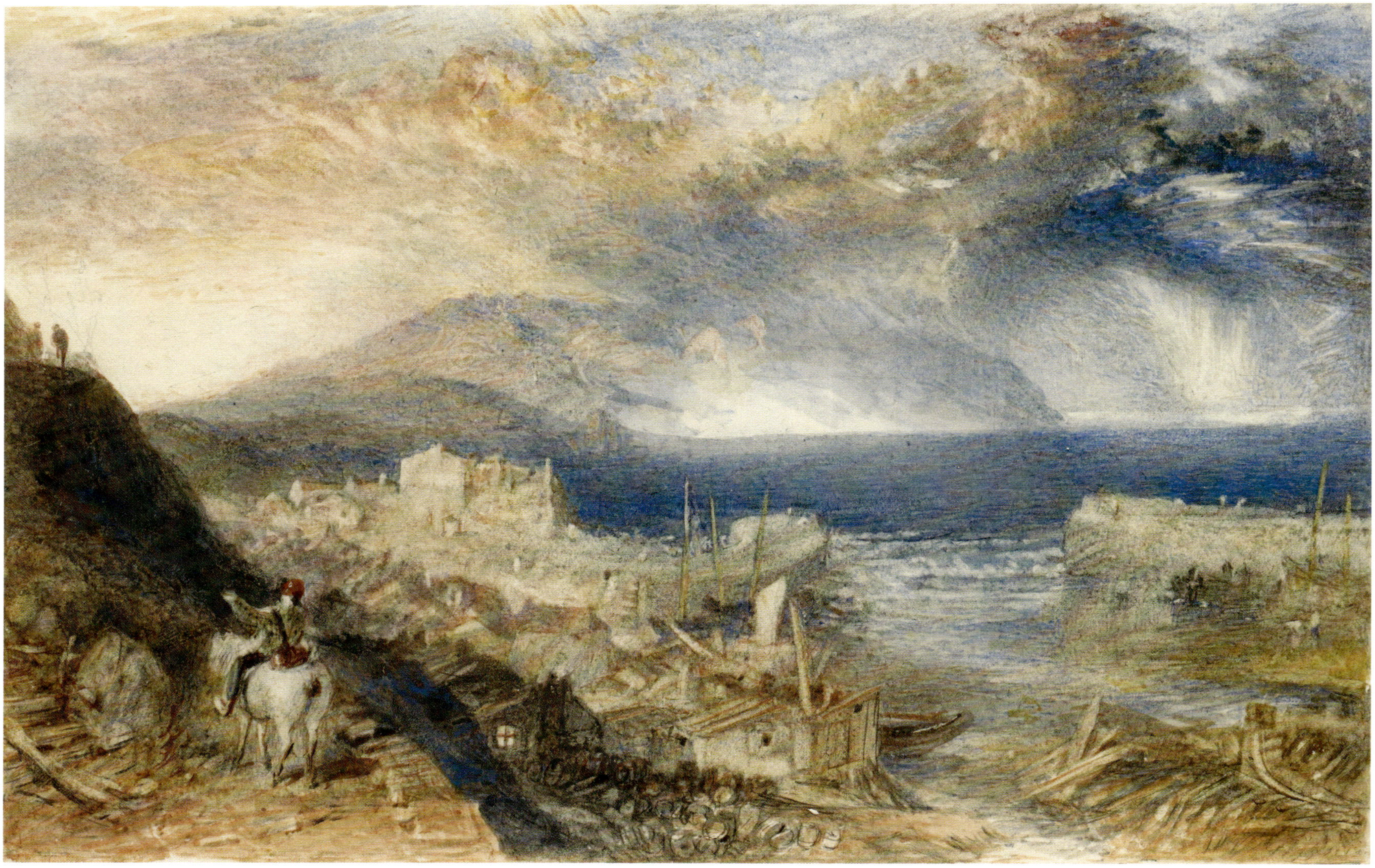

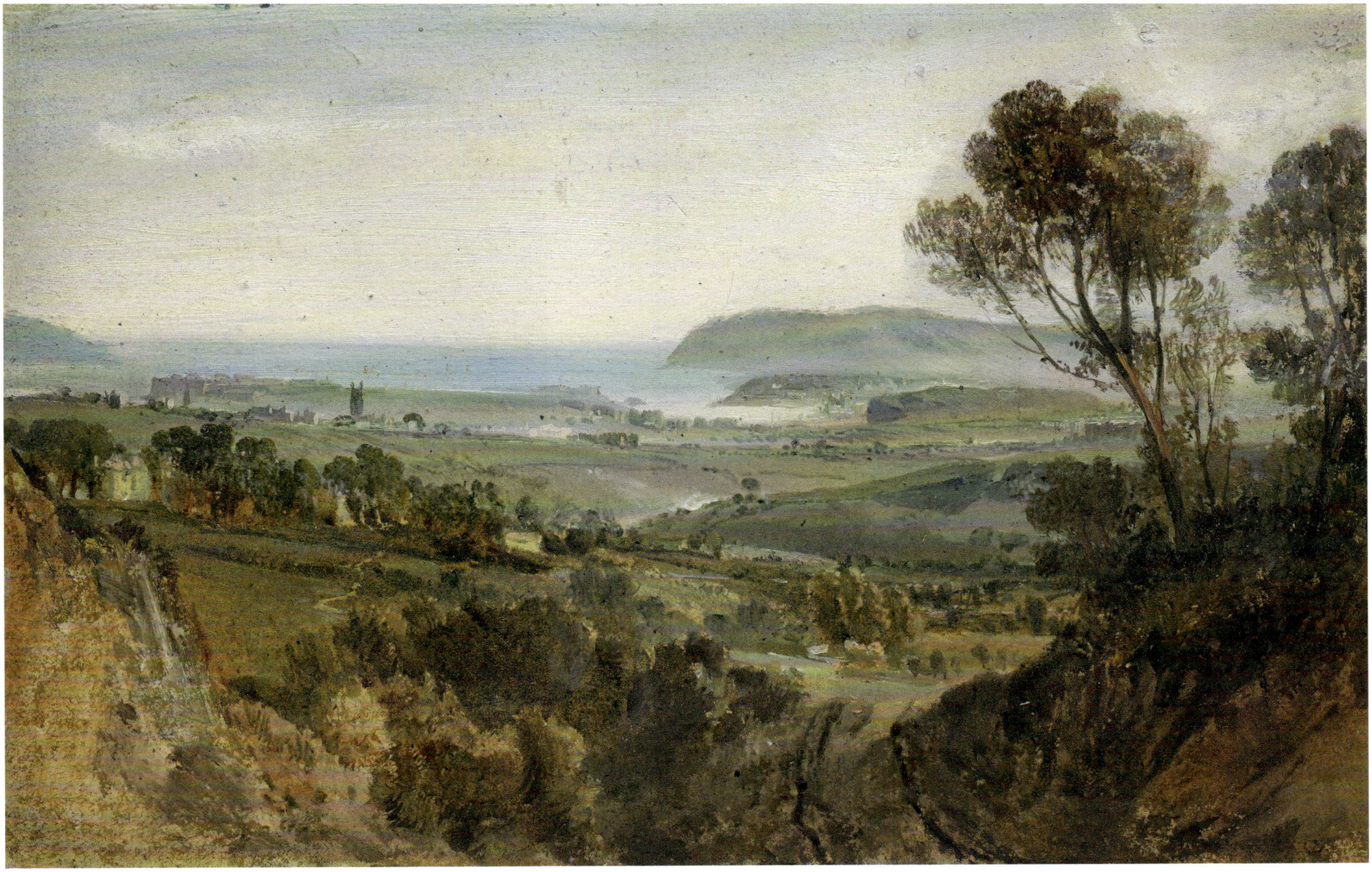

Fig. 91 Joseph Mallord William Turner, *Falmouth Harbor*, c. 1825. Watercolor and gouache, with scraping, on cream wove paper, 15.9 × 22.1 cm (no. 279)

Fig. 92 Joseph Mallord William Turner, *Entrance to Fowey Harbor, Cornwall*, c. 1827. Watercolor and gouache, with scraping, on cream wove paper, 28.6 × 39.4 cm (no. 281)

Illustrations of Lord Byron (1833–34), originally commissioned by Murray. Turner referred to drawings made during his second visit to Italy in 1828 for his view of the harbor and lighthouse that, rather than illustrating a specific text, shade in the background of a world where the experience of poet and painter interacts. Turner aimed to evoke Byron's life as much as his work, and chose subjects partly to accompany notes on places associated with the poet, proposed (but never delivered) by his friend John Cam Hobhouse. Evidently Genoa featured because Byron had spent part of his last months in Italy there, before sailing from Leghorn (Livorno) on his doomed expedition to Greece.[23]

In a similar project of topographical amplification, rather than illustration, for Sir Walter Scott, Turner's dramatically titled *Wolf's Hope, Eyemouth* (fig. 89), depicting a town on the Berwickshire coast, accompanied the poem *The Bride of Lammermoor* in the Revd. George Wright's *Landscape – Historical Illustrations of Scotland and the Waverley Novels* published by Fisher (1836–37). Just prior, in 1831, Scott's publisher Robert Cadell commissioned illustrations for a complete edition of the author's work, for which Turner made a two-month-long visit to Scotland, staying for part of the time with Scott at Abbotsford, his border estate. Their close acquaintance, if not actual friendship, gave Turner's illustrations a layer of empathy lacking in those he made to accompany the poems of Byron, whom he seems never to have met. Yet Turner's work for the poems of John Milton, one of his favorite poets, reaches across historical distance. The vignette *The Temptation of Christ on the Mountain* (no. 285), made for Milton's *Poetical Works*, compresses a prospect of valleys and rivers, cities and empires. That Satan uses such wonders to taunt Christ suffuses the little design with Romantic irony. As his publishers came to recognize, given the right conditions, Turner was the supreme master of landscapes of association that were rich in meaning yet instantly accessible, historically aware but utterly of their time.

If Turner's literary illustrations sprang from his mastery of topography, his explicitly topographical works were enriched by a sense of history and shared experience, encouraging viewers to "read" these too. The evident naturalism found in his many private studies of sea or sky should not mislead us into thinking that this was sufficient in itself. Turner was not Constable, and an exercise in plein air such as *Distant View of Plymouth* (fig. 90), painted in oil on paper during a visit to Devon in the sun-drenched summer of 1813, was in fact rare, the exception that proved the rule. More consistent in Turner's topography is the accumulation of associations and narrative, added to the love of buildings seen in his earliest antiquarian subjects. In *Falmouth Harbor* (fig. 91),

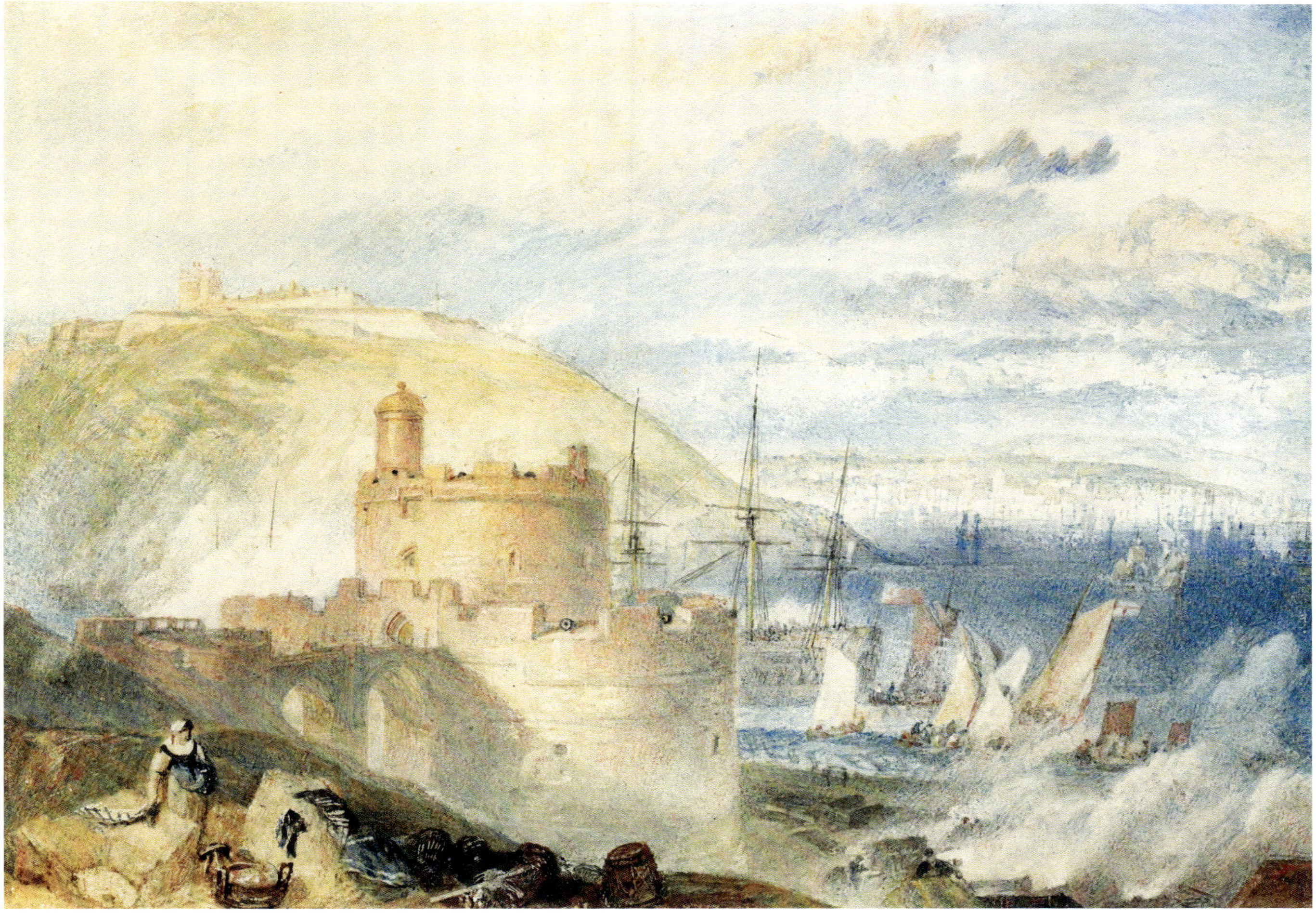

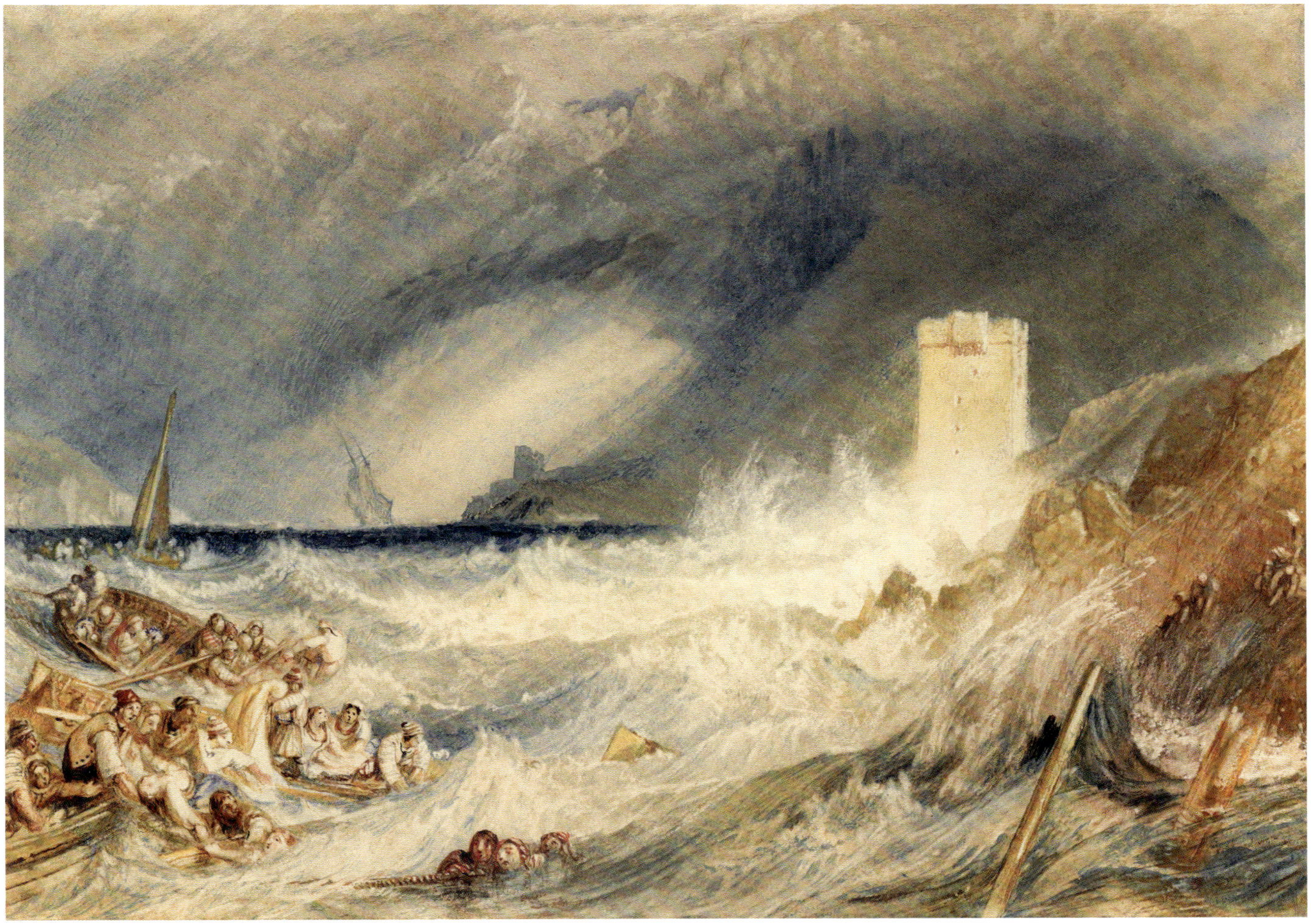

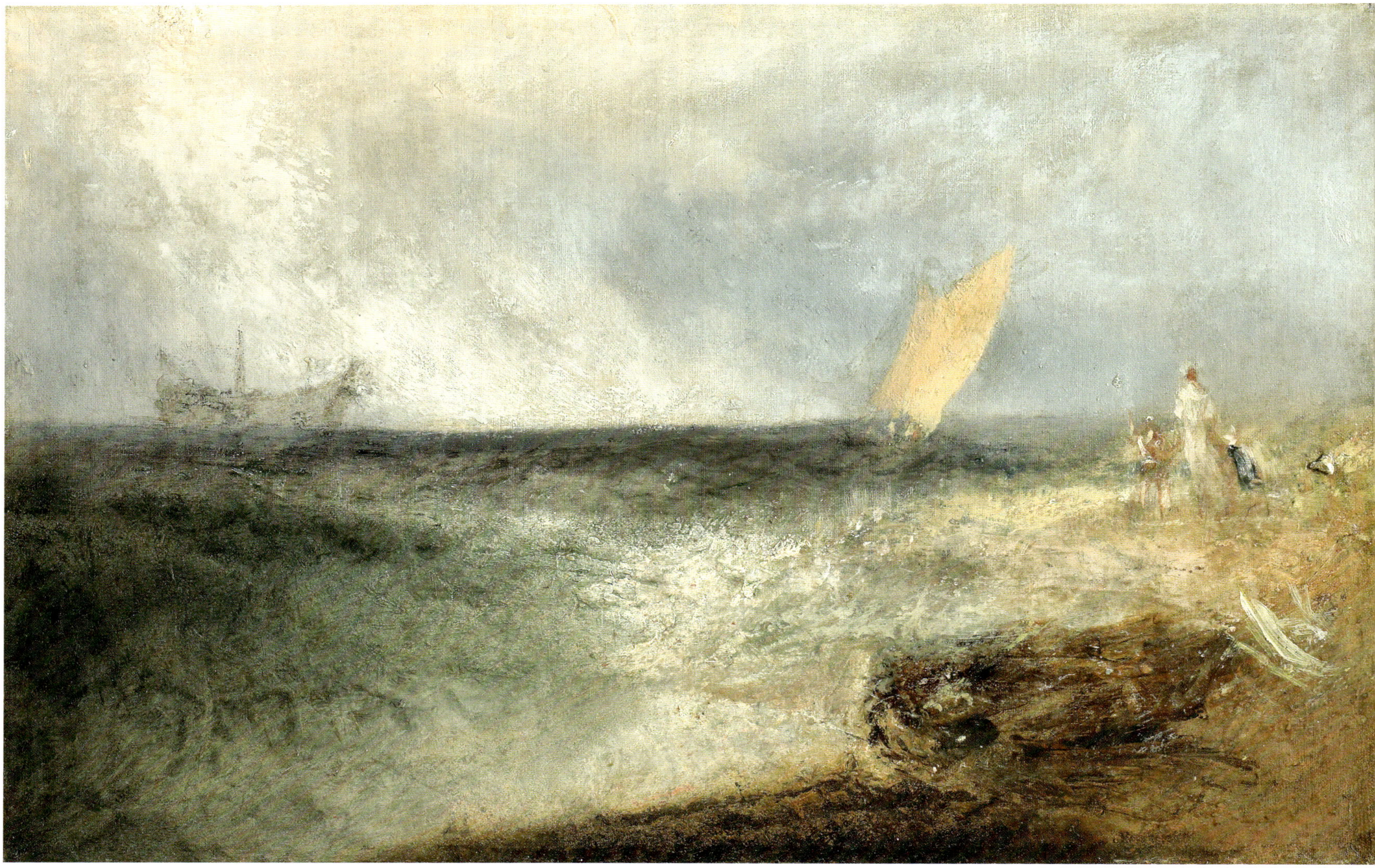

made in the mid-1820s from earlier drawings for a series of English ports,[24] the Tudor castle of St. Mawes fires its cannon to salute the modern naval vessels entering the harbor, while in the foreground a fishwife sorts a fresh catch. The composition seems to define this stretch of Cornish coast, but in fact Turner completely realigned the headlands of St. Mawes and Pendennis so that one is seen from the north and the other from the south,[25] and changed their relative scale – liberties inconceivable to the more empirical Constable. In *Entrance to Fowey Harbor*, *Cornwall* (fig. 92), another Cornish subject based on earlier material painted two years later,[26] forts still guard the coast, but Turner stirs up a violent storm and dramatic shipwreck to emphasize the natural dangers that have superseded threats of invasion. *Fowey Harbor* was engraved for the magisterial *Picturesque Views in England and Wales*, published by Charles Heath, which marked the peak of Turner's topographical career.[27] This great project, spanning more than a decade from 1827, enabled the artist to draw on a lifetime's impressions to build a picture of his country that was Shakespearean in scope and ambition.

Fig 93 Joseph Mallord William Turner, *View off Margate, Evening*, c. 1840
Oil on canvas, 32.1 × 48.9 cm
(no. 289)

If his splendid engraved watercolors, like his painting *What You Will!*, show the public aspects of Turner's art, *View off Margate, Evening* (fig. 93), the other Turner canvas in the Manton Collection and also a late acquisition, discloses his private side. It is related to various late oil sketches of the coast, and perhaps, in its motif of a woman and two children, to an exhibited picture, *The New Moon* or *"I've lost My Boat, You shan't have Your Hoop,"*[28] shown in 1840, as well as to explorations of medium and effect that he never showed. Even the history of this oil is intensely personal compared to other Manton Turners that belonged to such great collectors as John Ruskin or B.G. Windus, Turner's dealer Thomas Griffith, or his friends Fawkes and Chantrey. *View off Margate* was owned by Turner's mistress Mrs. Booth, who looked after him in his last years. It seems to represent the Kent resort where she lived overlooking the pier. Yet Turner would not be Turner if there were not also a sense of art, history, and the wider world as he looks out to sea; this time not south to the arts of France and Italy that joined Shakespeare in *What You Will!*, but north and east to the Dutch marine painters who he once said had made him an artist.

1 Alexander Joseph Finberg, *The Life of J. M. W. Turner, R.A.*, 2nd ed., rev., suppl. by Hilda F. Finberg (Oxford, U.K.: Oxford University Press, 1961), 156.

2 For reviews of *Rome from the Vatican*, see ibid., 264–65; and Martin Butlin and Evelyn Joll, *The Paintings of J. M. W. Turner*, rev. ed. (New Haven, Conn., and London: Yale University Press, 1984), 137–38.

3 For reviews of *What You Will!*, see Butlin and Joll, *Paintings of Turner*, 138.

4 Ibid., 106–7.

5 As suggested by Butlin in Martin Butlin, Mollie Luther, and Ian Warrell, *Turner at Petworth: Painter and Patron* (London: Tate Publishing, 1989), 52.

6 For a full discussion of Turner's knowledge of Watteau, see Selby Whittingham, "What You Will; or Some Notes Regarding the Influence of Watteau on Turner and other British Artists," *Turner Studies* 5, no. 1 (1985): 2–24; and *Turner Studies* 4, no. 2 (1985): 28–48.

7 Ian Warrell, *Turner on the Seine* (London: Tate Publishing, 1999), 22.

8 For example, *Vatican Fragments* sketchbook, 1819 (Tate, Turner Bequest CLXXX0, fol. 6, 31v, 52v, 53v); Cecilia Powell, *Turner in the South: Rome, Naples, Florence* (New Haven, Conn., and London: Yale University Press, 1987), 58–59.

9 Mrs. Bray, *The Life of Thomas Stothard, R.A., with personal reminiscences* (London, 1851), 70.

10 David Solkin et al., *Turner and the Masters* (London: Tate Publishing, 2009), 192–93.

11 George Jones, *Sir Francis Chantrey, R.A.: Recollections of His Life, Practice, and Opinions* (London, 1849), 104f.

12 John Constable to Maria Bicknell, East Bergholt, 30 June 1813, in *John Constable's Correspondence*, ed. Ronald Brymer Beckett, vol. 2, *Early Friends and Maria Bicknell (Mrs. Constable)* (Ipswich, U.K.: Suffolk Records Society, 1964), 110.

13 Andrew Wilton, *Turner, Girtin, and Bonington: A New York Private Collection; Paintings, Watercolours, and Drawings* (New York: published privately, 2001), 52.

14 Butlin and Joll, *Paintings of Turner*, 192.

15 Ian Warrell in Solkin, *Turner and the Masters*, 174–77; David Blayney Brown, "White and Gold: Turner in a Petworth Light," in Christopher Rowell, Ian Warrell, and David Blayney Brown, *Turner at Petworth* (Petworth, U.K.: National Trust; Tate Publishing, 2002), 75.

16 Ian Warrell, *Turner on the Loire* (London: Tate Publishing, 1997).

17 Andrew Wilton and David Blayney Brown, "Picture Notes: The Siege of Seringapatam," *Turner Studies* 8, no. 1 (1998): 59.

18 Anthony Cubberley and Luke Herrmann, *Twilight of the Grand Tour: A Catalogue of the Drawings by James Hakewill in the British School at Rome Library* (Rome: Istituto Poligrafico e Zecca della Stato, Libreria dell Stato, 1993).

19 Cecilia Powell, *Turner in Germany* (London: Tate Publishing, 1995).

20 Butlin and Joll, *Paintings of Turner*, 104–5.

21 Walter Thornbury, *The Life of J. M. W. Turner, R.A., Founded on Letters and Papers Furnished by his Friends and Fellow Academicians* (London: Chatto & Windus, 1877), 1:87.

22 For a discussion of these illustrations, see Jan Piggott, *Turner's Vignettes* (London: Tate Publishing, 1993), 32–34.

23 David Blayney Brown, *Turner and Byron* (London: Tate Publishing, 1992).

24 For example, *Devonshire Coast No.1* sketchbook, 1811 (Tate, Turner Bequest CXXIII, 145v).

25 As observed by Eric Shanes, *Turner's Rivers, Harbours and Coasts* (London: Chatto & Windus, 1981), 38.

26 For example, *Ivy Bridge to Penzance* sketchbook, 1811 (Tate, Turner Bequest CXXV, 18v, 19r); and an earlier watercolor engraved for *Picturesque Views on the Southern Coast of England*.

27 Eric Shanes, *Turner's Picturesque Views in England and Wales 1825–1838* (London: Chatto & Windus, 1979), 42–43.

28 Butlin and Joll, *Paintings of Turner*, 238.

Nature or Art?

Constable's Sketches and Studies

Anne Lyles

John Constable is usually regarded as England's quintessential painter of nature. While his contemporary Turner is admired for the extraordinary range of his subject matter, remarkable inventiveness, and expressive use of color, Constable is appreciated for something more measured, more accessible, and – because his paintings are apparently closer to the appearance of the visible world as we experience it – more "truthful."

Although Turner embarked on extensive travels throughout Europe during his lifetime, Constable regarded it as a badge of honor that he never visited the continent, admiring the Dutch seventeenth-century landscape painters for being "a *stay-at-home* people."[1] As Charles Robert Leslie noted in his famous biography of the artist, Constable never traveled expressly for his subject matter.[2] "I should paint my own places best," he told his great friend Archdeacon John Fisher, adding that it was the scenes of his Suffolk boyhood, "the sound of water escaping from Mill dams ... Willows, Old rotten Banks, slimy posts and brickwork ... [and] all that lies on the banks of the Stour" that had originally inspired him to become a painter.[3] Most of the locations featured in Constable's art – Hampstead, Brighton, Osmington, or Salisbury – are connected in some way with his family or close friends. Leslie perceptively observed that Constable's art formed "a history of his affections."[4]

Unlike Turner and the majority of his contemporaries, Constable was raised in the countryside. He was born in 1776 in the village of East Bergholt in Suffolk to respectable, prosperous, pious parents. His father, Golding, was a farmer as well as a corn and coal merchant who owned mills and barges in the vicinity of Flatford and Dedham. Constable was initially groomed to enter the church, and when this idea was abandoned he trained to enter the family milling business. This background was highly influential in shaping his subsequent career as an artist.

Growing up, Constable developed an acute eye for the workings of the land and changing weather patterns, as well as a deep appreciation for nature in all its manifestations. Meanwhile, his devout upbringing seems to have added a near-missionary zeal to his desire to reform landscape painting. The concept of artistic "truth to nature" recurs again and again in Constable's writings, and was something he perceived as having a moral basis.[5] Early in his career Constable told his fiancée Maria Bicknell (granddaughter to the rector of East Bergholt, Dr. Rhudde) that, when engaged in painting, he felt he was "performing a moral duty."[6]

Constable initially became aware of what he saw as the need to devote himself to a more naturalistic form of landscape painting in the spring of 1802, when he first submitted a painting to the Royal Academy. He felt dispirited by the work on view – such as Turner's large dramatic historical landscape, *The Tenth Plague of Egypt* – which he saw as contaminated with "the great vice of the present day … *bravura*, an attempt at something beyond the truth." In response, Constable resolved to return to East Bergholt and paint from Nature herself, "the fountain's head, the source from whence all originality must spring."[7] He remained committed to the idea of what he called "natural painture" for the rest of his artistic career.[8]

To have a profound ambition to produce a more naturalistic art was one thing, to achieve it was another. As art historian Ernst Gombrich so brilliantly argued in his *Art and Illusion: A Study in the Psychology of Pictorial Representation*, there is no such thing as absolute naturalism in painting.[9] All artists necessarily interpret to a greater or lesser degree. Constable understood this, and knew that it was important not to transcribe nature too literally if he was to achieve a powerful, innovative, and meaningful – "truthful" in an emotional sense – art. He spoke unfavorably of the landscapes of his contemporary, Frederick Richard Lee, describing them as of "the coldest and meanest kind" in large part because "they pretend to nothing but an imitation of nature."[10]

How, then, was Constable to achieve this new landscape art, with its "truth to nature"? The answer lay to some extent in the subject matter itself. Constable tended to paint landscapes with which he was either deeply acquainted or to which he had powerful associations. Examining the same particular area, or fragment, of landscape again and again enabled him to arrive at its very essence, something that struck a chord with the late British figurative artist Lucian Freud, who referred to this scrutinizing process as "downward travel."[11] It did not matter to Constable how humble his landscape subject might be; if anything, the more modest the better. He once claimed, "my limited and abstracted art is to be found under every hedge and in every lane, and therefore nobody thinks it worth picking up."[12]

The very process of painting was a vital tool for Constable in his endeavor to produce a more naturalistic art. As art historian Michael Kitson has pointed out, the extensive correspondence that survives between Constable and his friends, family, and artistic associates shows him preoccupied with the practical and aesthetic problems of representation and with the difficulty of trying to be an innovator in art. Above all, he was engaged with the act of painting: questions of execution and handling, painterly style and brushwork, and levels of finish.[13]

This dialogue between nature and art, whether manifested through choice of subject or mode of execution, is a constant theme in Constable's career, though it never runs in a straightforward path. Whether we are assessing his sketches and studies or the finished pictures made from them, we observe that his work seems to shift between a more mimetic representation of landscape and a more synthetic one. Generally, the art Constable produced in the first half of his career, before his marriage to Maria Bicknell in 1816 and permanent move to London that same year, tends to be more faithfully naturalistic, while that produced in the second half is more conceptual. However, it is not easy to read the purpose of his sketches on the basis of handling alone; an assessment of the context or period in which they were produced is an essential component in understanding their function.

Close examination of two sketches in the Manton Collection made by Constable during these two phases of his career, *Flailing Turnip-heads, East Bergholt* of c. 1812–15 (fig. 94) and *Salisbury Cathedral from the River Nadder* of c. 1829 (fig. 95), is highly illuminating in this respect. The former shows a scene in the Ryber Valley, close to the Rectory, on the edge of the village. In the foreground, laborers are threshing dried turnip-heads to remove the seeds, an activity usually carried out over cloths spread in the fields to avoid having to carry the heads very far and thus risk loss of seeds. The latter presents a distant view of Salisbury Cathedral from the southwest, and was made by Constable during a visit to his friend John Fisher. Fisher was offering comfort and moral support following the death of Maria the previous year, and suggested Constable paint a large composition of the cathedral as a distraction from grief.[14] Both sketches are rapidly executed, and show the vigorous and highly expressive brushwork Constable had begun to develop, initially in connection with outdoor sketching, around 1812. There is not a great deal to distinguish the two in their handling, though the Salisbury sketch has some white highlights that characterize Constable's later painting style. However, *Flailing Turnip-heads* is almost certainly a plein air study, while *Salisbury Cathedral* seems to be a composition sketch executed in the studio, as it closely resembles a pencil drawing that Constable made in a (now dismantled) sketchbook he used in Salisbury in 1829.[15]

Constable's plein air and composition sketches can often resemble each other in handling when, more confusingly, they relate to the same picture and were painted around the same time. For example, his study for *Flatford Mill from the Lock* in the Manton Collection (fig. 96) is one of five sketches relating to a painting that was exhibited at the Royal Academy in 1812.[16] Showing a lockkeeper, or boatman, in the process

Fig. 94 John Constable (English, 1776–1837), *Flailing Turnip-heads, East Bergholt*, c. 1812–15. Oil on canvas, 35.6 × 44.5 cm (no. 50)

Fig. 95 John Constable, *Salisbury Cathedral from the River Nadder*, c. 1829. Oil on beige wove paper, mounted on laminate cardboard, 19.8 × 27.8 cm (no. 73)

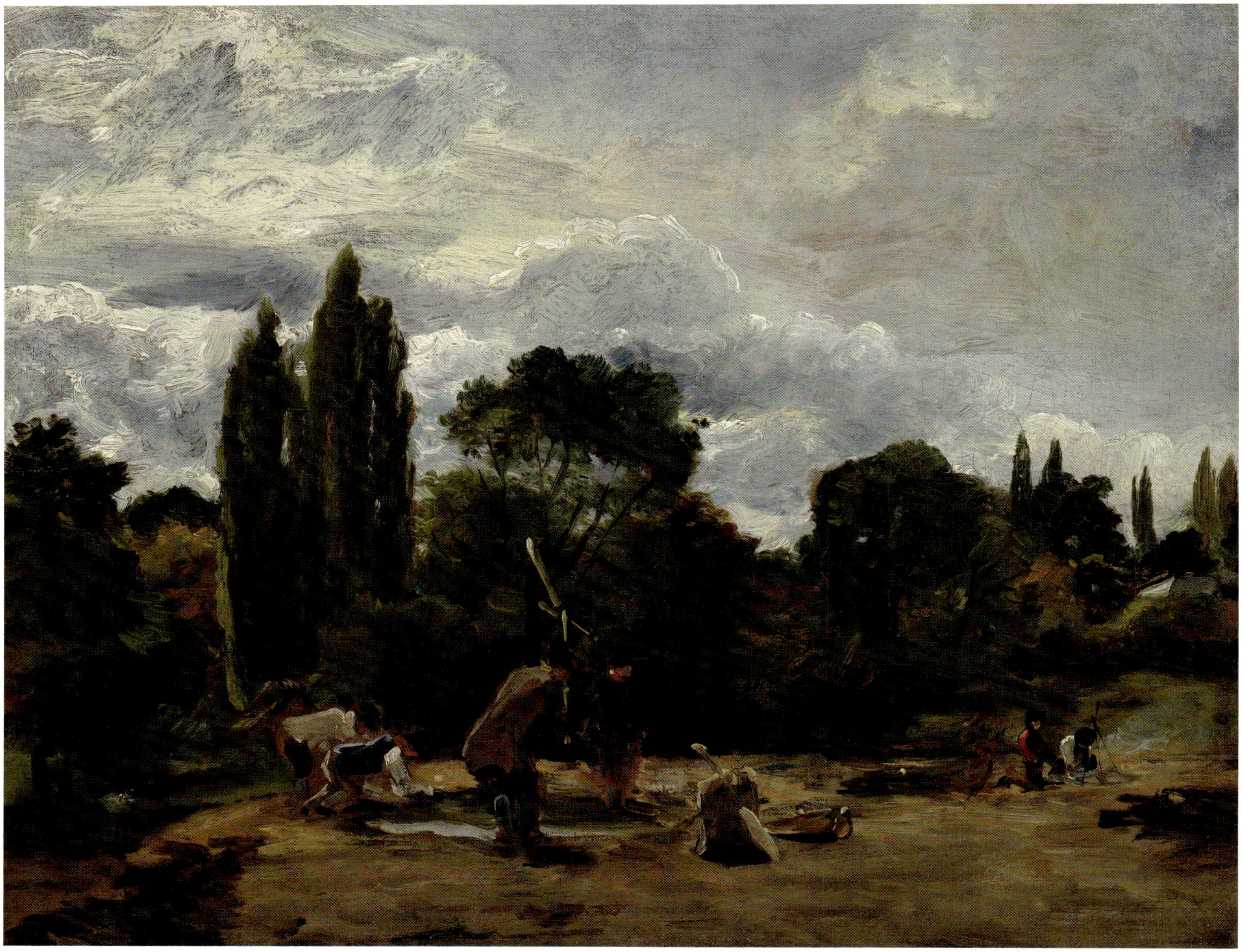

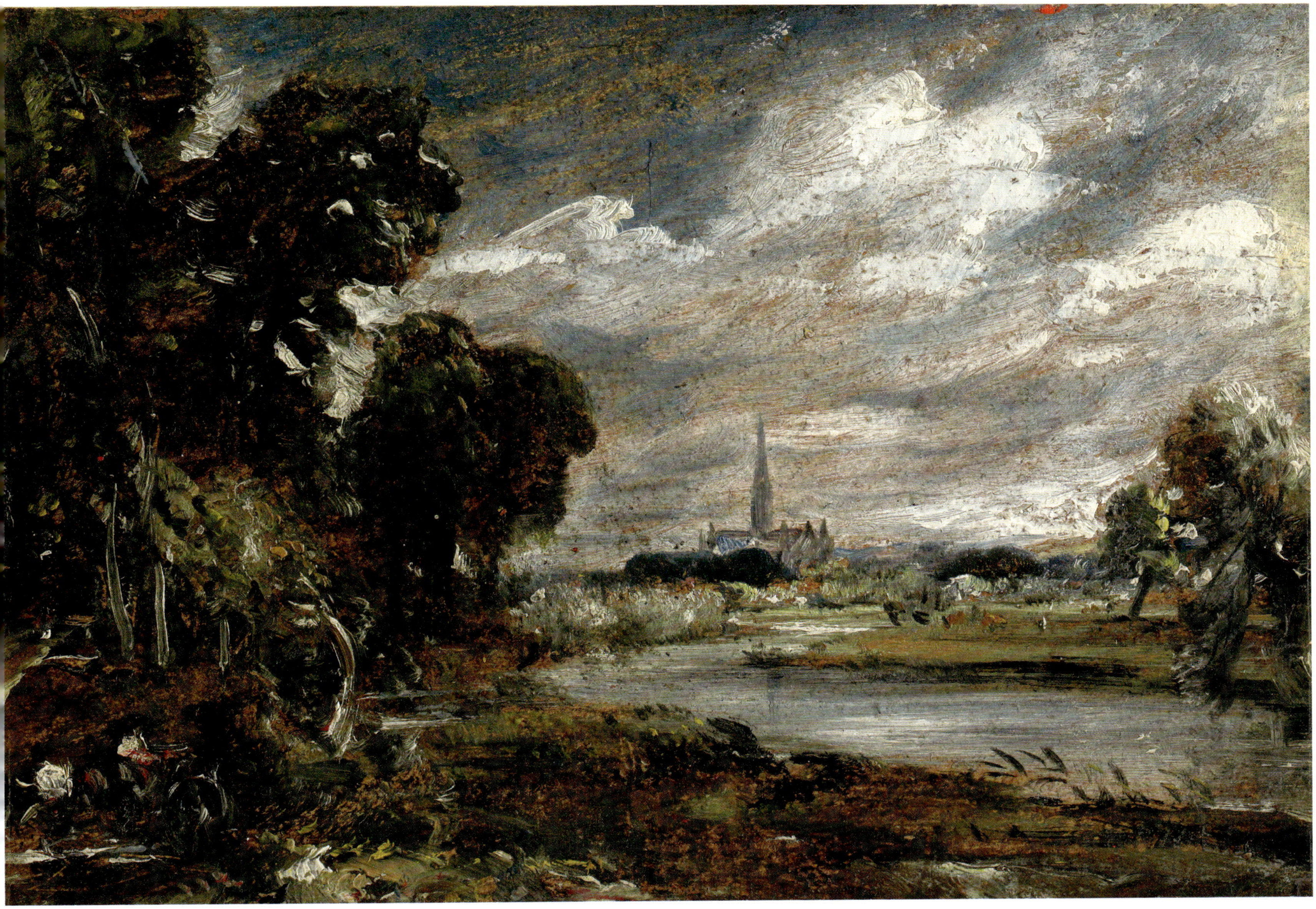

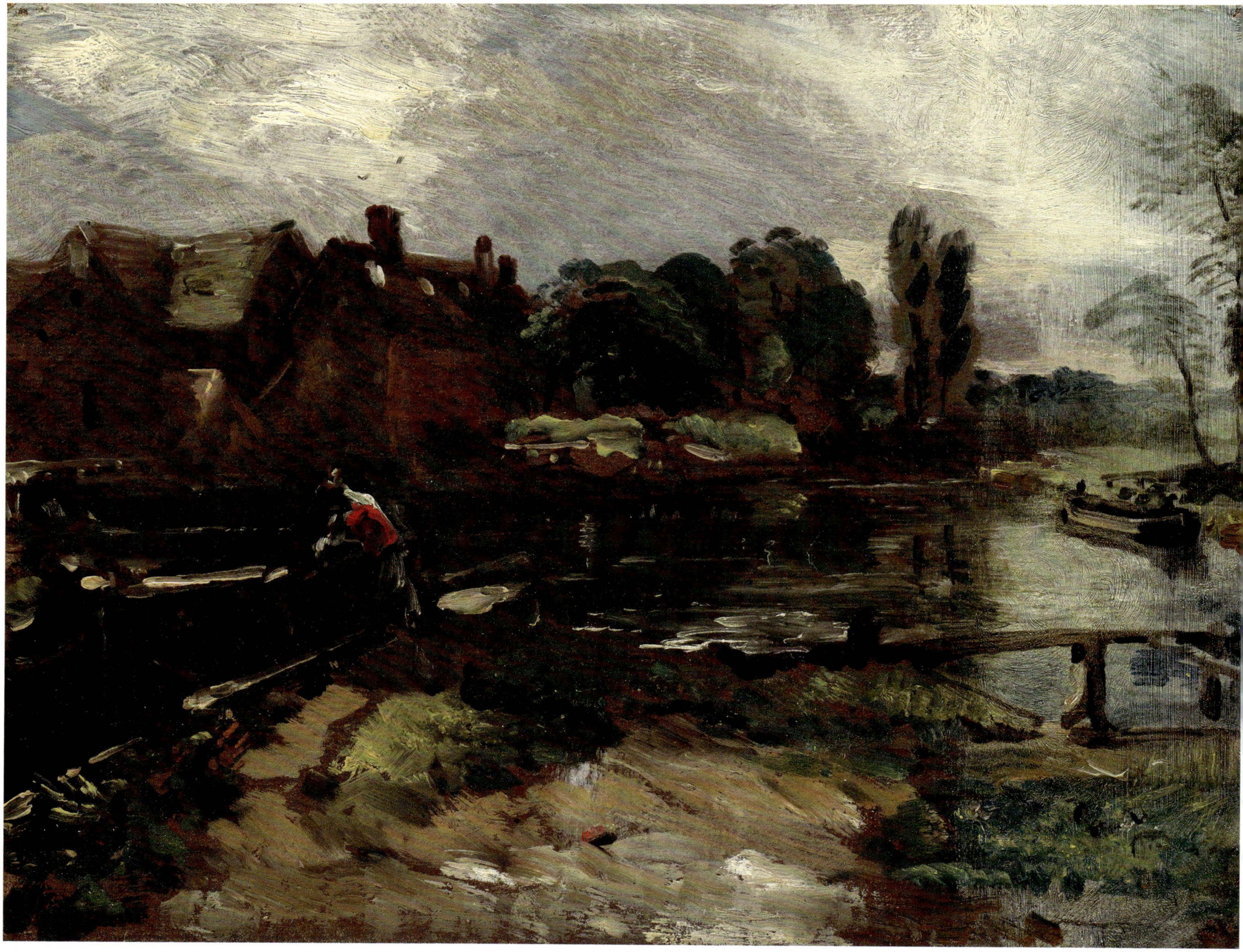

of opening a lock gate, the Manton study seems to be the first in the group, and was probably made on the spot. The others show Constable experimenting with the angle of vision in order to incorporate more of the features at left and right – the mill buildings, a stand of trees, and fields – to achieve a more scenic appearance as well as to deepen the perspective lines in a manner reminiscent of a seaport subject painted by Claude Lorrain. While three of these additional sketches are, like the first, probably plein air studies, the last one (fig. 97), which takes the most liberties with the topography of the site and is closest to the final painting, appears to be a composition sketch made in the studio. Together, they demonstrate Constable's transformation of nature into art.

In *Salisbury Cathedral from the River Nadder*, the existence of a related pencil drawing clarifies its role as a composition study. However, sometimes a pencil study has a more ambiguous relationship to an associated oil sketch, so other contextual factors must be investigated in order to resolve successfully the question of its function. This is the case with the oil study of *Willy Lott's House* (fig. 98) in the Manton Collection. It is one of a number of oil sketches relating to the evolution of an upright exhibition

Fig. 96 John Constable, *Flatford Mill from the Lock*, c. 1810. Oil on beige laid (?) paper, mounted on canvas, 19 × 24.1 cm (no. 47)

Fig. 97 John Constable, *Study for "Flatford Mill from the Lock,"* c. 1811. Oil on canvas, 24.8 × 29.8 cm. Victoria and Albert Museum, London

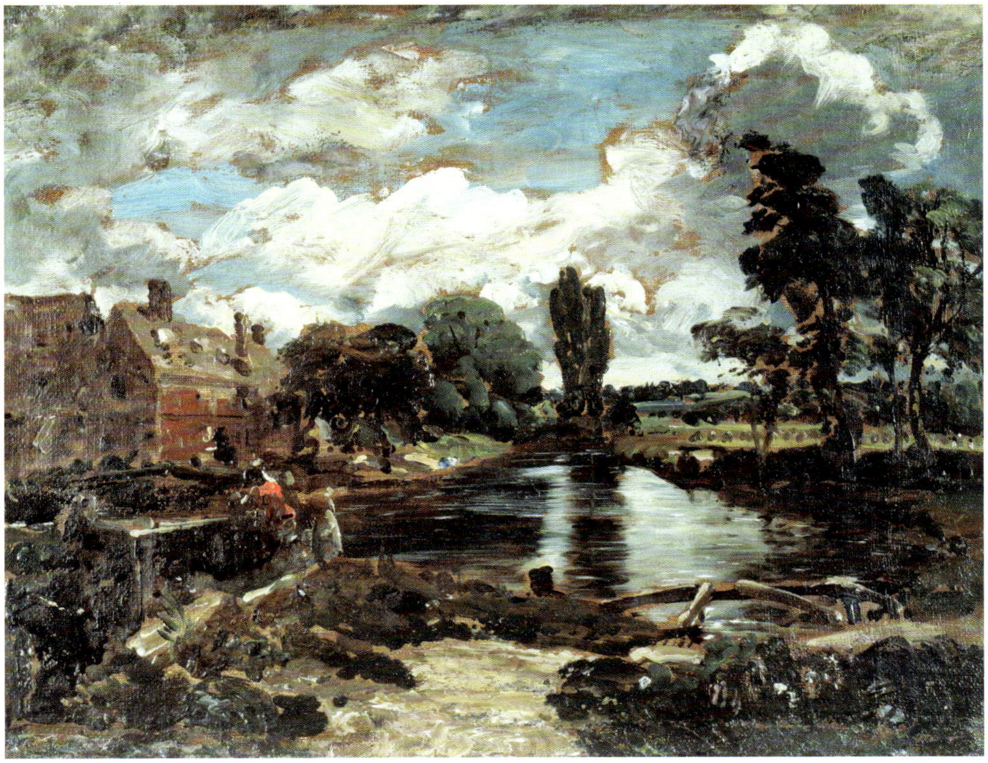

Fig. 98 John Constable, *Willy Lott's House* (recto), c. 1812–13. Oil on canvas, 34.9 × 43.5 cm (no. 49)

Fig. 99 John Constable, *The Ferry*, 1814. Oil on canvas, 125.7 × 100.3 cm. Tate, London. Lent by the Trustees of the Dupplin Trust, 2000

Fig. 100 John Constable, *Willy Lott's House*, c. 1812–13. Pencil on paper, 20 × 28.4 cm. The Courtauld Gallery, London. The Samuel Courtauld Trust

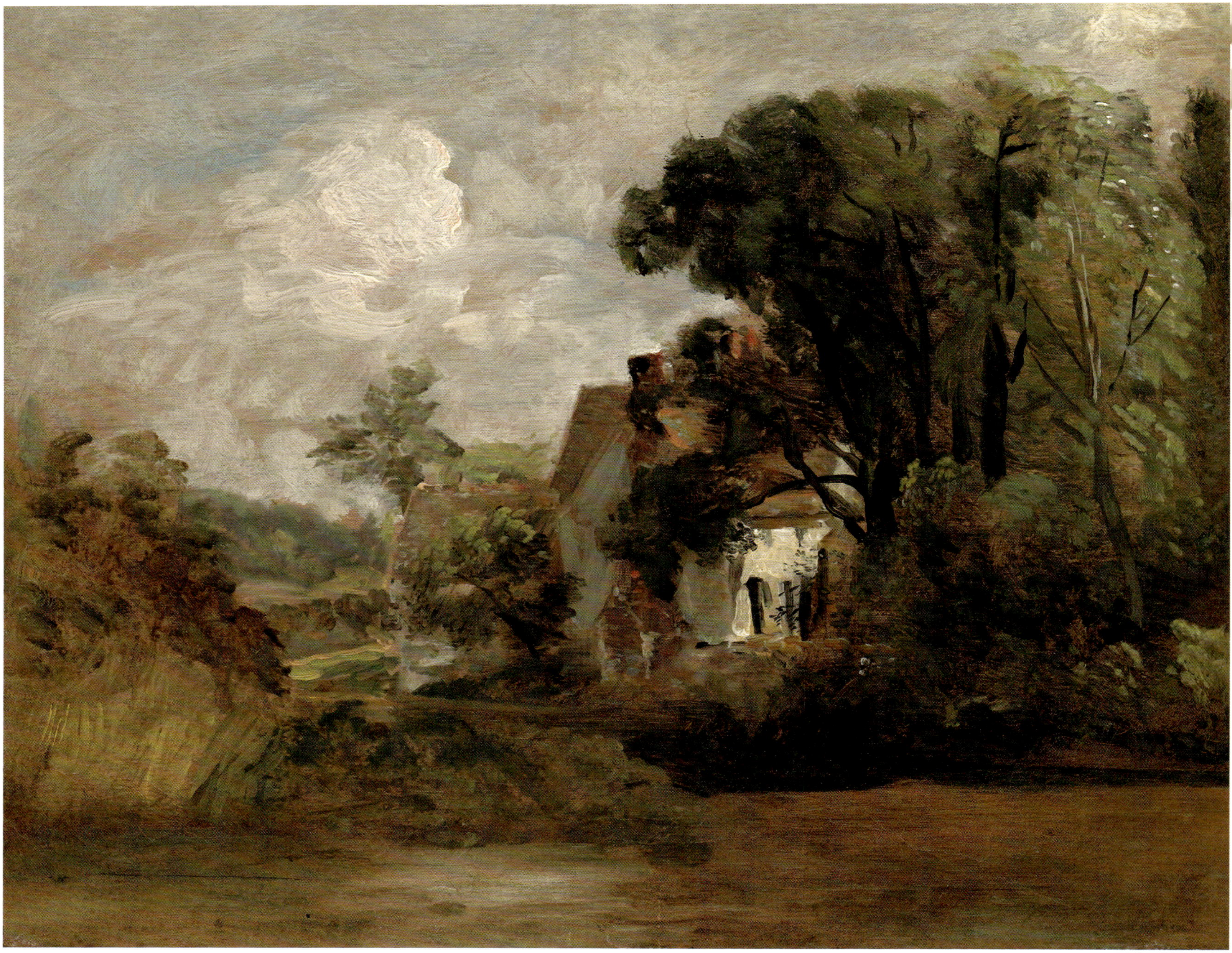

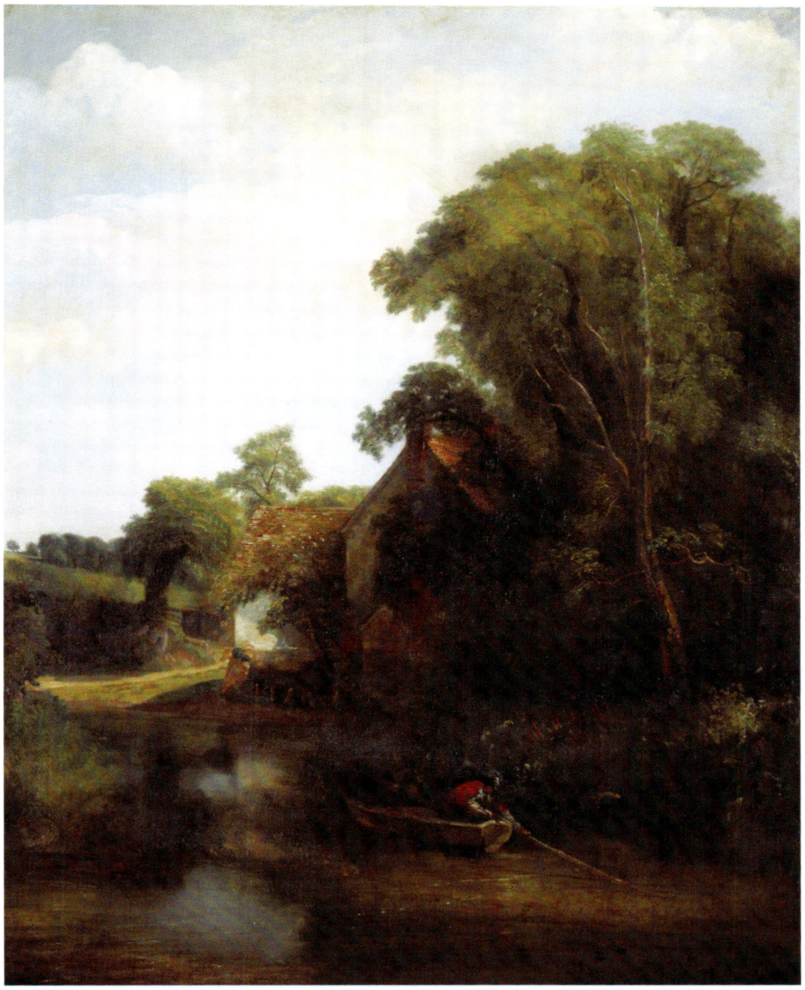

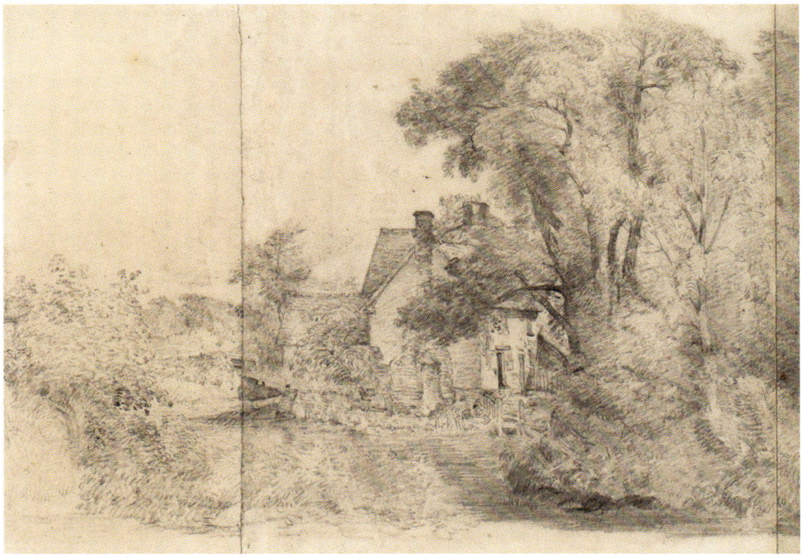

Fig. 101 John Constable, *The White Horse*, 1819. Oil on canvas (lined), 131.4 × 188.3 cm. The Frick Collection, New York

Fig. 102 John Constable, *Flatford Mill ("Scene on a Navigable River")*, 1816–1817. Oil on canvas, 101.7 × 127 cm. Tate, London

canvas, *The Ferry* (fig. 99), which Constable exhibited at the Royal Academy in 1814, and the only one of these sketches in a horizontal format.[17] It is so close to a detailed drawing by Constable of the same subject, in which the composition has been extended at the left through the addition of an extra slip of paper (fig. 100), that it seems logical to conclude that the oil sketch was based on the pencil drawing, and thus executed in the studio. On the other hand, the size of the canvas of *Willy Lott's House* is the same as that used for the plein air study of *Flailing Turnip-heads*, and this, together with its spontaneity of handling, points toward it having been produced out-of-doors. In attempting to resolve the likely status of *Willy Lott's House* as either plein air sketch or composition study, it is therefore necessary to consider other factors. First, it is important to remember that at this stage of his career, before Constable had embarked on his campaign to paint medium-sized canvases like *The Wheat Field* (see fig. 117) in the open air, he was primarily elaborating his compositions in the studio. Additionally, there is the matter of what would have been practical for the artist at the time. Constable's viewpoint for this particular composition appears to be from mid-stream, thus there would be a strong disincentive toward his returning to the spot to sketch a second time in oils.[18] Therefore, it is most likely that *Willy Lott's House* is a studio composition.

When Constable exhibited the final large, upright painting based on this sketch at the Royal Academy in the spring of 1814, titled *The Ferry*, it was criticized for a perceived lack of finish.[19] This criticism persuaded Constable to change his working methods. He decided to paint fully worked up, small- to medium-sized pictures almost entirely in the open air.[20] This was a practice Constable maintained for four consecutive summers in Suffolk, from 1814 until 1817, when he moved to London and gravitated to painting his "six-footers," such as *The Hay Wain* of 1821 (see fig. 118), for which he is today so famous. It was these ambitious large canvases that were eventually to win Constable recognition at the Royal Academy, where he became an Associate Member in 1819 following the exhibition of *The White Horse* (fig. 101), and a full member ten years later.[21]

The practice of painting medium-sized pictures on the spot was highly unusual in England at this time.[22] Returning to the same spot day after day meant that an artist needed to be able to store paints, brushes, canvas, and easel somewhere nearby, by no means easily done. Of course, Constable had the advantage over his metropolitan colleagues of painting on land owned by his father, which meant that he could leave his materials in one of the mills nearby, or else in the studio in East Bergholt that his father had acquired for him in 1802. Working in the open air was also labor-intensive as

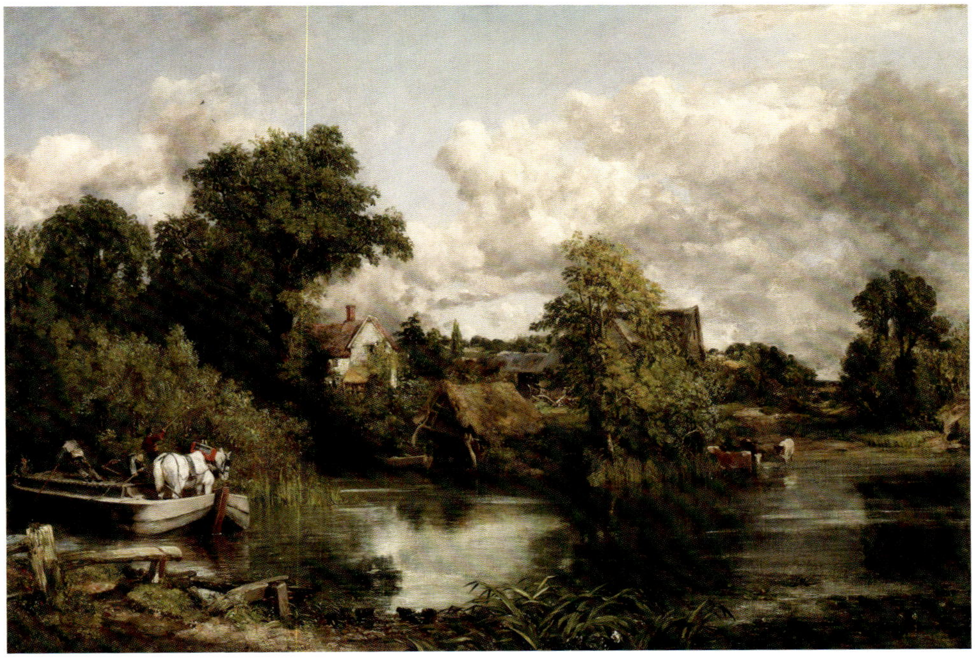

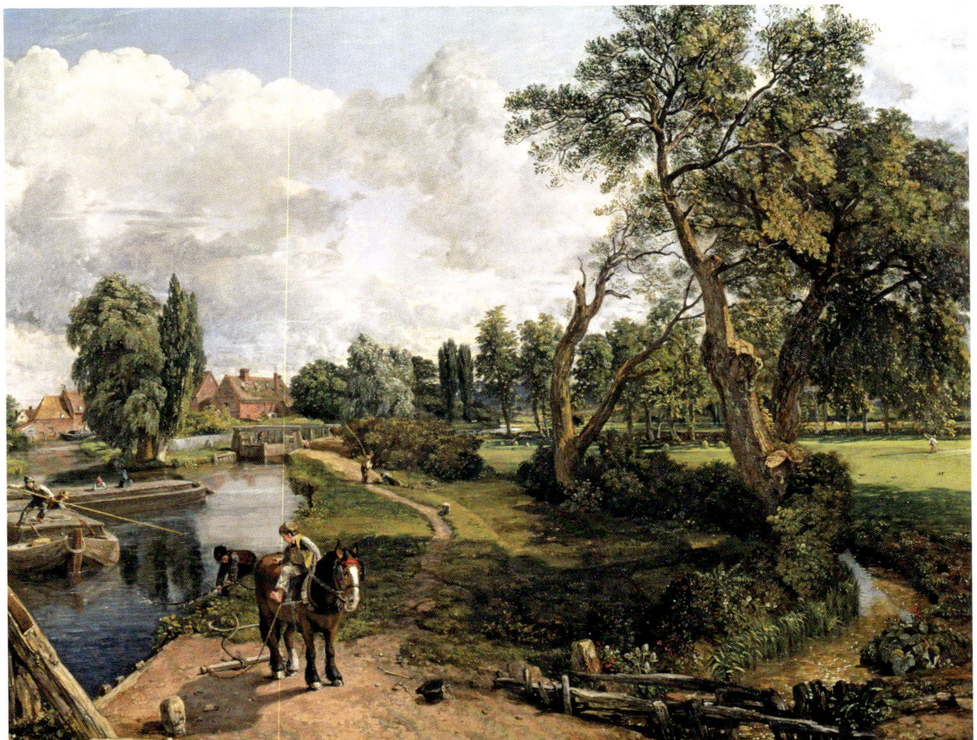

it required returning to the same spot at the same time of day to ensure that the light was accurate.[23] *Boat-Building near Flatford Mill* (1814–15), *Stour Valley and Dedham Church* (1814–15; see fig. 122), *The Wheat Field* (1815–16), *Flatford Mill* (1816–17; fig. 102), and *East Bergholt Church from the South-West* (c. 1817; fig. 103) are all plein air pictures with fewer related sketches than paintings Constable executed in the studio. However, this does not mean that he did not carefully plan in advance, whether by plotting their viewpoints through advance site visits or, perhaps, by starting some of the preliminary underdrawing in the studio.

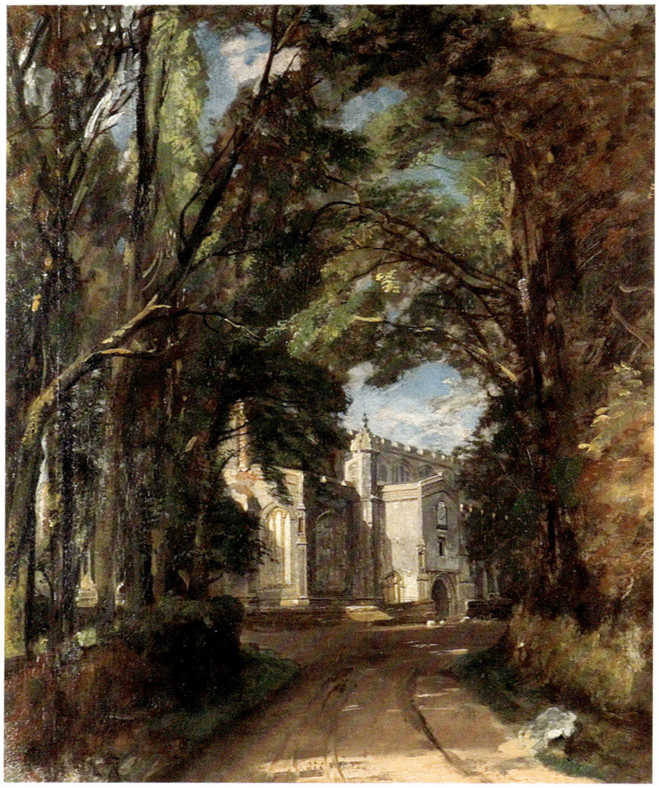

In recent years a number of pencil tracings by Constable have come to light that are connected with some of his medium-size plein air pictures, and that may have been made purposefully for them. One of these tracings, in the Manton Collection (fig. 104), relates to *East Bergholt Church from the South-West*, while another is tied to *Flatford Mill*. They are recognizable as tracings due to their rather flat, dead pencil lines and the telltale ink offprints on their reverse sides. The intriguing method that Constable used to make these tracings, said to derive from one described by Leonardo da Vinci in his *Treatise on Painting* (published posthumously in 1580), is described in a contemporary manual on perspective by Arthur Parsey:

The late Mr. Constable ... when studying the art of painting in his native place, unaided by others, that he might sketch correctly ... had attached to the upper part of his easel a frame with a pane of glass in it; this frame was attached by two screw nuts by the two upper corners; to the four corners he attached four strings, which he brought to his mouth in such a manner as to bring the centre of the glass perpendicular to his eye. *On this glass, thus held and secured from shifting by fixing the screw nuts, he traced with colour the outline of his painting and of course the drawing must have been true.*[24]

Fig. 103 John Constable, *East Bergholt Church from the South-West*, 1817. Oil on canvas, 53.6 × 43.8 cm. Durban Art Gallery, South Africa

Fig. 104 John Constable, *East Bergholt Church from the South-West* (recto), c. 1817. Graphite tracing on white laid paper, 18.7 × 18.9 cm (no. 57, recto)

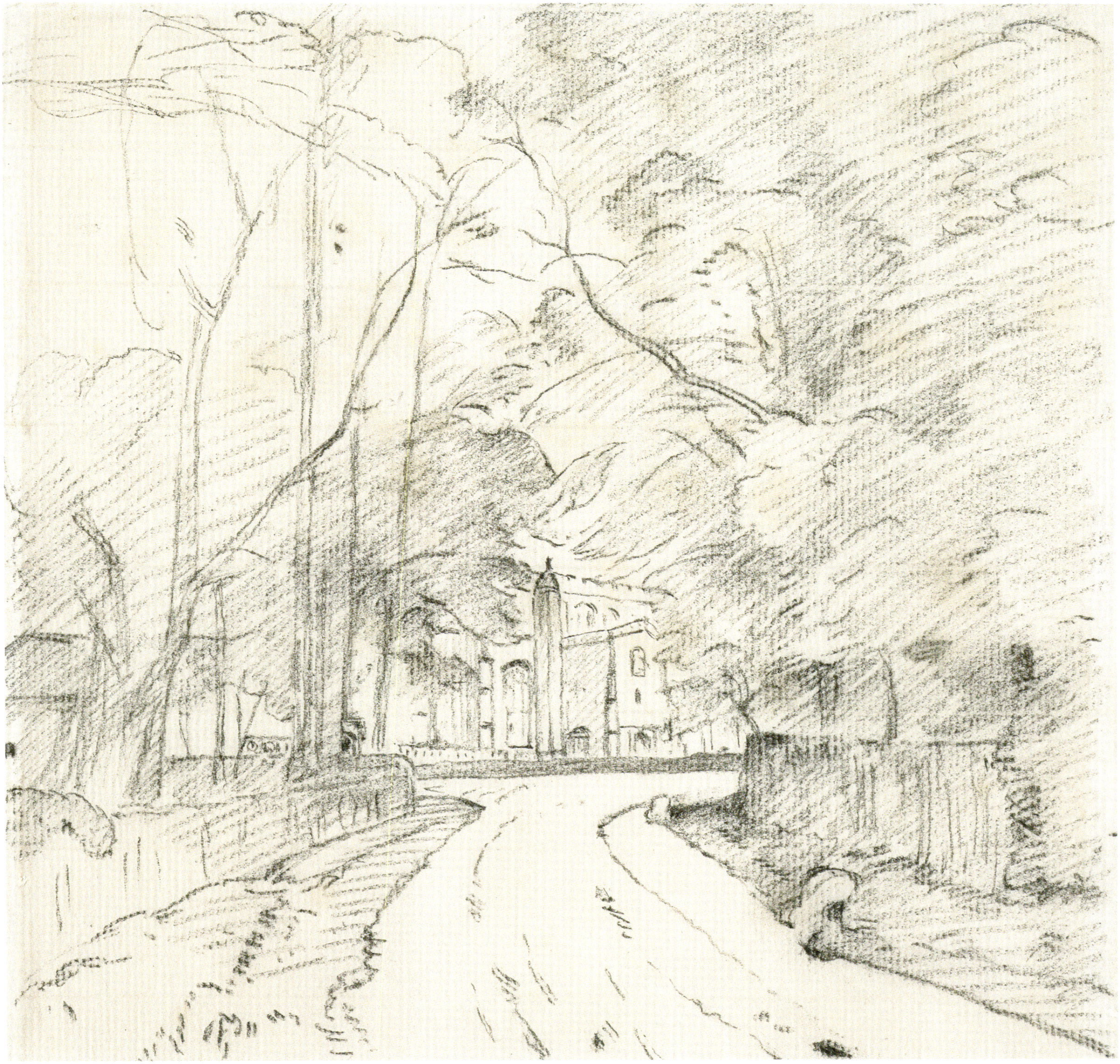

Having traced the outline of the scene directly onto the glass, probably with brush and printer's ink, Constable would then lay a sheet of paper on the glass and retrace the outline with pencil, perhaps holding both glass and paper up to the light. An offprint of the original ink tracing, in reverse, would be left on the back of the paper, presumably because the ink was still wet.[25] As Parsey commented, Constable's drawing "must have been true," with all its features recorded in correct relationship to each other as well as in accurate perspective, something that would otherwise have been hard for painters to gauge in the days before photography. Constable here applied a little science to art in his search for a more "natural painture."

Constable's tracing of *Flatford Mill* (fig. 105) was clearly used in the preparation of the related painting. Not only does it correspond very closely to the finished picture, but it is also squared for transfer: Constable drew a ruled grid over the tracing as a guide for enlarging the composition, section by section, onto the prepared canvas. Similar squaring grids are found on sketches by Constable held in the Manton Collection, as can be

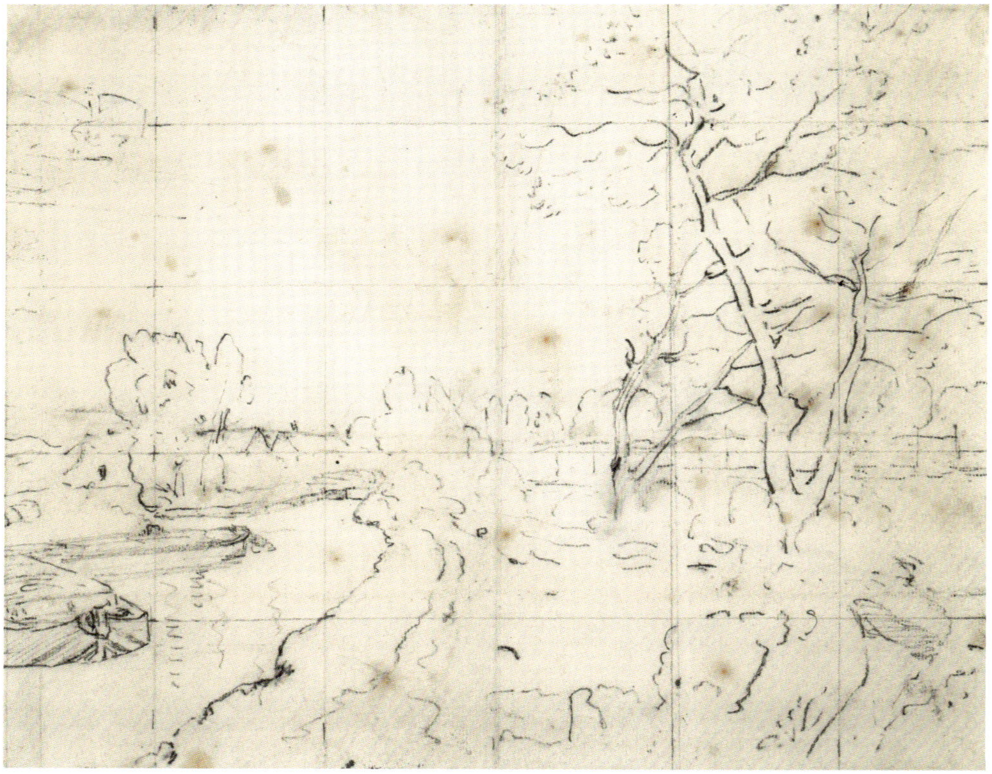

Fig. 105 *Study for "Flatford Mill"* (recto), c. 1814–16. Graphite tracing on paper, 25.5 × 31.2 cm. Tate, London

seen in the watercolor of *Bow Fell and Langdale Pikes* (1806; see fig. 65), which may relate to a lost painting of the same subject that was exhibited at the Royal Academy in 1807, and an oil *Sketch for "Dedham Vale"* (c. 1827; fig. 106), where the horizontal and vertical pencil lines are supplemented by diagonal ones, perhaps in homage to Claude.[26]

Constable's tracing of *East Bergholt Church* in the Manton Collection bears a similarly close relationship to its corresponding painting, but unlike the *Flatford Mill* tracing it is not squared for transfer. How Constable used the tracing in the preparation of the painting is less clear. He might have fixed a grid of threads over the drawing, an alternate method of squaring up in preparation for enlarging (or reducing) a composition onto another surface.[27] Another possibility is that this tracing was more experimental, a way for Constable to test the pictorial qualities of the view as well as a means of ensuring accurate perspective.[28] Whatever role the tracing of *East Bergholt Church* played, when he returned to the spot to paint, and even though Constable positioned himself slightly closer to the church, he appears in the painting to have been more liberal in his interpretation of the view than in the tracing drawing. In the painting the church appears on a relatively larger scale, indicating that when painting with the naked eye, Constable apparently succumbed to the instinctive tendency to bring distant objects, especially buildings, forward.

If some of Constable's plein air pictures were plotted by means of tracings, others were undeniably finished, or altered, in the studio after being worked on out-of-doors. Paintings conservator Sarah Cove has shown that *Boat-Building near Flatford Mill* not only contains a number of pentimenti, but it also has a finishing layer that Constable would have added indoors.[29] Similarly, although we know that he painted certain sections of *Flatford Mill* on the spot – he was continuing to work on the picture on the eve of his departure to London for his marriage to Maria Bicknell, much to her annoyance – other details (especially in the foreground) would have been added by him in the studio.[30]

Painting finished pictures substantially in the open air ultimately proved an unsustainable practice for Constable, although he continued to paint in oils in the open air until as late as 1829. This was partly for practical reasons, but also because, in the second half of his career, he turned to painting his more ambitious "six-footers," which might be considered worthy of comparison with those of the great artists of the past such as Claude, Titian, or Rubens. As his work became increasingly studio bound, his subjects were synthesized through the lens of nostalgia, albeit one always charged with emotion and powerfully expressed. If in Constable's early and mid-career

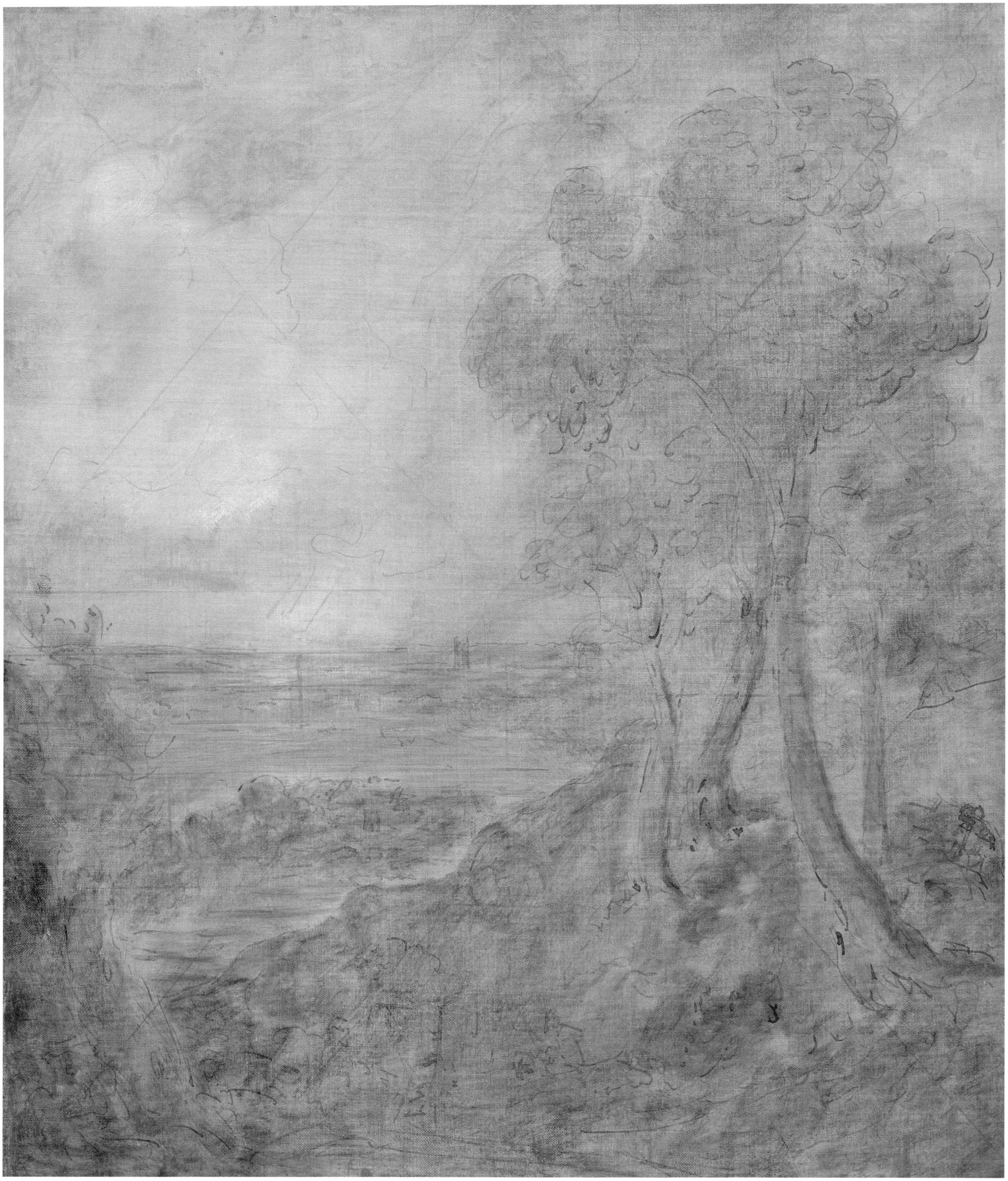

his landscapes can be seen to embrace art and nature in relative equilibrium, in his later career there can be no doubt that the pendulum swung toward art at the expense of nature.

Constable had never been in any doubt that it was in the public forum of the Royal Academy that his work would be judged and his reputation made. When presenting his lecture on the "History of Landscape" in the 1830s, he took pains to impress on his audience that, however diligent an artist might be in gathering his raw material from nature, he should not subsequently neglect to nurture it. Speaking of his favorite landscape artist, Claude, Constable emphasized how this great visual mentor had become a "real student of Nature" by diligently studying "in the fields all day" in Rome. However, Constable added, even Claude "drew at the Academy at night, for after all art is a plant of the conservatory, not of the desert."[31]

Fig. 106 John Constable, *Sketch for "Dedham Vale,"* c. 1827. Oil, ink, and graphite on canvas, 60.7 × 50.8 cm (no. 71)

1 "The Dutch and Flemish Schools" (draft of lecture for the Royal Institution, c. 1836), in Ronald Brymer Beckett, ed., *John Constable's Discourses* (Ipswich, U.K.: Suffolk Records Society, 1970), 65.

2 Charles Robert Leslie, *Memoirs of the Life of John Constable, Esq., R.A., Composed Chiefly of His Letters*, ed. Jonathan Mayne (1845; repr. London: Phaidon Press, 1951), 288.

3 John Constable to John Fisher, 23 October 1821, in *John Constable's Correspondence*, ed. Ronald Brymer Beckett, vol. 6, *The Fishers* (Ipswich, U.K.: Suffolk Records Society, 1968), 77–78.

4 Leslie, *Memoirs*, 288.

5 Michael Kitson, "The Inspiration of John Constable," Fred Cook Memorial Lecture, *Journal of the Royal Society of Arts* (November 1976): 740.

6 John Constable to Maria Bicknell, 30 June 1813, in Beckett, *John Constable's Correspondence*, vol. 2, *Early Friends and Maria Bicknell (Mrs. Constable)* (1964), 109–10.

7 John Constable to John Dunthorne the Elder, 29 May 1802, in ibid., 32. Although Beckett transcribed Constable's phrase to read that nature was "the source from whence all *originally* must spring," subsequent Constable scholars, such as Leslie Parris, have read this rather as "*originality* must spring."

8 Ibid., 32.

9 Ernst Gombrich, *Art and Illusion: A Study in the Psychology of Pictorial Representation* (London: Phaidon, 1960).

10 John Constable to C. R. Leslie, 20 January 1833, in Beckett, *John Constable's Correspondence*, vol. 3, *Correspondence with C. R. Leslie* (1965), 91.

11 *Lucian Freud on John Constable with William Feaver* (London: British Council, 2003), 37.

12 Letter from Constable to C. R. Leslie, 14 January 1832, in Beckett, *John Constable's Correspondence*, 3:59.

13 Kitson, "Inspiration of John Constable," 740.

14 The finished picture, *Salisbury Cathedral from the Meadows*, was exhibited at the Royal Academy in 1831; see Graham Reynolds, *The Later Paintings and Drawings of John Constable* (New Haven, Conn., and London: Yale University Press, 1984), no. 31.01, private collection. The picture is discussed in detail in Timothy Wilcox, *Constable and Salisbury: The Soul of Landscape* (London: Scala, 2011), 135–56.

15 The drawing, *Salisbury Cathedral from the Meadows*, 1829, is in the Yale Center for British Art; Reynolds, *Later Paintings and Drawings*, no. 29.42. See also Leslie Parris, *Constable: A New York Private Collection* (New York: published privately, 1994), 64–66.

16 All five sketches, and the exhibition picture, are discussed in Anne Lyles et al., *Constable: The Great Landscapes* (London: Tate Publishing, 2006), 92–97.

17 For *The Ferry*, see Graham Reynolds, *The Early Paintings and Drawings of John Constable* (New Haven, Conn., and London: Yale University Press, 1996), no. 14.02. Most of the related sketches, other than *Willy Lott's House*, in the Manton Collection, are discussed by Leslie Parris and Ian Fleming-Williams in *Constable* (London: Tate Gallery, 1991), 139–42.

18 Constable's exact viewpoint is ambiguous. However, the pencil study in the Courtauld Institute appears to have been drawn looking toward Willy Lott's House from midstream at Flatford, rather than from the southern bank of the River Stour – bearing in mind that the small wooded island on the right known as the Spong appears to be so close to the viewer. If so, it would most likely have been drawn by Constable from a boat.

19 The critic Robert Hunt wrote in *The Examiner*, 26 June 1814, that *The Ferry* demonstrated that Constable was "still deficient in finishing"; Judy Crosby Ivy, *Constable and the Critics, 1802–1837* (Woodbridge, U.K.: Boydell Press/Suffolk Records Society, 1991), 69.

20 Constable's original intention, as explained in a letter to John Dunthorne, was actually "to finish a small picture on the spot," in preparation, apparently, for a second larger picture that would be made by him in the studio. In the event, the small- to mid-sized plein air paintings became (or were destined to become) the finished products themselves; see Lyles et al., *Constable: The Great Landscapes*, 102.

21 The large canvases painted in the second half of Constable's career are fully discussed in Lyles, *Constable: The Great Landscapes*.

22 Plein air painting was more common on the continent, especially in Rome. See, for example, Phillip Conisbee et al., *In the Light of Italy: Corot and Early Open-Air Painting* (Washington, D.C.: National Gallery of Art; New Haven, Conn., and London: Yale University Press, 1996).

23 For example, *Boat-Building near Flatford Mill* (Victoria and Albert Museum, London) and *Stour Valley and Dedham Church* (Museum of Fine Arts, Boston) appear to have been painted concurrently in the same summer and fall of 1814, the latter in the mornings, and the former in the afternoons; see Parris and Fleming-Williams, *Constable*, 155.

24 Arthur Parsey, *The Science of Vision, Or Natural Perspective! Containing the True Language of the Eye, Necessary in Common Observation, Education, Art, and Science* (1840); cited in Ian Fleming-Williams, *Constable and His Drawings* (London: Philip Wilson, 1990), 118–19.

25 Ibid., 119–21.

26 Constable exhibited a painting titled *Bow Fell, Cumberland* at the Royal Academy in 1807, no. 150. The *Sketch for "Dedham Vale"* is a preliminary study for the large panting of *Dedham Vale* that he exhibited at the Royal Academy in 1828 under the title *Landscape* (National Gallery of Scotland, Edinburgh; Reynolds, *Later Paintings and Drawings*, no.28.1). For a discussion of the grid, and the possible connection with Claude, see Leslie Parris, *Constable: A New York Private Collection*, *Supplement* (New York: published privately, 1998), 32–35; and Mark Evans, "'A More Lasting Remembrance': Constable's Paintings of *Dedham Vale from the Coombs* and Claude's *Landscape with Hagar and the Angel*," *British Art Journal* 3, no. 3 (Fall 2012): 43–47.

27 Constable often used the method of creating a grid of threads when constructing his final paintings. See Sarah Cove, "The Painting Techniques of Constable's Six-Footers," in *Constable: The Great Landscapes*, ed. Anne Lyles et al. (London: Tate Publishing, 2006), 58–59.

28 Another tracing by Constable focusing on the porch of East Bergholt Church, in the Staatliche Graphische Sammlung, Munich, is inscribed by him: "To try the problem (by the Glass)/wether the side of any building/standing square on the base of/the picture does recede to the/point of distance or not"; Reynolds, *Early Paintings and Drawings*, no.14.59.

29 Sarah Cove, "Constable's Oil Painting Materials and Techniques," in Parris and Fleming-Williams, *Constable*, 511–12.

30 Maria Bicknell to John Constable, 16 September 1816, in Beckett, *John Constable's Correspondence*, 2:205; see also Parris and Fleming-Williams, *Constable*, 179–81.

31 Constable delivered lectures on the History of Landscape at Hampstead in 1833 and 1835, at Worcester in 1835, and at the Royal Institution in London in the spring and summer of 1836. Extensive drafts for the lectures were collated and published by Beckett in *John Constable's Discourses*; for Constable's comments on Claude, see "Lecture II: The Establishment of Landscape," in *Discourses*, 53.

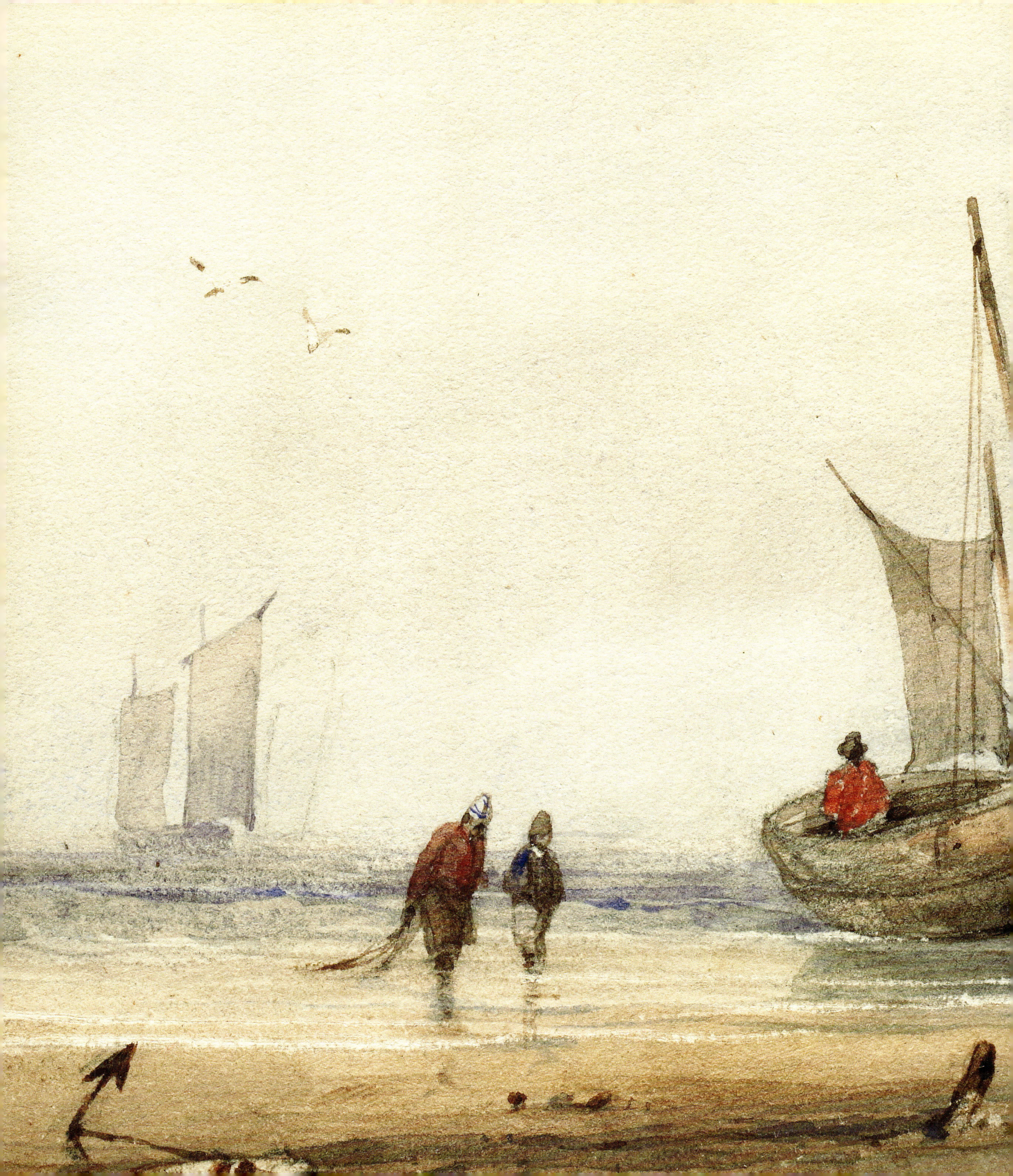

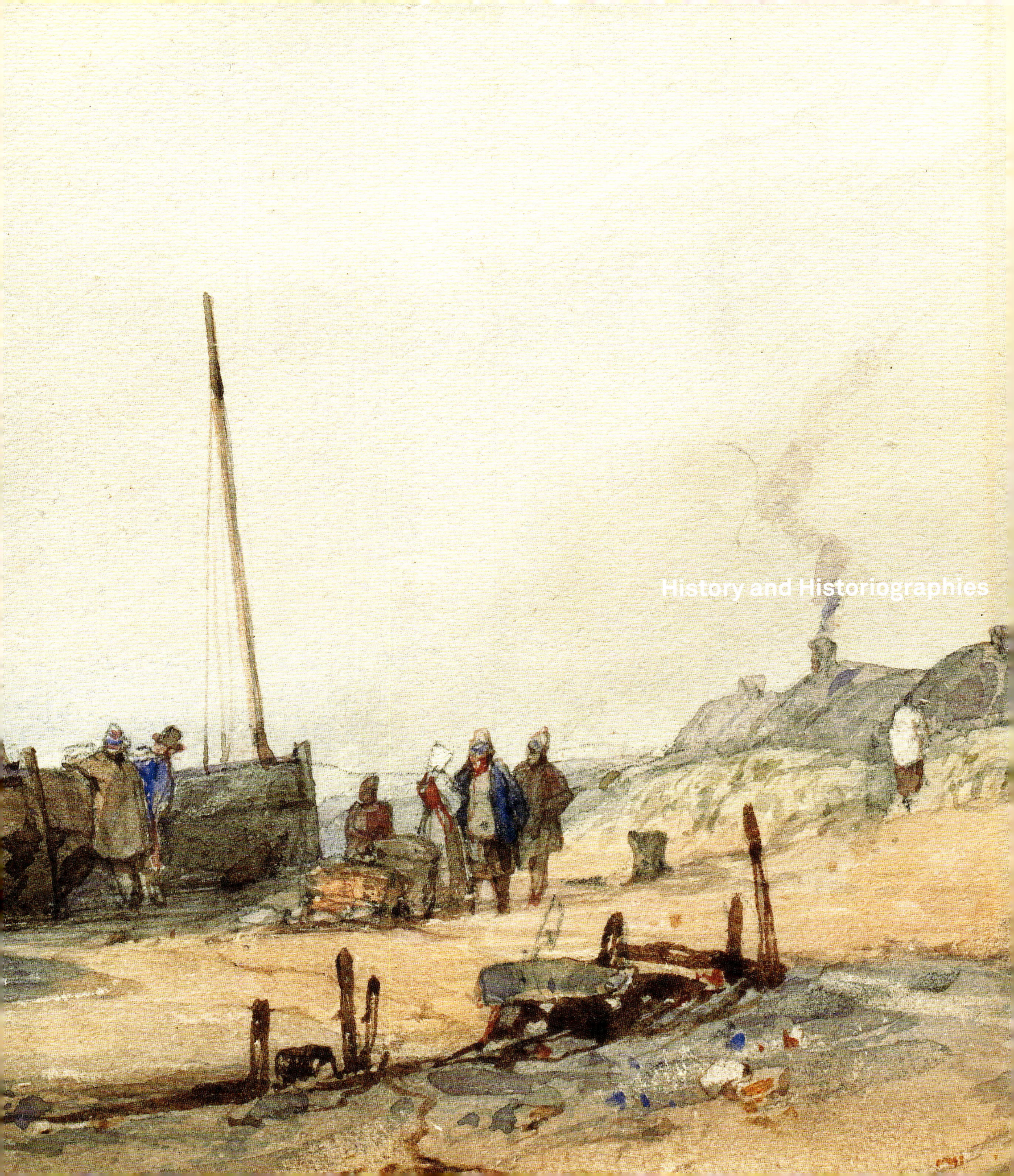

History and Historiographies

Encounters with Antiquity

Observation and Imagination in British Watercolors

Sam Smiles

The rise of watercolor as a serious creative practice is so often rehearsed in accounts of British art that we forget how quickly an orthodox history of it was constructed, and the effect that history has had on our understanding of topographical works. As early as 1812, when the essay "Observations on the Rise and Progress of Painting in Water Colours" was published, the ascendancy of "effect" over "outline" was presented as a laudable development.[1] "Outline" here refers to the practice typical of the early painters in watercolors in which the contours of objects were drawn neatly in ink or graphite, with color added principally as a means of differentiation rather than as a fully realized vehicle of expression. For these reasons, such watercolors were often referred to not as paintings but as "tinted drawings," as seen, for example, in Paul Sandby's *The Cemetery Gate of St. Augustine's Monastery, Canterbury* (fig. 107). "Effect," on the other hand, stands for later developments in watercolor technique, with artists attempting to produce convincing representations of atmosphere, varieties of weather, and fugitive phenomena of light and shade to capture the dynamism of nature, such as John Martin's *Landscape with Cattle Grazing in the Foreground* (fig. 108). Using the innate propensities of watercolor as a medium, especially its fluidity, transparency, and delicacy, the basis of design increasingly shifted away from the drawn outline to an exploration of light and color.

In 1823 the Society of Painters in Water Colours mounted a survey exhibition in London that looked back over the history of watercolor, from Alexander Cozens (1717–1786) to contemporary practitioners, both to celebrate past achievements and to demonstrate how the art had advanced. The articles on the history of watercolor William Henry Pyne contributed to the *Somerset House Gazette* in 1823 and 1824 further promoted the idea of steady evolution and improvement.[2] Watercolor artists working in the middle decades of the nineteenth century produced sheets whose range of subjects, size, and technical bravura vied with the best the Royal Academy could offer. As the Society declared, on its reestablishment in 1821: "the feeble tinted drawings formerly supposed to be the utmost efforts of this art, have been succeeded by pictures not inferior in power to oil paintings, and equal in delicacy of tint, and purity, and airiness of tone."[3] It was, in short, a triumphalist narrative that had emerged, with a strong teleological bent, and the "feeble tinted drawing" inevitably suffered in these comparisons.

Moreover, not only was the technique of early topographical watercolors presented as weak and uninspiring, the subject matter itself was considered to be inimical to the exercise of the imagination. Throughout the modern period, the idea has been sustained

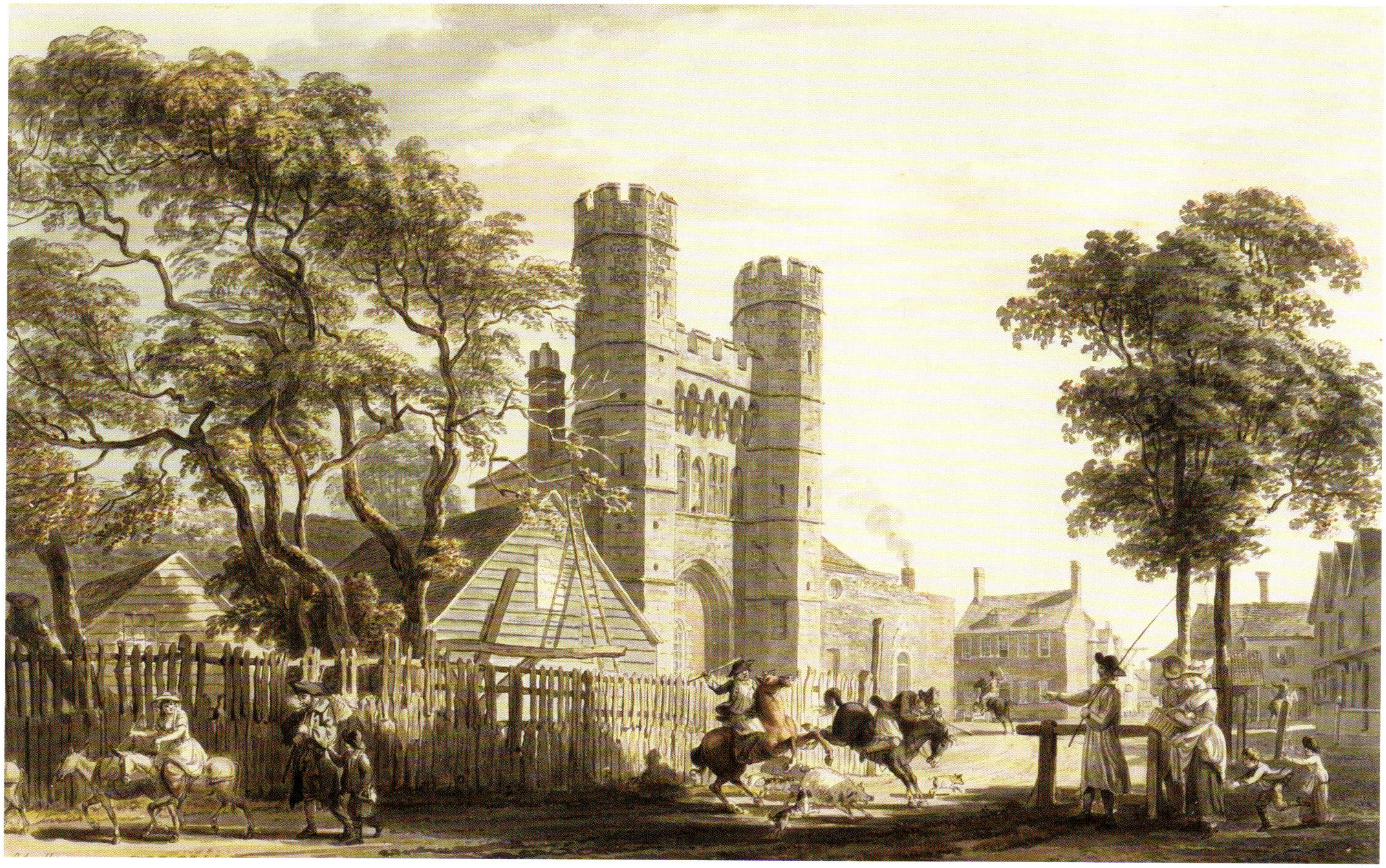

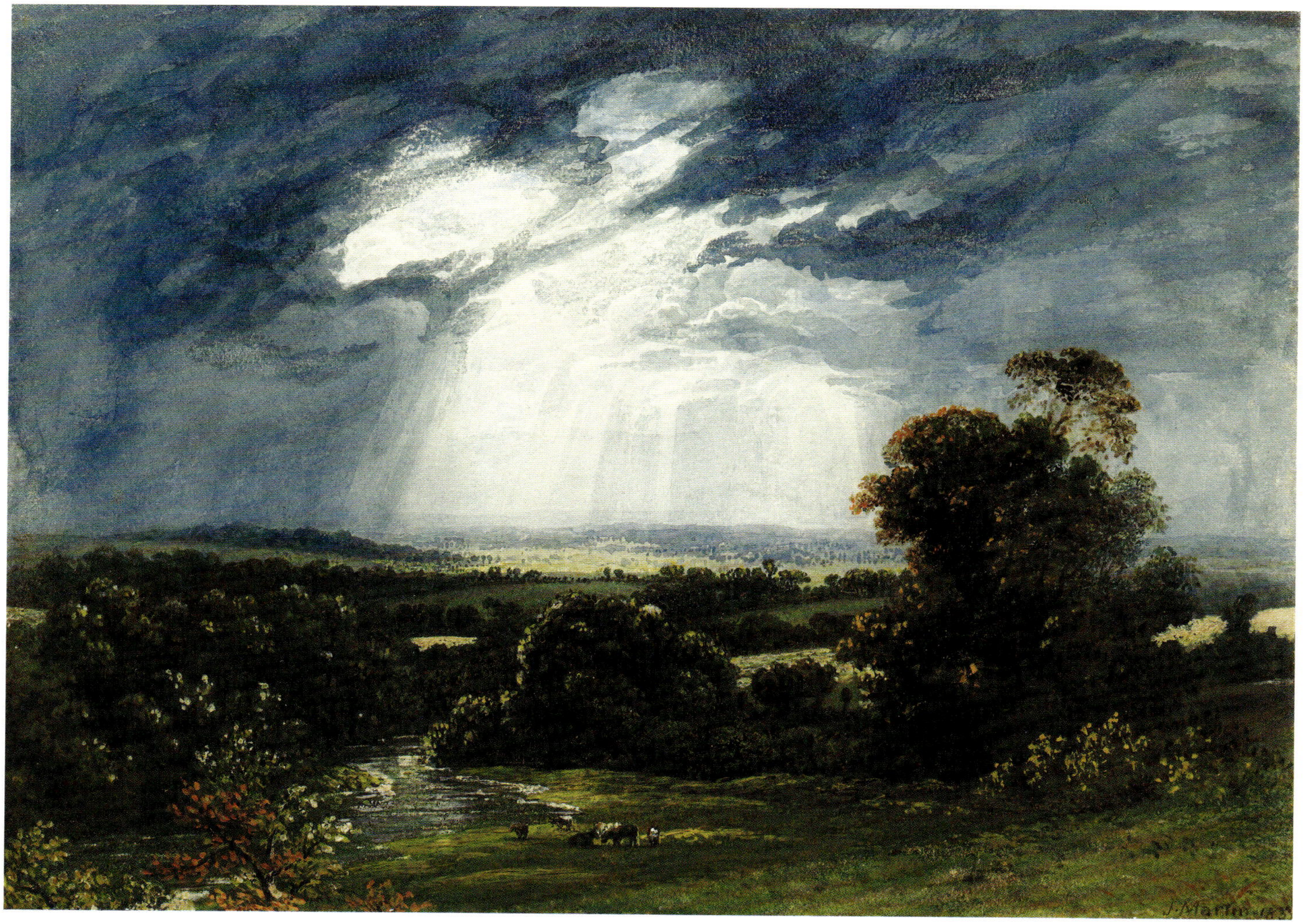

that any creative artist who worked in the antiquarian or topographical tradition would find its strictures chafing. Works with an antiquarian focus were intended to document archaeological sites, ancient buildings, and other survivors from the distant past; topographical watercolors recorded actual landscapes, no matter how mundane, with a viewpoint and precision of detail that was maximally informative. In each case the utility of the image lay in its fidelity to appearance. No matter how technically adept the performance, the need for accuracy elevated copying over invention. Copying, however, ran the risk of damaging the dignity of the artistic profession. Those who believed that painting was as worthy of respect as any other liberal art necessarily promoted it as an activity whose creativity and invention demonstrated the artist's intellectual capacities. Antiquarian and topographical views gave the artist scant opportunity to do so.

Henry Fuseli's well-known attack on view-painters, given in a lecture to the students of the Royal Academy in 1804, was characteristically brutal: "To portrait painting ... we subjoin, as the last branch of uninteresting subjects, that kind of landscape which is entirely occupied with the tame delineation of a given spot.... The landscape of Titian, of Mola, of Salvator, of the Poussins, Claude, Rubens, Elzheimer, Rembrandt, and Wilson, spurns all relation to this kind of mapwork."[4] Fuseli's sneering reference to "mapwork" highlights the fact that view-painters were expected to provide accurate transcriptions of real places, eschewing the play of imagination that dignified the Old Masters' approach to landscape. View-painters found a ready market, satisfying a taste that relished the local and particular as opposed to the idealized and imaginative. The antiquarian bent was most obviously fulfilled with images of Roman remains, medieval castles, abbeys, and churches; topography had a wider remit and added to these antiquarian subjects landed estates, vistas overlooking notable tracts of countryside, scenes of natural beauty, and urban panoramas. This enthusiasm for views was reinforced by the print market. At a time when many citizens had limited experience of travel, publishers capitalized on the growth of a wider reading public by providing illustrated surveys of the scenery and antiquities of the British Isles. Watercolor artists were in demand to supply these publications with designs for engraving. Fuseli's deprecating remarks are a measure of how menial many considered this work to be when compared to the creative potential of the fine arts.

Both practice and theory, then, tended to produce an understanding of watercolor's evolution that positioned the earlier topographical tradition as limited and limiting. According to this model, although topography had provided employment to artists and

Fig. 107 Paul Sandby (English, c. 1730–1809), *The Cemetery Gate of St. Augustine's Monastery, Canterbury*, 1782. Watercolor and pencil on paper, 32.4 × 50.8 cm. Tate, London

Fig. 108 John Martin (English, 1789–1854), *Landscape with Cattle Grazing in the Foreground*, 1833. Watercolor and gouache, with gum arabic and scraping, on cream wove paper, 16.5 × 22.9 cm (no. 185)

had seen numerous practitioners achieve a degree of competence in its pursuit, its demands were too strict to encourage the aesthetic qualities celebrated by Pyne and his contemporaries. Accuracy of record had been accomplished by means of careful draftsmanship and descriptive color in the tinted drawing, but the results were increasingly regarded as a mere prologue to the mature development of watercolor painting. Pyne summarized that history in 1823:

Hitherto, the topographical style of painting had been chiefly addressed to the antiquary, rather as a matter of curiosity than art. In this country, at least, architectural representations were viewed as subjects which did not afford sufficient scope for the display of much talent. Turner and Girtin, however, discerned in this pursuit, capacities which had escaped the most ingenious of their predecessors.[5]

Yet if we resist the teleology implicit in Pyne's and others' accounts, it is possible to approach the topographical watercolor from another point of view, one that is more sensitive to the institutional and intellectual protocols that determined its field of operations. Once its epistemic framework is restored, the topographical watercolor can be assessed not merely as a prelude to later developments but as a purposeful mode of practice in its own right. Most importantly, we have to remember that the topographical watercolor was poised between two demands, the picturesque and the antiquarian, which circumscribed its formal behavior. The relics of antiquity were subject to two understandings that were frequently, although not inevitably, antithetical. The picturesque, as a concept in aesthetics, came into prominence in the late eighteenth century when William Gilpin, Richard Payne Knight, and Uvedale Price promoted its use as a descriptive term to identify those qualities of irregularity, roughness, and variety that could not be adequately accommodated in Edmund Burke's well-known distinction between the sublime and the beautiful.[6] What we might call the pure picturesque reveled in the look of aged structures, with their crooked lines and timeworn masonry. Ruined structures, especially those variegated with lichen and ivy, and frequently found in remote situations, were differentiated from the everyday world and therefore ready to be transmuted into aesthetic objects, as seen in Edward Dayes's *Byland Abbey, Yorkshire* (fig. 109).

The pure antiquarian approach, in contrast, prided itself on its ability to reveal what nature and time had obscured, to ignore the aesthetic qualities of agedness or destruction and concentrate instead on the material evidence provided by what remained.

As the antiquarian draftsman John Carter proudly insisted of his own work, it was a serious contribution to historical research and should not be infected by

> *picturesque appearances produced by the skill of the Artist, in a certain disposal of light and shade toward what is called "effect" in drawing; an effect of that kind we perceive when gazing on an object with the eyes half open, in a sort of dim fascination of the senses, whereby we catch a momentary gleam of the sublime; such sort of pencilled performances tending more to accredit the modern Delineator than the antient Architect.*[7]

Between these two poles a third possibility emerged, where the contemplation of antique structures was neither purely aesthetic (picturesque) nor empirical (antiquarian) but, aided by association, became the occasion for a meditation on the past. As articulated by Archibald Alison in his *Essays on the Nature and Principles of Taste* (1790), associationism rationalized reactions to landscape as cognitive responses derived from remembered stimuli of pleasure and pain. In doing so, Alison effectively moved the contemplation of a scene in nature – or the contemplation of a work of art – from an outward sensitivity to form and structure as immediately experienced to an inner sensitivity to the beholder's state of mind and its train of memories. What associationism added to earlier writings on aesthetics was, first, the proposition that the imagination was stimulated by an association of ideas particular to each observer, and second, recognition that the legacy of culture could affect the beholder as profoundly as any natural feature or phenomenon. The historical connotations triggered by a particular site could inform the aesthetic response to it. In one sense, Alison was returning to the chorographic tradition

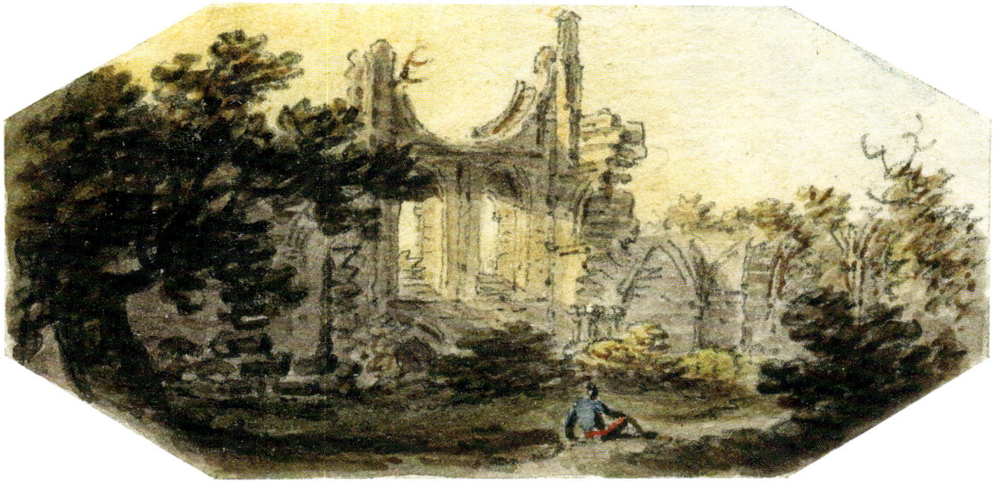

Fig. 109 Edward Dayes (English, 1763–1804), *Byland Abbey, Yorkshire* from *A Group of Eighteen Watercolors of Identified Castles, Abbeys, and County Seats*, c. 1790–1800. Watercolor over graphite on cream wove paper, 6.4 × 8.9 cm (no. 100)

of the early modern period that attended to topographical features not merely as they appeared to the contemporary observer but also in terms of their historical layering.[8] Informed by association, antique structures were approached not solely as objects of aesthetic delight in the present, nor as data banks of material evidence from the past, but instead as eddies in the flow of time where both present-day and ancient identities coexist.

The intellectual culture of the turn of the century witnessed the heyday of the topographical tradition. Advertising the publication of Dayes's collected writings, his posthumous editor, E. W. Brayley, spoke of the present time being "a Period when ... TOPOGRAPHICAL INQUIRIES so particularly accord with the prevailing Taste."[9] This was no exaggeration, for antiquarian researchers had flourished during the eighteenth century, especially in the last quarter. Writing in 1808, Nicholas Carlisle, at that time the Secretary of the Society of Antiquaries, cited some two hundred and fifty authoritative works for the study of topography in English counties. Looking at Carlisle's bibliography, what is immediately striking is the fact that well over half of his recommended publications had appeared between 1770 and 1805. Huntingdonshire was alone in lacking a reliable topographical publication, whereas all of the other counties boasted at least one, and some were blessed with a rich tradition of enquiry: notably Yorkshire, Kent, and Middlesex with over twenty studies each.[10]

Illustrated surveys, typified by the numerous series published by John Britton, combined antiquarian interest in topography with picturesque embellishment. As the *Quarterly Review* commented, by the 1820s the craze for the picturesque had produced a veritable avalanche of such publications.

Every nook in our island has now been completely ransacked, and described by our tourists and topographers.... It would be difficult to name any structure of the "olden time" which has not been transmitted into the portfolio and the library.[11]

In 1802 Britton asked Carter to contribute drawings to his *Beauties of England and Wales* (fig. 110) and attempted to tempt him away from his normal rectitude: "We must sometimes flatter in order to instruct ... Doctors sometimes gild the health-restoring pi[ll]." Carter, as we have seen, was ideologically opposed to picturesque embellishment and was adamant that he would not betray his calling: "I ... cannot be a means to help your efforts in the gilding part of the business ... being so unfashionable ... where the case of Antiquities is at stake."[12] His drawings therefore expunge all picturesque embellishments and concentrate on architectural detail with unswerving dedication. Carter's intransigence was isolated, however; most artists were quite content to receive commissions for this sort of work and, if necessary, would adjust the scene in view to produce a more pleasing composition. J. M. W. Turner's youthful *Rochester* (fig. 111), for example, was published by Walker and Storer in 1794 in *The Copper-Plate Magazine, or Monthly Cabinet of Picturesque Prints*. It marked the beginning of Turner's long association with topographical publications that extended into the 1830s.

Although Dayes hoped to gain acceptance to the Royal Academy by exhibiting historical pictures, he was unsuccessful in that endeavor, and his métier was dominated by the production of topographical works. He is known today chiefly for his association with Thomas Girtin – who was apprenticed to him in 1788 – and for his influence on Turner. Both artists imitated his manner in their early work. Dayes participated in the burgeoning market for illustrated topography, making annual sketching tours from 1790, recording country houses, abbeys, castles, cathedrals, and other historic structures as well as landscapes. His *View of Winchester Abbey* (fig. 112) is typical of these productions, showing the characteristic features of the building and setting it within its landscape environment. The composition may seem, at first glance, somewhat conventional, but its presentation

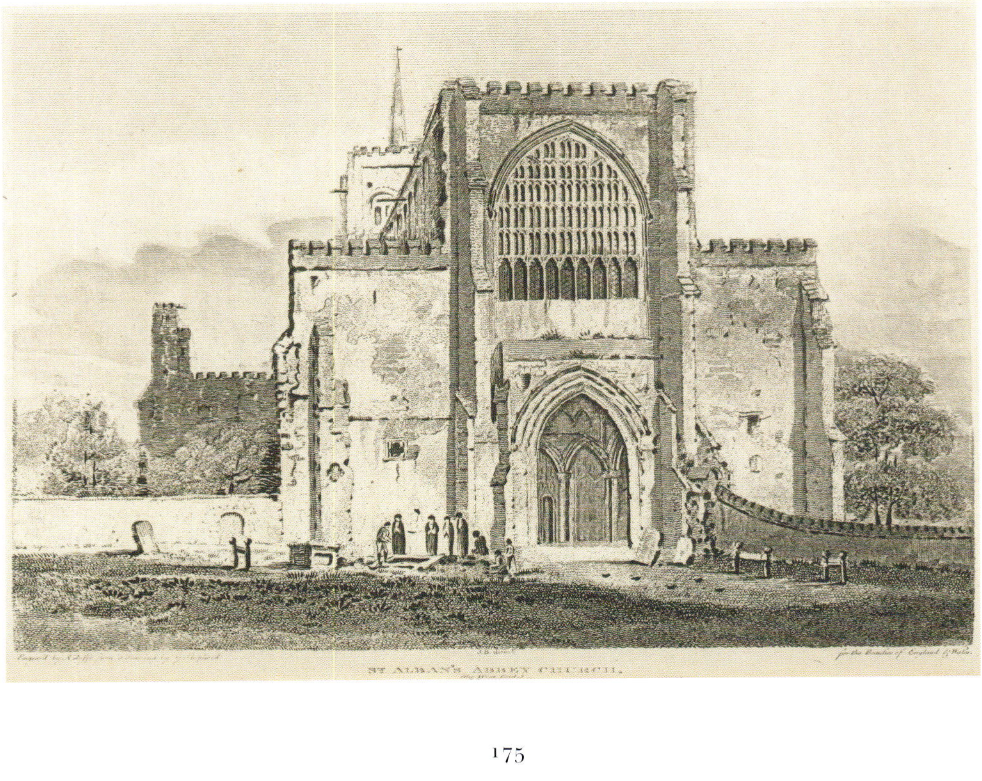

Fig. 110 Richard Roffe, after George Shepherd (1784–1862), *St. Alban's Abbey Church*, in John Britton and Edward Wedlake Brayley, *The Beauties of England and Wales: or Delineations, Topographical, Historical and Descriptive*, vol. 7 (London: Vernor, Hood & Sharpe, 1808), engraving. Yale Center for British Art, New Haven, Conn., Paul Mellon Collection (DA625 B38)

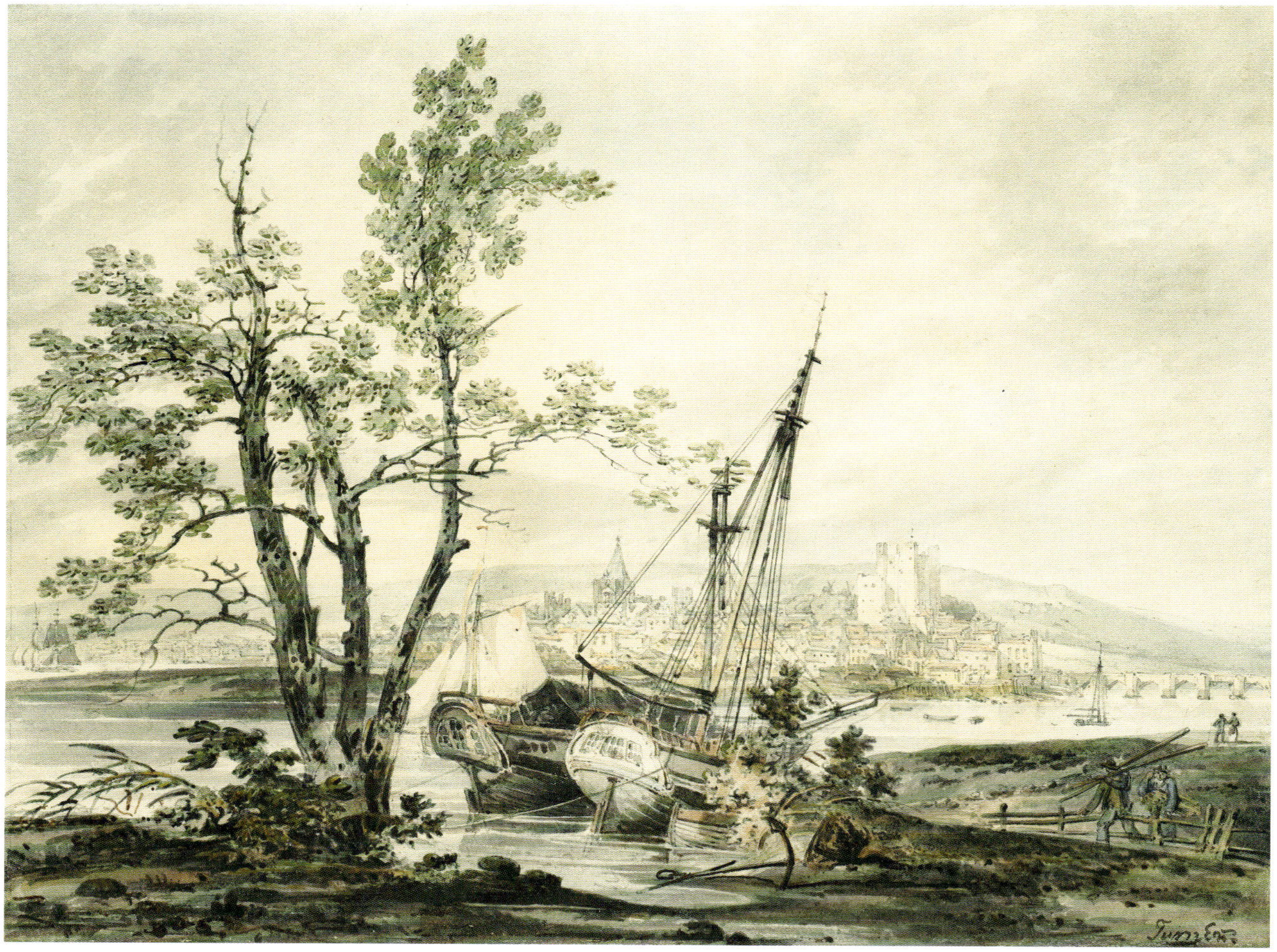

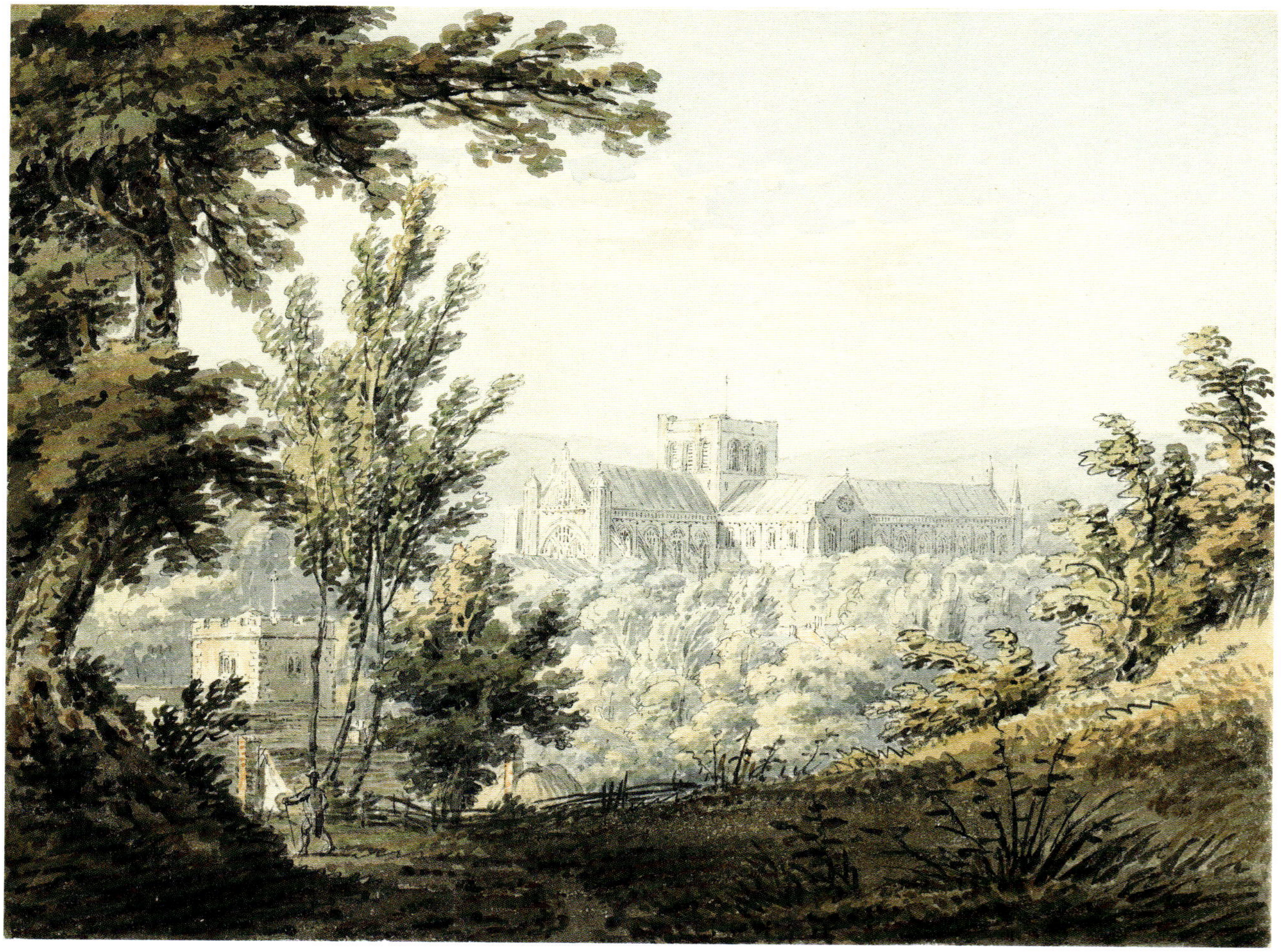

belies Dayes's commitment to visual representation as a species of knowledge. In his essay on drawing he speaks of the entertainment afforded by this skill, commending it to amateurs, but he goes on make a wider observation about its intellectual utility:

To every gentleman who travels, [ability in drawing] is absolutely necessary; for, independently of its teaching him to see accurately, the curious and ever-restless eye of the artist comprehends more, at one view, than the common observer will notice in an age. The volume of nature is laid open to him; his attention is alike directed to the vast and to the minute; men and manners are not concealed from his view, and his imagination clings to perfection with ineffable delight. It is not too much to say, that drawing opens the mind more than years devoted to the acquiring of languages or the mere learning of words: it teaches to think. The artist is a true logician: not content with producing effects he is ever enquiring after causes founded in a visible demonstration, to exhibit them in his works.[13]

Dayes asserts here that close observation inevitably requires the artist to investigate and understand the origin and interdependence of the phenomena, both natural and man-made, under his scrutiny. Topography is more than the mere surface imitation Fuseli and others considered it to be.

One of the subscribers to this volume was Turner, who also purchased a dozen of Dayes's drawings after the artist's death.[14] Turner shared with Dayes and with Britton a belief that topographical landscape drawings were far removed from Fuseli's caricature of them. Britton published a riposte to Fuseli's remarks on view-painters in his *Fine Arts of the English School* (1812), while Turner supported the original, more critical version of it, arguing:

I rather lament that the remark which you read to me ... is suppressed for it espoused the part of Elevated landscape against the aspersions of Map making criticism, but no doubt you are better acquainted with the nature of publication, and mine is a mistaken zeal.[15]

Elevated landscape, in Turner's sense, allowed the artist to use his knowledge of the artistic tradition and his understanding of natural phenomena to transfigure the commonplace.[16] In addition, Turner regularly chose subjects whose historical significance gave them an intrinsic value. The inclusion of *River Wye* (fig. 113) as one of the plates in his visual treatise on landscape, the *Liber Studiorum*, is a case in point. Chepstow Castle, looming above the river, was rich in historical associations. Built shortly after William the Conqueror was crowned King of England, it controlled one of

Fig. 111 Joseph Mallord William Turner (English, 1775–1851), *Rochester*, c. 1793. Watercolor with pen and gray ink on cream wove paper, 21.6 × 27.9 cm (no. 208)

Fig. 112 Edward Dayes, *A View of Winchester Abbey*, 1793. Watercolor and graphite on white wove paper, 16.1 × 22 cm (no. 95)

the key crossings from England into Wales, and was of strategic importance well into the seventeenth century. The engraving is identified with the letters EP, which most modern scholars agree as standing for "Elevated Pastoral," which Turner achieved by adopting a poetical treatment of the Wye in a manner reminiscent of seventeenth century Dutch landscapes.

Fig. 113 Joseph Mallord William Turner, *River Wye*, from *Liber Studiorum*, May 23, 1812. Etching and mezzotint printed in brown inks on cream wove paper, 20.9 × 29.1 cm (plate); 29.3 × 43.5 cm (sheet) (no. 260)

As has been frequently pointed out, the emergence of illustrated topography in Britain coincided with the long years of war with revolutionary and Napoleonic France (1793–1815). In that context vestiges of the past acquired further connotations: they spoke of long continuities in the nation's history, as opposed to the violent events across the Channel where the very fabric of society had been ruptured. An educated viewer would know of Winchester's associations with the Saxon monarch Alfred the Great and that king's successful defense of the kingdom against Danish aggression, or of Chepstow's strategic significance in the suppression of the Welsh. Battle Abbey, the subject of Girtin's watercolor, *The Gatehouse of Battle Abbey, Sussex* (fig. 114), was a building saturated in associations. It was erected on orders of William the Conqueror on the site of the Battle of Hastings, with its altar positioned at the very spot where King Harold was believed to have been killed. Taken into private ownership in 1538, it had fallen into disrepair until the late eighteenth century when a major program of building and refurbishment began. Girtin's presentation, making use of a low vantage point, emphasizes the massiveness of the gatehouse's construction. By taking the view, as did many artists, from inside the walls, thereby omitting the town's High Street on the other side of the building, he was able to separate the medieval remains from the quotidian, presenting them as isolated in their antiquity so as to become the object of contemplation or reverie.

Girtin's untimely death in 1802 saw Turner acknowledged as the major exponent of developments in watercolor practice. By the 1810s the tradition of topographical landscape in which he had worked initially was deemed to have underexploited the potential of watercolor as a creative medium, and he and Girtin were widely regarded as the two artists who had remedied the situation. Indeed, for all their too-hasty dismissal of that earlier topographical tradition, such accounts were correct in pointing to the radically new approach to watercolor that emerged in the early years of the nineteenth century.

Turner's image *Melrose Abbey* (fig. 115), makes this particularly clear. It was produced as one of a set of six watercolors illustrating verses by Walter Scott, Lord Byron, and Thomas Moore commissioned about 1822 by his friend and patron Walter Fawkes.

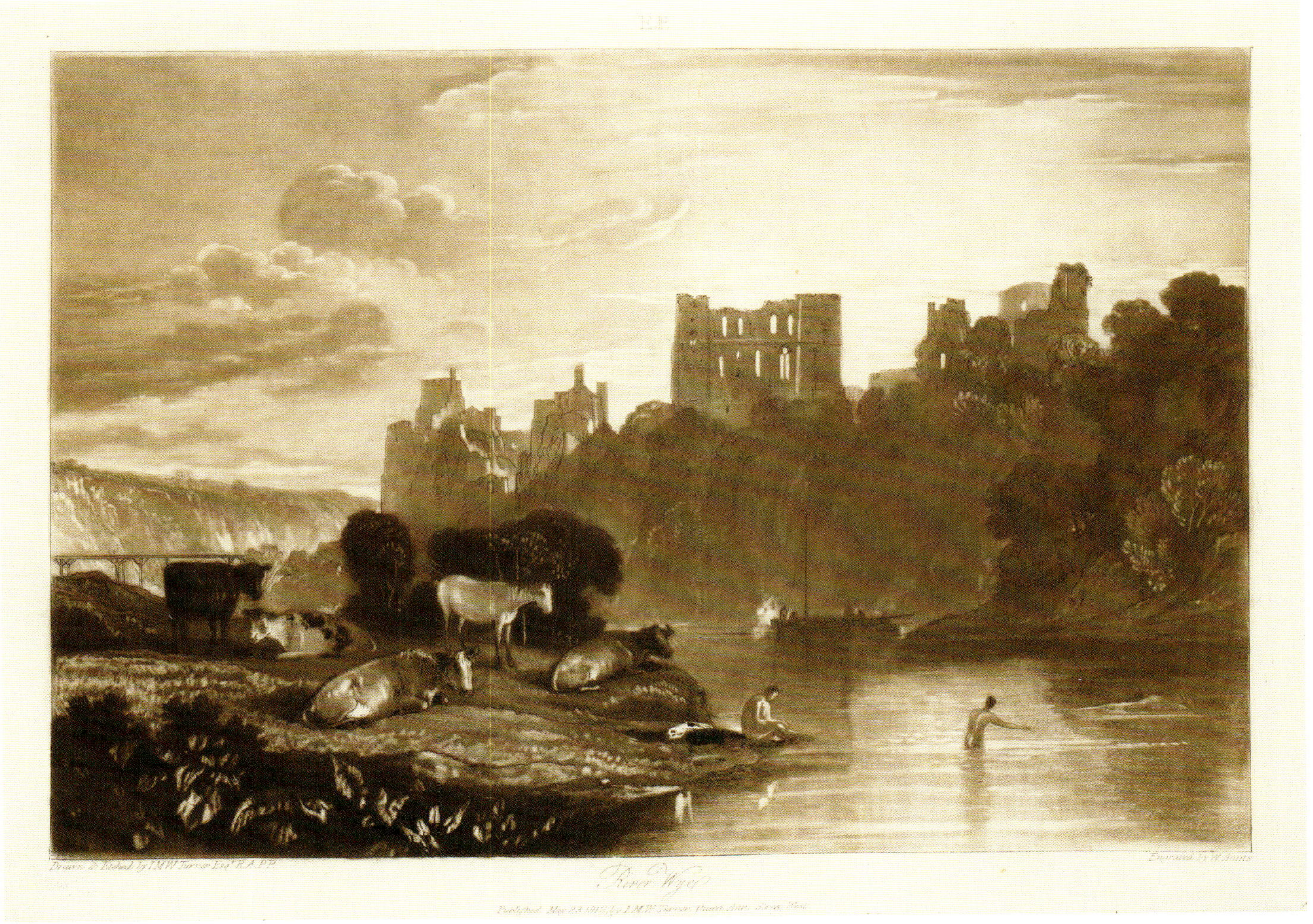
Drawn & Etched by I.M.W. Turner Esq.r R.A. P.P.
Engraved by W. Annis
River Wye
Published May 23 1812 by I.M.W. Turner, Queen Ann Street West

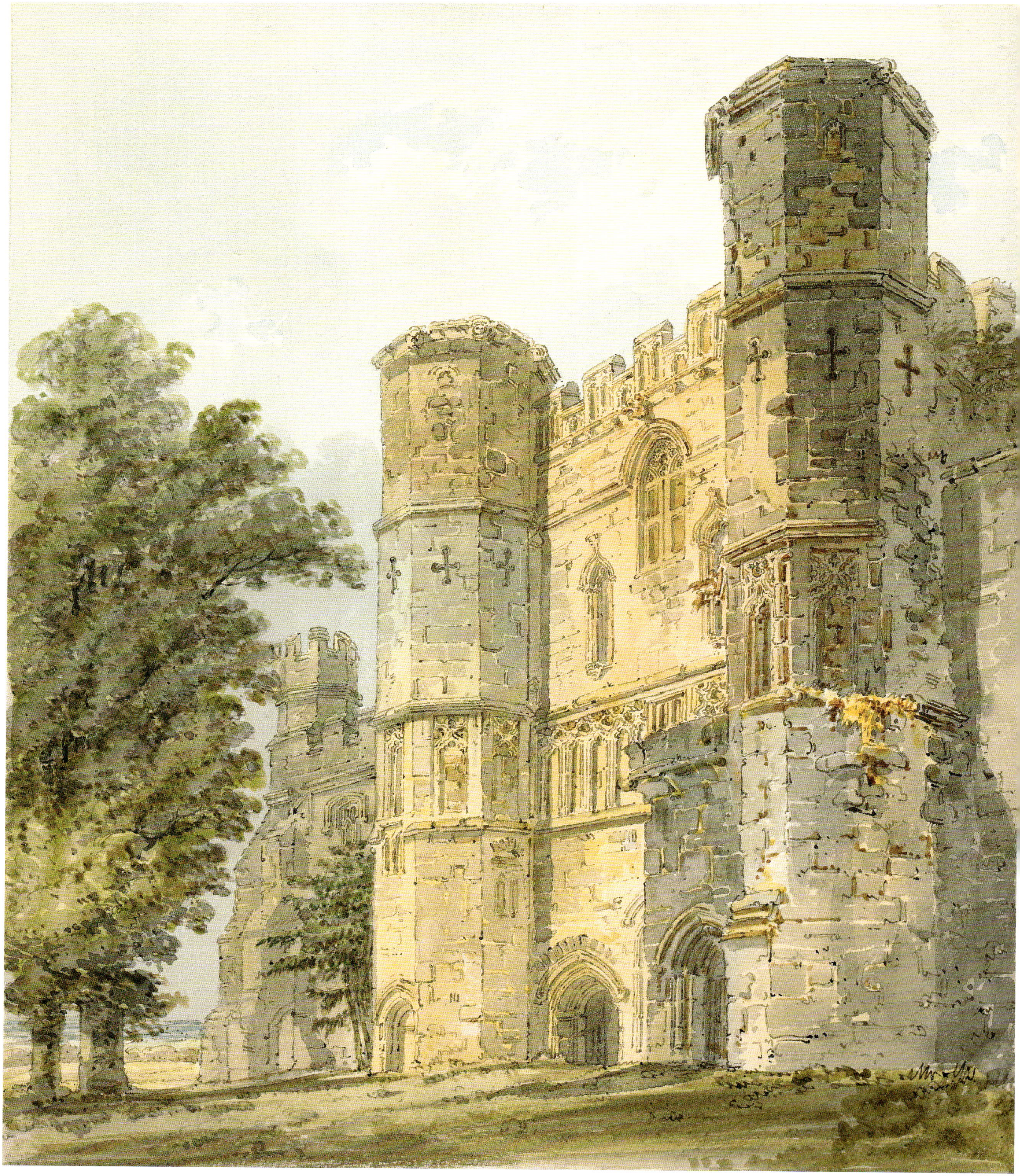

Turner had first visited Melrose Abbey in 1797 on his brief tour of the border country. He sketched four abbeys, Dryburgh, Jedburgh, Kelso, and Melrose, representing them in accordance with the antiquarian bent in his work of these years. All of these sites have deep historical roots; many Scottish nobles are buried at Melrose, and the heart of Robert the Bruce is reputed to have been interred in the abbey. The five pages devoted to Melrose in two of the sketchbooks Turner used on this excursion do not record an interior view, however,[17] and on his return trip in 1801 for a more extensive tour there is no evidence in the sketchbooks that he revisited Melrose. His visits of 1818, on commission to make drawings for Walter Scott's publication *Provincial Antiquities of Scotland*, and 1822, primarily to record George IV's visit to Edinburgh, would have given him the opportunity to study Melrose again; the site is some thirty-five miles from Edinburgh and close to Scott's home at Abbotsford, so it is more than likely that Turner visited the abbey again in this period.[18]

Fig. 114 Thomas Girtin (English, 1775–1802), *The Gatehouse of Battle Abbey, Sussex*, c. 1794. Pen and brown ink and watercolor over graphite on white wove paper, 27.3 × 23.5 cm (no. 139)

Similar to Girtin's watercolor of Battle Abbey, the presentation offered by Turner's watercolor of Melrose Abbey is a partial one. As with many sites, the abbey disappointed some tourists because of its proximity to the nearby village. Introducing the engraving after his own sketch that illustrated his account of the abbey, John Stoddart declared: "If this noble ruin stood, like Pluscardine [Abbey], in a solitary vale, instead of being elbowed by the village, it would be still more impressive. This effect is to a certain degree produced, by the exclusion of the adjacent buildings. . . ."[19] The interior view adopted in Turner's presentation obviously overcomes such difficulties. We should note, however, that a further selection is at work here. Melrose was not entirely ruined and open to the elements as this image suggests. A new vault and roof had been constructed over part of the crossing in 1610 (behind the vantage point of this watercolor) to allow local parishioners to worship. In the foreground Turner includes some of Scott's verses from his *Lay of the Last Minstrel* (1805), although he modifies them from Scott's direct "If thou would'st view" to the more neutral "Who'er would see." What Scott stresses and Turner reiterates is the transformation of the ruins by the light of the moon, whose particular illumination heightens the romance of the experience. Here, then, the topographical reality of the abbey is subordinated to a poetic interpretation, in which stone becomes malleable in moonlight. The transfiguration of the scene is the result of a natural phenomenon, but we are aware, too, that the ultimate transmogrification of the scene is produced by Turner's manipulation of the watercolor medium, using carefully calibrated registers of hue.

Fig. 115 Joseph Mallord William Turner, *Melrose Abbey*, 1822. Watercolor on cream wove paper, 19.7 × 13.5 cm (no. 277)

Fig. 116 Thomas Girtin, *Melrose Abbey: The East Window*, c. 1796. Watercolor and graphite on cream wove paper, 37.8 × 28.4 cm (no. 143)

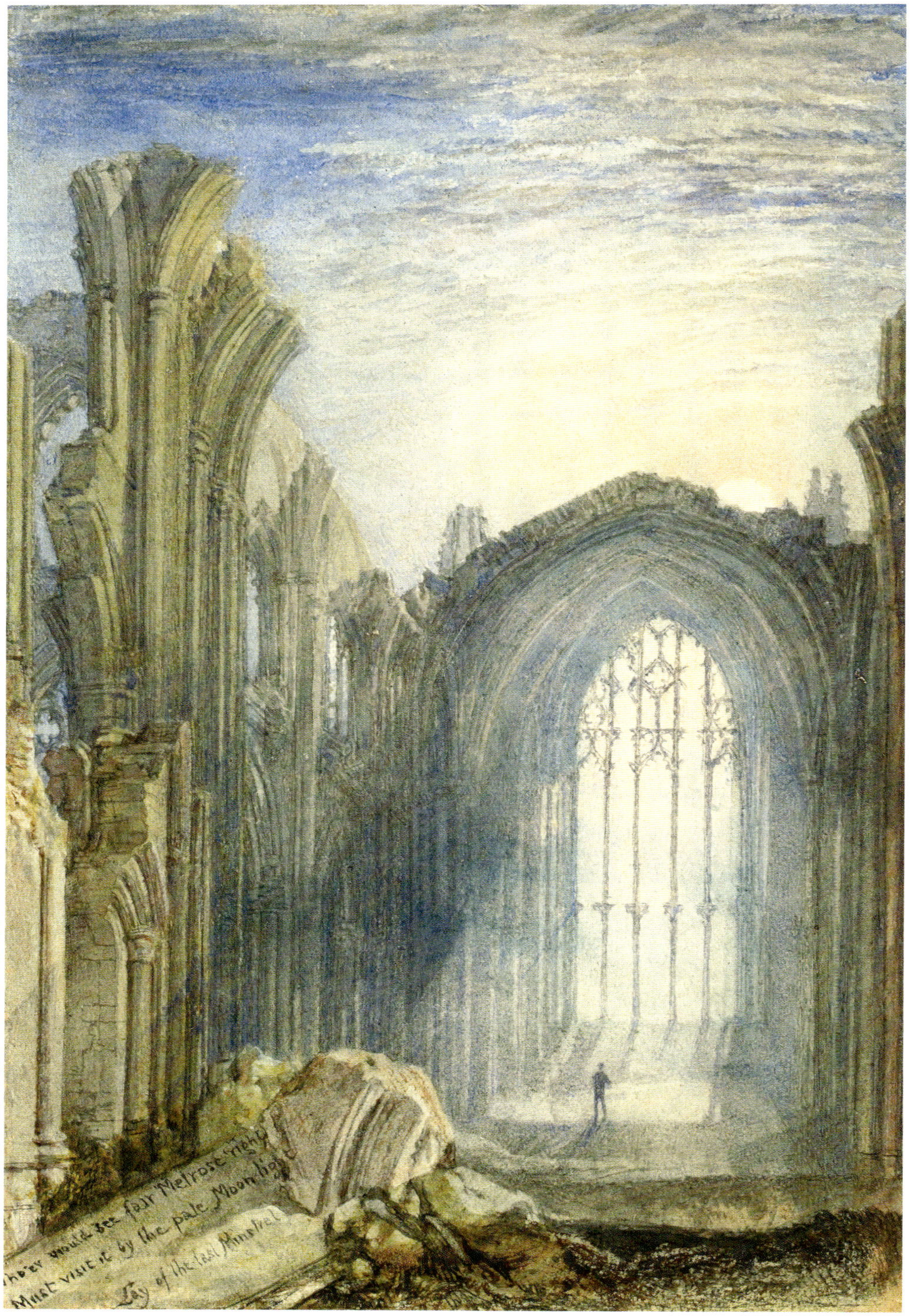

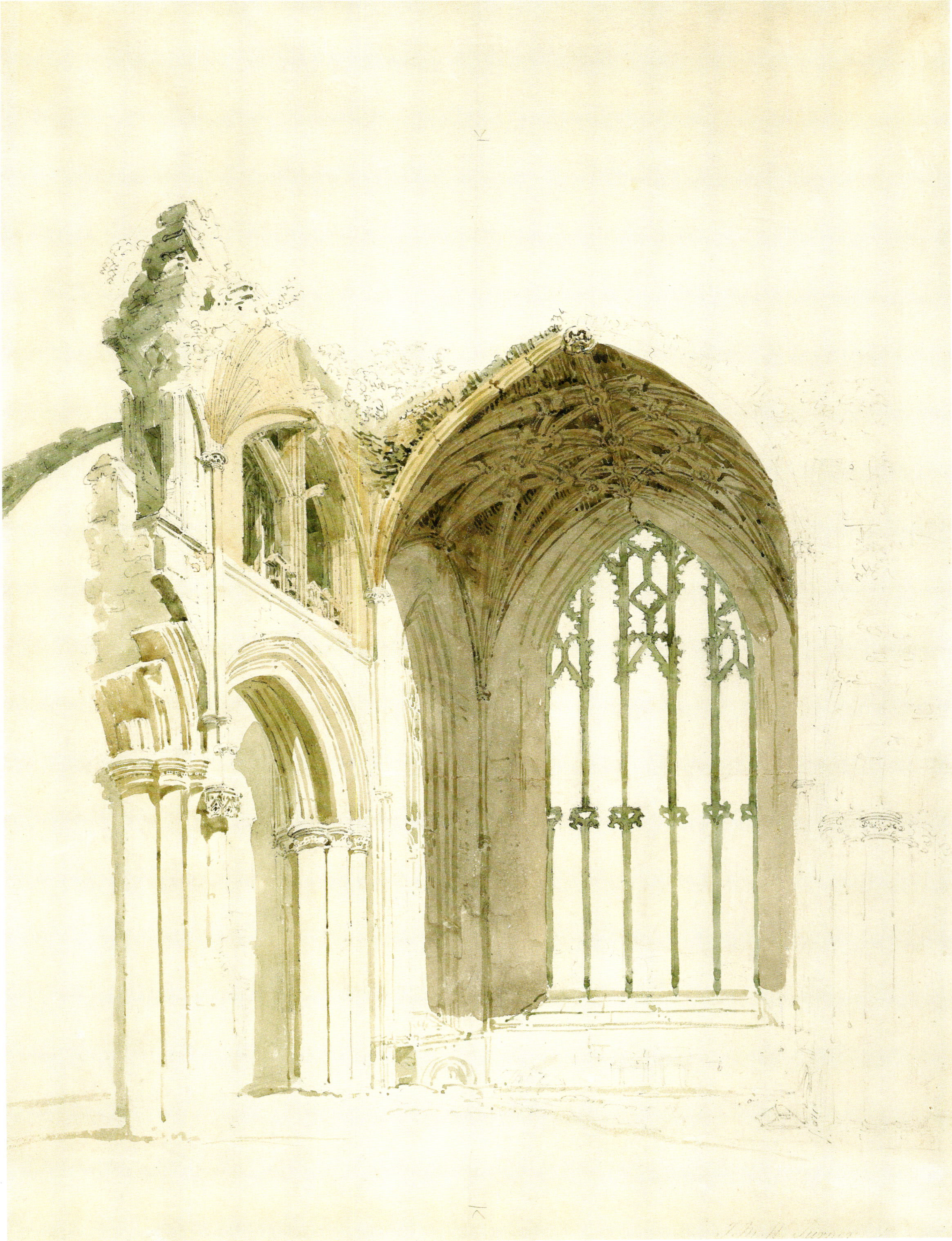

It is instructive here to examine Girtin's treatment of exactly the same view (fig. 116), produced some twenty years earlier. Girtin's painting is true to the topographical tradition insofar as it offers a precise account of the architectural remains seen from this vantage point. It is poised between the antiquarian rectitude demanded by Carter and the more picturesque approach to topography that has informed its point of view and the dramatic play of sunlight and shadow Girtin uses to animate the ruin. The watercolor is unfinished, tipping it toward the empirical, and leaving the historic associations of Melrose understated. It is an exercise in looking in much the way Dayes recommended, demonstrating, as only a skillful artist could, the architectural logic of Gothic masonry techniques for supporting the walls and bridging the vaults.

Turner's watercolor, in contrast, for all its sympathetic understanding of medieval stone construction, is not content merely to describe. The scene before us is heightened to encourage the play of the spectator's imagination, to meditate on this relic of the past. The evolution of watercolor, especially in Turner's case, might thus be characterized not simply as a product of increasing technical expertise and artistic ambition; it also witnessed a transition toward a practice that understood the scrutiny of the observable world to be a manifold behavior, combining psychological as well as physiological reactions. The acuity of empirical observation is evidently on display, but the image as a whole is also a visual correlative for the thoughts and feelings stimulated by antiquity.

1 [Anon, probably William Henry Pyne], "Observations on the Rise and Progress of Painting in Water Colours," in *Ackermann's Repository of Arts* 8, no. 47 (November 1812): 257–60.

2 William Henry Pyne [Ephraim Hardcastle], "The Rise and Progress of Water-Colour Painting in England," *Somerset House Gazette* 1 (1823–24): 65–67, 81–83, 97–99, 113–14, 129–30, 145–46, 161–63, 177–79, 193–95.

3 As quoted in John Lewis Roget, *A History of the "Old Water-Colour" Society* (London: Longmans, Green & Co., 1891), 1:426.

4 Henry Fuseli, "Lecture IV: On Invention, Part II," in John Knowles, ed. *The Life and Writings of Henry Fuseli, Esq., M.A., R.A.* (London, 1831), 2:217.

5 Pyne, "Rise and Progress of Water-Colour Painting," 98.

6 Edmund Burke, *A Philosophical Enquiry into the Origin of Our Ideas of the Sublime and Beautiful* (London: R. and J. Dodsley, 1757).

7 John Carter, "Publication of Cathedrals by the Antiquarian Society," *Gentleman's Magazine* 73, no. 1 (1803): 106–7.

8 See Howard Marchitello, *Narrative and Meaning in Early Modern England: Browne's Skull and Other Histories* (Cambridge, U.K.: Cambridge University Press, 1997), 78–85.

9 "Advertisement," in E. W. Brayley, ed., *The Works of the Late Edward Dayes* (London, 1805), n.p.

10 Nicholas Carlisle, *A Topographical Dictionary of England* (London: Longman, Hurst, Rees, and Orme, 1808), xviii–xxiv.

11 *The Quarterly Review* 25 (April and July 1821): 113.

12 British Library, add. ms 29944, fol. 73, John Britton to John Carter, 2 September 1802; Carter's reply is undated. This exchange is quoted in Bernard Nurse and J. Mordaunt Crook, "John Carter, FSA (1748–1817): 'The Ingenious, and Very Accurate Draughtsman,'" *Antiquaries Journal*, Cambridge Journals Online, published 31 May 2011, http://journals.cambridge.org/10.1017/S0003581511000047.

13 Edward Dayes, "On the Power and Usefulness of Drawing," in Brayley, *Works of the Late Edward Dayes*, 257–58.

14 Tate, London, Finberg CCCLXXI A–L.

15 J. M. W. Turner to John Britton, November 1811, in John Gage, ed., *Collected Correspondence of J. M. W. Turner* (Oxford, U.K.: Oxford University Press, 1980), 50.

16 Dayes, too, recommends study of the Old Masters in order to improve contemporary practice. See Brayley, *Works of the Late Edward Dayes*.

17 North of England Sketchbook (1797), Tate, London, Finberg XXXIV, 60, 61; Tweed and Lakes Sketchbook (1797), Tate, London, Finberg XXXV, 16, 17, 18, Tate, London.

18 The next records of the abbey, however, although recording the window, occur in sketchbooks of 1831, after this watercolor was produced. See Abbotsford Sketchbook, Tate, London, Finberg CCLXVII, 10,11, 12, 13a (including the window), 14, 14a, 15; Edinburgh Sketchbook, Tate, London, Finberg CCLXVIII, 53.

19 John Stoddart, *Remarks on Local Scenery and Manners in Scotland During the Years 1799 and 1800* (London: William Miller, 1801), 277.

The Wheat Field
Constable After Modernism

Tim Barringer

After John Constable's *The Wheat Field* (fig. 117) was taken down from the walls of the British Institution's exhibition in the Spring of 1817, it disappeared from public view for a century and three-quarters. No engraving or photograph of the painting existed, not even a sketch. Left with no more than its title, scholars could only speculate as to the nature of this pivotal work. It was painted in the summer of 1815, when Constable was still a struggling provincial artist. Neither the critics nor the members of the Royal Academy, where the work was first exhibited in 1816, had taken much interest in his work. However, by the time *The Wheat Field* was rediscovered in 1988, Constable had long been recognized as one of the greatest of British artists and a major figure in European Romanticism. The reappearance of *The Wheat Field* and its subsequent availability to a wide public on permanent view at the Clark significantly challenge accepted views of the artist and his work.[1]

Although Constable's legacy was treated with some disdain by the Victorians, by the dawn of the twentieth century it had achieved the unusual feat of becoming both canonical and popular with a wide public. Prominently enshrined in the National Gallery, Tate, and Victoria and Albert collections in London, as well as in major museums all over the world, his landscapes have become ubiquitous in reproduction on biscuit tins, tea towels, and plastic bags.[2] Scholarly scrutiny of every aspect of Constable's oeuvre has produced a large monographic historiography.[3] Constable has also taken his place within the wider narratives of the history of art. A familiar account emphasizes his influence on French painting through the exhibition of *The Hay Wain* (fig. 118) at the Paris Salon in 1824, where Delacroix, among others, found it revelatory. Moreover, Constable has been credited with foreshadowing, even influencing Impressionism through his practice of painting directly from nature in oils and from the spontaneous and performative character of his brushwork. The emergence in the late nineteenth century of Constable's private works – freely worked small oil sketches and turbulent full-size sketches for exhibited "six-footers" – ineluctably led to his canonization in the twentieth century as one of the distant forefathers of modernism.[4] Constable's work was prominent in the Museum of Modern Art's exhibition *Masters of British Painting* in 1956. The curator, Andrew Carnduff Ritchie, noted in the catalogue:

[Constable] tried to appease the Royal Academy and its authorities by "finishing" his canvases for exhibition – slicking over what appeared to the conventional eye to be the rough surface of his brushwork and the crude directness of his coloring. For example, it was the "finished" version of "The Haywain" [sic] which he sent to Paris for the exhibition

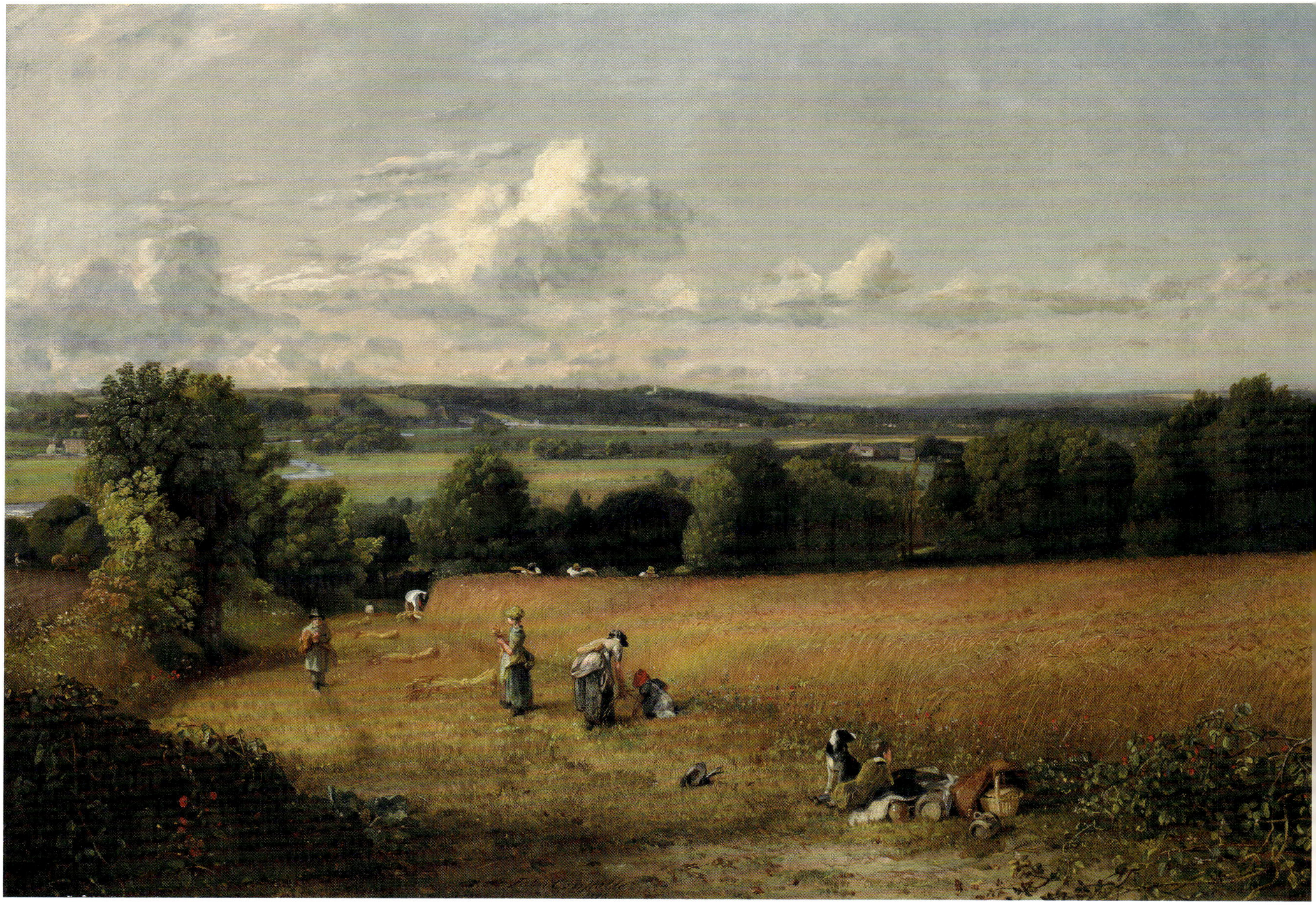

in 1824 and which so impressed Delacroix and is said to have led the latter to repaint his "Massacre of Chios." How much more impressed Delacroix might have been by the so-called sketch for "The Haywain," now in the Victoria and Albert Museum! (fig. 119)

A pioneering revisionist elsewhere, Ritchie here mobilizes the binary most brilliantly formulated by Clement Greenberg in his article, "Avant-Garde and Kitsch."[5] Constable's oeuvre presents an unusual dilemma, however, in that within his work both of these elements can allegedly be detected simultaneously. In characterizing Constable's exhibited work, Ritchie borrows from Greenberg's demonological lexicon terms such as "slick," "finish," "conventional," and "Academic," which implicitly contrast with the authentic, expressive brushwork and true coloring of the sketches. There is no doubting the power of this argument: the "good" painterly Constable seems to prefigure Abstract Expressionism and action painting, while the "bad" academic Constable is locked in arid dialogue with Claude Lorrain, creating meretricious, detailed, representational paintings contrived to appeal to the ignorant bourgeoisie. For Kenneth Clark, writing in 1949, Constable was "a bore only in his finished pictures."[6] The radical freedom of the sketch contrasts with the conservative repression of the finished work. Despite the undoubted persuasiveness of this rhetorical strategy, it entirely fails to acknowledge

Fig. 117 John Constable (English, 1776–1837), *The Wheat Field*, 1816. Oil on canvas, 54.6 × 77.2 cm (no. 52)

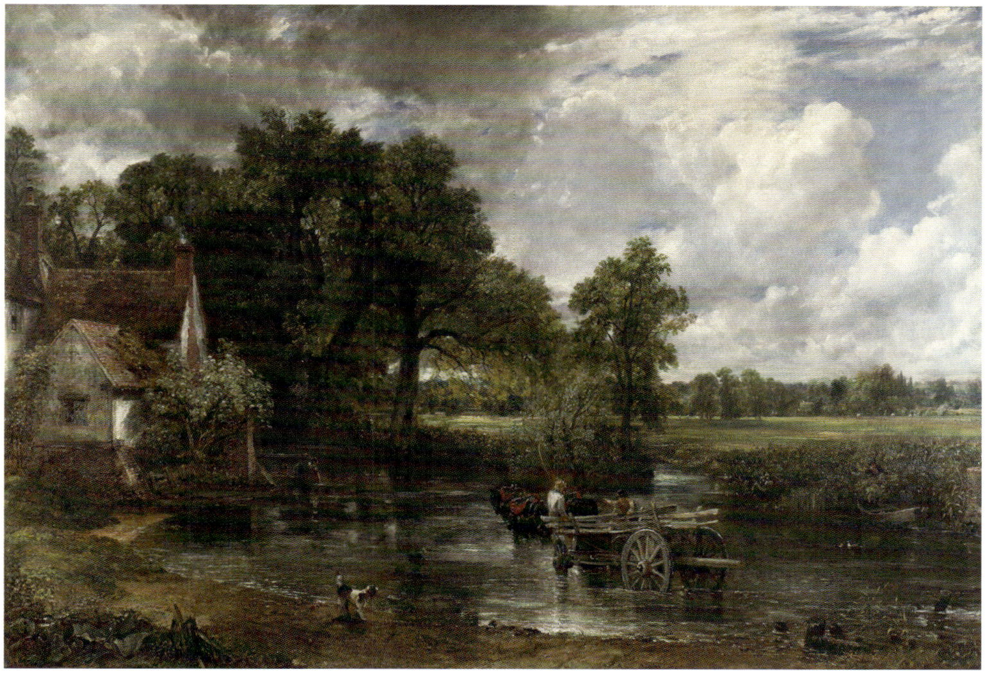

Fig. 118 John Constable, *The Hay Wain*, 1820–21. Oil on canvas, 130.2 × 185.4 cm. National Gallery, London. Presented by Henry Vaughan, 1886 (N61207)

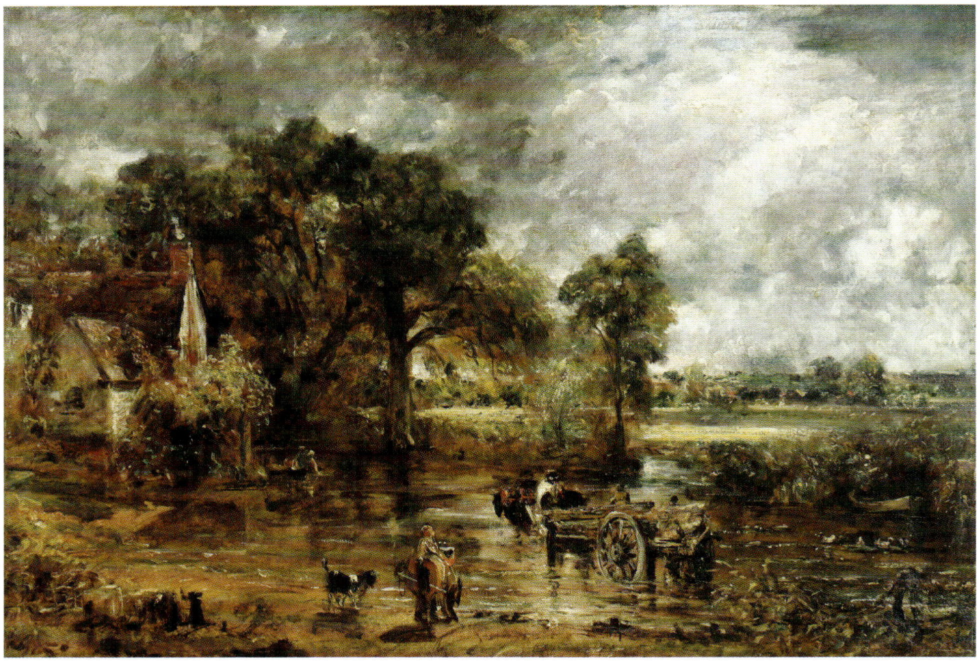

Fig. 119 John Constable, Full-Scale Sketch for *The Hay Wain*, 1820. Oil on canvas, 137 × 188 cm. Victoria and Albert Museum, London. Bequeathed by Henry Vaughan

the complexity of early nineteenth-century art theory, within which the significance, desirability, and status of "finish" were unstable and hotly debated, and it seriously skews our view of Constable's oeuvre. Modernism is now ended as a historical movement, even if its dead hand continues to shape the ways in which many museums approach their collections and art history is written and taught. Following the collapse of modernism's teleological narrative, thinking about the nineteenth century is belatedly entering a new phase. Impressionism is gradually taking its proper place as merely one of many important late nineteenth-century art movements. It can no longer be considered the sole benchmark of achievement, nor the inevitable *telos* of all worthwhile earlier art, nor the progenitor of everything good that followed. This new landscape of taste insists that we view Constable's work anew.

A close portraiture of our English scenery

It was an extraordinary quirk of fate that *The Wheat Field* should emerge from obscurity at just the moment when the critical tides were turning in its favor. *The Wheat Field* is not the kind of Constable that modernist criticism could endorse. Meticulously finished and laboriously worked, it does not display the rough, dramatic, or self-reflexive brushwork of the sketch. Instead, each ear of wheat, every fold of the reapers's dresses, all the chimneys of the distant cottages, every snaking turn of the river Stour is carefully replicated in disciplined, indexical brushstrokes. Rather than betraying traces of kinetic expressive energy, in the manner of action painting, *The Wheat Field* is a product of sustained and meticulous concentration, and of full and detailed elaboration, achieving a sense of hard-won verisimilitude, perhaps even an intentional contrivance. There is no striving after spontaneity. It is a work that makes no fetish of swift execution, but glories in the slow and laborious craft of painting. It would be easy, though wrong, to associate this with a "slick" studio finish, and thus a betrayal of the "good" Constable's true vision.

Though destined for public exhibition at the Royal Academy, this is not a studio piece. All the textual and visual evidence suggests that *The Wheat Field* was painted substantially, if not entirely, in the field during the harvest period of mid-August to early September 1815. The canvas is an unusual "small- to medium-scale, nonstandard format of 21 by 30 inches."[7] X-ray examination has shown that Constable significantly altered the composition as he was painting. In contrast to most other major works, there are no surviving compositional sketches in any medium; the entire process, from conception to high-finish completion, took place on the canvas. The art historian Robyn Asleson has further observed that, "as part of the finish process, Constable worked over the picture with fine touches of a stiff, granular paint that stands up from the surface of the canvas. The highlights add to the textured effect of the brushwork and create an impression of shimmering light and movement."[8] It is possible that this final layer of paint was added in the studio, but the painting's overall effect of luminosity and precision speaks of a direct, indexical link with the subject that the intervention of any mediating process might easily have killed.[9]

The Wheat Field surprised critics who had chastised Constable for his lack of polish. A reviewer for *The Repository of Arts* at the Royal Academy in 1816 remarked that, "from extreme carelessness this artist has gone to the other extreme, and now displays the most labored finish."[10] For the grandiose art critic Robert Hunt, "his finishing and drawing are a little better than formerly, though still far below the standard of his coloring and general effect. These are beautiful, in as much [sic] as they are a close portraiture of our English scenery."[11]

Constable's act of "close portraiture" was the direct result of intense experimentation over a period of several years. The practice of painting from nature has a long tradition in the history of art. However, the complexities of the oil painting technique, the time habitually taken to complete a work, and the lack of easily portable pigment and medium

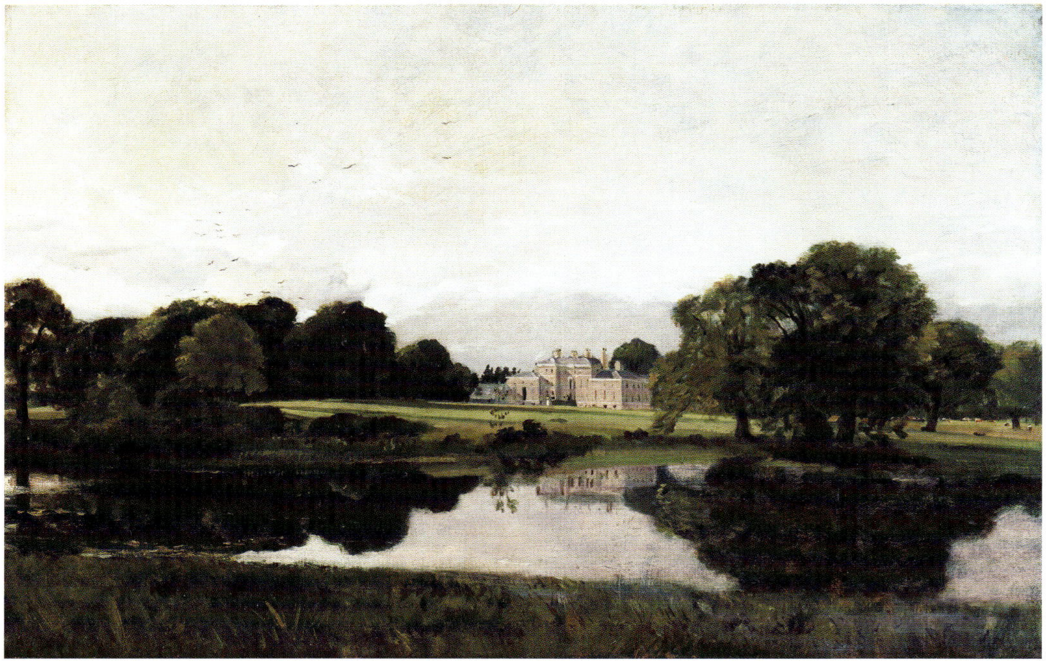

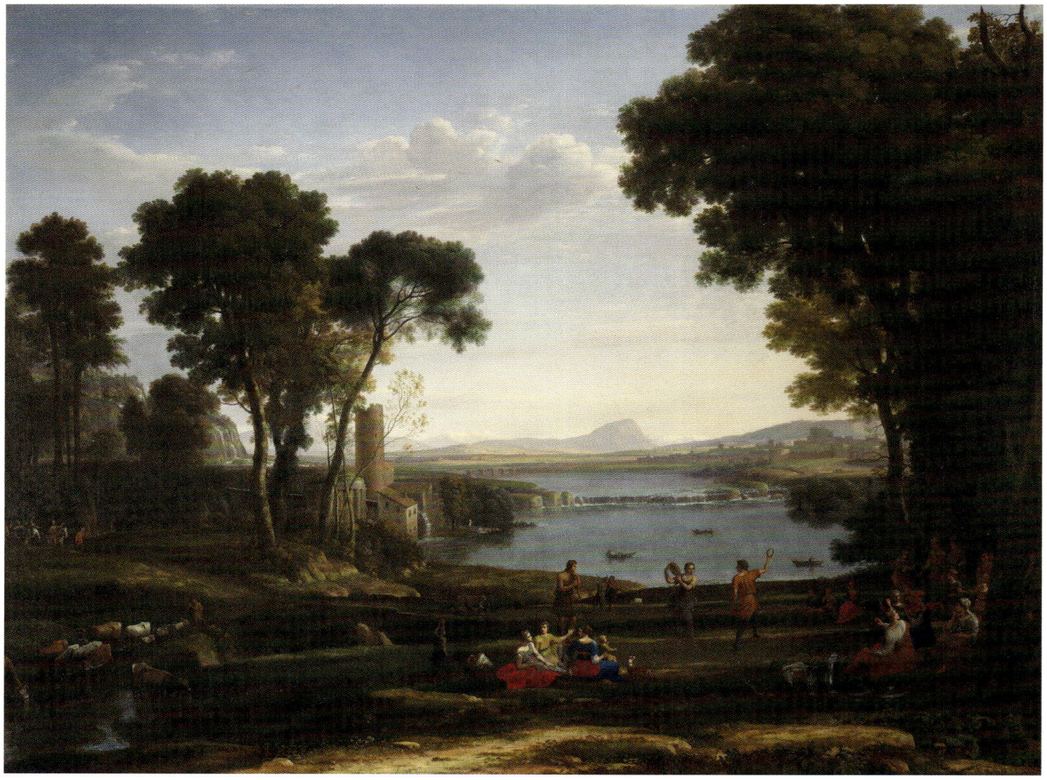

made the production of large-scale oil paintings in the open air highly unusual. More commonly, drawings in pencil and watercolor were made directly from the motif and later incorporated into the studio-based process of composing an oil painting, as in the case of Constable's great contemporary and perceived rival, Turner. From his earliest experiments in art making, Constable seems to have used oil paints outdoors, but it was only in 1809 that he completed a finished work, *Malvern Hall, Warwickshire* (fig. 120), entirely out-of-doors, possibly in a single day.[12] *Malvern Hall* shares the spontaneity and vibrancy of Constable's oil sketches of the period, but the composition, bearing the influence of Richard Wilson, and the size of the canvas declare that it is a work intended for public display.

Fig. 120 John Constable, *Malvern Hall, Warwickshire*, 1809. Oil on canvas, 51.4 × 76.8 cm. Tate, London

Constable did not produce another finished work outside until, in 1814, he set about two remarkable compositions that are the immediate predecessors of *The Wheat Field*. These paintings, of 1814–15, seem to have been conceived as a response to constructive criticism from an authoritative source, the Academician and diarist Joseph Farington, delivered in July 1814. Farington's diary records that he:

> *told [Constable] the objection made to His pictures was their being unfinished; that Thomson [Henry Thomson RA] gave Him great credit for the taste of His design … & for the indication shewn [sic] in the Colouring, but He had not carried His finishing far enough. – I recommended to Him to look at some of the pictures of* Claude *before He returns to His Country studies, and to attend to the admirable manner in which all the parts of His pictures are completed.*[13]

Fig. 121 Claude Lorrain (French, 1604/5–1682), *Landscape with the Marriage of Isaac and Rebecca*, 1648. Oil on canvas, 152.3 × 200.6 cm. National Gallery, London

Constable followed this advice, studying works of Claude Lorrain in the collection of John Julius Angerstein in London. It seems likely that he gave close attention to the *Landscape with the Marriage of Isaac and Rebecca* then known as *The Mill* (1648; fig. 121).

Thereafter, in July 1814, turning his back on London, but bearing with him a memory of the shimmering high finish of Claude's work, he returned to his family home in East Bergholt, Suffolk. When he next saw Farington, in November, Constable announced that he had been "long occupied in painting Landscapes from nature."[14] These were not mere sketches, but exhibition pictures: *Stour Valley and Dedham Church* (fig. 122) and *Boat-Building near Flatford Mill* (fig. 123). Of the latter, Constable's first biographer, C. R. Leslie, wrote, "I have heard him say he painted [it] entirely in the open air."[15] Constable seems to have worked on the two canvases simultaneously in East Bergholt, the former every morning, the latter every afternoon.[16] The two works were exhibited at the Royal

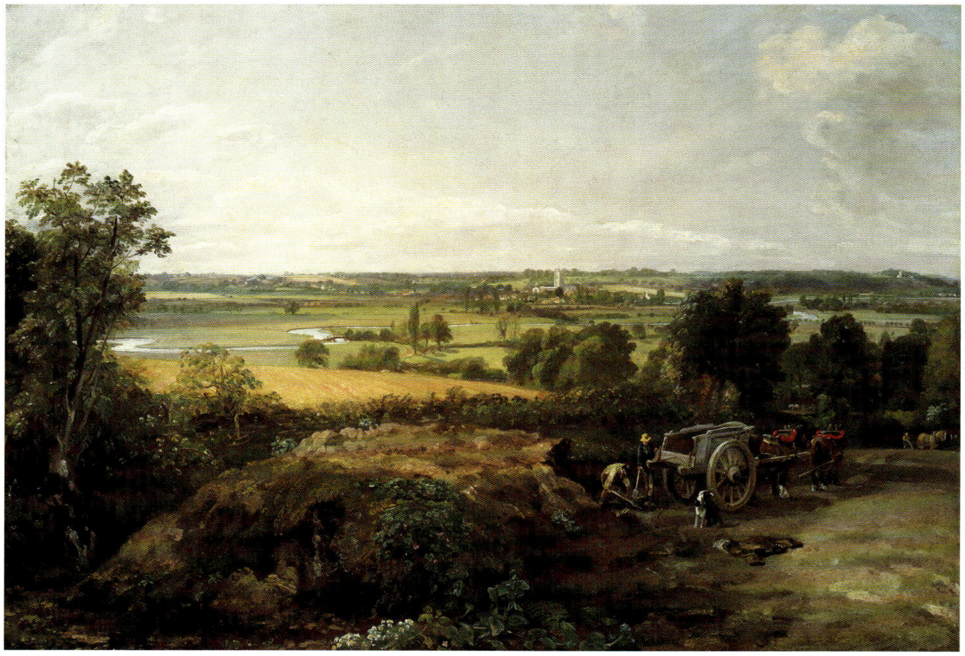

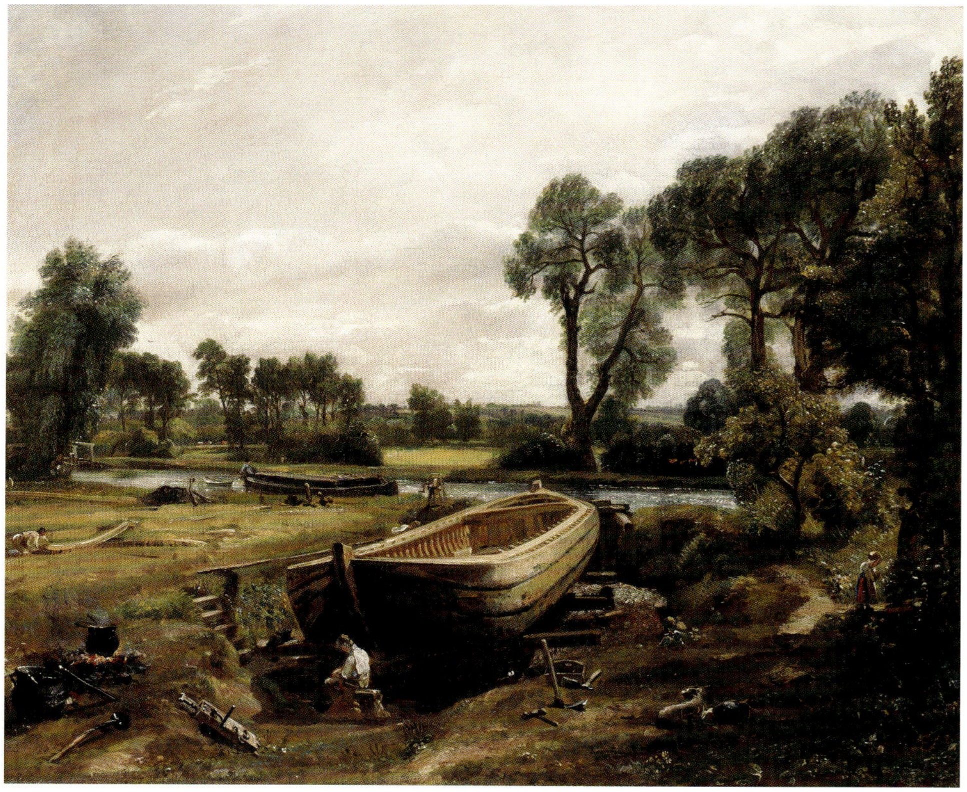

Academy in 1815. They do not form a pair, as they differ in size and tone. *Stour Valley and Dedham Church* has much closer connections with the Manton Collection *Wheat Field*, painted the following year; not only are the two canvases almost the same size, they also represent the very same field at different moments in the agricultural calendar.

Fig. 122 John Constable, *Stour Valley and Dedham Church*, 1814–15. Oil on canvas, 55.6 × 77.8 cm. Museum of Fine Arts, Boston. Warren Collection – William Wilkins Warren Fund (48.266)

Stour Valley and Dedham Church was commissioned by Thomas Fitzhugh for his much younger fiancée Philadelphia Godfrey, who was, like Constable, a native of the village of East Bergholt. As the squire's daughter, she held a higher status than Constable, the younger son of a prosperous miller. On leaving Suffolk to begin her married life in London, she wished to have a memento, a landscape of association, to remind her of the scenes of her early life. Accordingly, Constable was commissioned to paint the view on the Godfrey estate from just outside the grounds of her erstwhile home, Old Hall. Constable first prepared a freely executed preparatory oil sketch, dated 5 September 1814 (Leeds City Art Galleries), to work out the composition. The final canvas, just over 55 by 77 centimeters in size – and thus small enough to sit comfortably on a portable easel – was also painted painstakingly on the spot. The viewpoint allows Dedham village to be seen in the center of the canvas, but the most striking feature lies in the foreground: a large dunghill or "dungle" (as it was locally known) of manure from cattle, which would be ploughed into the fields after harvest to fertilize the land.[17] Whatever Constable learned from his study of Claude – and the new lucidity of detail in these finished paintings, as well as the distinctive character of the skies, may well owe something to the French master – the representation of dunghills was certainly not part of it. This insistence on the local and particular amounted to a resistance to conventional picturesque subject matter and a complete disavowal of academic theory as laid down in Joshua Reynolds's *Discourses*, where Dutch painters were castigated for their detailed representation of the vulgar details of everyday life.[18] Exceeding even Turner's radical naturalism in recent works like *Ploughing Up Turnips, near Slough ("Windsor")*, exhibited at the Royal Academy in 1809 (fig. 124), Constable focused on the precise activities of the harvest field.

Fig. 123 John Constable, *Boat-Building near Flatford Mill*, 1814–15. Oil on canvas, 50.8 × 61.6 cm. Victoria and Albert Museum, London. Given by John Sheepshanks, 1857

I see nobody but the harvest men

The Wheat Field represents both the completion of the agricultural cycle and the consummate achievement of Constable's early career. We are still in the field outside Old Hall depicted in *Stour Valley and Dedham Church*, but the view has shifted to the right. Fertilized by the nurturing manure ploughed into the stubble fields after the previous year's harvest, the thriving crop has grown to ripeness, and is now being collected under the late-summer sun. The dunghill, whose remnants form a dark mass in the lower-left corner of the painting, is reduced in size, while the foliage of the trees and fields has grown more opulent. In the distance, male harvesters, visible only from the waist up, are cutting the wheat with sickles, while women and children are gleaning in the foreground. *The Wheat Field* seems to bring to glorious fruition the project of a "natural painture," a purely realistic artistic style free of art-historical influence and true to nature. He had begun this project in his earliest works and further developed it in *Stour Valley and Dedham Church*. *The Wheat Field* marks his success in this daring gamble in painting a substantial, highly finished canvas from the motif. The fruits of Constable's work in the field, as much as that of the peasantry of East Bergholt, are on display.

The juxtaposition of Constable's method of working and the choice of imagery, agricultural work in fields belonging to one of his patrons, inevitably draws attention to the social worldview and commentary implicit in *The Wheat Field*. These issues were certainly on Constable's mind. On 27 August 1815, when work on *The Wheat Field* must have been at its most intense, he described himself as "occupied in my own pursuits," explaining that, "I live almost wholly in the feilds [sic] and see nobody but the harvest men."[19] The summer's labors had even transformed Constable's appearance: "I have as you guess been much out

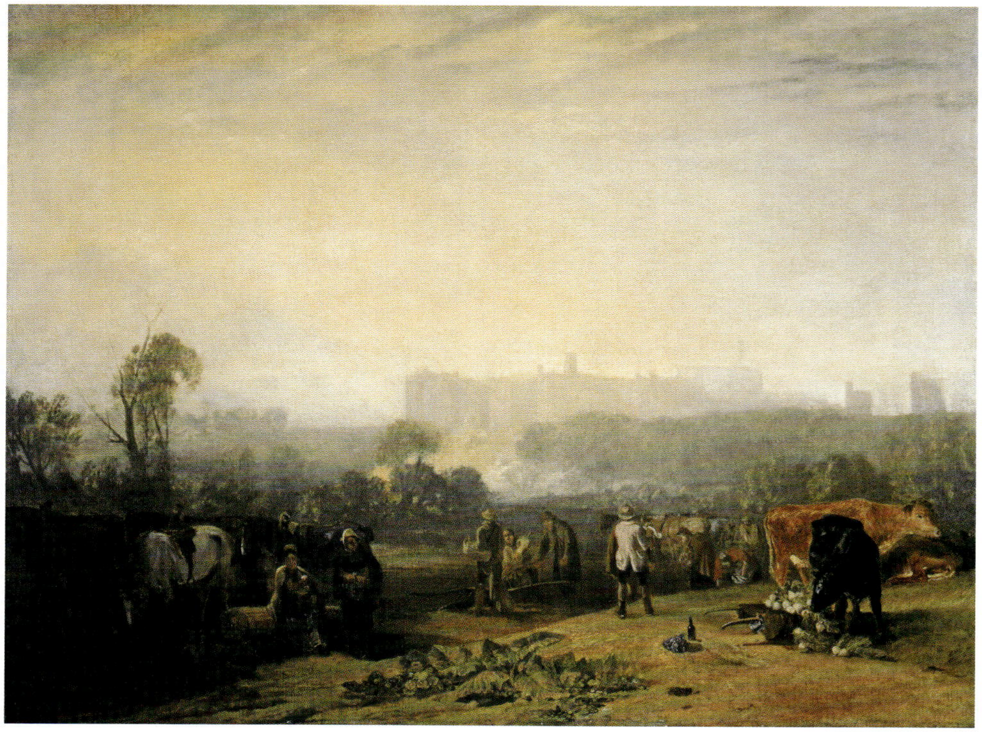

Fig. 124 Joseph Mallord William Turner (English, 1775–1851), *Ploughing Up Turnips, near Slough ("Windsor")*, 1809. Oil on canvas, 101.9 × 130.2 cm. Tate, London

of doors, indeed could you see me you would not want to be told that – I am so perfectly bronzed."[20] He was taking on something of the appearance of a field laborer rather than a gentleman or an artist.

This aspect of Constable's work became the unlikely site of genteel methodological and even ideological contention during the 1980s and early 1990s, as rival groups of British scholars representing the so-called new and the (de facto) old art history debated the political implications of his representations of agricultural laborers.[21] The first salvo was John Barrell's pathbreaking book, *The Dark Side of the Landscape*, of 1980. Barrell argued that, "in his attempt to recreate an older, georgic image of the fat and productive land of East Anglia," it was necessary for Constable:

to reduce his figures until they merge insignificantly with the landscape, to distance them, and even when they are in the foreground to paint them as indistinctly as possible, to evade the question of their actuality. The labourers ... keep their place, and it is a very small place, a long way away.[22]

Barrell's overall project was to juxtapose new writing about social conditions and class consciousness in the period, in the wake of E. P. Thompson's *Making of the English Working Class* (1963), with visual representations of the rural poor in order to reveal the ideological commitments underpinning the imagery of Gainsborough, George Morland, and Constable.[23] In a more detailed study, *Constable: The Painter and his Landscape* (1981), Michael Rosenthal drew on exhaustive research into local topography, farming practices, and social structures, as well as Constable's intellectual engagements with literature and contemporary politics, in order to provide a compelling interpretation of the artist's work. By contrast, a group of curators, led by Graham Reynolds of the Victoria and Albert Museum, Leslie Parris of the Tate Gallery, and the independent scholar Ian Fleming-Williams, naturalized Constable's conservative political beliefs (which perhaps they broadly shared) as common sense, and focused on questions of stylistic development and the details of the artist's career.

The reappearance of *The Wheat Field*, announced by Parris and Fleming-Williams in their monumental Tate exhibition catalogue of 1991, allowed their resentment to surface:

Even within his own terms the contrast drawn by John Barrell ... between the bold figuration of the latter and the – to him – nearly invisible workers in Constable's landscapes of the period clearly requires qualification now.[24]

The Wheat Field is indeed unusual, being (as Parris and Fleming-Williams acknowledge) "the most densely populated landscape Constable had so far painted."[25] But how should these prominent figures be understood? Responding to the newly discovered painting in 1991, Rosenthal noted that "a face is only given to one child: the proletariat is otherwise faceless."[26] Indeed, Constable, whose work as a portraitist has recently been reassessed, did not differentiate the faces of the poor as he did those of his social equals, and was not interested in their character or individual identities.[27] "The reappearance of this picture," he added, "has gone some way to confirming the thesis advanced by John Barrell that Constable, as one would expect from a person of his station, maintained a proper distance between himself and the proletariat."[28] Rosenthal's use of the term "proletariat" is tendentious, implying that the rural poor of 1815 were already incorporated into the kind of urban, industrial, cash economy that Marx and Engels analyzed a quarter century later.[29] His point, however, is an important one.

Constable understood the "harvesting men" to be members of the English peasantry. He drew attention to the human protagonists in *The Wheat Field* by placing them unusually close to the foreground, and representing their clothing and attitudes in great detail. Perhaps two of the white-shirted men in *The Wheat Field* are the same pair who, wearing rough jackets, dug muck from the dungle in *Stour Valley and Dedham Church*. The black-and-white sheepdog who attended them in *Stour Valley* reappears in *The Wheat Field*, its attitude unchanged.

In a gesture that is significant for our understanding of Constable's social vision, he added some lines of poetry to the title for its presentation at the British Institution in 1817:

Nature herself invites the reapers forth
....
No rake takes here what heaven to all bestows:
Children of want, for you, the bounty flows![30]

His choice of lines by Robert Bloomfield, the Suffolk-born, working-class poet, in preference to a standard work, such as James Thomson's *Seasons* (1726–30), was pointed. Bloomfield knew the rural world intimately, and wrote unflinchingly of poverty, yet when composing *The Farmer's Boy* in London in 1799–1800 he also nurtured a nostalgic sense of the delights of country life. Gleaners, women and children who would follow the reapers through the fields collecting any stems of wheat left behind by the harvesters, were a particular focus of interest for Constable and Bloomfield as the poorest members of the village community. Sanctioned by its presence in the Bible, gleaning was traditionally allowed as a measure to counter poverty. The use of a rake by the harvesters to catch stray stalks of wheat would have cut off this essential source of food and income to the very poor.[31] Constable selected an extract from Bloomfield's poem for his title precisely because of its endorsement of traditional farming practices as socially beneficial, in implicit contrast to the new profit-driven methods of industrial farming promoted since the 1770s by agricultural improvers such as Arthur Young. The artist made several detailed pencil sketches of women at work gleaning, including one sheet of tiny scribbles from which spring forth marvelously animated figures (fig. 125). In other sketches, the gleaners appear statuesque. One such, rendered with great care, relates directly to the stooping figure in a pink dress to the left of the center of *The Wheat Field* (fig. 126).

Despite its undeniable verisimilitude, Constable's painting offers an unrealistically rosy picture of the life of the agricultural laborer when measured, as Barrell would advise, against other archives and indexes. The prominent placing of a beer barrel and provisions for the harvesters' lunch suggests plenty and even prosperity, although recent research indicates that there was endemic poverty at the time.[32] Constable portrays specific labor practices typical of Suffolk at this date. Not only are the harvesters using the traditional sickle, a small, hook-shaped, handheld tool used to cut the stem of the corn at its base, but they are also arranged in traditional fashion, with a "lord" leading the group at the end of the row. An anecdote recorded in Charles Robert Leslie's *Memoirs of the Life of John Constable* records that Samuel Strowager, Head Porter at the Royal Academy, a Suffolk man who had worked as a farm laborer near East Bergholt, was "captivated" by this painting. Strowager "pointed out to the arranging committee [of Royal Academicians] its correctness, 'the *lord*,' as the leading man among reapers and mowers is called in Suffolk, being in due advance of all the rest."[33]

Like many Tories of the period, Constable decried the changes in rural life that have retrospectively been termed "the agricultural revolution," principal among them the process of enclosure, by which the medieval open-field system was replaced by modern patterns of ownership that consolidated the grip of larger landowners and marginalized smallholders.[34] This allowed a new bourgeoisie to increase its profits from farming, and prevented a Malthusian crisis by massively increasing the production of food. The cost was a dissolution of traditional social relations. Constable acknowledged this changing political and economic environment in a letter to his future wife, Maria Bicknell, on 14 January 1816:

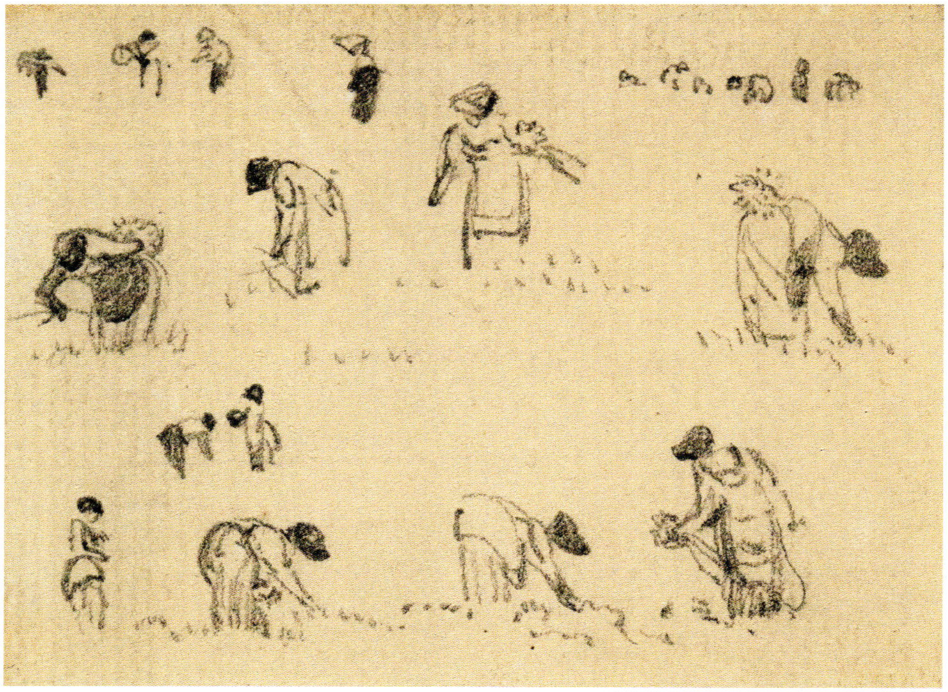

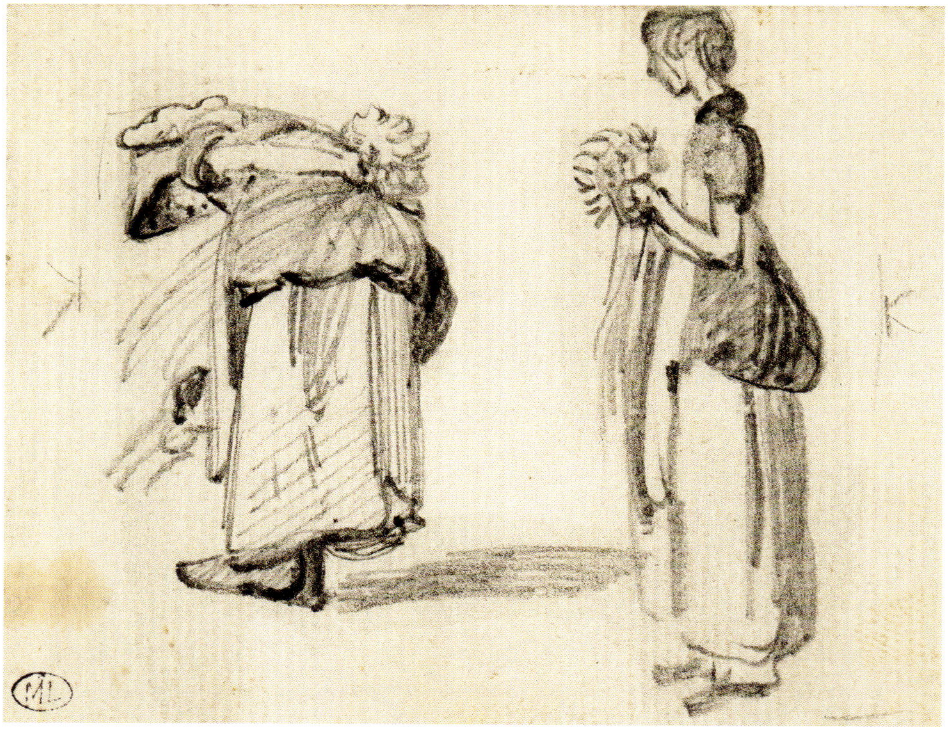
ML

Fig. 125 John Constable, *Studies of Gleaners*, 1816. Graphite on paper, 10.2 × 7.7 cm. Musée du Louvre, Paris

Fig. 126 John Constable, *Two Gleaners*, 1816. Graphite on paper, 10.1 × 5.6 cm. Musée du Louvre, Paris

The village has been quite in a bustle about the division of our Common, which is now being divided, besides many exchanges which are now taking place. I hope all will end amicably, but where so many interests are brought together, some may peradventure clash.... Some among us have shown such extreme greediness and rapacity to "lay feild to feild" as to make themselves obnoxious.[35]

Constable's choice of words indicates what was at stake. "Division," "exchanges," "greediness," "rapacity," "clash": this is the language of competition, of the free market, of the cash nexus. By quoting a specific Biblical reference, "lay feild to feild," Constable invokes the parable of the vineyard from the Book of Isaiah, a denunciation of selfish and oppressive behavior of the rich to the detriment of the wider community:

Woe unto them that join house to house, that lay field to field, till there be no place, that they may be placed alone in the midst of the earth!

In contrast, Constable's *Wheat Field* offers a timeless, georgic image of an organic society supported by social rather than economic relationships, blessed by natural bounty and benevolent rule. Implicit in this worldview is the notion that every inhabitant of the village – from the landowning Godfrey family and bourgeois landowners such as the artist's father Golding Constable to the tenant farmers, the laborers they employed and housed, and the village poor, the gleaners – knows his or her place. They are understood to be bound together in relations of mutual care and responsibility. Gleaning was the most significant emblem of rural charity, just as harvesting was the epitome of honest rural toil, hence the high symbolic stakes in Constable's painting. There is little evidence to suggest that actual social conditions ever really matched this roseate image. That being said, Constable's fears were well founded: as the nineteenth century progressed, the harvest field would become the scene of profound changes of labor organization and work discipline, leading by the 1850s to mechanization.[36] Constable's focus on gleaning in an unenclosed, open field indicates a deep commitment to a traditional, rural way of life that was doomed to extinction.

As Christiana Payne has noted, harvesting subjects became especially popular in the years around 1815, breaking the bounds of local significance to become emblematic of the resurgent British nation as the Napoleonic War drew to a close.[37] Constable would have seen Peter De Wint's panoramic *Cornfield* (fig. 127), depicting the flat and fertile landscape of Lincolnshire, at the Royal Academy exhibition of 1815, and may have been spurred to emulate this work. The scene is marked more by the luxuriance of nature than by the physical exertion of the harvesters, although it does record the practice of raking the field, in the center distance. Two gleaners, evidently allowed only modest pickings, are positioned in the right margin. The harvest of 1815, seen in *The Wheat Field*, which took place after De Wint's work was exhibited, was a particularly abundant one, widely taken as a symbol of the flourishing condition of the nation in the immediate aftermath of Wellington's victory at the Battle of Waterloo on Sunday 18 June 1815. Guns were fired in London to announce the victory on 22 June, though for Constable the news was tempered by anxiety about his relations serving in the forces.[38]

Constable's rural idyll, if it ever really existed, swiftly vanished. The postwar period saw deep economic depression and rapid social and economic change. By 1817, when *The Wheat Field* was shown with Bloomfield's text, East Bergholt had been enclosed, and a period of violent agricultural unrest descended on the southern counties of England. Constable, moreover, had married and moved to London, where he would spend most of the rest of his life.

Beginning in 1818, Constable embarked upon a series of large-scale works (the "six footers"), mainly painted in his London studio. Compositions of enormous ambition and resonance, these works were realized through the use of extensive preparatory works, particularly his freely painted full-size sketches. The "six-footers" are undoubtedly

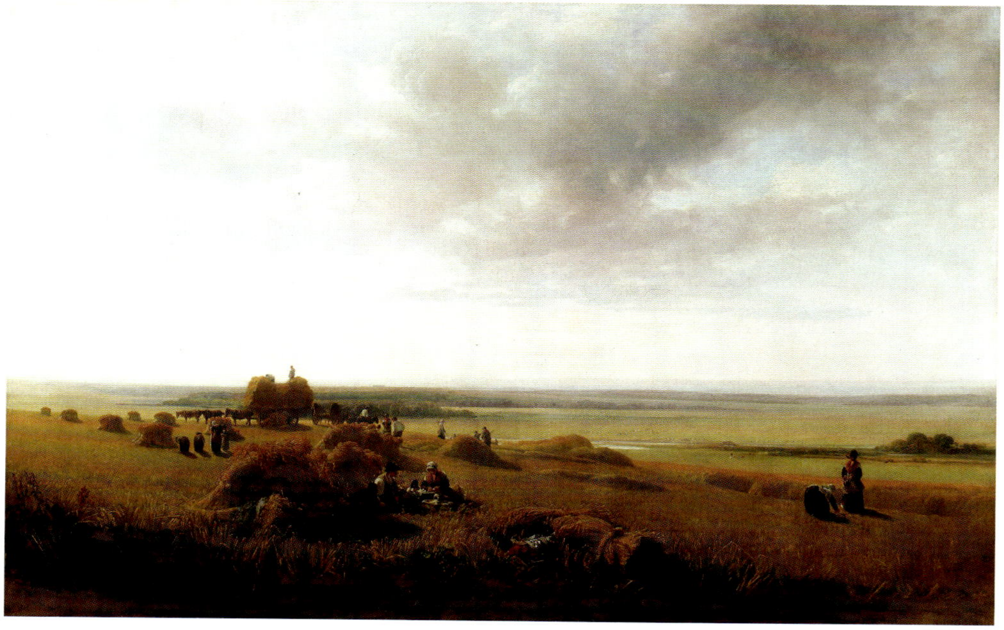

Fig. 127 Peter De Wint (English, 1784–1849), *Cornfield*, 1815. Oil on canvas, 104.8 × 163.8 cm. Victoria and Albert Museum, London. Given by Mrs. Helen Tatlock, daughter of the artist

his crowning achievement. Yet for a brief moment in the years around 1815, Constable achieved a feat of realism – a tour de force of manual, as well as intellectual, work – by completing revelatory finished canvases in the field. This singular labor of producing hard-won realist images places the bronzed figure of Constable among "the harvest men," and confers on the resulting works a degree of unvarnished integrity that can be readily observed in not only his natural, but also his social vision. The nostrums of the old and the new art histories both prove inadequate to provide an adequate response to Constable's profound statement. The painting refuses to be confined by modernism's restrictive account of artistic value. It is neither a treatise on social conditions nor a formal experiment. Rather, it is both a virtuoso demonstration of painting in the open air and a meditation on rural life and labor in the face of historical change; a personal testimony and a manifesto. Perhaps the last word should be left to that redoubtable man of Suffolk, the Royal Academy porter Samuel Strowager, who, "captivated" by the work, simply "pointed out its correctness."

1 The painting became known to Constable scholars in 1988 after it was discovered in an American private collection by Charles S. Rhyne. It was first publicly exhibited in modern times in the 1991 Tate Gallery exhibition on Constable. See Leslie Parris and Ian Fleming-Williams, eds., *Constable* (London: Tate Gallery, 1991), 160.

2 See Colin Painter, *At Home with Constable's Cornfield* (London: National Gallery, 1996). On Constable and the Victorians, see: Ian Fleming-Williams and Leslie Parris, *The Discovery of Constable* (New York: Holmes & Meier, 1984); Stephen Daniels, "John Constable and the Making of Constable Country," in *Fields of Vision: Landscape Imagery and National Identity in England and the United States* (Cambridge, U.K.: Polity Press, 1993), 200–42; and Tim Barringer, *Men at Work: Art and Labor in Victorian Britain* (New Haven, Conn., and London: Yale University Press, 2005), 104–6.

3 A useful selected bibliography of these works can be found in Anne Lyles, ed., *Constable: The Great Landscapes* (London: Tate Publishing, 2006), 208–9.

4 Sketches and studies by Constable belonging to the artist's son, Charles Golding Constable, were exhibited at the South Kensington (later Victoria and Albert) Museum between 1880 and 1883; in 1888, the artist's daughter, Isabel Constable, bequeathed a large collection of works, including the full-size oil study for *The Hay Wain*, to the South Kensington Museum.

5 Clement Greenberg, "Avant-Garde and Kitsch," first published in *Partisan Review*, 1939. The essay has been widely reproduced. See, for example, Clement Greenberg, *Art and Culture: Critical Essays* (Boston: Beacon Press, 1961), 3–21.

6 Kenneth Clark, *Landscape into Art* (London: John Murray, 1949), 77.

7 Anne Lyles, "The Open-Picture, 1814–1820," in Lyles, *Constable: The Great Landscapes*, 103.

8 Robyn Asleson, cat. entry in Malcolm Warner and Robyn Asleson, eds., *Great British Paintings from American Collections* (New Haven, Conn.: Yale Center for British Art, 2001), 159.

9 Constable enigmatically noted in a letter dated 15 November 1815, long after the harvest was gathered, as the winter evenings drew in: "It is my intention to continue here till I feel that I have secured such a picture as I mean for the Exhibition." John Constable to Maria Bicknell, East Bergolt, 15 November 1815, in *John Constable's Correspondence*, ed. Ronald Brymer Beckett, vol. 2, *Early Friends and Maria Bicknell (Mrs. Constable)* (Ipswich, U.K.: Suffolk Records Society, 1964), 160.

10 Judy Crosby Ivy, *Constable and the Critics, 1802–1837* (Woodbridge: Boydell Press/Suffolk Records Society, 1991), 71.

11 Ibid., 72.

12 Graham Reynolds, *The Early Paintings and Drawings of John Constable* (New Haven, Conn., and London: Yale University Press, 1996), 1:131–2; Parris and Fleming-Williams, *Constable*, 149.

13 Kathryn Cave, ed., *The Diary of Joseph Farington*, vol. 13, *January 1814–December 1815* (New Haven, Conn. and London: Yale University Press, 1984), entry for 23 July 1814, 4564.

14 Ibid., entry for 5 November 1814, 4603.

15 Charles Robert Leslie, *Memoirs of the Life of John Constable, Esq., R.A., Composed Chiefly of His Letters* (London: Longman, Brown, Green and Longmans, 1845), 53.

16 The account that follows owes much to Michael Rosenthal's excellent account in *Constable: The Painter and His Landscape* (New Haven, Conn., and London: Yale University Press, 1981), 78–89.

17 See Ian Fleming-Williams, "A runover dungle and a possible date for 'Spring,'" *Burlington Magazine* 114, no. 831 (June 1872): 386–93. See also Michael Rosenthal, "Constable at the Tate: The Bright Side of the Landscape," *Apollo*, August 1991, 77–84; quotation from p. 81.

18 Joshua Reynolds, "Fourth Discourse, Delivered to the Students of the Royal Academy on the Distribution of the Prizes, December 10, 1771," in Robert Wark, ed., *Joshua Reynolds: Discourses* (New Haven, Conn., and London: Yale University Press, 1997), 69.

19 John Constable to Maria Bicknell, East Bergholt, 27 September 1815, in Beckett, *John Constable's Correspondence*, 2:149.

20 John Constable to Maria Bicknell, East Bergholt, 14 September 1815, in Ibid., 152.

21 A flavor of these discussions can be gleaned from Martin Postle, "Not a happy lot: Constable symposium at the Tate," *Apollo* (September 1991): 209.

22 John Barrell, *The Dark Side of the Landscape: The Rural Poor in English Painting, 1730–1840* (Cambridge, U.K.: Cambridge University Press, 1980), 134.

23 E. P. Thompson, *The Making of the English Working Class* (Harmondsworth, U.K.: Penguin, 1963).

24 Parris and Fleming-Williams, *Constable*, 162.

25 Ibid.

26 Rosenthal, "Constable at the Tate," 80.

27 Martin Gayford and Anne Lyles, *Constable Portraits: The Painter and His Circle* (London: National Portrait Gallery, 2009).

28 Rosenthal, "Constable at the Tate," 80.

29 See for example, Frederick Engels, *The Condition of the Working-Class in England in 1844*, trans. by Florence Kelley Wischnewetzky (London: Swan Sonnenschein & Co. Paternoster Square, 1892).

30 Robert Bloomfield, *The Famer's Boy*, lines 132, 137–38.

31 Gleaning is referred to in the story of Ruth and Boaz in Ruth 2:15–16.

32 For a richly evidenced discussion, see Keith Snell, *Annals of the Laboring Poor: Social Change and Agrarian England, 1660–1900* (Cambridge, U.K.: Cambridge University Press, 1985).

33 Leslie, *Memoirs*, 13.

34 See J. D. Chambers and G. E. Mingay, *The Agricultural Revolution* (London: Batsford, 1966). The agricultural history of the period is explored in detail in G. E Mingay, ed., *The Agrarian History of England and Wales*, vol. 6, *1750–1850* (Cambridge, U.K.: Cambridge University Press, 1989).

35 John Constable to Maria Bicknell, East Bergholt, 14 January 1816, in Beckett, *John Constable's Correspondence*, 2:167.

36 See Tim Barringer, "The Harvest Field in the Railway Age," chap. 2 in *Men at Work*, 83–132.

37 Christiana Payne, "Boundless Harvests: Representations of Open Fields and Gleaning in Early Nineteenth Century England," *Turner Studies* 11, no. 1 (Summer 1991): 7–15.

38 Constable expressed "anxiety about our relations who were in the late dreadfull battle." John Constable to Maria Bicknell, East Bergholt, 28 June 1815, in Beckett, *John Constable's Correspondence*, 2:144. Indeed, his cousin, Captain James Gubbins of the 13th Light Dragoons, turned out to have been a casualty of the campaign.

Oil and Water

Richard Parkes Bonington, Eugène Delacroix, and Originality

Patrick Noon

Between the restoration of Louis XVIII to the French monarchy in 1815 and the accession of Queen Victoria to the British throne in 1837, but especially in the decade of the 1820s, an unprecedented engagement between two previously unsympathetic schools of painting would radically impact the course of modern art in Western Europe. The year 1824 was particularly momentous for the arts in France and England, as notable for its losses as for its triumphs. Among other events of import, it observed the birth of *Le Globe*, the official newspaper of the liberal French intelligentsia, and the foundation of the National Gallery in London, as well as the deaths of Théodore Géricault, Lord Byron, and Anne-Louis Girodet. The exhibition of the work of living artists that year in the Paris Salon, the "British Salon" as it later became known, was more than the "vile farrago of Bourbon restoration pictures" that William Hazlitt, the brilliant critic and essayist, summarily dismissed, or the "war of extermination against the classical purity of the French School" as the xenophobic French critic Charles Farcy lamented; rather, it marked a rapprochement between France and Britain of exceptional political and artistic consequence. After a hiatus of several decades, British artists were again invited to participate in this premier European cultural event. French visitors enjoyed, to be certain, a thoroughly disparate view of British painting. For example, nearly three-quarters of the fifty works submitted were watercolors by professional artists represented, not by the French establishment, but by a new class of Parisian commercial art dealers. There were no oils by J. M. W. Turner or David Wilkie, but what their French colleagues did experience was novel, challenging, and for many ultimately transforming. Among the British painters awarded gold medals for their efforts by the French Ministry were Sir Thomas Lawrence, President of Britain's Royal Academy; John Constable, the celebrated landscape painter; Copley Fielding, President of the Society of Painters in Water Colours; and a novice twenty-two-year-old virtuoso by the name of Richard Parkes Bonington, all of whom created a sensation with their patently British blend of bravura execution and penetrating naturalism.

This somewhat transitory accommodation between the two schools nevertheless rekindled the long-standing debate in France between those who delighted in the spontaneous inventions of fiery imaginations and those who valued more detailed and reflective compositions. This "sketch versus finish" debate would persist in dominating French aesthetic discourse through the nineteenth century, pitting a Romantic fascination with virtuosity, individuality, and spontaneity against a traditional respect for craftsmanship and lengthy apprenticeship, while raising the larger issue as to whether art could be taught at all. It set the French against the British, Delacroix against Ingres,

Ruskin against Whistler, and the Impressionists against their Pompier contemporaries. The rise to prominence of watercolor painting during this period, initially in Great Britain and then throughout Europe, was integral to amplifying that debate, especially in the realm of plein air landscape painting.

Jumping ahead fifty years, we will see just how crucial this oppositional debate would become. In 1876, Louis Edmond Duranty, novelist, critic, and principal apologist for Gustave Courbet, Edgar Degas, and Édouard Manet, issued a pamphlet in defense of the Impressionists, who had organized that year their second group exhibition in the galleries of Durand-Ruel in Paris.[1] It was essentially a critique of the stagnant system of art education and state patronage that had dominated French painting for the past century and that, despite the ferocious efforts of the Romantics and Realists to overhaul them, remained formidable and hostile forces against change. Duranty summoned, primarily, two historical voices to lay the groundwork for his definition of the originality of the "New Painting." The first was the highly regarded eighteenth-century encyclopedist, Denis Diderot, whom he credited with having defined, as early as 1765, the ideal of modern design; namely, design imaginatively, even naively derived solely from direct observation of nature. Something of what both authors were advocating is implicit in Diderot's Salon reviews, where he stated the case against entrenched academic process more broadly in an analysis of Hubert Robert's landscape oil sketches of 1767:

Why does a beautiful sketch please us more than a beautiful painting? It is because there is more life and less form. To the extent that one introduces form, life disappears. How can a young student, incapable of executing even a mediocre painting, make a marvelous sketch? Because the sketch is the work of heated inspiration and of genius, and the picture a work of toil and of patience, of long study and a consummate knowledge of art. . . . The sketch is so seductive because, being indeterminate, it affords greater freedom to our imaginations which see what pleases them. It is like the story of a child who ponders the clouds, and we are all that child more or less. . . . Movement, action, passion are indicated by a few characteristic traits, and my imagination does the rest. I am inspired by the divine breath of the artist.[2]

The second source upon which Duranty hinged his argument was an artist for whom both watercolor and oil sketches were also indispensable tools, John Constable, as transcribed and published posthumously in C. R. Leslie's biography of 1843.[3] "The execution of my pictures," Constable wrote, "I know, is singular, but I love that rule of Sterne's:

'Never mind the dogmas of the schools, but get at the heart as you can.'" Duranty extracted that sentence from Constable's letter of July 1824 to his patron the Archdeacon John Fisher, in which he also complained of the false criticism of the French in response to his pictures then on view in the 1824 Paris Salon. Duranty then skipped to another part of Leslie's biography, again quoting Constable at length:

My art is truly my own. Two routes can lead one to fame; the first is the art of imitation; the second is the art that relies only on itself, original art. The advantages of imitative art are that, since it repeats the works of known masters that the eye has been accustomed to admire for a long time, it is readily recognized and esteemed, while the art that sets out to copy no one, which desires to reveal only what one sees and senses in nature, can only attain estimation slowly.... When I am seated, crayon or brush in hand, before a scene in nature, my first care is to forget that I had ever seen a painting.[4]

That sentiment would reverberate through the musings of an entire generation of French landscape painters. Charles Daubigny, for instance, would tell his American pupil Dwight Tryon that he had no working method other than to paint as directly and as rapidly as possible what he saw and felt, without recourse to rules, memory, or models. The notion of deftly transcribing one's sensation of natural phenomena – "what one sees and senses" – pervades the declared ambitions of most later Impressionist and Postimpressionist painters.

But Duranty[5] was also echoing a more contemporary source – one equally indebted to both Diderot and British aesthetics and the bridge in practice and theory between them and the "New Painting" – the recently deceased Eugène Delacroix[6] who, in his published writings and his manuscript *Dictionary of Art*, grappled incessantly with the same notions of innate talent, execution, and finish as they pertained to artistic genius. As if paraphrasing Diderot, he would write in his *Journal* in 1859:

[Painting] is a science and an art all in one; in order to acquit oneself in a truly knowing manner, a long period of practice is indispensable ... [yet] born talents find by instinct the means of attaining the expression of their ideas; with them it is a mélange of spontaneous bursts and experimentations, through which the idea emerges with a charm perhaps more distinctive than the production offered by a consummate master. There is at the dawn of talent something naïf and daring at once, which recalls the charms of childhood and at the same time its happy lack of concern for the conventions that govern men of accomplishment.[7]

Fig. 128 Richard Parkes Bonington (English, 1801–1828). *Coast with Beached Boats and Figures*, c. 1823–24. Watercolor over graphite, with scraping, on cream wove paper, 15.2 × 21 cm (no. 25)

Thus, fifty years after the 1824 Salon, Duranty was able to rely on the collective memory of his own artistic community to bolster his defense of the Impressionist circle by invoking that decade and its celebrities. The British Salon represented a seminal moment in European painting, the lessons of which were disseminated with determination over the intervening decades.

It is the stuff of legend that Delacroix's response on seeing his first Constable painting in 1824 was to immediately rework the background of his *Massacre at Scios*, for which he was subsequently awarded a gold medal at the Salon. He also claimed to have divined in Constable's landscapes the "superiority" of his multitinted greens,[8] but the professional and personal relationship between the French painter and Constable's cadet rival, Richard Parkes Bonington, exhibited, even in its brevity, a creative intensity that was far richer and more consequential. Furthermore, if the 1820s were a defining moment in the history of modern art,[9] then Bonington and Delacroix were two of the principal architects, often acting in concert, despite their many differences in temperament, aspirations, nationality, and training.

Aside from their artworks, documentation of that professional relationship is sadly fragmentary at best. Delacroix claimed to have first met Bonington while both were painting copies in the Louvre, the former in oils after Veronese's *Wedding Feast at Cana* (1562–63) and the latter in watercolors after Metsu and other Dutch and Flemish artists. That would have been about 1820, shortly after Bonington moved to Paris from Calais with his family. Prior to the 1824 Salon, when he made his first public appearance as a landscape painter in oils, Bonington was engaged almost exclusively as a topographical draftsman and watercolorist. His initial forays from Paris were not in the traditional direction of Rome but to the picturesque coast of Normandy, which furnished him with material completely fresh to his Parisian patrons. In the quiescent *Coast with Beached Boats and Figures* (fig. 128), probably a view at Dunkerque, the seductively radiant aerial perspective; the lucid orthogonal composition, comprising a very low horizon line and a spare gathering of vertical masts against an expansive sky; and the dexterous insertion of secondary details capture the classic Bonington composition. Such brilliant exercises in Anglo-Dutch naturalism were without parallel in contemporary French practice.

The banishment of British artists from the continent during the Napoleonic conflict had the effect of generating on both sides of the channel the conviction that watercolor painting was a peculiarly English phenomenon. In France, where the Davidian taste for large Neoclassical pictures and strict hierarchical distinctions between works in different

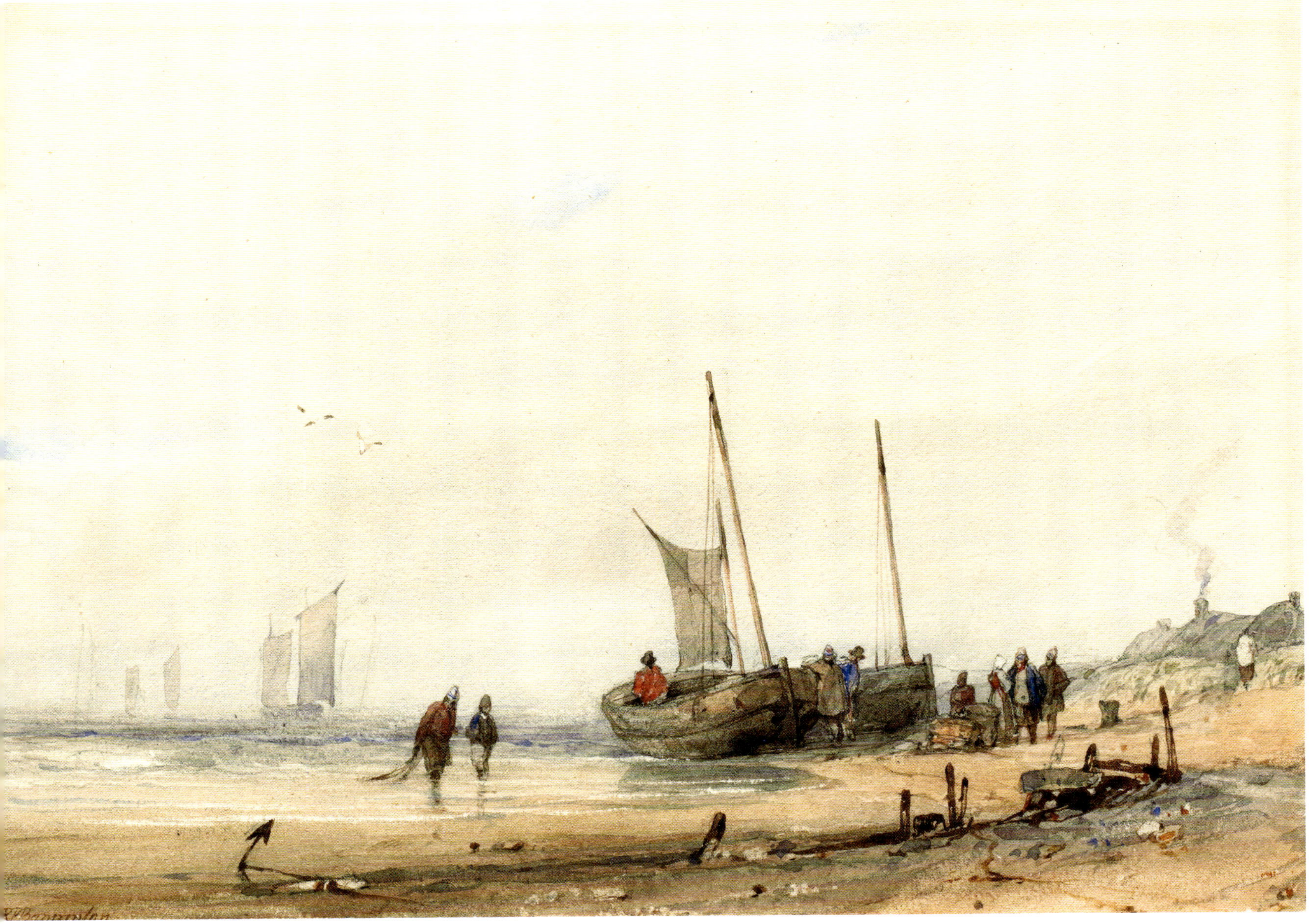

media, or between a sketch and a finished picture, continued to reign throughout the first quarter of the new century, watercolor painting gained recognition as a serious enterprise only after the 1824 Salon. By the mid-1830s, however, even the most skeptical critics were seduced by the virtues of the medium. The archconservative protégé of Jacques-Louis David, Étienne-Jean Delécluze, for instance, would allow the importance of watercolor:

Fig. 129 Richard Parkes Bonington, *Le Crotoy*, c. 1823. Watercolor, with scraping, on cream wove paper, 20.2 × 27.5 cm (no. 24)

Another significant accident in the history of landscape painting is the perfection with which we have succeeded in painting this genre in watercolors. Watercolor has an advantage over oil painting of conserving pure tints; and today, when we have succeeded in giving this process all the éclat of oil painting, it leaves little to desire when employed by men of talent.[10]

The more liberal banner, *L'Artiste*, elevated the medium with the cachet of social reform: "Landscape in watercolor is *the* new vehicle of taste. It avoids the apparatus of the Salon machine; moreover, it is democratic in its affordability, portability, and the accessibility of its subjects."[11] One phenomenon driving the popularity of watercolor painting in both England and France was the craze for creating albums of drawings and watercolors by living artists. *Coast with Beached Boats and Figures*, for instance, was commissioned for the album of Madame Valentine Delessert, sister-in-law of one of the wealthiest bankers in Paris, who hosted a liberal salon in Passy and was introduced to Bonington by Delacroix.

Bonington and Delacroix would also have frequented the ateliers of mutual acquaintances, in particular the British Fielding brothers, who had been brought to Paris as watercolorists by the Swiss publisher of deluxe illustrated books, J. F. d'Ostervald,[12] but there seems to have been no significant interaction until the 1824 exhibition thrust them both to the forefront of public notice. In addition to four oil paintings, Bonington's Salon entries included a significant number of landscape watercolors. *Le Crotoy* (fig. 129), which was etched in aquatint by Newton Fielding for Ostervald's *Excursions sur les côtes et dans les ports de France* (Paris, 1825) and may have been one of those entries, exemplifies the artist's adept fusion of broad, fluid execution and phenomenal realism. Similar works, when viewed in the window of a Paris art dealer, prompted Camille Corot to abandon his apprenticeship with a tailor and take up landscape painting as a profession.

The following summer Bonington and Delacroix traveled together with a coterie of young French artists to London, where, as Delacroix later mused, they were all "much in each other's company." The decisive event, however, occurred in the late fall, when

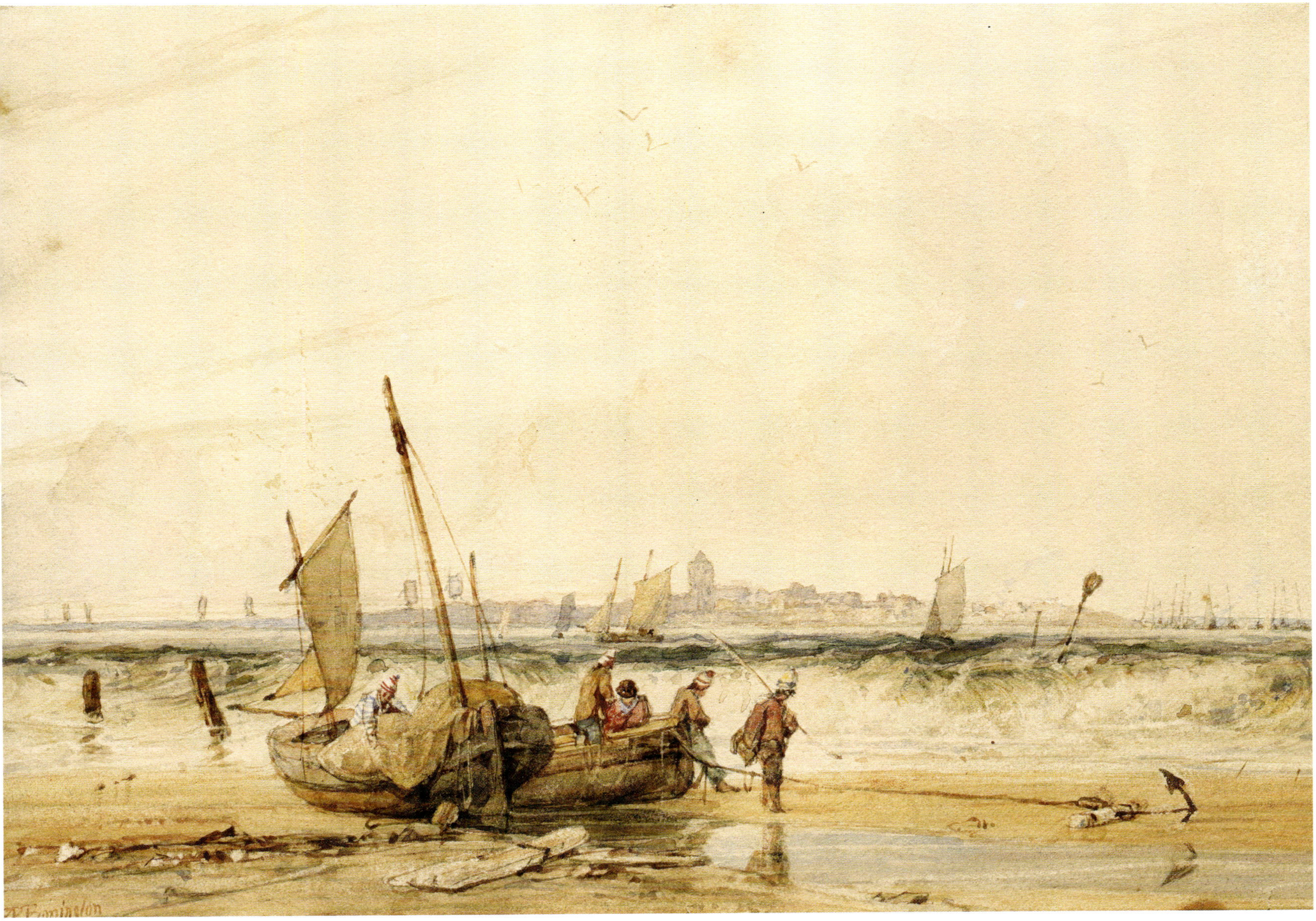

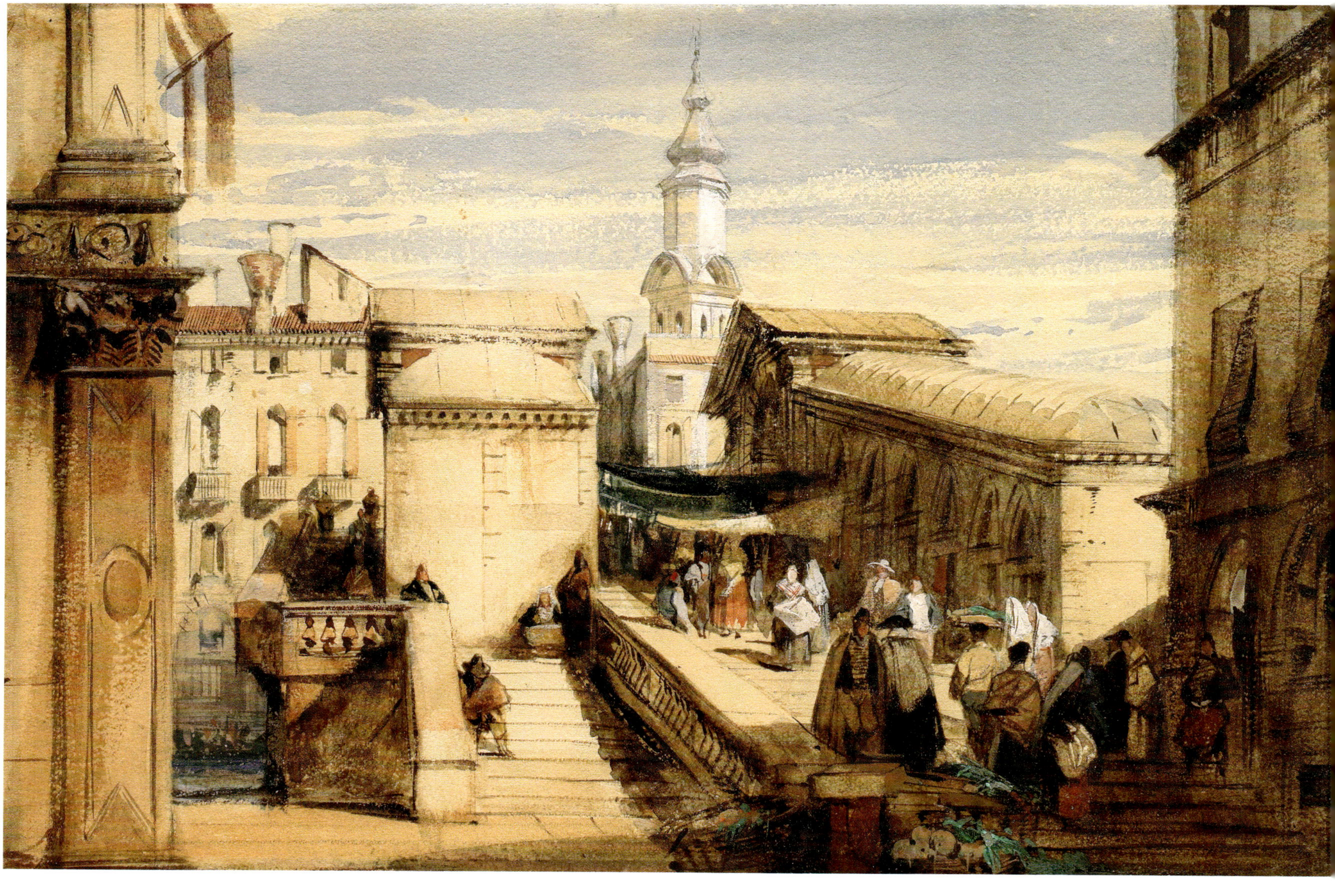

Bonington joined Delacroix for several months in the latter's Paris studio at 20 rue Jacob. Shortly thereafter Delacroix wrote to a friend that Bonington had been with him for some time. "There is much to be gained in the company of this chap," he announced, "and I assure you I am making the most of it."[13] Although Bonington would leave the studio in April 1826 to tour northern Italy (fig. 130), his cordial and serious *entente* with Delacroix would persist undiminished until his early death in 1828. Théophile Gautier first observed the lessons to which Delacroix probably referred in that letter: a new appreciation for dazzling, translucent color and an assured, vigorous execution that were first evident in his pictures of 1826, in particular his *Execution of Doge Marino Faliero* (Wallace Collection), which is usually described as his masterpiece in the Bonington manner.[14] Recalling his association with Bonington, Delacroix would write in his diary on New Year's Eve 1856:

Fig. 130 Richard Parkes Bonington, *The Rialto, Venice*, c. 1827. Watercolor and gouache, with gum arabic, on cream wove paper, 18.1 × 26.7 cm (no. 27)

Some talents come into the world fully armed and prepared. The kind of pleasure men of experience find in their work must have existed since the beginning of time. I mean a sense of mastery, sureness of touch going hand in hand with clear ideas. Bonington had that also, but especially in his hand: that hand was so skilled it ran ahead of his ideas: he altered his pictures because he had such facility that everything he put on canvas was charming.... Note also that, in this type of improvisation, there enters an element not occurring in Charlet's, an understanding of color.[15]

In 1861 he elaborated on this appreciation in an extensive note to the French art critic and poet Théophile Thoré, in which he observed:

When I met Bonington for the first time, I was very young and I was making studies in the Louvre.... I saw a tall adolescent in a short jacket, who was making watercolor studies. Already in this genre, which was an English novelty, he had astonishing ability.... No one in this modern school, and perhaps even before, has possessed that lightness of touch which, especially in watercolors, makes Bonington's work a type of diamond that flatters and ravishes the eye, independent of any subject and any imitative intent.[16]

The diamond allusion he had employed as early as 1829 to describe the appeal of Sir Thomas Lawrence's technique, while the subservience of subject matter to ophthalmic gratification, a principal tenet of art-for-art's-sake doctrine, is also at the core of his famous appreciation of Géricault's gruesome amphitheater studies[17] and derives ultimately from the writings of earlier British theorists such as Joseph Addison, Richard Payne Knight, and William Hazlitt, in which he was deeply steeped.

Fig. 131 Jean-Auguste-Domenique Ingres (1780–1867), *Entry into Paris of the Dauphin, the Future King Charles V*, 1821. Oil on canvas, 46.4 × 52.2 cm. Wadsworth Atheneum, Hartford, Conn.

Fig. 132 Richard Parkes Bonington, *François Ier and Marguerite of Navarre*, c. 1827–28. Oil on canvas, 45.7 × 34.5 cm. Wallace Collection, London

For Delacroix, French academic painting, in particular that of David and Ingres, was pedantic in its execution, overstudied, and overfinished, thus devoid of those qualities that stir the soul of the spectator. It suffered the "French defect" of overburdening the viewer's imagination with "too many facts" and offering a derivative experience of nature.[18] One strategy to combat the tedium of academic stylization was the *effect* attained through the power of expressive execution in the service of an inexhaustible imagination:

What Byron said. The poetry of Campbell smells too much of the lamp etc. He is never content with what he has done; he spoils his most beautiful productions in desiring to finish them; all of the brilliance of the first stroke is lost. It is with poetry as with painting. They should not be too finished. . . . I myself have said a hundred times that painting, materially speaking, was only a bridge thrown between the spirit of the painter and that of the spectator. Cold exactitude is not art: ingenious artifice, when it pleases and what it expresses, is art completely. The feigned conscientiousness of the majority of painters is only perfection laboriously applied to the art of being boring.[19]

In Delacroix's paradigm, Bonington was a superior artist because he was a master manipulator of color and expressive touch to emotive ends: "he extended the limits of the art."[20] In his last critical study on Romanticism, scholar Morse Peckham expanded on Delacroix's observation:

Bonington was the first instance of what was to prove the peculiar destiny and character of nineteenth-century painting, and above all of landscape painting, from which modern art emerged, the sense that one so often has, even with minor painters, that they are inventing painting, at least thinking about painting from its very foundations.[21]

Furthermore, by the "ingenious artifice" of technical virtuosity alone, Bonington was capable of imbuing any subject with sentiment and originality and therefore with the utmost aesthetic merit. As Gautier would claim for Delacroix, and Duranty for Constable, through the formal means of color and brushwork alone, Bonington could "give the sensation of the thing he is representing."[22] These points are made abundantly clear when we compare, for instance, Ingres's tableaux vivant, *Entry into Paris of the Dauphin, the Future King Charles V* (fig. 131), with one of Bonington's historical representations, *François Ier and Marguerite of Navarre* (fig. 132). One pretends toward a fastidious elucidation of history, the other toward its humanization.

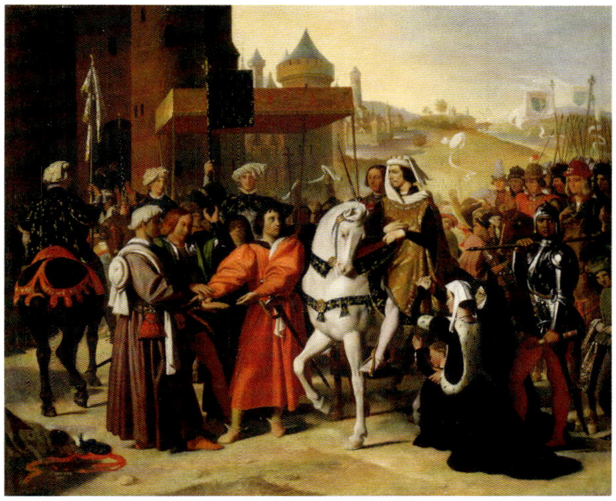

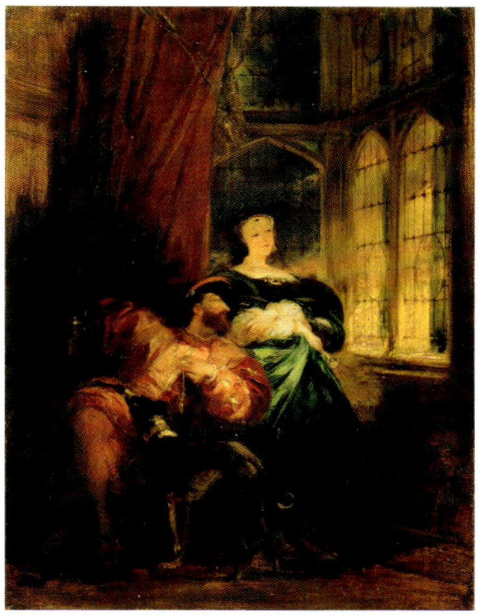

It is easily demonstrated that Bonington's approach to oil painting was intensely conditioned by his training and skills as a watercolorist, as he had no formal tuition in the former. It is also clear from Delacroix's diary and correspondence that Bonington's watercolor practice loomed large in the perception of his genius. Undoubtedly this is because watercolor painting, as a vehicle for helping to liberate and perfect technique, for narrowing the gulf separating the first inspiration from material realization, appealed fundamentally to Delacroix's passionate temperament and ambitions. It was his lifelong conviction that "to sketch and finish at the same time, to satisfy the imagination and judgment at one stroke, in the same breath! for a mortal that would be speaking the language of the gods."[23] The organizing principle of Delacroix's mature compositions, namely the simultaneous massing of color, form, and light, was intrinsic to much British watercolor technique through the nineteenth century, especially that of Turner and Bonington. In France, watercolor painting was also a reactionary tool for undermining institutional pedagogy, the hierarchy of genres, and the hierarchy of patronage, which had made the academy, the state, and the church the sole arbiters of taste. Finally, it anticipated one of the most significant characteristics of modernism: the aesthetic self-sufficiency of the very means of representation.

Even a cursory survey of Alfred Robaut's catalogue raisonné would confirm that at no time in Delacroix's long career did he use watercolor, and its corollary brown wash, to more varied ends than during the 1820s (fig. 133). This should not surprise, for the small cabinet picture in oils or watercolors represented a financial windfall for artists in that

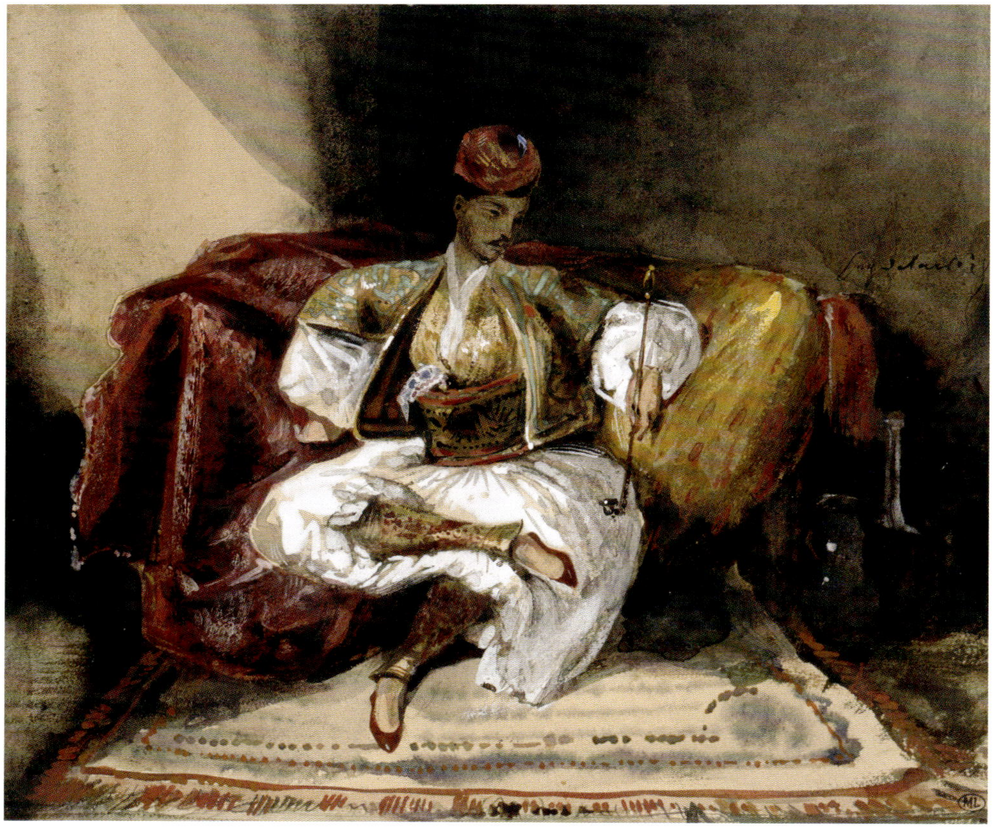

Fig. 133 Eugène Delacroix (1798–1863), *Seated Oriental*, c. 1827–28. Watercolor and gouache over graphite, 17.1 × 20.1 cm. Musée du Louvre, Paris

decade and, in Delacroix's case, a refreshing diversion from his Salon machines. Like Géricault before him, as well as Bonington and others, Delacroix welcomed the opportunity to exploit the new bourgeois audience for finished watercolors, album drawings, and lithographic suites. In fact, he corresponded extensively with Thales Fielding in London on the commercial potential of watercolors, going so far as to request copies of the articles of incorporation for the British Society of Painters in Water Colours in the hopes of founding a similar organization in Paris.[24] Watercolor remained, throughout Delacroix's career, a major weapon in his manifold artistic arsenal. In his most elaborate exercises, he would rival the masterworks of Bonington and prefigure those of Cézanne and Matisse.

Their mutual friend Paul Huet, who also evolved into an accomplished landscape watercolorist (fig. 134), once described Bonington as possessing the genius of "perception and touch" – the remarkable ability to precisely represent, with minimum effort and material, the most moving and varied naturalistic effects. He developed this purity and originality of vision as a watercolorist and then effortlessly transferred those lessons to his work in oils. *A Fisherman on the Banks of a River, a Church Tower in the Distance* of c. 1825–26 (fig. 135), for instance, a work deeply indebted to J. M. W. Turner for both its subject and the richness of its palette, reveals a sky treatment as a progression of blue and orange striations broadly applied and blending gradually into an expanse of yellow at the center and pale blue in the corners, which is identical to that in Bonington's contemporary oils (fig. 136). Indeed, it was Bonington's supreme virtue to be a master, as was Turner, of this technical and visual interplay between watercolor and oil painting, imbuing his oils with the translucency, breadth, and immediacy of touch of his watercolors, and his watercolors with the luminous equivalent of transparent oil glazes and bold gestural marking through the manipulation of gum arabic and opaque gouache, both innovations previously shunned by the watercolor purists in London and Paris. It was a style of painting that would influence artists for decades and even acquire the title of a school, *le Boningtonisme*. Between 1826 and 1828, when they were virtually sharing studios, Bonington and Delacroix and affiliated younger artists, from Paul Huet to Charles Gleyre, with whom most of the Impressionists would later study, explored this new relationship between watercolor and oil painting that had profound ramifications for French art, particularly in the arena of landscape painting.[25]

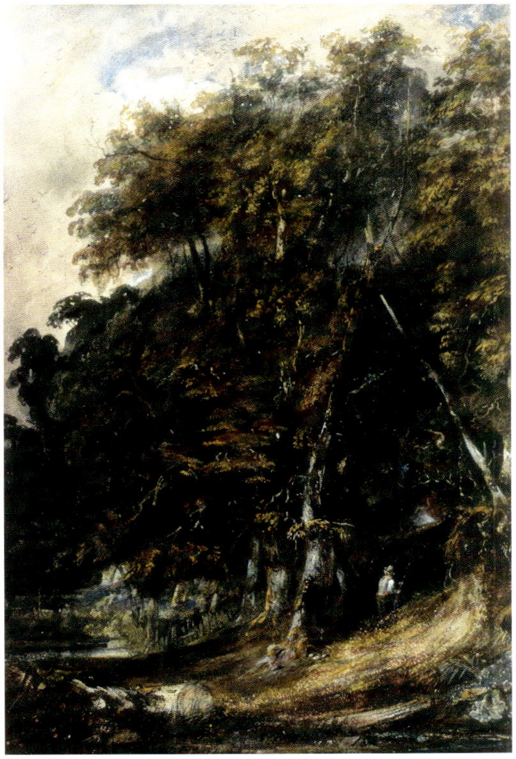

Fig. 134 Paul Huet (1803–1869), *After the Hunt*, c. 1830. Watercolor, gouache, and oil on laid paper, 52.5 × 34.5 cm. Private collection

As English painting was being celebrated at the 1824 Salon, the anglophilic French critic and Bonington patron, Amédée Pichot, was touring the British Isles. In 1825 he published in Paris his *Historical and Literary Tour of a Foreigner in England and Scotland*. In his cogent analysis of British landscape painting, Pichot formulated explicitly, as had Diderot before him and as would Duranty much later, an opposition – political, moral, and aesthetic – between a natural art based on experience and an artificial art generated

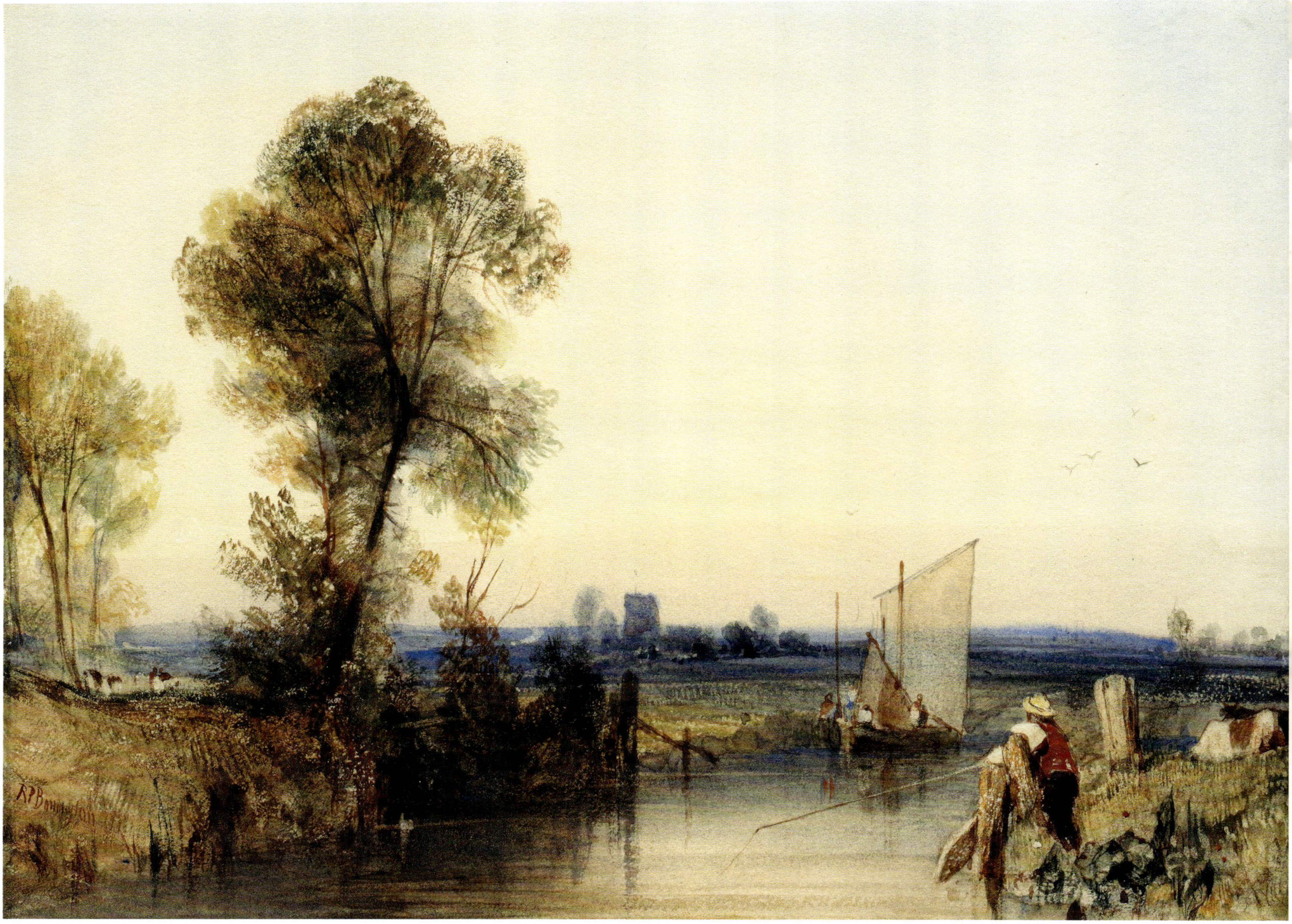

Fig. 135 Richard Parkes Bonington, *A Fisherman on the Banks of a River, a Church Tower in the Distance*, c. 1825–26. Watercolor and gouache, with traces of charcoal, with scraping, on cream wove paper, 17.5 × 23.6 cm (no. 26)

Fig. 136 Richard Parkes Bonington, *View on the Seine–Evening*, 1825. Oil on millboard, 30.5 × 40 cm. Virginia Museum of Fine Arts, Richmond. Gift of Mrs. Lincoln Davis in memory of her son, George Cole Scott, on behalf of the family

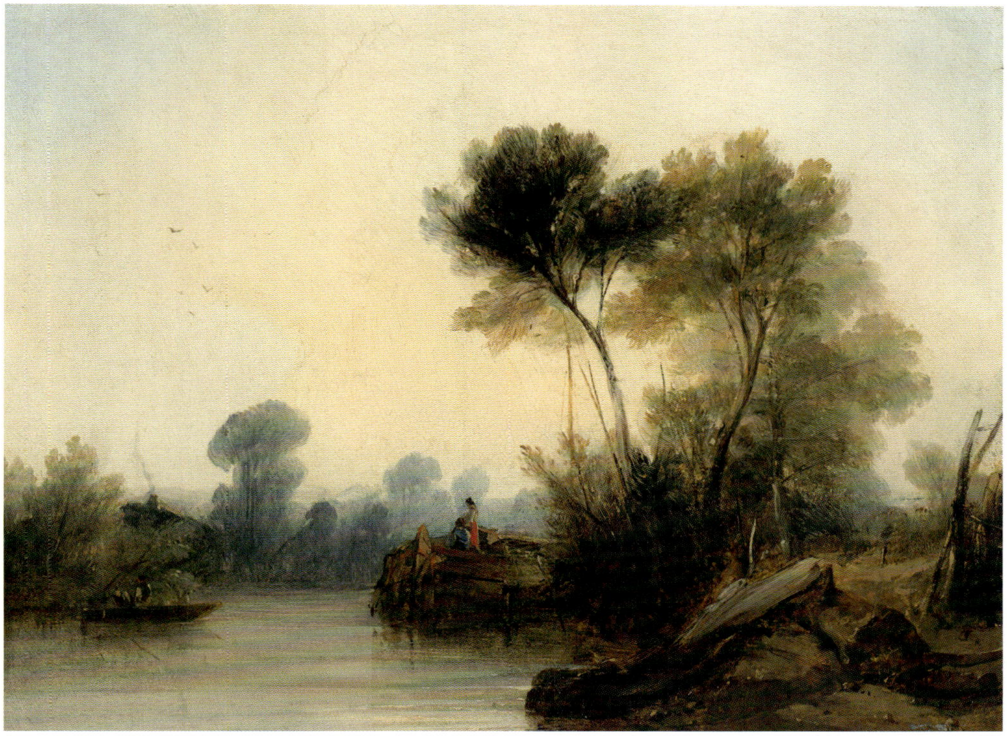

by academies. In Pichot's view, British landscape painters who had struggled, either in oils or watercolors or both, to represent the physical world in its complexity came to understand that world and themselves much better than their French colleagues, who simply regurgitated the tired studio formulas of traditional art or clung desperately to the prejudices of their antecedents and mentors.[26] It would not be an immediate conversion, but eventually the example of the British school – relearning how to see and depict nature, which Delacroix fully absorbed and advanced – would carry the day in the ardent pursuit of color and effect so prized by Duranty's "New Painters." As Cézanne famously put it, "Delacroix's palette is still the most beautiful in France, and I tell you no one under the sky had more charm and pathos combined than he, or more vibration of color. We all paint in his language."[27]

1 Louis Edmond Duranty, *La Nouvelle Peinture, à propos du groupe d'artistes qui expose dans les galleries Durand-Ruel* (Paris: Dentu, 1876).

2 Denis Diderot, *Salons*, ed. Jean Seznec and Jean Adhémar, 3 vols. (Oxford, U.K.: Clarendon Press, 1975–83), 3:241ff.; see also, Philippe Grunchec and Bruno Foucart, *Les Concours d'esquisses peintes, 1816–1863* (Paris: Ecole nationale supérieure des beaux-arts, 1986).

3 Charles Robert Leslie, *Memoirs of the Life of John Constable, Esq., R.A., Composed Chiefly of His Letters* (London: James Carpenter, 1843).

4 Duranty, *La Nouvelle Peinture*, 34–35.

5 In Fantin-Latour's celebrated *Homage à Delacroix (Musée d'Orsay)* of 1864, Duranty is the furthest-left standing figure.

6 As Paul Cézanne stated, "We all paint in his [Delacroix's] language." See *Joachim Gasquet's Cézanne: A Memoir with Conversations*, trans. Christopher Pemberton (London: Thames and Hudson, 1991), 197.

7 Eugène Delacroix, *Journal*, ed. Michèle Hannoosh, 2 vols. (Paris: Librarie José Corti, 2009), 2:1269 (1 March 1859). For an informative overview of Delacroix's pictorial theory, see Petra ten-Doesschate Chu, "A Science and Art at Once; Delacroix's Pictorial Theory and Practice," in *The Cambridge Companion to Delacroix*, ed. Beth S. Wright (New York: Cambridge University Press, 2001), 88ff. The first indication of Delacroix's familiarity with Diderot's critical writings appears in the *Carnet du Dante* (Louvre) of 1820–21, where he transcribes a passage from the *Salon de 1767*; see Delacroix, *Journal*, 2:1440.

8 Delacroix, *Journal*, 2:1652 (*Livres Bleus*, 1844–46).

9 Duranty implied the central importance of the 1820s in his use of Constable. For a thorough discussion of this important period of exchange between France and Great Britain, see Patrick Noon et al., *Crossing the Channel: British and French Painting in the Age of Romanticism* (London: Tate Publishing, 2003).

10 Étienne-Jean Delécluze, "Beaux Arts, Salon de 1833," *Journal des Débats* (1 May 1833): 3.

11 See, in particular, the articles in *L'Artiste* (1834): 175ff. and 298ff.

12 See Patrick Noon, *Richard Parkes Bonington: The Complete Paintings* (New Haven, Conn., and London: Yale University Press, 2008), 118ff.

13 *Correspondance générale d'Eugène Delacroix*, ed. André Joubin, 5 vols., (Paris: Plon, 1935–38), 1:172 (31 January 1826).

14 Théophile Gautier, *Histoire du Romantisme*, 2nd ed. (Paris: Charpentier, 1874), 212.

15 Delacroix, *Journal*, 1:1051.

16 MS letter, Bibliothèque Nationale, Paris, cited in full in Noon, *Richard Parkes Bonington*, 77.

17 "The originality of the painter gives novelty to his subjects. Painting does not always need a subject, etc. The painting of arms and legs by Géricault." Delacroix, *Journal*, 1:1080 (20 January 1857); and "This Géricault fragment is truly sublime.... It is the best argument for the beautiful as it ought to be understood." Ibid., 1120 (5 March 1857).

18 Delacroix, *Journal*, 1:1187 (29 October 1857). See also his comments of 26 May 1858 (Ibid., 1243): "Ingres, who has never known how to compose a subject as presented to him in nature, believes himself comparable to Raphael in aping certain gestures, certain forms which are characteristic of the latter and which have even in Ingres's work a certain grace recalling that of Raphael; but one senses strongly in the last that everything comes from within him and is not strained after."

19 Delacroix, *Journal*, 1:1092–93 (29 January 1857). In the context of a long discussion of Charlet, Delacroix also wrote: "His talent had no dawn. A marvelous facility found itself immediately in the service of an inexhaustible imagination. He had this in common with Bonington, charming talent too soon disappeared"; Ibid., 1182 (29 October 1857).

20 Delacroix, *Journal*, 2:1507 (*Carnet de Rouen*, 1841).

21 Morse Peckham, *The Romantic Virtuoso* (Hanover, N.H.: University Press of New England, 1995), 171.

22 Théophile Gautier, "Eugène Delacroix," *Le Moniteur* (18 November 1864).

23 Quoted in Charles Blanc, *Grammaire des Arts du Dessin*, 2nd ed. (Paris, 1870), 552. For the importance of watercolor in Delacroix's graphic oeuvre, see Maurice Sérullaz et al., *Inventaire Général des Dessins École Française, dessins d'Eugène Delacroix, 1798–1863*, 2 vols. (Paris: Éditions de la Réunion des Musées Nationaux, 1984), 2:14–15.

24 See Lee Johnson and Michèle Hannoosh, eds., *Eugène Delacroix, Nouvelles Lettres* (Bordeaux: William Blake and Co., 2000), 95ff.

25 Again, as Peckham (*The Romantic Virtuoso*, 171) contended: "Delacroix's burst into color, already evident in the paintings of the mid-1820s, and the freedom of his brush, so that the brushstroke itself becomes an emblem or sign of the artist's passion, springs from the examples and impact of Bonington."

26 Amédée Pichot, *Historical and Literary Tour of a Foreigner in England and Scotland*, 2 vols. (London: Saunders and Ottley, 1825), 1:131–32.

27 Pemberton, *Joachim Gasquet's* Cézanne, 197.

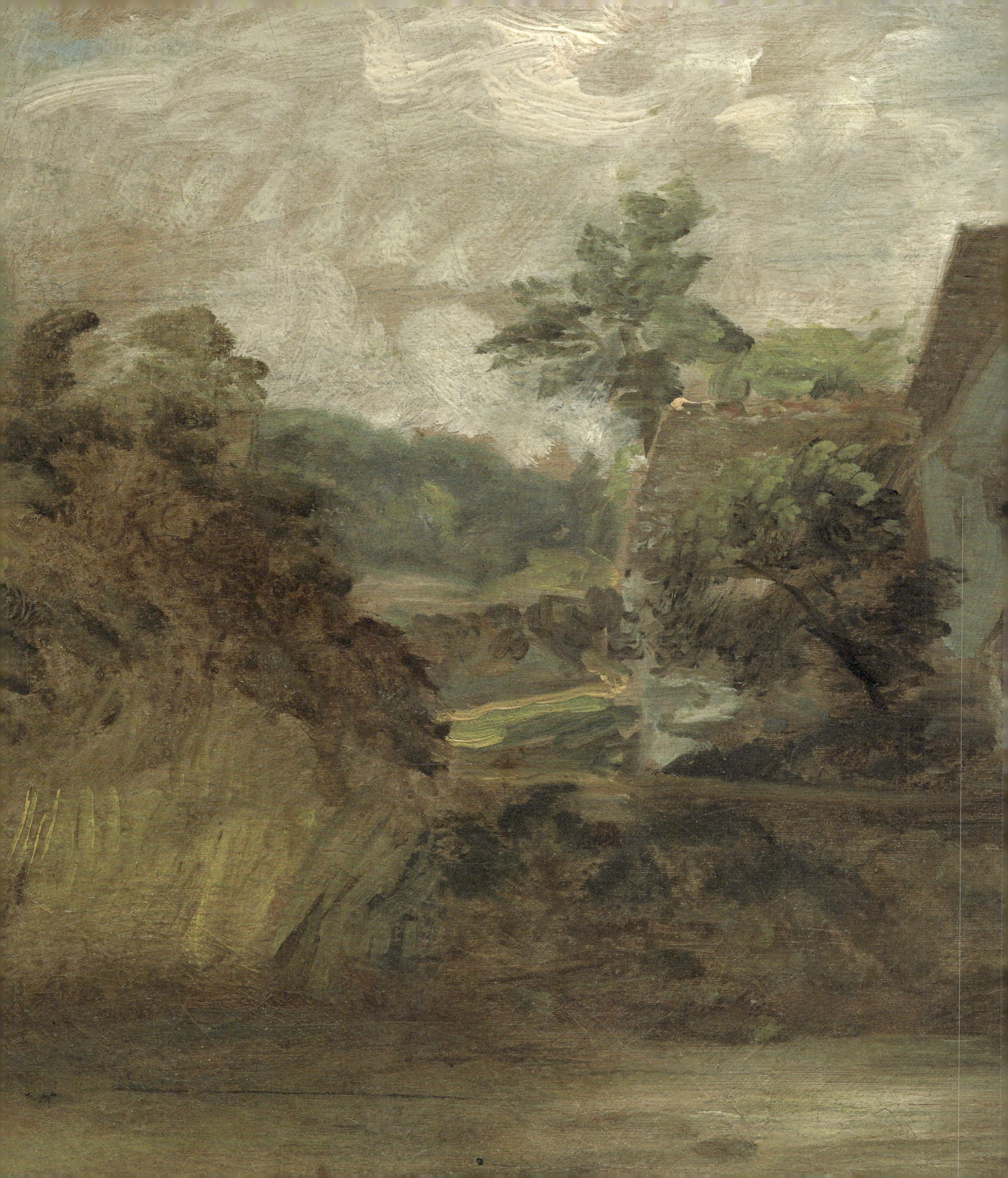

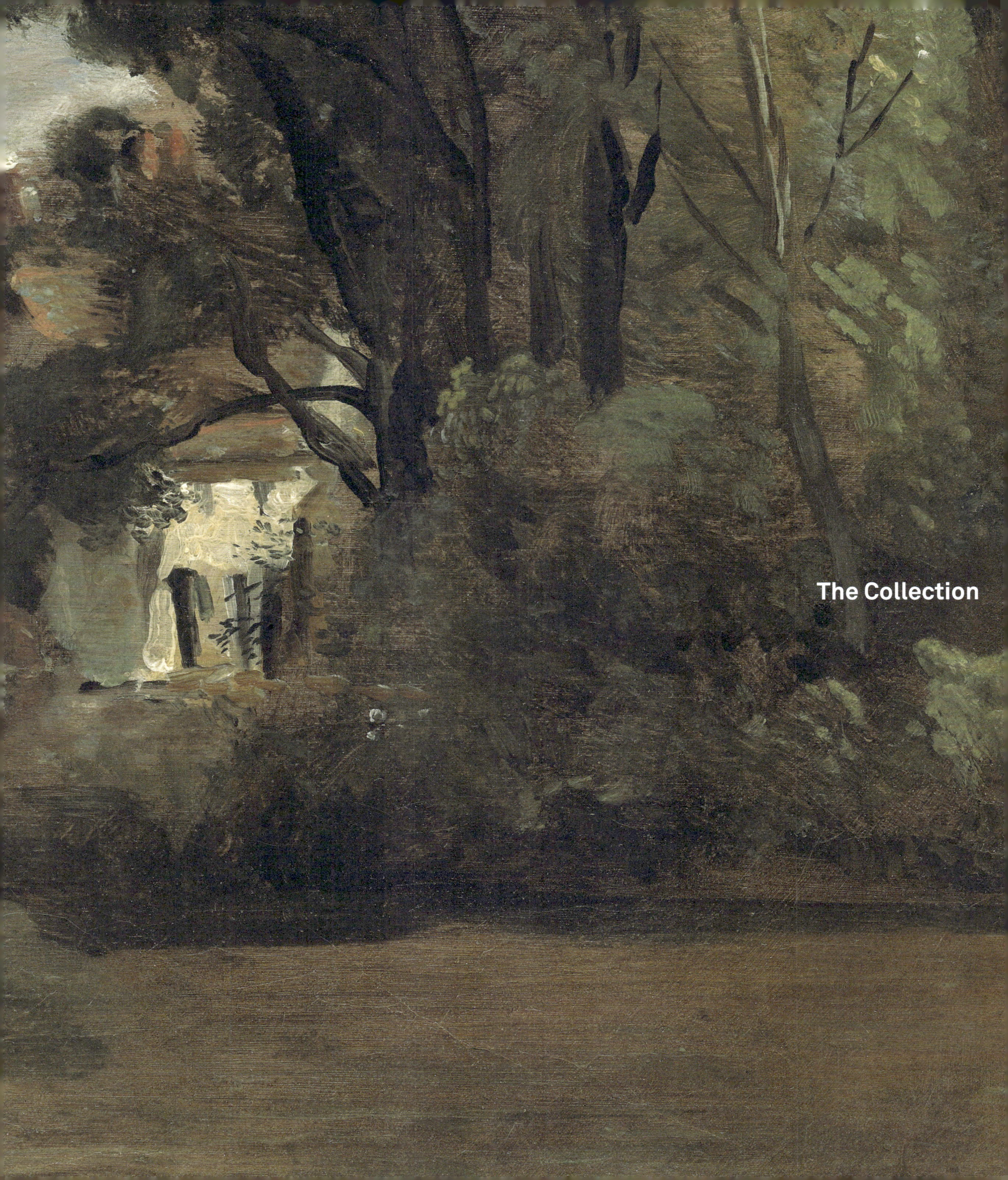

The Collection

List of Works in the Manton Collection

Susannah Blair
and Sarah Hammond

Notes to the Reader

Artists

Artists are listed alphabetically by last name. Unattributed works and works by non-British artists appear at the end of the checklist. The words "style of" encompass followers and students of the artist as well as works that may have been intended to deceive. "After" refers to works that were modeled on extant compositions.

Titles

Titles given by artists are preferred. When an artist's title is not available, we have deferred to historic titles, except in cases where new research has emerged. Foreign titles of works are given in English translation, and all titles have been edited to follow American practices for spelling.

Media

Paper color is listed according to the *Print Council of America Paper Sample Book* (1996). Gum fixatives on Gainsborough drawings are referred to generally, as the sources of the gum may vary. Gums found by conservators at the Williamstown Art Conservation Center include gum tragacanth, almond gum, and gum arabic.

Dimensions

Dimensions are listed in centimeters, height preceding width. Unless otherwise noted, dimensions refer to the primary support of the object.

Catalogues Raisonnés and Abbreviations

In the case that a publication (generally a catalogue raisonné) has become a standard reference for an artist, works by that artist are listed with the corresponding reference number, using the following abbreviations:

B: Binyon, Laurence. *The Engraved Designs of William Blake*. New York: Da Capo Press, 1967.

BJ: Butlin, Martin, and Evelyn Joll. *The Paintings of J. M. W. Turner*. Rev. ed. New Haven, Conn., and London: Yale University Press, 1984.

F: Finberg, A. J. *The History of Turner's Liber Studiorum, with a New Catalogue Raisonné*. London: E. Benn, 1924.

HD: Hayes, John. *The Drawings of Thomas Gainsborough*. 2 vols. New Haven, Conn., and London: Yale University Press, 1971.

HP: Hayes, John. *The Landscape Paintings of Thomas Gainsborough: A Critical Text and Catalogue Raisonné*. Ithaca, N.Y.: Cornell University Press, 1982.

HDS: Hayes, John. "Gainsborough Drawings: A Supplement to the Catalogue Raisonné." *Master Drawings* 21 (1983): 367–91.

L: Lister, Raymond. *Catalogue Raisonné of the Works of Samuel Palmer*. Cambridge, U.K.: Cambridge University Press, 1988.

NP: Noon, Patrick J. *Richard Parkes Bonington: The Complete Paintings*. New Haven, Conn., and London: Yale University Press, 2008.

ND: Noon, Patrick J. *Richard Parkes Bonington: The Complete Drawings*. New Haven, Conn., and London: Yale University Press, 2011.

R: Reynolds, Graham. *The Later Paintings and Drawings of John Constable*. New Haven, Conn., and London: Yale University Press, 1984.

R: Reynolds, Graham. *The Early Paintings and Drawings of John Constable*. New Haven, Conn., and London: Yale University Press, 1996.

W: Wilton, Andrew. *J. M. W. Turner: His Art and Life*. New York: Rizzoli, 1979.

Provenance

Unless otherwise specified, all works are the Gift of the Manton Foundation in memory of Sir Edwin and Lady Manton. The provenance section provides the most complete information currently available about the work's sequence of ownership. In cases where documentation is incomplete, the word "possibly" has been used as an indicator. Distinct owners are separated by semicolons, but if an object was purchased by an intermediary (e.g. Agnew for Manton) we have not listed the intermediate dealer in a separate line. Galleries and dealers are set off in brackets, while auction houses are listed without brackets. Wherever possible, the complete name of the gallery or dealer involved with a sale has been included. An exception to this is the use of "Christie's" to indicate Christie's London; any other location will be noted. Instances where a work was offered for sale but did not sell are not indicated, as ownership remained the same before and after the event. When ownership of a work is passed from one family member to another, the words "by descent" are used. Dates listed provide known dates of ownership; collector life dates have been excluded except where the date of death marks a change in ownership.

Further Reading

More complete information on the oil paintings in the Manton Collection of British Art, including references, exhibition histories, and technical notes, can be found in the forthcoming catalogue *Nineteenth-Century European Paintings at the Sterling and Francine Clark Art Institute*, to be published in the fall of 2012.

James Gubbins Archer-Burton English, 1800–1875

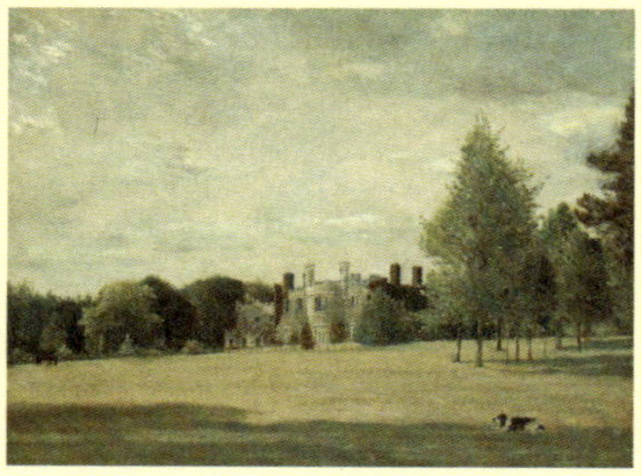

1
Woodlands, Emsworth, Hampshire, c. 1850
Oil on wood-pulp board, 22.8 × 30.3 cm
2007.20.1

Provenance: The artist, given or bequeathed to Archer-Burton; Florence Annie Archer-Burton, later Mrs. George Graves, his niece, by descent, by 1855; Mabel Earle Archer-Burton, Lady Crofton, her sister, by descent; [Newhouse Galleries, Inc., New York, by 1962, sold to Manton, as John Constable, 29 Jan. 1962]; Sir Edwin A. G. Manton, New York (1962–d. 2005); Diana Morton, his daughter, by descent (2005–2007, given to the Clark); Sterling and Francine Clark Art Institute, 2007.

William Blake English, 1757–1827

Illustrations of the Book of Job, 1825
Twenty-two engravings
2007.8.1.1–22 | B105–126

Provenance: Sale, Parke-Bernet Galleries, New York, 13 Mar. 1971, no. 129, sold to Manton; Sir Edwin A. G. Manton, New York (1971–d. 2005); Manton Family Art Foundation (2005–2007, given to the Clark); Sterling and Francine Clark Art Institute, 2007.

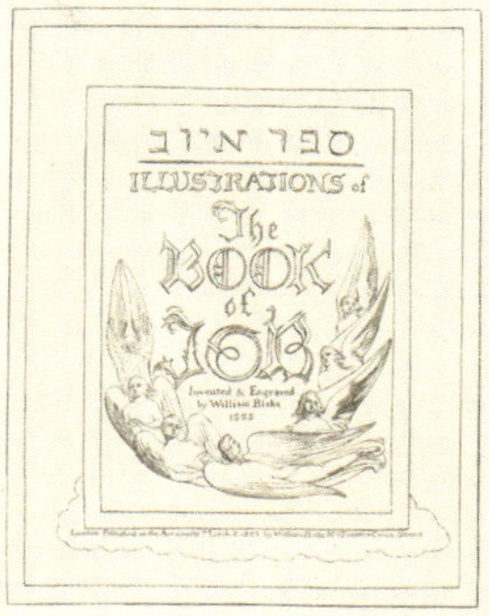

2
Title page, 1825
Engraving on chine collé on cream wove paper, 20.2 × 16 cm (chine); 21.3 × 16.5 cm (plate); 50.6 × 34.2 cm (sheet)
2007.8.1.1 | B105 II/II

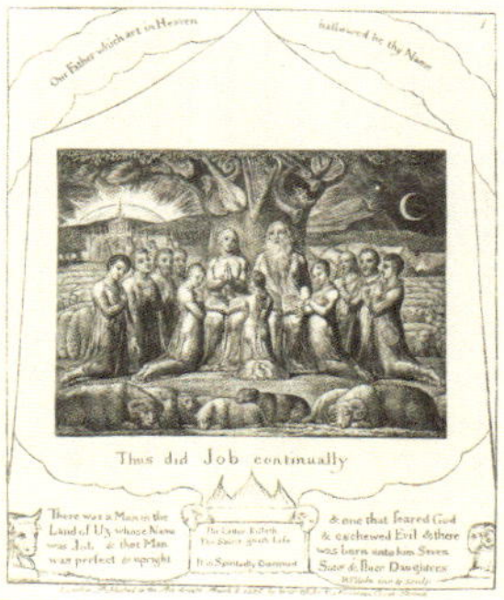

3
Job and His Family, 1825
Engraving on chine collé on cream wove paper, 19.5 × 15.7 cm (chine); 20 × 16.6 cm (plate); 50.1 × 34 cm (sheet)
2007.8.1.2 | B106 II/II

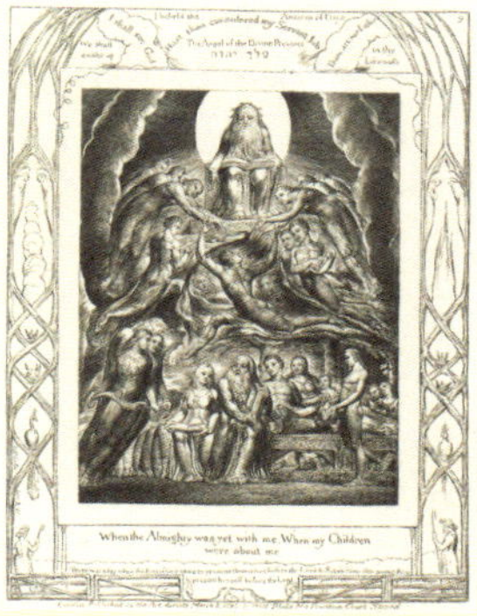

4
Satan before the Throne of God, 1825
Engraving on chine collé on cream wove paper, 20.3 × 15.4 cm (chine); 21.8 × 17 cm (plate); 50.7 × 34.8 cm (sheet)
2007.8.1.3 | B107 IV/IV

William Blake

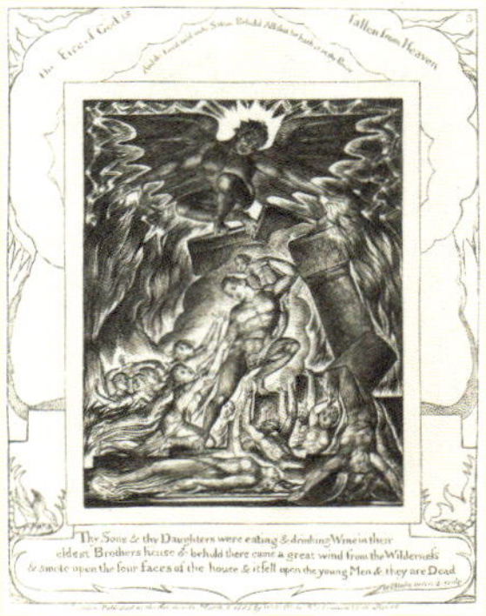

5
The Destruction of Job's Sons, 1825
Engraving on chine collé on cream wove paper, 20.9 × 16.2 cm (chine); 22 × 17.1 cm (plate); 50.2 × 34.4 (sheet)
2007.8.1.4 | B108 III/III

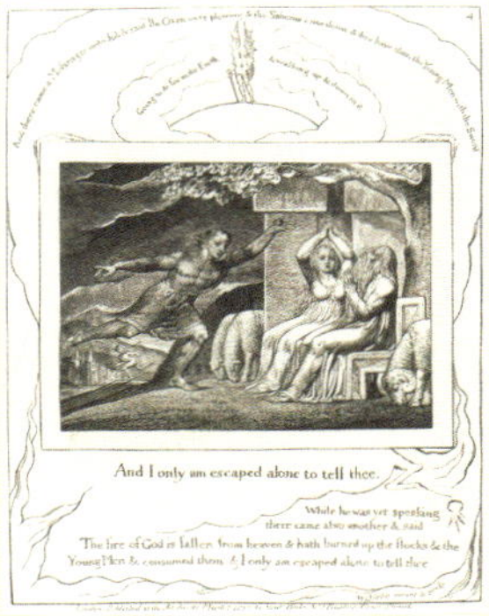

6
The Messengers Tell Job of His Misfortunes, 1825
Engraving on chine collé on cream wove paper, 20.6 × 15.7 cm (chine); 21.8 × 17.1 cm (plate); 50.8 × 34.4 cm (sheet)
2007.8.1.5 | B109 II/II

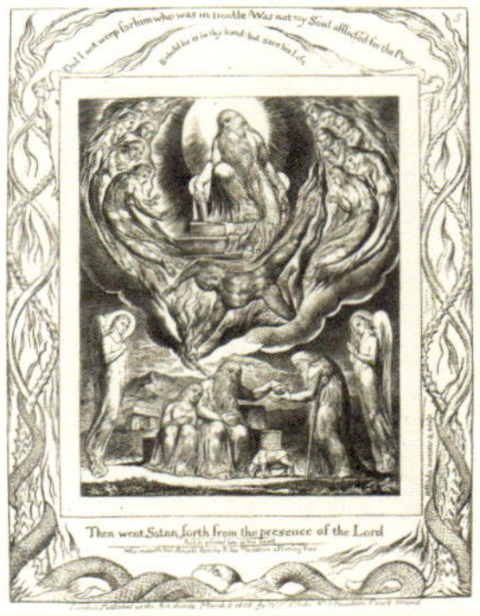

7
Satan Going Forth from the Presence of the Lord, 1825
Engraving on chine collé on cream wove paper, 20.6 × 15.6 cm (chine); 21.8 × 17.1 cm (plate); 50.6 × 34.3 cm (sheet)
2007.8.1.6 | B110 II/III

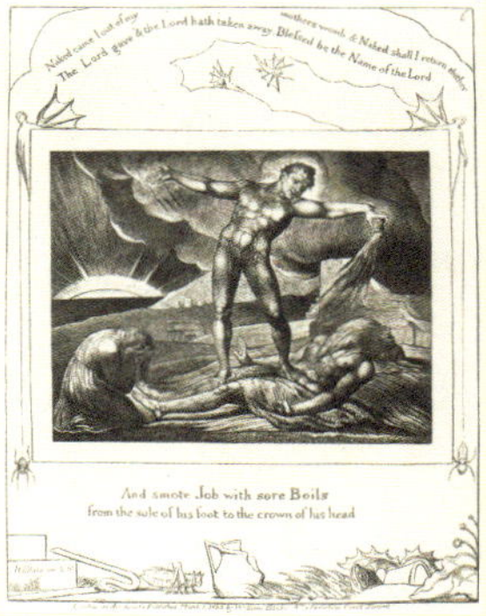

8
Satan Smiting Job with Boils, 1825
Engraving on chine collé on cream wove paper, 20.5 × 15.4 cm (chine); 21.8 × 17.1 cm (plate); 50.6 × 34.4 cm (sheet)
2007.8.1.7 | B111 II/II

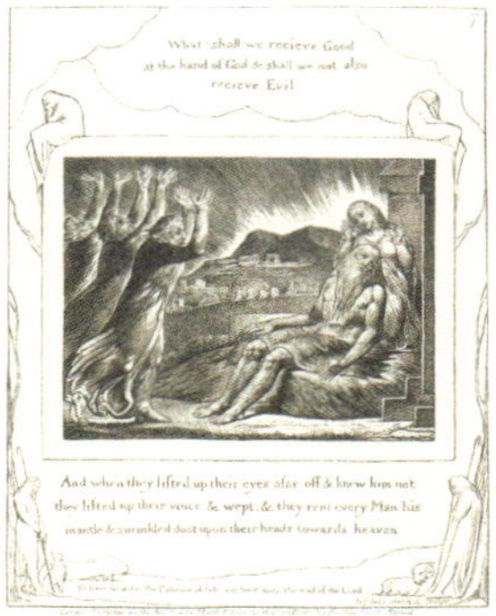

9
Job's Comforters, 1825
Engraving on chine collé on cream wove paper, 20.8 × 15.7 cm (chine); 22 × 17 cm (plate); 50.8 × 34.5 cm (sheet)
2007.8.1.8 | B112 II/II

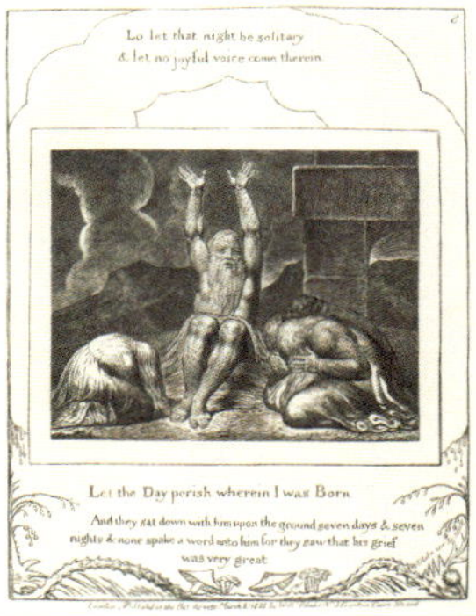

10
Job's Despair, 1825
Engraving on chine collé on cream wove paper, 21 × 16.5 cm (chine); 21.8 × 17 cm (plate); 50.8 × 34 cm (sheet)
2007.8.1.9 | B113 II/II

William Blake

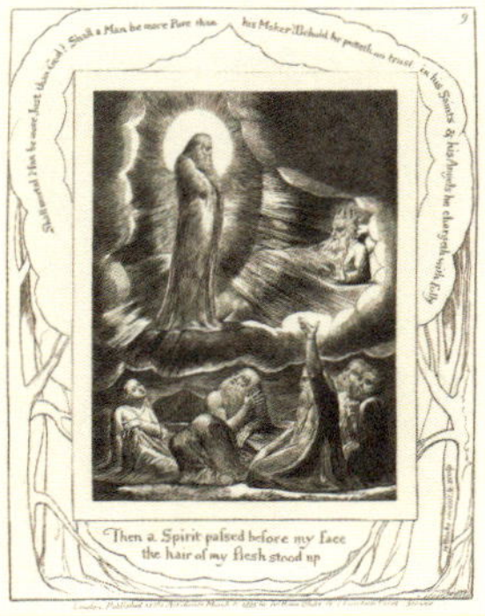

11
The Vision of Eliphaz, 1825
Engraving on chine collé on cream wove paper, 20.2 × 16.2 cm (chine); 21.7 × 17 cm (plate); 50.6 × 34.2 cm (sheet)
2007.8.1.10 | B114 II or III/III

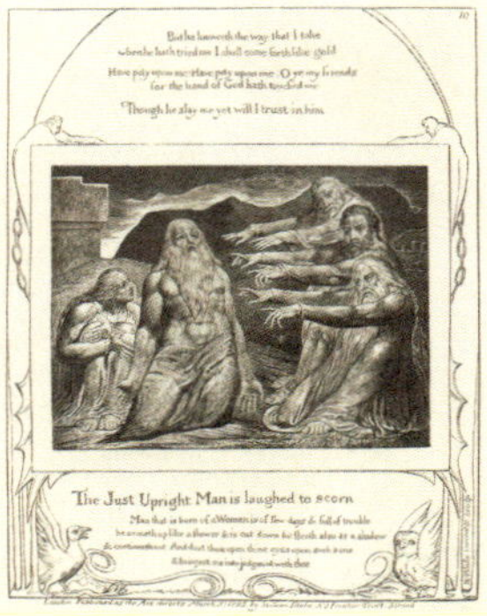

12
Job Rebuked by His Friends, 1825
Engraving on chine collé on cream wove paper, 20.2 × 16.2 cm (chine); 21.9 × 17 cm (plate); 50.8 × 34.5 cm (sheet)
2007.8.1.11 | B115 III/III

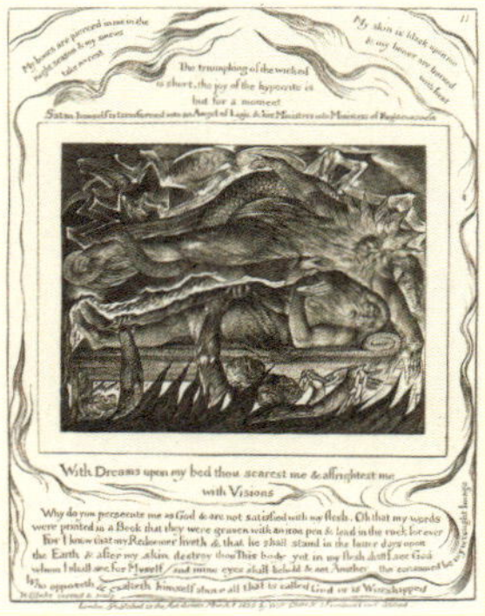

13
Job's Evil Dreams, 1825
Engraving on chine collé on cream wove paper, 21.2 × 16.7 cm (chine); 21.7 × 17.1 cm (plate); 50.8 × 34.2 cm (sheet)
2007.8.1.12 | B116 V/V

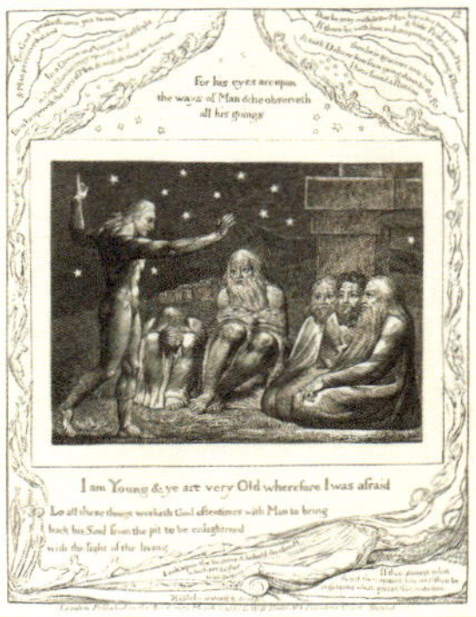

14
The Wrath of Elihu, 1825
Engraving on chine collé on cream wove paper, 20.7 × 16.2 cm (chine); 21.9 × 16.8 cm (plate); 50.8 × 34.5 cm (sheet)
2007.8.1.13 | B117 II/II

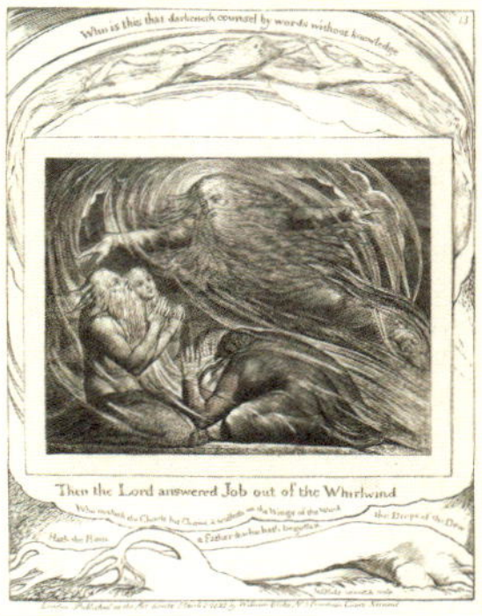

15
The Lord Answering Job out of the Whirlwind, 1825
Engraving on chine collé on cream wove paper, 20.6 × 15.7 cm (chine); 21.8 × 17 cm (plate); 51.2 × 34.5 cm (sheet)
2007.8.1.14 | B118 II/II

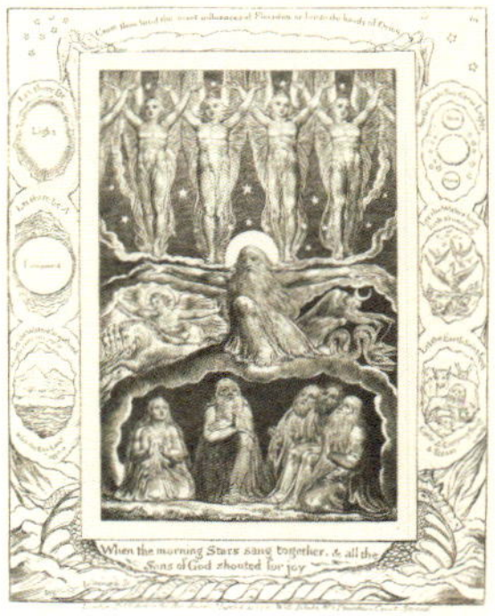

16
The Creation, 1825
Engraving on chine collé on cream wove paper, 20.3 × 15.6 cm (chine); 21.8 × 16.5 cm (plate); 50.8 × 34.5 cm (sheet)
2007.8.1.15 | B119 III/III

William Blake

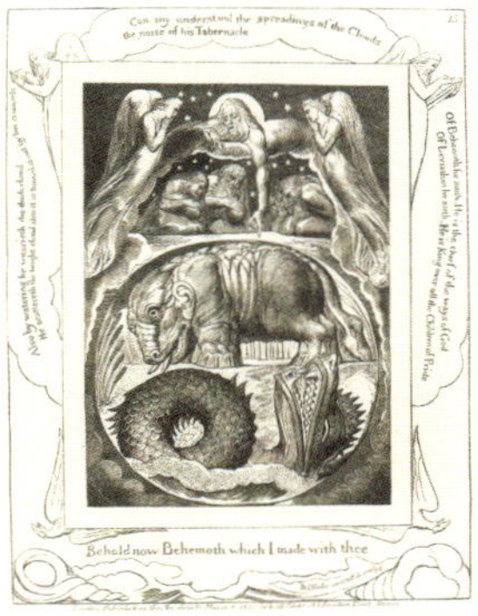

17
Behemoth and Leviathan, 1825
Engraving on chine collé on cream wove paper, 21 × 16.2 cm (chine); 21.8 × 17 cm (plate); 51 × 34.5 cm (sheet)
2007.8.1.16 | B120 II/II

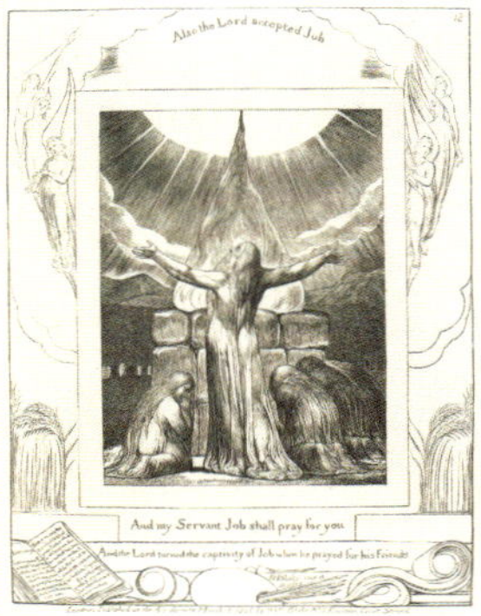

20
Job's Sons and Daughters Overwhelmed by Satan, 1825
Engraving on chine collé on cream wove paper, 21 × 16.2 cm (chine); 22 × 17.2 cm (plate); 50.4 × 34.7 cm (sheet)
2007.8.1.19 | B123 III/III

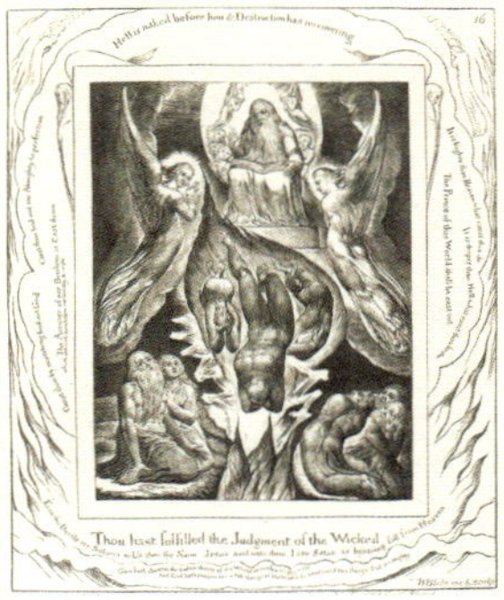

18
The Fall of Satan, 1825
Engraving on chine collé on cream wove paper, 19.6 × 16 cm (chine); 20.2 × 16.4 cm (plate); 50.8 × 34.2 cm (sheet)
2007.8.1.17 | B121 III/III

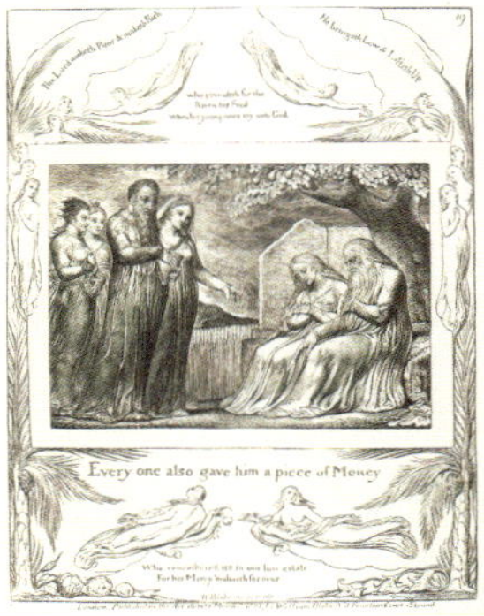

21
Job Accepting Charity, 1825
Engraving on chine collé on cream wove paper, 21 × 15.9 cm (chine); 22 × 17 cm (plate); 50.8 × 34.3 cm (sheet)
2007.8.1.20 | B124 IV/IV

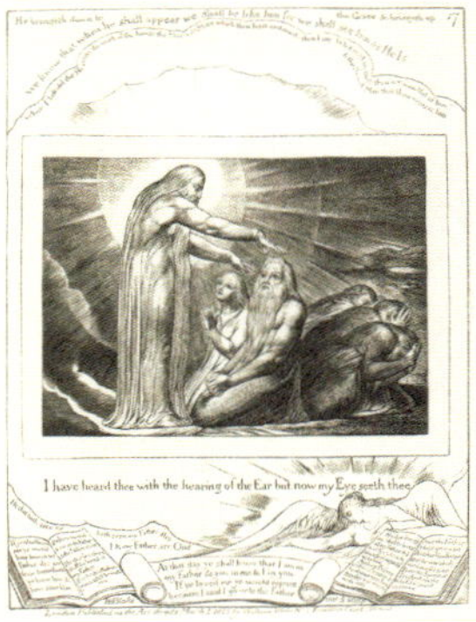

19
The Vision of God, 1825
Engraving on chine collé on cream wove paper, 21 × 16 cm (chine); 22 × 17 cm (plate); 50.5 × 34.5 cm (sheet)
2007.8.1.18 | B122 II/II

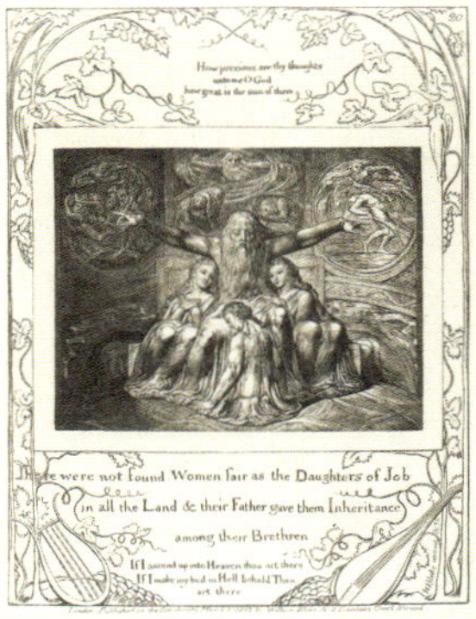

22
Job and His Daughters, 1825
Engraving on chine collé on cream wove paper, 21 × 16 cm (chine); 21.9 × 17 cm (plate); 50.5 × 34.5 cm (sheet)
2007.8.1.21 | B125 IV/IV

William Blake

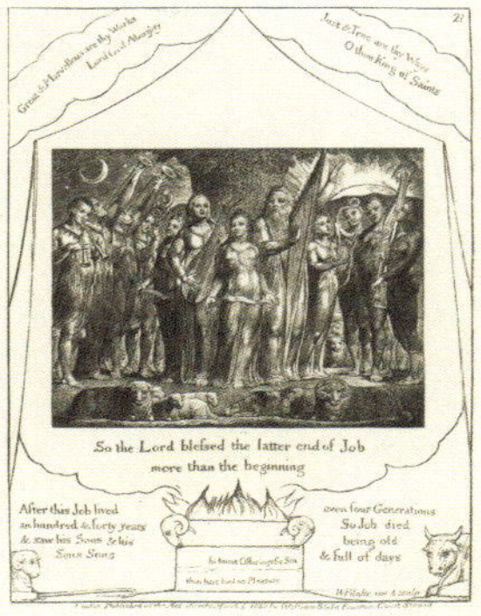

23
Job and His Wife Restored to Prosperity, 1825
Engraving on chine collé on cream wove paper, 21 × 18.1 cm (chine); 16.9 × 11.8 cm (plate); 50.9 × 34 cm (sheet)
2007.8.1.22 | B126 II or III/III

Richard Parkes Bonington English, 1801–1828

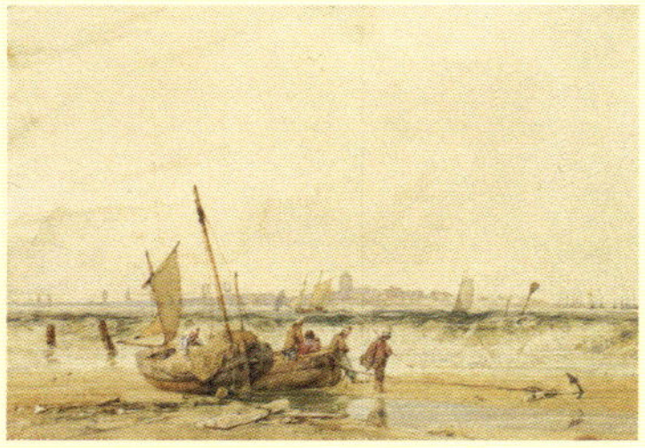

24
Le Crotoy, c. 1823
Watercolor, with scraping, on cream wove paper, 20.2 x 27.5 cm
2007.8.2 | NP75

Provenance: Sir Cuthbert Quilter; sale, Christie's, London, 28 June 1926, no. 82, sold to Davis; S. C. Davis; Walter Horace Samuel, 2nd Viscount Bearsted; Marcus Richard Samuel, 3rd Viscount Bearsted, probably by descent; Peter Montefiori Samuel, 4th Viscount Bearsted, probably by descent; Nicholas Alan Samuel, 5th Viscount Bearsted, probably by descent (1996–1997); sale, Christie's, London, 8 Apr. 1997, no. 63, sold to Ackermann & Johnson, London, as agent for Manton; Sir Edwin A. G. Manton, New York (1997–d. 2005); Manton Family Art Foundation (2005–2007, given to the Clark); Sterling and Francine Clark Art Institute, 2007.

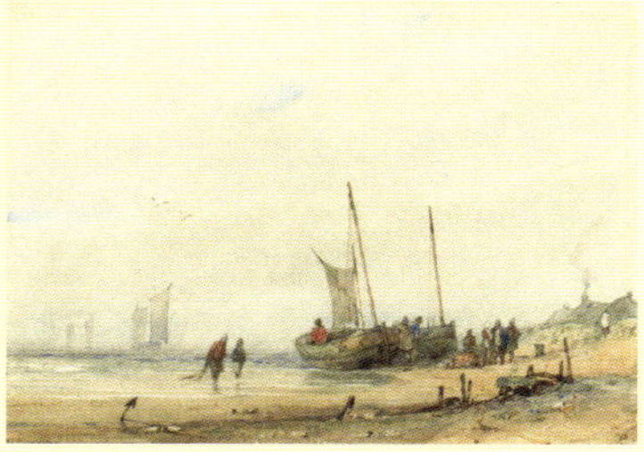

25
Coast with Beached Boats and Figures, c. 1823–24
Watercolor over graphite, with scraping, on cream wove paper, 15.2 x 21 cm
2007.8.3 | NP88

Provenance: The artist; sold or given to Madame Benjamin Delessert; Jean-Louis Lemerle, by descent; sale, Palais d'Orsay, Paris, 30 Nov. 1978, sold to Spink; [Spink & Son, Ltd., London, 1978–1979, no. K3 6832, sold to Manton, May 1979]; Sir Edwin A. G. Manton, New York (1979–d. 2005); Manton Family Art Foundation (2005–2007, given to the Clark); Sterling and Francine Clark Art Institute, 2007.

Richard Parkes Bonington

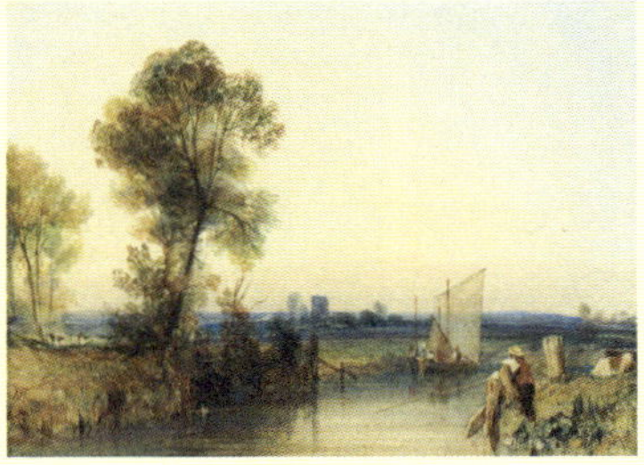

26
A Fisherman on the Banks of a River, a Church Tower in the Distance, c. 1825–26
Watercolor and gouache, with traces of charcoal, with scraping, on cream wove paper, 17.5 × 23.6 cm
2007.8.5 | NP139

Provenance: Possibly Lewis Brown, sale, Paris, 7 Mar. 1843, lot 25, sold to Odier; Sir Ernest R. Debenham; Dr. H. A. C. Gregory; C. R. N. Routh; Dr. William Brockbank (by 1951); sale, Sotheby's, London, 11 Nov. 1982, no. 168, sold to Leger Galleries, as agent for Manton; Sir Edwin A. G. Manton, New York (1983–d. 2005); Manton Family Art Foundation (2005–2007, given to the Clark); Sterling and Francine Clark Art Institute, 2007.

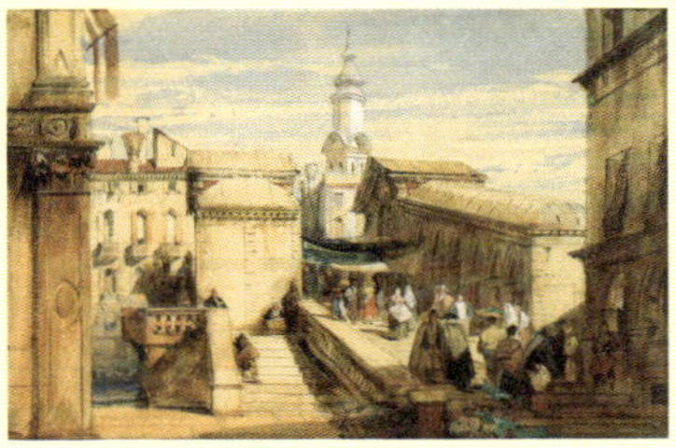

27
The Rialto, Venice, c. 1827
Watercolor and gouache, with gum arabic, on cream wove paper, 18.1 × 26.7 cm
2007.8.6 | NP248

Provenance: Possibly Lewis Brown, sale, Paris, 17 Apr. 1837, no. 69, sold to Hibbert; George Hibbert, sold to Agnew's; [Thomas Agnew and Sons, Ltd., London]; J. Knowles (possibly sold to Heugh, 1865); J. Heugh (1865–1878, sale, Christie's, London, 10 May 1878, no. 4, sold to Agnew's); [Thomas Agnew and Sons, Ltd., London, in 1878, sold to Hollingsworth]; A. T. Hollingsworth, sale, Christie's, London, 11 Mar. 1882, no. 53, sold to MacLean; MacLean; H. de Zoete, sale, Christie's, London, 8 May 1885, no. 7, sold to McLean; McLean (in 1885); E. V. Sturdy, sold to Leggatt, 23 Mar. 1960; [Leggatt Brothers Gallery, Mar.–June 1960, sold to Manton, June 1960]; Sir Edwin A. G. Manton, New York (1960–d. 2005); Manton Family Art Foundation (2005–2007, given to the Clark); Sterling and Francine Clark Art Institute, 2007.

Attributed to Richard Parkes Bonington

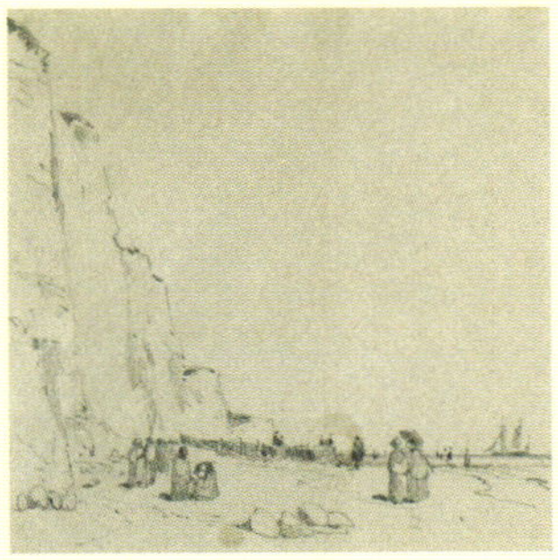

28
Ramsgate Looking East toward Broadstairs, c. 1824
Graphite on gray wove paper, 14.6 x 14.3 cm
2007.8.4 | ND351

Provenance: Possibly John Henderson or John Henderson Jr.; if the latter (his sale, Christie's, London, 16 Feb. 1882, no. 38, sold to Sewening); Norman D. Newall (his sale, Christie's, London, 14 Dec. 1979, no. 92, sold to Spink & Son, Ltd., London, as agent for Manton); Sir Edwin A. G. Manton, New York (1979–d. 2005); Manton Family Art Foundation (2005–2007, given to the Clark); Sterling and Francine Clark Art Institute, 2007.

Hercules Brabazon Brabazon English, 1821–1906

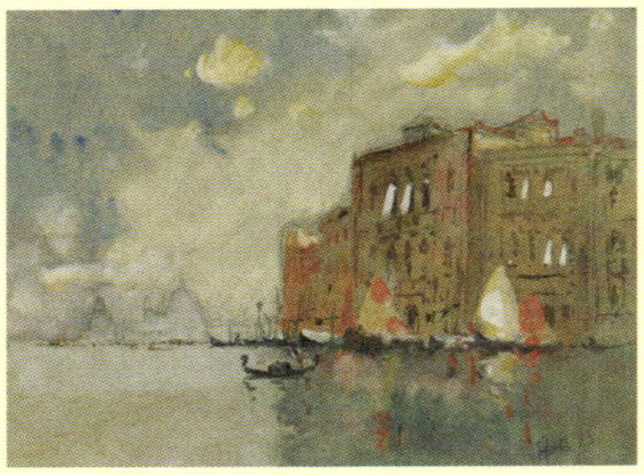

29
On the Grand Canal with Santa Maria della Salute in the Distance, c. 1890
Watercolor and gouache with graphite on blue-gray wove paper, 16.4 × 21.1 cm
2007.8.7

Provenance: [Spink and Son, Ltd., London, sold to Manton, June 1975]; Sir Edwin A. G. Manton, New York (1975–d. 2005); Manton Family Art Foundation (2005–2007, given to the Clark); Sterling and Francine Clark Art Institute, 2007.

Thomas Churchyard English, 1798–1865

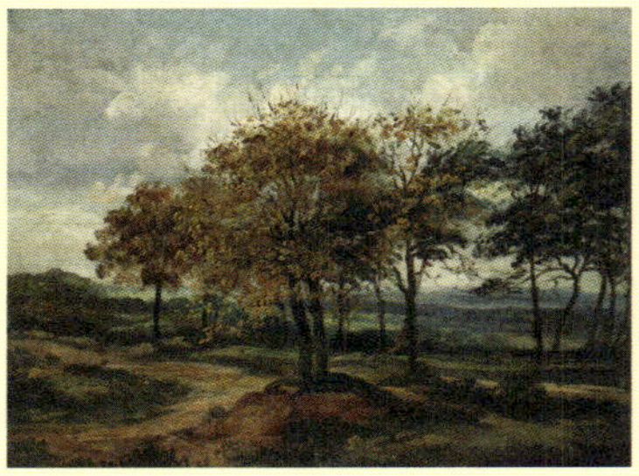

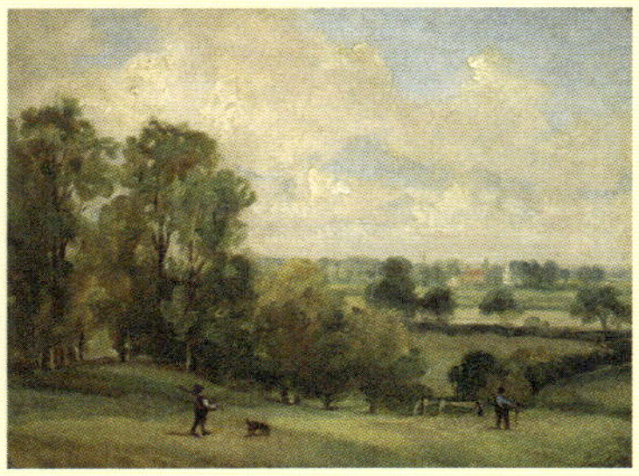

30
River Valley (recto); *Wooded Landscape* (verso), after 1830
Oil on wood-pulp board, 17.7 × 22.9 cm
2007.8.8

Provenance: [Ernest Leggatt, London, given to Johnson, 1899]; [Percy Johnson, London, from 1899]; Oscar Johnson, London, his son, by descent (d. 1965); [Peter Johnson, London, his son, by descent, sold to Oscar & Peter Johnson, Ltd., London, Feb. 1979, as agent for Manton, as John Constable]; Sir Edwin A. G. Manton, London (1979–d. 2005); Manton Family Art Foundation (2005–2007, given to the Clark); Sterling and Francine Clark Art Institute, 2007.

Attributed to Thomas Churchyard

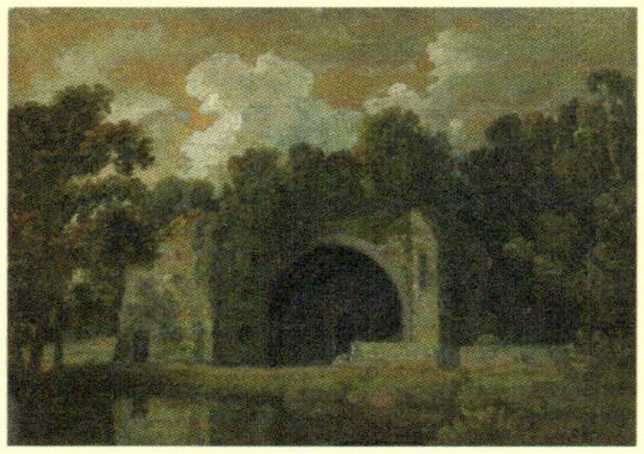

31
Ruins in a Landscape, c. 1840
Oil on beige laid paper, lined with Japanese tissue, 11 × 15.3 cm
2007.20.2

Provenance: Sir Edwin A. G. Manton, New York (d. 2005); Diana Morton, his daughter, by descent (2005–2007), given to the Clark; Sterling and Francine Clark Art Institute, 2007.

John Constable English, 1776–1837

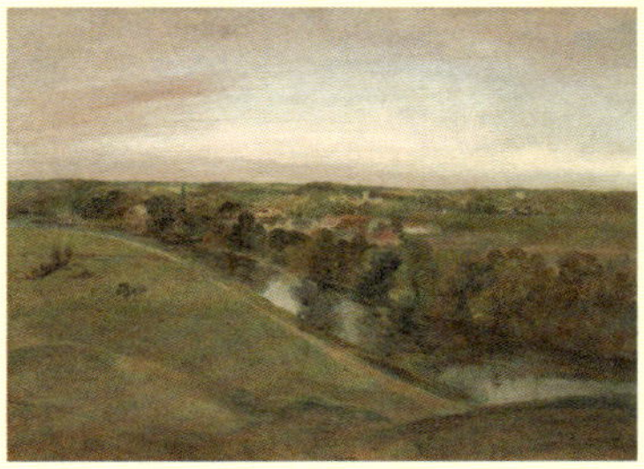

32
Stratford Saint Mary from the Coombs, c. 1800
Oil on canvas, 48.5 × 65.1 cm
2007.8.9 | R00.17

Provenance: Thomas Churchyard, perhaps in Churchyard's later sale, B. Moulton, Woodbridge, 26 Mar. 1866, no. 67, sold to Pearce; The Shipping Federation, London, given to Devitt; Thomas Land Devitt (1914–d. 1923); Miss Devitt, his daughter, by descent (from 1923); sale, Sotheby's, London, 20 Nov. 1985, no. 82; Elmerside, Ltd.; private collection, England; [Salander-O'Reilly Galleries, New York, sold to Manton, 9 June 1999]; Sir Edwin A. G. Manton, New York (1999–d. 2005); Manton Family Art Foundation (2005–2007, given to the Clark); Sterling and Francine Clark Art Institute, 2007.

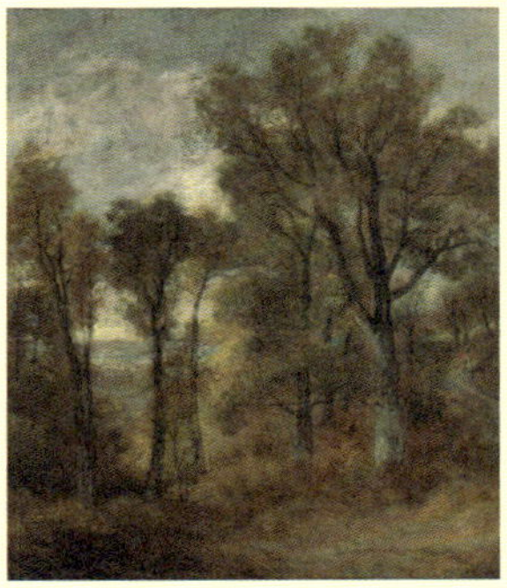

33
Woodland Scene Overlooking Dedham Vale, c. 1802–3
Oil on canvas, 77 × 65 cm
2007.8.10 | R03.59

Provenance: John Palmer, London; possibly F. J. Armitage; sale, Sotheby's, 1970s, sold to Dallas; [David Dallas, England]; [Deborah Gage (Works of Art), Ltd., London, sold to Manton, 22 Oct. 1993]; Sir Edwin A. G. Manton (1993–d. 2005); Manton Family Art Foundation (2005–2007, given to the Clark); Sterling and Francine Clark Art Institute, 2007.

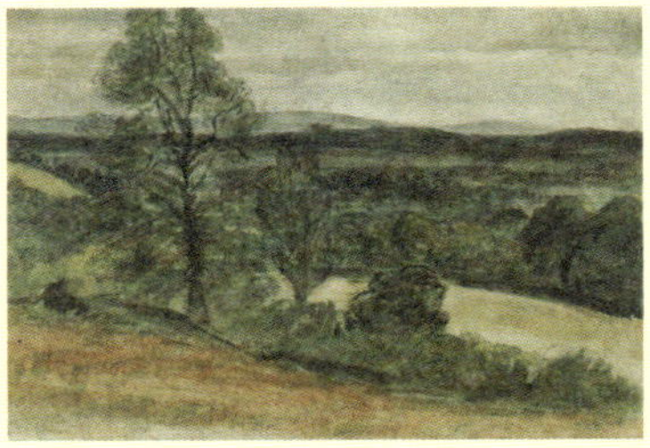

34
A View at Hursley, Hampshire, 1804
Watercolor with gouache and black chalk on white wove paper, 14.2 × 20.3 cm
2007.8.11 | R04.6

Provenance: Eustace Constable, probably by descent, sale, Christie's, London, 16 Apr. 1896, no. 33; Isaac (by 1896); Carlos Peacock, sale, Sotheby's, London, 11 Apr. 1991, no. 40, sold to The Gallery Downstairs; The Gallery Downstairs (in 1991); sale, Christie's, London, 7 Apr. 1998, no. 34, sold to Ackermann & Johnson, London, as agent for Manton; Sir Edwin A. G. Manton, New York (1998–d. 2005); Manton Family Art Foundation (2005–2007, given to the Clark); Sterling and Francine Clark Art Institute, 2007.

John Constable

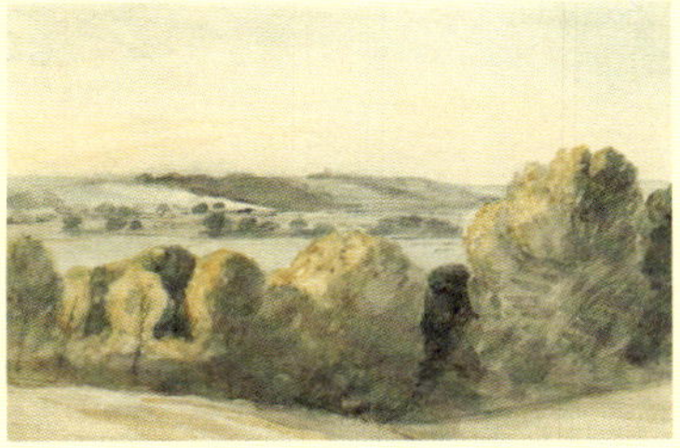

35
Dedham Vale, 1805
Watercolor and graphite on white wove paper, 15.5 × 22.6 cm
2007.8.12 | R05.25

Provenance: Suzanne Beadle, sale, Christie's, London, 15 June 1982, no. 100, sold to Phillips; John Phillips (in 1982, sold to Wyld); [Andrew Wyld, London, by 1985, no. K3 8832, sold to Spink, May 1985]; [Spink & Son, Ltd., London, 1985–1986, sold to Manton, Apr. 1986]; Sir Edwin A. G. Manton (1986–d. 2005); Manton Family Art Foundation (2005–2007, given to the Clark); Sterling and Francine Clark Art Institute, 2007.

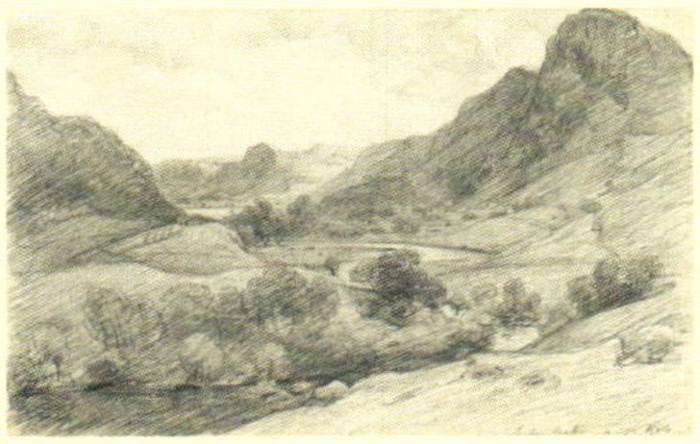

36
Leathes Water (Thirlmere), 19 Sept. 1806
Graphite on cream wove paper, 25.1 × 38.8 cm
2007.8.13 | R06.197

Provenance: Samuel Bostock; John Bostock, by descent; private collection, by descent, sale, Sotheby's, London, 9 Nov. 1995, no. 62, sold to Leger; [Leger Galleries, London, 1995–1996, sold to Manton, Jan. 1996]; Sir Edwin A. G. Manton, New York (1996–d. 2005); Manton Family Art Foundation (2005–2007, given to the Clark); Sterling and Francine Clark Art Institute, 2007.

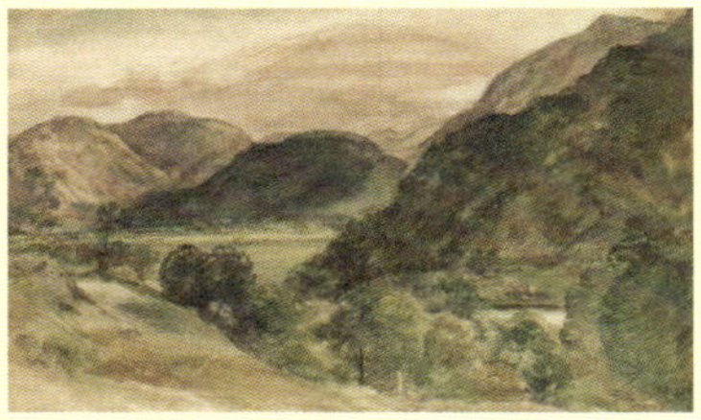

37
Borrowdale, 1806
Watercolor over graphite on cream wove paper, 28 × 46 cm
2007.8.14 | R06.256

Provenance: Sir Thomas Barlow; sale, Bonhams, London, 11 June 1997, no. 32, sold to Spink; [Spink-Leger Pictures, London, 1997–1998, sold to Manton, Feb. 1998]; Sir Edwin A. G. Manton, New York (1998–d. 2005); Manton Family Art Foundation (2005–2007, given to the Clark); Sterling and Francine Clark Art Institute, 2007.

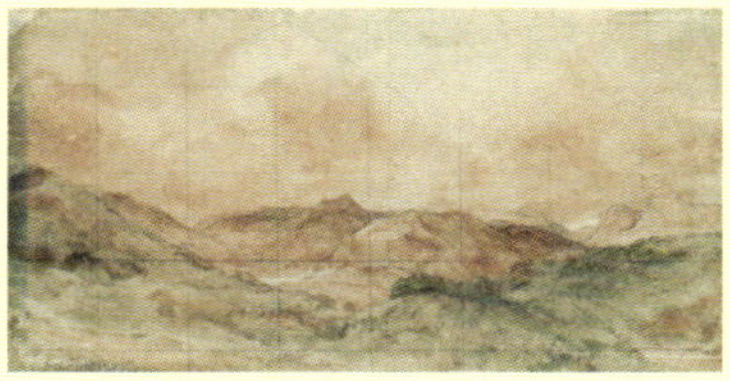

38
Bow Fell and Langdale Pikes, 1806
Watercolor and graphite, squared for transfer, on white laid paper, 20.3 × 38.8 cm
2007.8.56 | R06.249

Provenance: The artist; Captain Charles Golding Constable, his son, by descent (d. 1879); Constable family, by descent, sold to Salander-O'Reilly; [Salander-O'Reilly Galleries, Inc., New York, sold to Manton, Nov. 2000]; Sir Edwin A. G. Manton, New York (2000–d. 2005); Manton Family Art Foundation (2005–2007, given to the Clark); Sterling and Francine Clark Art Institute, 2007.

John Constable

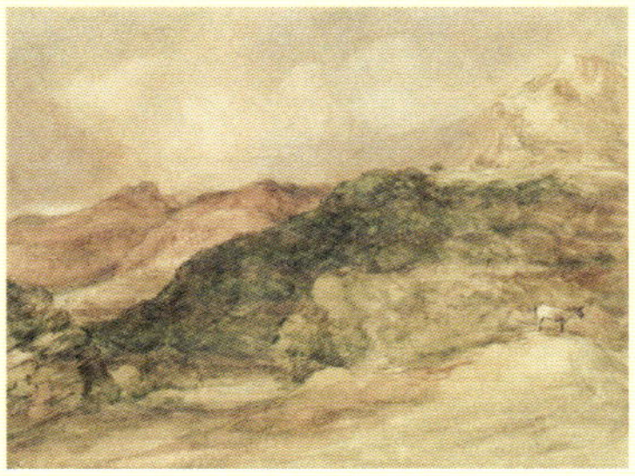

39
Bow Fell and Langdale Pikes, 1806
Watercolor over graphite on beige wove paper, 18.4 × 23.8 cm
2007.8.15 | R06.250

Provenance: Dr. and Mrs. Francis Springell (by 1965); sale, Sotheby's, London, 30 June 1986, no. 92, sold to Salander-O'Reilly; [Salander-O'Reilly Galleries, Inc., New York, 1986–1988, sold to Manton, Apr. 1988; Sir Edwin A. G. Manton, New York (1988–d. 2005); Manton Family Art Foundation (2005–2007, given to the Clark); Sterling and Francine Clark Art Institute, 2007.

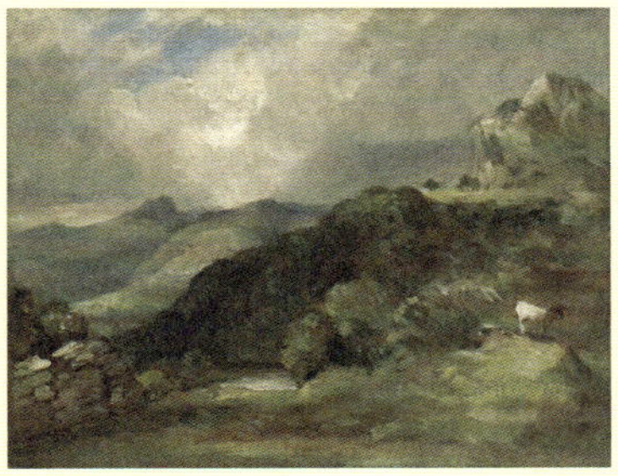

40
Bow Fell, Cumberland, 1807
Oil on canvas, 20.4 × 25.4 cm
2007.8.16 | R07.4

Provenance: The artist (d. 1837); John Hugh Constable, his great-grandson, by descent; Eileen Constable, his widow, by descent (1974–1977); [Spink, London, sold to Manton, 22 Sept. 1977]; Sir Edwin A. G. Manton, New York (1977–d. 2005); Manton Family Art Foundation (2005–2007), given to the Clark, Sterling and Francine Clark Art Institute, 2007.

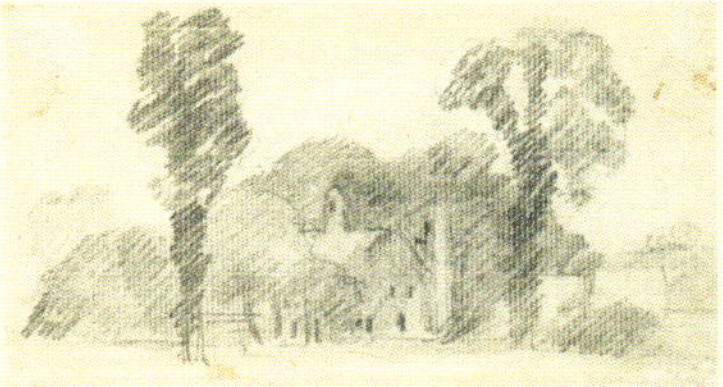

41
A House at Twyford, 1809
Graphite on beige laid paper, 8.3 × 15.1 cm
2007.8.17 | R09.13

Provenance: Sale, Sotheby's, London, 19 Nov. 1987, no. 27; sale, Sotheby's, London, 10 Apr. 1997, no. 22, sold to Ackermann & Johnson, London, as agent for Manton; Sir Edwin A. G. Manton, New York (1997–d. 2005); Manton Family Art Foundation (2005–2007, given to the Clark); Sterling and Francine Clark Art Institute, 2007.

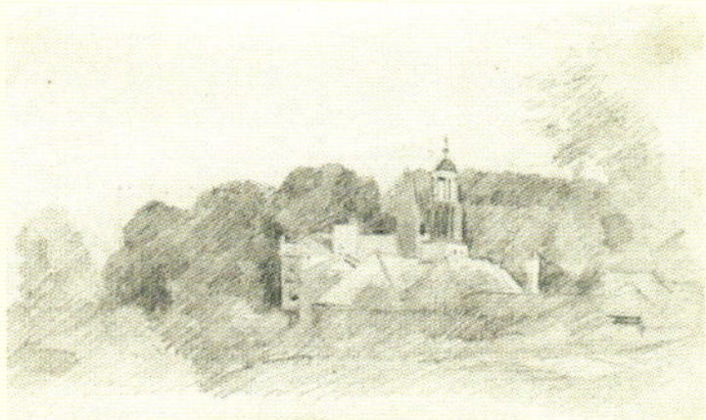

42
A House at Twyford, c. 1809
Graphite on white laid paper, 9.5 × 15.3 cm
2007.8.18 | R09.10

Provenance: Sir J. C. Robinson, sale, Christie's, London, 21 Apr. 1902, no. 80, sold to Reynolds; private collection, sale, Christie's, London, 12 July 1988, no. 9; [Salander-O'Reilly Galleries, Inc., New York, sold to Manton, Jan. 2002]; Sir Edwin A. G. Manton, New York (2002–d. 2005); Manton Family Art Foundation (2005–2007, given to the Clark); Sterling and Francine Clark Art Institute, 2007.

John Constable

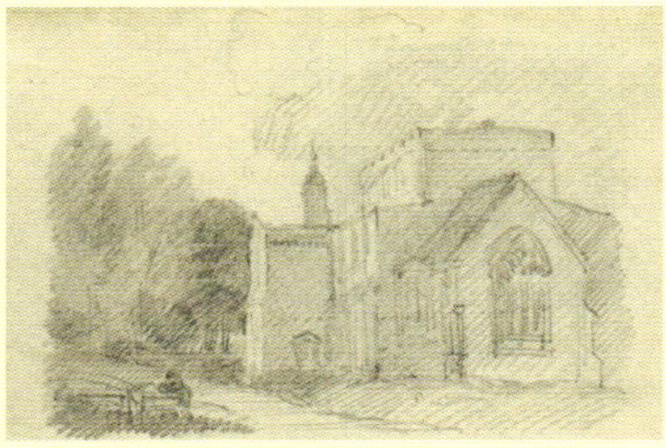

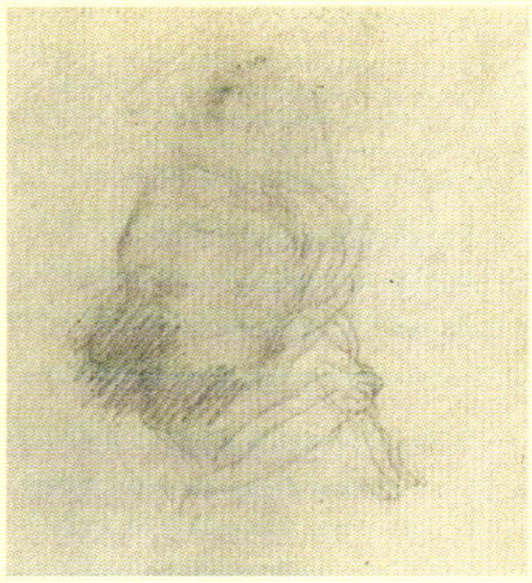

43
East Bergholt Church from the South-East (recto); *A Man's Head in Profile* (verso), c. 1809
Graphite on beige laid paper, 20.2 × 13.2 cm
2007.8.19 | R09.62

Provenance: Sale, Christie's, London, 12 July 1988, no. 7, sold to Oscar & Peter Johnson, Ltd., London, as agent for Manton; Sir Edwin A. G. Manton, New York (1988–d. 2005); Manton Family Art Foundation (2005–2007, given to the Clark); Sterling and Francine Clark Art Institute, 2007.

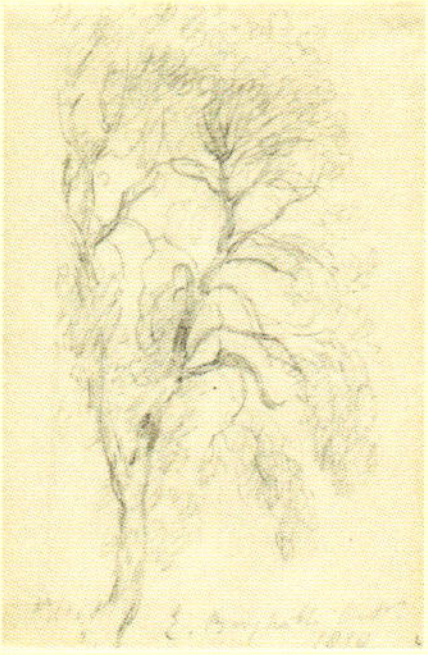

44
Study of an Ash Tree, East Bergholt, October 1810
Black chalk on white laid paper, 17.7 × 11.4 cm
2007.8.20 | R10.7

Provenance: Sale, Christie's, London, 12 July 1988, no. 16, sold to Salander-O'Reilly [Salander-O'Reilly Galleries, Inc., New York, 1988–before 1996, exchanged for a work or works in the collection of Richard Constable]; Richard Constable (before 1996–2001, sold to Deborah Gage [Works of Art], Ltd., London, as agent for Manton, Nov. 2001); Sir Edwin A. G. Manton, New York (2001–d. 2005); Manton Family Art Foundation (2005–2007, given to the Clark); Sterling and Francine Clark Art Institute, 2007.

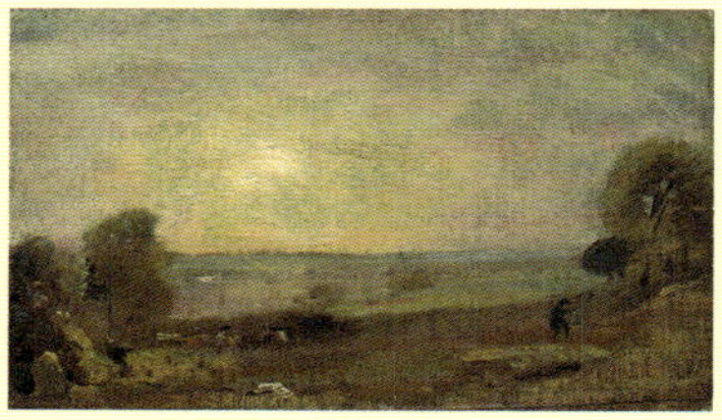

45
Dedham Vale from the Road to East Bergholt: Sunset, 1810
Oil on paper, mounted on board, mounted on panel, 15.4 × 26 cm
2007.8.21 | R11.3

Provenance: [Lloyd and Day, Effingham, Surrey, sold to Manton, 22 June 1983]; Sir Edwin A. G. Manton (1983–d. 2005); Manton Family Art Foundation (2005–2007, given to the Clark); Sterling and Francine Clark Art Institute, 2007.

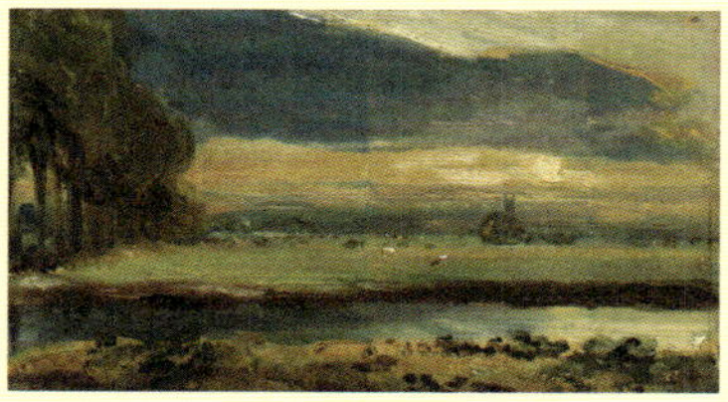

46
Dedham Church from Flatford, c. 1810
Oil on canvas, 10.6 × 19.4 cm
2007.8.22 | R10.60

Provenance: Perhaps Captain Charles Golding Constable, son of the artist (d. 1878); Mrs. A. M. Constable, his widow, by descent (1879–d. 1889, her sale, Christie's, London, 23 June 1890, no. 84, sold to Dowdeswell); [Dowdeswell Gallery, London]; private collection, Boston (1950s); [Deborah Gage (Works of Art), Ltd., London, sold to Manton, 25 Mar. 1993]; Sir Edwin A. G. Manton, New York (1993–d. 2005); Manton Family Art Foundation (2005–2007, given to the Clark); Sterling and Francine Clark Art Institute, 2007.

John Constable

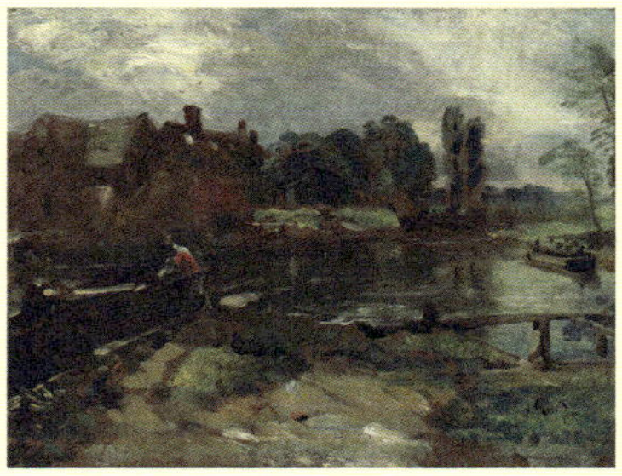

47
Flatford Mill from the Lock, c. 1810
Oil on beige laid (?) paper, mounted on canvas, 19 × 24.1 cm
2007.8.23 | R12.5

Provenance: Ella D. Constable, the artist's granddaughter, by descent; [Spink, London, sold to the Duke of Westminster]; Gerald Grosvenor, 6th Duke of Westminster (1983–at least 1996); [Hazlitt, Gooden & Fox, London, sold to Manton 20 Apr. 2002]; Sir Edwin A. G. Manton, New York (2002–d. 2005); Manton Family Art Foundation (2005–2007, given to the Clark); Sterling and Francine Clark Art Institute, 2007.

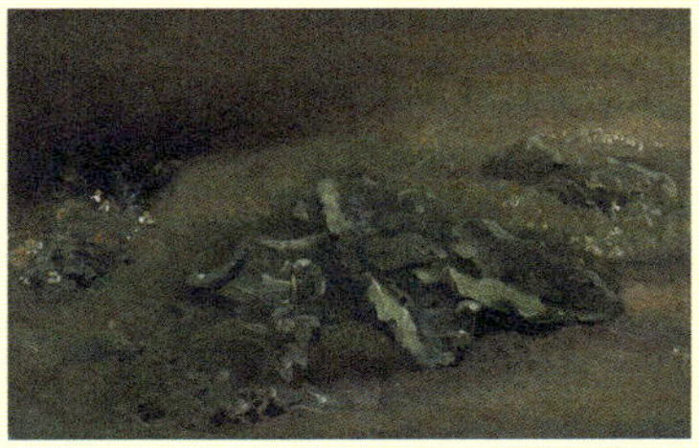

48
Study of a Burdock, c. 1810–14 or 1828
Oil on canvas, mounted on panel, 18.4 × 27.8 cm
2007.8.45 | R28.20

Provenance: Probably Isabel Constable, the artist's daughter, by descent, her sale, Christie's, London, 17 June 1892, possibly no. 240; Thomas J. Barratt (probably 1892–d. 1914); Baron Kohiro Matsukata (c. 1914–c. 1930, sold to private collection); private collection, Japan (c. 1930–1954, sold to Mizushima); Tokuzo Mizushima (1954–1983, sale, Sotheby's, London, 2 Mar. 1983, no. 72); sale, Sotheby's, London, 14 Mar. 1984, no. 103; sale, Christie's, 24 Apr. 1987, no. 49; sale, Christie's, London, 14 July 1994, no. 42, sold to Nahum; [Peter Nahum, London, sold to Manton, 26 Jan. 1996]; Sir Edwin A. G. Manton, New York (1996–d. 2005); Manton Family Art Foundation (2005–2007, given to the Clark); Sterling and Francine Clark Art Institute, 2007.

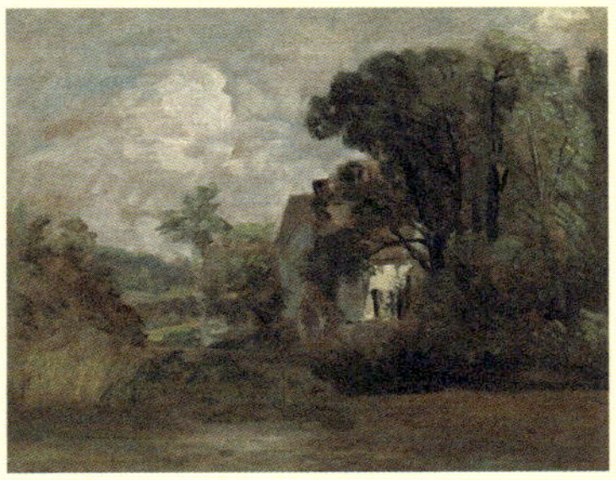

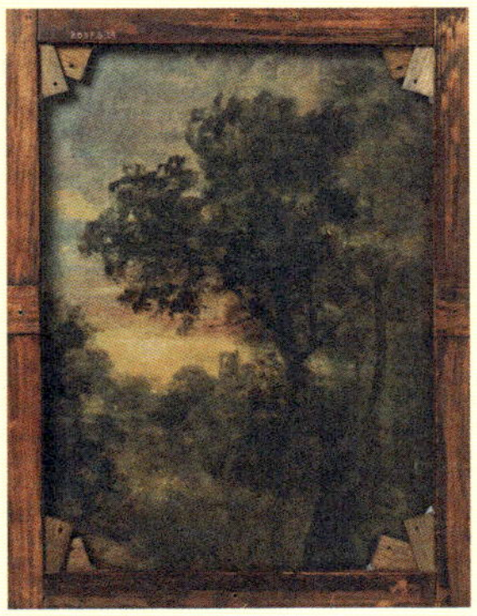

49
Willy Lott's House (recto), c. 1812–13; *Landscape Sketches with Trees and Church Tower* (verso), c. 1811–13
Oil on canvas, 34.9 × 43.5 cm
2007.8.24 | R13.21 (recto); R13.22 (verso)

Provenance: Sale, Sotheby's, London, 25 Sept. 1974, no. 35; private collection, Seattle; [Deborah Gage (Works of Art), Ltd., London, sold to Manton 2 Feb. 1993]; Sir Edwin A. G. Manton (1993–d. 2005); Manton Family Art Foundation (2005–2007, given to the Clark); Sterling and Francine Clark Art Institute, 2007.

John Constable

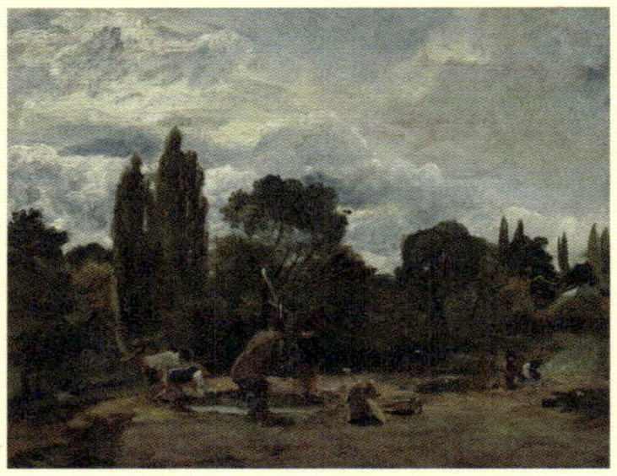

50
Flailing Turnip-heads, East Bergholt, c. 1812–15
Oil on canvas, 35.6 × 44.5 cm
2007.8.25 | R13.26

Provenance: Mr. Carpenter; private collection, London; sale, Sotheby's, London, 12 Mar. 1986, no. 96, sold to Leger; [Leger Galleries, London, sold to Manton, 9 June 1986]; Sir Edwin A. G. Manton, New York (1986–d. 2005); Manton Family Art Foundation (2005–2007, given to the Clark); Sterling and Francine Clark Art Institute, 2007.

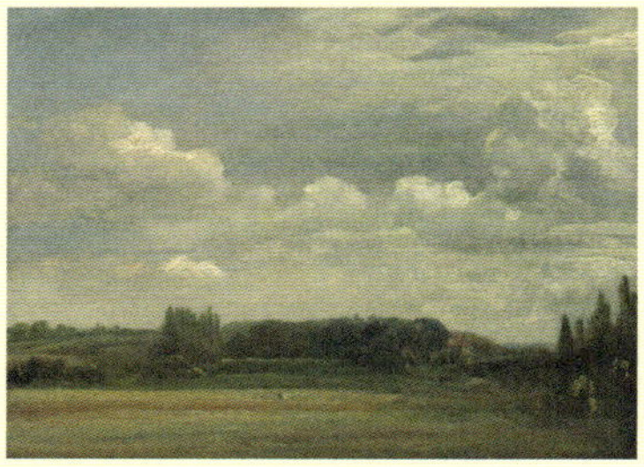

51
East Bergholt Common: View toward the Rectory, 18 Aug. 1813
Oil on canvas, mounted on panel, 22.5 × 29.3 cm
2007.8.26 | R13.13

Provenance: Isabel Constable, the artist's daughter, by descent (d. 1888, her sale, Christie's, London 28 May 1891, no. 124, bought in or sold to Colquhoun); Ernest Alfred Colquhoun (from 1891); Janet E. Colquhoun, by descent; sale, Sotheby's, London, 19 July 1978, no. 92; [Richard Green Gallery, London, by 1979]; sale, Sotheby's, London, 6 July 1983, no. 273; private collection, London; [Deborah Gage (Works of Art), Ltd., London, sold to Manton 10 Apr. 2002]; Sir Edwin A. G. Manton (2002–d. 2005); Manton Family Art Foundation (2005–2007, given to the Clark); Sterling and Francine Clark Art Institute, 2007.

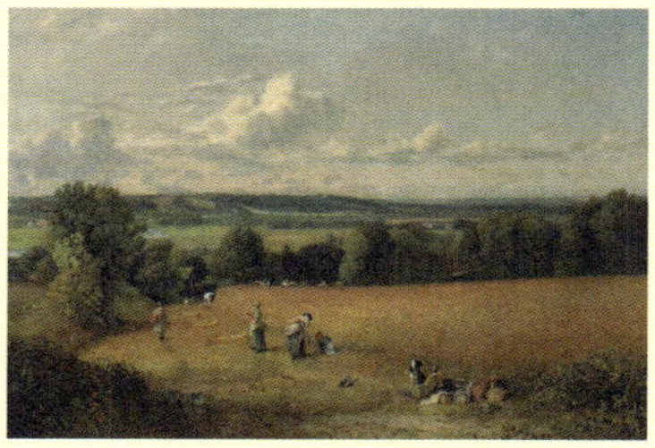

52
The Wheat Field, 1816
Oil on canvas, 54.6 × 77.2 cm
2007.8.27 | R16.1

Cheston family (possibly from the late nineteenth century); Morris Cheston, Jr., Philadelphia, by descent (until 1997); [Agnew's, London, sold through Salander-O'Reilly Galleries, New York, to Curtis Galleries, 1997]; [Curtis Galleries, Minneapolis, 1997–2000, sold through Salander-O'Reilly Galleries, New York, to Manton, 12 Dec. 2000]; Sir Edwin A. G. Manton, New York (2000–d. 2005); Manton Family Art Foundation (2005–2007, given to the Clark); Sterling and Francine Clark Art Institute, 2007.

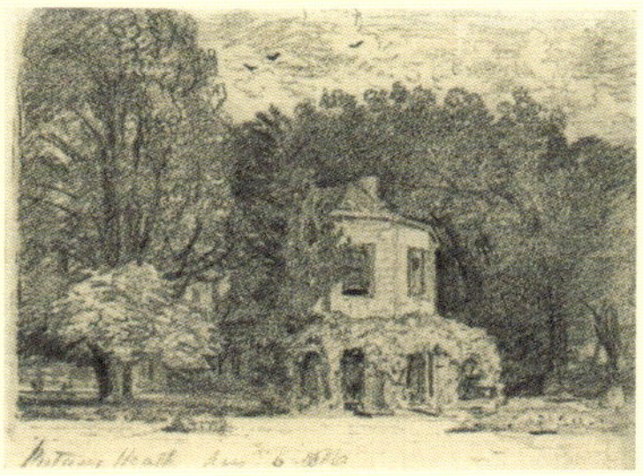

53
The Octagonal House, Putney Heath, 6 Aug. 1816
Graphite on cream wove paper, 8.9 × 12 cm
2007.8.28 | R16.26

Provenance: Arthur Hawley; bequeathed to Uppingham School, sold by the Trustees of Uppingham School to Oscar & Peter Johnson, Ltd., London, as agent for Manton, Apr. 1980; Sir Edwin A. G. Manton, New York (1980–d. 2005); Manton Family Art Foundation (2005–2007, given to the Clark); Sterling and Francine Clark Art Institute, 2007.

John Constable

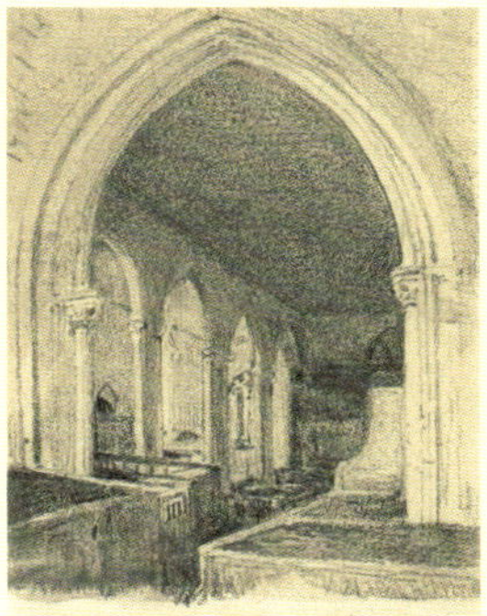

54
Saint Andrews Church, Preston: The Interior, 17 Oct. 1816
Graphite on cream wove paper, 11.5 × 8.6 cm
2007.8.29 | R16.49

Provenance: Arthur Hawley; bequeathed to Uppingham School, sold by the Trustees of Uppingham School to Oscar & Peter Johnson, Ltd., as agent for Manton, Mar. 1980; Sir Edwin A. G. Manton, New York (1980–d. 2005); Manton Family Art Foundation (2005–2007, given to the Clark); Sterling and Francine Clark Art Institute, 2007.

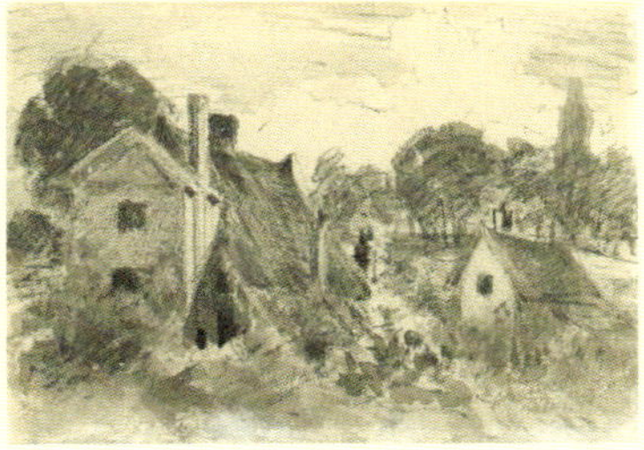

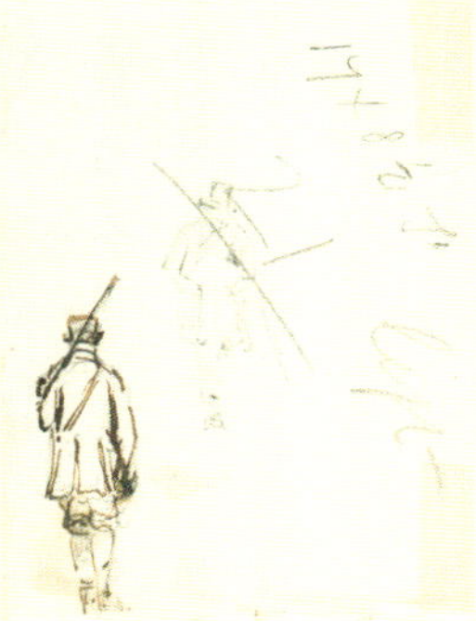

55
Cottages (recto); *Two Studies of a Shepherd* (verso), 1816
Graphite with brush and gray and brown inks and white chalk on cream wove paper (recto); pen and brown ink over graphite on cream wove paper (verso), 9.5 × 11.2 cm
2007.8.30 | R 16.35 (recto); R16.82 (verso)

Provenance: Arthur Hawley; bequeathed to Uppingham School, sold by the Trustees of Uppingham School to Oscar & Peter Johnson, Ltd., as agent for Manton, Mar. 1980; Sir Edwin A. G. Manton, New York (1980–d. 2005); Manton Family Art Foundation (2005–2007, given to the Clark); Sterling and Francine Clark Art Institute, 2007.

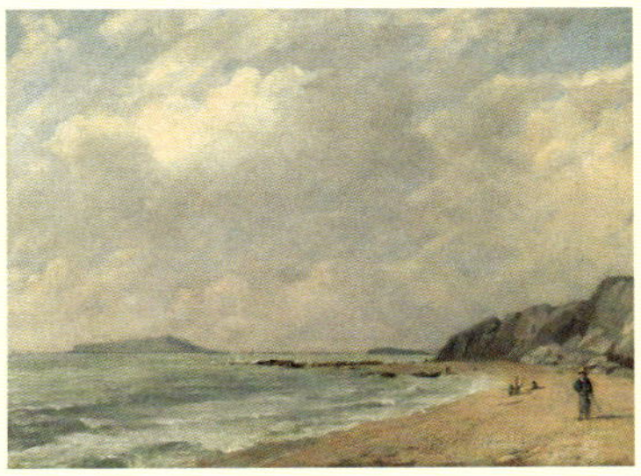

56
Osmington Bay, 1816
Oil on canvas, 23.3 × 30.6 cm
2007.8.31 | R16.80

Provenance: The artist, given to John (d. 1832) or Mary Fisher, Osmington; Osmond Fisher, their son, by descent (d. 1914); Osmond Philip Fisher, his son, by descent (1914–d. 1937); Mrs. Osmond Philip Fisher, his wife, by descent (1937–d. 1957); Hilda M. Burn, great-granddaughter of John and Mary Fisher, by descent; [Hazlitt, Gooden & Fox, London, sold to private collection, 1973]; private collection; sale, Christie's, London, 21 Nov. 1980, no. 73, sold to Spink; [Spink, Ltd., London, sold to Manton, 28 Feb. 1981]; Sir Edwin A. G. Manton, New York (1981–d. 2005); Manton Family Art Foundation (2005–2007, given to the Clark); Sterling and Francine Clark Art Institute, 2007.

John Constable

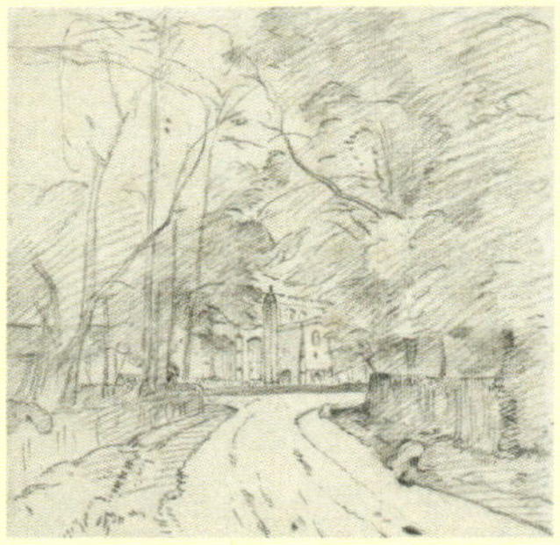

57
East Bergholt Church from the South-West (recto); *East Bergholt Church from the South-West* (verso), c. 1817
Graphite tracing on white laid paper (recto); black ink offprint (verso), 18.7 × 18.9 cm
2007.8.32 | R17.29A

Provenance: G. Smith; private collection, possibly with initials J. S.; sale, Christie's, London 19 Mar. 1985, no. 108, sold to Leger; [Leger Galleries, London 1985–1986, sold to Manton, Feb. 1986]; Sir Edwin A. G. Manton, New York (1986–d. 2005); Manton Family Art Foundation (2005–2007, given to the Clark); Sterling and Francine Clark Art Institute, 2007.

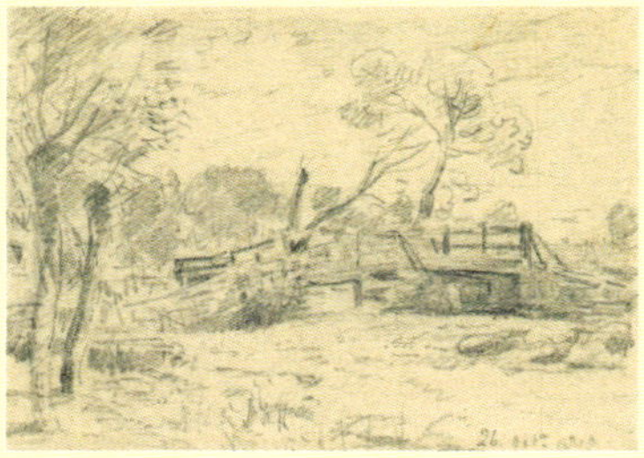

58
Flatford Bridge, 1818
Graphite on cream wove paper, 9.4 × 12.8 cm
2007.8.33 | R18.28A

Provenance: Major Leonard M. E. Dent (acquired in the 1940s); Peter Wise, his grandson, by descent, sold to Deborah Gage (Works of Art), Ltd., London, as agent for Manton, July 1997; Sir Edwin A. G. Manton, New York (1997–d. 2005); Manton Family Art Foundation (2005–2007, given to the Clark); Sterling and Francine Clark Art Institute, 2007.

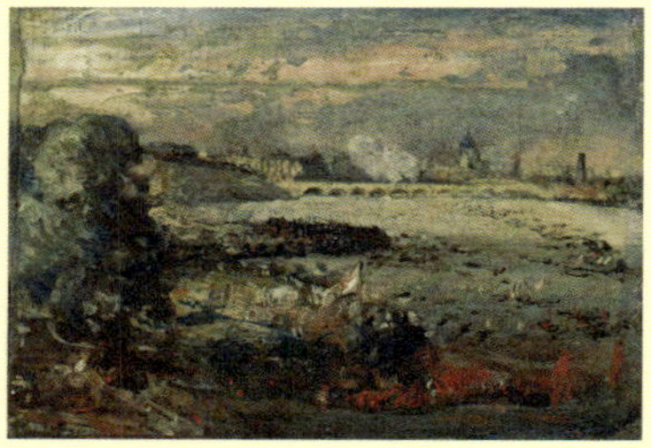

59
Sketch for "The Opening of Waterloo Bridge Seen from Whitehall Stairs, June 18th 1817," c. 1819
Oil on canvas, 15.2 × 22.2 cm
2007.8.48 | R19.22

Provenance: Possibly Edward Beaumont Venn, Freston Lodge, Freston, Ipswich (d. 1857); Lawrence E. Venn; sale, Sotheby's, London, 30 Nov. 1960, no. 122, sold to Leggatt; [Leggatt Brothers Gallery, London]; private collection, by descent (until at least 1991); given to Christ's College; Christ's College, Cambridge (by 1995, until 1997); private collection; [Spink, London, sold to Manton, 26 Oct. 1999]; Sir Edwin A. G. Manton, New York (1999–d. 2005); Manton Family Art Foundation (2005–2007, given to the Clark); Sterling and Francine Clark Art Institute, 2007.

John Constable

60
Cloud Study, c. 1821–22
Oil on cream laid paper, mounted on canvas, 27.5 × 32.7 cm
2007.8.34 | R22.57

Provenance: Constable family, by descent, sold to Kay, with T. MacLean as agent, 1896; Arthur Kay (from 1896); H. A. J. Munro of Novar; Capt. Briscoe, Longstowe Hall, sold to Leggatt; [Leggatt Brothers Gallery, London, sold to Manton, 2 June 1958]; Sir Edwin A. G. Manton, New York (1958–d. 2005); Manton Family Art Foundation (2005–2007, given to the Clark); Sterling and Francine Clark Art Institute, 2007.

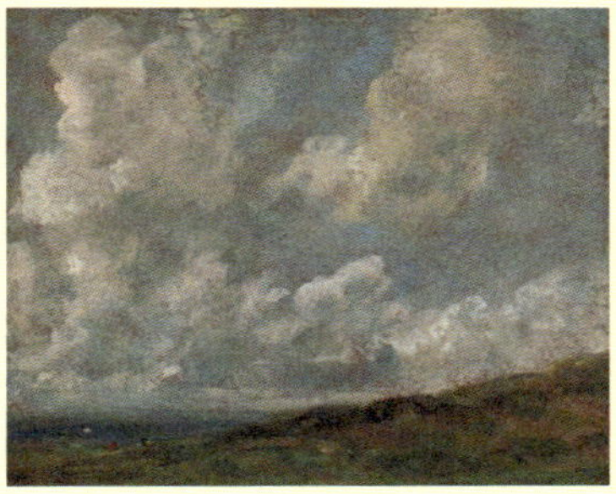

61
Study of Clouds over a Landscape, c. 1821–22
Oil on laminate cardboard, mounted on canvas, 24.4 × 29.5 cm
2007.8.35 | R22.73

Provenance: [Possibly Galerie Sedelmeyer, Paris]; private collection, sold by Deborah Gage (Works of Art), Ltd., London, to Manton, 4 Nov. 1993]; Sir Edwin A. G. Manton (1993–d. 2005); Manton Family Art Foundation (2005–2007, given to the Clark); Sterling and Francine Clark Art Institute, 2007.

62
High Clouds, c. 1821–22
Watercolor with graphite on white wove paper, 9 × 16.3 cm
2007.8.55 | R33.61

Provenance: [Cooling Galleries, London]; private collection (in 1937); Mrs. H. Brown, her daughter, by descent, sale, Christie's, 20 Mar. 1984, no. 116, sold to private collection; private collection (in 1984); [Salander-O'Reilly Galleries, Inc., sold to Manton, Jan. 2002]; Sir Edwin A. G. Manton, New York (2002–d. 2005); Manton Family Art Foundation (2005–2007, given to the Clark); Sterling and Francine Clark Art Institute, 2007.

63
Cloud Study, c. 1821–22
Oil on laminate cardboard, 23.8 × 30.2 cm
2007.8.58 | Not in Reynolds

Provenance: Private collection (c. 1960–1997), sale, Sotheby's, London, 9 July 1997, no. 90, sold to Ackermann & Johnson, Ltd., London, as agent for Manton; Sir Edwin A. G. Manton (1997–d. 2005); Manton Family Art Foundation (2005–2007, given to the Clark); Sterling and Francine Clark Art Institute, 2007.

John Constable

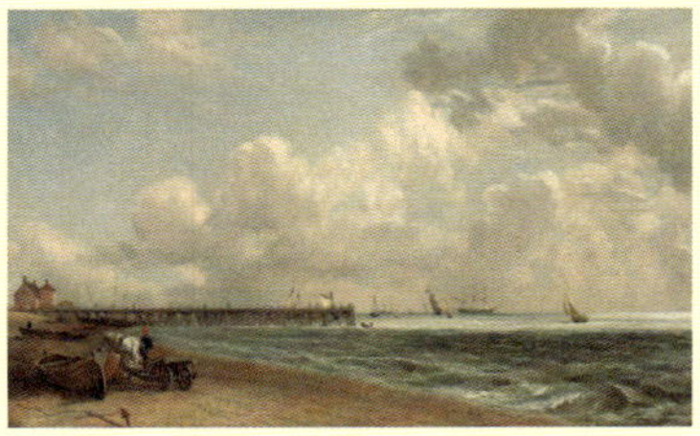

64
Yarmouth Jetty, c. 1822–23
Oil on canvas, 32.4 × 51.1 cm
2007.8.36 | R22.37

Provenance: The artist, possibly given to Gooch; possibly Dr. Robert Gooch (d. 1830); possibly bequeathed to George Jennings or to George Young; Frederick Winslow Young, George Young's brother, by descent (his sale, Rushworth and Jarvis, London, 30 Jan. 1857, no. 99, sold to Cundy); Charles Fishlake Cundy (from 1857); Rev. T. S. Cooper, his nephew, by descent; O. S. Cundy-Cooper, his son, by descent; Lord Ivor Spencer-Churchill; [Agnew's, 1949]; R. P. Silcock; Mrs. J. M. Stephens; [Leggatt Brother's Gallery, London]; Hon. Moira Nivison (1975–d. 1984); private collection, by descent, sold to Manton, 11 Dec. 2000, with R. M. Thune as agent; Sir Edwin A. G. Manton, New York (2000–d. 2005); Manton Family Art Foundation (2005–2007, given to the Clark); Sterling and Francine Clark Art Institute, 2007.

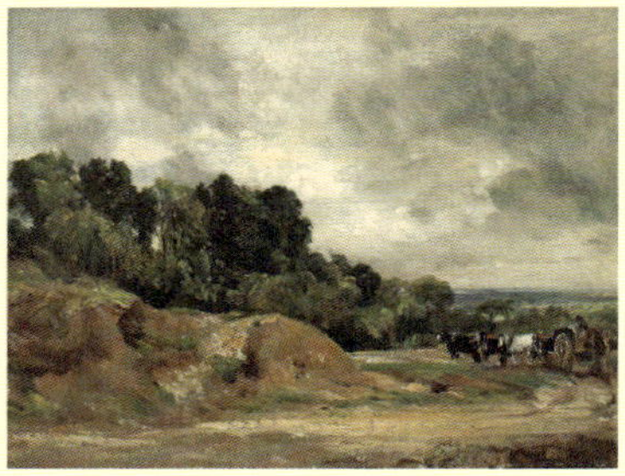

65
Sandbanks and a Cart and Horses on Hampstead Heath, c. 1820–25
Oil on canvas, 19.7 × 25.4 cm
2007.8.37 | Not in Reynolds

Provenance: Charles Golding Constable, the artist's son, by descent (d. 1878); Anna Maria Blundell Constable, his widow (1878–1887, Constable estate sale, Christie's, London, 11 July 1887, no. 73, sold to Permain); Permain; James Orrock (by 1888, his sale, Christie's, London, 27 Apr. 1895, no. 276, sold to Radcliffe); Radcliffe (from 1895); Mrs. Michaels (in1955); [Simon Dickinson, Ltd., London, sold to Thune]; Robert M. Thune, New York, sold to Leger; [Leger Galleries, London, sold to Manton, 18 Oct. 1996]; Sir Edwin A. G. Manton, New York (1996–d. 2005); Manton Family Art Foundation (2005–2007, given to the Clark); Sterling and Francine Clark Art Institute.

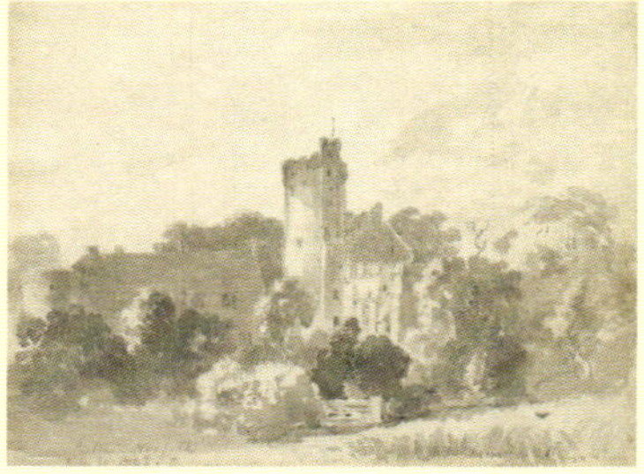

66
Caister Castle, Norfolk, 1823
Graphite and brush and gray wash on white laid paper, 20.3 × 26.3 cm
2007.8.38 | R23.34

Provenance: Victor Reinaecker, London; Percy Moore Turner; Dr. H. A. C. Gregory, sale, Sotheby's, London, 20 July 1949, no. 98, sold to Leggatt; [Leggatt Brothers Gallery (in 1949)]; Esmond Bulmer, sold to Johnson; [Oscar & Peter Johnson, Ltd., 1966–1967, sold to Manton, Feb. 1966]; Sir Edwin A. G. Manton, New York (1966–d. 2005); Manton Family Art Foundation (2005–2007, given to the Clark); Sterling and Francine Clark Art Institute, 2007.

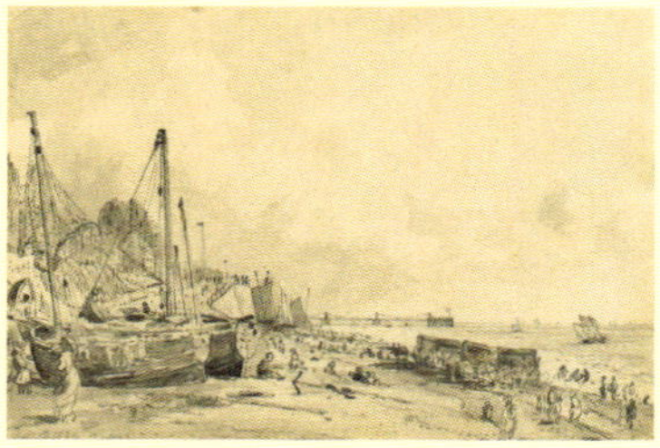

67
Brighton Beach, Looking East, 1824
Brush and gray wash with graphite on beige wove paper, 17.7 × 26.1 cm
2007.8.39 | R24.30

Provenance: The artist; Captain Charles Golding Constable, his son, by descent (d. 1879); Mrs. Anna Maria Constable, by descent (1879–1887), sold by court order, Christie's, London, 11 July 1887, no. 28 or 38, sold to Noseda, as agent for Heseltine; J. P. Heseltine, London (1887–1920, possible sale, Sotheby's, London, 25 Mar. 1920, no. 120, sold to Agnew's); [Thomas Agnew and Sons, Ltd., London]; A. Murray-Smith (in 1933); sale, Christie's, 28 June 1963, no. 11, sold to Johnson; [Oscar & Peter Johnson, Ltd., in 1963, sold to Manton, Aug. 1963]; Sir Edwin A. G. Manton, New York (1963–d. 2005); Manton Family Art Foundation (2005–2007, given to the Clark); Sterling and Francine Clark Art Institute, 2007.

John Constable

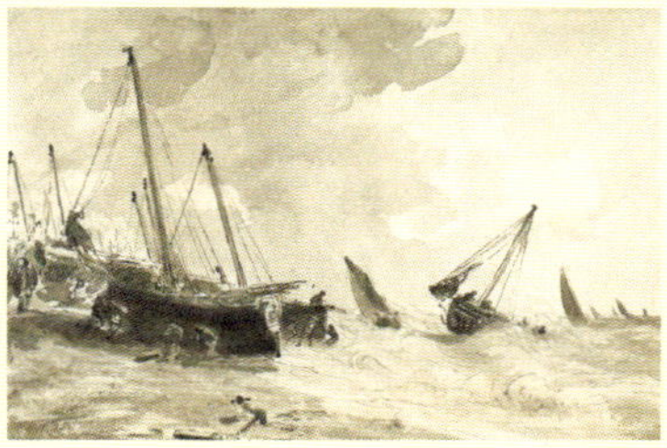

68
Shipping in a Stormy Sea at Brighton, 1824
Brush and gray ink over graphite on white wove paper, 17.5 × 25.6 cm
2007.8.40 | R24.91

Provenance: The artist; Captain Charles Golding Constable, his son, by descent (d. 1879); Mrs. Anna Maria Constable, by descent (in 1879, possibly held in trust for one of her children); sale, Bearnes and Waycotts, Torquay, 24 June 1969, no. 239, sold to Leger; [Leger Galleries, 1969–1971, sold to Homer]; T. W. B. Homer (1971–1981), sold to Leger; [Leger Galleries, in 1981]; private collection, sold to Leger Galleries, as agent for Manton, Oct. 1995; Sir Edwin A. G. Manton, New York (1995–d. 2005); Manton Family Art Foundation (2005–2007, given to the Clark); Sterling and Francine Clark Art Institute, 2007.

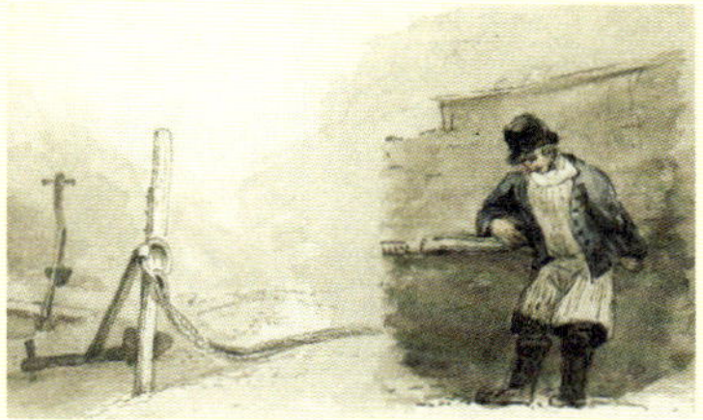

69
Studies of a Post and Anchors and of a Fisherman, Brighton (recto); *A Fishing Boat and Fishermen on Brighton Beach* (verso), c. 1824–26
Watercolor over graphite on white wove paper (recto); graphite on white wove paper (verso), 9.4 × 14.9 cm
2007.8.41 | R 27.1A (recto); R27.1B (verso)

Provenance: [Stephen Somerville, Ltd., London, sold to Harper, 1988]; Peter Harper (1988–after 1991, sold to Somerville); [Stephen Somerville, Ltd., London, sold to Spink]; [Spink-Leger Pictures, sold to Manton, Feb. 1998]; Sir Edwin A. G. Manton, New York (1998–d. 2005); Manton Family Art Foundation (2005–2007, given to the Clark); Sterling and Francine Clark Art Institute, 2007.

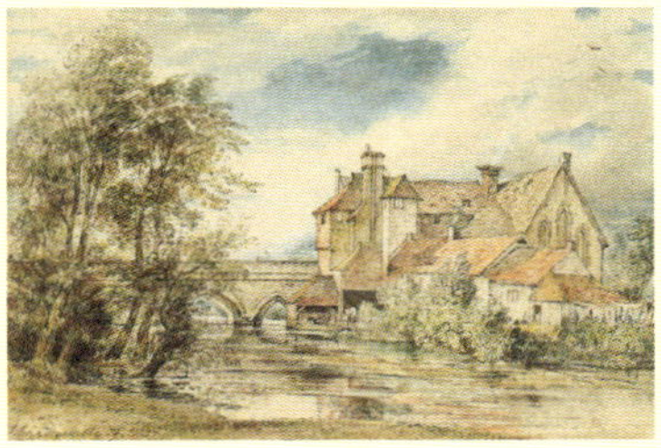

70
Old Houses on Harnam Bridge, Salisbury with the Ancient Hospital of Saint Nicholas, 1827
Pen and brown and gray inks with watercolor over graphite, with scraping, on white wove paper, 18.3 × 26.5 cm
2007.8.42 | R27.45

Provenance: Commissioned by George Fennell Robson on behalf of Mrs. George Haldimand (1827–1861, sale, Christie's, London, 21 June 1861, sold to Agnew's); [Thomas Agnew and Sons, Ltd., London, in 1861]; [Volkins Gallery, by 1883]; Stephenson Clarke (c. 1883–d. 1891); Stephenson Robert Clarke, his son, by descent (1891–1948); Ralph Stephenson Clarke, his son, by descent (1948–1980); private collection, his son, by descent, sale, Christie's, London, 18 Mar. 1980, no. 215, sold to Leger Galleries; [Leger Galleries, London, Mar.–Sept. 1980, sold to Manton]; Sir Edwin A. G. Manton, New York (1980–d. 2005); Manton Family Art Foundation (2005–2007, given to the Clark); Sterling and Francine Clark Art Institute, 2007.

John Constable

71
Sketch for "Dedham Vale," c. 1827
Oil, ink, and graphite on canvas, 60.7 × 50.8 cm
2007.8.43 | Not in Reynolds

Provenance: [Heinemann Gallery, Munich, 1906–1910, sold to Buhl, 16 Aug. 1910]; Dr. Franz Buhl, Deidesheim, from 1910, returned to Heinemann; [Heinemann Gallery, Munich, sold to Desclosières, 20 July 1911]; R. Desclosières, Paris (from 1911); Desclosières heirs, by descent, sold to Van Haeften, 1994; [Johnny Van Haeften, Ltd., London, sold to Manton, 1994, with Deborah Gage (Works of Art), Ltd., London, as agent]; Sir Edwin A. G. Manton, New York (1994–d. 2005); Manton Family Art Foundation (2005–2007, given to the Clark); Sterling and Francine Clark Art Institute, 2007.

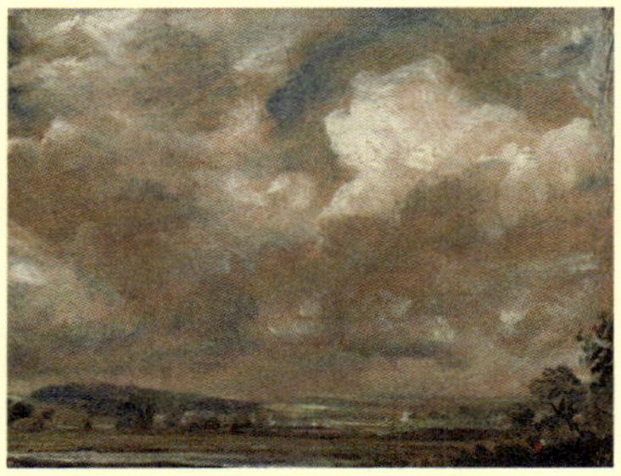

72
Harnham Ridge, Salisbury, c. 1829
Oil on beige wove paper, mounted on canvas, 19.7 × 24.8 cm
2007.8.44 | R29.39

Provenance: [Leggatt Brothers Gallery, London, sold to Manton, Sept. 1958]; Sir Edwin A. G. Manton, New York (1958–d. 2005); Manton Family Art Foundation (2005–2007, given to the Clark); Sterling and Francine Clark Art Institute, 2007.

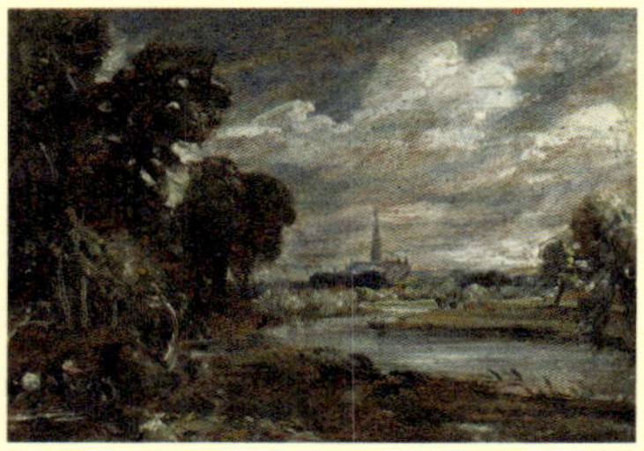

73
Salisbury Cathedral from the River Nadder, c. 1829
Oil on beige wove paper, mounted on laminate cardboard, 19.8 × 27.8 cm
2007.8.46 | R31.3

Provenance: The artist; Isabel Constable, his daughter, by descent, given to Fenwick; Alice Fenwick (c. 1880); Dora Harriet Fenwick, by descent; Major C. W. Maffett, her son, by descent; Joan Turville, his daughter, by descent (1981–1982), sale, Christie's, London, 19 Nov. 1982, no. 44, sold to Oscar & Peter Johnson, Ltd., as agent for Manton; Sir Edwin A. G. Manton, New York (1982–d. 2005); Manton Family Art Foundation (2005–2007, given to the Clark); Sterling and Francine Clark Art Institute, 2007.

John Constable

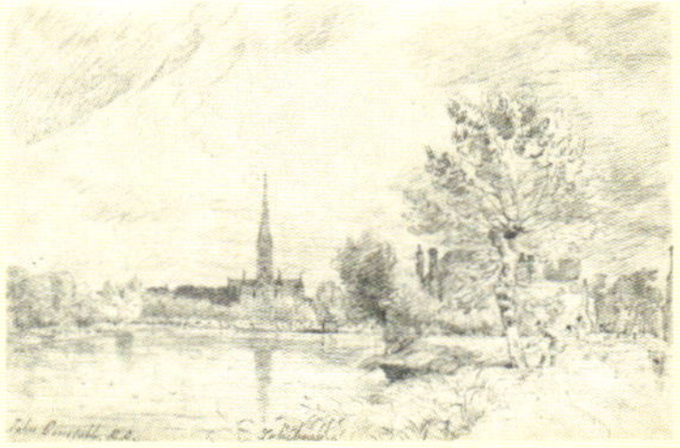

74
Salisbury Cathedral from the River Avon (recto); *Man Pulling a Rope* (verso), July 23, 1829
Graphite on cream wove paper, 23.1 × 33.6 cm
2007.8.47 | R29.20 (recto); Not in Reynolds (verso)

Provenance: Marietta Peabody Tree (her sale, Sotheby's, New York, 19 Oct. 1976, no. 196, sold to Manton); Sir Edwin A. G. Manton, New York (1976–d. 2005); Manton Family Art Foundation (2005–2007, given to the Clark); Sterling and Francine Clark Art Institute, 2007.

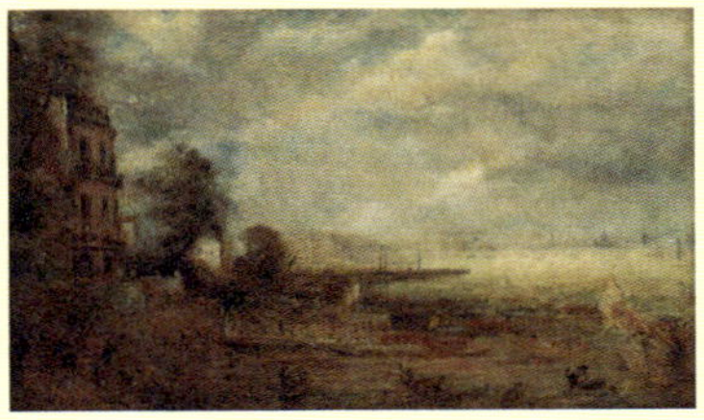

75
Waterloo Bridge Seen from Whitehall Stairs, c. 1829
Oil on canvas, 61 × 99.1 cm
2007.8.49 | R29.64

Provenance: [Legatt Brothers Gallery, sold to Hardy]; Lee Hardy (in 1940); John Hardy, his son, by descent, sold to Leger, 1988; [Leger Galleries, London, 1988–1989, sold to Manton, Mar. 1989]; Sir Edwin A. G. Manton, New York (1989–d. 2005); Diana Morton, his daughter, by descent (2005–2007), given to the Clark; Sterling and Francine Clark Art Institute, 2007.

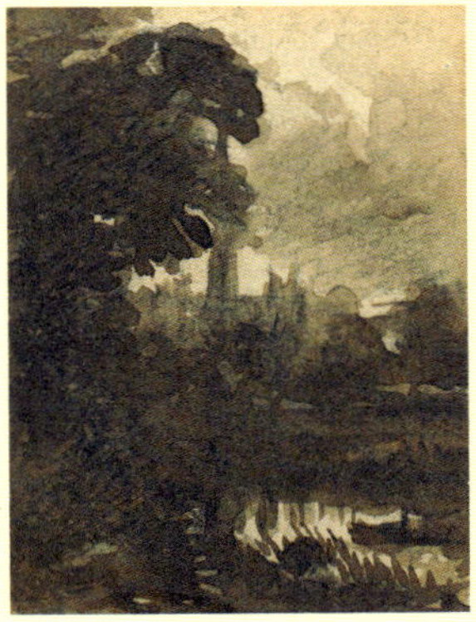

76
Salisbury Cathedral from the North-West, c. 1830–39
Brush and brown ink over graphite on cream wove paper, 7.7 × 5.6 cm
2007.8.50 | R36.31

Provenance: The artist; possibly Isabel Constable, his daughter, by descent (d. 1888); sale, Christie's, London, 17 June 1892, no. 183, sold to Rochefort; Rochefort (in 1892); Randall Davies; [P. & D. Colnaghi & Co., Ltd., London, sold to Appleby, 1964]; Appleby Bros., Ltd. (in 1964, sold to Day); Harold A. E. Day (sale, Christie's, London, 7 Apr. 1998, no. 28, sold to Ackermann & Johnson, as agent for Manton); Sir Edwin A. G. Manton, New York (1998–d. 2005); Manton Family Art Foundation (2005–2007, given to the Clark); Sterling and Francine Clark Art Institute, 2007.

John Constable

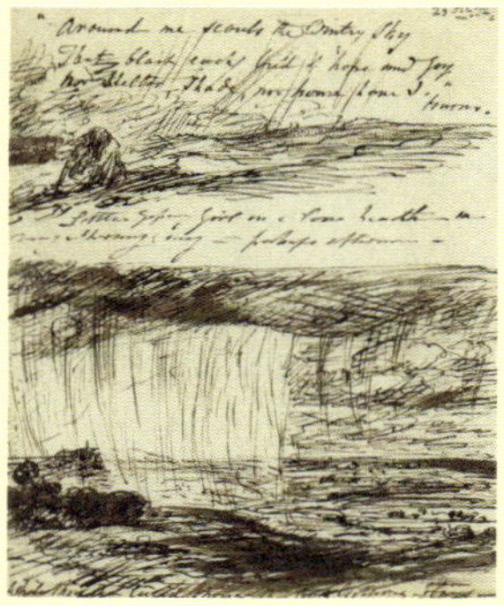

77
Sheet of Sketches with Verses from Burns, 23 Oct. 1832
Pen and brown ink and brush and brown wash on white laid paper, 19.4 × 15.7 cm
2007.8.51 | R32.31A

Provenance: Sale, Christie's, London, 12 July 1988, no. 19, sold to Oscar & Peter Johnson, Ltd., London, as agent for Manton; Sir Edwin A. G. Manton, New York (1988–d. 2005); Manton Family Art Foundation (2005–2007, given to the Clark); Sterling and Francine Clark Art Institute, 2007.

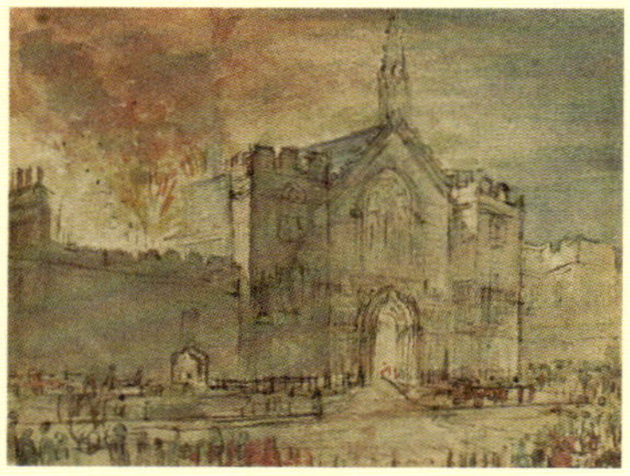

78
The Houses of Parliament on Fire, 1834
Pen and brown ink with watercolor on cream wove paper, 8.2 × 10.7 cm
2007.8.52 | R34.71

Provenance: The artist; John Hugh Constable, his great-great-grandson, by descent, sold to Spink, 1986; [Spink & Son, Ltd., London, 1986–1987, sold to Manton, June 1987]; Sir Edwin A. G. Manton, New York (1987–d. 2005); Manton Family Art Foundation (2005–2007, given to the Clark); Sterling and Francine Clark Art Institute, 2007.

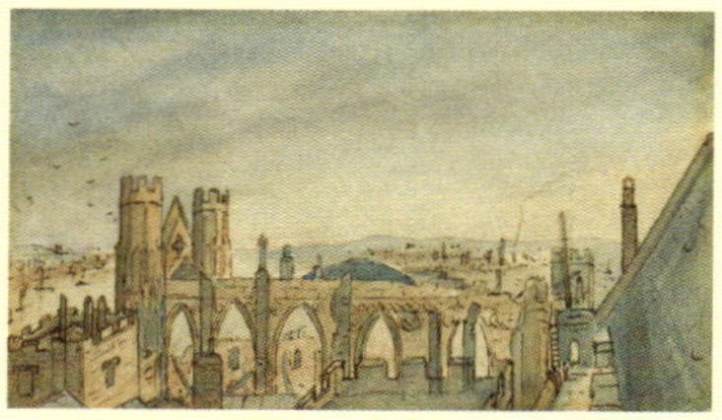

79
The Houses of Parliament after the Fire, 30 Oct. 1824
Pen and brown ink with watercolor on cream wove paper, 9.6 × 16.5 cm
2007.20.3 | R34.72

Provenance: Lt. Col. John Hugh Constable, sold to Spink, after 1984; [Spink & Son, Ltd., London, sold to Manton, July 1987]; Sir Edwin A.G. Manton, New York (1987–d. 2005); Manton Family Art Foundation (2005–2007, given to the Clark); Sterling and Francine Clark Art Institute, 2007.

John Constable

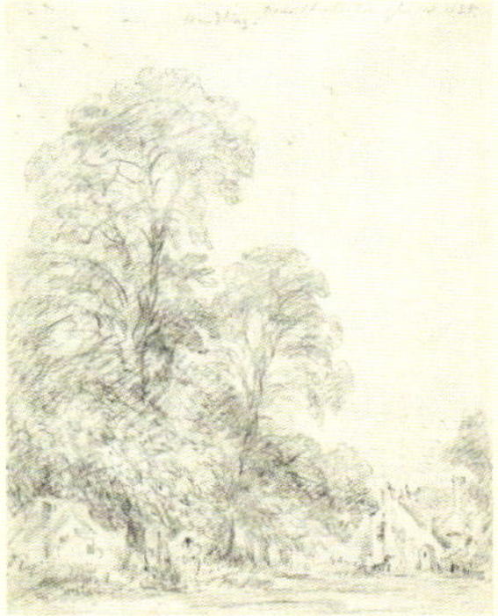

80
Maudlin, near Chichester, 18 July 1835
Graphite on cream wove paper,
28.4 × 22.1 cm
2007.8.53 | R35.17A

Provenance: The artist; Hugh Golding Constable, by descent, probably sold to Leggatt; [Leggatt Brothers Gallery, London, sold to Dent, 10 Aug. 1942]; Leonard M. E. Dent (in 1942); Mrs. Ian MacFarlane, his daughter, by descent, sold to Deborah Gage (Works of Art), Ltd., London, as agent for Manton, 1997; Sir Edwin A. G. Manton, New York (1997–d. 2005); Manton Family Art Foundation (2005–2007, given to the Clark); Sterling and Francine Clark Art Institute, 2007.

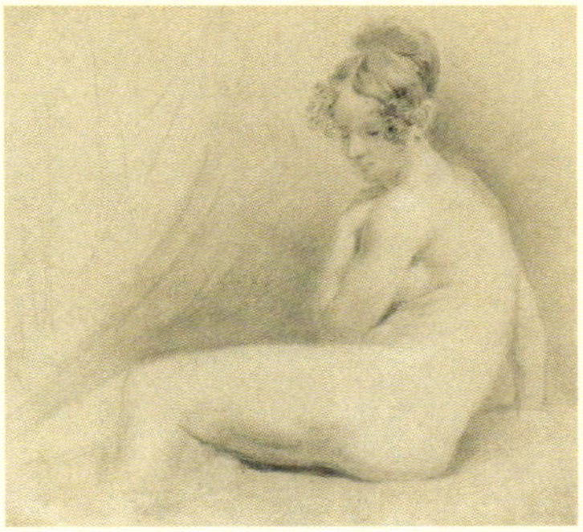

81
Academy Study (recto);
Figure Study (verso), c. 1820
Black and white chalks on beige wove paper (recto); black chalk on beige wove paper (verso), 25.4 × 27 cm
2007.8.54 | R08.50 (recto);
not in Reynolds (verso)

Provenance: Charles Fairfax Murray, London, according to label; [London dealer, possibly John Manning]; Charles B. N. Warren, sold to Spink; [Spink & Son, Ltd., London, no. K1930, sold to West, Jan. 1961]; Dame Rebecca West (1961–1983), sale, Christie's, London, 15 Nov. 1983, no. 133, sold to Leger; [Leger Galleries, London, 1983–1984, sold to Manton, Jan. 1984]; Sir Edwin A. G. Manton, New York (1984–d. 2005); Manton Family Art Foundation (2005–2007, given to the Clark); Sterling and Francine Clark Art Institute, 2007.

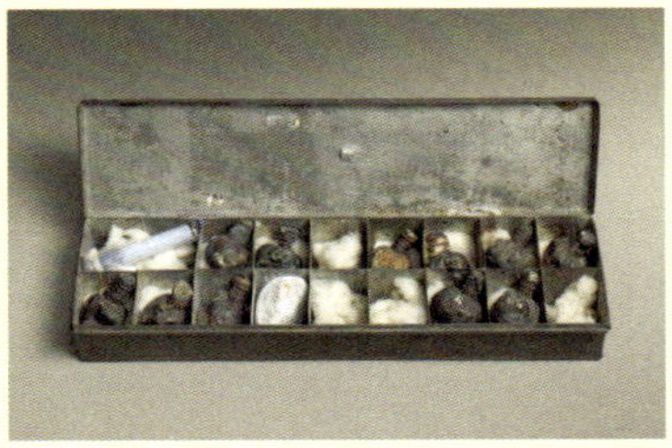

82
Paint Box, c. 1825
Tin box with hinged lid, and seventeen compartments containing oil paints and varnishes, 5.1 × 33 × 8.6 cm
2007.8.57

Provenance: The artist; John Charles Constable, his son, by descent; given to David Lucas between 1837 and 1839; Alfred Lucas, his brother, by descent, probably sale, Sotheby's, early 1920s; Henry S. Theobald; sale, Sotheby's, London, 14 Mar. 1984, no. 87, sold to Van Haeften; Johnny Van Haeften, Ltd., London (1984–1995, sold to Deborah Gage [Works of Art], Ltd., London, as agent for Manton, Oct. 1995); Sir Edwin A. G. Manton, New York (1998–d. 2005); Manton Family Art Foundation (2005–2007, given to the Clark); Sterling and Francine Clark Art Institute, 2007.

Attributed to John Constable

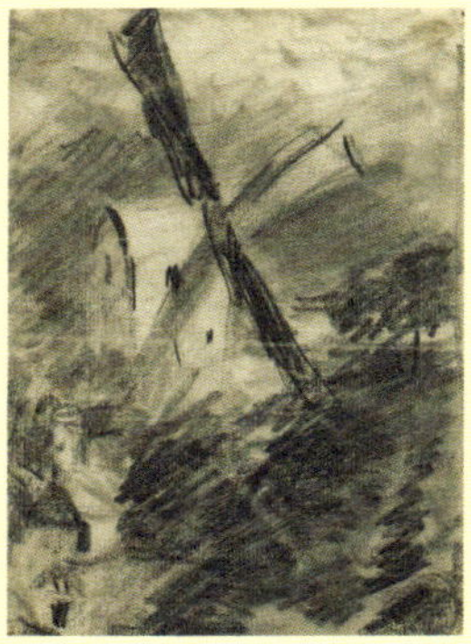

83
A Windmill, 19th century
Graphite with stumping, erasing, and scraping, on cream laid paper, 19.2 × 13.9 cm
2007.20.4

Provenance: R. H. Spurr, sold to Renshaw, Jan. 1966; Dr. Arnold Renshaw (in 1966); Janet E. Renshaw, his daughter, by descent; [Deborah Gage (Works of Art), Ltd., London, sold to Manton, Feb. 2002]; Sir Edwin A. G. Manton, New York (2002–d. 2005); Manton Family Art Foundation (2005–2007, given to the Clark); Sterling and Francine Clark Art Institute, 2007.

Style of John Constable British, 19th century

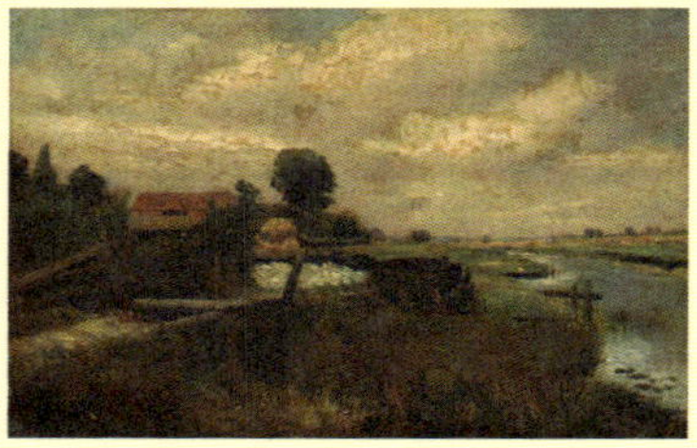

84
River View
Oil on canvas, 30 × 45.8 cm
2007.20.5

Provenance: Oscar Bondy, Vienna and New York (by 1938–d. 1944, seized by Nazi forces, 1938, recovered by the United States Fine Arts Commission and restituted to Bondy's widow); Elizabeth A. Bondy, his wife, by descent and restitution (1944–1949, Bondy sale, Kende Galleries, New York, 3 Mar. 1949, no. 75, sold to Manton); Sir Edwin A. G. Manton (1949– d. 2005); Diana Morton, his daughter, by descent (2005–2007, given to the Clark); Sterling and Francine Clark Art Institute, 2007.

Lionel Bicknell Constable English, 1828–1887

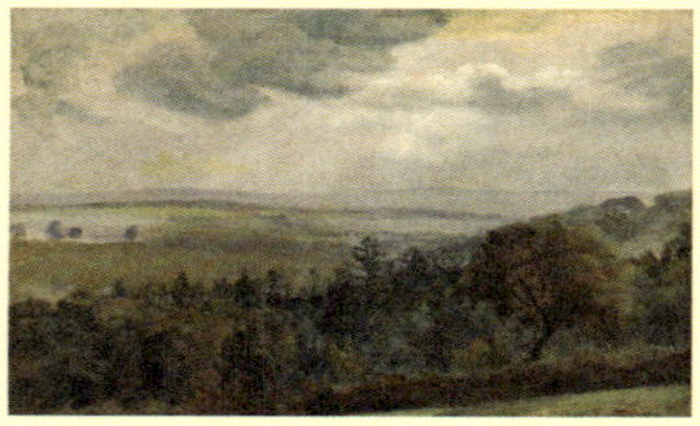

85
Extensive Landscape with Clouds, c. 1850
Oil on wood-pulp board, mounted on panel, 24.3 × 39.1 cm
2007.8.59

Provenance: Isabel Constable, the artist's sister, by descent (d. 1888, probably her sale, Christie's, London, 17 June 1892, no. 233, 234, or 238, as by John Constable, sold to Shepherd Bros.); Shepherd Bros. (probably from 1892); Victor Rienaecker, London; H. L. Fison (until 1969, his sale, Christie's, London, 6 Nov. 1969, no. 19, sold to Agnew's); [Agnew's, London, from 1969]; Mrs. A. Mackinnon; private collection, sold to Salander-O'Reilly, Nov. 2000; [Salander-O'Reilly Galleries, New York, sold to Manton, 30 May 2001]; Sir Edwin A. G. Manton, New York (2001–d. 2005); Manton Family Art Foundation (2005–2007, given to the Clark); Sterling and Francine Clark Art Institute, 2007.

Lionel Bicknell Constable

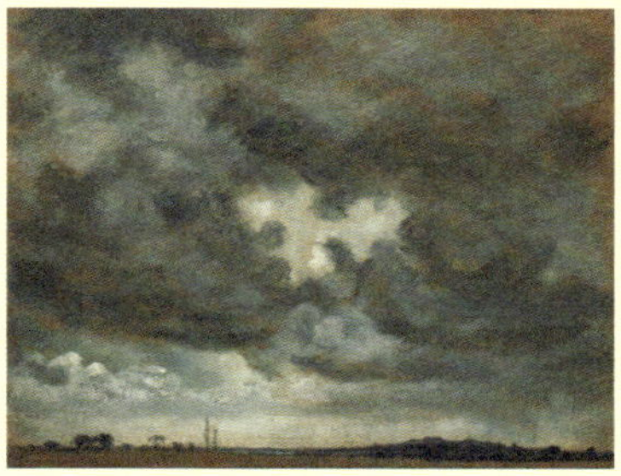

86
Cloud Study, c. 1850
Oil on beige wove paper, mounted on wood-pulp board, mounted on panel, 23.5 × 30 cm (original support); 24.5 × 31 cm (panel)
2007.8.60

Provenance: Hugh Golding Constable, the artist's nephew, by descent, sold to Leggatt, 1899; [Leggatt Brothers Gallery, London]; Mr. Waldron; G. B. Homewood; sale, Christie's, London, 18 Apr. 1986, no. 60, as by John Constable; Raymond Needler; sale, Sotheby's, London, 13 Nov. 1996, no. 100, as by Lionel Constable, sold to Ackermann & Johnson; [Ackermann & Johnson, London, as agent for Manton]; Sir Edwin A. G. Manton, New York (1996–d. 2005); Manton Family Art Foundation (2005–2007, given to the Clark); Sterling and Francine Clark Art Institute, 2007.

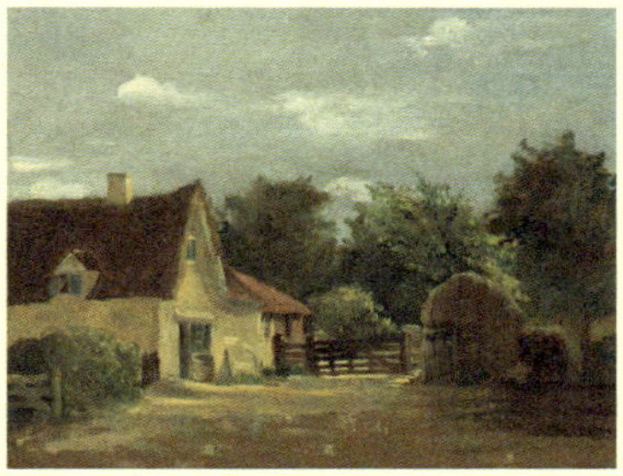

87
Cottage, c. 1850
Oil on wood-pulp board, mounted on linen, 22.5 × 28.3 cm
2007.8.61

Provenance: Constable family, by descent, sold to Leggatt; [Leggatt Brothers Gallery, London]; private collection, U.S.A., in 1959; private collection; sale, Phillips, Edinburgh, 2 Dec. 1983, no. 85; sale, Phillips, London, 11 Dec. 1984, no. 60, sold to Oscar & Peter Johnson, Ltd., as agent for Manton; Sir Edwin A. G. Manton, New York (1984–d. 2005); Manton Family Art Foundation (2005–2007, given to the Clark); Sterling and Francine Clark Art Institute, 2007.

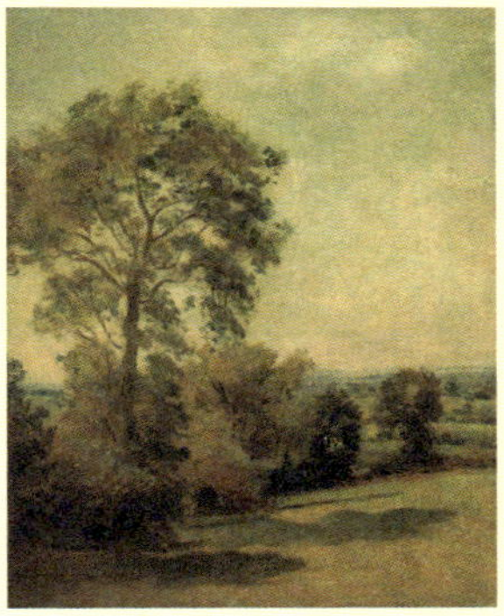

88
Tree in a Landscape, c. 1850
Oil on cream wove paper, mounted on panel, 33.5 × 26.1 cm (sheet); 34.3 × 27.2 cm (panel)
2007.8.62

Provenance: Sale, Christie's, c. 1958, sold to Leggatt; [Leggatt Brothers Gallery, London, sold to Mason]; Wing Commander Keith Mason; [Oscar & Peter Johnson, Ltd., London, sold to Manton, as John Constable, 4 Nov. 1971]; Sir Edwin A. G. Manton, New York (1971–d. 2005); Manton Family Art Foundation (2005–2007, given to the Clark); Sterling and Francine Clark Art Institute, 2007.

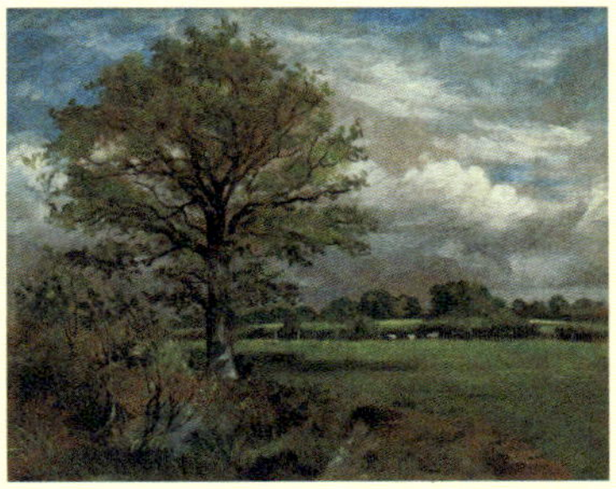

89
Tree in a Meadow, c. 1850
Oil on wood-pulp board, mounted on canvas, 24.3 × 31.3 cm
2007.8.63

Provenance: Hugh Golding Constable, the artist's nephew, by descent; [Leggatt, London, 1899, possibly sold to Young and Agnew's, 1899]; [Alexander Young and Agnew's, London, sold to Wallis, 6 May 1909]; [Wallis & Son (The French Gallery), London, from 1909]; John Edward Taylor; A. G. Penchen; sale, Parke-Bernet Galleries, New York, 7 Apr. 1966, no. 59, sold to Manton, as John Constable; Sir Edwin A. G. Manton, New York (1966–d. 2005); Manton Family Art Foundation (2005–2007, given to the Clark); Sterling and Francine Clark Art Institute, 2007.

Edward William Cooke English, 1811–1880

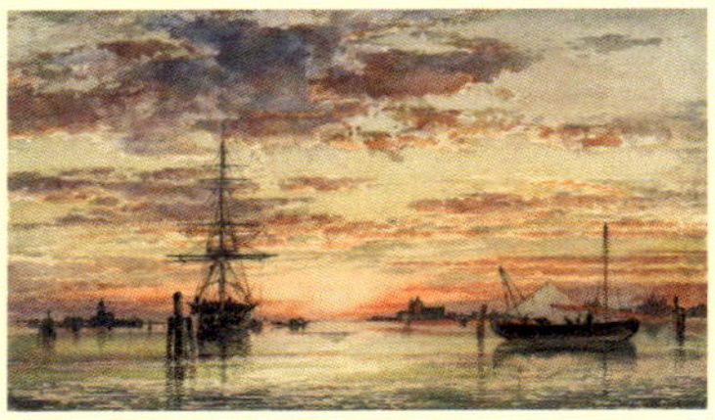

90
Venice at Sunset, 1864
Watercolor and gouache, with gum arabic, on cream wove paper, 19.6 × 32.2 cm
2007.20.13

Provenance: [Oscar & Peter Johnson, Ltd., sold to Manton, Mar. 1977]; Sir Edwin A. G. Manton, New York (1977–d. 2005); Manton Family Art Foundation (2005–2007, given to the Clark); Sterling and Francine Clark Art Institute, 2007.

Attributed to John Sell Cotman English, 1782–1842

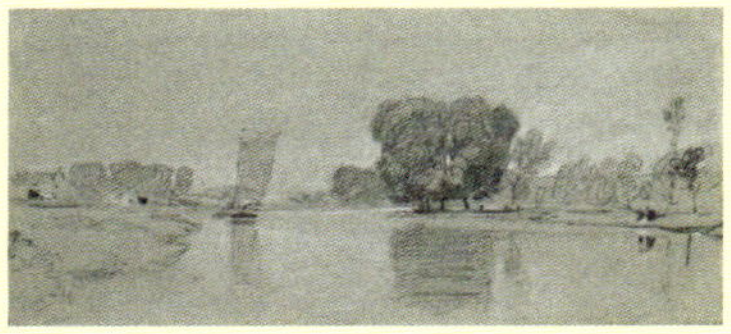

91
A Barge on a River, c. 1841
Black and white chalks on blue wove paper, 17.1 × 37.1 cm
2007.20.14

Provenance: Bruce Ingram (his sale, Sotheby's, London, 17 Feb. 1965, no. 546, sold to Johnson); [Oscar & Peter Johnson, Ltd., sold to Manton, Apr. 1967]; Sir Edwin A. G. Manton, New York (1967–d. 2005); Manton Family Art Foundation (2005–2007, given to the Clark); Sterling and Francine Clark Art Institute, 2007.

After John Sell Cotman British, 19th century

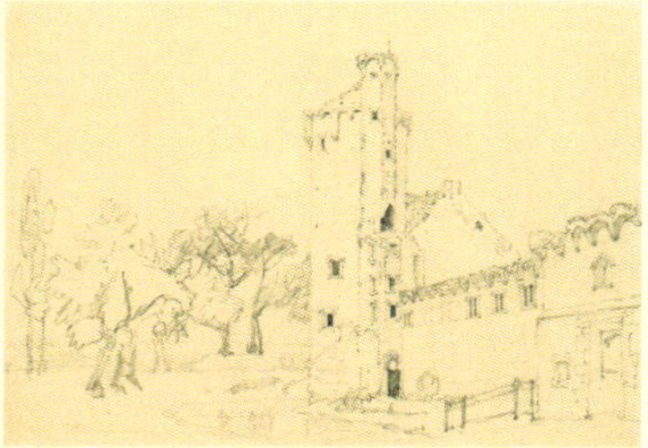

92
Falstaff Tower, Caister Castle
Graphite on beige wove paper, 24.4 × 33.2 cm
2007.20.52

Provenance: Sir Edwin A. G. Manton (d. 2005); Manton Family Art Foundation (2005–2007, given to the Clark); Sterling and Francine Clark Art Institute, 2007.

John Crome   English, 1768–1821

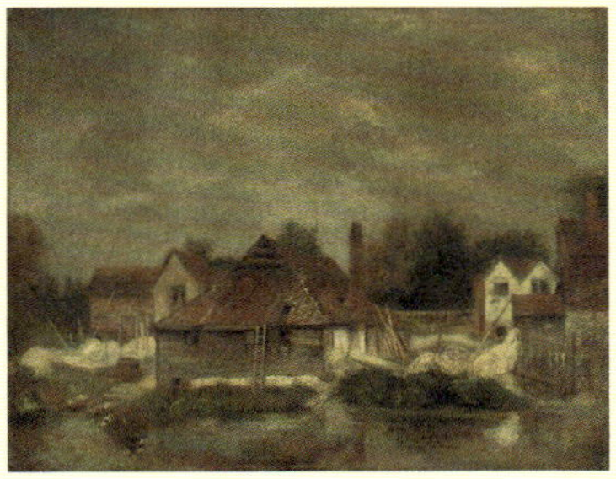

93
Sheds and Old Houses on the Yare, c. 1803
Oil on canvas, 50.8 × 63.3 cm
2007.8.64

Provenance: James Stark, Norwich (d. 1859); W. Wilde (possibly by 1860); Possibly L. or C. F. Huth; sale, Christie's, London, 30 June 1906, no. 119, sold to Gooden; Gooden; Leicester Harmsworth, Baronet (in 1921); [Tooth & Co., sold to Mackintosh, 1950]; arold Vincent Mackintosh, 1st Viscount Mackintosh of Halifax, Norfolk (1950–d. 1964); Viscountess Constance Mackintosh, his wife, by descent (1964–d. 1975); John Mackintosh, 2nd Viscount Mackintosh of Halifax, her son, by descent (from 1975); [Oscar & Peter Johnson, Ltd., London, sold to Manton, 6 May 1980]; Sir Edwin A. G. Manton, New York (1980–d. 2005); Manton Family Art Foundation (2005–2007, given to the Clark); Sterling and Francine Clark Art Institute, 2007.

George Dance the Younger   English, 1741–1825

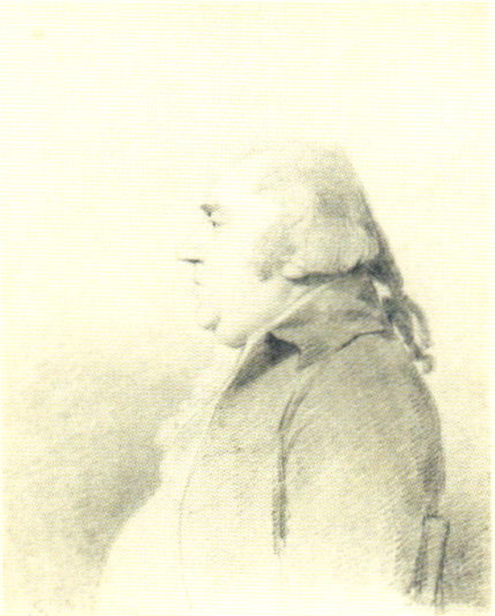

94
Portrait of George Stubbs, 22 Feb. 1794
Graphite on cream wove paper, 25.4 × 19.1 cm
2007.20.15

Provenance: [The Drawing Shop, sold to Manton, Dec. 1971]; Sir Edwin A. G. Manton, New York (1971–d. 2005); Manton Family Art Foundation (2005–2007, given to the Clark); Sterling and Francine Clark Art Institute, 2007.

Edward Dayes   English, 1763–1804

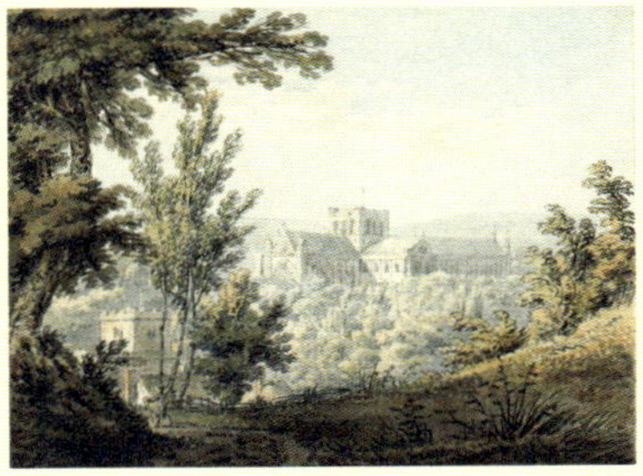

95
A View of Winchester Abbey, 1793
Watercolor and graphite on white wove paper, 16.1 × 22 cm
2007.20.16

Provenance: [Leger Galleries, London, sold to Manton, Mar. 1988]; Sir Edwin A. G. Manton, New York (1988–d. 2005); Manton Family Art Foundation (2005–2007, given to the Clark); Sterling and Francine Clark Art Institute, 2007.

Edward Dayes

A Group of Eighteen Watercolors of Identified Castles, Abbeys, and County Seats, c. 1790–1800, 6.4 × 8.9 cm
2007.20.17.1–18.

Provenance: John Constable, by descent until sold; gift to Sir Edwin A. G. Manton (d. 2005) from Spink-Leger, London in 1999; Manton Family Art Foundation (2005–2007, given to the Clark); Sterling and Francine Clark Art Institute, 2007.

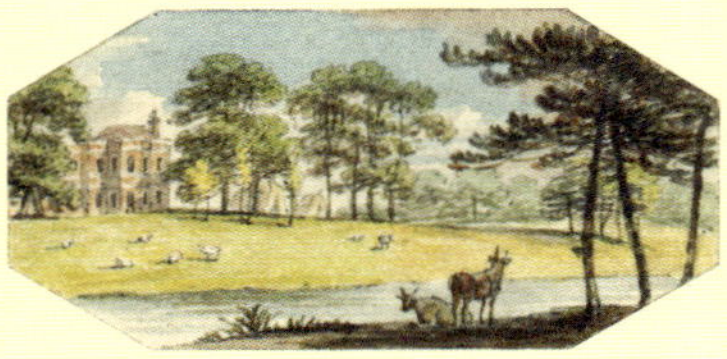

96
Oatlands, Surrey
Watercolor over graphite on beige wove paper
2007.20.17.1

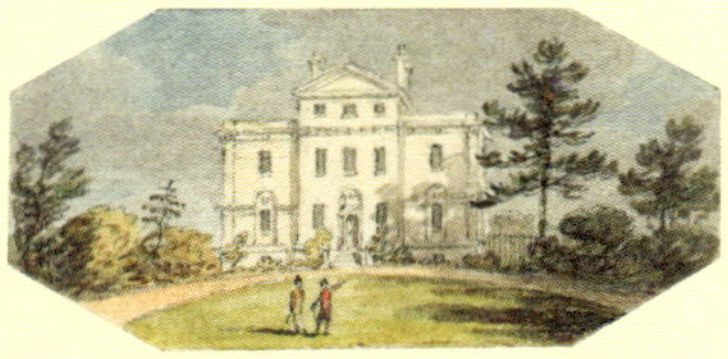

97
Bicknell, near Enfield, Middlesex
Watercolor over graphite on cream wove paper
2007.20.17.2

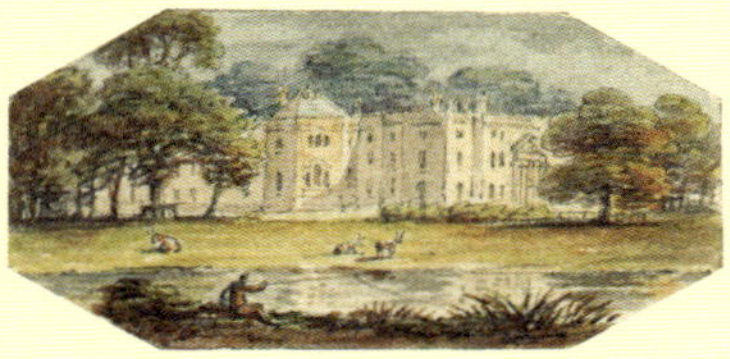

98
Poynton, Cheshire
Watercolor over graphite on cream wove paper
2007.20.17.3

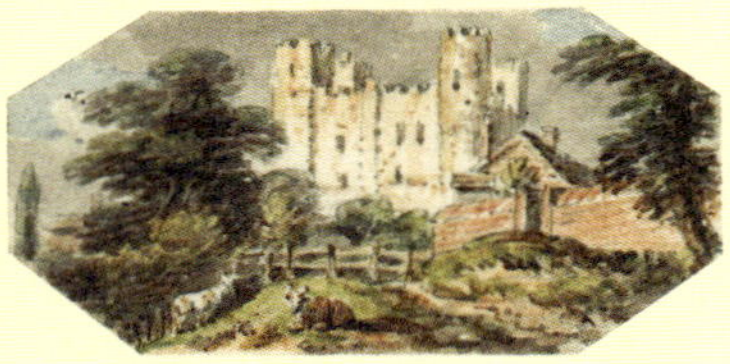

99
Rochester Castle, Kent
Watercolor over graphite on cream wove paper
2007.20.17.4

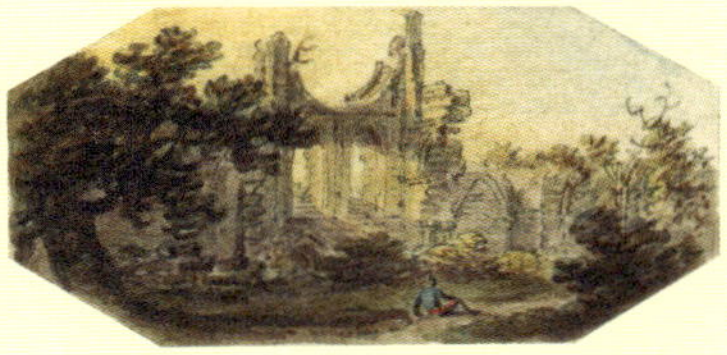

100
Byland Abbey, Yorkshire
Watercolor over graphite on cream wove paper
2007.20.17.5

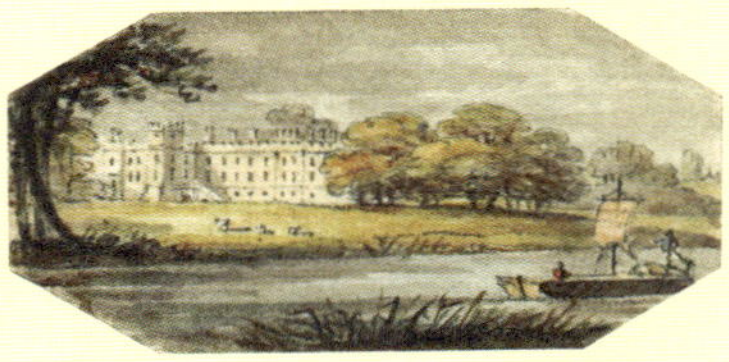

101
Syon House, Northumberland
Watercolor over graphite on white laid paper
2007.20.17.6

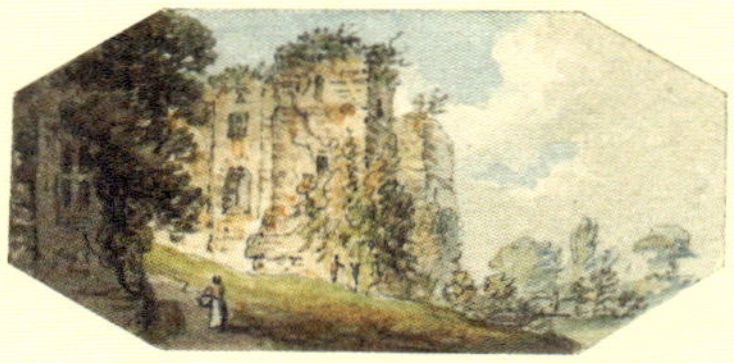

102
Kenilworth Castle, Warwickshire
Watercolor over graphite on cream wove paper
2007.20.17.7

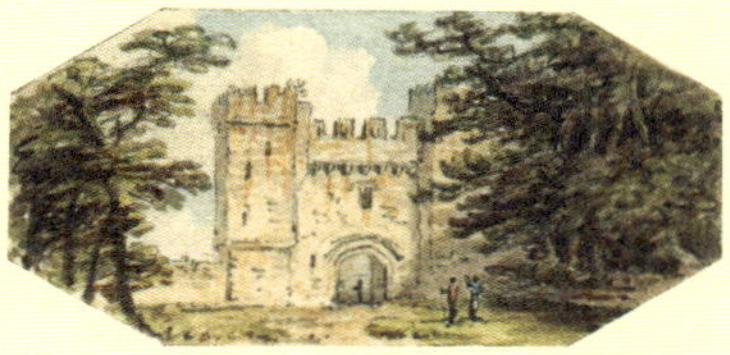

103
Alnwick Abbey, Northumberland
Watercolor over graphite on cream wove paper
2007.20.17.8

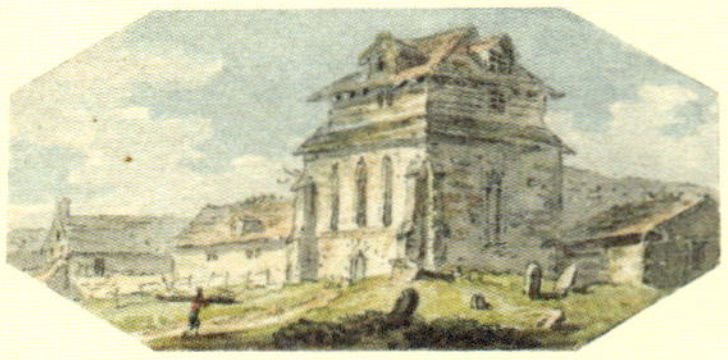

104
Romborough Priory Church, Norfolk
Watercolor over graphite with pen and brown ink on cream wove paper
2007.20.17.9

Edward Dayes

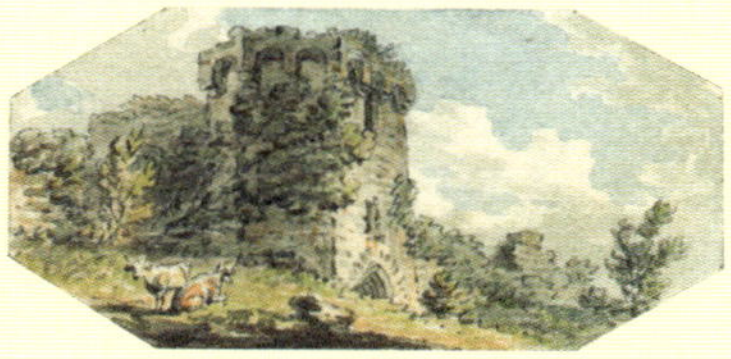

105
Caldicot Castle, Monmouthshire
Watercolor over graphite on cream wove paper
2007.20.17.10

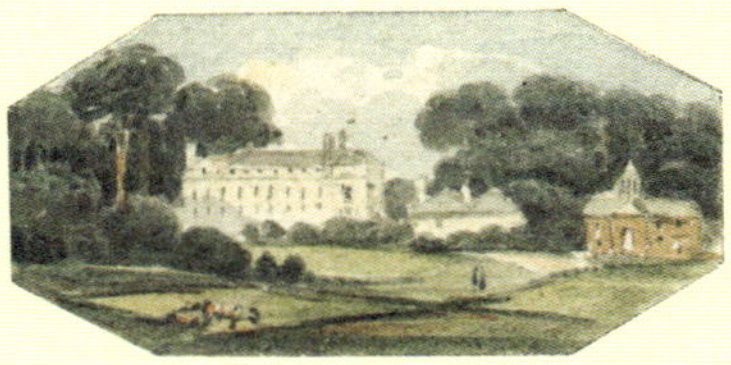

106
A House near Epsom, Surrey
Watercolor over graphite on cream wove paper
2007.20.17.11

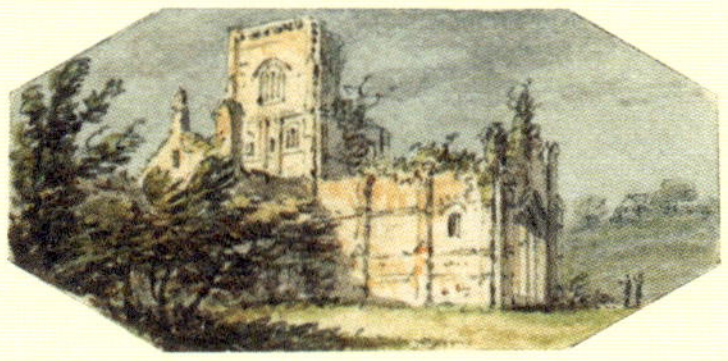

107
Kirkstall Abbey, Yorkshire
Watercolor over graphite on cream wove paper
2007.20.17.12

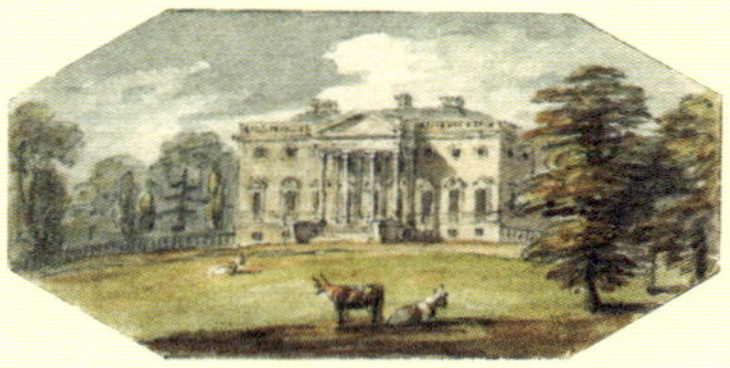

108
Claremont, Surrey
Watercolor over graphite on cream laid paper
2007.20.17.13

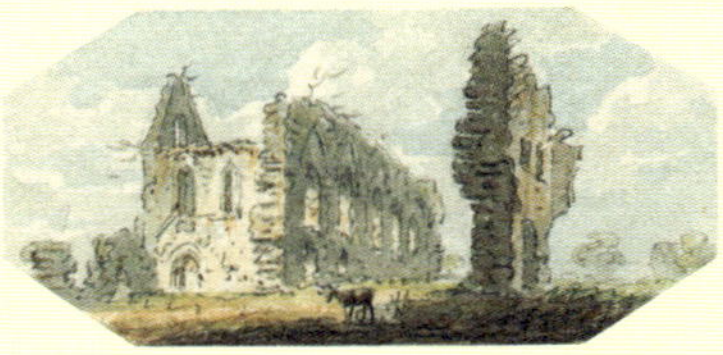

109
Newark Priory, Surrey
Watercolor over graphite on cream wove paper
2007.20.17.14

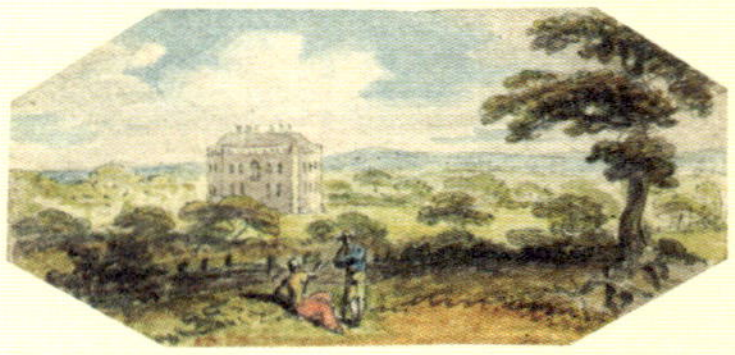

110
House in a Landscape
Watercolor over graphite on cream wove paper
2007.20.17.15

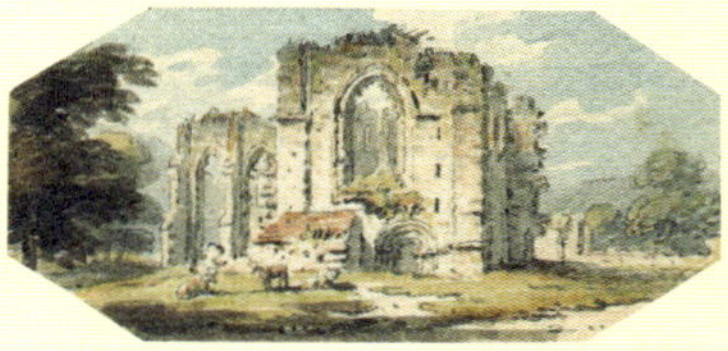

111
Furness Abbey, Lancashire
Watercolor over graphite on cream wove paper
2007.20.17.16

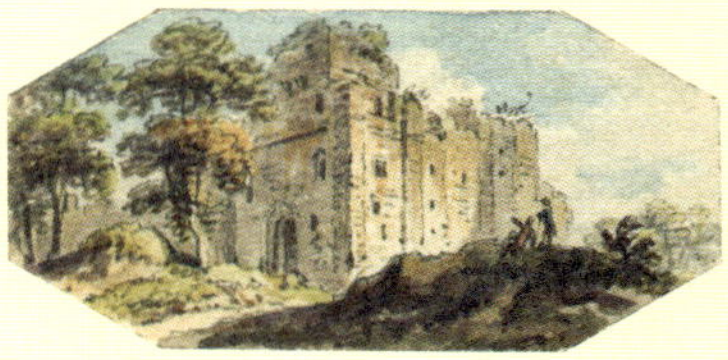

112
Brougham Castle, Westmorland
Watercolor over graphite on cream wove paper
2007.20.17.17

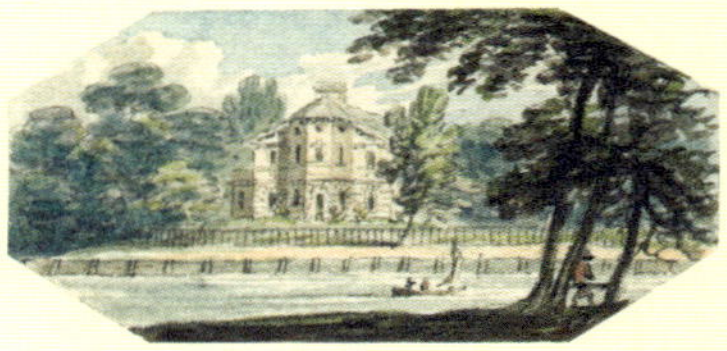

113
Richmond Place, Richmond, Surrey
Watercolor over graphite on cream wove paper
2007.20.17.18

Attributed to Peter De Wint English, 1784–1849

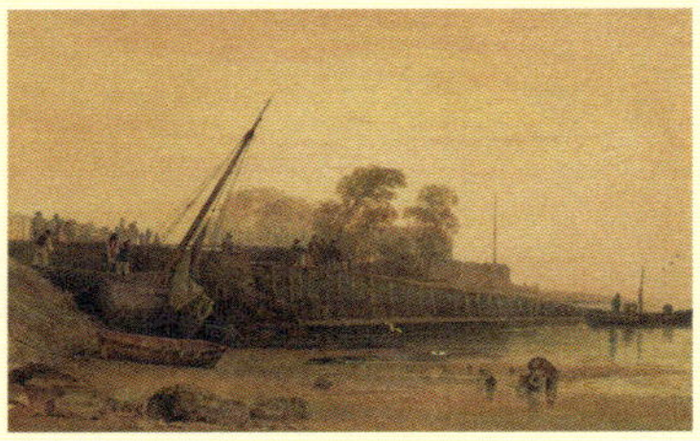

114
Figures by a Dock at Low Tide, c. 1825
Watercolor over graphite, with scraping, on beige wove paper, 24.5 × 38.7 cm
2007.20.45

Provenance: Sir Edwin A. G. Manton (d. 2005); Manton Family Art Foundation (2005–2007, given to the Clark); Sterling and Francine Clark Art Institute, 2007.

Thomas Gainsborough English, 1727–1788

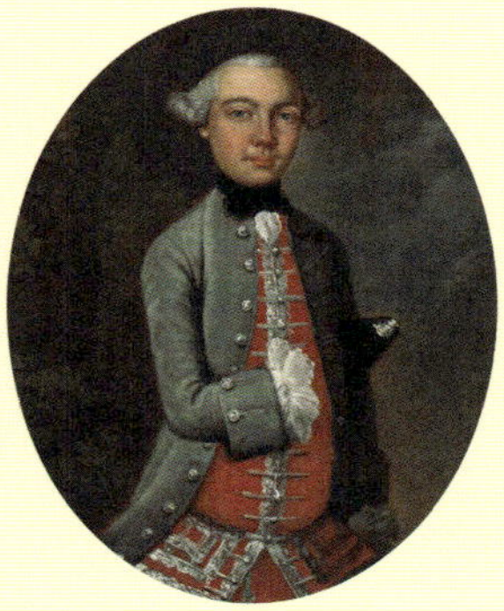

115
Portrait of a Gentleman, c. 1745–48
Oil on canvas on panel, 17.8 × 14 cm
2007.20.20 | Not in Hayes

Provenance: [Deborah Gage (Works of Art), Ltd., London, sold to Manton, Feb. 1994]; Sir Edwin A. G. Manton, New York (1994–d. 2005); Diana Morton, his daughter, by descent (2005–2007, given to the Clark); Sterling and Francine Clark Art Institute, 2007.

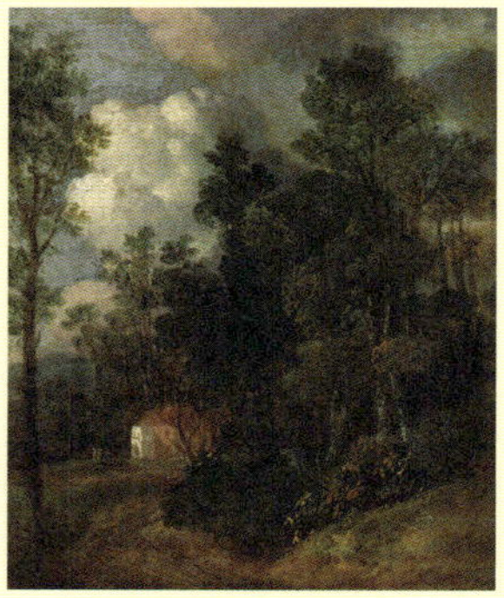

116
A Wooded Landscape with Figures by a House, c. 1752
Oil on canvas, 22.2 × 17.8 cm
2007.8.81 | Not in Hayes

Provenance: The artist; Mrs. Thomas Gainsborough, his wife, by descent; Margaret Gainsborough, the artist's daughter, by descent; Wynn Ellis, sale, Christie's, London, 27 Mar. 1858, no. 12; sale, Christie's, South Kensington, July 1998, as Thomas Churchyard, sold to Felder; [Felder Fine Art, London in 1998]; [Deborah Gage (Works of Art), Ltd., London, sold to Manton, Mar. 2000]; Sir Edwin A. G. Manton, New York (2000–d. 2005); Diana Morton, his daughter, by descent (2005–2007, given to the Clark); Sterling and Francine Clark Art Institute, 2007.

Thomas Gainsborough

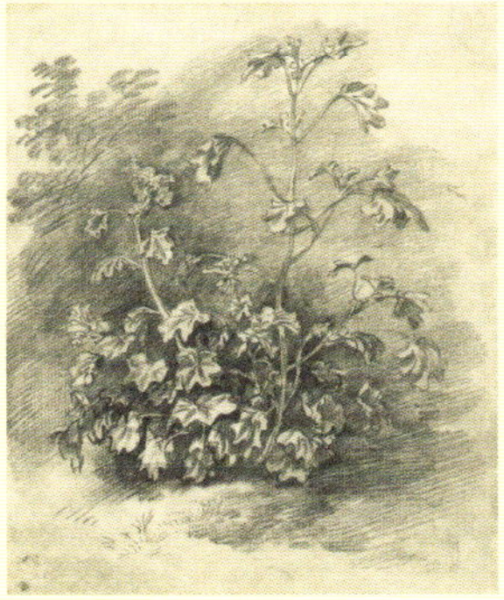

117
Study of Mallows, mid- to late 1750s
Graphite with stumping on white laid paper, with gum fixative, 19.3 × 15.5 cm
2007.8.65 | HD177

Provenance: Charles Fairfax Murray; Henry S. Reitlinger (his sale, Sotheby's, London, 27 Jan. 1954, no. 147, sold to Squire Gallery); [Squire Gallery, sold to Torbock by 1962]; H. Cornish Torbock (by 1962–1994, his sale, Sotheby's, London, 14 Apr. 1994, no. 63, sold to Spink); [Spink & Son, Ltd., London, 1994–1995, sold to Manton, Sept. 1995]; Sir Edwin A. G. Manton, New York (1995–d. 2005); Manton Family Art Foundation (2005–2007, given to the Clark); Sterling and Francine Clark Art Institute, 2007.

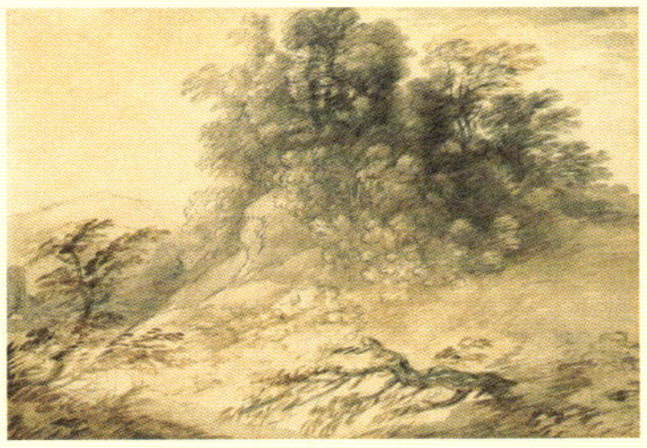

118
Landscape with a Clump of Trees on a Hillock, early 1760s
Watercolor and graphite, with coating, on beige laid paper, 26.1 × 36 cm
2007.8.66 | HD270

Provenance: Alfred de Pass, given to Uppingham School, 1920; Uppingham School (in 1920); [Oscar & Peter Johnson, Ltd., London, sold to Manton, Apr. 1980]; Sir Edwin A. G. Manton, New York (1980–d. 2005); Manton Family Art Foundation (2005–2007, given to the Clark); Sterling and Francine Clark Art Institute, 2007.

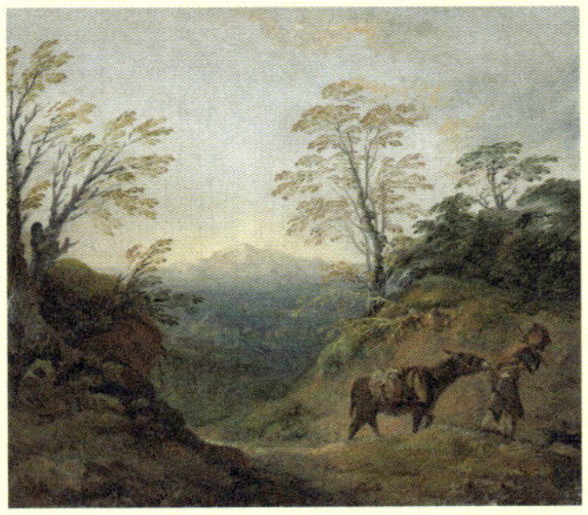

119
Wooded Landscape with a Boy Leading a Donkey and Dog, and an Extensive Panorama with Buildings and Distant Hills, early 1760s
Oil on canvas, 30.2 × 34.3 cm
2007.8.67 | HP78

Provenance: The artist, given to Somerville; Ann Vannam Somerville; John A. F. Somerville, by descent, sale, Sotheby's, London, 15 Mar. 1978, no. 119, sold to British Rail; British Rail Pension Fund, London (in 1978); sale, Sotheby's, London, 8 Mar. 1989, no. 70, sold to Leger; [Leger Galleries, London, 1989, sold to Manton, Mar. 1989]; Sir Edwin A. G. Manton, New York (1989–d. 2005); Diana Morton, his daughter, by descent (2005–2007, given to the Clark); Sterling and Francine Clark Art Institute, 2007.

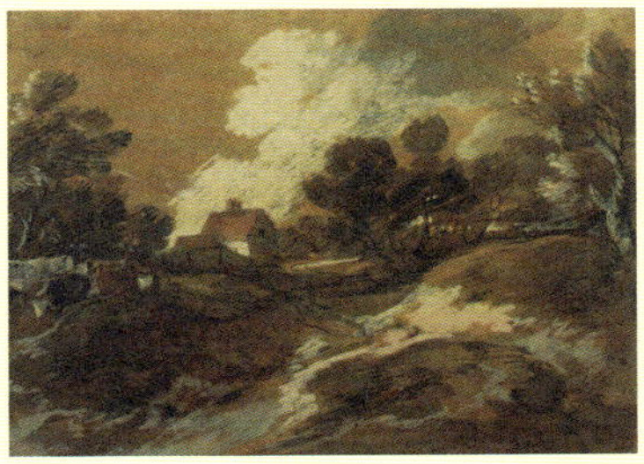

120
Wooded Landscape with a Cottage and Cows, mid-1770s
Brush and gray and red wash with black and blue chalks and lead white on tan laid paper, fixed with skim milk (?) and gum, varnished with mastic, 21.5 × 29.4 cm
2007.8.68 | HDS927

Provenance: [P. & D. Colnaghi & Co., Ltd., London, by 1977–1979]; Mrs. Charles Ward-Jackson; Kimbell Art Museum; Kimbell Art Foundation, sale, Sotheby's, London, 16 July 1987, no. 96, sold to Spink; [Spink & Son, Ltd., London, 1987–1994, no. K3 9477, sold to Manton, May 1994]; Sir Edwin A. G. Manton, New York (1994–d. 2005); Manton Family Art Foundation (2005–2007, given to the Clark); Sterling and Francine Clark Art Institute, 2007.

Thomas Gainsborough

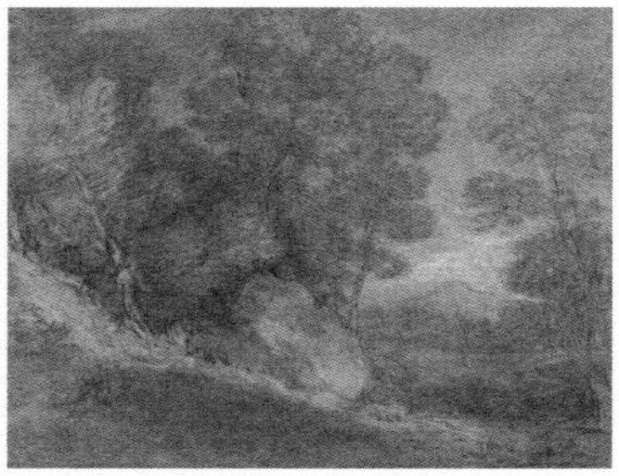

121
Wooded Landscape with Rocks, Stream, and Distant Hill, mid- to late 1770s
Black and white chalks on blue laid paper, fixed with skim milk (?), 25.7 × 32.1 cm
2007.8.69 | Not in Hayes

Provenance: H. C. Laurence; [Squire Gallery]; Norman Baker (in 1951); [Oscar & Peter Johnson, Ltd., London, sold to Manton, Sept. 1964]; Sir Edwin A. G. Manton, New York (1964–d. 2005); Manton Family Art Foundation (2005–2007, given to the Clark); Sterling and Francine Clark Art Institute, 2007.

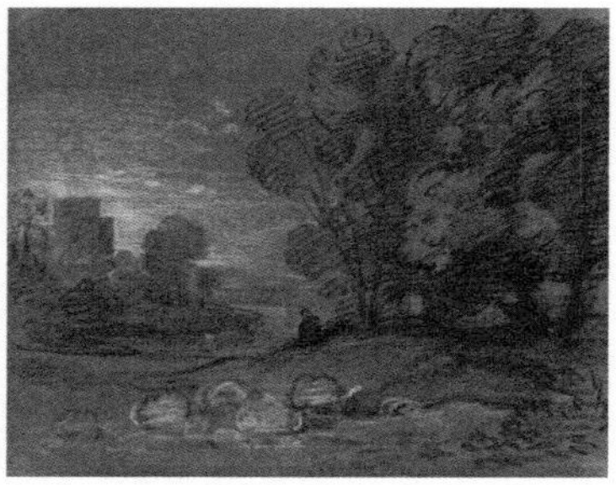

122
Wooded Landscape with Shepherd and Sheep, Winding River, and Tower, mid- to late 1770s
Black and white chalks on brown laid paper, 18.2 × 21.8 cm
2007.8.70 | HD625

Provenance: The artist, probably given to Gardiner; Susannah Gardiner, the artist's sister; Miss R.H. Green, by descent, sale, Christie's, 1 Apr. 1949, no. 36, sold to Colnaghi; [P. & D. Colnaghi & Co., Ltd., London, sold to Bliss]; J. Howard Bliss (in 1949, sold to The Leicester Galleries, 1949); [The Leicester Galleries, London, 1949–1950, sold to Lewsen]; Dr. Sidney Charles Lewsen (1950–1995), sale, Sotheby's, London, 12 Apr. 1995, no. 50; sale, Sotheby's, London, 10 Apr. 1997, no. 25, sold to Ackermann & Johnson, as agent for Manton; Sir Edwin A. G. Manton, New York (1997–d. 2005); Manton Family Art Foundation (2005–2007, given to the Clark); Sterling and Francine Clark Art Institute, 2007.

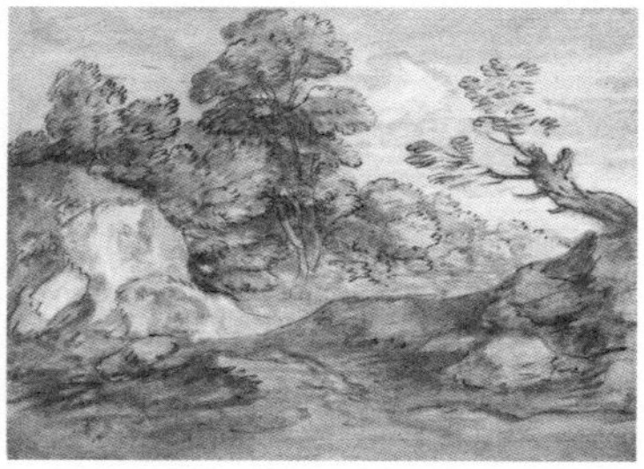

123
Rocky Wooded Landscape with Winding Track, late 1770s
Pen and black ink with brush and gray wash and white chalk on blue laid paper, 26.7 × 34.4 cm
2007.8.71 | Not in Hayes

Provenance: [The Leicester Galleries, London, in 1950]; J. Howard Bliss (in 1950, sold to Spink); [Spink & Son, Ltd., London, 1950, no. K3 9185 sold to Andrews]; Mrs. Andrews (in 1950); [Burlington Paintings, London, May–June 1987, sold to Manton, June 1987]; Sir Edwin A. G. Manton, New York (1987–d. 2005); Manton Family Art Foundation (2005–2007, given to the Clark); Sterling and Francine Clark Art Institute, 2007.

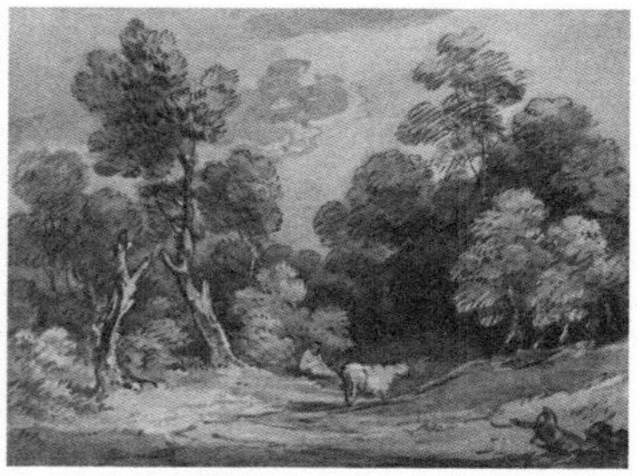

124
Wooded Landscape with Herdsman and Cow, early 1780s
Brush and black and gray wash with black and white chalks on cream laid paper, fixed with skim milk and/or gum, 26.7 × 35.6 cm
2007.8.80 | HD536

Provenance: Randall Davies; [P. & D. Colnaghi & Co., Ltd., London, sold to Egerton, 1938]; Mrs. J. Egerton (in 1938); private collection, by descent, sold to Deborah Gage (Works of Art), Ltd., London, as agent for Manton, Dec. 1999; Sir Edwin A. G. Manton, New York (1999–d. 2005); Manton Family Art Foundation (2005–2007, given to the Clark); Sterling and Francine Clark Art Institute, 2007.

Thomas Gainsborough

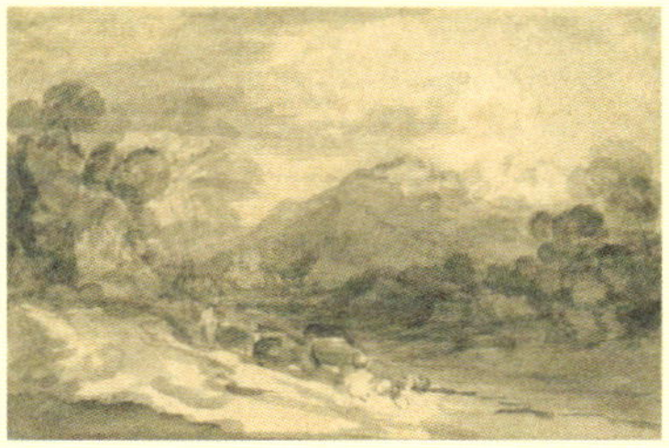

125
Rocky Wooded Landscape with Herdsman Driving Cattle along a Valley and Distant Mountains, c. 1783
Brush and gray wash on beige laid paper, 21.1 × 30.8 cm
2007.8.72 | HDS973

Provenance: Mary Ann Revett; Miss Joan Revett Higginson, her great-granddaughter, by descent, sale, Sotheby Parke Bernet & Co., New York, 17 Nov. 1983, no. 92, sold to Spink; [Spink & Son, Ltd., London, 1983–1984, sold to Manton, Apr. 1984]; Sir Edwin A. G. Manton, New York (1984–d. 2005); Manton Family Art Foundation (2005–2007, given to the Clark); Sterling and Francine Clark Art Institute, 2007.

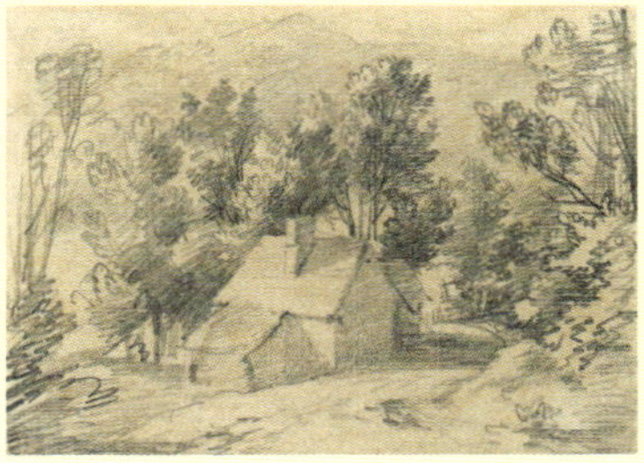

126
Study of a House and Shed in a Wooded Valley, c. 1783
Graphite on beige laid paper, fixed with gum, 14.1 × 18.9 cm
2007.8.73 | Not in Hayes

Provenance: Possibly, sale, Christie's, 11 May 1799, no. 82, 84, or 88, sold to Hibbert; George Hibbert (in 1799); Princess Adelgunde Marie Auguste Therese von Hohenzollern, given to von Werner; given to Anna von Werner, her lady-in-waiting (in 1943); sale, Christie's, London, 8 Apr. 1997, lot 3, sold to Ackermann & Johnson, as agent for Manton; Sir Edwin A. G. Manton, New York (1997–d. 2005); Manton Family Art Foundation (2005–2007, given to the Clark); Sterling and Francine Clark Art Institute, 2007.

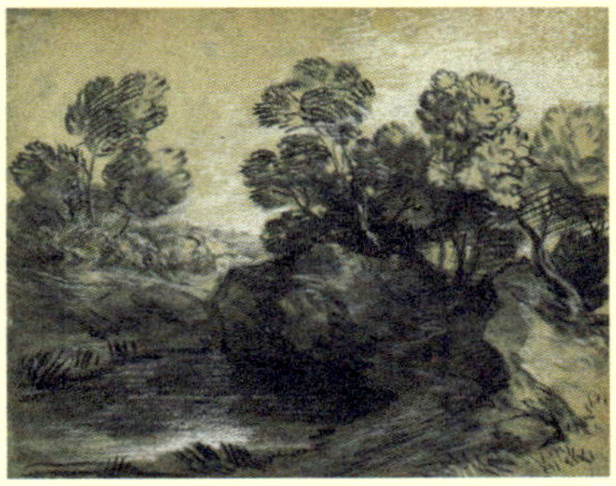

127
Wooded Landscape with Rocks Overhanging a Pool, mid-1780s
Black chalk and lead white with stumping on beige laid paper, fixed with skim milk (?), 26.5 × 32.7 cm
2007.8.74 | HD673.

Provenance: Sale, Sotheby's, London, 15 Apr. 1953, no. 6, sold to Colnaghi; [P. & D. Colnaghi & Co., Ltd., London, in 1953, sold to Blaiberg]; Edgar J. Blaiberg, sale, Christie's, London, 20 June 1978, no. 29, sold to Spink; [Spink & Son, Ltd., London, 1978–1979, no. K3 6647, sold to Manton, May 1979]; Sir Edwin A. G. Manton, New York (1979–d. 2005); Manton Family Art Foundation (2005–2007, given to the Clark); Sterling and Francine Clark Art Institute, 2007.

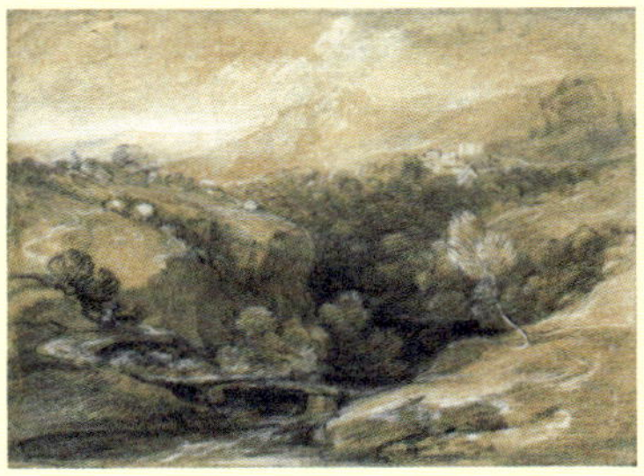

128
Extensive Wooded Landscape with a Bridge over a Gorge, Distant Village, and Hills, c. 1786
Black and white chalks with stumping on beige laid paper, fixed with skim milk and/or gum, 25.9 × 34.8 cm
2007.8.75 | HD771

Provenance: Dr. Dibdin; L. W. Neeld (his sale, Christie's, London, 13 July 1945, no. 106, sold to Agnew's); [Thomas Agnew and Sons, Ltd., London, 1945–1949, sold to Bliss]; J. Howard Bliss (in 1949); [The Leicester Galleries, London, in 1949, sold to Spink]; [Spink & Son, Ltd., London, sold to Walton]; Sir William Walton; Lady Walton, his widow, sale, Sotheby Parke Bernet & Co., New York, 12 July 1984, no. 82, sold to Spink; [Spink & Son, Ltd., London, 1984–1986, sold to Manton, Jan. 1986]; Sir Edwin A. G. Manton, New York (1986–d. 2005); Manton Family Art Foundation (2005–2007, given to the Clark); Sterling and Francine Clark Art Institute, 2007.

Thomas Gainsborough

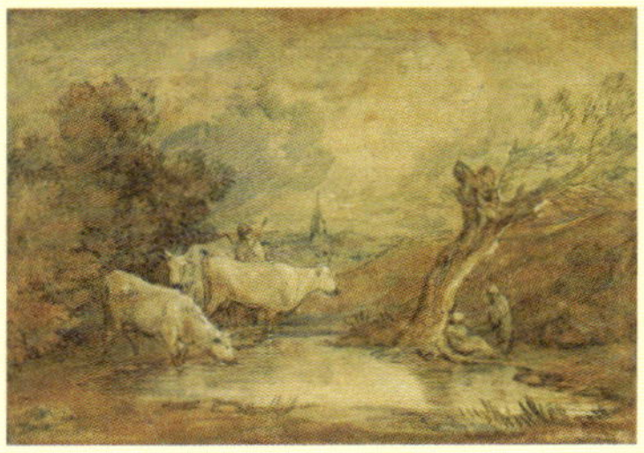

129
Landscape with Figures, Herdsman and Cattle at a Pool, and Distant Church, mid- to late 1780s
Watercolor and gouache with lead white on beige laid paper, fixed with gum, varnished with mastic, 22.1 × 30.7 cm
2007.8.76 | HD665

Provenance: Fitzwilliams of Wiganthorpe; Miss Elsie Fitzwilliam, by descent, sold to Worsley, 1956; Sir William Worsley (in 1956, given to Kent); Katharine Lucy Mary Worsley, later Duchess of Kent, his daughter; [Spink & Son, Ltd., London, no. K3 8389 and P8416, sold to Manton, May 1991]; Sir Edwin A. G. Manton, New York (1991–d. 2005); Manton Family Art Foundation (2005–2007, given to the Clark); Sterling and Francine Clark Art Institute, 2007.

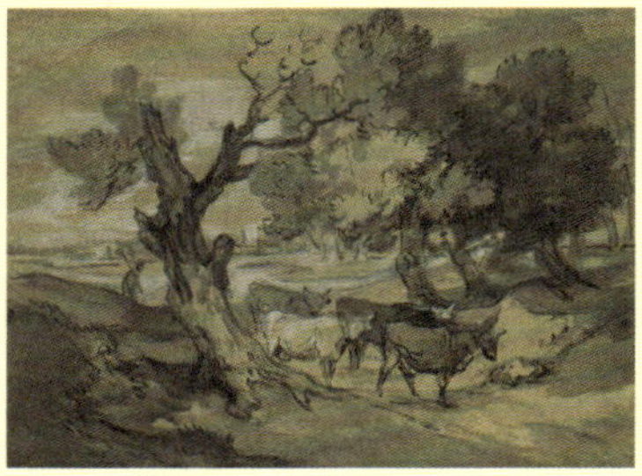

130
Landscape with Herdsman Driving Cows and Distant Buildings, mid- to late 1780s
Black chalk over brush and gray wash with lead white on beige laid paper, fixed with gum (?), 24.6 × 32.4 cm
2007.8.77 | Not in Hayes

Provenance: Sale, Sotheby's, 24 Nov. 1965, no. 27, sold to Tunnard; Tunnard (in 1965); Mr. And Mrs. Lester Avnet, sold to Manton, July 1973; Sir Edwin A. G. Manton, New York (1973–d. 2005); Manton Family Art Foundation (2005–2007, given to the Clark); Sterling and Francine Clark Art Institute, 2007.

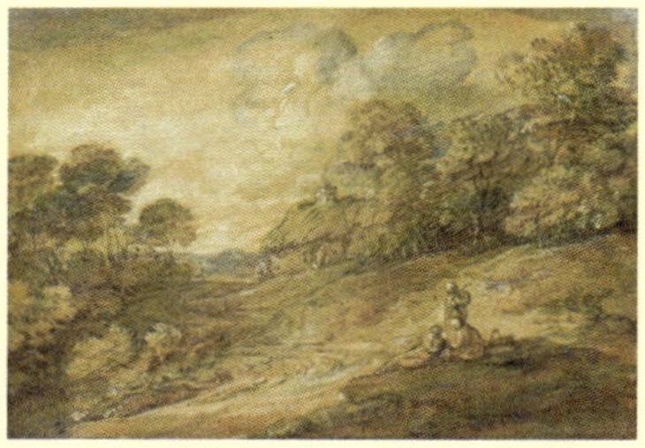

131
Wooded Landscape with Figures and Winding Track Leading to a Cottage, mid- to late 1780s
Watercolor and gouache with lead white on beige laid paper, fixed with gum and skim milk (?), varnished with mastic, 22.1 × 37 cm
2007.8.78 | HD739

Provenance: Fitzwilliams of Wiganthorpe; Miss Elsie Fitzwilliam, by descent, sold to Worsley, 1956; Sir William Worsley (in 1956, given to Kent); Katharine Lucy Mary Worsley, later Duchess of Kent, his daughter; [Spink & Son, Ltd., London, no. K3 10334, sold to Manton, July 1992]; Sir Edwin A. G. Manton, New York (1992–d. 2005); Manton Family Art Foundation (2005–2007, given to the Clark); Sterling and Francine Clark Art Institute, 2007.

Attributed to Thomas Gainsborough

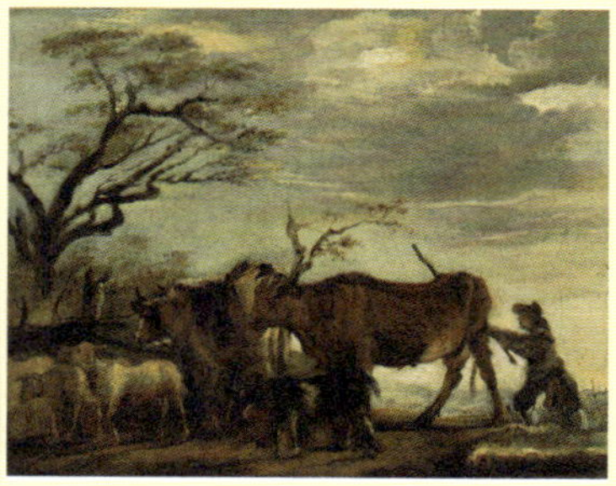

132
A Peasant Driving Cattle, Sheep and Goats in a Landscape, c. 1785
Oil on canvas, 17.8 × 22.2 cm
2007.8.79

Provenance: Probably Wynn Ellis; [Felder Fine Art, London]; [Deborah Gage (Works of Art), Ltd., London, sold to Manton, Nov. 2000]; Sir Edwin A. G. Manton, New York (2000–d. 2005); Diana Morton, his daughter, by descent (2005–2007, given to the Clark); Sterling and Francine Clark Art Institute, 2007.

After Thomas Gainsborough British, 18th century

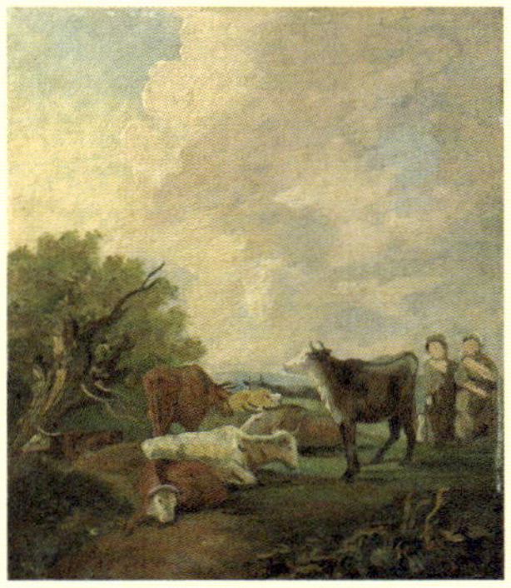

133
Figures and Cattle in a Landscape
Oil on canvas mounted on panel, 19.1 × 17.1 cm
2007.20.19

Provenance: Sir Edwin A. G. Manton, New York (d. 2005); Diana Morton, his daughter, by descent (2005–2007, given to the Clark); Sterling and Francine Clark Art Institute, 2007.

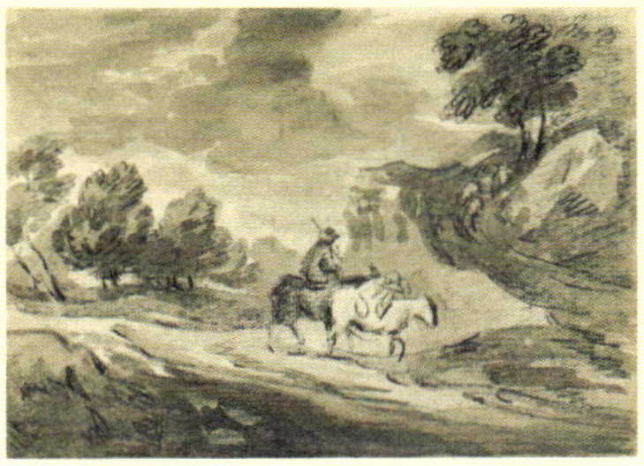

134
Rocky Landscape with Horseman and Packhorse
Graphite over brush and gray washes on cream laid paper, 17 × 23 cm
2007.20.22

Provenance: Lord Nathan of Churt; [Spink & Son, Ltd., London]; [Oscar & Peter Johnson, Ltd., London, sold to Manton, June 1964]; Sir Edwin A. G. Manton, New York (1964–d. 2005); Manton Family Art Foundation (2005–2007, given to the Clark); Sterling and Francine Clark Art Institute, 2007.

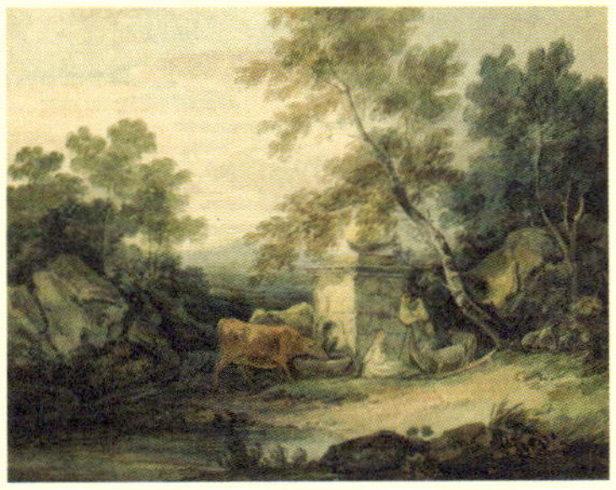

135
Rocky Landscape with Herdsman Conversing with a Girl, Goats, Cows Drinking at a Fountain and Distant Hills
Watercolor over graphite on cream wove paper, 31.6 × 38.7 cm
2007.20.23

Provenance: J. Huth (his sale, Christie's, London, 8 July 1895, no. 64); [Oscar & Peter Johnson, Ltd., London, sold to Manton Oct. 1966]; Sir Edwin A. G. Manton, New York (1966–d. 2005); Manton Family Art Foundation (2005–2007, given to the Clark); Sterling and Francine Clark Art Institute, 2007.

Style of Thomas Gainsborough British, 18th century

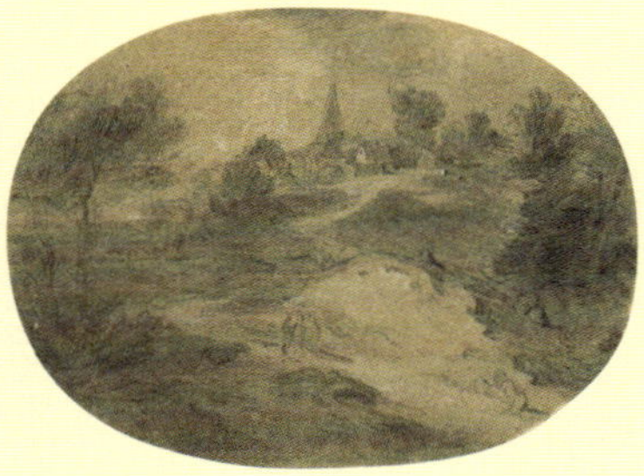

136
A Wooded Landscape with a Village on a Hilltop and Figures on a Lane in Front
Black and white chalks with stumping on beige laid paper, 25.5 × 34 cm
2007.20.21

Provenance: [Oscar & Peter Johnson, Ltd., London, sold to Manton, Jan. 1966]; Sir Edwin A. G. Manton, New York (1996–d. 2005); Manton Family Art Foundation (2005–2007, given to the Clark); Sterling and Francine Clark Art Institute, 2007.

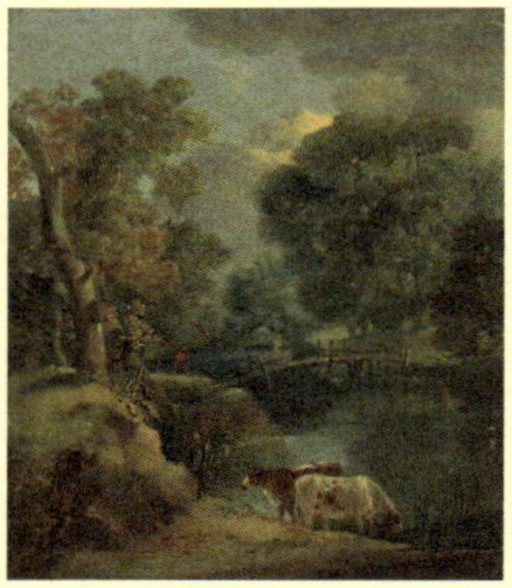

137
A River Landscape with Two Cows and a Figure on a Bridge
Oil on canvas, 35.9 × 28.9 cm
2007.8.82

Provenance: Sir Edwin A. G. Manton, New York (June 2005–d. 2005); Diana Morton, his daughter, by descent (2005–2007, given to the Clark); Sterling and Francine Clark Art Institute, 2007.

Thomas Girtin English, 1775–1802

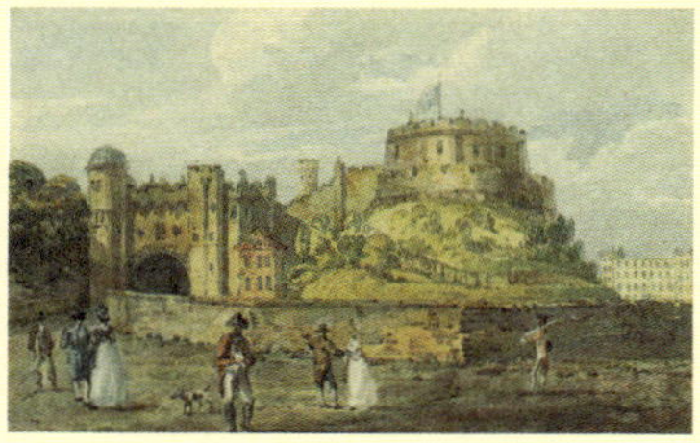

138
Windsor Castle, c. 1792
Watercolor over graphite with pen and brown ink on cream wove paper, 12.4 × 18.3 cm
2007.8.83

Provenance: Sale, Christie's, London, 15 Nov. 1983, no. 155, sold to Leger; [Leger Galleries, 1983–1984, sold to Manton, Feb. 1984]; Sir Edwin A. G. Manton, New York (1984–d. 2005); Manton Family Art Foundation (2005–2007, given to the Clark); Sterling and Francine Clark Art Institute, 2007.

Thomas Girtin

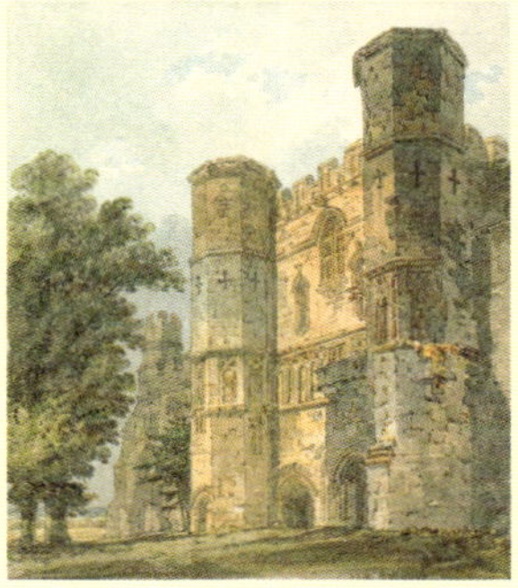

139
The Gatehouse of Battle Abbey, Sussex, c. 1794
Pen and brown ink and watercolor over graphite on white wove paper, 27.3 × 23.5 cm
2007.8.84

Provenance: W. C. Alexander (in 1912); private collection, by descent, sold to Spink, 1998; [Spink-Leger Pictures, 1998–1999, no. K3 11560, sold to Manton, June 1999]; Sir Edwin A. G. Manton, New York (1999–d. 2005); Manton Family Art Foundation (2005–2007, given to the Clark); Sterling and Francine Clark Art Institute, 2007.

Thomas Girtin English, 1775–1802 and Joseph Mallord William Turner English, 1775–1851

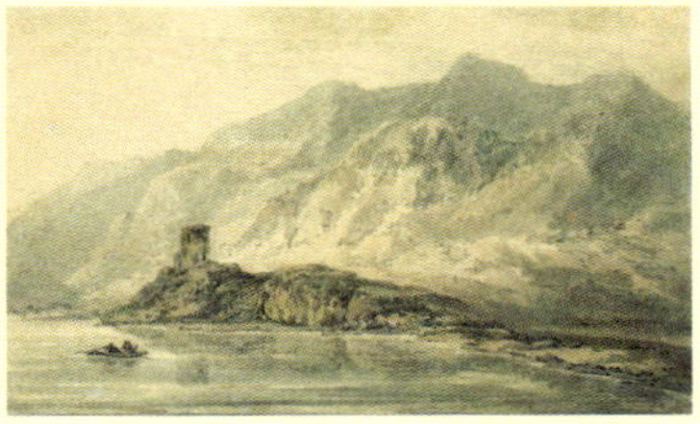

140
Dolbadarn Castle, c. 1795
Watercolor over graphite on cream wove paper, 14.9 × 23.8 cm
2007.8.120

Provenance: Possibly Dr. Thomas Monro, sale, Christie's, London, 26-28 June and 1-2 July 1833; Joseph Mayer, sale, Sotheby's, London, 23 July 1887, no. 551, sold to Hibbert; Hibbert (in 1887); Alexander Abraham; sale, Parke-Bernet Galleries, New York, 7 Apr. 1966, no. 83, sold to Manton, as Joseph Mallord William Turner; Sir Edwin A. G. Manton, New York (1966–d. 2005); Manton Family Art Foundation (2005–2007, given to the Clark); Sterling and Francine Clark Art Institute, 2007.

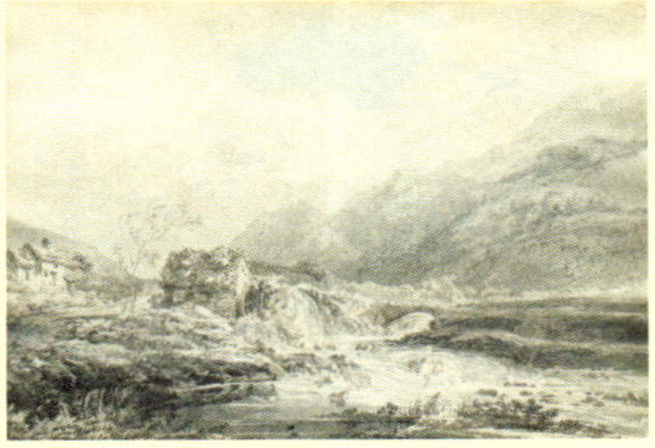

141
Mountainous Landscape with Overshot Mill and Bridge, c. 1795
Watercolor and graphite on cream wove paper, 26.4 × 37.8 cm
2007.8.121

Provenance: Possibly Dr. Thomas Monro, sale, Christie's, London, 26-28 June and 1-2 July 1833; John Dobbs Berger, sale, Sotheby's, London, 16 July 1981, no. 45; sale, Sotheby's, New York, 23 Oct. 1990, no. 6; sale, Christie's, London, 7 Apr. 1998, no. 26, to Ackermann; [Ackermann & Johnson, London, Apr.–Nov. 1998, sold to Manton, Nov. 1998]; Sir Edwin A. G. Manton, New York (1998–d. 2005); Manton Family Art Foundation (2005–2007, given to the Clark); Sterling and Francine Clark Art Institute, 2007.

Thomas Girtin and Joseph Mallord William Turner

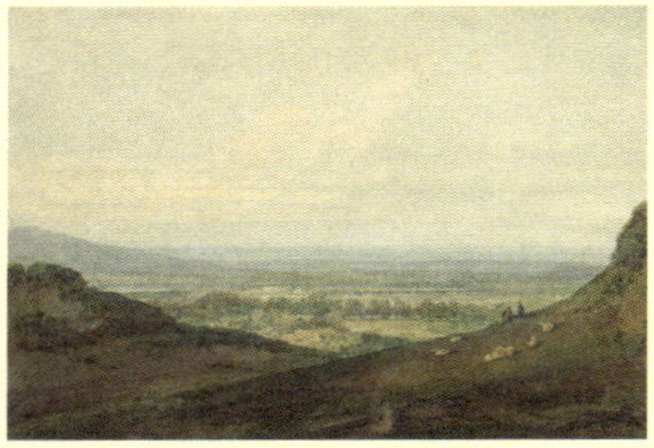

142
View in Westmorland, near Ireton, c. 1796
Watercolor over graphite on cream wove paper, 15.9 × 22.9 cm
2007.8.122

Provenance: [Thomas Agnew and Sons, Ltd., London]; private collection, Berkshire; [Spink & Sons, Ltd., London, sold to Manton, 1986]; Sir Edwin A. G. Manton, New York (1986–d. 2005); Manton Family Art Foundation (2005–2007, given to the Clark); Sterling and Francine Clark Art Institute, 2007.

Thomas Girtin

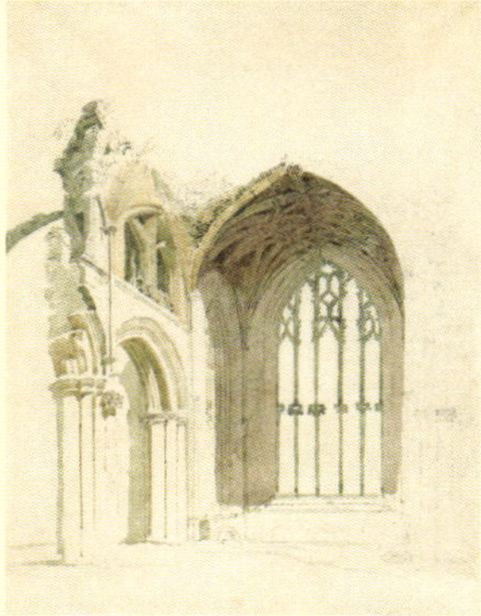

143
Melrose Abbey: The East Window, c. 1796
Watercolor and graphite on cream wove paper, 37.8 × 28.4 cm
2007.8.85

Provenance: Col. H. S. Eeles, sale, Christie's, London, 14 Nov. 1989, no. 91; [Spink & Son, Ltd., London, no. K3 10079, sold to Manton, Apr. 1995]; Sir Edwin A. G. Manton, New York (1995–d. 2005); Manton Family Art Foundation (2005–2007, given to the Clark); Sterling and Francine Clark Art Institute, 2007.

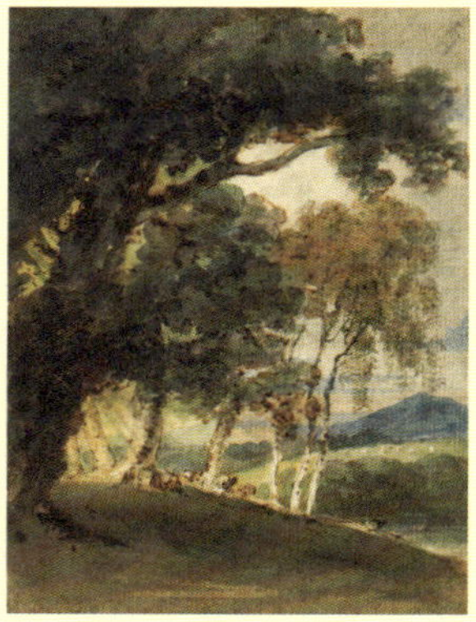

144
A River Valley and Distant Hill Seen through Trees, c. 1800
Watercolor with pen and brown ink over graphite on cream laid paper, 22.5 × 16.8 cm
2007.8.86

Provenance: C. E. Hughes; by descent until sold to Deborah Gage (Works of Art), Ltd., London, as agent for Manton, Aug. 1998; Sir Edwin A. G. Manton, New York (1998–d. 2005); Manton Family Art Foundation (2005–2007, given to the Clark); Sterling and Francine Clark Art Institute, 2007.

Thomas Girtin

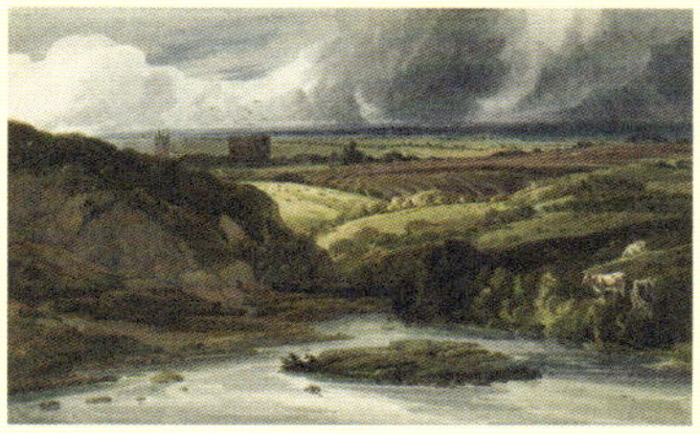

145
Lydford Castle, c. 1800
Watercolor and gouache over graphite on white laid paper, 31.8 × 52.1 cm
2007.8.87

Provenance: The artist, sold to Ramsden; Sir John Ramsden; by descent until sale, Sotheby's, London, 11 July 1990, no. 92, sold to Leger; [Leger Galleries, London, July–Oct. 1990, sold to Manton, Oct. 1990]; Sir Edwin A. G. Manton, New York (1990–d. 2005); Manton Family Art Foundation (2005–2007, given to the Clark); Sterling and Francine Clark Art Institute, 2007.

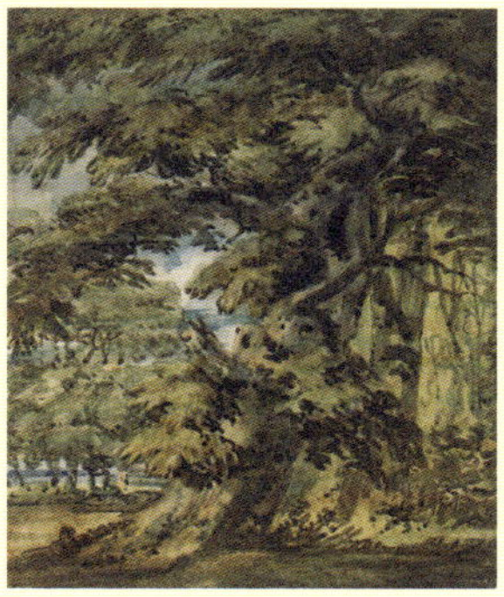

146
A Wooded Landscape, c. 1800
Watercolor over graphite on cream wove paper, 15.2 × 12.4 cm
2007.8.88

Provenance: [Spink-Leger Pictures, London, sold to Manton, May 2000]; Sir Edwin A. G. Manton, New York (2000–d. 2005); Manton Family Art Foundation (2005–2007, given to the Clark); Sterling and Francine Clark Art Institute, 2007.

Albert Goodwin English, 1845–1932

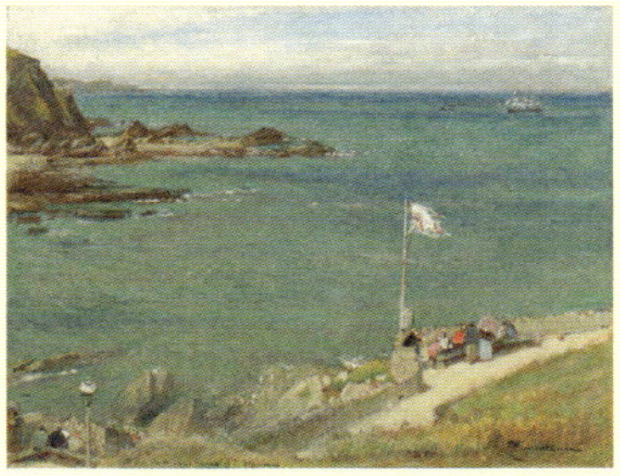

147
The Bristol Channel from Ilfracombe, 1890s
Oil on board, 31.1 × 40.2 cm
2007.8.89

Provenance: [Ackermann & Johnson, Ltd., London, sold to Manton, 17 Nov. 1994]; Sir Edwin A. G. Manton, New York (1994–d. 2005); Manton Family Art Foundation (2005–2007, given to the Clark); Sterling and Francine Clark Art Institute, 2007.

Albert Goodwin

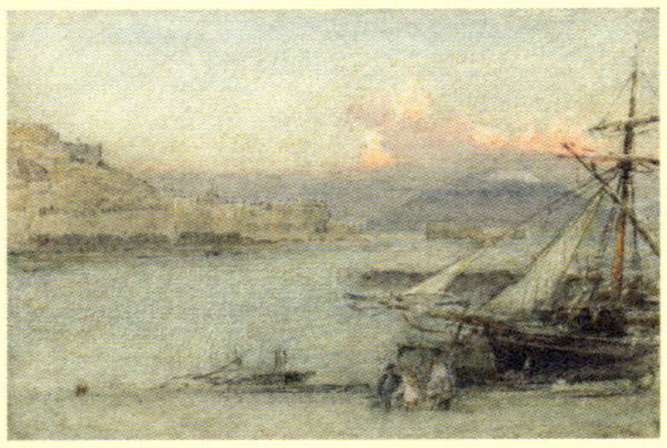

148
Naples, c. 1910
Watercolor and pen and ink over graphite, with scraping, on cream wove paper, 19.7 × 28 cm
2007.20.25

Provenance: [Oscar & Peter Johnson, Ltd., London, sold to Manton, Mar. 1977]; Sir Edwin A. G. Manton, New York (1977–d. 2005); Manton Family Art Foundation (2005–2007, given to the Clark); Sterling and Francine Clark Art Institute, 2007.

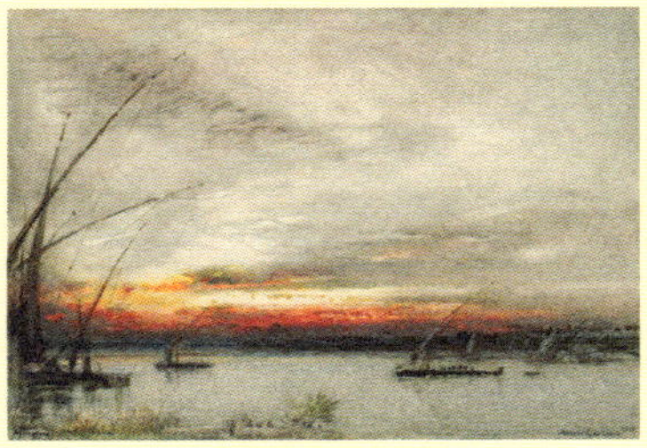

149
Afterglow on the Nile, 1911
Watercolor and gouache, with scraping, on white wove paper, 28.5 × 38.8 cm
2007.20.24

Provenance: [Oscar & Peter Johnson, Ltd., London, sold to Manton, Feb. 1983]; Sir Edwin A. G. Manton, New York (1983–d. 2005); Manton Family Art Foundation (2005–2007, given to the Clark); Sterling and Francine Clark Art Institute, 2007.

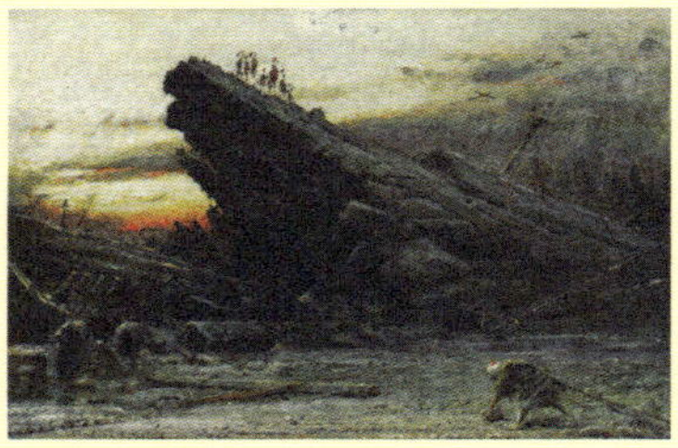

150
Sinbad the Sailor, 1929
Gouache on black wove paper, 26.6 × 38.5 cm
2007.20.26

Provenance: [Oscar & Peter Johnson, Ltd., London, sold to Manton, Dec. 1979]; Sir Edwin A. G. Manton, New York (1979–d. 2005); Manton Family Art Foundation (2005–2007, given to the Clark); Sterling and Francine Clark Art Institute, 2007.

Attributed to Amelia Long, Lady Farnborough English, 1772–1837

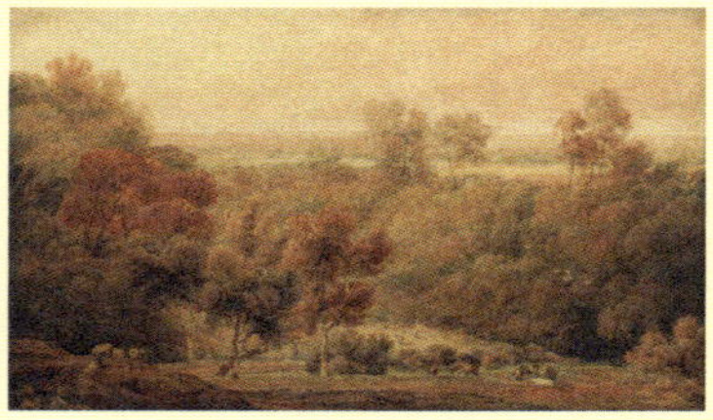

151
An Extensive Wooded Landscape with Cattle in the Foreground, early 19th century
Watercolor and graphite, with scraping, on cream laid paper, 32.4 × 54 cm
2007.20.42

Provenance: Sir Edwin A. G. Manton (d. 2005); Manton Family Art Foundation (2005–2007, given to the Clark); Sterling and Francine Clark Art Institute, 2007.

David Lucas English, 1802–1881 after John Constable English, 1776–1837

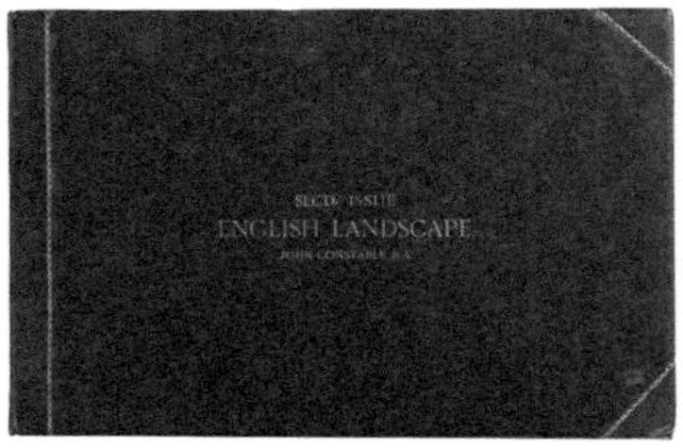

English Landscape portfolio, 1826–46
Fifteen mezzotints in various states, first published in 1838 and 1846, two etchings dated 1826, and four pages of text in a gold-stamped, green leather album, compiled by Hugh Golding Constable. Lettered in gilt on the front cover "Secd. Issue | English Landscape. | John Constable, R.A."

Provenance as follows unless otherwise stated: Hugh Golding Constable; John Constable, his grandson, by descent, sold to Salander O'Reilly Galleries, as agent for Manton, May 1993; Sir Edwin A. G. Manton, New York (1995–d. 2005); Manton Family Art Foundation (2005–2007, given to the Clark); Sterling and Francine Clark Art Institute, 2007. 2007.20.6.1–17

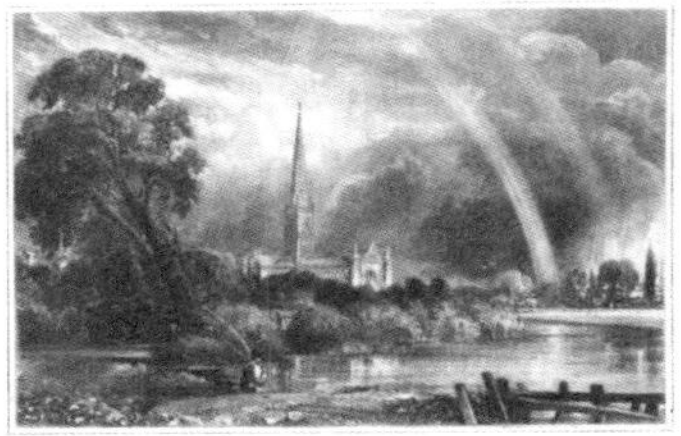

152
Salisbury Cathedral from the Meadows, 1838
Mezzotint on chine collé on cream wove paper, 15.9 × 23.4 cm (chine); 17.5 × 25 cm (plate); 27.2 × 42.3 cm (sheet)
2007.20.6.1 | S30 proof n

Provenance: John Constable; Alfred Constable, his son, by descent; Hugh Golding Constable; John Constable, his grandson, by descent, sold to Salander O'Reilly Galleries, as agent for Manton, May 1993; Sir Edwin A. G. Manton, New York (1995–d. 2005); Manton Family Art Foundation (2005–2007, given to the Clark); Sterling and Francine Clark Art Institute, 2007.

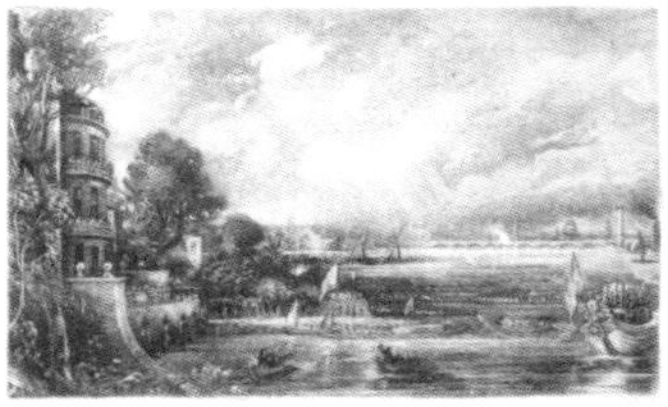

153
Opening of Waterloo Bridge, 1838
Mezzotint on cream wove paper, 17.5 × 24.5 cm (plate); 27.8 × 42.5 cm (sheet)
2007.20.6.2 | S31 I/II

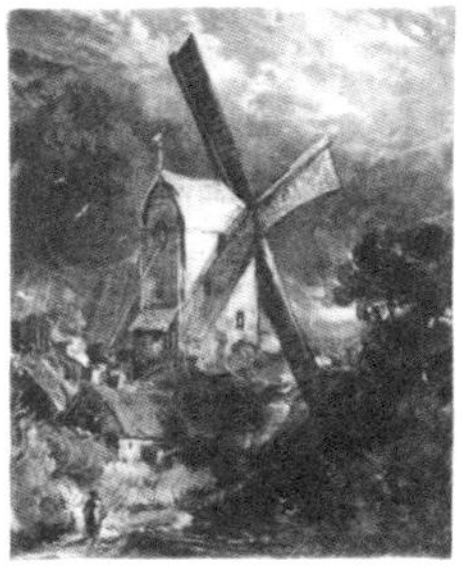

154
A Mill near Brighton, 1838
Mezzotint on cream wove paper, 17.7 × 12 cm (plate); 27.8 × 42.5 cm (sheet)
2007.20.6.3 | S4 I/II

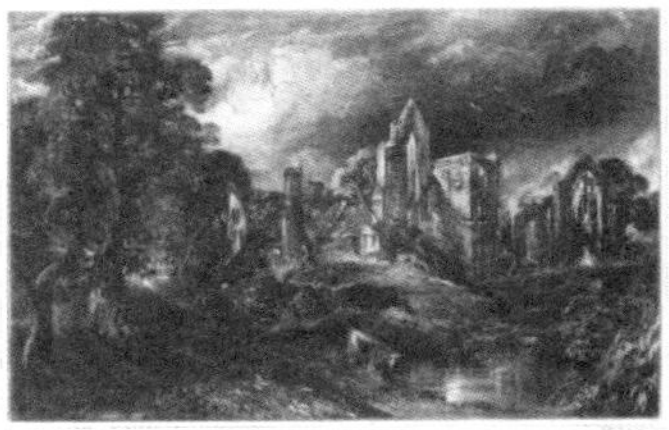

155
Castle Acre Priory, 1838
Mezzotint on cream wove paper, 17.5 × 25.2 cm (plate); 7.8 × 42.4 cm (sheet)
2007.20.6.4 | S22 I/III

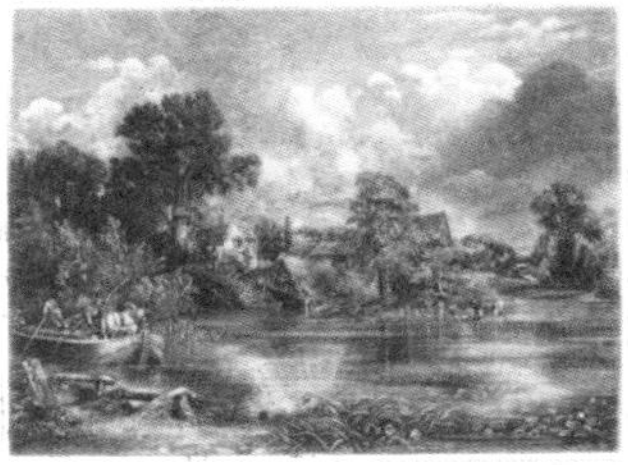

156
View on the River Stour, 1838
Mezzotint on cream wove paper, 17.8 × 22 cm (plate); 27.8 × 42.4 cm (sheet);
2007.20.6.5 | S21 I/II

David Lucas after John Constable

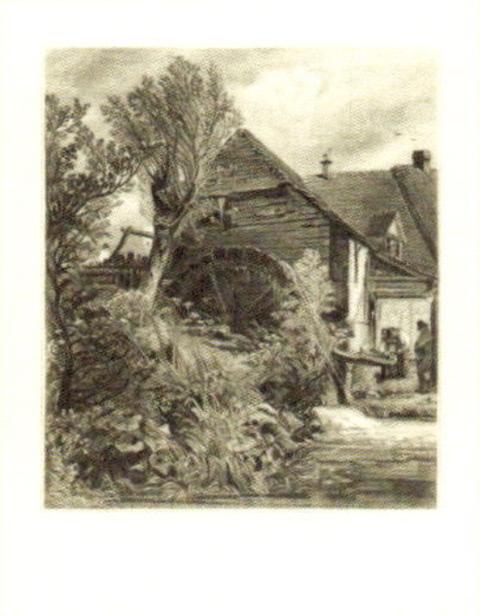

157
Gillingham Mill, Dorsetshire, 1846
Mezzotint on cream wove paper,
25 × 19 cm (plate);
27.8 × 42.5 cm (sheet)
2007.20.6.6 | S43 proof h

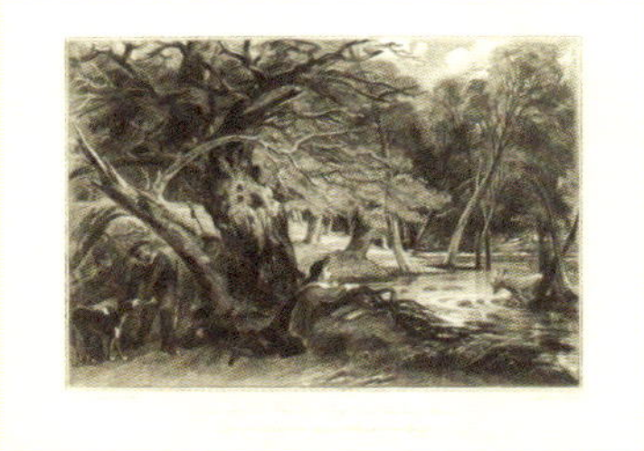

158
Jacques and the Wounded Stag, 1846
Mezzotint on cream wove paper,
17.4 × 24.2 cm (plate);
27.8 × 42.3 cm (sheet)
2007.20.6.7 | S15 I/II

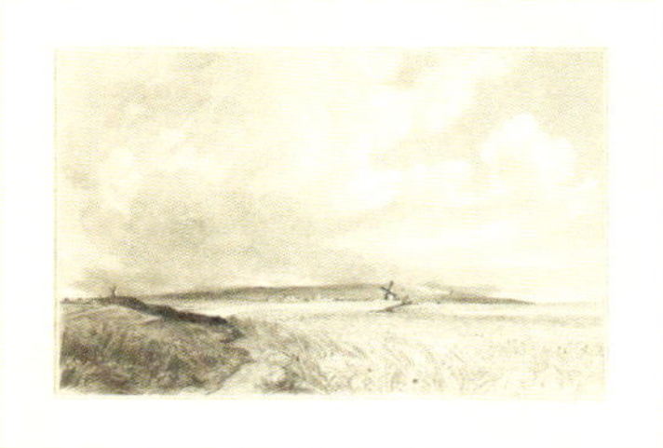

159
Cornfields near Brighton, 1846
Mezzotint on cream wove paper,
18.3 × 25.4 cm (plate);
27.8 × 42.5 cm (sheet)
2007.20.6.8 | S44 proof k

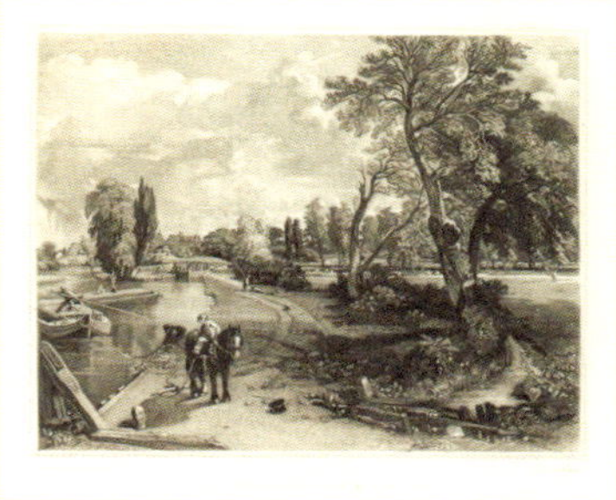

160
Flatford Mill, 1846
Mezzotint on chine collé on cream wove paper, 17.7 × 20.9 cm (chine);
17.5 × 20.7 cm (plate);
27.8 × 42.5 cm (sheet)
2007.20.6.9 | S46 I/II

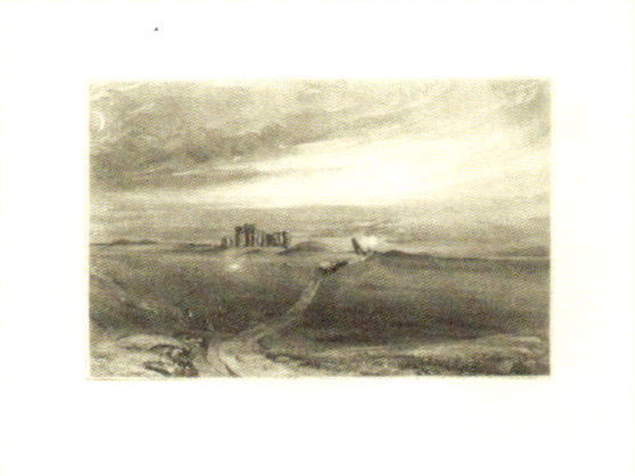

161
Stonehenge, 1846
Mezzotint on cream wove paper,
21.1 × 27.6 cm (plate);
27.8 × 42.5 cm (sheet)
2007.20.6.10 | S41 proof e

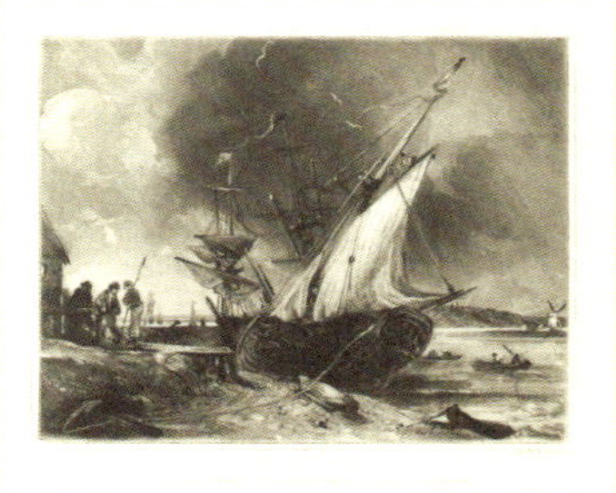

162
View on the Orwell near Ipswich, 1838
Mezzotint on cream wove paper,
17.8 × 21.8 cm (plate);
27.8 × 42.4 cm (sheet)
2007.20.6.11 | S24 I/III

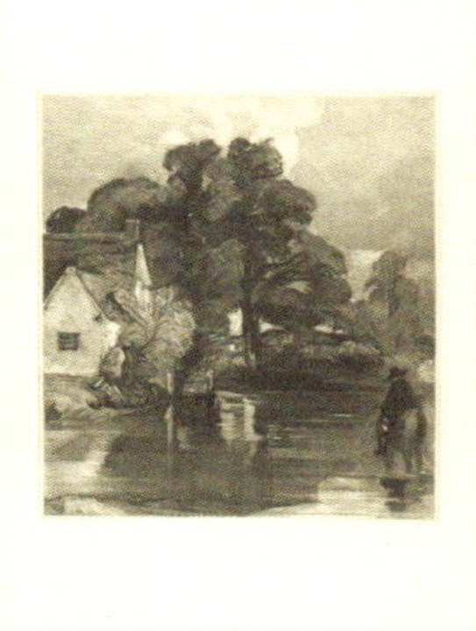

163
Willy Lott's House, 1846
Mezzotint on beige wove paper,
18.5 × 25.5 cm (plate);
27.8 × 42.4 cm (sheet)
2007.20.6.12 | S33 proof h

David Lucas after John Constable

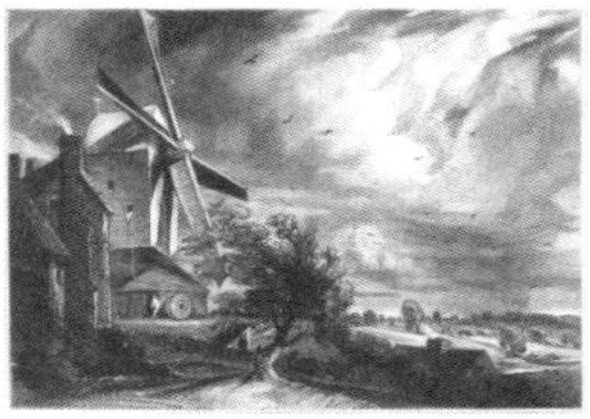

164
Mill near Colchester, 1846
Mezzotint on beige wove paper,
19 × 24.1 cm (plate);
27.8 × 42.2 cm (sheet)
2007.20.6.13 | S50 proof t

Provenance: David Lucas, presented to Alfred Constable; Alfred Constable; Hugh Golding Constable, by descent; John Constable, his grandson, by descent, sold to Salander O'Reilly Galleries, as agent for Manton, May 1993; Sir Edwin A. G. Manton, New York (1995–d. 2005); Manton Family Art Foundation (2005–2007, given to the Clark); Sterling and Francine Clark Art Institute, 2007

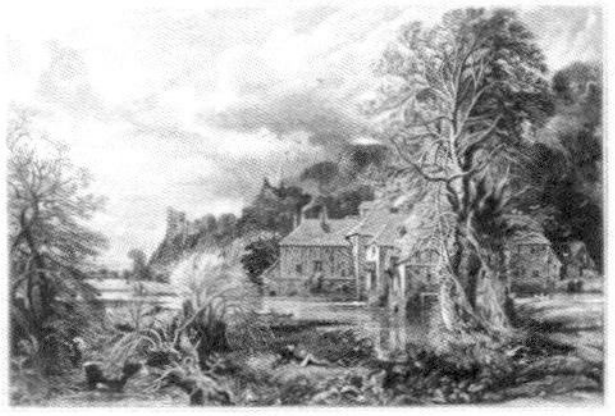

165
Arundel Mill and Castle, 1846
Mezzotint on beige wove paper,
19.1 × 24.1 cm (plate);
27.8 × 42.5 cm (sheet)
2007.20.6.14 | S49 proof q

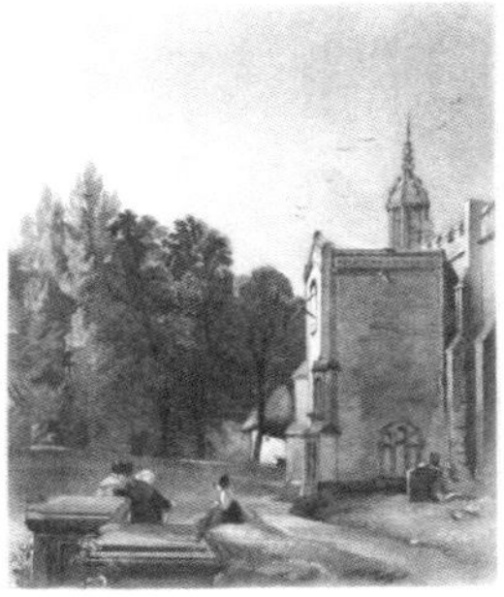

166
Porch of the Church at East Bergholt, Suffolk, 1846
Mezzotint on cream wove paper,
24.1 × 19.1 cm (plate);
27.8 × 42.3 cm (sheet)
2007.20.6.15 | S42 proof f

Provenance: David Lucas, presented to Alfred Constable; Alfred Constable; Hugh Golding Constable, by descent; John Constable, his grandson, by descent, sold to Salander O'Reilly Galleries, as agent for Manton, May 1993; Sir Edwin A. G. Manton, New York (1995–d. 2005); Manton Family Art Foundation (2005–2007, given to the Clark); Sterling and Francine Clark Art Institute, 2007.

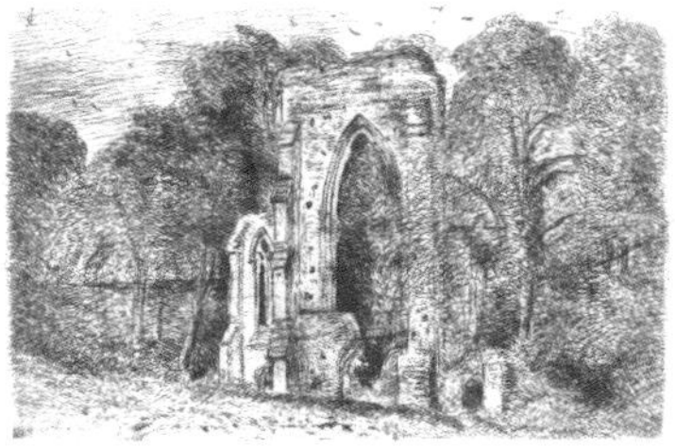

167
Netley Abbey, 1826
Etching on cream wove paper,
13.2 × 18.8 cm (plate);
27.8 × 42.1 cm (sheet)
2007.20.6.16

Provenance: John Constable; Hugh Golding Constable, by descent; John Constable, his grandson, by descent, sold to Salander O'Reilly Galleries, as agent for Manton, May 1993; Sir Edwin A. G. Manton, New York (1995–d. 2005); Manton Family Art Foundation (2005–2007, given to the Clark); Sterling and Francine Clark Art Institute, 2007.

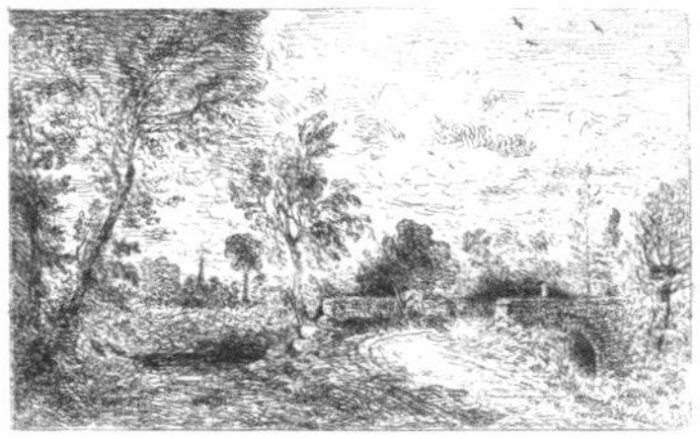

168
Milford Bridge, 1826
Etching on chine collé on cream wove paper, 12.7 × 18.4 cm (chine);
13.4 × 19 cm (plate);
27.8 × 42.1 cm (sheet)
2007.20.6.17

Provenance: John Constable; Hugh Golding Constable, by descent; John Constable, his grandson, by descent, sold to Salander O'Reilly Galleries, as agent for Manton, May 1993; Sir Edwin A. G. Manton, New York (1995–d. 2005); Manton Family Art Foundation (2005–2007, given to the Clark); Sterling and Francine Clark Art Institute, 2007.

David Lucas after John Constable

Three prints from *English Landscape* trimmed and mounted to one sheet

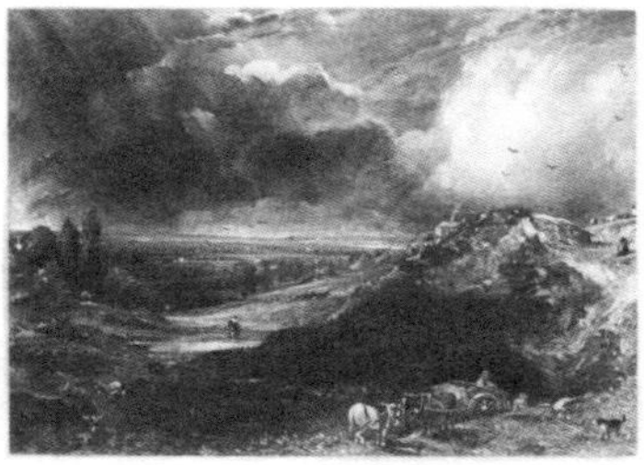

169
A Heath, from *English Landscape*, 1831
Mezzotint, trimmed to image and laid within false platemark, on cream wove paper, 13.1 × 18.7 cm (image); 23.1 × 77.8 cm (sheet).
2007.20.7 | S23 I/IV

Provenance: Percy Johnson; Peter Johnson, his grandson, by descent, sold to Manton, Feb. 1985; Sir Edwin A. G. Manton, New York (1999–d. 2005); Diana Morton, his daughter, by descent (2005–2007, given to the Clark); Sterling and Francine Clark Art Institute, 2007.

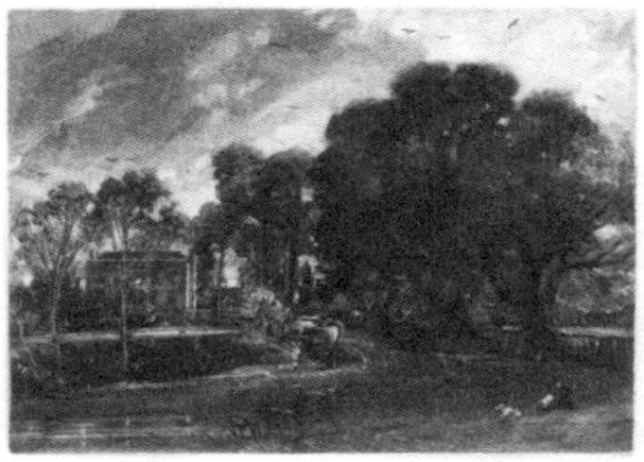

170
East Bergholt, Suffolk from *English Landscape*, June 1832
Mezzotint, trimmed to image and laid within false platemark, on cream wove paper, 14.7 × 22.2 cm (image); 23.1 × 77.8 cm (sheet)
2007.20.8 | S27 II/IV

Provenance: Percy Johnson; Peter Johnson, his grandson, by descent, sold to Manton, Feb. 1985; Sir Edwin A. G. Manton, New York (1999–d. 2005); Diana Morton, his daughter, by descent (2005–2007, given to the Clark); Sterling and Francine Clark Art Institute, 2007.

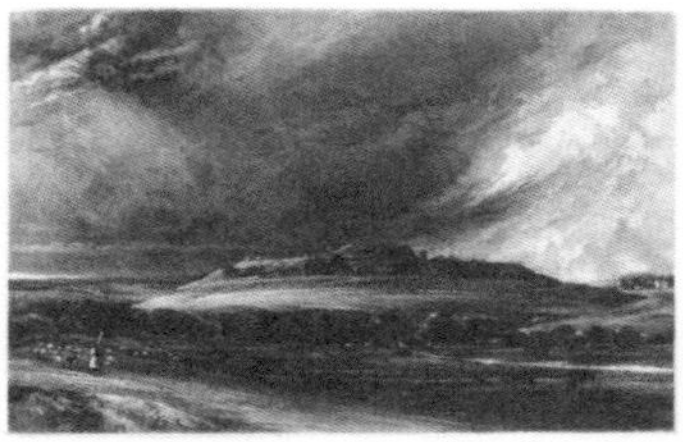

171
Old Sarum, from *English Landscape*, 1833
Mezzotint, trimmed to image and laid within false platemark, on cream wove paper, 13.6 × 18.4 cm (image); 23.1 × 77.8 cm (sheet)
2007.20.9 | S32 I/III

Provenance: Percy Johnson; Peter Johnson, his grandson, by descent, sold to Manton, Feb. 1985; Sir Edwin A. G. Manton, New York (1999–d. 2005); Diana Morton, his daughter, by descent (2005–2007, given to the Clark); Sterling and Francine Clark Art Institute, 2007.

David Lucas after John Constable

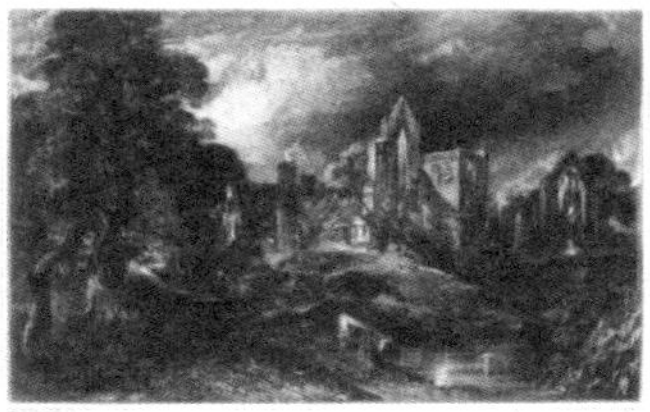

172
Castle Acre Priory, from *English Landscape*, 1846
Mezzotint on white wove paper,
12.3 × 17.8 cm (plate);
27.9 × 33.1cm (sheet)
2007.20.10 | S33 III/III

Provenance: Possibly Percy Johnson; Peter Johnson, his grandson, by descent, sold to Manton, May 1986; Sir Edwin A. G. Manton, New York (1999–d. 2005); Diana Morton, his daughter, by descent (2005–2007, given to the Clark); Sterling and Francine Clark Art Institute, 2007.

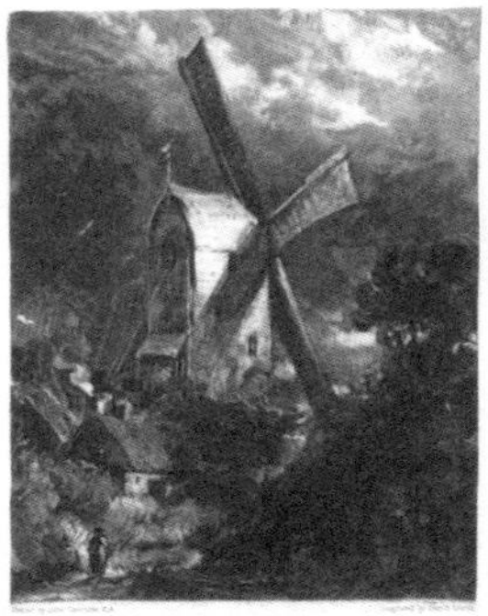

173
A Mill near Brighton, from *English Landscape*, 1838
Mezzotint on cream wove paper,
25.1 × 17.3 cm (plate);
32.5 × 24 cm (sheet)
2007.20.11 | S4 II/II

Provenance: Sir Edwin A. G. Manton, New York (1995–d. 2005); Manton Family Art Foundation (2005–2007, given to the Clark); Sterling and Francine Clark Art Institute, 2007.

Set of eleven prints loose in a green fabric-covered portfolio, printed 1992–93 by Ian Bain and Leslie Parris at the Tate from plates originally published by John Constable and David Lucas in 1830, 1831, and 1846.
2007.20.12.1–11

Provenance: Sir Edwin A. G. Manton, New York (1995–d. 2005); Manton Family Art Foundation (2005–2007, given to the Clark); Sterling and Francine Clark Art Institute, 2007.

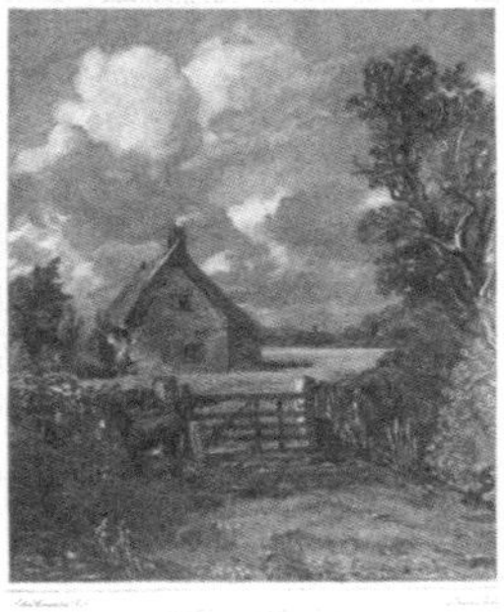

174
A Cottage in a Cornfield, 1846, printed 1992–93
Mezzotint on white wove paper,
24 × 19 cm (plate);
37.9 × 33 cm (sheet)
2007.20.12.1.1 | S45 II/II

David Lucas after John Constable

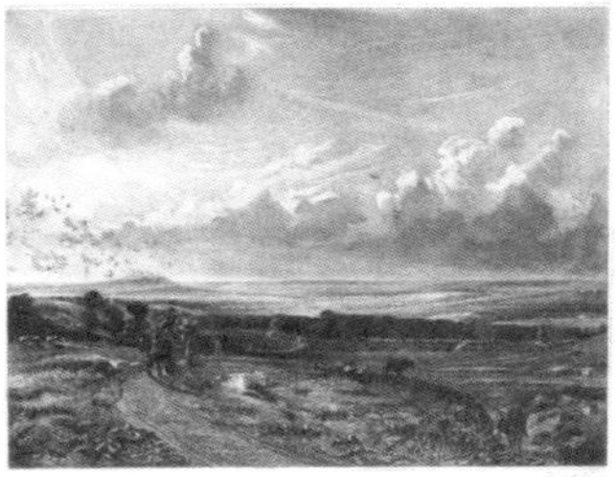

175
Hampstead Heath, Harrow in the Distance, 1846, printed 1992–93
Mezzotint on white wove paper,
17.5 × 20.9 cm (plate);
33.6 × 37.7 cm (sheet)
2007.20.12.2 | S47 II/II

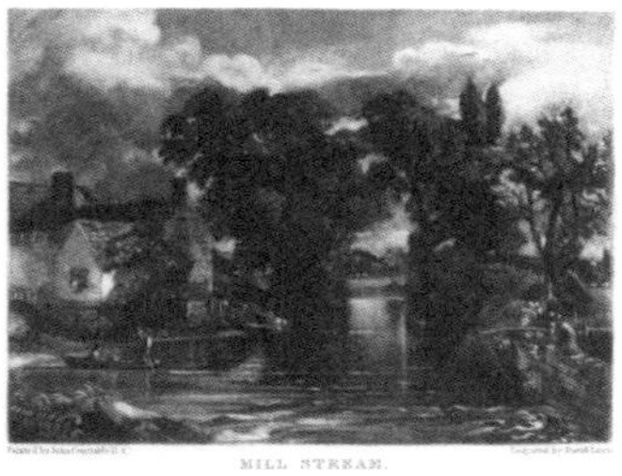

176
Mill Stream, 1831, printed 1992–93
Originally published in 1831
Mezzotint on white wove paper,
17.4 × 21.4 cm (plate);
33.2 × 37.5 cm (sheet)
2007.20.12.3 | S25 V/V

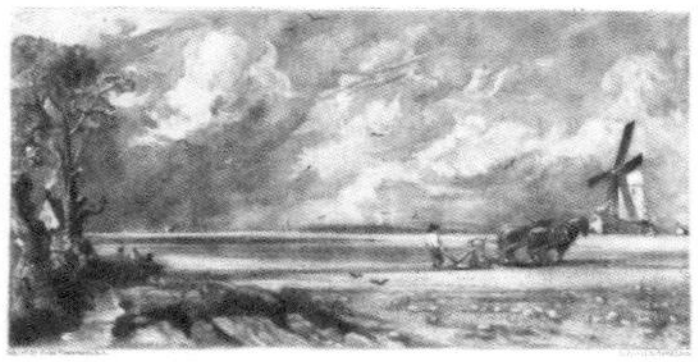

177
Spring, 1830, printed 1992–93
Mezzotint on white wove paper,
15.2 × 25.4 cm (plate);
33.2 × 37.5 cm (sheet)
2007.20.12.4 | S7 V/V

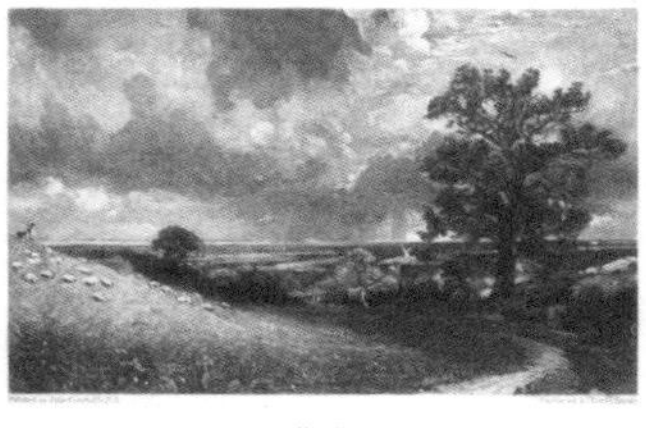

178
Noon, 1831, printed 1992–93
Mezzotint on white wove paper,
18.8 × 25.3cm (plate);
33.3 × 37.2 cm (sheet)
2007.20.12.5 | S16 VI/VI

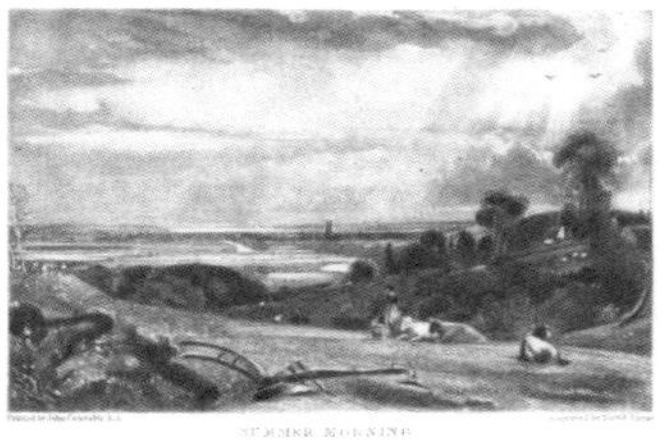

179
Summer Morning, 1831,
printed 1992–93
Mezzotint on white wove paper,
17.3 × 25.1 cm (plate);
33.2 × 37.2 cm (sheet)
2007.20.12.6 | S26 VI/VI

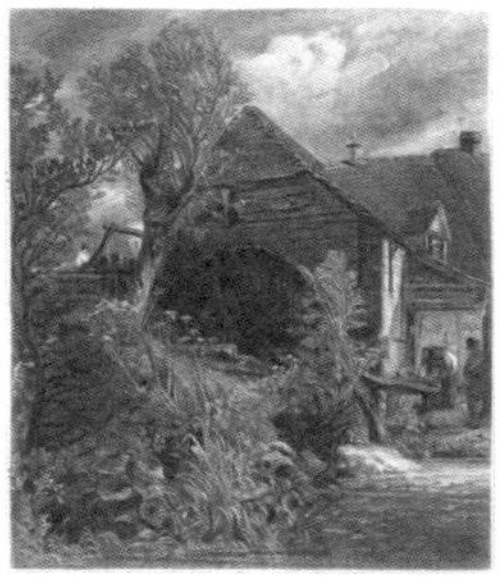

180
Gillingham Mill, Dorsetshire,
1846, printed 1992–93
Mezzotint on white wove paper,
24.6 × 19 cm (plate);
37.9 × 32.8 cm (sheet)
2007.20.12.7 | S43 II/II

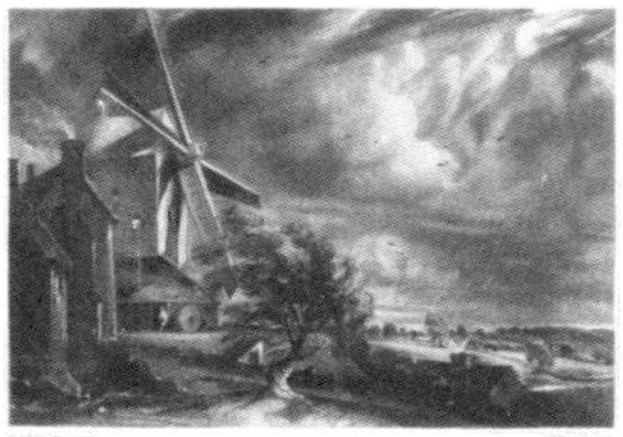

181
Mill near Colchester, 1846,
printed 1992–93
Mezzotint on white wove paper,
18.2 × 24 cm (plate);
33.2 × 37.3 cm (sheet)
2007.20.12.8 | S50 I/I

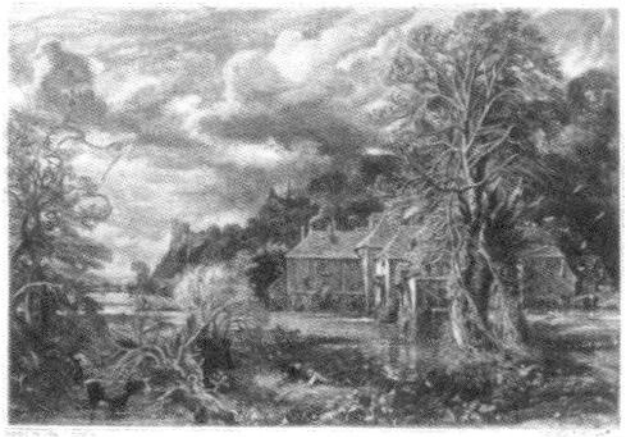

182
Arundel Mill and Castle, 1846,
printed 1992–93
Mezzotint on white wove paper,
18.8 × 24 cm (plate);
37.1 × 33.1 cm (sheet)
2007.20.12.9 | S49 I/I

David Lucas after John Constable

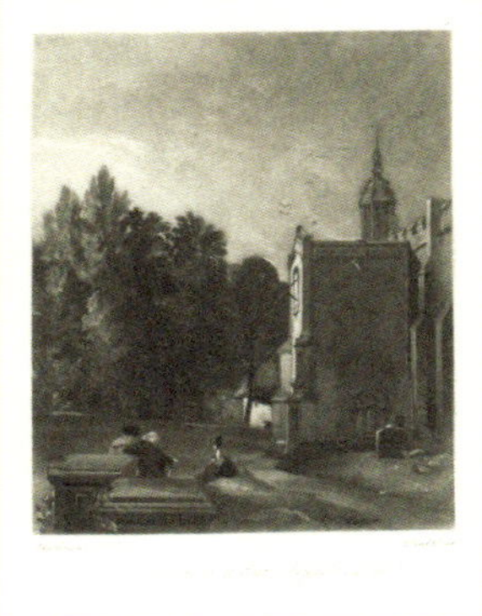

183
Porch of the Church at East Bergholt, Suffolk, 1846, printed 1992–93
Mezzotint on white wove paper, 24.3 × 18.6 cm (plate); 37.9 × 33.1 cm (sheet)
2007.20.12.10 | S42 II/II

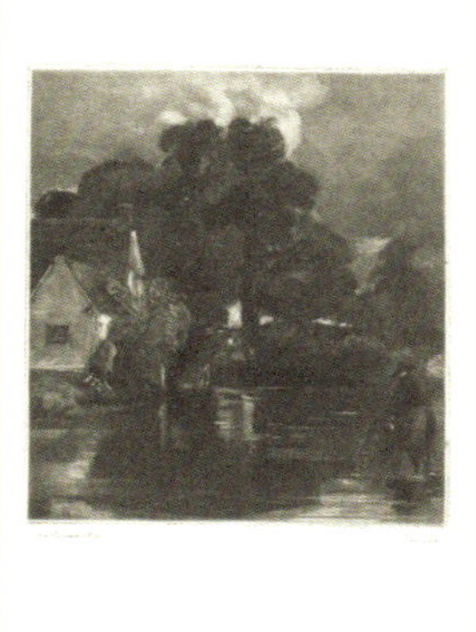

184
Willy Lott's House, 1846, printed 1992–93
Mezzotint on white wove paper, 25.3 × 18.4 cm (plate); 37.2 × 33.1 cm (sheet)
2007.20.12.11 | S33 II/II

John Martin English, 1789–1854

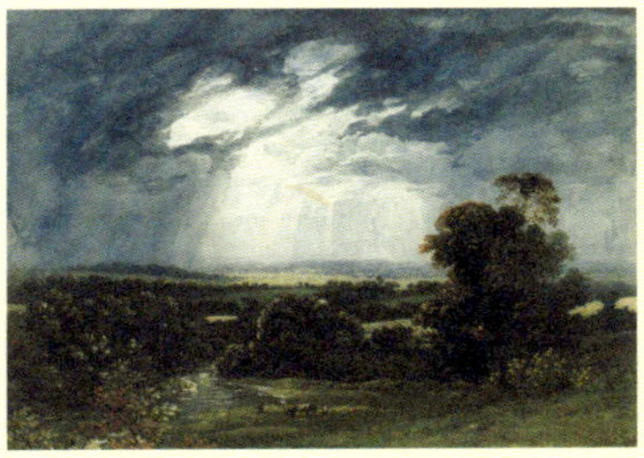

185
Landscape with Cattle Grazing in the Foreground, 1833
Watercolor and gouache, with gum arabic and scraping, on cream wove paper, 16.5 × 22.9 cm
2007.8.90

Provenance: James Armitage, JP; [Spink & Son, Ltd., London, no. K3 10928, sold to Manton, May 1996]; Sir Edwin A. G. Manton, New York (1996–d. 2005); Manton Family Art Foundation (2005–2007, given to the Clark); Sterling and Francine Clark Art Institute, 2007.

Thomas Monro English, 1759–1833

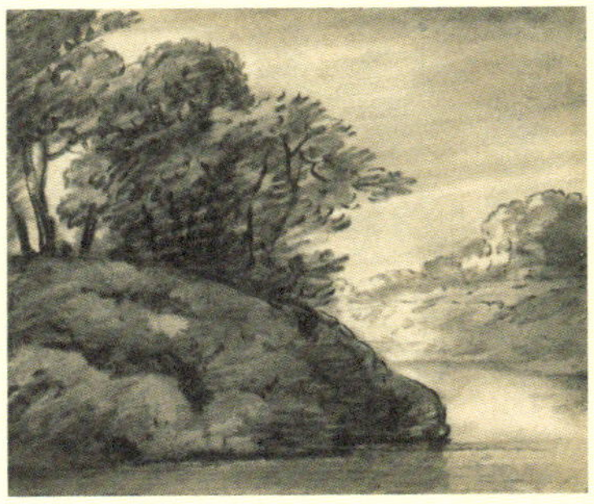

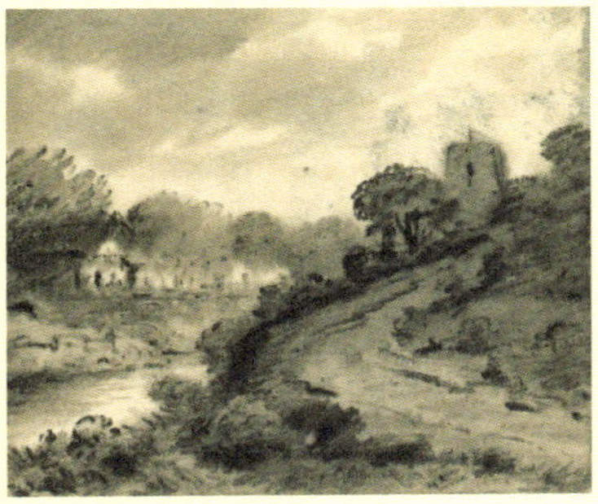

186
A Wooded River Landscape with a Rock in the Left Foreground (recto); *A Wooded River Landscape with a Path and Tower* (verso), c. 1800
Graphite and black chalk with watercolor on cream laid paper, 15.2 × 17.8 cm
2007.20.27

Provenance: [Oscar & Peter Johnson, Ltd., London, sold to Manton, Aug. 1968]; Sir Edwin A. G. Manton, New York (1968–d. 2005); Manton Family Art Foundation (2005–2007, given to the Clark); Sterling and Francine Clark Art Institute, 2007.

Samuel Palmer English, 1805–1881

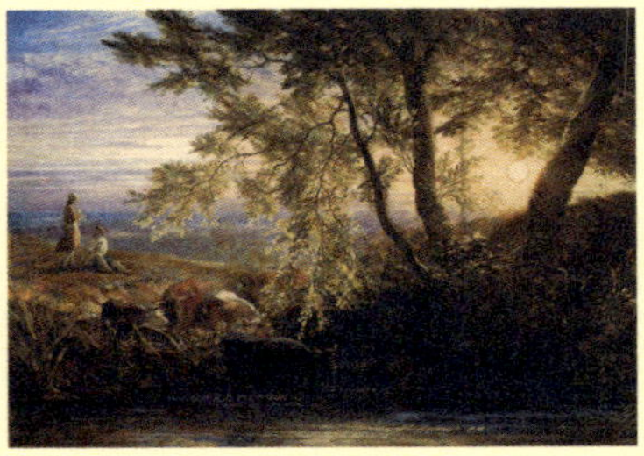

187
The Setting Sun, c. 1862
Watercolor and gouache, with touches of shell gold and scraping, on cream wove paper, 52.5 × 72.5 cm
2007.8.91 | L595

Provenance: Brian G. Hamilton (1948–1968); private collection, sold to Leger, 1985; [Leger Galleries, sold to private collection, 1985]; private collection (1985–1992, sold to Leger); [Leger Galleries, 1992, sold to Manton, June 1992]; Sir Edwin A. G. Manton, New York (1992–d. 2005); Manton Family Art Foundation (2005–2007, given to the Clark); Sterling and Francine Clark Art Institute, 2007.

Henry Redmore English, 1820–1887

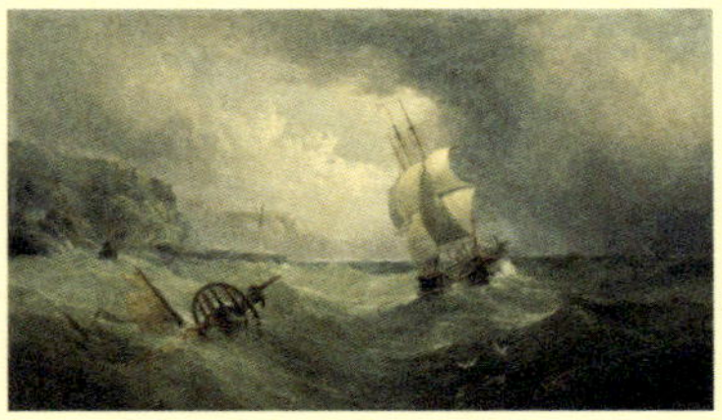

188
Shipping off the Coast in a Stormy Sea, 1874
Oil on canvas, 61 × 102.2 cm
2007.8.92

Provenance: [Ackermann & Johnson, Ltd., London, sold to Manton. 17 Nov. 1994]; Sir Edwin A. G. Manton, New York (1994–d. 2005); Manton Family Art Foundation (2005–2007, given to the Clark); Sterling and Francine Clark Art Institute, 2007.

Thomas Rowlandson English, 1756–1827

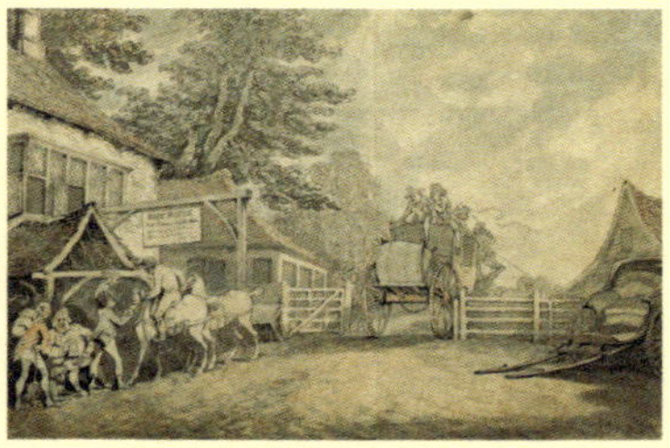

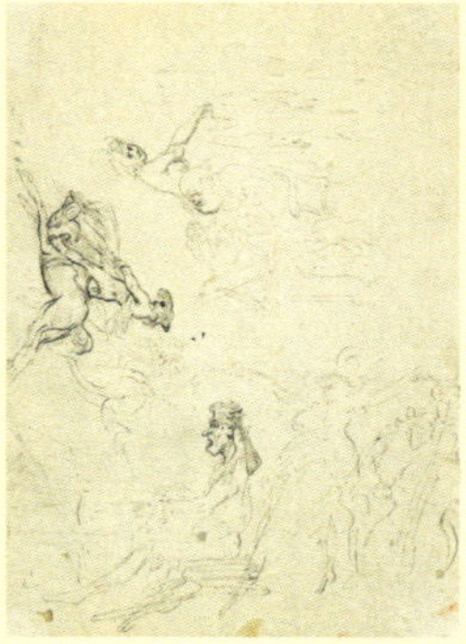

189
The Post House (recto); *Studies of a Musical Trio, Two Riders and a Domestic Scene* (verso), c. 1778–80
Pen and black ink over watercolor with traces of graphite on cream laid paper (recto); pen and black ink on cream laid paper (verso), 28.9 × 41.9 cm
2007.20.28

Provenance: [Frank Sabin (by 1948)]; [Ackermann & Johnson, Ltd., London, by 1989–1992, sold to Manton, Apr. 1992]; Sir Edwin A. G. Manton, New York (1992–d. 2005); Manton Family Art Foundation (2005–2007, given to the Clark); Sterling and Francine Clark Art Institute, 2007.

Thomas Rowlandson

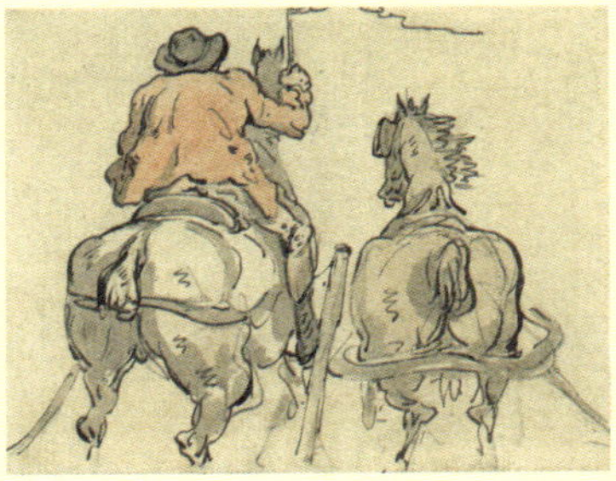

190
An English Postillion, c. 1784–90
Pen and gray ink with graphite and watercolor on white laid paper, 11.8 × 15 cm
2007.20.29

Provenance: Sale, Sotheby Parke Bernet & Co., New York, 26 Jan. 1978, no. 203, sold to Spink; [Spink & Son, Ltd., London, Jan.–Mar. 1978, sold to Manton, Mar. 1978]; Sir Edwin A. G. Manton, New York (1978–d. 2005); Manton Family Art Foundation (2005–2007, given to the Clark); Sterling and Francine Clark Art Institute, 2007.

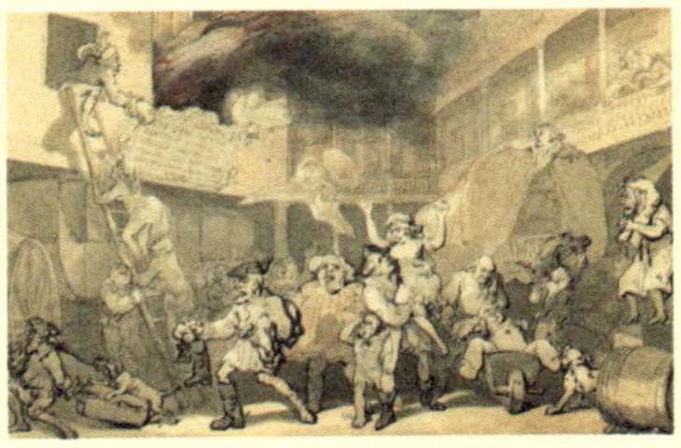

191
Peregrine Rescuing Emilia from the Inn Fire, c. 1786
Pen and black and gray inks and watercolor over graphite on cream wove paper, 21.6 × 32.8 cm
2007.8.94

Provenance: Sale, Christie's, London, 20 Nov. 1984, no. 98, sold to Spink; [Spink & Son, Ltd., London, 1984–1985, no. K3 8722 sold to Manton, May 1985]; Sir Edwin A. G. Manton, New York (1985–d. 2005); Manton Family Art Foundation (2005–2007, given to the Clark); Sterling and Francine Clark Art Institute, 2007.

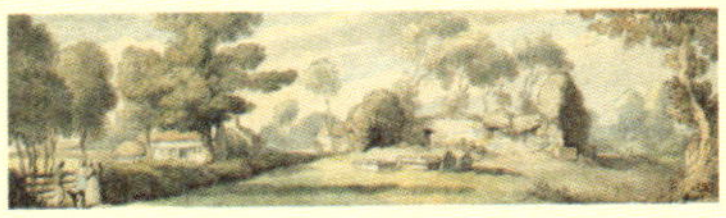

192
New Town, Old Church (Isle of Wight), c. 1790–98
Pen and brush and gray ink and watercolor over graphite on cream wove paper, 13.3 × 46.6 cm
2007.8.95

Provenance: Possibly Sir John Crampton (by 1923); Major Leonard M. E. Dent (1936–1984, his sale, The Dent Collection of Watercolours and Drawings by Thomas Rowlandson, Christie's, London, 10 July 1984, no. 3, sold to Leger); [Leger Galleries, London, July–Nov. 1984, sold to Manton, Nov. 1984]; Sir Edwin G. Manton, New York (1984–d. 2005); Manton Family Art Foundation (2005–2007, given to the Clark); Sterling and Francine Clark Art Institute, 2007.

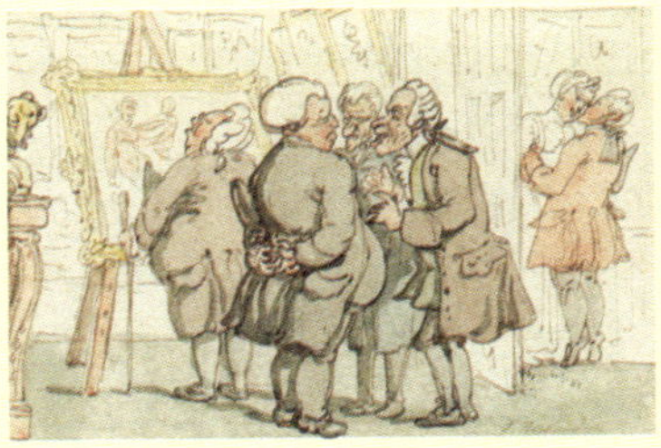

193
The Art Gallery, c. 1790–98
Pen and brown ink over graphite and watercolor on white wove paper, 9.1 × 13.6 cm
2007.20.30

Provenance: Sale, Sotheby's, London, 14 July 1994, no. 34, sold to Spink; [Spink & Son, Ltd., London, 1994–1995, sold to Manton, Apr. 1995]; Sir Edwin A. G. Manton, New York (1995–d. 2005); Manton Family Art Foundation (2005–2007, given to the Clark); Sterling and Francine Clark Art Institute, 2007.

Thomas Rowlandson

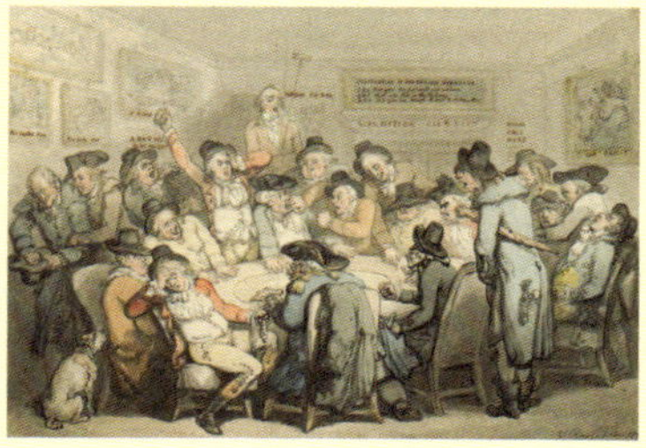

194
The Subscription Club Room, 1791
Pen with black and brown inks over graphite and watercolor with additions in pen and brush and black ink on cream wove paper, 32.6 × 46.5 cm
2007.8.93

Provenance: [Frank Sabin (by 1943)]; Bernard Landau; Philip Pinsof (in 1972); [Spink & Son, Ltd., London, no. K3 6945/7]; [Thomas Agnew and Sons, Ltd., London, sold to Manton, Oct. 2003]; Sir Edwin A. G. Manton, New York (2003–d. 2005); Manton Family Art Foundation (2005–2007, given to the Clark); Sterling and Francine Clark Art Institute, 2007.

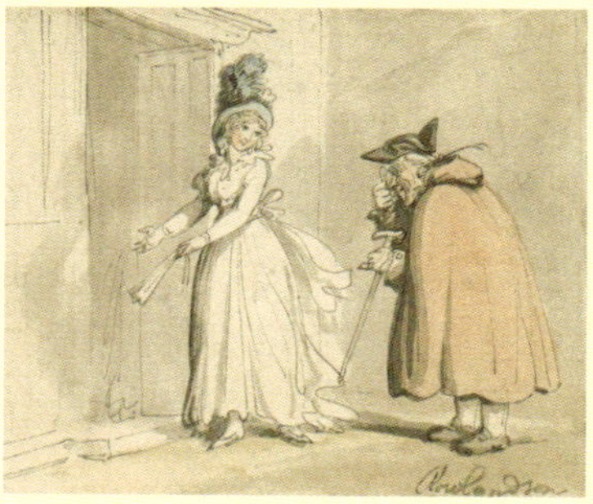

195
The Courtesan, c. 1795–1800
Pen and gray ink and watercolor over graphite on cream laid paper, 10 × 11.6 cm
2007.20.31

Provenance: Sale, Christie's, London, 9 Apr. 1991, no. 79, sold to Ackermann]; [Ackermann & Johnson, Ltd., London, 1991–1992, sold to Manton, Sept. 1992]; Sir Edwin A. G. Manton, New York (1992–d. 2005); Manton Family Art Foundation (2005–2007, given to the Clark); Sterling and Francine Clark Art Institute, 2007.

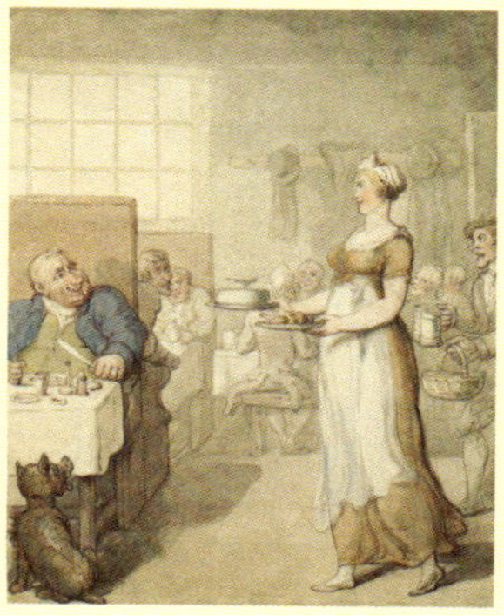

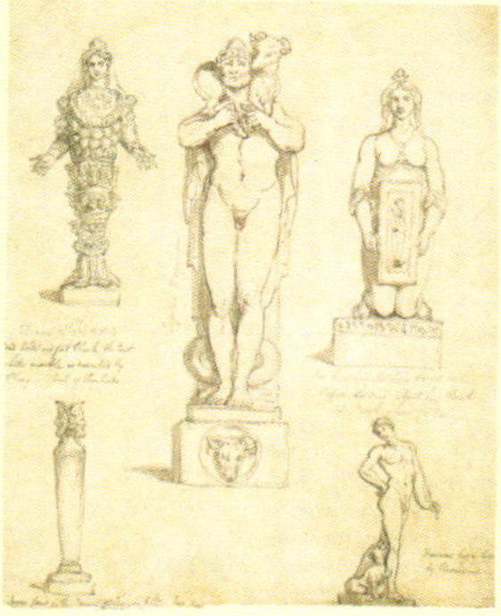

196
Mutton Chops in Maiden Lane (recto), c. 1798–1810; *Studies of Classical and Egyptian Figures* (verso), c. 1817–21
Pen with vermilion and gray inks and watercolor on cream wove paper (recto); pen with brown and gray inks, graphite, and watercolor on cream wove paper (verso), 27.8 × 21.7 cm
2007.20.32

Provenance: [Lefevre Fine Art, Ltd., London]; [The Leicester Galleries, London, sold to Manton, May 1958]; Sir Edwin A. G. Manton, New York (1958–d. 2005); Manton Family Art Foundation (2005–2007, given to the Clark); Sterling and Francine Clark Art Institute, 2007.

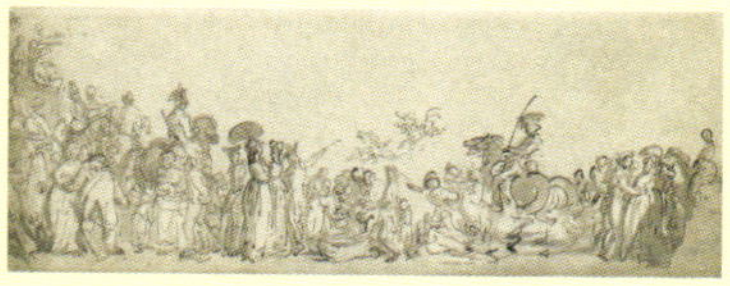

197
A Review in Hyde Park, c. 1800
Pen and gray ink and brush and gray wash over graphite on white laid paper, 17.5 × 45.8 cm
2007.8.96

Provenance: Sale, Sotheby's, c. 1961, sold to Colnaghi; [P. & D. Colnahi & Co., Ltd., London, sold to Warren]; Dr. Charles B. N. Warren; [Spink & Son, Ltd., London, 1978–1991, no. K3 10222, sold to Manton, May 1991]; Sir Edwin A. G. Manton, New York (1991–d. 2005); Manton Family Art Foundation (2005–2007, given to the Clark); Sterling and Francine Clark Art Institute, 2007.

Thomas Rowlandson

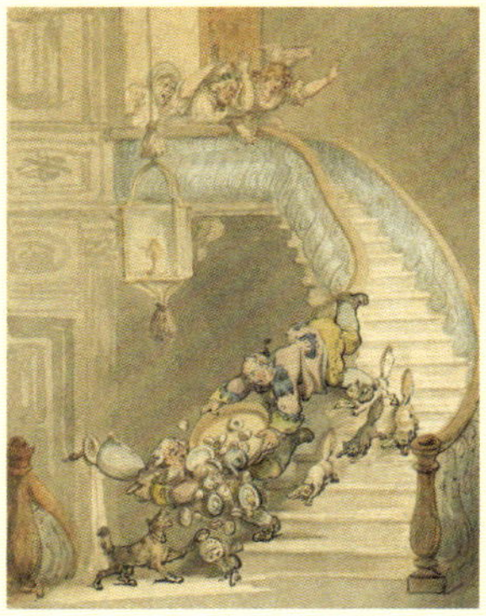

198
The Cat-astrophy, or Crash to My Grandmother's Old China, c. 1800
Brush and dark brown ink with touches of pen and vermilion ink and watercolor over graphite on cream wove paper, 34.5 × 26.2 cm
2007.8.97

Provenance: Philip Pinsof, Chicago; [Spink & Son, Ltd., London, sold to Manton, Feb. 1981]; Sir Edwin A. G. Manton, New York (1981–d. 2005); Manton Family Art Foundation (2005–2007, given to the Clark); Sterling and Francine Clark Art Institute, 2007.

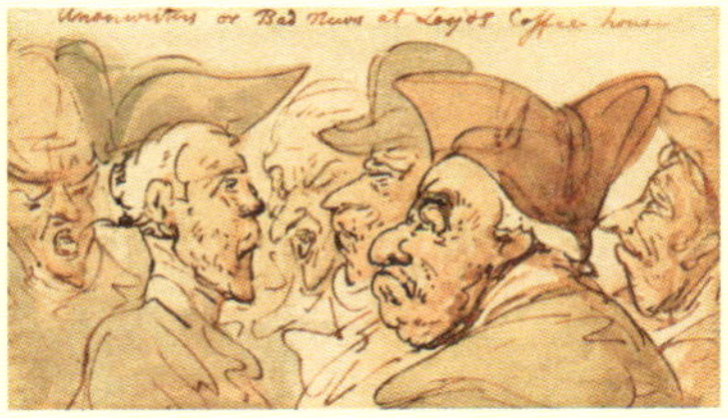

199
Underwriters or Bad News at Lloyd's Coffee House, c. 1800–10
Pen and vermilion ink with watercolor over graphite on cream wove paper, 11.45 × 19.3 cm
2007.20.33

Provenance: Sale, Sotheby's, London, 19 Nov. 1981, no. 105, sold to Spink; [Spink & Son, Ltd., London, 1981–1982, sold to Manton, May 1982]; Sir Edwin A. G. Manton, New York (1982–d. 2005); Manton Family Art Foundation (2005–2007, given to the Clark); Sterling and Francine Clark Art Institute, 2007.

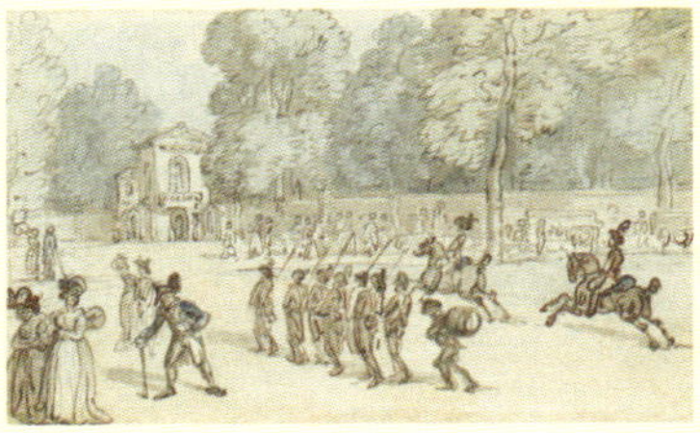

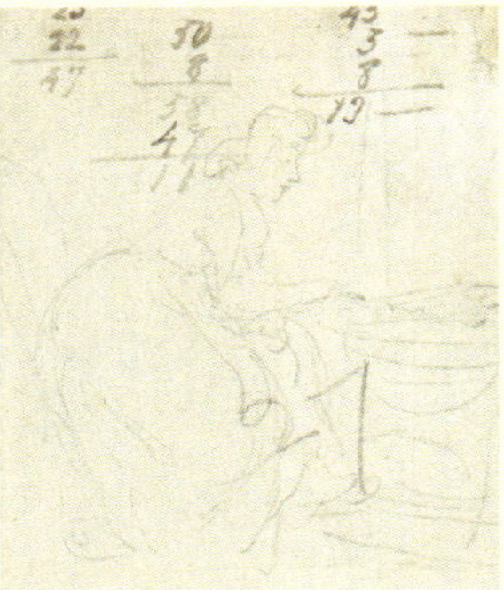

200
Guardsmen Marching through St. James's Park (recto); *Study of a Woman with Arithmetic* (verso), c. 1820
Pen and gray and brown and vermilion inks with watercolor over graphite on cream laid paper (recto); graphite and gray ink on cream laid paper (verso), 10.8 × 17.2 cm
2007.20.34

Provenance: Sale, Sotheby's, London, 11 Nov. 1993, no. 72, sold to Spink; [Spink & Son, Ltd., London, 1993–1995, sold to Manton, Sept. 1995]; Sir Edwin A. G. Manton, New York (1995–d. 2005); Manton Family Art Foundation (2005–2007, given to the Clark); Sterling and Francine Clark Art Institute, 2007.

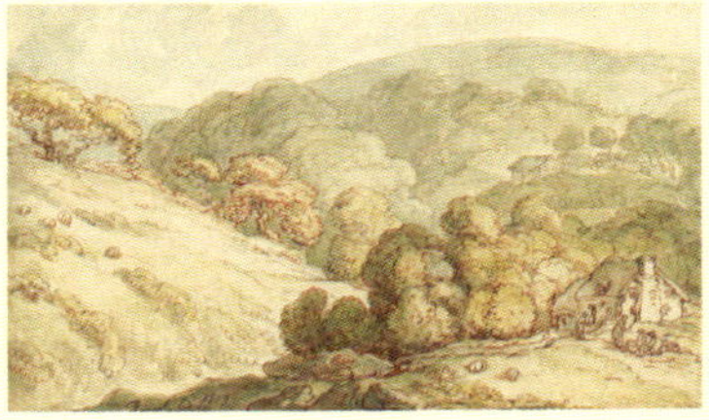

201
Wooded Hilly Landscape with Cottage and Figures, 1809
Pen and vermilion ink with graphite and watercolor on cream wove paper, 15.6 × 25.8 cm
2007.20.35

Provenance: Sale, Sotheby's, London, 24 Mar. 1977, no. 127, sold to Spink; [Spink & Son, Ltd., London, 1977–1978, sold to Manton, Mar. 1978]; Sir Edwin A. G. Manton, New York (1978–d. 2005); Manton Family Art Foundation (2005–2007, given to the Clark); Sterling and Francine Clark Art Institute, 2007.

Thomas Rowlandson

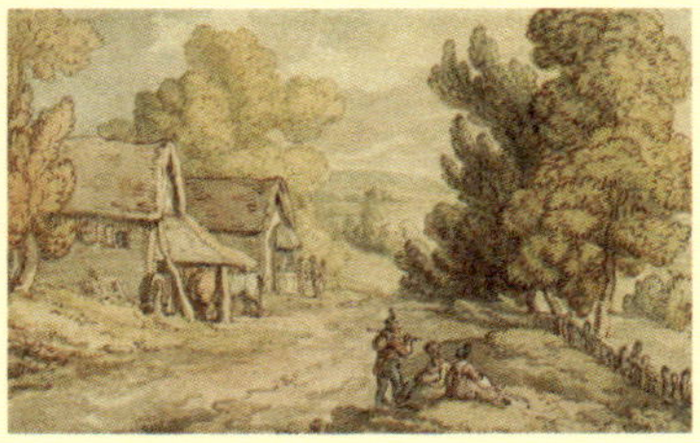

202
Cottage and Barn with Figures Resting by the Side of a Country Road, c. 1810–20
Pen with gray and vermilion ink and watercolor on cream wove paper, 13.1 × 20.5 cm
2007.20.36

Provenance: [Walker Galleries, Harrogate]; [Leger Galleries, London, sold to Manton, Feb. 1986]; Sir Edwin A. G. Manton, New York (1986–d. 2005); Manton Family Art Foundation (2005–2007, given to the Clark); Sterling and Francine Clark Art Institute, 2007.

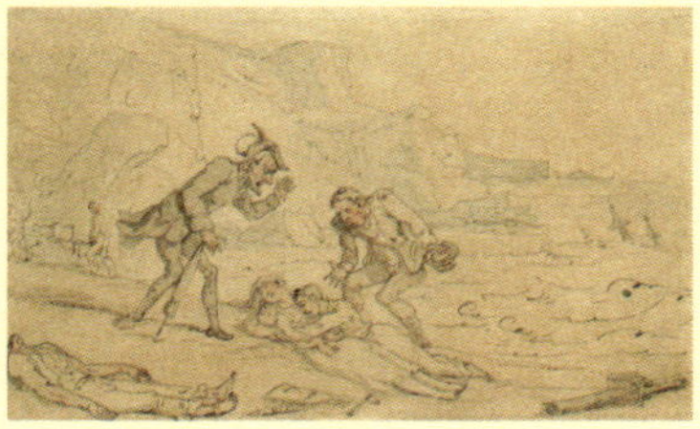

203
Doctor Syntax at the Scene of a Shipwreck, c. 1815–20
Pen and brown ink over watercolor and graphite on tan wove paper, 12.1 × 19.4 cm
2007.20.37

Provenance: [Morris Gallery, New York, sold to Manton]; Lady Gretchen Manton, given to E. A. G. Manton; Sir Edwin A. G. Manton (d. 2005); Manton Family Art Foundation (2005–2007, given to the Clark); Sterling and Francine Clark Art Institute, 2007.

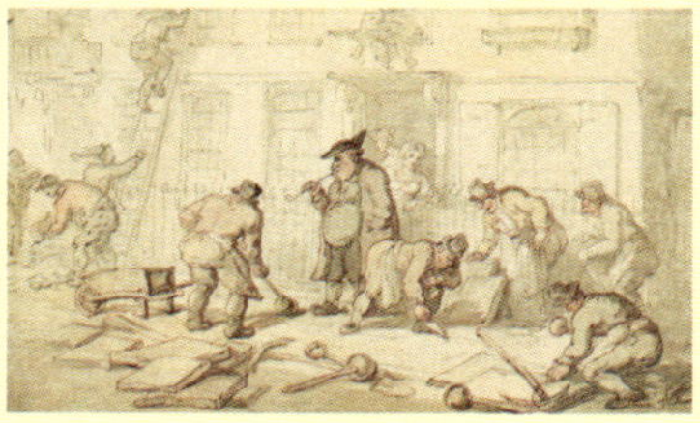

204
Laborers Laying a Pavement, c. 1815–20
Pen and gray and vermilion ink over watercolor and graphite on cream wove paper, 14.2 × 23 cm
2007.20.38

Provenance: Sale, Christie's, London, 8 Apr. 1997, no. 23, sold to Ackermann & Johnson, as agent for Manton; Sir Edwin A. G. Manton, New York (1997–d. 2005); Manton Family Art Foundation (2005–2007, given to the Clark); Sterling and Francine Clark Art Institute, 2007.

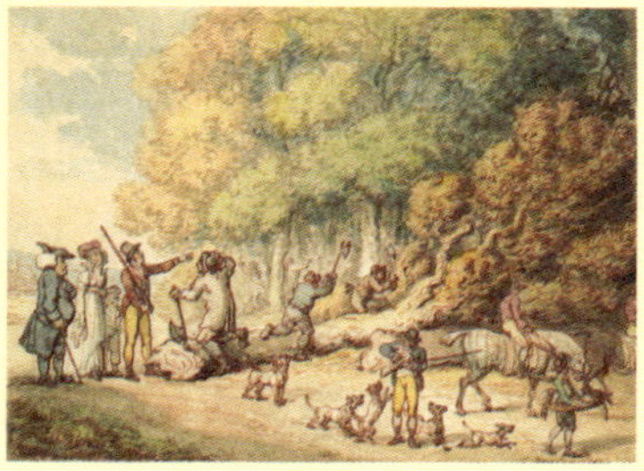

205
A Sportsman with His Family Instructing Woodmen to Chop up a Felled Tree, c. 1816
Pen and brush and vermilion and gray inks with watercolor over graphite on beige wove paper, 21.2 × 28.4 cm
2007.20.39

Provenance: Sale, Sotheby Parke Bernet & Co., New York, 4 Apr. 1973, no. 64, sold to Manton; Sir Edwin A. G. Manton, New York (1973–d. 2005); Manton Family Art Foundation (2005–2007, given to the Clark); Sterling and Francine Clark Art Institute, 2007.

John Ruskin English, 1819–1900

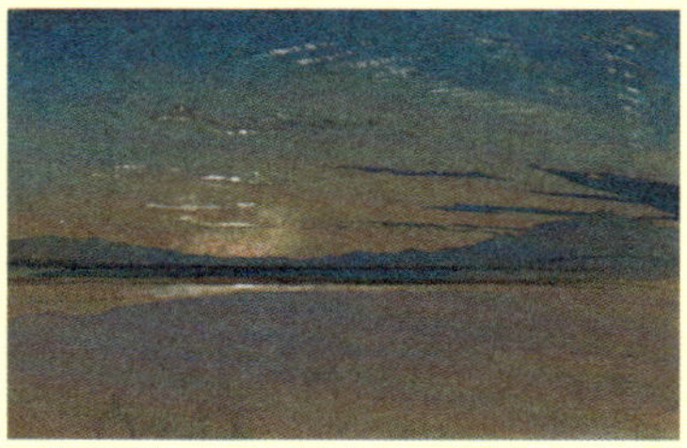

206
Sunset over the Mountains, c. 1845
Watercolor and gouache with graphite on beige wove paper, 14.3 × 22.2 cm
2007.20.43

Provenance: [Spink Leger Pictures sold to Manton, May 1997]; Sir Edwin A. G. Manton, New York (1997–d. 2005); Manton Family Art Foundation (2005–2007, given to the Clark); Sterling and Francine Clark Art Institute, 2007.

Daniel Turner English, active 1782–1817

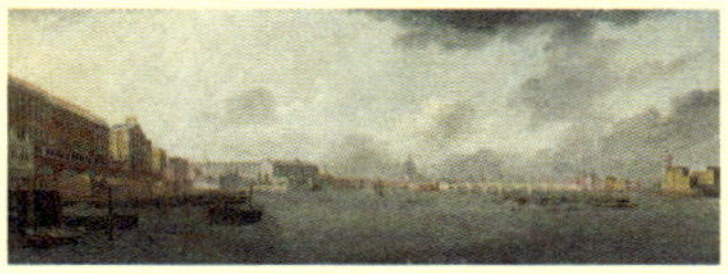

207
A View of the Thames Looking East with the Adelphi Somerset House and Saint Paul's Cathedral, c. 1806
Oil on panel, 17.2 × 45.2 cm
2007.8.99

Provenance: George Price Boyce (d. 1897, his sale, Christie's, London, 1–3 July 1897, no. 281, sold to White); Frederick Anthony White, London (1897–d. 1934, his sale, Christie's, London, 20 Apr. 1934, no. 148, sold to Raikes); Raikes (from 1934); [Oscar & Peter Johnson, Ltd., London, sold to Manton, 6 Nov. 1970]; Sir Edwin A. G. Manton, New York (1970–d. 2005); Manton Family Art Foundation (2005–2007, given to the Clark); Sterling and Francine Clark Art Institute, 2007.

Joseph Mallord William Turner English, 1775–1851 (See also Girtin)

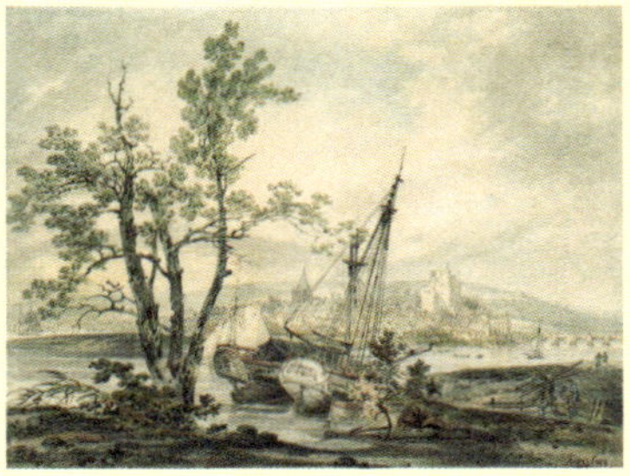

208
Rochester, c. 1793
Watercolor with pen and gray ink on cream wove paper, 21.6 × 27.9 cm
2007.8.100 | W187

Provenance: John Walker, sold to private collection; private collection (in 1993); [Thomas Agnew and Sons, Ltd., London, sold to Ackermann & Johnson]; [Ackermann & Johnson, London, sold to Manton, June 1997]; Sir Edwin A. G. Manton, New York (1997–d. 2005); Manton Family Art Foundation (2005–2007, given to the Clark); Sterling and Francine Clark Art Institute, 2007.

Joseph Mallord William Turner

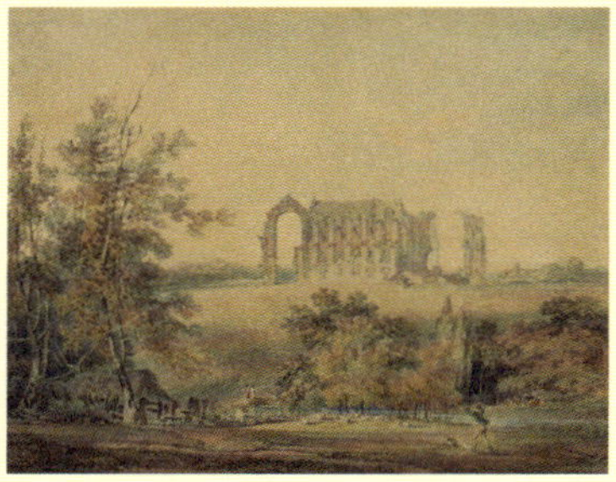

209
Malmesbury Abbey from the South, c. 1794
Watercolor with traces of graphite on tan wove paper, 20.8 × 26 cm
2007.8.101

Provenance: [A. J. Finberg, Cotswold Gallery, sale, 28 July 1927, no. 1209, sold to Campbell]; Alexander Campbell (in 1927); Duncan Campbell, his son, by descent, sold to Johnson, 1971; [Oscar & Peter Johnson, Ltd., 1971–1977, sold to Manton, Jan. 1977]; Sir Edwin A. G. Manton, New York (1977–d. 2005); Manton Family Art Foundation (2005–2007, given to the Clark); Sterling and Francine Clark Art Institute, 2007.

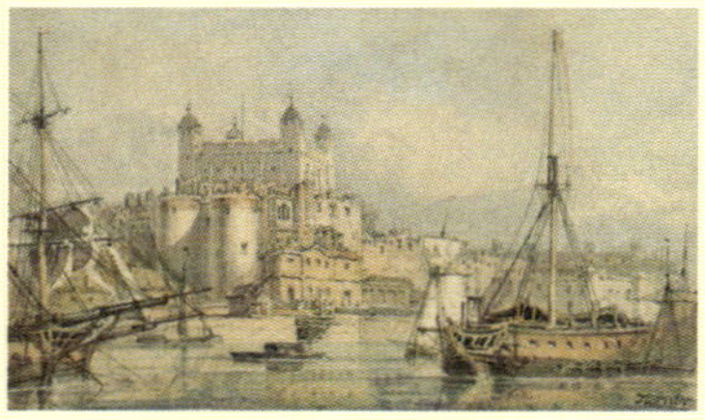

210
The Tower of London, c. 1794
Watercolor over graphite on cream wove paper, 12.4 × 17.1 cm
2007.8.102

Provenance: The artist, probably given to Flaxman; John Flaxman, R.A., probably his sale, Christie's, London 10–11 Apr. 1862; Grundy, his sale, Oct. 1881, no. 134; Sir Robert Witt (d. 1952); Sir John Witt, his son, by descent; Mrs. S. Darbyshire-Robert, sale, Sotheby Parke Bernet & Co., New York, 19 Mar. 1981, no. 111; [Leger Galleries, London, sold to private collection]; private collection (1981–1995, sold to Leger); [Leger Galleries, London, sold to Manton, Apr. 1995]; Sir Edwin A. G. Manton, New York (1995–d. 2005); Manton Family Art Foundation (2005–2007, given to the Clark); Sterling and Francine Clark Art Institute, 2007.

211
The Tower of London, c. 1794
Graphite on white wove paper, 13 × 21 cm
2007.20.40 | W103

Provenance: The artist, given to Flaxman; John Flaxman, R. A., probably sold at his sale, Christie's, 10–11 Apr. 1862, sold to Grundy; Grundy (in 1862, probably sale, Grundy, Oct. 1881, no. 134); Sir Robert Witt (d. 1952); Sir John Witt; Miss S. Darbyshire-Robert, sale, Sotheby Parke Bernet & Co., New York, 19 Mar. 1981, no. 111, sold to private collection; private collection (1981–1995, sold to Leger); [Leger Galleries, sold to Manton, Apr. 1995]; Sir Edwin A. G. Manton, New York (1995–d. 2005); Manton Family Art Foundation (2005–2007, given to the Clark); Sterling and Francine Clark Art Institute, 2007.

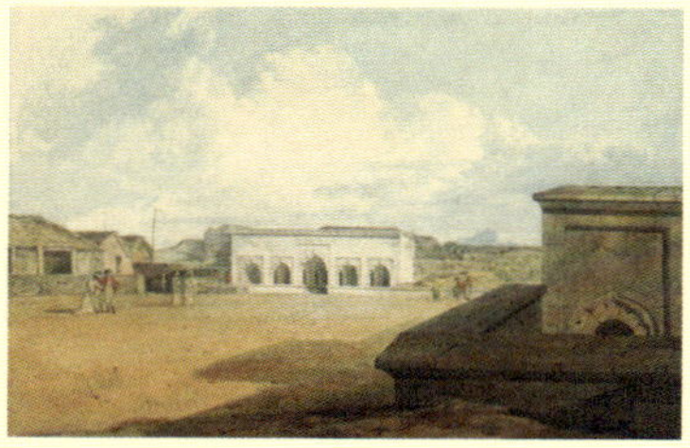

212
Hoolay Deedy, Seringapatam, c. 1800
Watercolor over graphite on white wove paper, 42.1 × 65.4 cm
2007.8.119

Provenance: [P. & D. Colnaghi & Co., Ltd., London, sold to Murphy as attributed to Williams Daniell, 1948]; Ray Livingston Murphy (1948–1986, sale, Christie's, London, 18 Mar. 1986, no. 107, sold as attributed to Turner, sold to Leger); [Leger Galleries, Mar.–Nov. 1986, sold to Manton, Nov. 1986]; Sir Edwin A. G. Manton, New York (1986–d. 2005); Manton Family Art Foundation (2005–2007, given to the Clark); Sterling and Francine Clark Art Institute, 2007.

Joseph Mallord William Turner

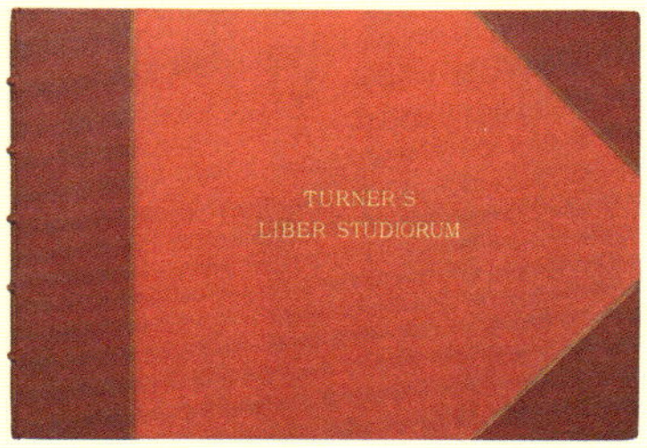

Liber Studiorum, originally published 1808–11
Sixty-one of the first seventy published etchings, bound in a collector's album
Purchased with funds contributed by the Manton Foundation in memory of Sir Edwin and Lady Manton
2008.5.1–61

Provenance: Henry Arthur Clowes; probably Legh Algernon Clowes, by descent; James A. Bergquist, sold to Clark; Sterling and Francine Clark Art Institute, 2008.

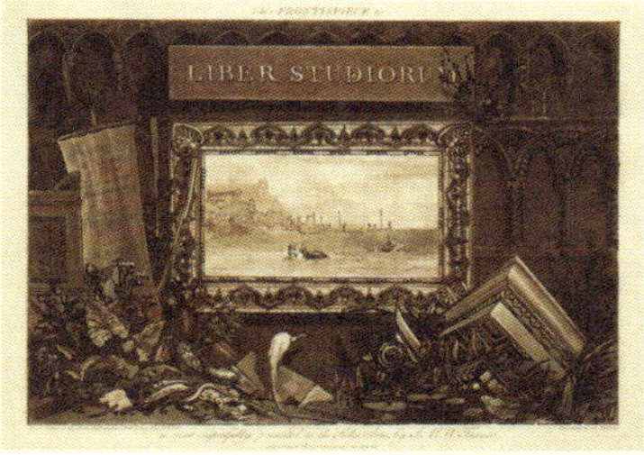

213
Frontispiece, May 1812
Etching and mezzotint printed in brown inks on cream wove paper,
21 × 29.3 cm (plate);
29 × 43.5 cm (sheet)
2008.5.1 | F1 I/V

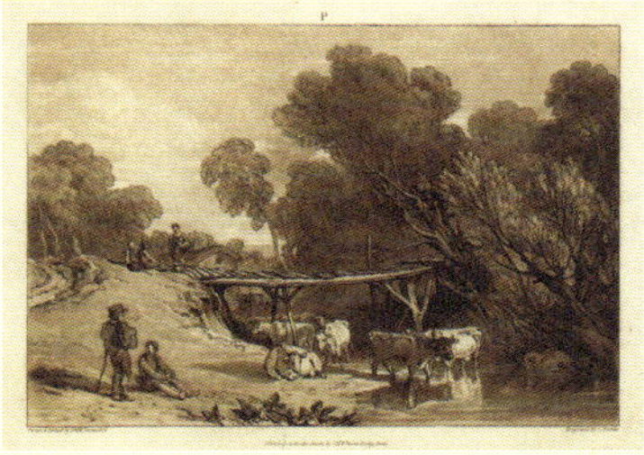

214
Bridge and Cows, 11 June 1807
Etching and mezzotint printed in brown inks on cream laid paper,
20.5 × 28.2 cm (plate);
29.2 × 42 cm (sheet)
2008.5.2 | F2 II/V

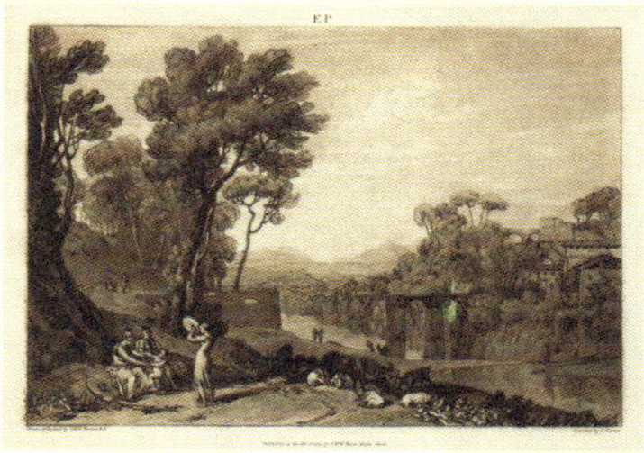

215
The Woman and the Tambourine, 11 June 1807
Etching and mezzotint printed in brown inks on cream laid paper,
20.3 × 28.9 cm (plate);
29.1 × 42.7 cm (sheet)
2008.5.3 | F3 II/V

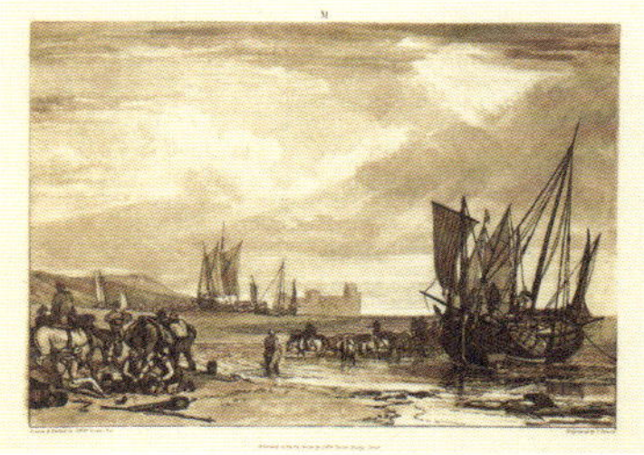

216
Scene on the French Coast, 11 June 1807
Etching and mezzotint printed in brown inks on cream laid paper,
20.6 × 28.6 cm (plate);
29.8 × 40.8 cm (sheet)
2008.5.4 | F4 II/III

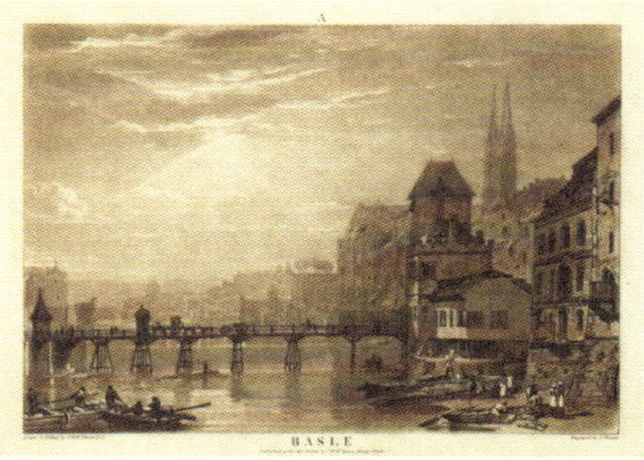

217
Basle, 11 June 1807
Etching and mezzotint printed in brown inks on cream laid paper,
20.6 × 28.1 cm (plate);
29.4 × 40.7 cm (sheet)
2008.5.5 | F5 II/VI

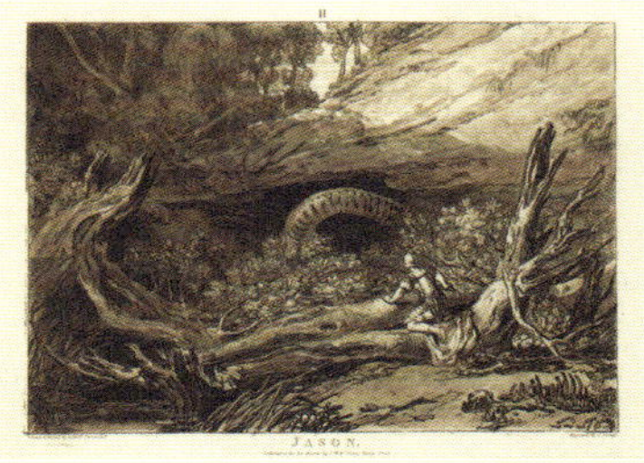

218
Jason, 11 June 1807
Etching and mezzotint printed in brown inks on cream laid paper,
20.6 × 28.7 cm (plate);
29 × 42.4 cm (sheet)
2008.5.6 | F6 III/V

Joseph Mallord William Turner

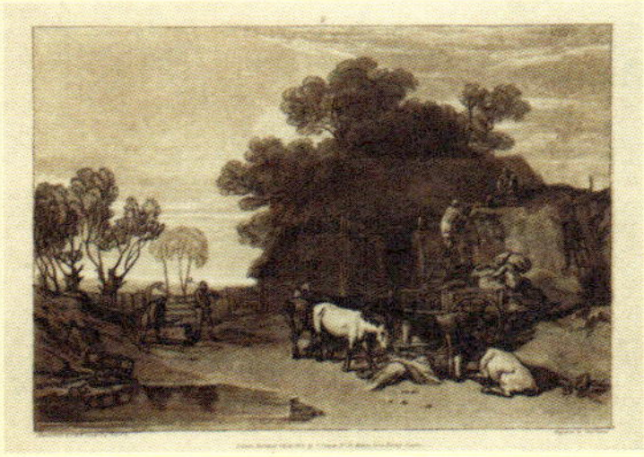

219
The Straw Yard, 20 Feb. 1808
Etching and mezzotint printed in brown inks on cream laid paper, 20.6 × 28.2 cm (plate); 28 × 41.5 cm (sheet)
2008.5.7 | F7 III/IV

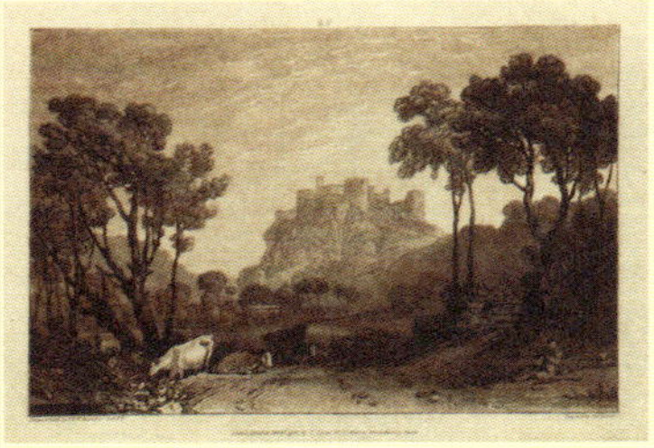

220
The Castle above the Meadows, 20 Feb. 1808
Etching and mezzotint printed in brown inks on cream laid paper, 20.5 × 28.8 cm (plate); 28 × 40.9 cm (sheet)
2008.5.8 | F8 III/IV

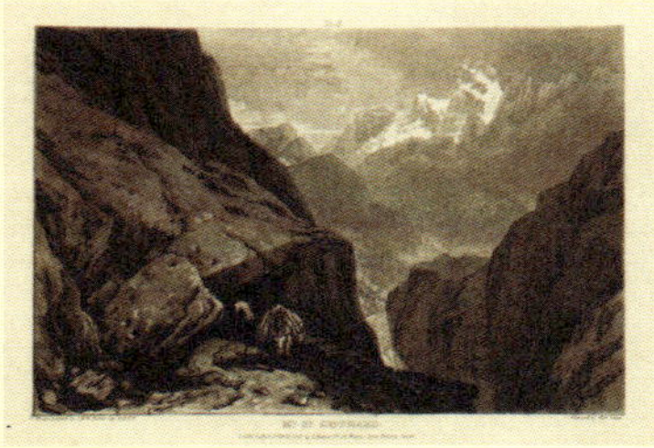

221
Mt. St. Gothard, 20 Feb. 1808
Etching and mezzotint printed in brown inks on cream laid paper, 20.7 × 28.7 cm (plate); 28.6 × 41.4 cm (sheet)
2008.5.9 | F9 I/VI

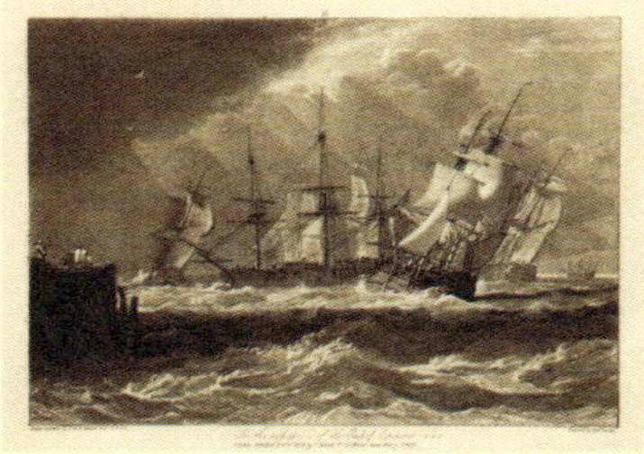

222
Ships in a Breeze, 20 Feb. 1808
Etching and mezzotint printed in brown inks on cream laid paper, 20.4 × 28.9 cm (plate); 28.5 × 42 cm (sheet)
2008.5.10 | F10 IV/V

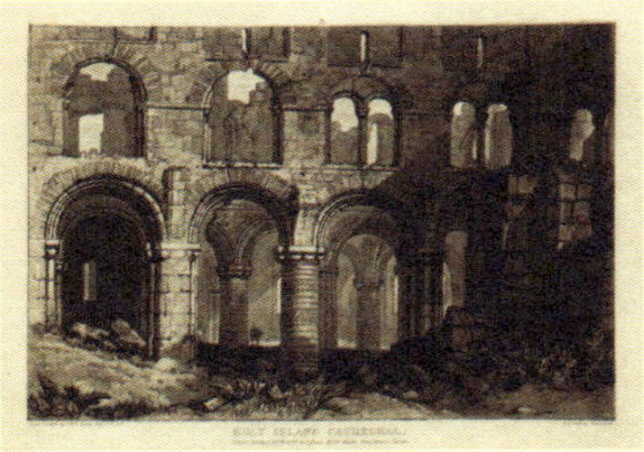

223
Holy Island Cathedral, 20 Feb. 1808
Etching and mezzotint printed in brown inks on cream laid paper, 20.7 × 28.8 cm (plate); 29.7 × 41.6 cm (sheet)
2008.5.11 | F11 I/IV

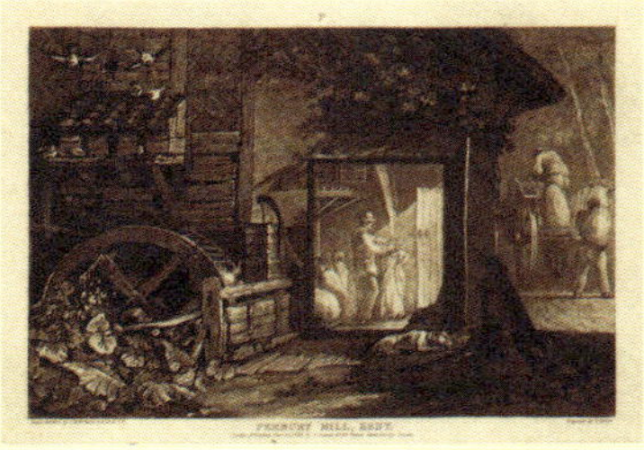

224
Pembury Mill, Kent, 10 June 1808
Etching and mezzotint printed in brown inks on cream laid paper, 20.8 × 29 cm (plate); 29.5 × 42.5 cm (sheet)
2008.5.12 | F12 I/IV

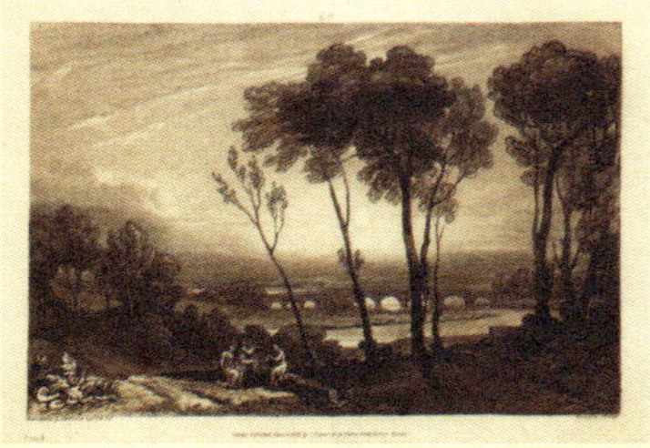

225
The Bridge in Middle Distance, 10 June 1808
Etching and mezzotint printed in brown inks on cream laid paper, 20.8 × 28.8 cm (plate); 29 × 42.3 cm (sheet)
2008.5.13 | F13 I/V

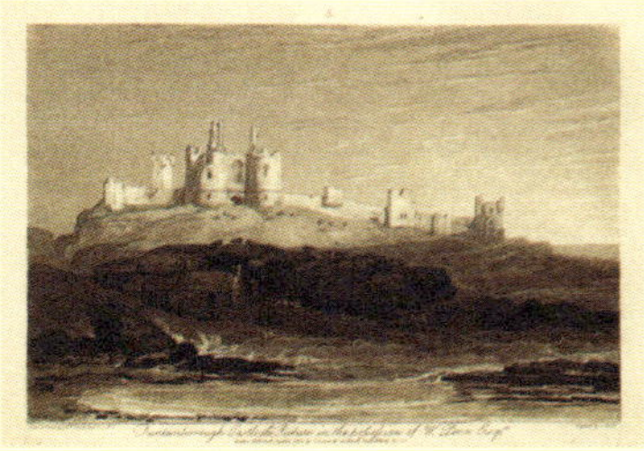

226
Dustanborough Castle, 10 June 1808
Etching and mezzotint printed in brown inks on cream laid paper, 20.8 × 28.9 cm (plate); 28.9 × 41.8 cm (sheet)
2008.5.14 | F14 I/III

Joseph Mallord William Turner

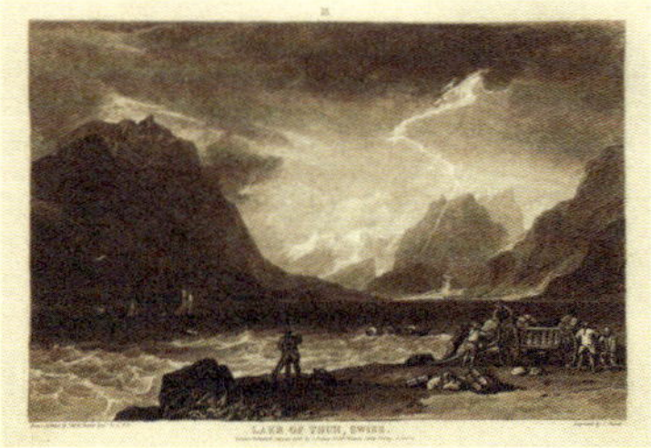

227
Lake of Thun, 10 June 1808
Etching and mezzotint printed in brown inks on cream laid paper,
20.8 × 28.9 cm (plate);
29.5 × 42.2 cm (sheet)
2008.5.15 | F15 I/III

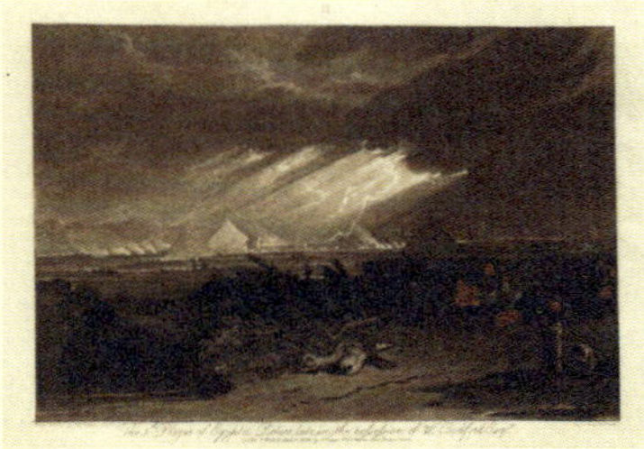

228
The Fifth Plague of Egypt,
10 June 1808
Etching and mezzotint printed in brown inks on cream laid paper,
20.7 × 28.7 cm (plate);
29.1 × 41.8 cm (sheet)
2008.5.16 | F16 I/III

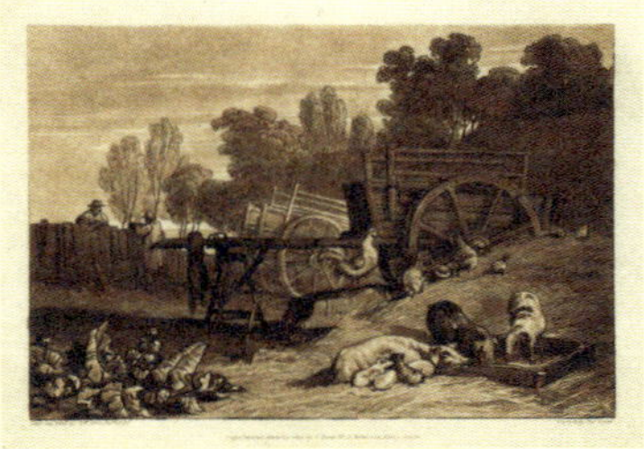

229
The Farm Yard with the Cock,
29 Mar. 1809
Etching and mezzotint printed in brown inks on cream laid paper,
20.8 × 28.9 cm (plate);
29 × 42 cm (sheet)
2008.5.17 | F17 I/III

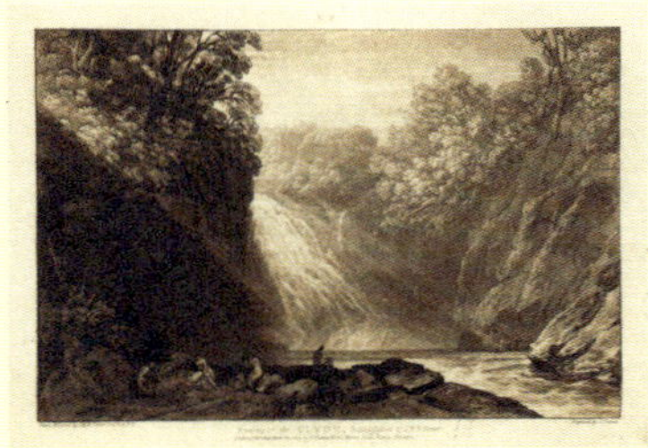

230
The Fall of the Clyde, 29 Mar. 1809
Etching and mezzotint printed in brown inks on cream laid paper,
20.8 × 29 cm (plate);
29.1 × 42.5 cm (sheet)
2008.5.18 | F18 I/III

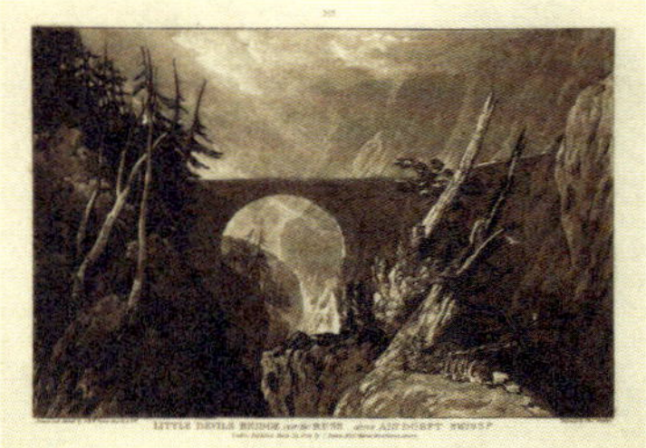

231
Little Devil's Bridge, 29 Mar. 1809
Etching and mezzotint printed in brown inks on cream laid paper,
20.9 × 28.6 cm (plate);
29.4 × 42.2 cm (sheet)
2008.5.19 | F19 III/III

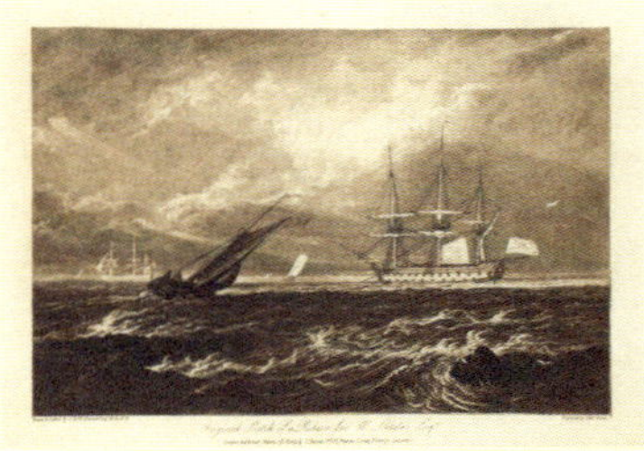

232
The Leader Sea Piece, 29 Mar. 1809
Etching and mezzotint printed in brown inks on cream laid paper,
20.9 × 28.7 cm (plate);
29.8 × 42.2 cm (sheet)
2008.5.20 | F20 I/III

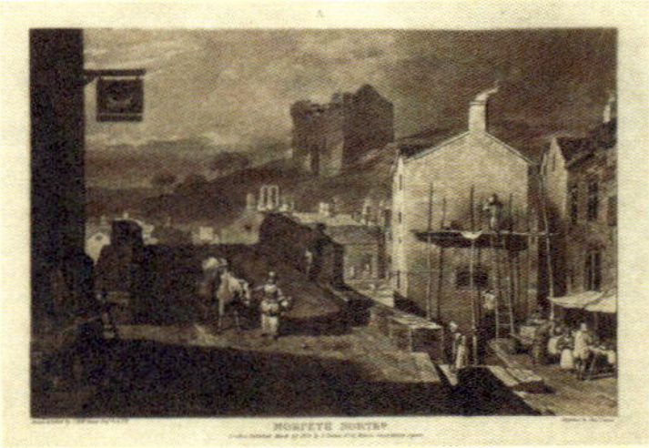

233
Morpeth, 29 Mar. 1809
Etching and mezzotint printed in brown inks on cream laid paper,
20.6 × 28.7 cm (plate);
29.5 × 20.6 cm (sheet)
2008.5.21 | F21 III/IV

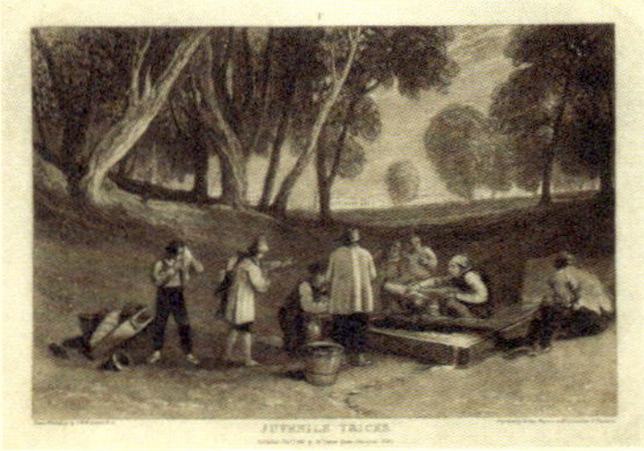

234
Juvenile Tricks, 1 Jan. 1811
Etching and mezzotint printed in brown inks on cream wove paper,
20.6 × 28.6 cm (plate);
29.7 × 43.1 cm (sheet)
2008.5.22 | F22 I/III

Joseph Mallord William Turner

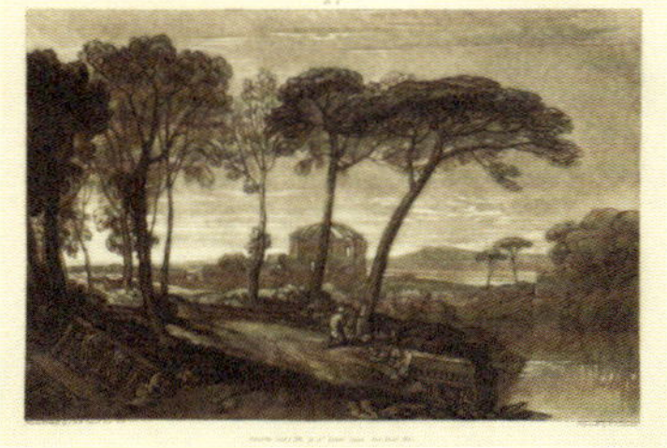

235
The Temple of Minerva Medica, 1 Jan. 1811
Etching and mezzotint printed in brown inks on cream wove paper,
20.5 × 28.7 cm (plate);
29.9 × 42.7 cm (sheet)
2008.5.23 | F23 I/V

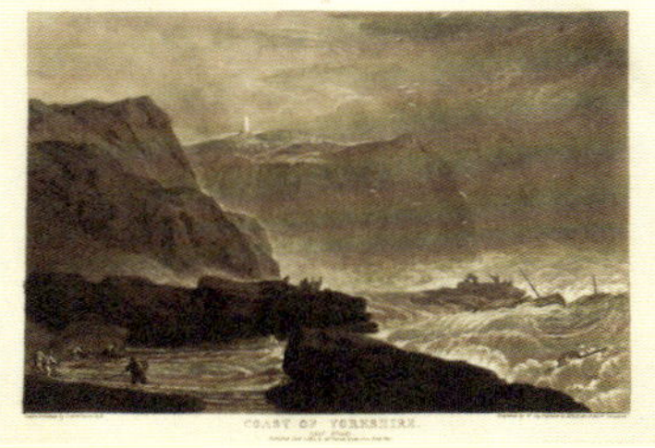

236
Coast of Yorkshire, 1 Jan. 1811
Etching and mezzotint printed in brown inks on cream wove paper,
20.6 × 28.7 cm (plate);
29.1 × 43.2 cm (sheet)
2008.5.24 | F24 I/IV

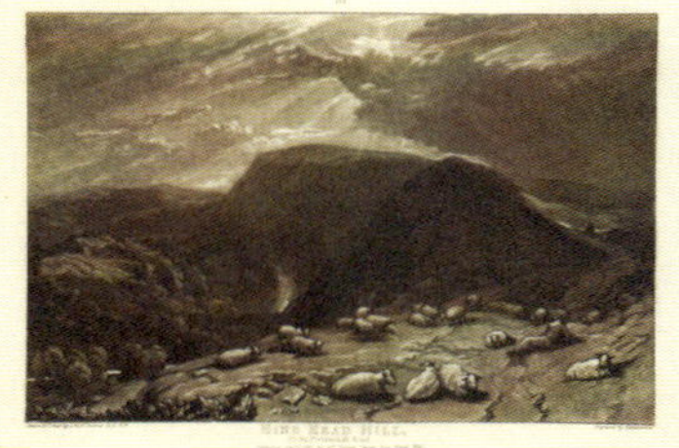

237
Hind Head Hill, 1 Jan. 1811
Etching and mezzotint printed in brown inks on cream wove paper,
20.6 × 28.7 cm (plate);
29.3 × 41.9 cm (sheet)
2008.5.25 | F25 II/IV

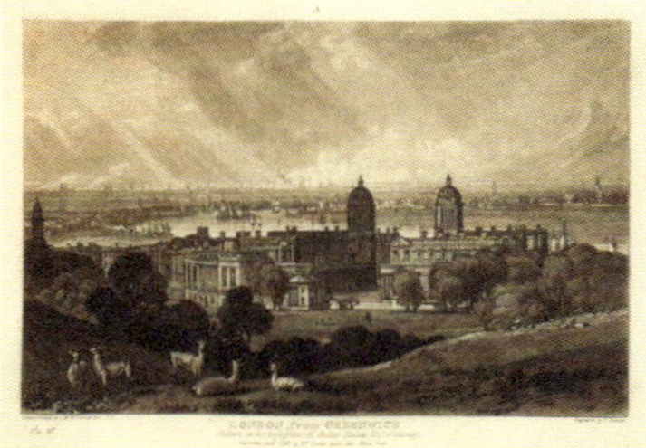

238
London from Greenwich, 1 Jan. 1811
Etching and mezzotint printed in brown inks on cream wove paper,
20 × 28.8 cm (plate);
28.7 × 42 cm (sheet)
2008.5.26 | F26 II/IV

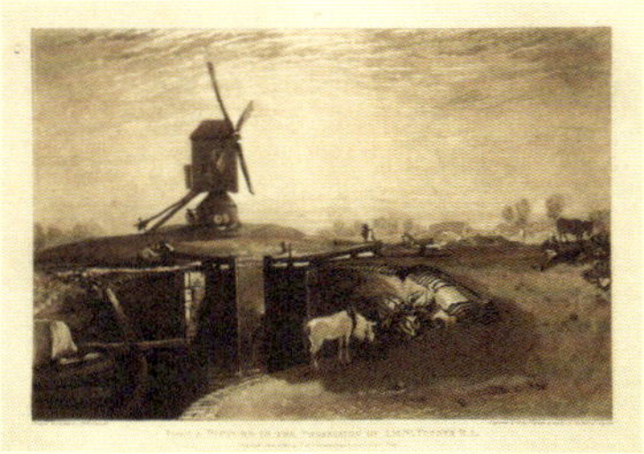

239
Windmill and Lock, 1 June 1811
Etching and mezzotint printed in brown inks on cream wove paper,
20.9 × 28.9 cm (plate);
29.9 × 42.7 cm (sheet)
2008.5.27 | F27 I/III

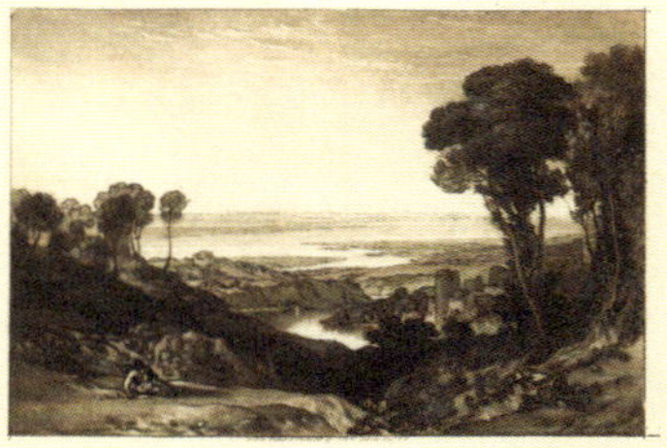

240
Junction of Severn and Wye, June 1811
Etching and mezzotint printed in brown inks on cream wove paper,
20.7 × 28.7 cm (plate);
29.1 × 42.9 cm (sheet)
2008.5.28 | F28 I/III

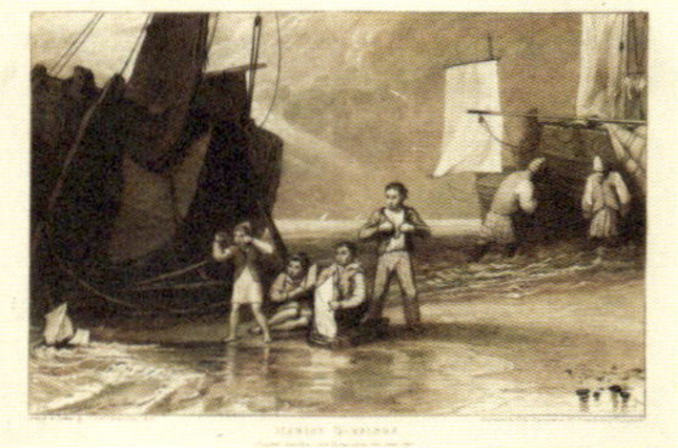

241
Marine Dabblers, June 1811
Etching and mezzotint printed in brown inks on cream wove paper,
20.8 × 28.9 cm (plate);
29.2 × 43.2 cm (sheet)
2005.5.29 | F29 I/II

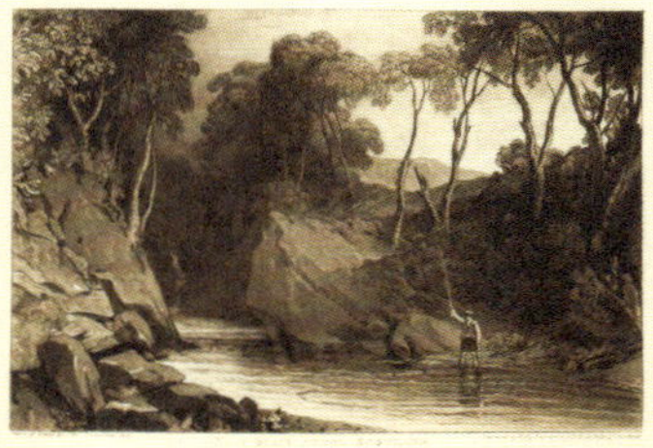

242
Near Blair Athol, 1 June 1811
Etching and mezzotint printed in brown inks on cream wove paper,
20.7 × 29 cm (plate);
29.3 × 42.9 cm (sheet)
2008.5.30 | F30 I/III

Joseph Mallord William Turner

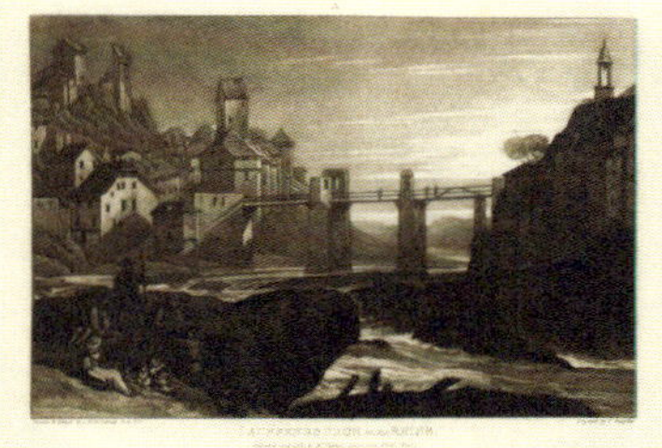

243
Lauffenbourgh on the Rhine, 1 Jan. 1811
Etching and mezzotint printed in brown inks on cream wove paper, 20.1 × 28.7 cm (plate); 28.7 × 43.4 cm (sheet)
2008.5.31 | F31 II/VI

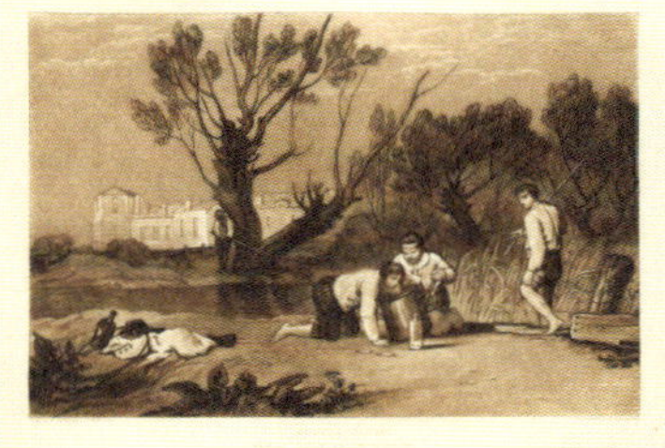

244
Young Anglers, 1 June 1811
Etching and mezzotint printed in brown inks on cream wove paper, 20.8 × 29 cm (plate); 29.8 × 42.9 cm (sheet)
2008.5.32 | F32 III/III

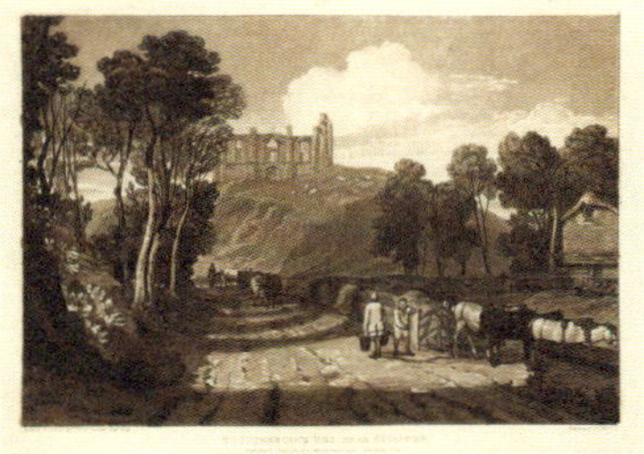

245
St. Catherine's Hill near Guildford, June 1811
Etching and mezzotint printed in brown inks on cream wove paper, 21.1 × 28.8 cm (plate); 30.1 × 43.2 cm (sheet)
2008.5.33 | F33 II/III

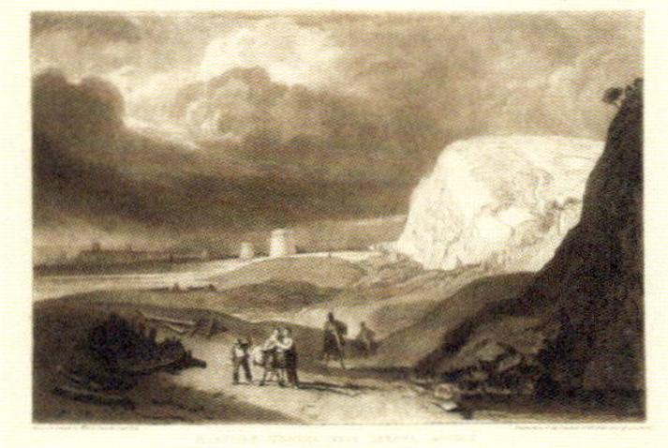

246
Martello Towers near Bexhill, Sussex, June 1811
Etching and mezzotint printed in brown inks on cream wove paper, 21.1 × 28.8 cm (plate); 29.1 × 43.2 cm (sheet)
2008.5.34 | F34 III/IV

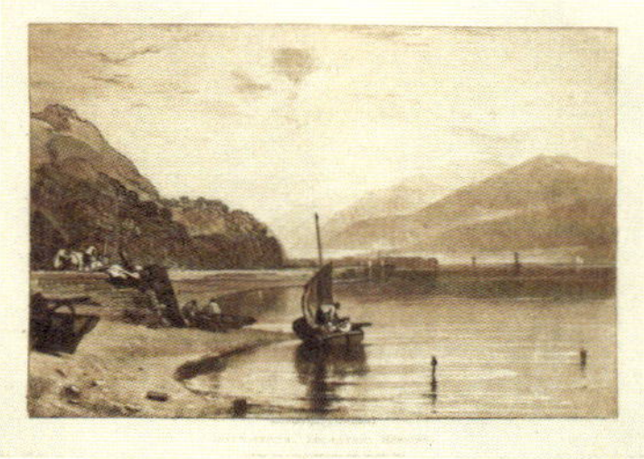

247
Inverary Pier, 1 June 1811
Etching and mezzotint printed in brown inks on cream wove paper, 20.9 × 28.9 cm (plate); 29.8 × 42.8 cm (sheet)
2008.5.35 | F35 III/VI

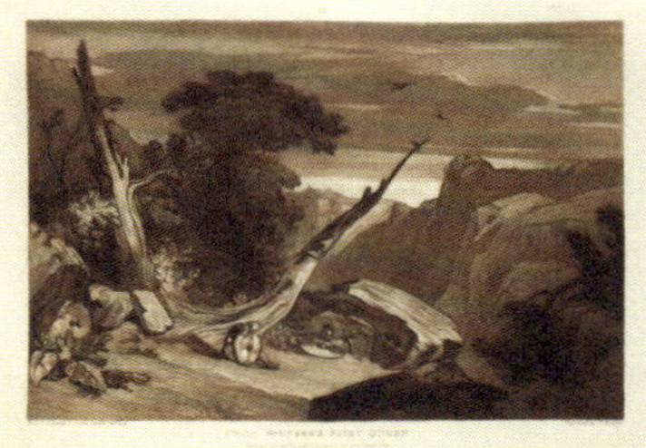

248
From Spenser's "Fairy Queen," June 1811
Etching and mezzotint printed in brown inks on cream wove paper, 20.7 × 28.9 cm (plate); 30 × 43.6 cm (sheet)
2008.5.36 | F36 III/IV

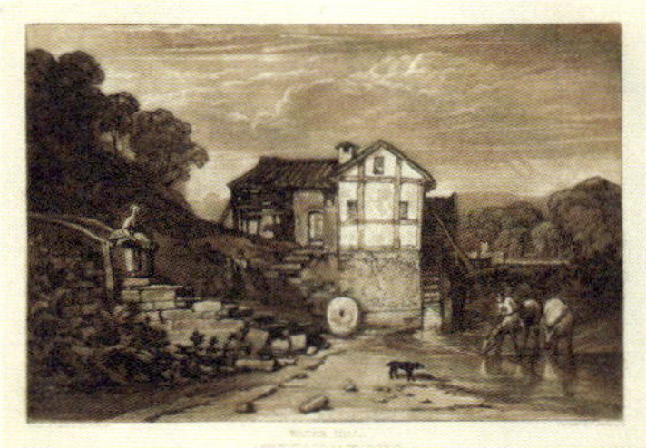

249
Water Mill, 1 Feb. 1812
Etching and mezzotint printed in brown inks on cream wove paper, 20.9 × 28.8 cm (plate); 28.8 × 42.9 cm (sheet)
2008.5.37 | F37 I/III

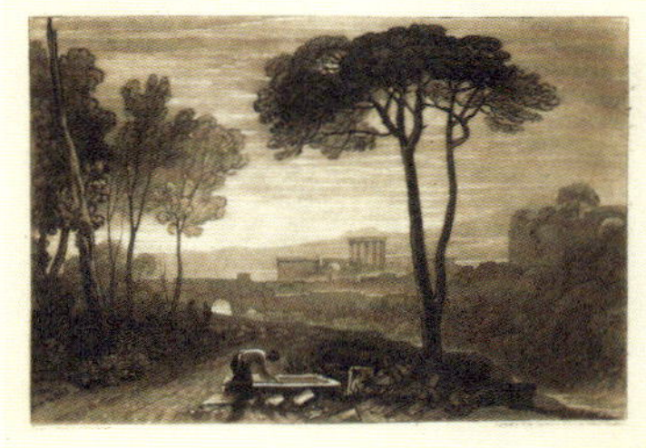

250
Scene in the Campagna, 1 Feb. 1812
Etching and mezzotint printed in brown inks on cream wove paper, 20.9 × 28.7 cm (plate); 29.5 × 43 cm (sheet)
2008.5.38 | F38 I/II

Joseph Mallord William Turner

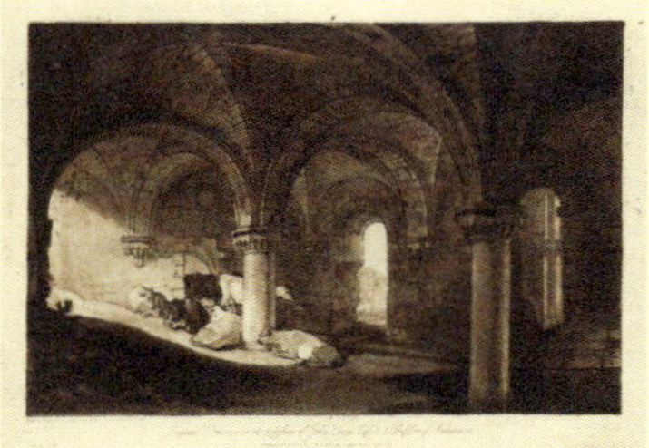

251
Crypt of Kirkstall Abbey, 11 Feb. 1812
Etching and mezzotint printed in brown inks on cream wove paper,
20.8 × 29 cm (plate);
29.4 × 43.4 cm (sheet)
2008.5.39 | F39 proof c

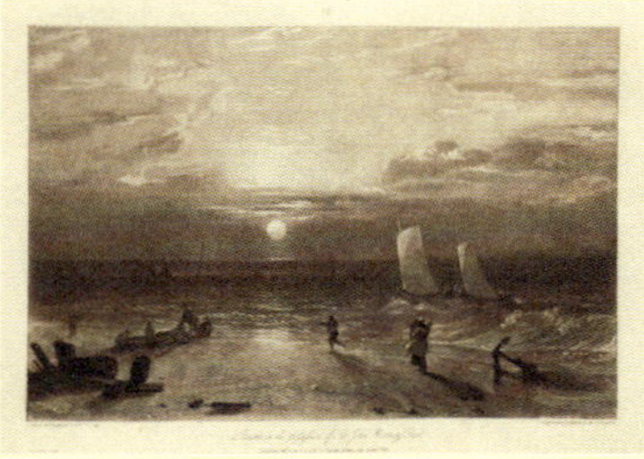

252
The Mildmay Sea Piece, 11 Feb. 1812
Etching and mezzotint printed in brown inks on cream wove paper,
20.9 × 29.2 cm (plate);
29 × 42.7 cm (sheet)
2008.5.40 | F40 II/IV

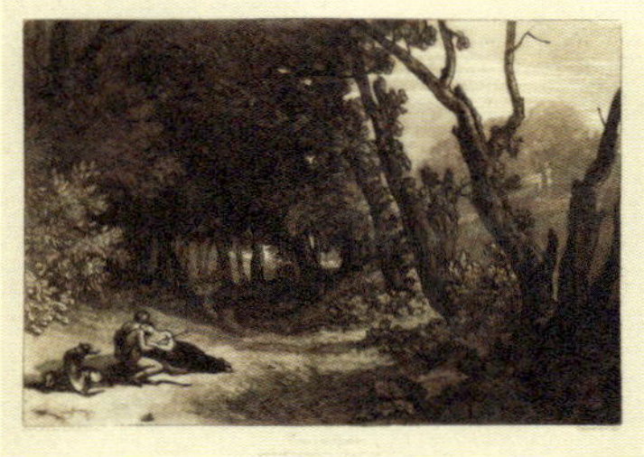

253
Procris and Cephalus, 14 Feb. 1812
Etching and mezzotint printed in brown inks on cream wove paper,
21.6 × 29 cm (plate);
29.7 × 43.4 cm (sheet)
2008.5.41 | F41 II/III

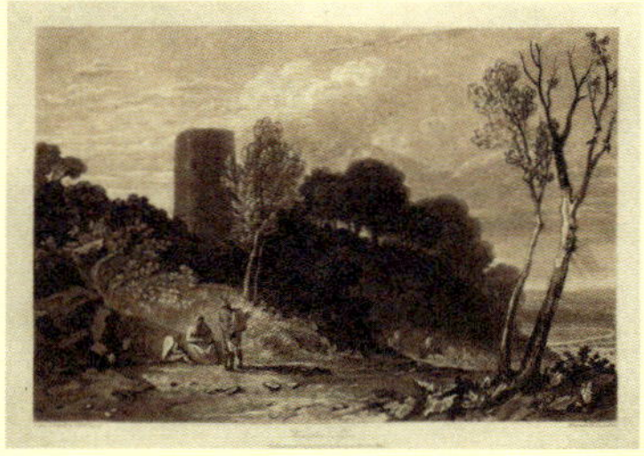

254
Winchelsea, Sussex, 23 Apr. 1812
Etching and mezzotint printed in brown inks on wove laid paper,
20.7 × 28.8 cm (plate);
29 × 42.8 cm (sheet)
2008.5.42 | F42 II/III

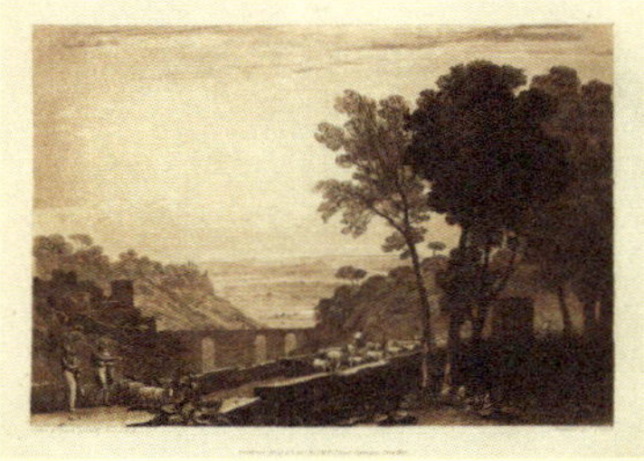

255
The Bridge and Goats, 23 Apr. 1812
Etching and mezzotint printed in brown inks on cream wove paper,
21.1 × 29 cm (plate);
29.3 × 43.4 cm (sheet)
2008.5.43 | F43 III/V

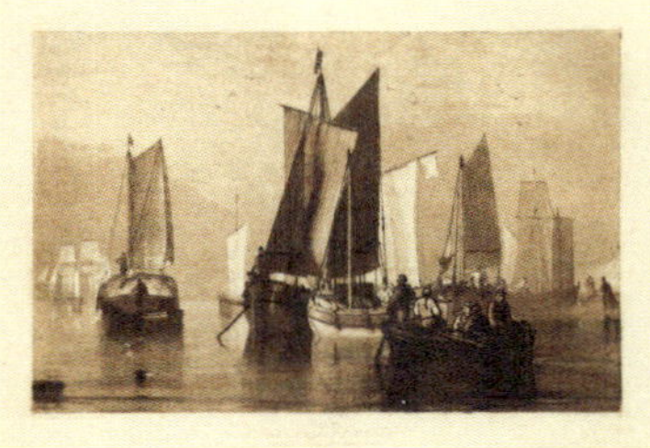

256
Calm, 23 Apr. 1812
Etching and mezzotint printed in brown inks on cream wove paper,
21.4 × 30.2 cm (plate);
29.5 × 43.6 cm (sheet)
2008.5.44 | F44 III/VII

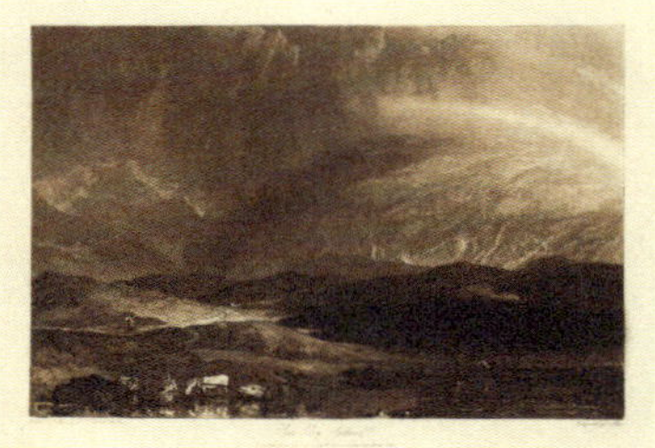

257
Peat Bog, Scotland, 23 Apr. 1812
Etching and mezzotint printed in brown inks on cream wove paper,
20.7 × 28.9 cm (plate);
29.5 × 43.4 cm (sheet)
2008.5.45 | F45 III/V

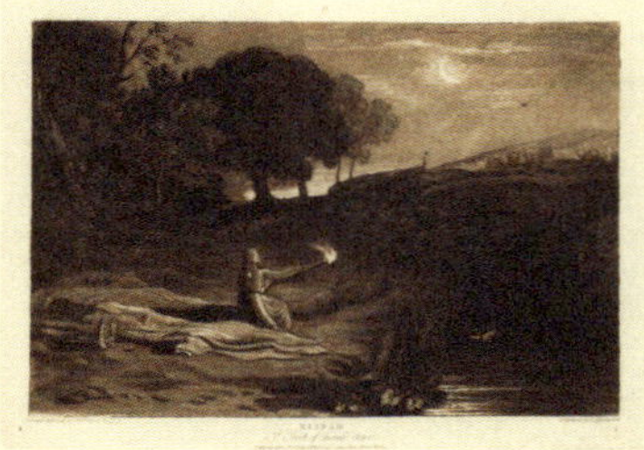

258
Rispah, 23 Apr. 1812
Etching and mezzotint printed in brown inks on cream wove paper,
20.9 × 29.1 cm (plate);
29.4 × 43.9 cm (sheet)
2008.5.46 | F46 II/IV

Joseph Mallord William Turner

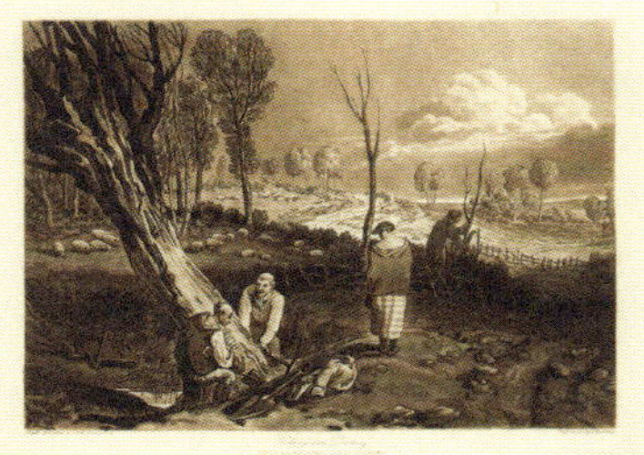

259
Hedging and Ditching, 23 May 1812
Etching and mezzotint printed in brown inks on cream wove paper, 21 × 29.1 cm (plate); 29.3 × 43.1 cm (sheet)
2008.5.47 | F47 I/IV

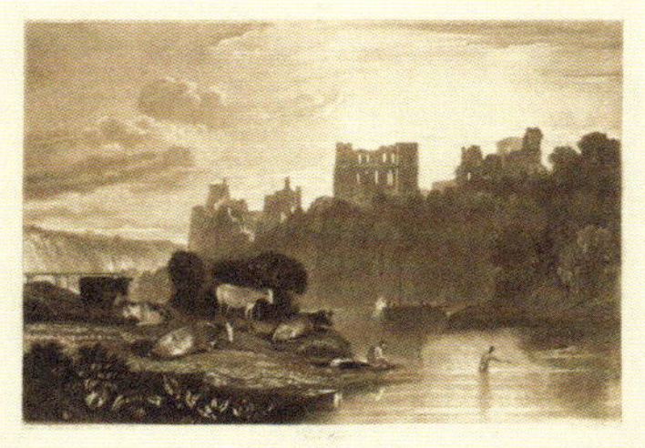

260
River Wye, 23 May 1812
Etching and mezzotint printed in brown inks on cream wove paper, 20.9 × 29.1 cm (plate); 29.3 × 43.5 cm (sheet)
2008.5.48 | F48 I/V

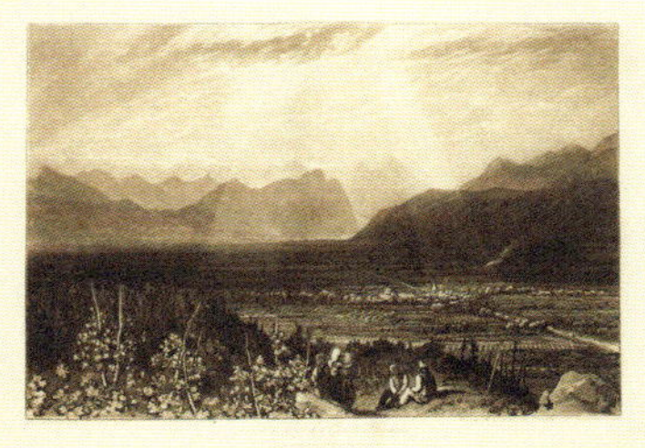

261
Chain of Alps from Grenoble to Chamberi, 23 May 1812
Etching and mezzotint printed in brown inks on cream wove paper, 20.8 × 28.8 cm (plate); 29.6 × 43.5 cm (sheet)
2008.5.49 | F49 I/IV

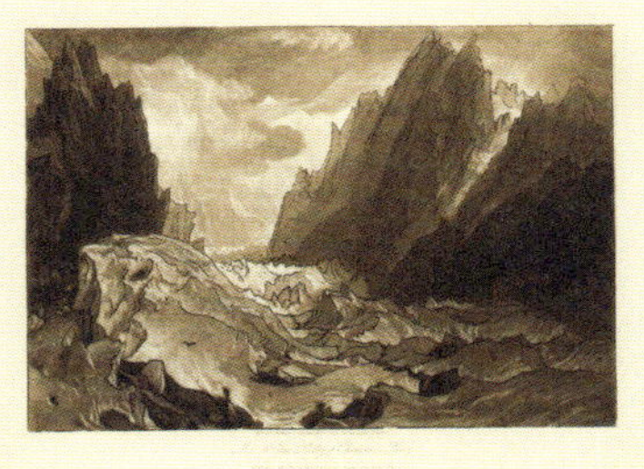

262
Mer de Glace, 23 May 1812
Etching and mezzotint printed in brown inks on cream wove paper, 21.2 × 29.2 cm (plate); 29.1 × 44 cm (sheet)
2008.5.50 | F50 I/V

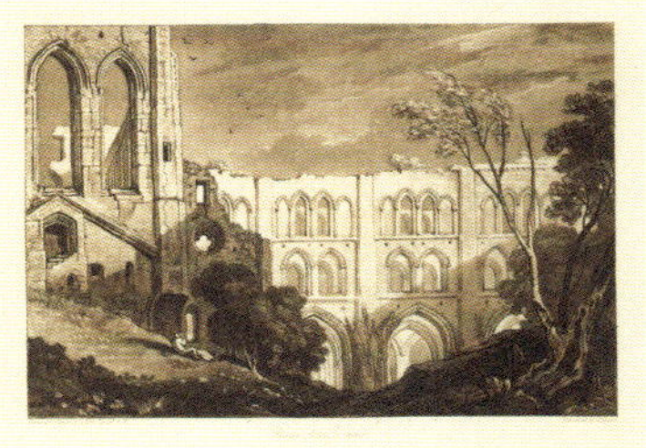

263
Rivaux Abbey, 23 May 1812
Etching and mezzotint printed in brown inks on cream wove paper, 21.8 × 29.8 cm (plate); 29.4 × 43.5 cm (sheet)
2008.5.51 | F51 I/IV

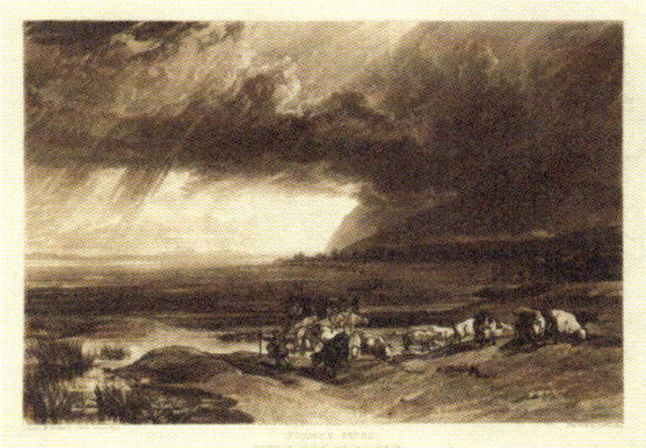

264
Solway Moss, 1 Jan. 1816
Etching and mezzotint printed in brown inks on cream laid paper, 20.9 × 29 cm (plate); 29.3 × 42.5 cm (sheet)
2008.5.52 | F52 III/V

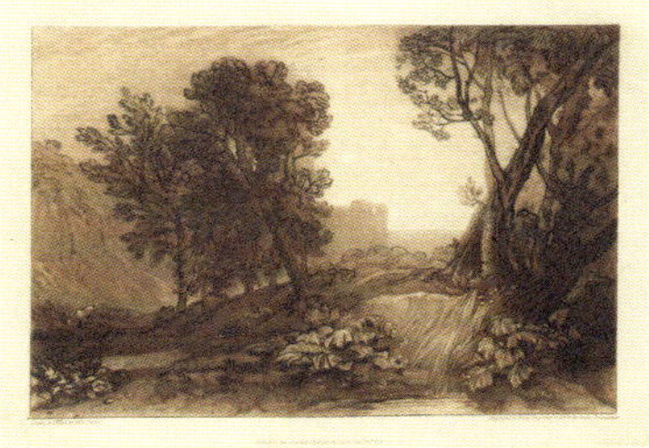

265
Solitude, 12 May 1814
Etching and mezzotint printed in brown inks on cream laid paper, 20.5 × 28.8 cm (plate); 29 × 42.3 cm (sheet)
2008.5.53 | F53 II/VII

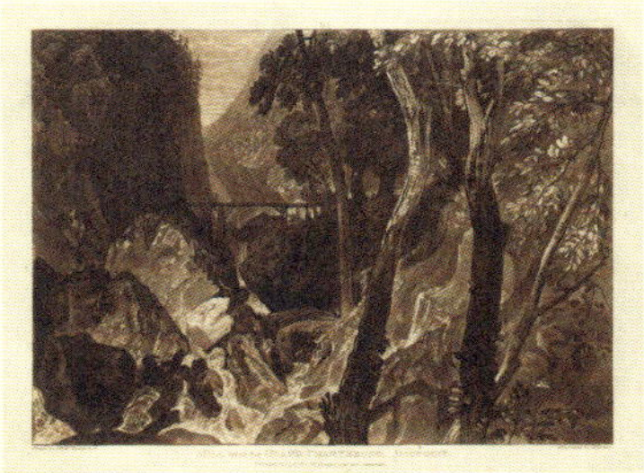

266
Mill near the Grand Chartreuse, 1 Jan. 1816
Etching and mezzotint printed in brown inks on cream laid paper, 20.7 × 29 cm (plate); 30.2 × 42.2 cm (sheet)
2008.5.54 | F54 II/IV

Joseph Mallord William Turner

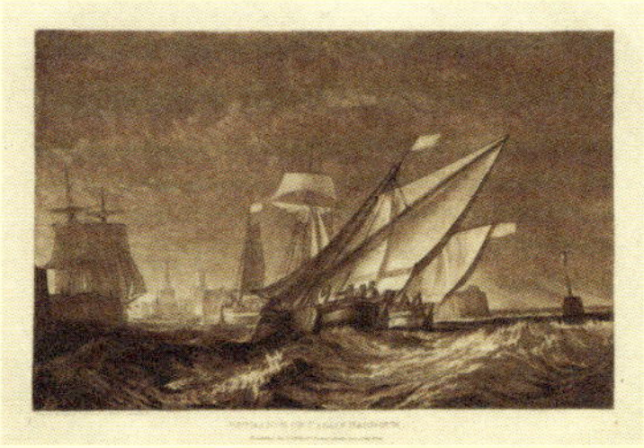

267
Entrance of Calais Harbor,
1 Jan. 1816
Etching and mezzotint printed in brown inks on cream laid paper,
21.9 × 30.2 cm (plate);
29.3 × 42.4 cm (sheet)
2008.5.55 | F55 III/VI

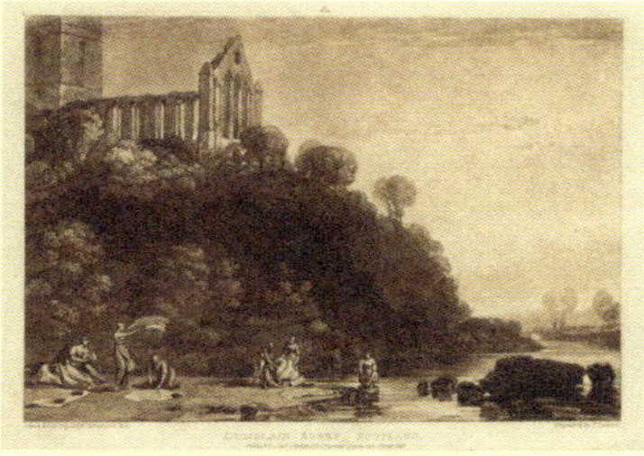

268
Dumblain Abbey, 1 Jan. 1816
Etching and mezzotint printed in brown inks on cream laid paper,
20.6 × 28.7 cm (plate);
29.8 × 41.6 cm (sheet)
2008.5.56 | F56 II/IV

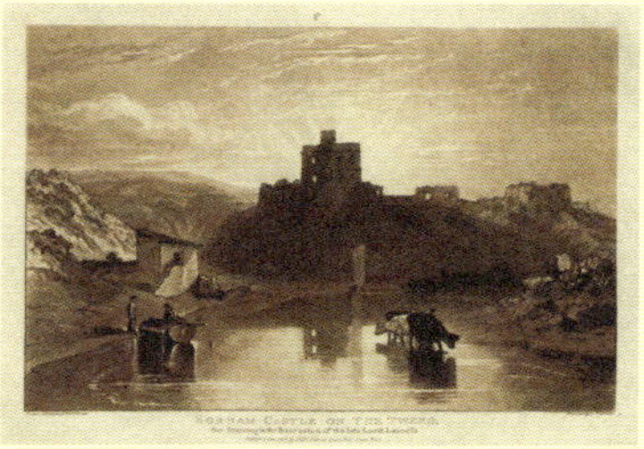

269
Norham Castle, 1 Jan. 1816
Etching and mezzotint printed in brown inks on cream laid paper,
20.7 × 28.8 cm (plate);
29.7 × 42.4 cm (sheet)
2008.5.57 | F57 II/III

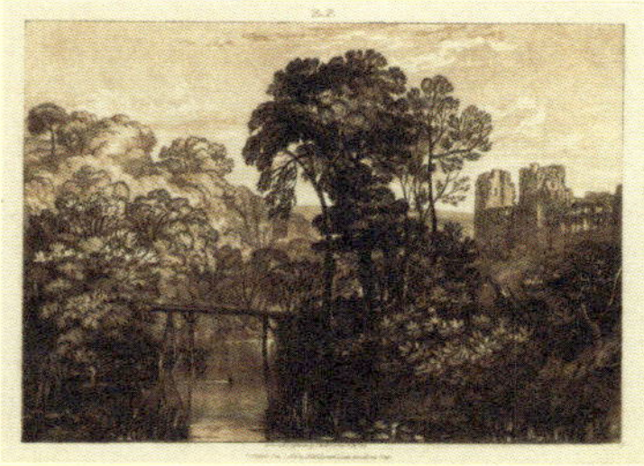

270
Berry Pomeroy Castle, 1 Jan. 1816
Etching and mezzotint printed in brown inks on cream laid paper,
21.4 × 29 cm (plate);
29.5 × 43 cm (sheet)
2008.5.58 | F58 II/III

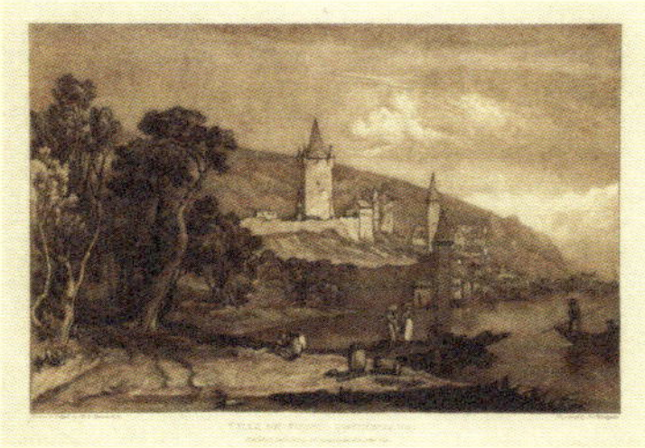

271
Ville de Thun, 1 Jan. 1816
Etching and mezzotint printed in brown inks on cream laid paper,
20.6 × 29.2 cm (plate);
29.4 × 41.9 cm (sheet)
2008.5.59 | F59 II/III

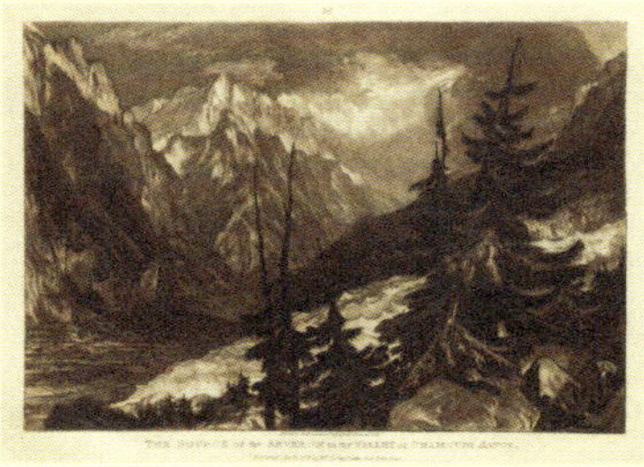

272
Source of the Arveron, 1 Jan. 1816
Etching and mezzotint printed in brown inks on cream laid paper,
21.5 × 29.1 cm (plate);
29.1 × 42.2 cm (sheet)
2008.5.60 | F60 II/III

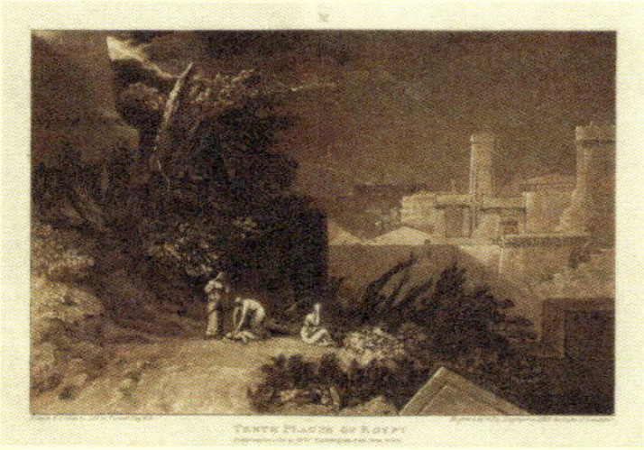

273
Tenth Plague of Egypt, 1 Jan. 1816
Etching and mezzotint printed in brown inks on cream laid paper,
20.8 × 28.9 cm (plate);
29.5 × 40.9 cm (sheet)
2008.5.61 | F61 III/IV

Joseph Mallord William Turner

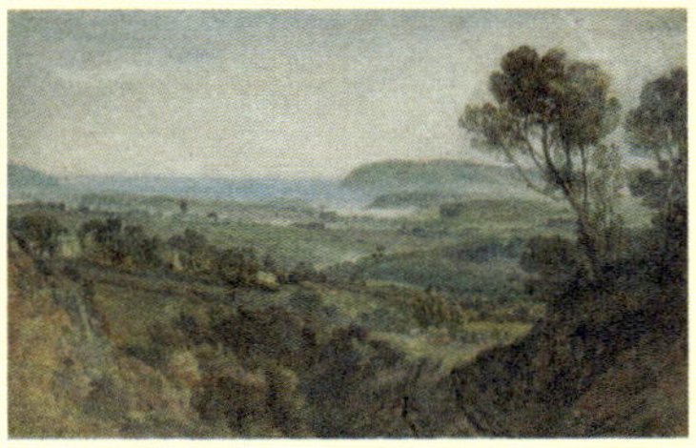

274
Distant View of Plymouth, 1813
Oil on cream wove paper, 15.2 × 23.5 cm
2007.8.103 | BJ225

Provenance: John Edward Taylor (his sale, Christie's, London, 5 July 1912, no. 100, sold to Wallis & Son); [Wallis & Son (The French Gallery), London, from 1912]; [Knoedler, London, by 1939]; Charles E. Russell; sale, Christie's, London, 30 June 1981, no. 88, sold to Leger; [Leger Galleries, London, sold to Manton, 8 Dec. 1981]; Sir Edwin A. G. Manton, New York (1981–d. 2005); Manton Family Art Foundation (2005–2007, given to the Clark); Sterling and Francine Clark Art Institue, 2007.

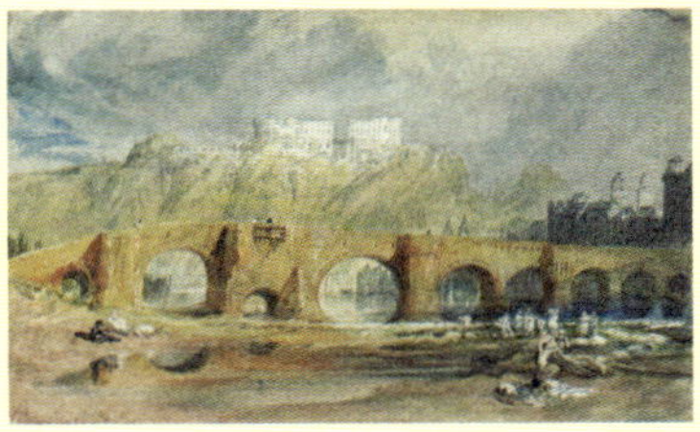

275
The Moselle Bridge at Coblenz, 1817
Watercolor and gouache, with scraping, on white wove paper, 20 × 31.4 cm
2007.8.104 | W187

Provenance: The artist, sold to Fawkes, Nov. 1817; Walter Ramsden Hawksworth Fawkes (in 1817); Rev. Ayscough Fawkes, by descent; sale, Christie's, London, 27 June 1890, no. 25, sold to Agnew's; [Thomas Agnew and Sons, Ltd., London, in 1890, sold to MacGregor]; Rev. W. MacGregor, sale, Christie's, 23 Apr. 1937, no. 14, sold to The Fine Art Society, Ltd.; [The Fine Art Society, Ltd., in 1937, sold to Astor]; Lord Astor of Hever; given to Laurence Irving (1962–1984, sold to Agnew's, as agent for private collection); private collection (1984–1998, sold to Spink-Leger); [Spink-Leger Pictures, no. K3 11266, sold to Manton, June 1999]; Sir Edwin A. G. Manton, New York (1999–d. 2005); Manton Family Art Foundation (2005–2007, given to the Clark); Sterling and Francine Clark Art Institute, 2007.

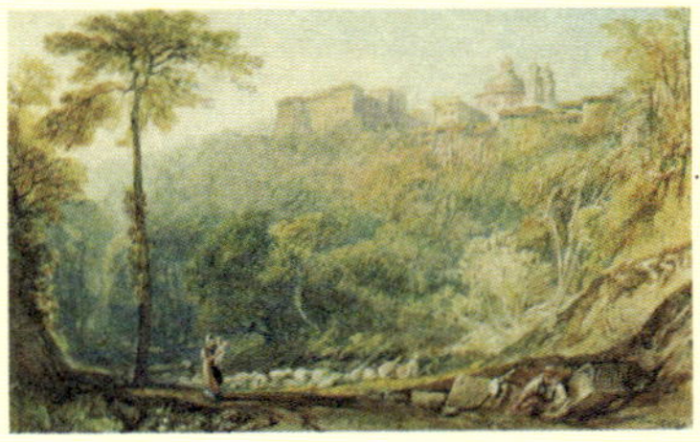

276
View of La Riccia (Ariccia), 1817
Watercolor and gouache, with scraping, on cream wove paper, 13.6 × 21.5 cm
2007.8.105 | W710

Provenance: Benjamin Godfrey Windus; Sara Austen, sale, Christie's, London, 10 Apr. 1889, no. 197, sold to Volkins; [Volkins Gallery]; Robert Strauss; Edward Steinkopff, Esq., sold 24 May 1935 to Thomson; Thomson; Dr. Marc Fitch, sold to Leger; [Leger Galleries, sold to Manton, July 1987]; Sir Edwin A. G. Manton, New York (1987–d. 2005); Manton Family Art Foundation (2005–2007, given to the Clark); Sterling and Francine Clark Art Institute, 2007.

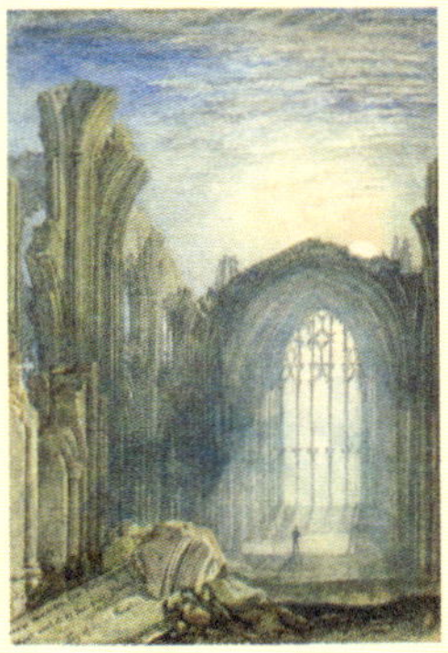

277
Melrose Abbey, 1822
Watercolor on cream wove paper, 19.7 × 13.5 cm
2007.8.106 | W1056

Provenance: The artist, commissioned by Walter Ramsden Hawksworth Fawkes; Major Lt. G. G. W. Horton-Fawkes, by descent (by 1967–1988, sale, Christie's, London, 12 July 1988, no. 193); sale, Sotheby's, London, 19 Nov. 1992, no. 152, sold to Arthur Ackermann & Peter Johnson, Ltd., as agent for Manton; Sir Edwin A. G. Manton, New York (1992–d. 2005); Manton Family Art Foundation (2005–2007, given to the Clark); Sterling and Francine Clark Art Institute, 2007.

Joseph Mallord William Turner

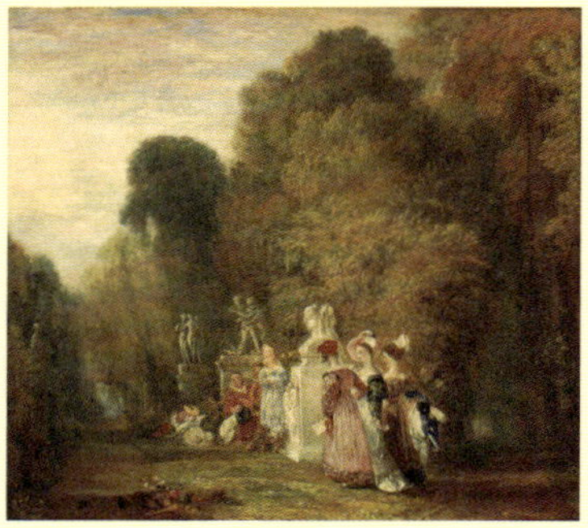

278
What You Will!, 1822
Oil on canvas, 49.8 × 54.3 cm
2007.8.107 | BJ229

Provenance: Royal Academy, sold to Chantrey, 1822; Francis Leggatt Chantrey (1822–d.1841); Chantrey, his wife, by descent (1842–1861, sale, Christie's, London, 15 June 1861, no. 91, sold to Agnew's); [Thomas Agnew and Sons, Ltd., in 1861]; R. Newsham or Newisham; J. H. Nettleford, sale, Christie's, London, 12 Feb. 1910, no. 68, sold to Vicars; [Vicars Brothers, London, 1910]; [Thomas Agnew and Sons, Ltd., in 1910, sold to Darrell-Brown]; H. Darrell-Brown, sold by his executors to Rofé, with Agnew's as agent; Albert Rofé (1927–1959, sold to Agnew's); [Thomas Agnew and Sons, Ltd., 1959, no. 19732, sold to Sobell]; Michael Sobell (1959–1994, sale, Christie's, 15 Apr. 1994, no. 60, sold to Pilkington); Brian Pilkington; [Salander-O'Reilly Galleries, Inc., New York, sold to Manton, Dec. 1999]; Sir Edwin A. G. Manton, New York (1999–d. 2005); Diana Morton, his daughter, by descent (2005–2007), given to the Clark; Sterling and Francine Clark Art Institute, 2007.

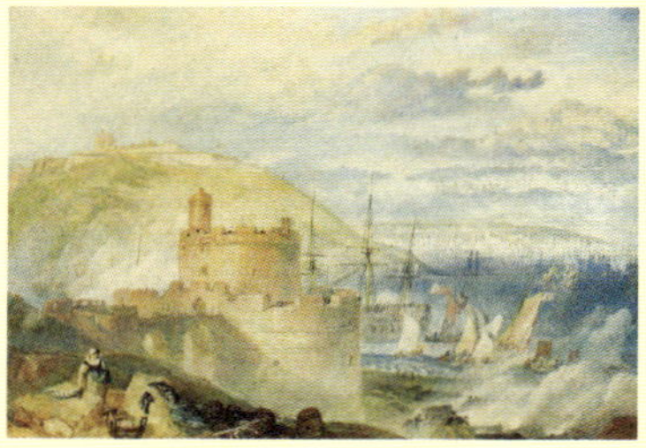

279
Falmouth Harbor, c. 1825
Watercolor and gouache, with scraping, on cream wove paper, 15.9 × 22.1 cm
2007.8.108 | W762

Provenance: Robert Stirling Newall; Frederick Stirling Newall, his son, by descent (by 1879); Norman D. Newall, his son, by descent; Mrs. Norman D. Newall, his widow, by descent (1952–1979, sale, Christie's, London, 13 Dec. 1979, no. 75, sold to Spink & Son, Ltd., London, as agent for Manton); Sir Edwin A. G. Manton, New York (1979–d. 2005); Manton Family Art Foundation (2005–2007, given to the Clark); Sterling and Francine Clark Art Institute, 2007.

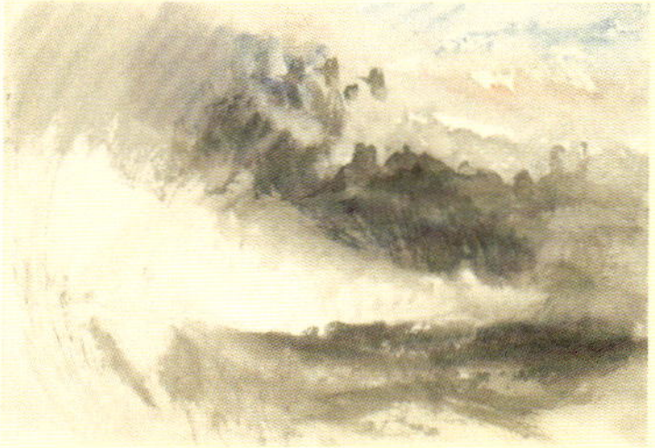

280
Sky and Sea, c. 1826–29
Watercolor and graphite on white wove paper, 22.4 × 31.3 cm
2007.8.109 | Not in Wilton

Provenance: John Rutson (c. 1850); private collection, by descent, sold to Leger, 1993; [Leger Galleries, in 1993, sold to Manton, Oct. 1993]; Sir Edwin A. G. Manton, New York (1993–d. 2005); Manton Family Art Foundation (2005–2007, given to the Clark); Sterling and Francine Clark Art Institute, 2007.

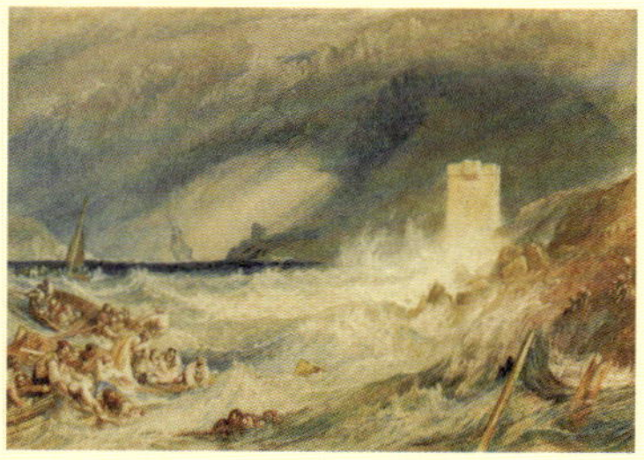

281
Entrance to Fowey Harbor, Cornwall, c. 1827
Watercolor and gouache, with scraping, on cream wove paper, 28.6 × 39.4 cm
2007.8.110 | W801

Provenance: Benjamin Godfry Windus (by 1833); E. Atkinson; Marquess of Landsdowne (by 1908); sale, Christie's, London, 22 July 1955, no. 83, sold to The Fine Art Society, Ltd.; [The Fine Art Society, Ltd., London, in 1955]; [Knoedler & Co., New York]; [Oscar & Peter Johnson, Ltd., sold to Manton, Oct. 1967]; Sir Edwin A. G. Manton, New York (1967–d. 2005); Manton Family Art Foundation (2005–2007, given to the Clark); Sterling and Francine Clark Art Institute, 2007.

Joseph Mallord William Turner

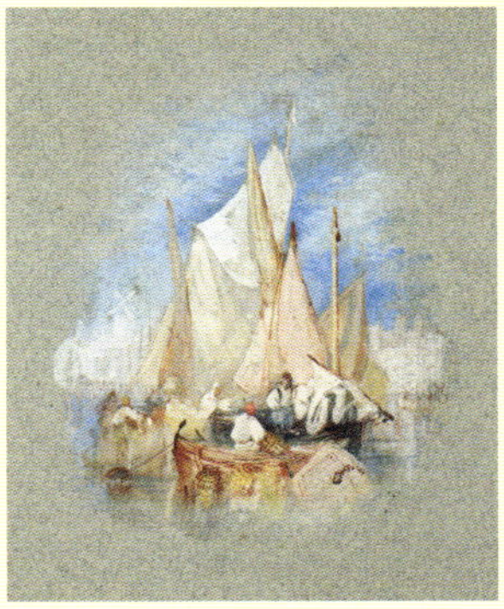

282
Great Yarmouth Fishing Boats, c. 1827
Gouache on blue wove paper, 24.6 × 18.1 cm
2007.8.111 | Not in Wilton

Provenance: Lewis Loyd, Esq. (by 1857); Captain E. N. F. Loyd, his grandson, by descent, sale, Christie's, London, 30 Apr. 1937, no. 67, sold to Fontansay; Fontansay (in 1937); [Thomas Agnew and Sons, Ltd., London]; Norton Simon, sale, Parke Bernet Galleries, New York, 8 May 1971, no. 216a, sold to Manton; Sir Edwin A. G. Manton, New York (1971–d. 2005); Manton Family Art Foundation (2005–2007, given to the Clark); Sterling and Francine Clark Art Institute, 2007.

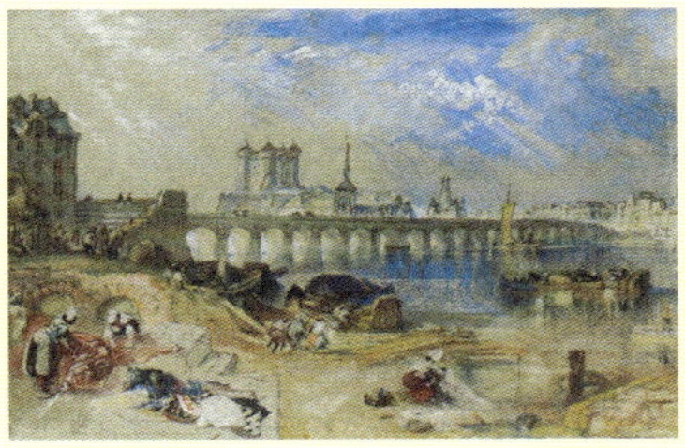

283
Saumur from the Île d'Offart, with the Pont Cessart and the Château in the Distance, c. 1830
Watercolor and gouache with pen and black and brown ink over traces of graphite on blue wove paper, 12.7 × 19.2 cm
2007.8.112 | W941

Provenance: [Thomas Griffith, sale, 31 May 1850 as part of a group of 24 Loire subjects for 600 guineas, sold to Stokes]; Charles Stokes (1850–d. 1853); Lewis Loyd, Esq. (by 1857); Captain E. N. F. Loyd, sale, Christie's, London, 30 Apr. 1937, no. 68, sold to MacConnell; Rayner MacConnell (in 1937, sold to Fattorini); T. Edward Fattorini (1937–1966, sale, Sotheby's, London, 13 July 1966, no. 47, sold to Lusk); A. R. Lusk (1966–1981, sold to Agnew's); [Thomas Agnew and Sons, Ltd., London, in 1981]; John Madden, Colorado, sold to Agnew's, 1991; [Thomas Agnew and Sons, Ltd., London]; [Spink-Leger Pictures, 1996–1997, no. K3 11266, sold to Manton, Feb. 1997]; Sir Edwin A. G. Manton, New York (1997–d. 2005); Manton Family Art Foundation (2005–2007, given to the Clark); Sterling and Francine Clark Art Institute, 2007.

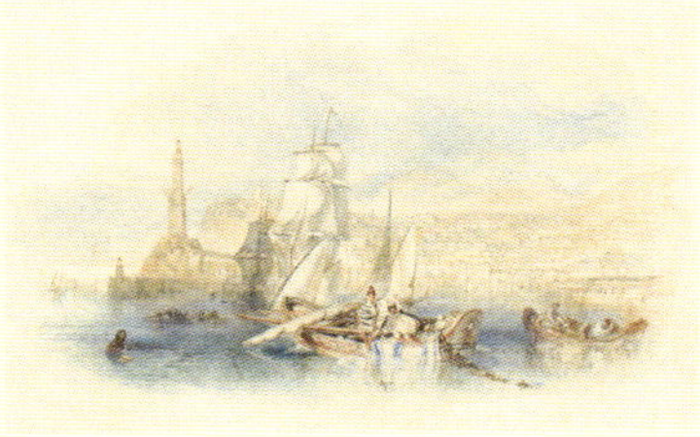

284
Genoa, c. 1832
Watercolor and gouache over graphite on cream wove paper, 12.7 × 21 cm
2007.8.113 | W1231

Provenance: John Edward Taylor, sale, Christie's, London, 5 July 1912, no. 160, sold to Agnew's; [Thomas Agnew and Sons, Ltd., London, in 1912]; A. A. Allen (his sale, Sotheby's, London, 4 Apr. 1935, no. 112); Mrs. Benskin; Mrs. John Fergusson-Cuninghame, her granddaughter, by descent, sale, Christie's, London, 1 Nov. 1966, no. 151, sold to Johnson; [Oscar & Peter Johnson Ltd., Nov.–Dec. 1966, sold to Manton, Dec. 1966]; Sir Edwin A. G. Manton, New York (1966–d. 2005); Manton Family Art Foundation (2005–2007, given to the Clark); Sterling and Francine Clark Art Institute, 2007.

Joseph Mallord William Turner

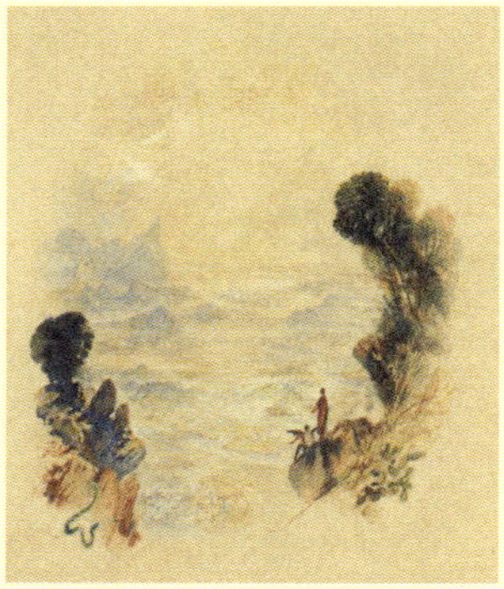

285
The Temptation of Christ on the Mountain, c. 1834
Watercolor and gouache with graphite on cream wove paper, 20.3 × 15.7 cm
2007.8.114 | W1267

Provenance: The artist, commissioned by Sir Egerton Brydges; Hugh Andrew Johnstone Munro of Novar, sale, Christie's, London, 2 June 1877, no. 29, sold to Agnew's; [Thomas Agnew and Sons, Ltd., London, 1877–1882, possibly sold to Hollingsworth]; A. T. Hollingsworth, sale, Christie's, London, 11 Mar. 1882, no. 74, possibly sold to Clements; possibly Clements (in 1882); George Gurney (by Mar. 1883); S. Sandars; H. L. Fison (in or by 1934, sale, Christie's, London, 6 Nov. 1959, no. 2, sold to Leggatt Brothers Gallery, as agent for Manton); Sir Edwin A. G. Manton, New York (1959–d. 2005); Manton Family Art Foundation (2005–2007, given to the Clark); Sterling and Francine Clark Art Institute, 2007.

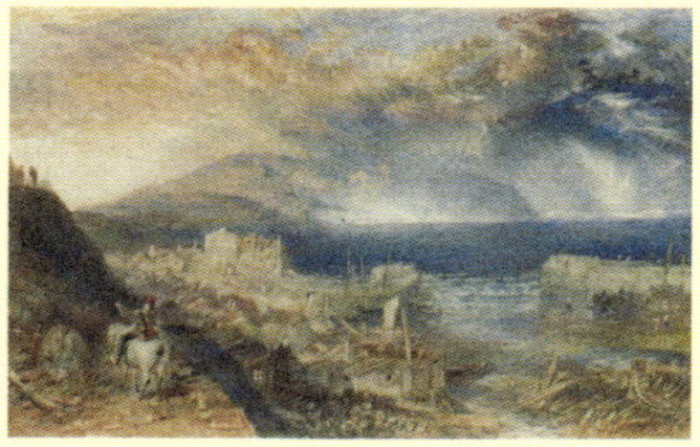

286
Wolf's Hope, Eyemouth, c. 1835
Watercolor and gouache over graphite, with scraping, on cream wove paper, 10.5 × 16.5 cm
2007.8.115 | W1138

Provenance: The artist, sold to John Ruskin; J. R. Williams, sale, Christie's, London, 10 June 1865, no. 35, sold to Shaw; Matthew T. Shaw (1865–1880, sale, Christie's, 20 Mar. 1880, no. 52, sold to Lloyd); Theodore Lloyd (1880–1911, sale, Christie's, London, 4 Feb. 1911, no. 17, sold to King); James King (in 1911); Lt. Col. James B. Gaskell (by 1912–1926, sale, Christie's, London, 30 Apr. 1926, no. 78, sold to King); James King (in 1926); Frank Gaskell; Joan Gaskell, his daughter, by descent, sale, Sotheby's, London, 9 Apr. 1992, no. 56, sold to Spink; [Spink & Son, Ltd., London, 1992–1993, no. K3 10353, sold to Manton, June 1993]; Sir Edwin A. G. Manton, New York (1993–d. 2005); Manton Family Art Foundation (2005–2007, given to the Clark); Sterling and Francine Clark Art Institute, 2007.

287
Ivrea, 1836 or c. 1845
Watercolor and resist on cream wove paper, 22.9 × 30.5 cm
2007.8.116

Provenance: Possible sale, Christie's, c. 1860, no. 103; sale, Sotheby's, London, 20 Nov. 1986, no. 90, sold to private collector; private collection (1986–1997, sold to Spink); [Spink-Leger Pictures, 1997–1998, no. K3 11408, sold to Manton, Feb. 1998]; Sir Edwin A. G. Manton, New York (1998–d. 2005); Manton Family Art Foundation (2005–2007, given to the Clark); Sterling and Francine Clark Art Institute, 2007.

Joseph Mallord William Turner

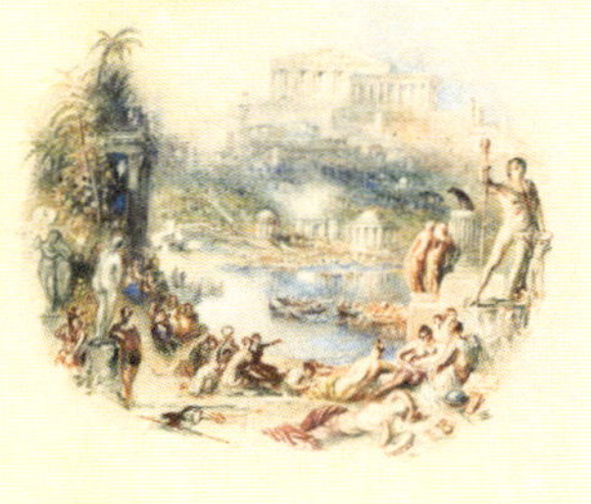

288
The Garden: An Illustration to Thomas Moore's "The Epicurean," c. 1837–39
Watercolor over graphite, with scraping, on cream wove paper, 18.7 × 14.9 cm
2007.8.118 | W1298

Provenance: Hugh Andrew Johnstone Munro of Novar, sale, Christie's, 2 June 1877, no. 25 or 125, sold to Agnew's; [Thomas Agnew and Sons, Ltd., London]; Mrs. Prater, sale, Christie's, London, 9 Apr. 1880, no. 95, sold to White; White (in 1880); Major U. P. Misa (in 1919); J. R. Smith (in 1921); Lord Derby (in 1926); [Thomas Agnew and Sons, Ltd., London, sold to Manton, Nov. 2003]; Sir Edwin A. G. Manton, New York (2003–d. 2005); Manton Family Art Foundation (2005–2007, given to the Clark); Sterling and Francine Clark Art Institute, 2007.

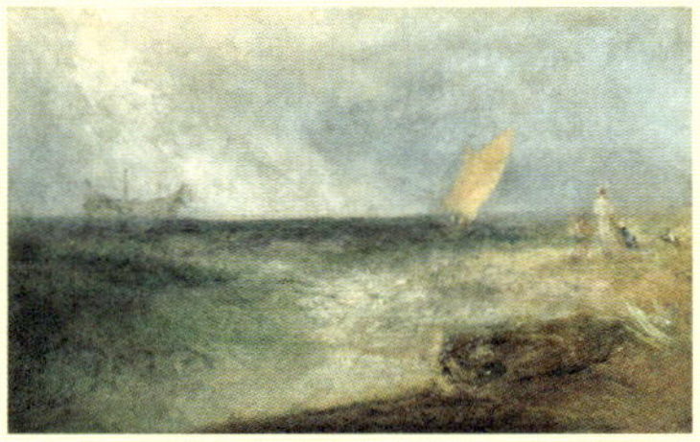

289
View off Margate, Evening, c. 1840
Oil on canvas, 32.1 × 48.9 cm
2007.8.117 | BJ479

Provenance: The artist, probably given to Booth; Sophia Caroline Booth, Margate; John Pound, her son, by descent (until 1865, sale, Christie's, London, 24–25 Mar. 1865, no. 205, sold to Agnew's); [Agnew's, London, sold to Holdsworth, 1866]; W. J. Holdsworth (1866–1881, sold to Agnew's, Jan. 1881); [Agnew's, London, sold to Blake, Dec. 1881]; T. W. Jex Blake (from 1881, probably given to Rugby School, 1887); Rugby School Art Museum (probably 1887–1982, sale, Sotheby's, London, 17 Mar. 1982, no. 51, sold to Leger Galleries); [Leger Galleries, London, sold to Flacks, probably Sept. 1983]; Alan Flacks (probably from 1983, sold to Spink); [Spink, London, sold to Manton, 2 Nov. 1998]; Sir Edwin A. G. Manton, New York (1998–d. 2005); Manton Family Art Foundation (2005–2007, given to the Clark); Sterling and Francine Clark Art Institute, 2007.

Attributed to Joseph Mallord William Turner

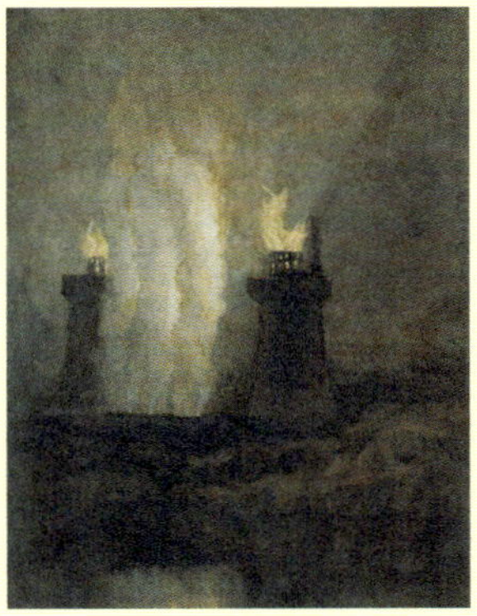

290
Carron Iron Works, c. 1800
Watercolor and gouache over graphite, with gum arabic, on beige (?) wove paper, mounted on cream paperboard, 34.8 × 25.1 cm
2007.20.41

Provenance: Sale, Kende Galleries, New York, 29–30 Apr. 1949, sold to Manton; Sir Edwin A. G. Manton, New York (1949–d. 2005); Manton Family Art Foundation (2005–2007, given to the Clark); Sterling and Francine Clark Art Institute, 2007.

Alfred Vickers English, 1786–1868

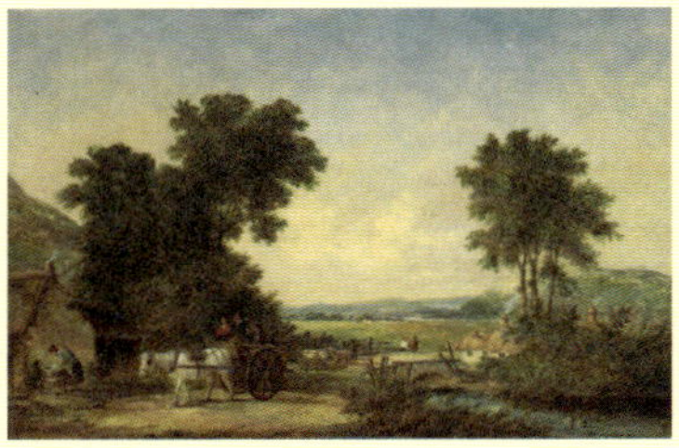

291
Wooded Country Landscape with Figures in a Cart, 1855
Oil on canvas, 63.2 × 93.3 cm
2007.8.123

Provenance: Sale, Sotheby's, London, 9 Apr. 1997, no. 100, sold to Ackermann & Johnson, Ltd., London, as agent for Manton; Sir Edwin A. G. Manton (1997–d. 2005); Manton Family Art Foundation (2005–2007, given to the Clark); Sterling and Francine Clark Art Institute, 2007.

Hugh Williams Williams Scottish, 1773–1829

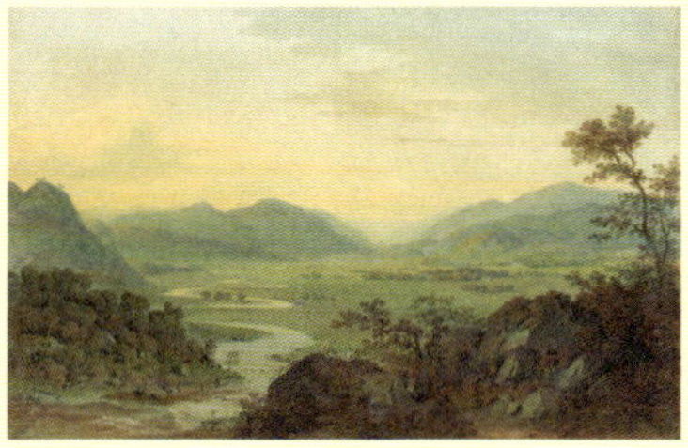

292
Carne River from Loudoun Castle, Ayrshire, 1804
Watercolor over graphite on cream wove paper, lined with fabric, mounted on canvas, 61.6 × 67.3 cm
2007.8.124

Provenance: [Oscar & Peter Johnson, Ltd., sold to Manton, Sept. 1969]; Sir Edwin A. G. Manton, New York (1969–d. 2005); Manton Family Art Foundation (2005–2007, given to the Clark); Sterling and Francine Clark Art Institute, 2007.

Hugh Williams Williams

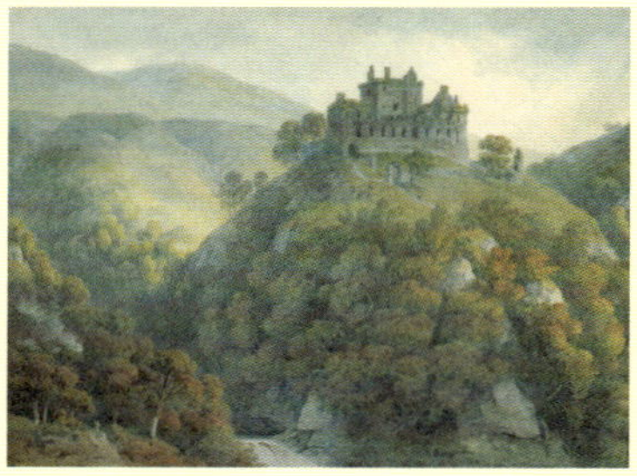

293
Castle Campbell, Clackmannanshire, 1813
Watercolor over graphite on cream wove paperboard, 59.7 × 78.1 cm
2007.8.125

Provenance: [Oscar & Peter Johnson Ltd., sold to Manton, Feb. 1985]; Sir Edwin A. G. Manton, New York (1985–d. 2005); Manton Family Art Foundation (2005–2007, given to the Clark); Sterling and Francine Clark Art Institute, 2007.

Richard Wilson Welsh, 1713–1782

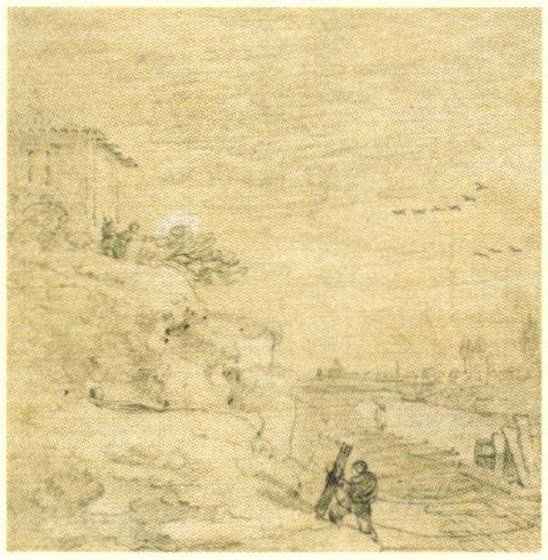

294
On the Banks of the Tiber, 1751–52
Black and white chalk over tan prepared ground on cream laid paper, 22.9 × 22.2 cm
2007.20.44

Provenance: Willem Anne Van Keppel (1751–d. 1754); Hon. Augustus Keppel, his son, by descent (Dec. 1754); S. Wooding; Aimee Wooding; [Leger Galleries, sold to Manton, Sept. 1984, as Joshua Reynolds]; Sir Edwin A. G. Manton, New York (1984–d. 2005); Manton Family Art Foundation (2005–2007, given to the Clark); Sterling and Francine Clark Art Institute, 2007.

Artist unknown British, 19th century

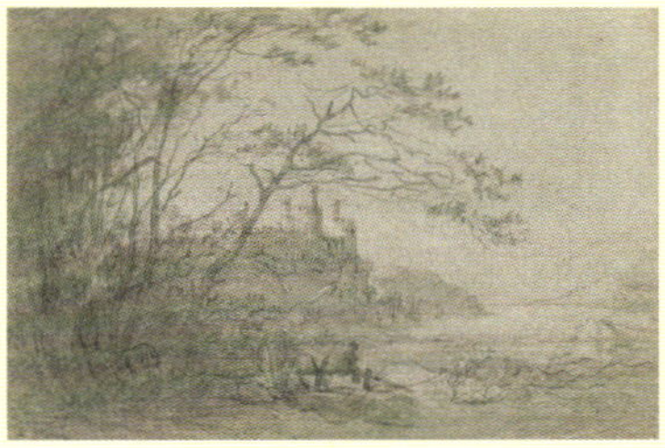

295
A Figure Seated on a Stile with Conwy Castle in the Distance (recto); *Mountain View by a Lake* (verso)
Black chalk over brush and gray wash on blue wove paper (recto); black chalk on blue wove paper (verso), 25 × 35.1 cm
2007.20.18

Provenance: Sir Edwin A. G. Manton (d. 2005); Manton Family Art Foundation (2005–2007, given to the Clark); Sterling and Francine Clark Art Institute, 2007.

Artist unknown British, 19th century

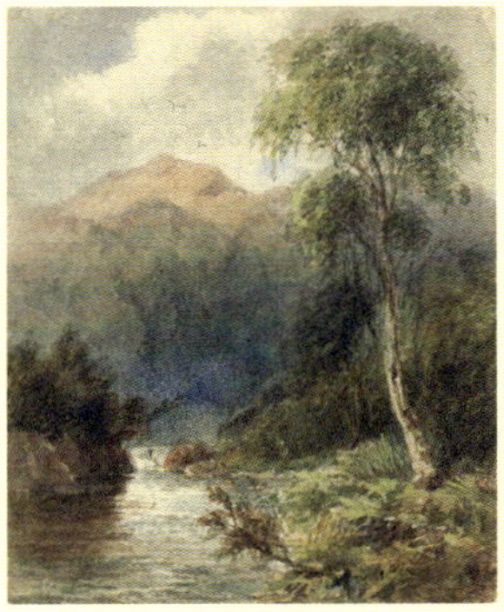

296
In the Trossachs, Scotland
Watercolor on cream wove paper, 23.1 × 18 cm
2007.20.46

Provenance: John Anderson, Jr., sale, Edward P. and William H. O'Reilly, 18 Mar. 1937, no. 54; Geoffrey Oliver, New York, sold to Manton, Feb. 1982; Sir Edwin A. G. Manton, New York (1982–d. 2005); Manton Family Art Foundation (2005–2007, given to the Clark); Sterling and Francine Clark Art Institute, 2007.

Artist unknown British, 19th century

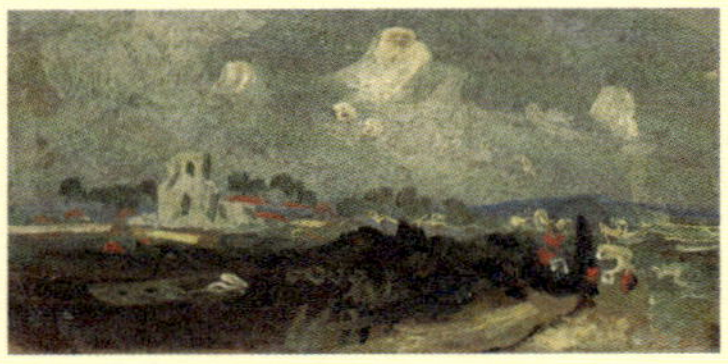

297
Landscape with Church
Oil on laminate cardboard, 4.5 × 9.1 cm
2007.20.47

Provenance: Walter P. Chrysler, Jr. (his sale, Parke-Bernet Galleries, New York, 30 Apr. 1960, no. 172, sold to Manton, as John Constable); Sir Edwin A. G. Manton, New York (1960–d. 2005); Manton Family Art Foundation (2005–2007, given to the Clark); Sterling and Francine Clark Art Institute, 2007.

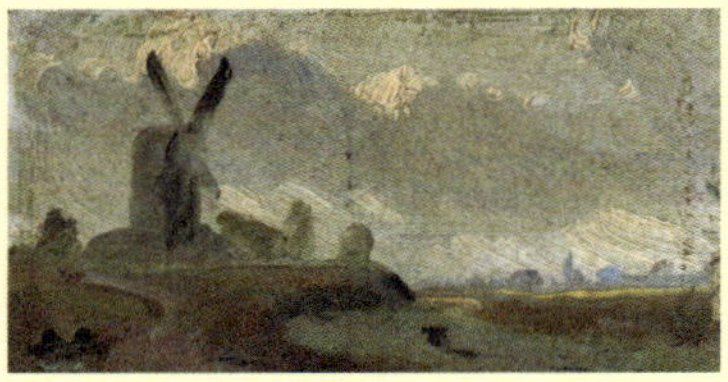

298
Landscape with Windmill
Oil on laminate cardboard, 5.1 × 9.7 cm
2007.20.48

Provenance: Walter P. Chrysler, Jr. (his sale, Parke-Bernet Galleries, New York, 30 Apr. 1960, no. 172, sold to Manton, as John Constable); Sir Edwin A. G. Manton, New York (1960–d. 2005); Manton Family Art Foundation (2005–2007, given to the Clark); Sterling and Francine Clark Art Institute, 2007.

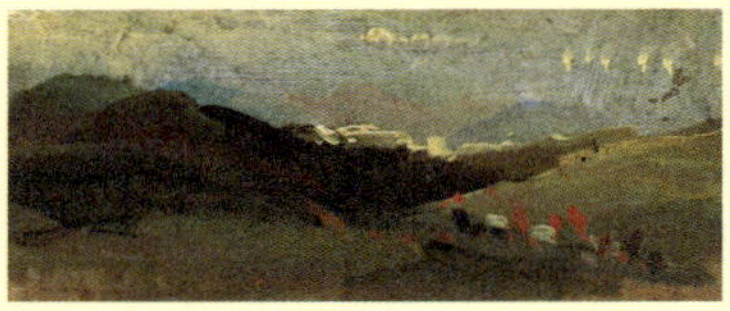

299
Mountain Landscape
Oil on laminate cardboard, 4 × 9.1 cm
2007.20.49

Provenance: Walter P. Chrysler, Jr. (his sale, Parke-Bernet Galleries, New York, 30 Apr. 1960, no. 172, sold to Manton, as John Constable); Sir Edwin A. G. Manton, New York (1960–d. 2005); Manton Family Art Foundation (2005–2007, given to the Clark); Sterling and Francine Clark Art Institute, 2007.

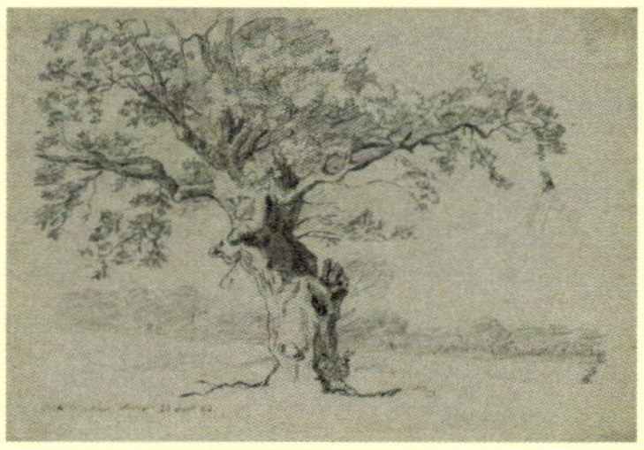

300
Oak Tree, Windsor Forest, 22 Oct. 1823
Black chalk over graphite with stumping and pen and brown ink on blue-gray wove paper, 27.8 × 37.8 cm
2007.20.50

Provenance: [Oscar & Peter Johnson, Ltd., London, sold to Manton, June 1972, as James Stark]; Sir Edwin A. G. Manton, New York (1972–d. 2005); Manton Family Art Foundation (2005–2007, given to the Clark); Sterling and Francine Clark Art Institute, 2007.

Artist unknown

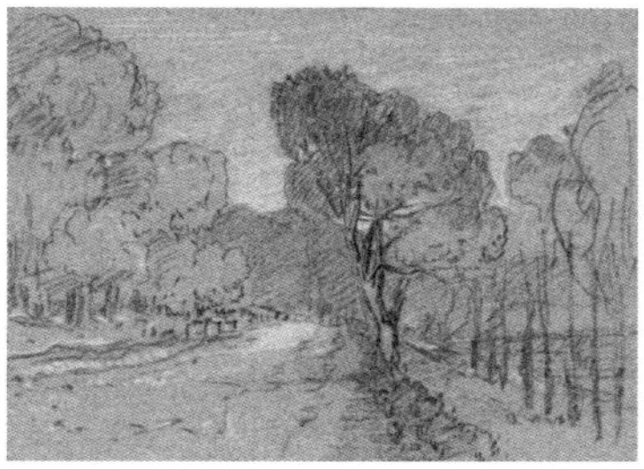

301
Petersham (recto); *Tree Branches* (verso)
Black and white chalks on blue wove paper, 13.9 × 18.6 cm
2007.20.51

Provenance: [Oscar & Peter Johnson, Ltd., sold to Manton, Feb. 1973, as John Sell Cotman]; Sir Edwin A. G. Manton, New York (1973–d. 2005); Manton Family Art Foundation (2005–2007, given to the Clark); Sterling and Francine Clark Art Institute, 2007.

John Singer Sargent American, 1856–1925

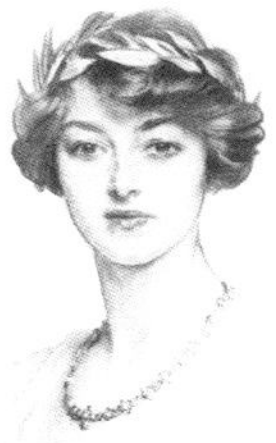

302
Portrait of Mrs. Gilbert Russell, 1911
Charcoal on cream laid paper, 61.4 × 46.5 cm
2007.8.98

Provenance: Sale, Sotheby Parke Bernet & Co., New York, 25 May 1983, no. 72; Sale, Christie's, New York, 30 Apr. 1997, no. 146, sold to Ackermann & Johnson, as agent for Manton; Sir Edwin A. G. Manton, New York (1997–d. 2005); Manton Family Art Foundation (2005–2007, given to the Clark); Sterling and Francine Clark Art Institute, 2007.

Selected Bibliography

Asleson, Robyn. *British Paintings at the Huntington*. New Haven, Conn., and London: Yale University Press, 2001.

Barrell, John. *The Dark Side of the Landscape: The Rural Poor in English Painting, 1730–1840*. Cambridge, U.K.: Cambridge University Press, 1980.

———, ed. *Painting and the Politics of Culture: New Essays on British Culture, 1700–1850*. Oxford, U.K.: Oxford University Press, 1992.

Barringer, Tim, Geoff Quilley, and Douglas Fordham, eds. *Art and the British Empire*. Manchester, U.K.: Manchester University Press, 2007.

Bermingham, Ann. *Landscape and Ideology: The English Rustic Tradition, 1740–1860*. Berkeley: University of California Press, 1986.

———. *Learning to Draw: Studies in the Cultural History of a Polite and Useful Art*. New Haven, Conn., and London: Yale University Press, 2000.

Bindman, David. *The Complete Graphic Works of William Blake*. London: Thames and Hudson, 1978.

Broughton, Michael, William Clarke, and Joanna Selbourne. *The Spooner Collection of British Watercolours at the Courtauld Institute Gallery*. London: Courtauld Institute of Art, 2005.

Brown, David Blayney. *Turner Watercolours*. London: Tate Publishing, 2007.

———, Andrew Hemingway, and Anne Lyles. *Romantic Landscape: The Norwich School of Painters*. London: Tate Gallery Publishing, 2000.

Cohn, Marjorie B. *Wash and Gouache: A Study in the Development of the Materials of Watercolor*. Cambridge, Mass.: Center for Conservation and Technical Studies, Fogg Art Museum, 1977.

Crowley, John E. *Imperial Landscapes: Britain's Global Visual Culture, 1745–1820*. New Haven, Conn. and London: Yale University Press, 2011.

Fleming-Williams, Ian. *Constable and His Drawings*. London: Philip Wilson, 1990.

———, Anne Lyles, Jane McAusland, and Patrick Heron. *Constable: A Master Draughtsman*. London: Dulwich Picture Gallery, 1994.

Forrester, Gillian. *Turner's "Drawing Book": The Liber Studiorum*. London: Tate Publishing, 1996.

Gage, John. *J. M. W. Turner: "A Wonderful Range of Mind."* New Haven, Conn., and London: Yale University Press, 1987.

Griffiths, Antony, ed. *Landmarks in Print Collecting: Connoisseurs and Donors at the British Museum since 1753*. London: British Museum Press, 1996.

———. *Prints and Printmaking: An Introduction to the History and Techniques*. Berkeley: University of California Press, 1996.

Hamilton, James. *Turner: The Late Seascapes*. New Haven, Conn., and London: Yale University Press; Williamstown, Mass.: Sterling and Francine Clark Art Institute, 2003.

Hargraves, Matthew. *Great British Watercolors: From the Paul Mellon Collection at the Yale Center for British Art*. New Haven, Conn., and London: Yale University Press, 2007.

Harris, Theresa Fairbanks, and Scott Wilcox. *Papermaking and the Art of Watercolor in Eighteenth-Century Britain: Paul Sandby and the Whatman Paper Mill*. New Haven, Conn., and London: Yale University Press, 2006.

Hayes, John. *The Art of Thomas Rowlandson*. Alexandria, Va.: Art Services International, 1990.

———. *Gainsborough and Rowlandson: A New York Private Collection*. New York: published privately, 1998.

Hemingway, Andrew. *Landscape Imagery and Urban Culture in Early Nineteenth-Century Britain*. Cambridge, U.K.: Cambridge University Press, 1992.

Hoozee, Robert, ed. *British Vision: Observation and Imagination in British Art, 1750–1950*. Brussels: Mercatorfonds, 2007.

Kriz, Kay Dian. *The Idea of the English Landscape Painter: Genius as Alibi in the Early Nineteenth Century*. New Haven, Conn., and London: Yale University Press, 1997.

Lord, John, ed. *Peter DeWint, 1784–1849: "For the Common Observer of Life and Nature."* Burlington, Vt.: Lund Humphries, 2007.

Lyles, Anne, and Robin Hamlyn. *British Watercolours from the Oppé Collection*. London: Tate Gallery, 1997.

Monrad, Kasper, ed. *Turner and Romantic Nature*. Copenhagen: Statens Museum for Kunst, 2004.

Myrone, Martin. *Gothic Nightmares: Fuseli, Blake, and the Romantic Imagination*. London: Tate Publishing, 2006.

———, ed. *John Martin: Apocalypse*. London: Tate Publishing, 2011.

Noon, Patrick. *Crossing the Channel: British and French Painting in the Age of Romanticism*. London: Tate Publishing, 2003.

———. *Richard Parkes Bonington: "On the Pleasure of Painting."* New Haven, Conn. and London: Yale University Press, 1991.

Parris, Leslie. *Constable*. London: Tate Gallery, 1991.

———. *Constable: A New York Private Collection*. New York: published privately, 1994.

———. *Constable: A New York Private Collection: Supplement*. New York: published privately, 1998.

———. *The "English Landscape" Prints of John Constable and David Lucas*. London: Tate Gallery, 1986.

———, and Ian Fleming-Williams. *Lionel Constable*. London: Tate Gallery, 1982.

Pointon, Marcia. *Hanging the Head: Portraiture and Social Formation in Eighteenth-Century England*. New Haven, Conn., and London: Yale University Press, 1993.

Rauser, Amelia. *Caricature Unmasked: Irony, Authenticity, and Individualism in Eighteenth-Century English Prints*. Newark: University of Delaware Press, 2008.

Rosenthal, Michael. *The Art of Thomas Gainsborough: A Little Business for the Eye*. New Haven, Conn., and London: Yale University Press, 1999.

———, Christiana Payne, and Scott Wilcox, eds. *Prospects for the Nation: Recent Essays in British Landscape, 1750–1880*. New Haven, Conn., and London: Yale University Press, 1997.

Sloan, Kim. *"A Noble Art": Amateur Artists and Drawing Masters, c. 1600–1800*. London: British Museum Press, 2000.

Sloman, Susan. *Gainsborough in Bath*. New Haven, Conn. and London: Yale University Press, 2002.

Smiles, Sam. *The Image of Antiquity: Ancient Britain and the Romantic Imagination*. New Haven, Conn. and London: Yale University Press, 1994.

Smith, Greg. *The Emergence of the Professional Watercolourist: Contentions and Alliances in the Artistic Domain, 1760–1824*. Aldershot, U.K. and Burlington, Vt.: Ashgate, 2002.

———, Peter Bower, Anne Lyles, and Susan Morris. *Thomas Girtin: The Art of Watercolour*. London: Tate Publishing, 2002.

Solkin, David H., ed. *Art on the Line: The Royal Academy Exhibitions at Somerset House, 1780–1836*. London: Yale University Press for the Paul Mellon Centre for Studies in British Art; Courtauld Institute Gallery, 2001.

———. *Richard Wilson: The Landscape of Reaction*. London: Tate Gallery, 1982.

Stratis, Harriet K., and Britt Salveson, eds. *The Broad Spectrum: Studies in the Materials, Techniques, and Conservation of Color on Paper*. London: Archetype Publications, 2002.

Tedeschi, Martha. *How Prints Work: Reproductions, Originals, and their Markets in England, 1840–1900*. Ph.D. diss., Northwestern University, 1994.

Vaughan, William, Elizabeth E. Barker, and Colin Harrison. *Samuel Palmer, 1805–1881: Vision and Landscape*. Burlington, Vt.: Lund Humphries, 2005.

Wilcox, Scott, Gillian Forrester, Morna O'Neill, and Kim Sloan, eds. *The Line of Beauty: British Drawings and Watercolors of the Eighteenth Century*. New Haven, Conn., and London: Yale Center for British Art, 2001.

Wilton, Andrew. *Turner, Girtin, and Bonington: A New York Private Collection: Paintings, Drawings, and Watercolors*. New York: published privately, 2001.

———, and Anne Lyles. *The Great Age of British Watercolours: 1750–1880*. London: Royal Academy of the Arts, 1993.

Contributors

Tim Barringer

Tim Barringer is Paul Mellon Professor of the History of Art at Yale University. His publications include *Reading the Pre-Raphaelites* (1999; revised 2012), *Men at Work: Art and Labour in Victorian Britain* (2005), and *Broken Pastoral: Art and Music in Britain, Gothic Revival to Punk Rock* (forthcoming). He coedited *American Sublime: Landscape Painting in the United States 1820–1880* (2002), *Art and Emancipation in Jamaica* (2007), and *Art and the British Empire* (2009), and is co-curator of *Pre-Raphaelites: Victorian Avant-Garde* (Tate, 2012).

Ann Bermingham

Ann Bermingham is Professor of the History of Art and Architecture and Director of the Interdisciplinary Humanities Center at the University of California, Santa Barbara. She is the author of *Landscape and Ideology: The English Rustic Tradition, 1760–1860* (1989) and *Learning to Draw: Studies in the History of a Polite and Useful Art* (2000), and editor of *Sensation and Sensibility: Viewing Gainsborough's "Cottage Door"* (2005) and, with John Brewer, *The Consumption of Culture: Image, Object, Text, 1600–1800* (1997). Her research interests include the history of landscape painting and art of the eighteenth and nineteenth centuries, aesthetic theory, and popular visual culture.

Susannah Blair

Susannah Blair is a graduate student at the Williams College Graduate Program in the History of Art, with a concentration in European art of the nineteenth and twentieth centuries. She is a graduate curatorial intern in the Manton Study Center for Prints, Drawings, and Photographs at the Sterling and Francine Clark Art Institute. She graduated with high honors from Swarthmore College in Pennsylvania in 2008.

Mary Broadway

Mary Broadway received her M.A., with an advanced certificate of study in art conservation, from Buffalo State College in the fall of 2011. She worked with Leslie Hill Paisley, Head of Paper Conservation, at the Williamstown Art Conservation Center (WACC) from 2010 to 2011. While at WACC, Broadway conducted analysis and research on several pieces in the Manton Collection from the Sterling and Francine Clark Art Institute.

David Blayney Brown

David Blayney Brown is Curator of British Art 1790–1850 at Tate Britain, where he has led a major online catalogue project for the drawings in the Turner Bequest, and is co-convenor of Tate's Research Centre for British Romantic art. He is an authority on Samuel Palmer, David Wilkie, and British and European art of the Romantic period, and has published and lectured extensively on these areas of expertise. He has curated and contributed to numerous exhibitions and catalogues. His many publications include *Romanticism* (2001) and *Turner in the Tate Collection* (2002). He is also vice president of the Byron Society.

Jay A. Clarke

Jay A. Clarke is Manton Curator of Prints, Drawings, and Photographs at the Sterling and Francine Clark Art Institute and a lecturer in the Graduate Program in the History of Art at Williams College. Her publications include *Becoming Edvard Munch: Influence, Anxiety, and Myth* (2009) and essays on the critical reception of Käthe Kollwitz and Max Beckmann, Munch's use of repetition, and Julius Meier-Graefe as an art dealer. She was the editor of *Negotiating History: German Art and the Past* (2002) and coeditor of *The Spiritual Landscapes of Adrienne Farb, 1980–2006* (2006).

Antony Griffiths

Antony Griffiths was Keeper of the Department of Prints and Drawings at the British Museum from 1991 to 2011, having been with the museum since 1976. His specialty is the history of printmaking, and he has contributed essays on the subject to numerous exhibition catalogues and periodicals. He is author of *Prints and Printmaking*, first published in 1980 and still in print. He is now working on a book to be titled *The Print before Photography: An Introduction to European Printmaking 1550–1820*.

Sarah Hammond

Sarah Hammond is Special Projects Assistant for the department of Publishing and Information Resources at the Sterling and Francine Clark Art Institute. She received her B.A. in art history and archaeology from Washington University in Saint Louis and her M.A. from the Williams College Graduate Program in the History of Art. She was an affiliate student at University College London. Her research focuses on British artists of the eighteenth through twentieth centuries, with a particular focus on prints and graphic satire. She has held positions in the prints, drawings, and photographs departments at the Saint Louis Art Museum and at the Clark.

Anne Lyles

Anne Lyles is a leading authority on the art of John Constable. She was a curator at Tate Britain between 1987 and 2012, specializing in late eighteenth- and early nineteenth-century landscape painting. Her curatorial and publication projects include *Turner and Natural History: The Farnley Project* (1988), *Colour into Line: Turner and the Art of Engraving* (1989), *The Great Age of British Watercolours: 1750–1880* (1993), *British Watercolours from the Oppé Collection* (1997), *Constable's Clouds* (2000), and *Constable: Le choix de Lucian Freud* (2002–3). Most recently, she co-curated *Constable: The Great Landscapes* (2006) and *Constable Portraits* (2009).

Patrick Noon

Patrick Noon is the Patrick and Aimee Butler Chair of Paintings at the Minneapolis Institute of Arts. From 1977 to 1997, he was Curator of Prints, Drawings, and Rare Books at the Yale Center for British Art. An acknowledged scholar of Romanticism, his most recent publications include *Crossing the Channel: British and French Painting in the Age of Romanticism* (2003) and the catalogues raisonnés *Richard Parkes Bonington: The Complete Paintings* (2008) and *Richard Parkes Bonington: The Complete Drawings* (2011).

Leslie Hill Paisley

Leslie Hill Paisley received her early conservation training at the Center for Conservation and Technical Studies, Harvard University Art Museums. She has been a practicing conservator and head of the paper conservation department at the Williamstown Art Conservation Center since 1989. A professor in the Williams College Graduate Program in the History of Art, Paisley has trained numerous graduate conservation interns. She is a fellow of the American Institute for Conservation of Historic and Artistic Works.

Amelia Rauser

Amelia Rauser is Associate Professor of Art History at Franklin and Marshall College. She has contributed articles to numerous journals and spoken at many professional conferences. Rauser's publications include *Caricature Unmasked: Irony, Authenticity, and Individualism in Eighteenth-Century English Prints* (2008) and the forthcoming *Living Statues: Neoclassical Culture and Fashionable Dress in the 1790s*, which relates the vogue for the antique style in London, Paris, and Naples to a cultural fascination with transparency, sensibility, and the mystery of the life force.

Sam Smiles

Sam Smiles is Emeritus Professor of Art History at the University of Plymouth. He has lectured and published widely on British art after 1750. Smiles's numerous publications include *J. M. W. Turner: The Making of a Modern Artist* (2007), *The Turner Book* (2006), *Eye Witness: Artists and Visual Documentation in Britain 1770–1830* (2000), and *The Image of Antiquity: Ancient Britain and the Romantic Imagination* (1994), among many others. He has coauthored many exhibition catalogues, including *Landscapes of Retrospection: The Magoon Collection of British Prints and Drawings 1739–1860* (1999) and *Into the Light: French and British Painting from Impressionism to the Early 1920s* (2011). He is currently completing a study of Turner's last paintings (c. 1835–50).

Index

Note: Works of art are listed at the end of each entry for artists. Large portfolios are listed separately. Pages with illustrations are given in *italics*.

V

W

Y

Photography Credits

Permission to reproduce illustrations is provided by courtesy of the owners listed in the captions. Unless otherwise noted, photos of works in the Manton Collection and other works belonging to the Sterling and Francine Clark Art Institute are by Michael Agee. Additional photography credits are as follows:

The Courtauld Gallery, London, The Samuel Courtauld Trust: fig. 100
Durban Art Gallery, South Africa: fig. 103
© The Frick Collection, New York: fig. 101
Photograph by Blake Gardner: p. 8
Photograph by Scott Lapham: fig. 21
Courtesy of The Lewis Walpole Library, Yale University: fig. 78
Courtesy of the Manton family: p. 5, figs. 1, 3, 4, 5, 7
Photograph by J. T. Matijevich, New York: fig. 6
Photograph © 2012 Museum of Fine Arts, Boston: fig. 122
© National Gallery, London / Art Resource, New York: figs. 118, 121
Réunion des Musées Nationaux / Art Resource, New York: fig. 125, 126
Réunion des Musées Nationaux / Art Resource, New York (photograph by Jean-Gilles Berizzi): fig. 133
Ruskin Foundation, Ruskin Library, University of Lancaster: fig. 16
Courtesy of Skinner Inc., www.skinnerinc.com: fig. 12
Collection of the Skyscraper Museum, New York: fig. 2
Smith College Museum of Art, Northhampton, Mass. © 2012 Artists Rights Society (ARS), New York / ADAGP, Paris: fig. 11
© Tate, London 2012: figs. 22, 81, 82, 83, 102, 105, 107, 120, 124
© Tate, London 2012. Lent by the Trustees of the Dupplin Trust, 2000: fig. 99
Tate, London / Art Resource, New York; Art © Louise Bourgeois Trust / Licensed by VAGA, New York: fig. 23
© The Trustees of the British Museum: figs. 43, 47, 76, 79
By kind permission of the Trustees of the Wallace Collection, London / Art Resource, New York: fig. 132
V&A Images, London / Art Resource, New York: fig. 97
© Victoria and Albert Museum, London: figs. 119, 123, 127
© Virginia Museum of Fine Arts (photograph by Katherine Wetzel): fig. 136
Wadsworth Atheneum Museum of Art / Art Resource, New York: fig. 131
Williamstown Art Conservation Center: figs. 51, 52, 57, 62, 71
Yale Center for British Art, New Haven, Conn.: fig. 32
Yale Center for British Art, Paul Mellon Collection, New Haven, Conn.: fig. 110